INFORMATION SYSTEMS MANAGEMENT IN PRACTICE

Seventh
Edition

INFORMATION SYSTEMS MANAGEMENT IN PRACTICE

Barbara C. McNurlin

Writer–Information Systems

Ralph H. Sprague, Jr.

University of Hawaii

PARK LEARNING CENTRE
UNIVERSITY OF GLOUCESTERSHIRE
PO Box 220, The Park, Cheltenham, GL50 2QF
Tel: (01242) 532721

PEARSON EDUCATION INTERNATIONAL

Executive Editor: Robert Horan
VP/Editorial Director: Jeff Shelstad
Project Manager: Lori Cerreto
Senior Media Project Manager: Nancy Welcher
Executive Marketing Manager: Debbie Clare
Marketing Assistant: Joanna Sabella
Managing Editor: John Roberts
Production Editor: Renata Butera
Permissions Supervisor: Charles Morris
Manufacturing Buyer: Michelle Klein
Cover Design: Karen Salzbach
Composition: Integra Software Services
Full-Service Project Management: BookMasters, Inc./Jennifer Welsch
Printer/Binder: Phoenix Color Corp.
Cover Printer: Phoenix Color Corp.

Credits and acknowledgments borrowed from other sources and reproduced, with permission, in this textbook appear on appropriate page within text.

If you purchased this book within the United States or Canada you should be aware that it has been wrongfully imported without the approval of the Publisher or the Author.

Pearson Education LTD.
Pearson Education Singapore, Pte. Ltd
Pearson Education, Canada, Ltd
Pearson Education–Japan
Pearson Education Australia PTY, Limited

Pearson Education North Asia Ltd
Pearson Education de Mexico, S.A. de C.V.
Pearson Education Malaysia, Pte. Ltd
Pearson Education Upper Saddle River, NJ

10 9 8 7 6 5 4 3 2 1
0-13-196877-7

This book is dedicated to our parents

Dick and Peggy Canning
and
Ralph and Virginia Sprague

for all their inspiration, guidance, and support.

Brief Contents

Contents

CHAPTER 4 INFORMATION SYSTEMS PLANNING   134

**CHAPTER 7 MANAGING INFORMATION
RESOURCES   263**

CHAPTER 8 MANAGING OPERATIONS   298

Preface

This book deals with the management of information technology (IT) as it is being practiced in organizations today. Successfully managing IT has become crucial for several reasons:

- IT is now a strategic asset that is being used to mold competitive strategies and change organizational processes.
- The situations in which organizations are applying IT have increased in complexity, including more interorganizational environments.
- The capabilities of IT and the complexities of using the technologies are also growing at an accelerating rate.
- As IT and its uses become more complex, developing strategies and systems to deliver the technology has become more difficult.

The net result is a growing need for guidance on the issues, strategies, and tactics for managing the use of IT. To partially satisfy this need, universities and colleges have developed courses that focus on the management of IT. Textual material for these courses has been sparse for two particularly troublesome reasons.

First, IT is changing so rapidly that textbook authors, practitioners, researchers, and academics have a difficult time staying current. For example, two major developments stand out. One has been the fast uptake of business uses of the World Wide Web. This dramatic shift appears to be a precursor of a current revolution—wireless handheld computing—which is beginning to change how we all work, live, and play. Thus, while information systems (IS) departments are busily creating an Internet-based platform for their enterprises, they must also be experimenting with another computing platform: small wireless devices.

The second major development is the changes in the business world itself. Terrorism, corporate malfeasance, cybercrime, regional conflicts, and outsourcing are changing how profit and nonprofit enterprises conduct business. As a result, the work of IS organizations and the roles CIOs need to fill are changing as well. Keeping abreast of these business-world changes, and the responses businesses are making to them, is also difficult.

Another reason for the paucity of IT textual material for these courses is that the principles and strategies of effective management are evolving out of the experiences of practicing managers. Merely collecting reports from current literature fails to provide the interaction needed to decipher principles from the lessons learned in practice. Current developments and experiences need interpretation and coalescence to provide the guidance that new and practicing managers need to further develop their knowledge and managerial skills.

CONTRIBUTION OF THIS BOOK

We believe this book makes a major contribution to addressing both of these challenges. One resource for this book is work we have performed for several organizations — Gartner EXP, the Sourcing Interests Group, and the Hawaii International Conference on System Sciences (HICSS), in particular. Our work for these organizations does not merely report current developments and practices; it includes thoughtful interpretation to provide guidance, principles, and strategies for IS executives.

Our objective in this book is to capture the material of most current importance to IS executives and to organize it around a framework that provides guidance for IS organizations. A key element of our writing continues to be examples of actual work in companies. This book includes over 90 case examples.

USE OF THIS BOOK BY PRACTICING MANAGERS AND CONSULTANTS

In the management of IT, this book is useful to several levels of managers:

- To senior business executives who want an overview of the issues and strategies in managing IT, with examples of what other enterprises are doing
- To CIOs who must implement IT as a strategic resource to help their enterprises attain their overall goals and objectives
- To IS managers who are responsible for major technical areas, such as system development, technology planning, and architecture
- To managers of functional units who (1) want to better understand the issues and processes of providing IT support for their areas of responsibility, (2) want to promote the use of IT in their organization, or (3) are now responsible for overseeing the management of IT in their function

We believe that managers of all types will find this book valuable. By focusing on issues and strategies while explaining technical concepts, this book provides an overview of IS management for business executives and managers. By combining the experiences of successful executives this book provides a real-world perspective for all IS managers.

Consultants to executives and managers will also find this book a useful reference for staying up-to-date on important issues in the field.

USE OF THIS BOOK AS A TEXT

Future IS managers who are graduate or undergraduate students will find that this book presents a view of what "the real world" has in store. As a text, it is intended for students who have had at least one IS course.

At the graduate level, it has been used since its first edition in 1986 for the second course, beyond the required IS course. It is especially well suited for the final course in a graduate curriculum on IS management. In addition, as MBA students have become more computer literate, the book has been increasingly used as the text in the MBA IS core course. In both uses, the book gives students conceptual and practical guidelines for dealing with the management of today's IS function.

At the undergraduate level, the book can serve as the text for a course dealing specifically with the management of IT or in the capstone course that summarizes the practice of IS for students about to begin their careers. Most undergraduate majors in IT take entry-level positions in the IS organization and then proceed into management. In the short term, they work with IS managers who are facing the problems and using the principles dealt with in this book.

Although this book has not been aimed at students majoring in other areas, non-IS majors are taking IS courses in increasing numbers to better understand how to work with systems professionals. All the chapters are pertinent to them because the theory is illustrated by real-life case studies, which are easily understood by students in all business disciplines.

At the end of each chapter are three types of questions and exercises to reinforce the material in the text.

- *Review questions* are based directly on the material in the chapter, allowing the reader to assess comprehension of the chapter's key principles, topics, and ideas.

- *Discussion questions* are based on a few topics in the chapter for which there is a legitimate basis for a difference of opinion. These questions focus discussion on these issues when the book is used in a seminar or classroom setting.

- *Exercises* provide an opportunity for the reader to put some of the concepts and ideas into practice on a small scale. In particular, one exercise in each chapter requires a student, or a team of students, to visit a local company and discover how the ideas in the chapter are being implemented in that company.

THE INSTRUCTOR'S GUIDE

We accompany this seventh edition with an Instructor's Guide, originally prepared by Jerry McBride of Marist College in Poughkeepsie, New York. Again, Jerry supplies the all-important critical questions in the guide. The purposes of the guide are (1) to help instructors prepare a strategy and outline for conducting an advanced systems course using this text and (2) to provide support materials and techniques to enhance the course.

We believe there are six approaches for using this text. The six course modes are:

1. A lecture-based course
2. A seminar-based course
3. A directed study course
4. An independent study course
5. An action research course
6. An Internet-based course

In the Instructor's Guide, Jerry suggests some interesting resources to use in these approaches. For example, he explains how he has used a computer-based simulation game to help his students understand the consequences of their actions as they try to introduce technology innovation into an organization.

The Instructor's Guide includes:

- Outlines for the six course approaches
- An expanded outline of each chapter
- Answers to the review questions in each chapter
- Study notes for the Part Discussion Cases
- A listing of case studies appropriate for each chapter
- An Image Library of all the figures in the text
- Suggestions on how to conduct site visit exercises
- Several sample syllabi
- An approach to using simulation software
- Critical questions for each chapter and how to create them
- A PowerPoint presentation for each chapter by Michael Matthew. (See Web site description below.)
- Test Item File in Microsoft Word. (See Web site description below.)

These critical questions deserve a short explanation. Like the discussion questions in the text, critical questions are designed to stimulate critical thinking and discussion among students. In the Instructor's Guide, we present critical questions for each chapter, as well as an explanation of how Jerry has helped his students create them, thereby stimulating their critical thinking.

A course in IS management can be exciting—to teach and to take. We have provided the Instructor's Guide to make this one of those exciting courses.

WEB SITE: WWW.PRENHALL.COM/MCNURLIN

The Web site for this text, provided by Prentice Hall, houses the Instructor's Guide, the Test Item File in Word, TestGen and TestGen in WebCT/BlackBoard-ready files, and the Image Library in a secure area for faculty download only. PowerPoint slides are available in the student area of the Web site. In addition, other items relevant to this text can be found at www.cal.net/~mcnurlin.

FORMAT AND CONTENTS

This book is divided into five major parts, each dealing with a major portion of the field of IT. Chapter 1 precedes Part I because it serves as the framework around which the rest of the book is built. It traces the growing importance of IS management and presents a conceptual model to show the key areas, how they fit together, and the principal issues for executives in each area. It also presents a very interesting longitudinal case example of how these ideas have been implemented in a company over the lifetime of this book—since 1986. In a nutshell, it presents a 19-year historical view of the evolution of IS management.

Part I deals with *leadership issues*, including the top IS jobs, strategic uses of IT, and approaches to systems planning. Part II treats the all-important issues in *managing the essential technologies*, including distributed systems, telecommunications, information resources, and operations. Part III deals with *managing system development*; its evolution continues to present management with important, yet risky, challenges. Part IV explores *systems for supporting decision making, collaboration, and knowledge work*. Part V concludes the book and discusses the challenges ahead. At the end of Parts I through IV is a Part Discussion Case, which is meant to give students an open-ended case with real-life quandaries that require decisions. These cases are intended to elicit creative thinking and class discussion.

Throughout the book, our objectives have been to keep the material practical, to give examples, and to derive guidance for today's and tomorrow's IS executives based on the experiences of others. To that end, chapters are sprinkled with company examples. These are not so much case studies that require solutions or recommendations; rather, they are case examples of how companies have put some of the ideas in a chapter into practice.

ACKNOWLEDGMENTS

We wish to acknowledge the contribution of Richard G. Canning, Barbara's father. His insight and foresight originally made this book possible in 1986. In the early 1960s, he recognized the data processing executive's need for case studies, practical research findings, and thoughtful analysis. Through publishing and editing *EDP Analyzer* from 1963 until his retirement in 1986, Dick Canning devoted a major portion of his professional career to that purpose. His legacy continues in this book.

We also wish to thank the organizations that have allowed us to draw on work we performed for them—Gartner EXP, the Sourcing Interests Group, and HICSS in particular.

Reviewers for this edition were:

Phil Beck, University of Texas

Rajiv Kohli, University of Notre Dame

Roberta Lamb, University of Hawaii

Mark Lewis, University of Mississippi

Chunlei Liu, Troy State University

Karen Reaves, High Point University

Finally, we thank Bill Chismar, Jerry McBride, Michael Matthew, and Tracia McNurlin Barbieri. Bill Chismar was a significant contributor to the fifth and sixth editions. His ideas live on. Jerry was again instrumental in creating the all-important Instructor's Guide. Michael has contributed the thorough PowerPoint slides on the Prentice Hall Web site. And without Tracia's assistance, the Instructor's Guide would not be so thorough.

Barbara Canning McNurlin
Ralph H. Sprague, Jr.
July 2004

INFORMATION SYSTEMS MANAGEMENT IN PRACTICE

CHAPTER

1

THE IMPORTANCE OF INFORMATION SYSTEMS MANAGEMENT

INTRODUCTION

Information technology (IT)—computers and telecommunications—is having the kind of revolutionary, restructuring impact that has been expected and touted for years. The rapid advances in the speed and capacity of computing devices, coupled with the pervasiveness of the Internet, digital storage, wireless and portable devices, and multimedia content, are causing major changes in the way we live and work.

Although IT affects nearly all aspects of human endeavor, this book emphasizes its use in managing and operating organizations, including business enterprises, government organizations, and social and charitable organizations. Any time people work together to jointly pursue objectives, IT is changing the way they work.

Managing and operating IT for these purposes has been a field of practice for some 50 years. First known as *business data processing* and later as *management information systems* (MIS), the field is now called *information technology* (IT). In this book, we distinguish between *IT* (the technology) and the organization that manages the technology, which we call the *IS* (information systems) organization. IS combines the technologies, people, processes, and organizational mechanisms for fostering the use of IT to improve organizational performance.

Themes of This Book

Due to the growth and pervasiveness of IT, organizations are operating in a different environment from just a few years ago. The nature of this environment is explored in several themes in this edition of the book. The following three themes are woven through the book:

- *Globalization.* Have you noticed? The world seems to be getting smaller. Events in a faraway land can impact others in another part of the globe. As a result, a major theme in today's world is globalization, whereby companies seek to offer their goods and services around the world. However, the worldwide spread of brands and the emergence of global institutions are encountering major backlashes from groups, and even nations, that want to maintain their local identity. Companies feel this backlash in their use of IT: locales and regions want systems that suit their culture, preferences, or ways of working. In addition, they want jobs to stay put, not move to a far-off country. In response, IS executives are seeking to achieve a balance between implementing a single enterprisewide IT infrastructure and tailoring systems to fit local needs—and locating work where it is best performer.

- *E-enablement.* Doing business electronically has been a fundamental use of computers since the 1950s, but now the Internet has become a hub for conducting business. The before-Internet economy is transforming into an electronic economy where clicks and bricks exist side by side. The dot-com crash might have seemed a hiccup in the increasing use of the Internet for business and commerce. However, it has not deterred companies from e-enabling their businesses, that is, integrating the Internet into how they work. In general, the term *e-business* has the broad connotation of doing business electronically. E-business has much to do with building e-enabled relationships with consumers and other enterprises, not just performing transactions electronically. *E-commerce*, on the other hand, is being used in the more limited sense of buying and selling electronically, as in handling commerce transactions.

  The vision is full interconnectivity among everyone on earth, with the ability to communicate electronically, transfer multimedia files, and access information from around the world at the touch of a button on a wireless device in the blink of an eye.

- ***Knowledge Sharing and Knowledge Management.*** The third major theme is how to deal with all the world's knowledge. One aspect of this is the transfer of knowledge between people (sharing), because the most important asset in enterprises is the people and the knowledge they possess. The other aspect is the transfer of knowledge from people's heads into lasting things, such as processes, products, practices, databases, directories, software, and such. People walk out the door each night (or leave the company); these other artifacts do not, but they do grow stale and outdated. This second area is called *knowledge management*. Both aspects have to do with managing people and the knowledge they possess. IT can be used for both.

Later in this chapter, we discuss two kinds of knowledge work: procedure based and goal based. Emphasis on knowledge work is shifting from the former to the latter. At the same time, a major shift is taking place from information access to content management, which includes searching, filtering, synthesizing, assimilating, and sharing knowledge resources. The importance of content management is reinforced by the fact that intellectual assets are considered by many to be the only source of sustainable competitive advantage for organizations.

Management of IS

Although IT is used in space exploration, weapons systems, medicine, entertainment, and many other aspects of human activity, the majority of information technologies are used to manage organizations.

The process of managing IT in organizations is becoming increasingly complex as it becomes more important. To illustrate why, here are just three major trends that impact IT management:

- Governance of IT, that is, deciding who makes which IT decisions, is shifting from being handled exclusively by IS executives to being a collaborative effort between IS and the business.
- The role of IS is shifting from application delivery to system integration and infrastructure development.
- Outsourcing is becoming a way of life for many IS organizations, to the extent that a major responsibility of IS is developing and managing relationships with external service providers (ESPs).

The purpose of this book is to describe how IT is being managed today in leading-edge enterprises. Thus, this book is appropriate for anyone who is using IT to improve organizational performance—IS executives, technical managers, top executives, business unit executives, line managers, and employees at all levels of an organization.

This chapter briefly reviews the recent history of IT and its management in organizations. Then it identifies a number of organizational and technical trends that are affecting IT management. Finally, it presents a framework for thinking about how IT is used and managed in organizations. This framework serves as the road map for the rest of the book.

A LITTLE HISTORY

Most people are surprised to learn that the United States passed from the industrial era to the information era in 1957. In that year, the number of U.S. employees whose jobs were primarily to handle information (information workers) surpassed the number of industrial workers. Figure 1-1 shows Marc Porat's well-known division of the economy.

In the late 1950s and early 1960s, though, information technology to support information work hardly existed. Only the telephone was widespread, and even it did not reach every desk. Computers were just beginning to be used in data processing applications, replacing electric accounting machines. Even where computers were in use, their impact was modest.

Most other information work in general offices was done without much support from technology. Xerographic office copiers were introduced in 1959. Electric typewriters were commonplace, but the first word processor would not arrive until 1964. Facsimile machines were used only in specialized applications and would not be in general office use until the 1970s. However, the future of technology support for information workers was extremely bright. Many of the foundations of IT had been invented, and costs were starting their steady long-term fall.

Another milestone was reached in about 1980, when the number of U.S. information workers surpassed the number of U.S. workers in all other sectors combined. In other words, information workers exceeded 50 percent of the U.S. work force. However, the technology to support these information workers remained slow, expensive, and segmented into special-purpose categories.

IT was initially used to perform manual information work more quickly and more efficiently. Then it was used to manage work better. Now we are well into the third stage of technology assimilation in which IT makes pervasive changes in the structure and the operation of work, business practices, organizations, industries, and the global economy.

The next two sections explore the changes in the work environment and the technical environment.

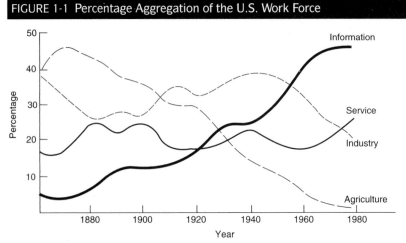

FIGURE 1-1 Percentage Aggregation of the U.S. Work Force

Source: Marc U. Porat, *The Information Economy* (Washington, D.C.: Office of Telecommunications Policy, U.S. Department of Commerce, 1977).

THE ORGANIZATIONAL ENVIRONMENT

How IT is used depends on the environment surrounding the organization that uses it. This environment includes economic conditions, characteristics of principal resources (especially labor), management philosophies, societal mores, and other factors. This environment changes constantly. Simultaneously, technological advances affect the way IT is used. An ongoing debate centers around whether technology drives change in organizations or merely supports it. This "chicken or egg" debate is giving way to the realization that IT and its use and management coevolve, each influencing the other.

This section explores two aspects of the organizational environment: the external forces that are causing executives to reexamine how their firms compete and the internal structural forces that affect how organizations operate or are managed. It then considers how these environmental trends have led to a new set of goals for the new work environment.

The External Business Environment

Today, the turbulent business world includes shorter and shorter product cycles, a U.S. telecommunications industry in turmoil, investor doubts about corporate truthfulness, and terrorism. IT contributes to this turbulence because it allows information to move faster, increasing the pace at which individuals and organizations can respond to events. One result is higher peaks and lower valleys, caused by an IT-charged herd instinct. The following are the main changes taking place in our global marketplace.

The Internet Economy.   This economy began with business-to-consumer (B2C) retailing, selling over the World Wide Web (Web). The pioneer of the Web-only business model was Amazon.com. The action then moved to business-to-business (B2B), with buyers and sellers using Internet exchanges (or e-marketplaces) to find and consummate business deals. eBay is the most well-known exchange, but there are other industry-specific exchanges. The main point is that today's economy is encompassing both old and new ways of operating, and IT is a major underpinning of the way these two worlds interface with each other.

Global Marketplace.   The entire world has become the marketplace. To succeed, large companies believe they need to be global, meaning huge and everywhere. Merger mania is occurring across industries as companies aim for this goal. Mergers even cross national boundaries. It is not unusual for a British food company to own U.S., French, and other food and beverage companies, or for a Swiss pharmaceutical company to buy out its American and Japanese counterparts.

In addition, the Internet enables companies to work globally—with three main operating arenas, Asia/Pacific, the Americas, Europe and the Middle East and Africa (EMEA)—and work around the clock by passing work from one region to the next, following the sun.

The global marketplace has become a two-way street. Firmly entrenched companies find unexpected competitors from halfway around the world bidding on work via the Internet. Parts and subassemblies are being manufactured in many countries to cut overall labor costs and then shipped to other countries for final assembly.

The Internet also allows small firms to have a global reach. Norwegians can order extra-hot chili sauce from Texas. Europeans can order books over the Internet from U.S. companies before those books become available in their own country's bookstores. And so on. The business environment is now global, but local tastes still matter. As noted earlier, local backlashes against globalization are a factor global enterprises need to include in their planning.

Business Ecosystems.   A new term is creeping into the business lexicon: *ecosystem*. An ecosystem is a web of relationships surrounding one or a few companies. For example, Microsoft and Intel are the center of the Wintel ecosystem that has dominated the PC world. Yet, although they dominate the PC ecosystem, they are far less dominant in other ecosystems, such as the Internet ecosystem and the wireless communications ecosystem. The point about ecosystems is that they appear to follow biological rules rather than industrial-age, machine-like rules. They require flexibility because relationships change more frequently; they are more organic. Relationships and coevolution require a different corporate mindset from the command-and-control mindset of the past.

Decapitalization.   Tangible items, such as capital, equipment, and buildings, were the tenets of power in the industrial age. Today, intangible items, such as ideas, intellectual capital, and knowledge, have become the scarce, desirable items. You could say that the business world is moving from tangible to intangible; it is decapitalizing. For this reason, managing talent has become as important as managing finances. Without talent, ideas dwindle, the new-product pipeline shrivels up, and the company becomes less competitive. More and more talk focuses on managing intellectual capital (the knowledge in people's heads).

Faster Business Cycles.   The tempo of business has accelerated appreciably; companies do not have as much time to develop new products or services and move them into the marketplace. Once on the market, their useful lives tend to be shorter as well, so speed has become of the essence. Efforts to accelerate time to market or to reduce cycle time often depend on innovative uses of IT.

Accountability and Transparency.   The rise and fall of dot-coms probably should have been expected; some of their business plans truly could not make money. However, the ensuing debacle in the overbuilt telecommunications industry and the corporate financial shenanigans in several industries around the world have shaken investor confidence and led to calls for greater transparency of corporate operations and greater accountability of corporate officers. These events are likely to increase the pressure for corporate ethics. IT will surely play a role in implementing the ensuing regulations and fostering transparency. Discussions of IT ethics might also increase.

Rising Societal Risks of IT.   Since the last edition of this book, IT has negatively affected millions of people—through network shutdowns, computer viruses, identity thefts, e-mail scams, movement of white-collar jobs to lower-cost countries, and such—which has led to increasing calls for government regulation and for vendors and corporations to take action. This edition includes more discussion of the societal risks that accompany the societal benefits of IT.

Now, more than in the past, CIOs need to address the dark side of IT, which includes protecting the privacy of individuals whose information they store and securing their networks, databases, and computers from cybercrime, computer viruses, and such. They also need to consider the societal effects of outsourcing, and ease, as much as possible, the human misery that comes from employees losing their job or having to oversee work performed in distant places.

The Internal Organizational Environment

The work environment is also changing, and the art of managing people is undergoing significant shifts. These changes are profound enough to change organizational structures. Frances Cairncross,[1] management editor at the *Economist*, writes in her book *The Company of the Future* that the relationship between IT and enterprise structure is growing more widespread and deeper. She believes that the company of the future will look much like the Japanese *keiretsu* (the associations of independent and interdependent businesses working in concert). Here are some of the changes we see affecting how people work and how organizations operate. Some support Cairncross's belief.

From Supply-Push to Demand-Pull.   In the industrial age, companies did their best to figure out what customers wanted. Firms were organized to build a supply of products or services and then "push" them out to end customers on store shelves, in catalogs, and such. The Internet, which allows much closer and one-to-one contact between customer and seller, is moving the business model to demand-pull. In this model, companies offer customers the components of a service or product, and the customers create their own personalized versions, creating the demand that pulls the specific product or service they want through the supply chain, or rather, the demand chain.

To move to this consumer-pull mass customization business model, companies need to essentially reverse their business processes to be customer facing. In fact, this model can lead to suppliers and customers cocreating products and services. For example, book buyers who put their critiques of books on Amazon.com's Web site are, in a sense, cocreating part of Amazon's service to other book buyers.

Here's another bookseller example. Borders is the second-largest book retailer in the United States. Its president has decided to replace the industry's supply-push approach with a new demand-pull approach. Traditionally, and still today, booksellers push those books that publishers pay them to promote in their bookstore windows, on near-the-door tables, and in other high-traffic areas.

Borders' president thinks these short-term incentives might actually hurt overall sales in categories, so he is shifting Borders to "category management," which means publishers will help comanage 250 book categories, reports Trachtenberg.[2] In return for being part of the decision-making process by recommending titles to Borders, the publishers will help pay for the market research Borders will do to find out what book buyers want. For instance, Borders wants to find out which books are bought on impulse, which ones sell better when the cover is showing, which types should be grouped together, where sections should be located, and even how to price books.

Borders' competitors are watching this demand-pull experiment with great interest. Some doubt that it will work, reports Trachtenberg, arguing that selling books is not like selling screwdrivers or prescription drugs. One thing Borders has already learned through its market research, though, is that one-fourth of its cookbooks are bought as gifts.

Customer-centricity is another term for this trend. It means replacing product-centric thinking with customer-centric thinking. The result: Organizational structures shift from product groups to customer groups. One way to view this shift is to see it as turning traditional thinking inside out. When companies focus on products, they are thinking inside-out. When they think about customers and customer groups, they think outside-in.

Although you might think this shift means keeping customers happy, it can actually have the opposite effect for some customers. When companies create customer clusters using data warehousing and data mining techniques, they find out which clusters are profitable and which are not. They may then institute policies that cater to the profitable customers and charge or let go the unprofitable ones.

Self-Service.   Bank automated teller machines (ATMs) were an early example of customer self-service. The 1990s saw an increase in systems that let consumers access corporate computer systems to purchase products, inquire about the state of an order, and, in general, do business with the firm online on their own. FedEx was one of the first companies to leverage the Web by allowing customers to directly access its package-tracking system via its homepage. Today, companies that ship products via FedEx have links to the same homepage, providing that service to their customers. When customers serve themselves, employees can do other kinds of work.

Real-Time Working.   A term that has been around for at least 15 years but has only recently gained traction (and use in vendor marketing materials) is the *real-time enterprise*. The genesis of this notion, we believe, was the military, whose personnel fly planes and drive tanks using instrument panels. These panels show the pilots and soldiers the surrounding terrain as it exists at the moment, so that they can respond to changes and threats in real time. The term has been adopted in business and means operating a business in as close to real time as possible, using computer systems to indicate the state of the "business terrain" as it exists at the moment.

For example, members of a sales team about to talk to a potential global customer can have up-to-the-minute information about that customer—late-breaking news about the company, recent management changes, latest orders to the company (if any), sales tips from other employees—all gathered for them from many sources.

Other examples of real-time working are knowing inventories as of right now (not 1 week or 1 month ago), knowing cash on hand right now (not at the end of last month), and being able to reach someone when you need them, perhaps via instant messaging. With accurate, current information on company operations, customer orders, inventory stocks, and on-demand access to others, people have better information to make decisions. Thus, businesses are making a major push to have real-time information in hand and real-time access to people, which are not easy feats, especially for enterprises with global operations.

Team-Based Working.   The trend is toward people working together on projects. Rather than depending on chains of command and the authority of the boss, many organizations emphasize teams to accomplish major tasks and projects. Peter Drucker's classic article in the *Harvard Business Review*[3] uses the analogy of a symphony, where each member of the team has a unique contribution to make to the overall result. Task-oriented teams form and work together long enough to accomplish the task, then disband. This project-based working, where people sometimes work simultaneously on several projects with different teams across different organizations, is generating major interest in information systems called *groupware*. Groupware provides IT support for meetings, collaborative work, and communications among far-flung team members. Cairncross[1] believes the increased ability to collaborate in new ways using IT is one of the forces driving the changes in organizational structures and that enterprises that use the technology to work in new collaborative ways will be the winners.

Anytime, Anyplace Information Work.   Information workers are increasingly mobile, so computers are needed not just for accessing information, but also for communicating with others. One of the hallmarks of IT today is that the communication capabilities of computers are seen as more important than their computing capabilities. Communication technology has developed to the point where information work can be done anywhere with a laptop computer, cell phone, or PDA. Electronic mail, voice mail and instant messaging (IM) cross time zones to allow work to be conducted anytime, anywhere. People sporadically work from home, rather than commute every day, and they work in their preferred geographical location, even if it is remote from the main office. The advances in wireless technology enable people to work in an airport, at a customer site, while walking, and so on.

Outsourcing and Strategic Alliances.   To become more competitive, organizations are examining which work they should perform internally and which they should give to others. *Outsourcing*, having a third party perform information work for you, may be a simple contract for services or a long-term strategic alliance. Between these two extremes are a variety of relationships that are redefining the way organizations work together. The thinking is: We should focus on what we do best and outsource the other functions to people who specialize in them to make us more world-class in all our functions. The result is becoming known as the *extended enterprise*. IT is providing the information and communication means to manage complex sets of relationships.

Demise of Hierarchy.   In the traditional hierarchy, people performing the same type of work are grouped together and overseen by a supervisor. The supervisor allocates the work, handles problems, enforces discipline, issues rewards, provides training, and so on. Management principles such as division of labor and chain of command define this traditional work environment.

This structure is no longer best in many instances. Self-managed groups, whether working on an assembly line or in an insurance company, provide much of their own management. They have lower absenteeism, yield higher productivity, produce higher quality work, and are more motivated than workers in traditional settings.

A major reason for the demise of hierarchy is that the more turbulent business environment—represented by the changes just noted—challenges the premises of a hierarchical structure because it cannot cope with rapid change. Hierarchies require a vertical chain of command where lines of responsibility do not cross and approval to proceed on major initiatives is granted from above. This communication up and down the chain of command can take too much time in today's environment. IT enables team-based organizational structures by facilitating rapid and far-flung communication.

Goals of the New Work Environment

As a result of these changes in the internal and external organizational environment, enterprises around the world are redefining their work environment—a tumultuous proposition, at best—without any true guidance. We see the following overarching goals for thriving in the new work environment:

- Leverage knowledge globally
- Organize for complexity
- Work electronically
- Handle continuous and discontinuous change

Leverage Knowledge Globally.   Knowledge is now being called *intellectual capital* to signify its importance. This is not the knowledge in an expert system or a Lotus Notes database, but rather the knowledge in people's heads. Knowledge that people know but cannot really explain to others is called *tacit knowledge*, as opposed to explicit explainable knowledge. Companies that are able to leverage tacit knowledge globally will be successful—provided, of course, its use is directed by a sound strategy.

Brook Manville and Nathaniel Foote of McKinsey & Company[4] point out that knowledge-based strategies begin with strategy, not knowledge. Intellectual capital is meaningless unless companies have the corporate fundamentals in place, such as knowing what kind of value they want to provide and to whom.

They also point out that executing a knowledge-based strategy is not about managing knowledge but about nurturing people who have the knowledge, tapping into the knowledge that is locked in their experience. Although companies have numerous systems in place to share explicit knowledge, the key to unlocking tacit knowledge is a work environment in which people want to share. A manufacturer that tried to foster greater knowledge transfer while downsizing discovered that the combination was impossible. Why would employees share what they know when the bosses were looking for ways to consolidate expertise?

The means to tap tacit knowledge is to foster sharing and to support the sharing with technology. E-mail and groupware can provide the interconnection, but the driving force is the culture. When people want to share, they form *worknets*—informal groups whose collective knowledge is used to accomplish a specific task. The sharing and leveraging of knowledge happens through organizational "pull"—people needing help from others to solve a problem—rather than organizational "push," which overloads people with information. Therefore, leveraging knowledge is all about raising the aspirations of each individual, say Manville and Foote.

Organize for Complexity.   A second overarching goal of companies, whether they recognize it or not, is to be able to handle complexity. Why? One reason is that the world has become so interconnected that simple solutions no longer solve a problem. Another reason is that issues are systemic. Corporate decisions can have an environmental impact, a human resources impact, an economic impact, and even an ethical impact. Furthermore, capturing marketshare oftentimes requires allying with others who have complementary expertise. Alliances increase complexity; so does specialization. Have you bought shampoo, crackers, or tires lately? These used to be fairly straightforward decisions. Today, the choices are so numerous that consumers can spend an inordinate amount of time making a selection. To thrive in such an age, companies need to be organized to be able to handle complexity.

Work Electronically.   Just as the marketplace is moving to the market*space*, the workplace is moving to the work*space*. Taking advantage of the Internet, and networks in general, is a third major goal of enterprises these days. But just as the move from horse and buggy to train to automobile to jet plane each was not simply a change in speed, but a change in kind, so, too, is the move to working in a space rather than a place a change in kind. It requires different organizing principles, management tenets, compensation schemes, organizational structures, and such. It also changes how organizations interact with others, such as their customers.

George Gilder,[5] columnist and author, noted that business eras are defined by the plummeting price of the key factor of production. During the industrial era, this key factor was horsepower, as defined in kilowatt hours. It dropped from many dollars to 7.5 cents. For the past 40 years, the driving force of economic growth has been transistors, translated into millions of instructions per second (MIPS) and bits of semiconductor memory. The latter has fallen 68 percent a year, from $7 per bit to a millionth of a cent. Gilder thinks that we are now at yet another "historic cliff of cost" in a new factor of production, bandwidth. "If you thought the price of computing dropped rapidly in the last decade, just wait until you see what happens with communications bandwidth," said Gilder, referencing a remark by Andy Grove, CEO of Intel.

MIPS and bits have been used to compensate for the limited availability of bandwidth. The microchip moved power *within* companies, allowing people to vastly increase their ability to master bodies of specialized learning. Microchips both flattened corporations and launched new corporations. Bandwidth, on the other hand, moves power all the way to consumers. That is the big revolution of the Internet, Gilder contends, and the reason behind the move to relationship marketing with consumers.

In an era of bandwidth abundance, the economy changes. For example, TV is based on a top-down hierarchical model with a few broadcast stations (transmitters) and millions of passive broadcast receivers (televisions). The result is "lowest-common-denominator" entertainment from Hollywood. The Internet, on the other hand, is a "first-choice" culture, much like a bookstore. You walk in and get your first-choice book. First-choice culture is vastly different from lowest-common-denominator culture, says Gilder. As the Internet spreads, the culture will move from what we have in common to one in which our aspirations, hobbies, and interests are manifested.

Handle Continuous and Discontinuous Change.   Finally, to keep up, companies will need to innovate continually—something most have generally not been organized to do. Continual innovation, however, does not mean continuously steady innovation. Innovation occurs in fits and starts. Change takes two forms: continuous change (the kind espoused by total quality management techniques) or discontinuous change (the kind espoused by reengineering). When a product or process is just fine, but needs some tuning, continuous change improves its efficiency. However, when it is not fine, discontinuous change is needed to move to an entirely new way of working. The two often form a cycle. Companies need to be able to handle both for their products and processes.

These four major goals underlie the new work environment. This organizational environment sets the backdrop for exploring the emerging technology environment.

THE TECHNOLOGY ENVIRONMENT

The technology environment enables advances in organizational performance. The two have a symbiotic relationship; IT and organizational improvements coevolve. IT evolution can be described using the four traditional areas of hardware, software, data, and communication.

Hardware Trends

In the 1950s and 1960s, the main hardware concerns of data processing managers were machine efficiency and tracking new technological developments. Batch processing was predominant; online systems emerged later. At that time, hardware was centralized, often in large showcase data centers behind glass walls.

In the mid-1970s, processing power began to move out of the central site, but only at the insistence of users who bought their own departmental minicomputers and word processors. In the 1980s, mainly due to the advent of personal computers (PCs), this trend accelerated far beyond the expectations of most people, especially IS managers.

Now this trend is well established. Client-server computing forms the underlying structure. A *client* machine on the desktop, a laptop, or a handheld provides the user interface, and a *server* on the network holds the data and applications. This same client-server model is used for interacting with the Web.

The major development in hardware toward mobile and handheld devices is led by two factions: telecommunications companies (and the cell phone manufacturers that serve them) and handheld computer manufacturers, such as Palm and Microsoft. Functionality is expanding with devices handling both voice and data. Use of wireless hardware has become the norm for the anytime-anyplace workforce.

These hardware trends are further distributing processing beyond organizational boundaries to suppliers and customers. The result is the movement of enterprisewide hardware and processing power out of the control—although perhaps still under the guidance—of the IS organization.

Software Trends

The dominant issue in software and programming in the 1960s was how to improve the productivity of in-house programmers—those who created mainly transaction processing systems. Occasionally, IS management discussed using outside services, such as time-sharing services, application packages, and contract programming from independent software houses. The software industry was still underdeveloped, though, so application development remained the purview of IS managers.

Later, programming issues centered first around modular and structured programming techniques. Then the topic expanded to life cycle development methodologies and software engineering, with the goals of introducing more rigorous project management techniques and getting users more involved in early stages of development. Eventually, prototyping (quick development of a mock-up) became popular.

Then two other software trends appeared. One, purchased software became a viable alternative to in-house development for many traditional, well-defined systems. Two, IS managers began to pay attention to applications other than transaction processing. Software to support decision support systems (DSS), report generation, and database inquiry shifted some programming from professional programmers to end users.

During the 1990s, the push for open systems was driven primarily by software purchasers who were tired of being locked in to proprietary software (or hardware). The open systems movement continues to demand that different products work together, that is, *interoperate*. Vendors initially accommodated this demand with hardware and software black boxes that performed the necessary interface conversions, but the cost of this approach is lower efficiency.

Another major trend in the 1990s was toward enterprise resource planning (ERP) systems, which tightly integrate various functions of an enterprise so that management can see cross-enterprise financial figures and order and manufacturing volumes. Some firms implemented ERP to replace legacy systems that were not Y2K compliant (i.e., the systems would think that an "02" would mean 1902 rather than 2002). Implementing ERP involves integrating components, which is called systems integration, rather than application development. Implementation has been expensive and troublesome, especially for companies wanting to modify the ERP software to fit their unique processes. However, for many large corporations, their ERP system has become their foundation information system, in essence, defining their IT architecture.

Like hardware, software is becoming more network-centric. Rather than replace legacy systems, many companies are adding Web front ends to broaden access to the systems to employees, customers, and suppliers. Companies are establishing corporate portals where employees log into their company intranet to use software housed at that site. This approach moves the software from being decentralized (on PCs) to being centralized (on a server somewhere).

Another change in software is the move to Web Services. Web Services are packages of code that each perform a specific function and have a URL (Uniform Resource Locator; an address on the Internet) so that they can be located via the Internet to fulfill a request. For example, if you have accessed FedEx's Web site to track a package, you have used a Web Service. MacAfee's virus protection also is delivered to PCs using a Web Services approach. The software industry is morphing into a Web Services industry.

The significance of Web Services is that it moves software and programming to being truly network-centric; the network becomes the heart of the system, linking all Web Services. Packages of code can be concatenated to produce highly tailored and quickly changed processes. In the past, once software was programmed to handle a process in a specific way, it essentially cast that process in electronic concrete because the process could not change until the software was modified. The tenet of Web Services is that a process is defined at the time it is executed, because each Web Service decides at that time which of its many options to use to answer the current request. The world of Web Services entails its own jargon, standards, and products. Importantly, it builds on the past—functions in legacy systems can be packaged to become Web Services.

Data Trends

The evolution of the third core information technology area—data—has been particularly interesting. At first, discussions centered around file management and techniques for organizing files to serve individual applications. Then generalized file management systems emerged for managing corporate data files. This more generalized approach led to the concept of corporate databases to serve several applications, followed a few years later by the concept of establishing a data administration function to manage these databases.

In the 1970s, the interest in data turned to technical solutions for managing data—database management systems. As work progressed, it became evident that a key element of these products was their data dictionary. Dictionaries now store far more than data definitions; they store information about relationships between systems, sources and uses of data, time cycle requirements, and so on.

For the first 20 years of information processing, discussions about data concerned techniques to manage data in a centralized environment. It was not until the advent of fourth-generation languages and PCs that interest in letting employees directly access corporate data began. Then users demanded it.

In addition to distributing data, the major trend in the early 1990s was expanding the focus from data resources to information resources, both internal and external to the firm. Data management organizes internal facts into data record format. Information management, on the other hand, focuses on concepts (such as ideas found in documents, especially digital documents such as Web pages) from both internal and external sources. Thus, *information resources* encompass digitized media, including voice, video, graphics, animation, and photographs.

Managing this expanded array of information resources requires new technologies. Data warehousing has arisen to store huge amounts of historical data from such systems as retailers' point-of-sale systems. Data mining uses advanced statistical techniques to explore data warehouses to look for previously unknown relationships in the data, such as which clusters of customers are most profitable. Similarly, massive amounts of document-based information are organized into document repositories and analyzed with document mining techniques. In addition, as noted earlier, businesses now emphasize intellectual capital management. Some believe knowledge can reside in machines; others believe it only resides in people's heads. Either way, knowledge management is of major importance in the new economy because intangibles hold competitive value.

The Web has, of course, broadened the term *data* to mean "content," which encompasses text, graphics, animation, maps, photos, film clips, and such. Initially, Web content was managed by the content creators, such as marketing departments. However, with the huge proliferation of sites, enterprises realized they needed to rein in all the exuberance in order to standardize formats, promote their brands in a common manner, establish refresh cycles for their content, and create approval and archival processes. Content management has become very important, and as one manager observed, it is a lot like running a newspaper.

Two major data issues now facing CIOs are security (protecting data from those who should not see it) and privacy (safeguarding the personal data of employees and customers). Furthermore, regulations (such as the Sarbanes-Oxley Act in the United States) now require company officers to verify their financial data. Because the processes that handle financial data are undoubtedly automated, CIOs need to document and ensure the accuracy of these processes. Thus, numerous aspects of data safeguarding have become important.

Communications Trends

The final core information technology is telecommunications. This area has experienced enormous change and has now taken center stage. Early use of data communications dealt with online and time-sharing systems. Then interest in both public and private (intracompany) data networks blossomed.

Telecommunications opened up new uses of information systems, and thus it became an integral component of IS management. Communications-based information systems were used to link organizations with their suppliers and customers. In the early 1980s, a groundswell of interest surrounded interorganizational systems, because some provided strategic advantage. Also during the 1980s, the use of local area networks (LANs) to interconnect PCs began. PCs started out as stand-alone devices, but that only took advantage of their computing capabilities. It soon became clear that they had communication capabilities as well, so companies jammed even more wires in their wiring ducts to connect desktops to each other and then to the corporate data center.

Until the Internet appeared, enterprises leased lines from telecommunications carriers to create wide area networks (WANs) that linked their offices and factories. The only publicly available telecommunication system was the voice telephone system. Transmitting data from PCs in small offices that did not have leased lines generally entailed using a modem to dial-up a computer at another site.

The Internet changed all that. Internet Service Providers (ISPs) appeared seemingly overnight to provide PC users with a local number for dialing into the Internet to search the Web, converse in a chat room, play text-based games, send e-mail, and transfer files. The Internet provided for data the equivalent of the worldwide voice network. Today, the Internet's protocol has become the worldwide standard for LANs and WANs. In fact, it will soon be the standard for voice as well.

The latest development in telecommunications technology is wireless—wireless long distance, wireless local loops (the last-mile connection of a home or office), wireless LANs (increasingly handled by Wi-Fi technology), and even wireless personal area networks (PANs). Wireless does not just enable mobility; it changes why people communicate, how they live, and how they work. It is a paradigm shift, and we are in the early days of wireless.

THE MISSION OF IS ORGANIZATIONS

With the organizational and IT environments as backdrops, we now turn to the mission of the IS organization. In the early days, transaction processing systems acted as "paperwork factories" to pay employees, bill customers, ship products, and so on. During that era, the performance of the IS organization was defined by efficiency (or productivity) measures such as the percentage of uptime for the computer, throughput (number of transactions processed per day), and the number of lines of program code written per week.

Later, during the MIS era, the focus of IS departments shifted to producing reports for "management by exception" or summary reports for all levels of management. This era gave us the classic IS objective to "get the right information to the right person at the right time." In this era, IS was judged on effectiveness measures (in addition to the efficiency measures of the previous era).

For today's environment, the mission of IS organizations has broadened to the following:

To improve the performance of people in organizations through the use of IT.

The objective is improvement of the enterprise, not IS, so, ideally, IS performance is based on business outcomes and business results. IT is but one contributor to improving enterprise performance. This book focuses on the resources used by IS organizations.

A SIMPLE MODEL

We propose a simple model to describe the IS function in organizations. Figure 1-2 represents the process of applying IT to accomplish useful work. On the left is the technology, and on the right are the users who put it to work. The arrow represents the process of translating users' needs into systems that fill that need. In the early days of IT, this translation was performed almost entirely by systems analysts.

Figure 1-3 is a simple representation of what has happened over the past 50 years. Technology has become increasingly complex and powerful; uses have become increasingly sophisticated. Information systems are now viewed as system *products* and users have become *customers*. The increased distance between the two boxes represents the increasingly complex process of specifying, developing, and delivering these system products. It is no longer feasible for one system analyst to understand the fine points of all the technologies needed in an application as well as the nuances of the application. More specialization is required of systems professionals to bridge this wider gap.

Systems professionals are not the only ones who can help bridge this gap between the technology and its users. Technology has become sophisticated enough to be used by many employees and consumers. At the same time, they are becoming increasingly computer literate; many employees even develop their own applications. Figure 1-4 depicts this trend. Today, some of the technology is truly user-friendly, and some applications, such as Web page development, database mining, and spreadsheet manipulation, are handled by non-IT staff. Transaction systems, however, are still developed by professional developers, either inside or outside the firm.

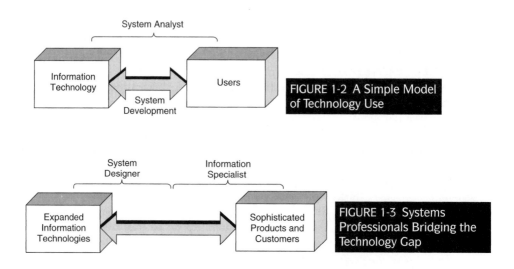

FIGURE 1-2 A Simple Model of Technology Use

FIGURE 1-3 Systems Professionals Bridging the Technology Gap

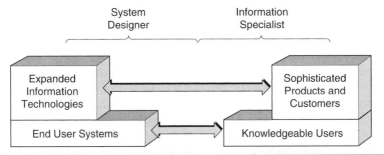

FIGURE 1-4 Users Bridging the Technology Gap

The main point of this discussion is that technology is getting more complex, applications are becoming more sophisticated, and users are participating more heavily in the development of applications. The net result is that management of the process is becoming more complex and difficult as its importance increases.

A BETTER MODEL

Expanding the simple model gives us more guidance into managerial principles and tasks. We suggest a model with four principal elements:

1. A set of technologies that represent the IT infrastructure installed and managed by the IS department
2. A set of users who need to use IT to improve their job performance
3. A delivery mechanism for developing, delivering, and installing applications
4. Executive leadership to manage the entire process of applying the technology to achieve organizational objectives and goals

Let us look more carefully at each of these elements.

The Technologies

Several forces contribute to the increased importance and complexity of IT. One, of course, is the inexorable growth in computing and communications capacity accompanied by significant reductions in cost and size of computers and telecommunications components. Another is the merging of the previously separate technologies of computers, telephones/telecom/cable TV, office equipment, and consumer electronics. Still a third contributor is the ability to store and handle multiple forms of data—including voice, image, and graphics—and integrate them, resulting in multimedia. Here is a brief list of some rapidly growing technology areas:

- Handheld wireless devices and multifunction cell phones
- Web Services

- Wireless networks
- Convergence of voice, data, and video
- Integration of consumer electronics and IT

These technologies form products that are useful to employees, customers, suppliers, and consumers. No longer relegated primarily to automating transactions, information systems now fill major roles in management reporting, problem solving and analysis, distributed office support, customer service, and communications. In fact, most activities of information workers are supported in some way by IT; the same is becoming true of suppliers, customers, business trading partners, and consumers.

The Users

As IT becomes pervasive, user categories expand. The users of electronic data processing and MIS once were relatively easy to identify; they were inside the company. These systems performed clear-cut processes in specific ways. Now, though, many people want open-ended systems that allow them to create their own processes on the fly. They want systems that act as a tool, not dictate how to perform a task.

If we concentrate only on business use of IT, one helpful dichotomy divides the activities of information workers into two: procedure-based activities and knowledge-based (or goal-based) activities. The value of this model is that it focuses on the important characteristics of information workers—their job procedures and knowledge—rather than on the type of data (e.g., numbers versus text) or the business function (production versus sales), or even job title (managerial versus professional).

Procedure-based activities are large-volume transactions, where each transaction has a relatively low cost or value. The activities are well defined; therefore, the principal performance measure is efficiency (units processed per unit of resource spent). For a procedure-based task, the information worker is told what to accomplish and the steps to follow. Procedure-based activities mainly handle data.

Knowledge-based activities, on the other hand, handle fewer transactions, and each one has higher value. These activities, which can be accomplished in various ways, must therefore be measured by results, that is, attainment of objectives or goals. Therefore, the information worker must understand the goals because part of the job is figuring out how to attain them. Knowledge-based activities are based on handling concepts, not data. Figure 1-5 summarizes these two kinds of information-based work, giving several examples from banking.

Some authors use the words *clerical* and *managerial* to refer to these two types of activities. Looking at the attributes, however, it is clear that managers often do procedure-based work, and many former procedure-based jobs now have knowledge-based components. Furthermore, the distinction between manager and worker is blurring.

The most important benefit of this dichotomy is that it reveals how much of a firm's information processing efforts have been devoted to procedure-based activities, which is understandable because computers are process engines that naturally support process-driven activities. As important as they are, though, it is clear that

Procedure Based	*Knowledge Based*
• High volume of transactions	• Low volume of transactions
• Low cost (value) per transaction	• High value (cost) per transaction
• Well-structured procedures	• Ill-structured procedures
• Output measures defined	• Output measures less defined
• Focus on process	• Focus on problems and goals
• Focus on efficiency	• Focus on effectiveness
• Handling of data	• Handling of concepts
• Predominantly clerical workers	• Managers and professionals
• Examples	• Examples
Back office	Loan department
Mortgage servicing	Asset/liability management
Payroll processing	Planning department
Check processing	Corporate banking

FIGURE 1-5 A Dichotomy of Information Work

procedure-based activities are the wave of the past. The wave of the future is applying IT to knowledge-based activities. For the task "pay employees" or "bill customers," the system analyst can identify the best sequence of steps. On the other hand, the task "improve sales in the Asian market" has no best process. People handling the latter work need a variety of support systems to leverage their knowledge, contacts, plans, and efforts.

System Development and Delivery

In our model, system development and delivery bridge the gap between technology and users, but systems for procedure-based activities differ from systems for knowledge-based information work.

The left side of Figure 1-6 shows the set of technologies that form the IT infrastructure. Organizations build systems on these technology resources to support both procedure-based and knowledge-based activities. The three main categories, called *essential technologies*, are computer hardware and software, communication networks, and information resources. We call the management of them *infrastructure management*, which includes operations, that is, keeping the systems that use these technologies up and running.

The right side of Figure 1-6 shows the two kinds of information work: procedure based and knowledge based. These two categories are not distinct or separate, of course, but it is helpful to keep their major differences in mind because they lead to different approaches, and frequently different teams, in the bridging of systems development and delivery.

In between the technologies and the information workers is the work of developing and delivering both procedure-based systems and support systems.

IS Management

The fourth component of this book's model is executive leadership. IT leadership comes from a chief information officer (CIO) who must be high enough in the enterprise to influence organizational goals and have enough credibility to lead the harnessing of the technology to pursue those goals. However, the CIO, as the top technology executive,

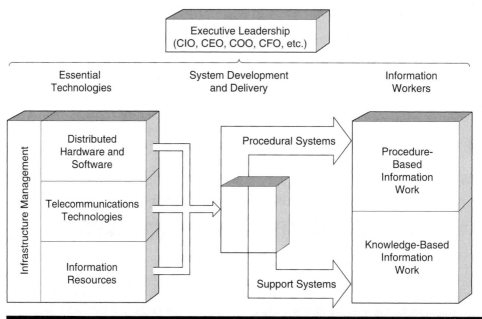

FIGURE 1-6 A Framework for IS Management

does not perform the leadership role alone, because IT has become too important to enterprise success to be left to one individual. Thus, CIOs work with their business peers, C-level executives—CEO, COO, CFO—and the heads of major functional areas and business units. The technology is becoming so fundamental and enabling that this executive team must work together to govern and leverage it well.

To summarize, this model of the IS function has four major components:

1. The technology, which provides the electronic and information infrastructure for the enterprise

2. Information workers in organizations, who use IT to accomplish their work goals

3. The system development and delivery function, which brings the technology and users together

4. The management of the IS function, with the overall responsibility of harnessing IT to improve the performance of the people and the organization

ORGANIZATION OF THIS BOOK

This book is designed to meet the needs of IS executives—current ones and students who could become IS executives in the future. The organization of the book corresponds to the major parts of Figure 1-6.

- Part I (Chapters 2 through 4) deals with the strategic issues that are the responsibility of the top systems executive—the CIO—and the IT governing boards established by the organization. Chapter 2 deals with the evolution of the IS function and the CIO's job. Chapter 3 looks at strategic uses of IT. Chapter 4 treats the subject of IS planning.

- Part II (Chapters 5 through 8) deals with the management of the essential information technologies (the left side of Figure 1-6). The chapters discuss, in turn, the distributed systems architecture that now dominates computing, building and managing telecommunications, managing corporate information resources, and managing day-to-day operations.

- Part III contains two chapters that deal with developing and delivering systems, primarily procedure-based systems. Chapter 9 describes the evolution of system development, tools and approaches, the trend toward system integration, and the growth of Internet-based development. Chapter 10 discusses important issues in managing system development and delivery.

- Part IV consists of three chapters that discuss different types of systems that support knowledge work. Chapter 11 looks at using IT to support decision making. Chapter 12 discusses systems that support collaborative work. Chapter 13 looks at supporting knowledge work.

- Part V, the final chapter of the book, looks to the future.

To illustrate how one IS organization has evolved over the years, following is the case of MeadWestvaco. The story begins with the first edition of this book, in 1985. The evolution of the case study to the present seventh edition mirrors the changes that have taken place in many IS organizations over the past 20 years.

CASE EXAMPLE

MEADWESTVACO CORPORATION

MeadWestvaco, with headquarters in Stamford, Connecticut, is an $8-billion company that produces specialty and coated paper, packages specialty chemicals, and manufactures consumer and office products. It owns and manages some 3 million acres of forest using sustainable forestry practices. The company operates in 33 countries, has about 30,000 employees around the world, and serves customers in approximately 100 nations.

Mead Corporation and Westvaco, two comparably-sized forest products companies, merged in early 2002 to form

MeadWestvaco Corporation. This case study begins in 1985 and follows the evolution of Mead's IT function up to the present time, in its newly merged form. The IT organization has remained in Dayton, Ohio, the former headquarters of Mead Corporation.

THE 1960s AND 1970s: DECENTRALIZE SOME FUNCTIONS

In the 1960s, Mead's corporate information services (CIS) department provided

(Case Continued)

all divisions with data processing services. By 1967, the department's budget had grown so large that management decided to spin off some of the functions to the divisions. Divisions could establish their own data processing and process engineering groups or they could continue to purchase data processing services from CIS. Many of the divisions did establish their own IS departments, but all continued to use the corporate data center for their corporate applications. In the late 1970s, the CIS department had six groups, as illustrated in Figure 1-7. The director reported to the vice president of operations services. The six groups under the director were:

- *Computer Operations* to manage the corporate data center

- *Telecommunications* to design the telecommunications network and establish standards
- *Technical Services* to provide and maintain systems software
- *Developmental Systems* to handle traditional system development
- *Operational Systems* to maintain systems after they become operational
- *Operations Research* to perform management science analysis

THE 1980s: FOCUS ON END USER COMPUTING

In 1980, management realized that its CIS organizational structure would not serve the needs of the rapidly growing

---

FIGURE 1-7 Mead Corporation's Pre-1980 Information Services Department

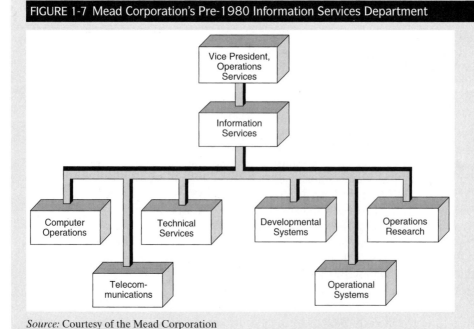

Source: Courtesy of the Mead Corporation

(Case Continued)

end user community. Furthermore, to become an "electronic-based" organization, Mead needed a corporatewide network. Therefore, the department reorganized, as shown in Figure 1-8, so that the director of corporate information resources (CIR) reported directly to the company president. This change signaled the increased importance of information resources to Mead.

CIR was responsible for creating hardware, software, and communication standards for the entire corporation; it ran the corporate data center; and it operated the network. All the divisions used the network and corporate data center, and they followed the corporate standards; some operated their own small, distributed systems as well, which linked into the corporate network. The

FIGURE 1-8 Mead Corporation's 1980s Information Services Department

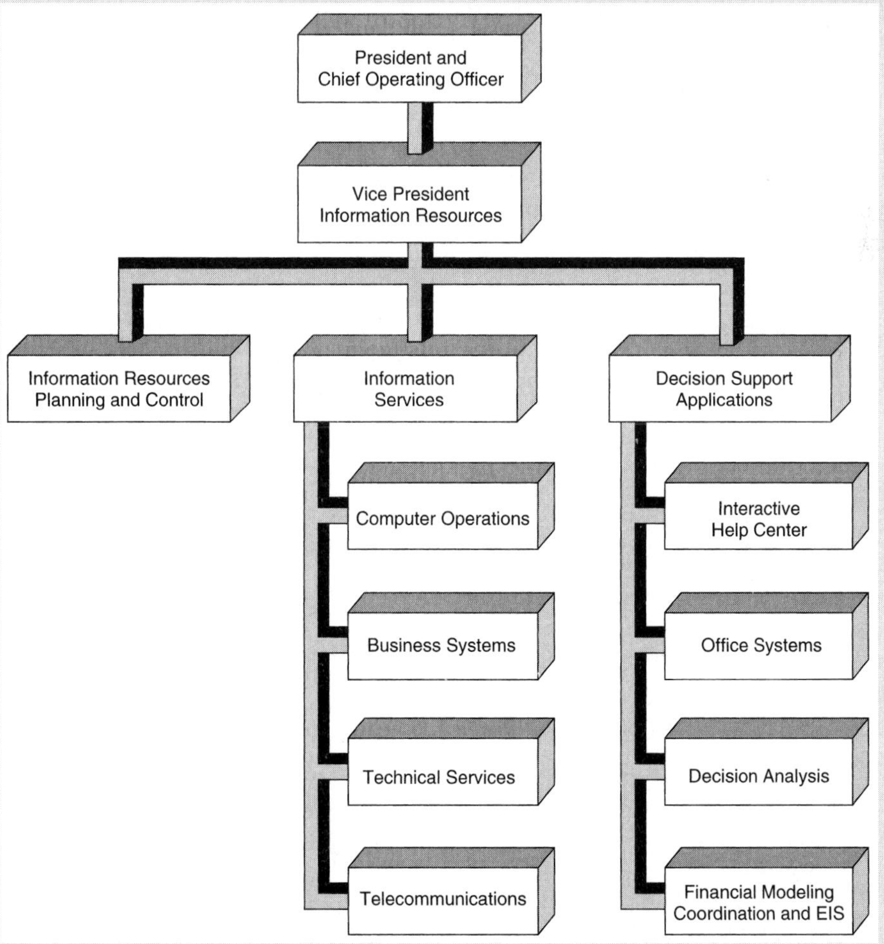

Source: Courtesy of the Mead Corporation

(Case Continued)

three departments within the new group were as follows.

Information Resources Planning and Control was responsible for planning future information systems and technology. This department grew out of the company's strong planning culture. The decentralization in the 1970s highlighted the need for a coordinating IT body. Although it was small, it had two important roles. First, it took the corporate perspective for IT planning to ensure that Mead's IT plans meshed with its business plans. Second, it acted as planning coordinator, helping various groups and divisions coordinate their plans with corporate and CIR plans.

Information Services was responsible for most of the traditional IS functions from the old information services department—companywide telecommunications support, data center operations, development of corporatewide systems, database administration, system software support, and technical support for end user computing.

Most divisions developed their own applications, following the guidelines created by this department. The IS steering committee—composed of the president and group vice presidents—established a policy that applications should be transportable among the various computing centers and accessible from any Mead terminal. The company's telecommunications network established the guidelines for making this interconnection possible.

Decision Support Applications (DSA) provided all end user computing support for the company. At the time of the reorganization, DSA had no users, no products, no common applications among multiple locations, and only five staff members in operations research and two in office

systems support. By 1985, they were serving 1,500 users in some 30 Mead locations with 10 staff members. DSA offered 14 products and 8 corporate-wide applications through the following 4 groups:

- *Interactive help center* provided hotline support and evaluated new end user computing products.
- *Office systems* supported the dedicated word processing systems and IBM's Professional Office System (PROFS), which Mead used as the gateway to end user computing. Divisions were free to select any office system, but most followed the recommendations of this group to ensure corporatewide interconnection.
- *Decision analysis* built a number of companywide decision support systems, such as a corporate budgeting model and a graphics software system. It also used operations research tools to develop linear programming models and simulations for users needing such sophisticated analysis tools.
- *Financial modeling coordination and EIS* was in charge of Mead's integrated financial system. It also supported executive computing through IBM PCs used by corporate executives and an executive information system (EIS) accessed through PROFS.

LATE 1980s: ADJUST THE STRUCTURE

The 1980 reorganization separated the more people-oriented activities under DSA from the more technical activities

(Case Continued)

under the information services department. The technology was better managed, and relations with users improved. However, this split caused two problems. The first was that traditional programmers and systems analysts felt that DSA received all the new and exciting development work. The second problem was coordinating the two departments. A matrix arrangement evolved to handle both problems, with both information services and DSA people staffing most projects.

The departmental structure implemented in 1980 remained essentially intact throughout the 1980s with only two major changes. In early 1988, the vice president of information resources began reporting to Mead's chairman and CEO. Second, the DSA group was reorganized, as shown in Figure 1-9.

FIGURE 1-9 Mead Corporation's 1989 Corporate Information Resources Group

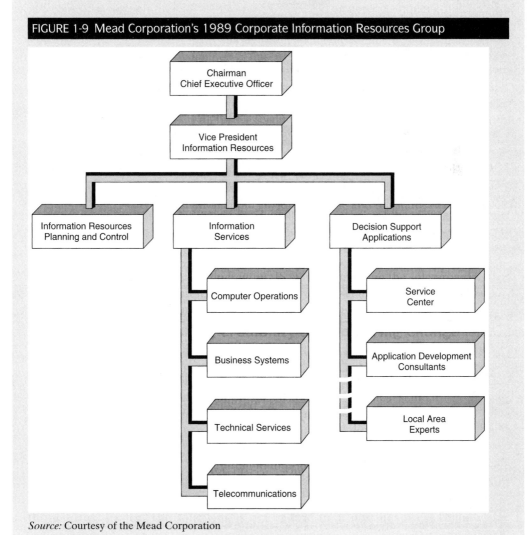

Source: Courtesy of the Mead Corporation

(Case Continued)

As users became more sophisticated and less generic, the department created small groups with expertise in specific areas. By the end of the 1980s, they were supporting more than 5,000 users corporatewide in three ways:

- The *service center* continued to introduce new users to technology and provide telephone hotline assistance to experienced users.

- The *application development consultants* helped users develop more sophisticated applications and guided maintenance of user-written applications, which had become a noticeable problem. They also updated traditional applications to permit end user systems to access the data.

- The *local area experts* worked in the functional departments supporting users in their area. They reported directly to their area manager and indirectly to CIR. Due to the growing number of user-written applications, they, too, helped users keep their applications up-to-date.

During the 1980s, Mead found its end user computing focus shifting from introducing new technology to making more effective use of the technology in place. By the end of the decade, Mead was concentrating on harvesting its investment in IT by using it as a lever to change the way it was doing business.

1990: LEVERAGE THE IT INFRASTRUCTURE

In 1990, CIR underwent another reorganization to bring it in line with a new strategy. We first discuss the reorganization, then the strategy.

Management realized that the end user systems and large-scale business systems needed to cross-pollinate each other. Users needed one place to go for help; therefore, application development was placed in one group, which was renamed *information services*, as shown in Figure 1-10.

The emphasis of the reorganization was to strengthen Mead's mainframe-based infrastructure that the corporatewide network depended on. Although the network had been created in 1983, its value in connecting Mead to vendors and customers had not been recognized until the late 1980s. Therefore, in 1990, CIR created a new group—network services—to handle computer operations, technical services, and telecommunications. The 1990 reorganization also consolidated administrative functions (such as chargeback) into the technology planning and control group.

Although the 1990 reorganization did not add any new functions, it shifted emphasis from end user computing to building an infrastructure and integrating development of all sizes of applications.

1990 Strategy

In the early 1980s, Mead installed its first information resources business plan, which emphasized networking and end user computing. By the late 1980s, the objectives had been accomplished. In hindsight, management realized the 1980 plan had been a technology plan, not a business plan, because its goal had been to get control of IT. Having accomplished this goal, Mead decided to create a true business plan, one that addressed employing its IT resources.

(Case Continued)

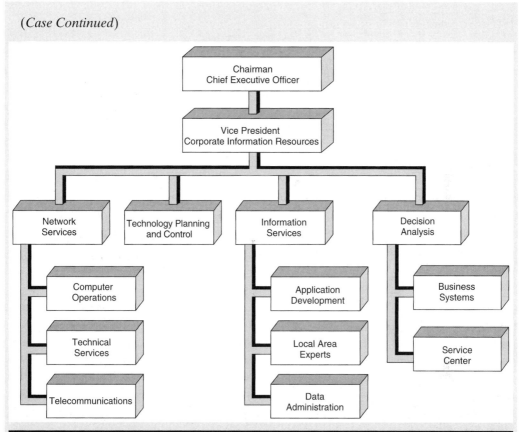

FIGURE 1-10 Mead Corporation's 1990 Corporate Information Resources Group

Source: Courtesy of the Mead Corporation

Using the two-by-two matrix shown in Figure 1-11, management realized that Mead had only been building systems that fit into the lower-right quadrant—systems to support traditional products and internal business processes. Rather than focus on company operations, management decided to shift emphasis in two directions: (1) toward reengineering company operations and (2) toward using IT to work better with suppliers and customers.

Business process reengineering—that is, significantly restructuring the internal operations in a business—became a major

strategic direction, with the companywide network playing a key role. Because IT removes many time and distance barriers associated with business processes, Mead decided to use IT to build new processes rather than simply accelerate existing ones.

One of the major processes carved out to be recentralized and reengineered was purchasing. The reengineering group discovered, for example, that 240 people handled accounts payable, mainly reconciling mismatches between goods received and purchase orders. By reengineering purchasing, the need for such

(Case Continued)

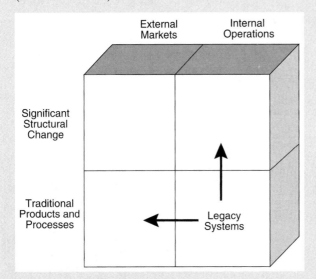

FIGURE 1-11 Mead Corporation's Strategic Opportunities Framework

Source: Courtesy of the Mead Corporation

reconciliations was eliminated. Mead outsourced the function while developing the new purchasing system.

Putting in the corporate purchasing system was Mead's first big venture into reengineering. The company learned a lot from that experience. It also accomplished something few others had achieved: standard part numbers for all 800,000 MRO (maintenance, repair, and operations) parts. This excruciating data cleansing exercise was done so that Mead could automatically consolidate parts orders from all 10 divisions and reap larger discounts due to the higher volumes. The result was large savings.

The second emphasis involved doing business electronically by extending current business processes and products to suppliers and customers. The motto was: "It is easy to do business with us," meaning that customers could specify the transaction format they wished to use, from electronic data interchange (EDI) for application-to-application transactions across company boundaries to terminals at customer sites linked to Mead's computers to the telephone using voice response. In essence, Mead installed various front-ends on its mainframe applications. For the purchasing system, Mead went to major parts suppliers and required them to use EDI as a condition of selling to Mead. The system was fully automatic. If a part was in stock, it was supplied; if not, an order was generated.

Thus, the basic strategy set forth in 1980 remained in force in 1990—to retain central control of the IT infrastructure and distribute responsibility for building and maintaining applications in the operating divisions. As the uses of IT changed, CIR reorganized to focus on those new uses: end user computing in the 1980s, business reengineering and customer-oriented systems in 1990.

THE 1990s: IMPLEMENT VISION 2000

In 1993, CIR management recognized that client-server computing was a paradigm

(Case Continued)

shift in computing; therefore, Mead's mainframe-based structure would (at long last) need to be changed—and changed significantly. Thus, CIR launched Vision 2000 to develop a vision of what Mead computing and communications would look like in the year 2000.

Vision 2000 foresaw three tiers of computing: the mainframe, midrange servers, and desktops. Workstations were to be users' "window to the world" for information access, analysis, and communication. Interfaces, data, and applications would be at the appropriate level. Applications would be of three types: enterprisewide, division, and local; and they would use a global network that reached out beyond Mead.

CIR continued to focus on shared services (providing the infrastructure and supporting enterprise applications), whereas divisions would tailor systems to their customers and business. Users would not need to worry about where processing occurred, where data was housed, or how the mechanics of information processing were handled; CIR would handle all of these details. Data was to be viewed as a resource and managed accordingly, balancing access with integrity and security. Users would have greater geographic independence than in the past.

This vision is based on a demanding partnership in which the divisions buy into the infrastructure and its standards while CIR provides a flexible and responsive infrastructure.

CIR made the following five major assumptions when developing Vision 2000 in 1993:

1. The mainframe would continue to be the best platform for large-volume transaction systems or systems requiring massive computing power. In addition, it could become an enterprise server. This role was consistent with the adoption of an enterprisewide client-server architecture.

2. Integration of voice, image, video, and so on would occur at desktops, servers, and portable devices; therefore, higher-capacity networks would be needed to transmit and route these massive amounts of data.

3. Although unit costs of technology would continue to decline, overall IT usage at Mead would increase.

4. PCs presented a hidden cost that was at least as large as the visible IT costs.

5. Technology advancements would increase; therefore, the challenge was to balance the need for standards while keeping up with the pace of change.

New Organizational Structure

To implement Vision 2000, Mead had two organizational options. One was to set up a *skunk works* (a secret development group) to create the new infrastructure and systems. The other was to absorb the new client-server paradigm into CIR's organizational structure. CIR chose the latter; thus, the entire CIR group was reorganized to match the client-server model, as shown in Figure 1-12.

The core was the *Vision 2000 Project*, which was managed by a high-level CIR executive. Around this core was the technology layer of the CIR organization—the four core technologies that provided the IT infrastructure on which Mead

(*Case Continued*)

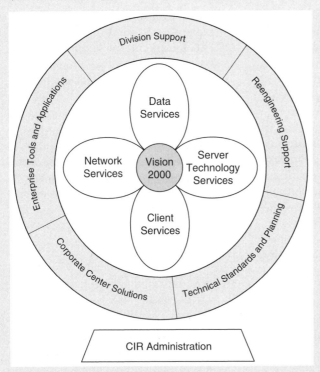

FIGURE 1-12 Mead Corpo-
ration's 1993 Corporate
Information Resources
Structure

Source: Courtesy of the Mead
Corporation

operated. *Data Services* provided data and information. *Server Technology Services* handled all servers on the network, from mainframes on down. *Client Services* handled all devices that customers touched, which included desktop workstations, fax machines, and telephones. CIR defined their customers as Mead employees as well as others who interfaced with Mead. *Network Services* handled everything that tied these other pieces together, both voice and data communications, as well as the Internet, intranet, gateways, firewalls, and interactions with their ISP.

All four groups reported to then vice president of CIR, John Langenbahn, who, by the way, has led Mead's IS department since the first edition of this book in 1985. All four groups had two jobs: (1) to run current operations and

(2) to build Vision 2000. Langenbahn noted that the move from mainframe to client-server shifted CIR from managing hundreds of components to managing thousands of them—an order-of-magnitude change.

On the outside layer of the organization chart, closer to the customer, were the application groups. To serve their constituencies, they drew on Vision 2000 and the IT infrastructure provided by the inner layers. *Division Support* supported the applications developed by Mead's 10 operating divisions. *Reengineering Support* was concerned with a few companywide business processes that had been recentralized and reengineered to improve efficiency and lower costs. These processes included Mead's financial systems and purchasing system, which did

(Case Continued)

not touch customers. *Enterprise Tools and Applications* provided a common desktop toolkit to all Mead staff, which consisted of hardware and a suite of software products, such as spreadsheet, e-mail, word processing, graphics, browser, EDI, and knowledge tools (such as Lotus Notes). *Corporate Center Solutions* handled application development and main-tenance of corporate applications. *Technical Standards and Planning* was a one-person think tank devoted to determining the standards that would underlie Vision 2000, whereas everyone else worked on the day-to-day issues. Finally, *CIR Administration*, shown beneath the circle, handled contracting and financials.

Like other companies, Mead encountered the typical staff problems of getting the mainframe staff to move into the client-server environment and getting new client-server talent to follow the discipline needed to develop enterprisewide systems.

Progress Made by 2000

The Internet had a large impact on Vision 2000 in that more and more of the vision was being served by it. For example, the vision foresaw storing lots of data on servers, so that CIR, not users, could handle backup. However, with so much information on the Internet, CIR did not need to acquire, install, or maintain as much public information as was originally planned. For instance, CIR had planned to install the U.S. telephone directory on a CD-ROM server. After it became available on the Internet, CIR simply added an icon to the standard desktop for quick access to the directory.

Mead learned that client-server computing was not cheaper than mainframe computing, as was touted in the early 1990s. In 1993, Mead placed the cost of a PC at $9,024 a year ($2,517 hard costs, $6,507 soft costs). With the Vision 2000 standards, Mead believed the soft costs had been cut to $3,005 a year.

The vision was conceived in 1993, implementation began at the end of 1994, and by 2000, right on schedule, the company rolled out 8,000 workstations. During that time, only one change was made to the organization structure: adding Vision Support Services to handle operations (Figure 1-13).

INTO THE 2000s: LEVERAGE CENTRALIZATION

The "leverage the infrastructure" viewpoint begun in 1990 persisted through the 1990s and was expected to yield significant business results in 2003 when Mead would have installed the SAP ERP system in all eight divisions to manage operations companywide. At that time, Mead would use one image of SAP to run the entire company. This accomplishment has been the goal of ERP since its inception in the early 1990s, but it is a vision that few companies have actually attained. By 2003, Mead would have spent $124 million dollars on the endeavor. The first division went live in late 1999, the second in 2000, and so on. Thus, from the 1960s to 2000, Mead's Information Resources division would have moved from significant decentralization to significant centralization of systems.

Implementing ERP

In the early 1990s, Mead looked at SAP, the leading ERP system, but decided that the software was not appropriate for the forest products industry. In 1995, Mead

(*Case Continued*)

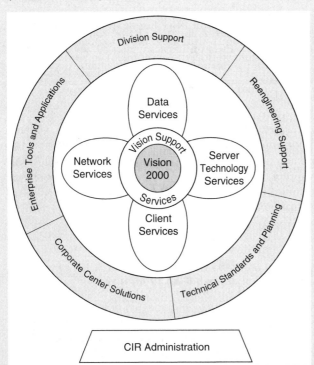

FIGURE 1-13 Mead Corpo-
ration's Current Corporate
Information Resources
Structure

Source: Courtesy of the Mead
Corporation

looked again, and although the software was better, management felt the company did not have the necessary companywide standards, so it declined to move forward on ERP again.

In 1997, though, management forced the issue. The company had increasingly been using a shared-services vision, where functions were taken out of divisions and centralized, making them best-of-breed. Logistics, purchasing, finance, and information resources were provided via shared services. This collaboration left the divisions with the customer-facing work. Management saw a train wreck coming once the first division wanted to install an ERP system. The company would then have to decide, "Do we want to be good at satisfying customers or have good shared services?" Management decided, "We have to do both." To do so, they had to put in the same ERP system companywide to leverage back-end shared services and be number one in customer satisfaction.

Mead spent 1998 determining the design of the enterprisewide system and began implementation in the first division in 1999. From the reengineering work on the purchasing system in the 1990s, Mead learned that significant company change required business leadership, thus the SAP effort was led by a business executive, and 70 of the 100 team members also came from the business; only 30 came from CIR. In addition, some 80 IBM consultants were involved. Mead chose IBM as its SAP implementation partner because IBM had helped Monsanto

(Case Continued)

implement SAP and had created the IBM/Monsanto Solution Center. Mead was able to draw on that center and Monsanto's experience and even reuse 80 percent of Monsanto's business design, down to the general ledger, giving Mead a running start. ERP implementations are huge and expensive, and many have failed. Mead avoided those pitfalls by learning from others.

Mead used the entire suite of SAP modules except human resources, which was handled by PeopleSoft; it was installed in the mid-1990s and has worked well. Mead was one of the first to install a recent module, Advanced Optimization Planning (AOP), which handles all planning and scheduling. SAP was originally designed to support build-to-inventory manufacturing, which is 60 percent of Mead's business. AOP is for the other 40 percent, which is build-to-order manufacturing.

Lotus Notes, a sophisticated database system from IBM and part of Vision 2000, was invaluable in providing the building blocks for defining the new ways of working under SAP. SAP required Mead to define 800 roles and describe the work flows and security flows among these roles. This task was not handled by SAP, so Mead used Lotus Notes for it and other SAP support work.

SAP unified the company, but it is a large and complex system. In addition, it requires strict adherence to its rules, which is its downside. A division can no longer tailor its own systems to meet its market's changing needs; in some instances, changes can be accommodated easily, but for major changes it must get concurrence from the other seven divisions to change SAP. This *could* make Mead less nimble; it remains to be seen.

As SAP was turned on, old systems were turned off. In fact, SAP replaced the last generation of systems Mead built itself. Now, all software work is integrating packages, or systems integration. Nothing is coded from scratch. Once SAP was implemented, the development work done by the divisions went away through natural attrition. However, each division has an executive information officer, who mentors the division and coaches it on how to use IT. They focus on reengineering to leverage SAP. They are business people with IT exposure and IT people with business exposure.

E-Commerce

The Internet has, of course, changed many things. The greatest effect has been internal. Mead's intranet has become how the company conducts its business processes. The homepage is employees' gateway to most of what they need to do at Mead. SAP is browser based.

Mead would have preferred to implement e-commerce on SAP because e-commerce exposes all of a company's legacy-system inefficiencies. However, the company could not wait until 2003, and because its legacy systems still functioned in 2000, it put browser-based front ends on its legacy systems. Once SAP was in place, only the system interfaces needed to change.

In some sense, Mead sees B2B e-commerce as old wine in new bottles. In 1986, Mead built a cluster terminal system for its paper business. The system was proprietary; it ran on Mead's network, and Mead gave proprietary terminals to customers to order paper. Even though the terminals were only character based, with no graphics, customers could

(Case Continued)

see Mead's stock levels, delivery times, and prices. One-third of its business came through this system. In 2000, the system became Internet based. All a customer needed was a browser to log into Mead's extranet to place orders.

However, Mead discovered that although it broke down its own internal silos in installing SAP, it encountered silos in customers' operations. True end-to-end e-commerce will not occur until these partners improve their internal operations.

Peering into the Future in 2000

In 2000, Mead's industry, like most others, was experiencing unprecedented global competition. To survive, companies needed to become larger or become a niche player. Mead expected to be one of the survivors, and management saw SAP aiding in achieving that goal. If, for example, Mead acquired another company, it would be able to merge operations within 90 days because of SAP. That capability made SAP a valuable acquisition tool.

"The CIO job has definitely changed since 1985," says Langenbahn. "In the 1990s, we always talked about IT being strategic, but it was really a wish. In 2000, it is reality. The role of the CIO has become more strategic and the role has grown, but at the end of the day, information technology is inherently valueless. Value is created by business change and true business change cannot be led by the IT side; it must spring from the business side. The major role of the CIO is to bridge the gap between the business and technology, and to have the enabling technology in place to deliver what the business requires, although the business might not as yet realize what it requires."

2002: MEAD AND WESTVACO MERGE

The global landscape that Langenbahn talked about in 2000 did, indeed, lead to a merger. On January 28, 2002, Mead and Westvaco merged.

To understand why, it is necessary to understand the industry. It is fragmented. Whereas the oil and gas industry has 5 global suppliers, forest products has 30—and they represent just 60 percent of the market. Demand for paper and paperboard in developed countries is slowing, or declining; thus, the promising markets are in developing countries. However, regional competition has arisen in those areas. In South America and Indonesia, for example, which both have robust fiber supplies, local companies have invested in pulp mills and paper and finishing machines. Thus, products that Mead and Westvaco formerly exported to these and other developing countries faced local competition. The result: a worldwide glut.

To be a leader in this fragmented market, Mead had to grow. One route would be to grow internally, but with too much capacity already in the market, this option made little sense. A second route would be to acquire companies and consolidate. Management declined this option because of its unfavorable economics, saying, "You always overpay when you buy another company." The third choice was to merge with a comparably-sized competitor. That was the route chosen; Mead and Westvaco combined their assets without taking on any debt.

A Merger of Equals

John Langenbahn saw the merger through and then retired, turning over the CIO job to Jim McGrane. McGrane

(Case Continued)

had been in charge of Mead's SAP implementation, but he had not reported to Langenbahn. They had been peers, on purpose. When the SAP project was being discussed in 1997–1998, Langenbahn wanted to ensure that it was viewed as a business investment, not an IT investment. Therefore, the project lead, McGrane, worked for the business executive who chaired the SAP steering committee. Both McGrane and Langenbahn were on that committee.

As the SAP implementation progressed, Langenbahn and McGrane talked about the need to bring the SAP work into the CIR fold once the system had been implemented in all the plants—sometime in 2003. Their goal was to create a process-centered IT organization, because with the implementation of SAP and its focus on processes, CIR's new role was becoming working on business process design enabled by IT.

The merger accelerated that move by 1 year. In becoming CIO, McGrane brought the SAP team with him. Fortunately, Westvaco planned to implement SAP. Mead was further ahead, though, so MeadWestvaco adopted Mead's plan, extending deployment by several years to include all Westvaco's sites. The merger also forced the issue of restructuring CIR, which was renamed Enterprise Information Solutions (EIS) to reflect its scope and its mission: process solutions, rather than systems.

Evolving to a New Process-Centered Structure

Balancing centralization (and standardization) with local autonomy caused an age-old tension. McGrane dealt with this tension through a "strategic conversation between the corporation and EIS" to decide how MeadWestvaco would address this tension. The issue was governance: Who would be making which decisions? "Restructuring EIS is very akin to what the framers of the U.S. Constitution struggled with," noted McGrane, "instituting a federal government while preserving states' rights. IT has moved from a mysterious, technical backroom activity into the mainstream, so we now need to hold this business-EIS conversation to do the same."

As an interim step, McGrane put in place the outlines of a new EIS organizational structure, one that would facilitate the creation of a process-based, business-driven organization. He viewed the former Vision 2000 structure as taking a techno-centered view of the world—with a workstation in the center, surrounded by services, and then an application layer. The new structure took a process view.

The interim organization, as shown in Figure 1-14, included:

- *Planning and Administration*, which included an information standards and policy quarterback
- *Technical Services*, which was in charge of application design and staging processes
- *Chief Technology Officer*, who was in charge of architecture
- *Operations*, which was in charge of the deployment process
- *Manufacturing Solutions*, which built and maintained mill and manufacturing support systems
- *Business Solutions*, which included ERP, emerging solutions, and other

(Case Continued)

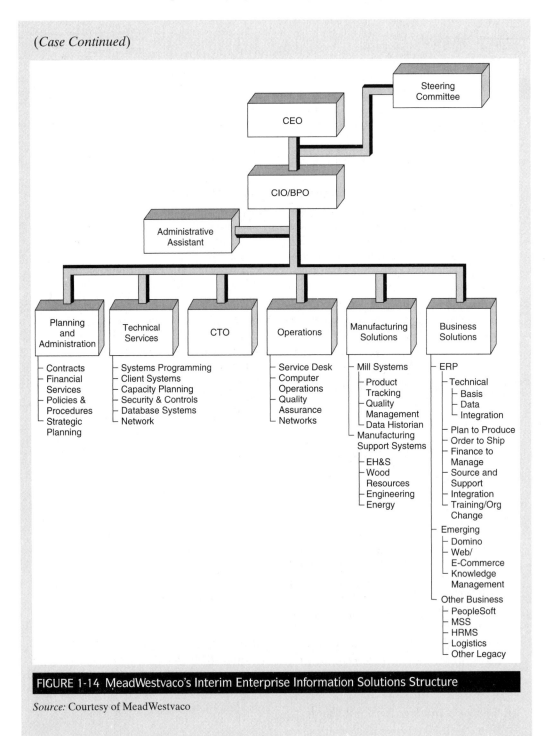

FIGURE 1-14 MeadWestvaco's Interim Enterprise Information Solutions Structure

Source: Courtesy of MeadWestvaco

(*Case Continued*)

business systems. Members of this group also handled sunrise/sunset systems, which means they were in charge of managing down ("sunsetting") legacy systems as SAP was implemented in plants and replaced those systems and explored emerging ("sunrising") technologies.

McGrane's goal was eventually to evolve EIS along three major areas of focus:

1. *Business Processes and Applications* so that EIS was viewed as a business enabler.

2. *Infrastructure* so that by designing and developing the right kind of infrastructure, business processes could be automated using advanced software applications.

3. *Administration* to ensure return on investments, end user education and support, asset management, information security, and business continuity, to name just a few.

Within these three areas, a series of processes needed to be defined. For example, one administrative process was security. Creating this process started with defining it, stating policies and procedures (that is, what was to be protected), and then creating tasks to ensure execution. Today, people who do security work reside in different functions throughout the company. The question McGrane asked was "Do we organize them around a security process or use a matrix, with a security quarterback?" The business goal was end-to-end security and protection of vital information. To achieve that, the company had to move from viewing security as an activity to viewing it as a process. This was the organizational challenge.

This three-area focus was actually in use since preplanning for the merger. The integration teams were organized around these three areas. Each team's objectives were to find synergies and adopt standards. Adopting Mead's SAP model, for example, shaved millions of dollars off future expenses.

During the first 4 months following the merger, the new EIS team closed down Westvaco's data center and migrated the systems to Dayton. Desktops, networks, and e-mail systems were migrated to one standard each. In integrating the two IS organizations, EIS saved additional millions of dollars and freed resources to focus on more strategic investments.

Creating a Governance Structure

A major issue was investment. How could the company ensure that the EIS portfolio was aligned with the business strategy? And how could EIS engage the business units in constructive conversations about what to do next? How would the company decide between, say, an investment in infrastructure and an investment in a Web-based application? Should they be measured the same way? What should the measurements be?

Based on research outside the organization, McGrane estimated that perhaps only 50 percent of an IT organization's investments were aligned with the business's goals because there have been few mechanisms for holding conversations with the business. MeadWestvaco knew it could not afford that level of misalignment. Now that EIS spending was more

(Case Continued)

than 3 percent of sales (rather than 0.5 percent in the 1970s) and embodied how the business operated (such as how orders were filled), business-IT conversations had to become the norm. From the mechanisms used to hold these conversations, EIS's organizational structure would emerge.

Thus, EIS experimented with some governance structures. To govern overall IT investments, for example, an executive steering committee was formed. It consisted of the executive vice presidents of the business units, the CFO, CIO, and head of manufacturing research and development. These seven executives meet monthly to review and approve new investments and resolve conflicts. MeadWestvaco moved toward an IT investment portfolio with four "buckets":

1. *Infrastructure*: Value is measured by total cost of ownership (TCO) benchmarked against the world.

2. *Utility applications*: These included payroll, compliance software, and such; value is measured by benchmarked TCO.

3. *Business applications*: Value is measured by return on investment (ROI). The total cost of the application will be made visible. Thus, if it requires modifying or expanding the infrastructure, that cost will be made visible.

4. *Emerging and experimental applications*: No expectations are made of these investments, which deal with technologies that might transform the business but have associated technology risks. ERP was experimental in 1995; reverse auctions and Web applications were experimental in 2002. This category is no more than 5 to 10 percent of EIS's budget.

Extending Standardization

Administration of most of the development resources was centralized. Formerly, business units managed their own IT developers. "We are finding that as we engage in conversations that make total cost visible, and we provide alternatives that deliver equal value at lower cost, we have arrived at a point where the business units are willing to give centralization of development a try," says McGrane. SAP has actually driven this move; its development was centralized and its configuration is centrally controlled. As SAP replaces the legacy systems, the business units' need for local developers has gone away. EIS extended that central model to Web technology; most development was central.

To balance the tension between centralization and local needs, EIS worked with business leadership to create governing councils, which include business leaders. These councils "own" specific processes and direct the technology enhancements required to improve those processes. The benefit of these councils, notes McGrane, is that once a council approves an enhancement, that enhancement happens across the corporation at one time. Thus, an improvement in plant maintenance occurs at all the plants. Thus, the businesses decide the priorities, and they occur companywide.

Implementing ERP drove MeadWestvaco to leverage resources to solve problems as a joint entity. The company came to see that a problem for one is generally a problem for all. Thus, central

(Case Continued)

design is leveraged. The result is that a business unit that wants to make a change needs to have conversations with the others, and those conversations revolve around what is good for the whole.

"The answer might not be reached as quickly, but it is a more effective answer," states McGrane. "Our business does not change at Web speed. So needing to make a decision quickly is often a red-herring argument. Standardization has forced real business discussions to occur. And it is forcing our business leaders to become more technology literate, and those of us in EIS to become more literate about the business issues we are trying to solve. That's all for the good."

2004: CREATING THE PROCESS-BASED, BUSINESS-DRIVEN EIS ORGANIZATION

In mid-2004, McGrane was 2 years into his 5-year plan to turn EIS into a process-based and business-driven organization. "It's a bit tougher than I expected," he admits. According to McGrane:

It's essentially reengineering the organization from being functionally oriented to being process oriented. We are moving from managing work to managing outcomes.

We characterize our future state as 'nimble,' where IT is embedded in our business strategies and we in EIS can support change without disrupting our operation, which is global, mobile, and always-open-for-business.

If you look at what it will take to survive, CIOs have to figure out (1) how to achieve better strategic alignment across the corporation, the business units, and IT investments;

(2) how to deliver high-quality service while driving out costs; and (3) what the right organizational model for IS should be. We don't yet know the right organizational model for EIS, but we do know we must transition our skill set from managing subordinates to negotiating and delivering services.

During their due diligence on how to put the theory of process orientation into practice, McGrane's team discovered ITIL (Information Technology Infrastructure Library), a process-based framework for managing IT service delivery. Rather than start from scratch on defining IT processes, ITIL has been adopted.

"We chose ITIL because it supports our strategy. It focuses on service management—aligning services with future needs, improving service quality, and improving long-term costs—just the issues we need to solve," says McGrane.

ITIL

ITIL was developed by the U.K. Office of Government Commerce (OGC) in the late 1980s to improve IT service delivery by the U.K. central government. The result was a set of books that describes best practices in IT service delivery. The books, edited by OGC, were written by numerous organizations and verified by others.[6] An entire industry has grown up around ITIL, providing training, consulting, certification, and even trade associations.

The main tenet of ITIL is that the IT infrastructure—which includes not only hardware and software but also skills, communications, and documentation—supports the delivery of IT services and thus needs to be managed professionally. ITIL calls this management *IT service*

(Case Continued)

management, and it has two main sets of IT management processes: *service delivery* and *service support*. The two ITIL books on these subjects describe the key components of these processes and provide guidance on how to create and operate them.

Service delivery is composed of five tactical processes, all aimed at the long-term planning and improvement of IT services:

- *Availability management* is the process of optimizing the capacity of the IT infrastructure.
- *Capacity management* is the process of managing resources at a time of high demand (such as a crisis) and predicting the need for extra capacity in advance.
- *IT service continuity management* is the process of managing the organization's ability to continue providing an IT service after a business interruption.
- *Service-level management* is the process of continually improving the quality of an IT service.
- *Financial management for IT services* is the process of being a good steward of the organization's money.

Service support is composed of one operational function and five operational processes. All aim to ensure that customers have access to the services they need to support their business. The processes differ from the function in that they are measured by their outcome:

- *Service desk* (a function, not a process) provides one point of contact for users.
- *Incident management* is the process of restoring a disrupted service.

- *Problem management* is the process of diagnosing the causes of incidents and preventing them.
- *Change management* is the process of handling changes efficiently.
- *Release management* is the process of managing new versions of a service.
- *Configuration management* is the process of managing all the components of a service or the infrastructure.

The five other ITIL books deal with the processes of security management, infrastructure management (such as managing network services), application management, planning to implement service management, and three books for business managers on integrating IT into the business in times of change, dealing with transitions in the IT infrastructure, and understanding the role of managers in improving IT service delivery.

Implementing ITIL at MeadWestvaco

According to McGrane:

We like ITIL's business perspective of *delivering* a service (which involves negotiating a service, its characteristics, the financials, the availability agreements, and such) and *supporting* a service (via a service desk, incident management, release management, etc.), and the notions of enterprisewide infrastructure and security management. We also like drawing on the intellectual property ITIL has accumulated, such as the precise definitions of IT terminology.

Procter & Gamble adopted ITIL service management 6 years ago to

(Case Continued)

get the same kinds of benefits we are looking for. They also, as a result, prepared themselves for a major outsourcing initiative. While outsourcing might become an attractive option for MeadWestvaco in the future, we are taking this direction because we must become outcome focused, to bring more discipline to the "interface points" in our relationships with the business, and to handle the increased complexity we face in the technologies, service delivery, and processes.

The EIS structure McGrane implemented in 2002 has not changed. He is transforming EIS within that context. Four major steps toward this transformation have been to (1) put IT governance

in place, (2) assign the first business relationship manager, (3) begin creating the service catalog, and (4) pilot test three ITIL-based processes.

IT Governance Is in Place. "In our industry, the economics dictate that we centralize IT to cut costs. We cannot afford decentralization. To achieve business alignment, we are using IT governance structures," notes McGrane.

The overall model is one of stewardship; that is, actively managing the assets that have been entrusted to us for the good of the organization. As shown in Figure 1-15, three bodies handle IT governance:[7]

- The *EIS Steering Committee* acts as an internal board of directors for

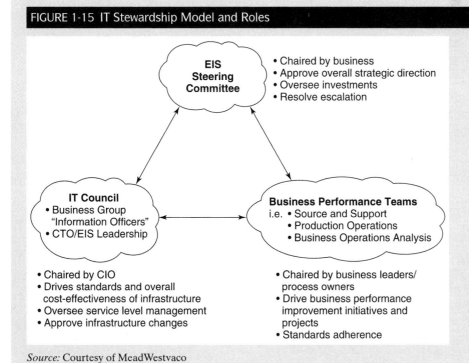

FIGURE 1-15 IT Stewardship Model and Roles

EIS Steering Committee
- Chaired by business
- Approve overall strategic direction
- Oversee investments
- Resolve escalation

IT Council
- Business Group "Information Officers"
- CTO/EIS Leadership

- Chaired by CIO
- Drives standards and overall cost-effectiveness of infrastructure
- Oversee service level management
- Approve infrastructure changes

Business Performance Teams
i.e. • Source and Support
- Production Operations
- Business Operations Analysis

- Chaired by business leaders/ process owners
- Drive business performance improvement initiatives and projects
- Standards adherence

Source: Courtesy of MeadWestvaco

(Case Continued)

IT. It is chaired by the business, approves IT's strategic direction, oversees IT investments, and resolves disputes.

- The *IT Council* represents the interests of the business units and the corporation. It is chaired by the CIO and includes information officers from the units. On the one hand, the members advocate projects that drive unique value for a particular business. On the other hand, they represent decisions back to their respective areas to ensure alignment. The council also drives standards, oversees service level management, and approves the IT infrastructure.

- *Business Performance Teams* represent the interests of business process teams. They are chaired by process owners or business leaders, they drive initiatives aimed at improving business performance, and they ensure that standards are being followed.

The First Business Relationship Manager Has Been Assigned.   Says McGrane, "In essence, we will be running EIS like a business, focused on delivering services. In so doing, we need to distinguish *users* (people who request enhancements) from *customers* (organizations that approve investments and pay for the services). Users will be served by the service desk; customers will be served by business relationship managers."

One business relationship manager has been assigned so far to a Mead-Westvaco business unit. This senior IT executive acts as both coach and account executive for that unit—a step toward improving "the interface point" between EIS and the unit. Together, McGrane and the business unit's head (who was very open to having such an intermediary) decided on the new appointment. He was chosen for his business–IT acumen. Others will be chosen for the same capability.

"The benefit of this new position is that the business unit gets a single point of contact," says McGrane. "Later, these managers will become their unit's advocate within EIS. The benefit to us in EIS is that we will get better information coming back to us from the business units. The goal is more efficient and effective relationships."

The EIS Service Catalog Is Being Developed.   The service catalog essentially documents the EIS–business conversation about what services EIS provides and what users and customers expect. It is a major part of the transformation, so EIS is going through formal planning stages to create it.

It will contain a high-level listing of EIS's services, productivity tools, connectivity options, applications, consulting, and application development services. Each service will have a service-level agreement that tells users and customers what to expect and the cost. To support these services, EIS will put in place the formal ITIL support processes noted earlier.

ITIL is actually very complex. Each process has subprocesses (activities and tasks). Tasks become roles. Roles are aggregated into jobs. Once defined, McGrane faces the challenge of introducing this process-based organization into his current function-based organization. Exactly how that will be done is currently unclear, so he has started some pilot programs.

(Case Continued)

Three ITIL-Based Processes Are Being Pilot Tested. To test the ITIL concepts, three senior EIS leaders are on 18- to 24-month assignments to lead three process teams: service-level management, IT service continuity management, and change and release management. Each has subordinate leaders for the ITIL subprocesses. They are designing their processes and running pilots to educate the EIS organization internally and then to roll out these concepts to the entire organization.

Take change and release management, for example. Like most organizations, EIS currently has 12 change management systems. "We are not atypical," notes McGrane. "Like others, these have grown up over the years. Our goal is to have one change system with formalized approval levels and defined severity levels within 6 months' time. One of the pilot teams is working on this."

Being process oriented, the teams combine business and EIS staff. For example, the secure-to-pay process is a business process owned by the business but having a large IT component. EIS's processes must interweave with this business process. One team is working to refine this process and the EIS-to-business interfaces.

"It's difficult to tell where this process orientation will take us, from a structural point of view. We could end up with an organization that is vertical and horizontal. Or we could end up with one that is only horizontal. We just don't know yet," notes McGrane.

As a result, McGrane is spending about 50 percent of his time on this internal reorganization, 40 percent of his time on corporate and business unit issues, and 10 percent with MeadWestvaco

customers. He says, "That's not enough time outside the company. Once the internal reorganization is accomplished, I hope to be working more externally with our larger customers, to exploit supply-chain technologies. At the moment, that work is happening at a lower level."

The Role of the Business

"For business executives to be truly involved in guiding IT, they must have a fairly high level of IT maturity," notes McGrane. He continues:

> In essence, they need to know as much about using IT to run their business as they already know about finance. They must be able to judge the value of an IT investment and balance that value against the operational changes they will need to make (in processes, people, investments).
>
> IT investment decisions are complex, and IT vendors' commercials do not portray this complexity. I wish they would stop promising simple silver bullets—like "Just outsource everything to us and we'll handle it for you"—because they are creating a hostile environment between IT and the business. In reality, we could not afford to outsource all IT to a vendor—nor would we.

The IT governance structure, the business relationship managers, and the process teams are creating the context for the in-depth IT–business conversations that need to take place for the business executives to understand the IT issues and become truly involved in guiding IT. They are a start to MeadWestvaco's emerging ITIL model. ∎

QUESTIONS AND EXERCISES

Review Questions

Review questions are based directly on the material in the chapter, allowing the reader to assess comprehension of the chapter's key principles, topics, and ideas.

1. What changes are taking place in the external business environment?
2. What changes are occurring in the internal organizational environment?
3. What are the goals of the new work environment?
4. Give two or three characteristics of the technology trends in hardware, software, data, and communications.
5. What is the mission for the IS organization recommended by the authors? How does it differ from earlier perceptions of the purpose and objectives of information systems?
6. Summarize the four main components of the model of the IS function (Figure 1-6).
7. List several attributes of procedure-based and knowledge-based information activities. Which do you think are most important? Why?
8. How did Mead focus on end user computing in the 1980s?
9. What was Mead's 1990 strategy?
10. Why did Mead choose to implement ERP?
11. Give an example of a MeadWestvaco governance structure to govern overall IT investments.
12. What four "buckets" is MeadWestvaco moving toward to define its IT investment portfolio?
13. What has been the effect of ERP on MeadWestvaco's decision making?
14. As of mid-2004, what four steps had McGrane taken to transform EIS into an ITIL-like, process-driven organization? Briefly describe each step.
15. Describe the three IT governance bodies at MeadWestvaco and what each does.

Discussion Questions

Discussion questions are based on a few topics in the chapter that offer a legitimate basis for a difference of opinion. These questions focus discussion on these issues when the book is used in a seminar or classroom setting.

1. Even though the PC dispersed control of processing power out of the IS organization, the Internet is returning control to the department. Do you agree or disagree? Discuss.
2. Do we really need a major change in the way the IS function is structured? Are the necessary changes just minor modifications to accommodate normal growth in computer uses? Discuss.
3. The procedure–knowledge dichotomy does not add much beyond the clerical–managerial distinction. Do you agree or disagree? Give reasons for your opinion.
4. The Internet-based economy is going to end up just like the old economy with the huge conglomerates controlling everything. Do you agree or disagree? Is this situation desirable or not?

Exercises

Exercises provide an opportunity for the reader to put some of the concepts and ideas into practice on a small scale. In particular, one exercise in each chapter requires a student, or a team of students, to visit a local company and discover how the ideas in the chapter are being implemented in that company.

1. Show how MeadWestvaco's 2002 interim organizational structure compares with the model in Figure 1-6 by entering its functions on the figure.
2. Contact a company in your community and prepare a diagram and narrative to describe the structure of its IS function. Compare it with Figure 1-6 and with MeadWestvaco's current structure.
3. Find an article about how companies are melding the Internet with their traditional ways of working. Present those ideas to the class.

REFERENCES

1. Cairncross, Frances, *The Company of the Future: How the Communications Revolution Is Changing Management*, Harvard Business School Press, Boston, 2002.
2. Trachtenberg, Jeffrey, "Borders Sets Out to Make the Book Business Businesslike," *The Wall Street Journal*, May 20, 2002, pp. B1, B6.
3. Drucker, Peter F., "The Coming of the New Organization," *Harvard Business Review*, January/February 1988.
4. Manville, Brook, and Nathaniel Foote, "Strategy as if Knowledge Mattered," *Fast Company*, 1996.
5. Gilder, George, "The Coming Telecosm," (speech, Aspen Institute, Aspen, CO, July 18, 1996).
6. Pink Elephant was one of the organizations involved in the initial ITIL effort and is now a leading ITIL consulting and training firm. It provides a good overview of ITIL on its Web site. For instance, see *The ITIL Story*, Pink Elephant, Version 3.1, April 2004. Available at www.pinkelephant.com. Accessed June 2004.
7. For more discussion of MeadWestvaco's IT governance structure, see Peter Weill and Jeanne Ross, *IT Governance: How Top Performers Manage IT Decision Rights for Superior Results*, Harvard Business School Press, 2004, pp. 94–96.

PART

I ‖ LEADERSHIP ISSUES

Part I consists of three chapters that address leadership issues of managing the IT arena, which includes information, IS, and IT. This part deals with the shaded portion of the following figure—executive leadership—which is based on Figure 1-6 of Chapter 1, the conceptual framework for this entire book.

Leadership of the IS function is no longer limited to CIOs and their subordinates. Increasingly, CIOs share the top leadership role with the CEO and other C-level executives. Managing and nurturing this shared relationship is an underlying theme of this book.

Chapter 2 discusses the changing structure of the IS organization and four areas of responsibility for CIOs. Chapter 3 discusses strategic uses of IT. Chapter 4 completes this leadership part by discussing the changing world of IS planning and a number of planning approaches and techniques.

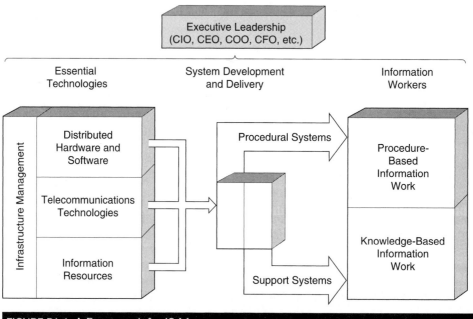

FIGURE P1-1 A Framework for IS Management

CHAPTER 2

THE TOP IS JOB

INTRODUCTION

The management of IT in organizations has changed drastically over the past 50 years. In the early years, the big job was to manage the technology—get it working, keep it running, and reduce the cost of doing business. Later, the main thrust was to manage the information resources of the organization, particularly to support management decision making by delivering information when and where it was needed. Today, IT is pervasive in organizations and is a mandatory link between enterprises. Hence, it affects every aspect of organizational performance and is leading to the formation of "business ecosystems" in which organizations operate. Proper deployment of IT can determine an organization's growth, direction, structure, and viability.

In this book, the term *IT* is used to denote the technology, whereas *IS* is used to denote the organization that manages IT. The responsibilities of the head of IS now go far beyond operating highly efficient "production programming shops." These executives are now part of top management and help form the goals of the enterprise in partnership with the CEO, CFO, and other C-level members of top management. Yet, the CIO is the focal point for IT deployment.

In this chapter, we look at two dimensions of the top IS job. First, we ask the question, "Where is the IS organization headed?" Second, we look at the responsibilities of CIOs.

WHERE IS THE IS ORGANIZATION HEADED?

The roles and responsibilities of the IS organization have been evolving since the first electronic data processing departments were formed in companies in the 1950s. We set the context for discussing this evolution by looking at the escalating benefits of IT, which in turn change the way executives view IS's role in the business.

The Escalating Benefits of IT

Kenneth Primozic, Edward Primozic, and Joe Leben, authors of *Strategic Choices*,[1] present one view of the evolution of IT and the escalating benefits it provides firms. They introduce the notion of "waves of innovation," which they define as how IT is used by industries and by enterprises. They identify five waves of innovation, as shown in Figure 2-1, with *time* on the horizontal axis and *benefit* on the vertical access. The waves are

- Wave 1: Reducing costs
- Wave 2: Leveraging investments

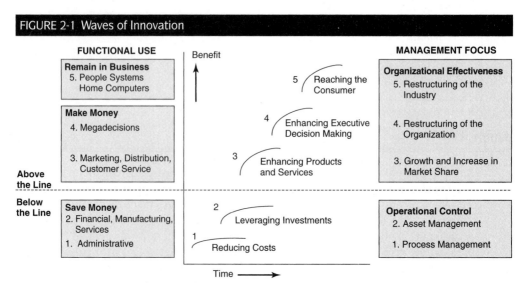

FIGURE 2-1 Waves of Innovation

Source: Kenneth Primozic, Edward Primozic, and Joe Leben, *Strategic Choices: Supremacy, Survival, or Sayonara* (New York: McGraw-Hill, 1991).

- Wave 3: Enhancing products and services
- Wave 4: Enhancing executive decision making
- Wave 5: Reaching the consumer

Wave 1: Reducing costs.   This wave began in the 1960s when use of IT focused on increasing the productivity of individuals and business areas. The goal was to achieve clerical and administrative savings by automating manual processes.

Wave 2: Leveraging investments.   This wave began in the 1970s and concentrated on making more effective use of corporate assets to increase profitability. Systems were justified on return on investment and increasing cash flow.

As shown in Figure 2-1, both Wave 1 and Wave 2 are below the line, which means both focus on saving money, not making money, through better management of processing and assets. Systems are developed mainly for administration, finance, and manufacturing.

Wave 3: Enhancing products and services.   This wave began in the 1980s and was the first time that attention shifted to using IT to produce revenue by gaining strategic advantage or by creating entirely new businesses. In conjunction with the new goals of using IT to grow the business or increase market share, IT was used to improve outward-looking functions, such as marketing, distribution, and customer service.

Wave 4: Enhancing executive decision making.   This wave began later in the 1980s and focused on changing the fundamental structure of the organization as well as creating real-time business management systems.

The authors point out that Waves 1 and 2 can be implemented at any time, because of their internal focus, but Waves 3 and 4 can only be implemented once an industry leader has set the precedent. Companies that do not follow suit cease to be competitive.

Wave 5: Reaching the consumer.   This wave began in the 1990s. IT is used to communicate directly with consumers, leading to new marketing, distribution, and service strategies. This wave changes the rules of competition, which has been precisely the focus of leading-edge firms—to restructure their industry by creating new businesses using the Internet, e-commerce, and now wireless technologies.

Waves 3, 4, and 5 are above the line because they concentrate on making money and staying in business. Due to the worldwide ubiquity of the Internet and the standard browser software for accessing the Web, most organizations have jumped to Wave 5.

Once companies cross "the line," top management must be involved in guiding IT use, say the authors of *Strategic Choices*, because they must steer the company in the new business environment. The risks of inappropriately using IT for competitive purposes are too great for the senior executives to abrogate leadership to technicians. Therefore, joint planning by top management and IS management must take place.

To illustrate how one company has maneuvered through these five waves, consider the example of the American Airlines SABRE system.

CASE EXAMPLE

THE SABRE SYSTEM

The American Airlines computer reservation system—SABRE—represents a prime example of a system that has progressed through the five waves of innovation.

Waves 1 and 2

SABRE was initially built to reduce the costs of making airline seat reservations and to leverage the reservation-making assets of the airline. The system moved American from a manual-based reservation operation to a computer-based one.

Wave 3

American then expanded the system so that it could be used by travel agents, giving them a means of making reservations directly through online terminals. American enhanced the offering by adding functions of importance to travel agents, such as tools for preparing trip itineraries. SABRE was a win-win proposition—the travel agents liked the direct access and American increased the barriers to agents switching to another carrier's reservation system.

Wave 4

American later expanded its reservation service to include hotels and rental cars. In so doing, American was transforming itself, and perhaps the entire industry, from an airline company to a travel company. At about the same time, American also added a yield-management component to SABRE, which enabled the company to reprice seats more dynamically to maximize revenue.

Wave 5

American extended its reach to the consumer in three major moves. First, it introduced EAASY SABRE, a computer reservation system that consumers can access through their PCs.

Second, American introduced its frequent flyer program, AAdvantage, thereby encouraging frequent business flyers to fly American and gain points redeemable for free trips. In addition, the airline began allying the program with credit card and long-distance telephone companies, giving AAdvantage members free airline miles when they use those credit cards and telephone companies.

Third, American enhanced its Wave 5 connections to consumers via the Web. As reported by Patricia Seybold in her book *Customers.com*,[2] American was the first major airline to develop a Web site. This meant that passengers could not only plan their trip via the Internet, but could also buy tickets online and obtain real-time flight information, such as arrival and departure information. Even the name of the movie(s) being shown on flights could be accessed. Before the Web site, some 85 percent of telephone calls to the SABRE call center were not booking related. After the Web site, this percentage dropped significantly.

Importantly, writes Seybold, American targeted its site at the most profitable

(Case Continued)

customers—its 32 million AAdvantage members—practically all of whom had access to a computer. The goal was to give them better control of their travel planning and rescheduling. Thus, on the site, AAdvantage members can see their accumulated frequent flyer points, make reservations, book electronic tickets, and so on. American promoted use of the site by offering extra frequent flyer miles; bookings spiked every time a promotion was run, notes Seybold. American has continued to enhance the functionality of the site, helping flyers find hotels and restaurants.

In addition, American has used the site to experiment with different offerings to flyers in general. One experiment proved to be a real winner. John Samuel, a marketing manager at AMR, American's parent company, asked, "How can we market to fill seats?" He and his team decided to offer to send an e-mail message every Wednesday listing "the specials of the week"—empty seats on flights the upcoming weekend—to anyone who signed up for the Net-SAAver service. Not knowing what to expect, they were overwhelmed with the response—20,000 subscribers within 30 days, 100,000 in 60 days, and 775,000 in 1 year, notes Seybold.

This marketing strategy not only lets American remind subscribers of their service each week, at the subscribers' own request, but it also enables American to sell distressed inventory (the unsold seats). This additional revenue drops directly to the bottom line.

Both uses of the Internet, the AAdvantage Web site and the Net-SAAver e-mail service, have required American to appropriately manage knowledge about flyers, use the Internet to interact with them, and create an e-commerce engine to support the financial interactions involved. In the knowledge management arena, for example, the airline learned that keeping Web sites pertinent requires operating like a newspaper publisher, with strict deadlines, publishing guidelines, dispersed accountability, and so forth, notes Seybold.

This example makes clear that management had to be involved as soon as SABRE moved into money-making, beginning with Wave 3, when it began offering the system to customers, the travel agents. That was a heart-of-the-business move, and it had to be led by the business executives, not the IS executives. The same has been true of its use of the Web. ∎

This SABRE example illustrates that as the benefits of IT increase, the importance of executive guidance also increases. It also raises the question, "What's the job of the IS organization?" That's the topic discussed next.

Traditional Functions Are Being Nibbled Away

As SABRE demonstrates, IT has become an essential piece of business strategy; therefore, the speed of IT deployment affects when and how companies can carry out their strategy. Not keeping up in IT can even mean going out of business. The role of the IS organization is thus expanding. At the same time, management is realizing that traditional operational portions may not all need to be performed in-house. They can be performed by others. The traditional set of responsibilities for IS has included:

- Managing operations of data centers, remote systems, and networks
- Managing corporate data
- Performing system analysis and design and constructing new systems
- Planning systems
- Identifying opportunities for new systems

Although all these functions still need to be performed, the following trends are moving their performance out of IS into other parts of the organization or to other enterprises:

- *Distributed systems* have led to the migration of software applications to user areas. These applications are controlled by the users and generally purchased with their funds. Sometimes these applications are acquired following guidelines (or even standards) promulgated by the IS department; sometimes they are not.

- *Ever more knowledgeable users* have taken on increased IS responsibilities. They often identify high-leverage applications and lead multifunctional teams (which include IS staff) that acquire these systems.

- *Better application packages* have resulted in less need for armies of programmers and analysts to develop systems in-house from scratch. The job of IS has changed to *system integration*, which means integrating purchased applications so that they function together as a system. A case in point is ERP systems. Implementing these purchased systems has involved system integration rather than system development.

- *Outsourcing* has spread widely, perhaps more than most people expected, because companies see value in turning IS functions over to specialist companies. Outsourcing can be an effective strategy, based on fiscal and managerial considerations, for handling data center operations, application maintenance, network management, and PC support.

Thus, as shown in Figure 2-2, the work of the IS department is being "nibbled away." On the other hand, the IS job also is expanding.

New Roles Are Emerging

Gartner Executive Programs (EXP), part of the well-known Gartner IT analysis firm, presents analyses of the evolving IS situation and provides useful insights into the structure of IS organizations and where they are likely to be headed. In one report, George Cox[3] (of Wentworth Research Program, which is now part of Gartner EXP) stated that IS is not a single monolithic organization, but rather a cluster of four functions:

1. *Run operations:* Running computers and networks
2. *Develop systems:* Developing and maintaining systems, designing new systems, and updating existing ones

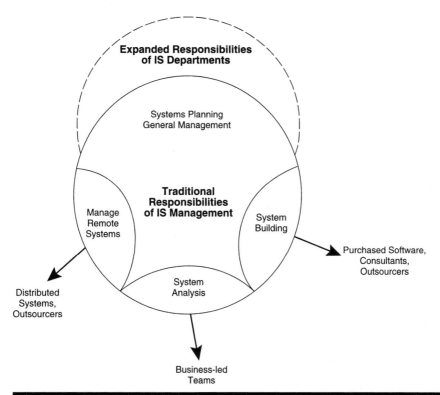

FIGURE 2-2 Traditional Responsibilities Being "Nibbled Away" from IS Departments

3. *Develop architecture:* Setting a strategy and maintaining an architecture for both IT and information, providing a framework or standard for systems operations

4. *Identify business requirements:* Helping articulate what the business needs from IT

Each of these functions requires a different set of skills and a different management strategy. A function that aims for cost efficiency and requires technical skills (such as running operations) needs to be managed differently from one that aims to add business value and requires business expertise (such as identifying business requirements).

Figure 2-3 shows the four functions on a matrix with two dimensions: the kind of impact an activity has on the organization (from cost efficiency to value added) and the type of expertise needed by the activity (from technical to business expertise).

Two technical activities that focus on cost efficiency—operations and system development and maintenance—are of less importance to the business, hence they are smaller bubbles. Meanwhile, the business-oriented activities that seek to add value to the enterprise are of far greater importance to the enterprise, hence the larger bubbles.

Companies that have failed to recognize the differences among these four areas—the relative importance of each and how to manage each properly—have, in some cases, misplaced their resources or underdeveloped their expertise. Until recently, most IS organizations invested heavily in computer operations and system development/maintenance, while neglecting the other two (developing architectures and identifying

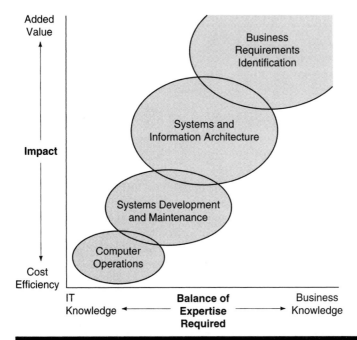

FIGURE 2-3 Four Major IS Activities

Source: George Cox, *Time to Reshape the IS Department?*, Wentworth Research Program (now part of Gartner EXP, Stamford, CT), June 1994.

business requirements). Operations and systems development can be purchased because they are commodity-like; architecture development and business requirements identification cannot because they are unique to each organization.

Most IS organizations have had to reskill their staffs to move to these more value-added kinds of work. As they have, they see a "squeeze" similar to the "nibbling" discussed earlier. As shown in Figure 2-4, external services in the form of outsourcing compete well in the lower left of the matrix, the technical arena. Meanwhile, increasingly knowledgeable users assume more of the responsibility and initiative in the upper-right area of the matrix, the business-centric arena.

Will these trends continue? Will the IS organization be squeezed into oblivion, outsourced on one end and absorbed into business units on the other? Cox thinks not! Two roles will emerge as dominant for the IS function.

First, it is not reasonable to expect an outsourcing service provider to understand and satisfy all the needs of the organization without active management and counsel. They sell commodities. Therefore, the IS organization is needed to develop and manage these contractual relationships with a variety of external suppliers. Thus, IS is becoming the broker between technical service providers and business units.

Second, a crucial role for IS organizations is development and management of the IT architecture for the enterprise, providing the framework for IT to support the business. Architecture is the biggest challenge, especially given IS organizations' systems development and operations heritage. As Cox notes, "The precious baby of a coherent framework for systems should be differentiated from the bath water of

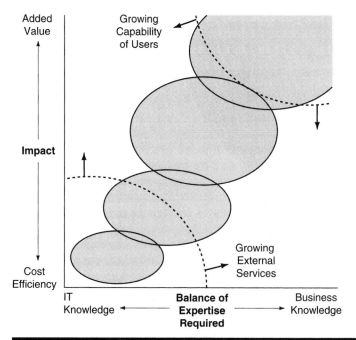

Added Value

Growing Capability of Users

Impact

Growing External Services

Cost Efficiency

IT Knowledge ← **Balance of Expertise Required** → Business Knowledge

FIGURE 2-4 The Squeeze on Traditional IS Activities

Source: George Cox, *Time to Reshape the IS Department?*, Wentworth Research Program (now part of Gartner EXP, Stamford, CT), June 1994.

system delivery and operation." Figure 2-5 shows these two new roles and how they overlap the past roles.

In short, Cox describes the metamorphosis of IS departments as follows:

- *In computer and network operations*, IS started out being the sole provider, then moved to being the preferred provider, next was seen as a competing supplier, and finally is becoming broker and contract manager for outsourcing this work.

- *In system development and maintenance*, in-house programmers initially wrote the code, then they became software product specialists, next systems integrators, and finally brokers and contract managers for acquiring software.

- *In systems and information architecture*, IS began as technology guru and standards setter, then evolved into being custodian of technical standards, later became specialist in IT trends, and most recently morphed into IT strategist.

- *In business requirements identification*, IS initially defined the specifics of computer programs, then focused on analyzing information flows and business systems, later moved to contributing to multidisciplinary analysis teams, and finally has been partnering with the business in looking at business processes.

In short, IS organizations have moved in Figure 2-3 from lower left to upper right in their role in the business, from efficiency to value added and from technical to business expertise.

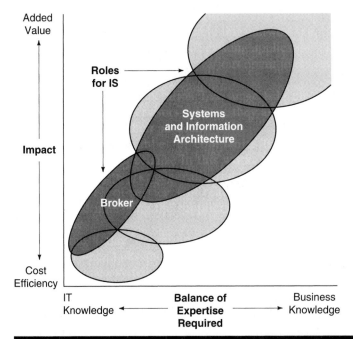

FIGURE 2-5 Roles for IS

Source: George Cox, *Time to Reshape the IS Department?*, Wentworth Research Program (now part of Gartner EXP, Stamford, CT), June 1994.

Toward IS Lite

Roger Woolfe[4a] has furthered the thinking at Gartner EXP about the role of IS departments by studying how they have responded to this evolution. He notes that whereas IS may have started as a single centralized organization, it has evolved into a federal model, where some activities (such as standards setting and operations) are handled centrally because they can be leveraged across the enterprise, whereas other activities (such as application development) have been dispersed to business units so they can best meet local needs. Unfortunately, making this split has been far from easy and has produced continual swings between centralizing and decentralizing specific activities to try to best fit the current business environment.

As an example, where should Web sites be developed? Initially, most were built by enterprising business people in marketing and other functions, without standards or guidance. When the importance of these sites was recognized, and the diversity began to impinge on "creating a single, powerful corporate image on the Web," Web site development was often pulled into a newly created e-commerce group. Yet the job is too large for one group, so those with responsibility for the content (in marketing, operations, and other functions) have added Web content management to their job—thus distributing that job—whereas Web site standards and operations are handled by central groups. The end result is the federal model.

However, that is not the end of the story. As Web sites take on new uses and greater importance, some companies have outsourced Web site development to specialist firms, others outsource Web operations to hosting specialists (who can provide vaultlike security and handle large spikes in demand, for instance), and they perhaps outsource hosting of Web events to still others who specialize in that activity. In short, the federal model can become quite complex with lots of players.

To make the federal model work better, companies are shifting attention from roles to processes. In this view, the IS organization can be viewed as managing three overall processes:

- Driving innovation
- Managing change
- Supporting infrastructure

Applying the federal model to these processes sharpens the distinction between IS activities performed centrally and those performed in business units. Woolfe sees the division coming from distinguishing supply-side activities from demand-side ones. *Supporting infrastructure* and aspects of *managing change* (such as delivering applications) are supply side. They involve providing networks, databases, and processing; they are best centralized because they can leverage economies of scale.

Most *managing change* and all *driving innovation*, on the other hand, are demand side. They create the demand for IT services; they are best localized in business units, which can tailor services to their needs.

To serve this split, some IS organizations have created centers of excellence to pool expertise and leverage it across the enterprise. Such centers now exist for such areas as e-commerce, supply chain management, policies and standards, help desk support, and systems integration.

The result is that much of the supply and demand sides of IS's work is being given up, as noted previously, to outsourcers and knowledgeable users. The result is that IS organizations are moving to *IS Lite*, as shown in Figure 2-6.

The remaining processes are *driving innovation*, which includes information and systems architecture, and *managing supplier and user relationships*, which includes brokering.

A company that is moving in this direction is LifeScan. Here is what its information management (IM) department is doing, as described in the paper submitted to the Society for Information Management's annual paper competition.[5]

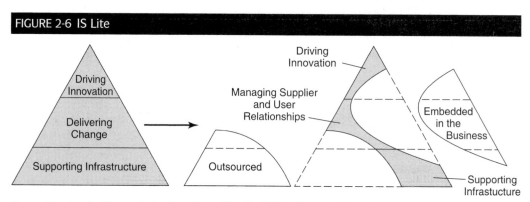

FIGURE 2-6 IS Lite

Source: Reprinted with permission from Roger Woolfe, *IS Lite*, Gartner EXP, July 2000.

CASE EXAMPLE

LIFESCAN

LifeScan, a wholly owned subsidiary of Johnson & Johnson, is a world leader in blood glucose monitoring for diabetes management. Located in Silicon Valley, the company offers an array of consumer and hospital products. In 1981, LifeScan pioneered the modern era of blood glucose monitoring by eliminating wiping and timing procedures. This breakthrough took blood glucose testing out of the laboratory and into the hands of patients. LifeScan's mission is to improve the quality of life for people with diabetes.

In 1986, Johnson & Johnson acquired LifeScan, and in 1996 it began promoting greater use of IT in business strategy. The company created the board-level position of CIO and encouraged all 188 affiliates (including LifeScan) to do the same. At the time, LifeScan Information Management (IM) was led by a director—two levels below the president.

In 1998, LifeScan appointed its first CIO, Hugo Yepez, who brought with him an agenda to align the department with the business. This agenda is leading the IM department to an IS Lite type of structure.

The Alignment Road Map

Yepez has drawn on a three-stage maturation of IM departments as his road map to moving his department from supporting the business to partnering with the business. His framework defines maturity by the value the IM department delivers at each stage:

- Stage 1 IM organizations are backroom in nature. Their purpose is to keep the business running. Their value is defined through the internal IM measures of faster/better/cheaper.

- Stage 2 IM organizations work closely with business units. Hence, their value is measured from the business units' viewpoint in terms of delivery and execution. In measuring their success, some use the Balanced Scorecard because it measures performance on four dimensions—financial, internal performance, customer satisfaction, and health and growth.

- Stage 3 IM organizations partner with business units and have direct influence on business strategy. Their value is therefore gauged through the business's own performance measures. The two are integrated; there are no separate measures for IM.

Yepez believed the LifeScan IM department was at stage 1 when he arrived, but he believed it could move into stage 2 in a couple of years and into stage 3 in several more years.

To progress toward stage 2, Yepez focused on execution and measurement to gain credibility with the business units. Execution meant bringing in IM projects on time and within budget. Focusing on project execution would help move the department to a stage-2 mindset because IM staff would view

(Case Continued)

their performance from the results they deliver to the business.

To deliver on their promises in implementing new systems, IM staff learned that they had to have strong project management and not allow *scope creep* (users asking for additional functions in applications as development proceeded). To deliver on promises in maintenance, IM began outsourcing work on several major systems. They use Tata Computing Systems in Calcutta, India, which has impressive software quality processes and high-quality software maintenance programmers.

LifeScan also outsourced maintenance of its desktop machines, drawing on the corporate outsourcing agreement negotiated by Johnson & Johnson's IM department. Furthermore, LifeScan has turned over computer operations to Johnson & Johnson's corporate operations department, National Computing Service. Outsourcing these supply-side IT areas has freed IM staff from *doing* the work to *overseeing* the work—performing the brokering and relationship management role in the IS Lite model.

IM also began measuring new projects, to make execution visible, by giving LifeScan employees an IM scorecard on the company intranet to show which milestones were being hit or not. The scorecard is expanded, as appropriate, to include stage 2 and stage 3 measures, such as the business impact of new systems on customer service, opera-

tions, and so on. The goal is for the board of LifeScan to be able to link IM measures to LifeScan's corporate measures to identify where IM is best supporting the business.

In the areas of driving innovation and managing change, Yepez has undertaken several initiatives to involve business units in IM work. For example, he brought in an alignment process that assists business unit executives both to determine the priority of LifeScan's business drivers and then to rank IM projects in their support of those drivers.

Being a manufacturer, LifeScan has instituted quality processes. IM is aligning itself with that quality-driven culture so that the entire company speaks the same language. In one initiative, IM is working with three other departments that develop software (for products, services, and quality assurance) to implement a company-wide, quality-based software development life cycle.

In addition, all IM projects are business led, which moves ownership of systems to the business people.

Finally, IM staff members who have the skills needed in a stage 3 IM organization—those with strong project management, business process, change management, and interpersonal skills—are being promoted and given opportunities to partner with business peers. In so doing, these employees present a leadership model, one that emphasizes relationship management and brokering skills, as noted in the IS Lite model. ∎

Given these descriptions of how the IS department is evolving, we now look at the responsibilities of CIOs.

THE CIO'S RESPONSIBILITIES

In line with the evolution of IS departments, the emphasis of the top IS job has changed through the seven editions of this textbook as follows.

In 1986, when the first edition of this book was published, the leading IS executives were talking about their new role as architects of the enterprisewide IT infrastructure. Much of the talk centered around the strategic use of IT.

In 1989, attention shifted to helping formulate corporate policy, with an emphasis on creating a vision of the role of IT in the future. In other words, from 1986 to 1989, the focus of the top IS job had swung significantly toward addressing business issues.

In 1992, the challenge for IS executives was to use IT as a catalyst for revamping the way enterprises worked. To accomplish this task, they needed to be in a high enough position to influence the use of IT as a major underpinning of the enterprise of the future. Reflecting this higher level of responsibility, the title Vice President of MIS or Information Systems Director evolved into Chief Information Officer (CIO), a position often occupied by someone with general management expertise, rather than a traditional technology manager.

In 1998, the need to revamp business operations using IT continued with the Internet expanding the CIO's horizon beyond company boundaries out to potential customers. IT began playing a more front-office role, especially in the rapidly changing Internet marketspace.

In 2002, the CIO had become the technical member of top management. The emphasis of the job was to make sure that the electronic infrastructure for e-commerce and e-business was being put into place, to ensure that IS staff were working as partners with business units on value-adding initiatives, and to rapidly deploy new IT uses.

In 2004, IS executives had a more sobering role than the high-flying "let's get into e-commerce fast" days of the late 1990s and early 2000s. Far more emphasis was placed on justifying IT investments, building a portfolio of IT projects that balanced risk and return, ensuring that the right people were involved in making IT decisions, and working outward with customers and suppliers to build interlinking systems.

Today, the cost emphasis remains, thus the use of outsourcing continues to grow (amid controversy). However, CIOs are expected to do much more with not much more money. They are under pressure to implement protective measures to safeguard the privacy of customer data, to install increasingly sophisticated security so that viruses and other attacks do not cripple systems, and to add new financial reporting features to satisfy government regulations, such as the Sarbanes-Oxley Act in the United States. At the same time, they have to keep the IT innovations coming. It's a tall order.

CIO Roles in Three Eras

In looking at the role of CIOs, Jeanne Ross of MIT and David Feeny of Templeton College, Oxford University,[6] divide the world of computing into three eras: mainframe, distributed, and Web based. They distinguish between the three eras because they see discontinuities between them. Each era is defined by technology innovations, resulting in new uses of IT, and consequently new roles for CIOs. Figure 2-7 shows how these eras intersect.

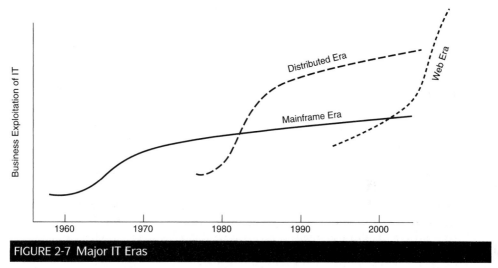

FIGURE 2-7 Major IT Eras

Source: Reprinted with permission from Pinnaflex Educational Resources, Cincinnati, Ohio 2002.

The Mainframe Era. This era dominated from the 1960s to the early 1980s. Ross and Feeny see the role of the data processing or information systems manager (the top IS job titles back then) as being the *operational manager* of a specialist function, IS. The focus was delivery. Deliver applications on time and within budget. Make sure operations run reliably. In short, as functional heads, they needed to deliver on promises to be credible.

The Distributed Era. This era started at the end of the 1970s and saw major changes. PCs became commonplace. LANs and WANs proliferated, linking computers of all sizes. The client-server concept arose (a client requests a service of a server). Eventually, companies recentralized IT by establishing standards for desktop machines and implementing ERP systems to coordinate companywide data. This turbulent era was very different from the stable mainframe era. Thus, the role of CIOs was very different, say Ross and Feeny. In fact, they believe CIOs took on four more roles (in addition to being the operational manager): organizational designer, technology adviser, technology architect, and informed buyer.

As *organizational designer*, the CIO's job was to make the IS organization responsive to the business. The result, in general, was to create a federal structure, with a central IS organization responsible for corporatewide IT and business-unit IS groups mainly developing applications for their business unit.

As *technology advisor*, the CIO's job was to align business and IS by educating business management on IT opportunities and helping the business solve their problems. In this job, CIOs spent a lot of their time outside the IS organization, working with their business peers as a technology advisor.

As *technology architect*, the CIO's role was to understand future capabilities, design the IT architecture for the entire enterprise, and then sell the business on adopting the appropriate technical standards. However, the role still had an operational aspect, ensuring that service levels remained high, no matter how many external service providers were involved.

Finally, as *informed buyer*, the CIO's role was to draw on external resources (third parties) by offloading work to them to leverage internal IS resources, such as expertise, money, space, location, and such, and thereby lower the overall cost of IS.

CIOs who mastered all four roles came to enjoy the status of being a member of the executive team, generally reporting to the CEO. Of the four roles, the most important was technology advisor, because that role provided the CEO and other top executives with an understanding of IT, its role in the enterprise, and their role in guiding its use. In short, as a strategic partner with the business, the CIO's job was to align IT with the business.

The Web Era.   This era started in the mid-1990s for some. It arose, of course, from the emergence of the Internet, and especially the Web, as a business tool. With this era in its infancy, Ross and Feeny speculate that the main role of CIOs will be that of *business visionary*. By that, they mean that the CIO will need to believe and then convince others that the Internet will lead to new business models. The Internet is about fundamental business change, not technology. The challenge for enterprises is to think through possible business models; CIOs could lead this charge. Ross and Feeny even go so far as to say that CIOs who do well in this era will become leading contenders to become CEOs. Of course, CIOs still need to draw on the five former roles, but their key role will be to help the business leverage the Internet. In short, as a business visionary, their role is to be a main driver of strategy.

Obviously, this cut-and-dried pattern is an approximation of reality, note Ross and Feeny, but it demonstrates the thrust of change in the CIO's role.

Chuck Gibson,[7] who has presented executive education seminars for years and is coauthor of an article on the Stages of Growth theory described in Chapter 4, notes that the relationship between CIOs and other senior executives, especially CEOs, has changed over time as well. In essence, it has diversified.

At one end of the relationship spectrum is the traditional relationship between CEOs and CIOs. The CIO is expected to implement technology to support business plans in a boss–subordinate, and somewhat distant, relationship. Behind this relationship is the view and practice of business and IT services as separable, and IT in a support role.

The emergence of dot-coms, though, demonstrated a much closer relationship between technologists and CEOs, Gibson points out. This closeness represents the other end of the spectrum. In dot-coms, the business is inseparable from IT. Acting as a team to respond to change and build the infrastructure and applications quickly, CEOs know a lot more about IT and dot-com CIOs know a lot more about running the business because both see the two as inseparable.

One of the reasons for the breadth of this relationship spectrum is our current place in history, says Gibson. We are at the technological discontinuity on the Stages of Growth diagram (Figure 4-5 on page 147) where the Micro Era is ending and the Network Era is beginning. Today, both eras coexist, but the relationships, issues, and discussions of Micro Era executives are different from those of Network Era executives. Whereas Micro Era executives are talking about implementing and extending their ERP system (inside-out view), Network Era executives are talking about how to achieve customer-led product design (outside-in view).

Of course, these approaches fall along a spectrum, but the point is that not all CEO–CIO teams today talk about the same issues they did, say, 5 years ago before the dot-coms merged IS and business. Moreover, the issues, roles for IS, and relationships required between CEOs and CIOs across businesses are more diverse. As a result, it is far less appropriate to generalize about CEO–CIO discussions; the context now sets the agenda, and agendas now vary. Gibson speculates that as established companies integrate their business operations with their Internet operations, the relationship between CEO and CIO will become closer and discussion points may coalesce as the requirements of the Network Era come into clearer focus and apply more generally to all businesses.

Given these two historical overviews, we look at four aspects of the CIO role these days:

1. *Leading*: Creating a vision by understanding the business
2. *Governing*: Establishing an IS governance structure
3. *Investing*: Shaping the IT portfolio
4. *Managing*: Establishing credibility and fostering change

Leading: Creating a Vision by Understanding the Business

If CIOs are to play an important role in shaping a business's use of IT, they must understand the business. With that understanding, they can then create a vision of their firm's use of IT.

Understanding the Business.   In the past, studying a business generally meant learning how it was run. However, studying internal operations is no longer enough. Today, it is important to understand the environment in which the business operates because the business's close relationships with other firms affect how the business competes. Here are seven approaches CIOs are using to understand a business and its environment.

- Encourage project teams to study the marketplace
- Concentrate on lines of business
- Sponsor weekly briefings
- Attend industry meetings with line executives
- Read industry publications
- Hold informal listening sessions
- Partner with a line executive.

Encourage project teams to study the marketplace.   To learn about the business, broaden the kinds of information that project teams seek in their study of the business. Then have them describe their findings to IT management. For example, the project study might begin with a broad overview of the company, gathering the following information about the company and its industry:

- Current industry environment
- Business goals and objectives
- Major practices of competitors
- Pertinent government regulations
- The inputs, outputs, and resources of the firm

Such an overview study can be conducted for a business unit or a product in a few weeks. The study is apt to uncover some surprises, revealing things about the industry and the company that even business unit people might not know, especially now that e-commerce initiatives are no longer being touted, but are going on nevertheless. IT management can be briefed on the findings, educating them about the markets in which their firm participates.

Concentrate on lines of business.   IT researchers Robert Benson and Marilyn Parker[8] have long studied how to manage information on an enterprisewide basis. IT needs to serve individual lines of business rather than the entire company, they found, because planning for an entire enterprise overlooks both competitive and performance matters. They believe that a line of business is where business and technology planning can be linked.

A *line of business* is an organizational unit that conducts business activities with common customers, products, and market characteristics, says Benson. For example, certain schools in a university have one line of business—undergraduate education. Others have two—undergraduate and graduate education. The customers, products, and market characteristics for the two schools are different, thus they are different lines of business.

Information technology can serve lines of business in two ways. One is by supporting current operations, which Benson and Parker call *alignment*. The second is by using systems to influence future ways of working, which they call *impact* (Figure 2-8). They recommend asking the following questions about each line of business to decide what each one needs:

1. Are we in IT organized to serve that line of business?

2. Do we have an account manager in IS who has responsibility for that line of business?

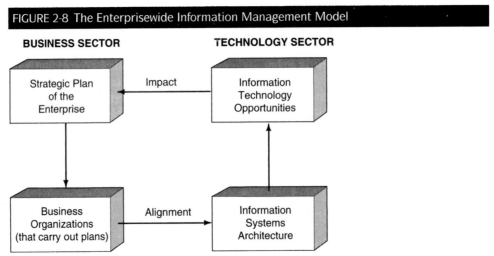

FIGURE 2-8 The Enterprisewide Information Management Model

Source: Marilyn Parker and Robert Benson with Ed Trainor, *Information Economics: Linking Information Technology and Business Performance* (Upper Saddle River, NJ: Prentice Hall, 1988).

3. Do we have someone within that line of business who oversees IT activity and talks the business language?

4. Do we have a sponsor in the line of business?

5. Do we have the attention of the line's management?

6. Does the line of business offer an opportunity to use systems in new ways?

By becoming familiar with lines of business, CIOs can better help them use IT to support current operations and influence the future, say Benson and Parker.

Sponsor weekly briefings. Another way to learn about the business is to sponsor short briefings for IT management and staff that are presented by line management or staff. We have attended such meetings and have found them to be most informative. They were about one-half hour long, with one speaker describing a part of the business. Managers and staff from different departments were invited to talk to a small group of IS managers and staff about their business and its marketplace: the products and services they offered versus what the competitors offered, the strengths and weaknesses of the firm and competitors, growth projections, possible changes in the market, and so on.

For example, in the aircraft industry an engineer could give the basics of the commercial aircraft business: sizes of planes, passenger capacity, distance capability, expected competition, changes in the industry, 5-year market projections, and so on. In the financial services industry, a manager could describe various types of customers and how each is using the Internet, products now offered by the firm and competitors, the impact of globalization and the Internet on financial markets, and so on. At such briefings, it is helpful if the presenter provides a written summary of the ideas presented, so attendees can take something away with them. A brief question-and-answer period also is useful.

To understand the business, people need to understand the marketplace. Few employees are given exposure to this breadth of knowledge. By sponsoring short presentations by the people closest to a business, IS management can help fix that problem without cutting into work time too greatly.

Attend industry meetings with line executives. Another way to learn about the business is to accompany a line executive to an industry conference — not a computer conference. We have found that attending a conference is one of the quickest ways to uncover issues currently facing an industry. These conferences contain the jargon used in the industry and the approaches others have used to market products, handle regulations, respond to competition, and so on. Attending a conference with a line executive can be even more enlightening because he or she can explain what the company is or is not doing in areas discussed by the speakers. Such joint attendance also is likely to foster a new friendship.

Read industry publications. One of the best ways to stay abreast of an industry is to read its publications, perhaps those that are online. Getting a well-rounded view of an industry may require reading several publications a month. News publications can provide information on new products, current issues, company changes, and so on. Newsletters, reports, and research journals generally provide better analyses of industry trends, discussions of ongoing research, and projections about the future.

One CIO spreads this job around in his department. Every staff member is responsible for reading certain periodicals and routing interesting articles and URLs to others.

Hold informal listening sessions.   In his book *Thriving on Chaos*,[9] consultant Tom Peters presents hundreds of suggestions on how managers can learn to not just cope with a chaotic business environment, but to thrive on it. In numerous places in the book, Peters urges people to simply listen and learn. His ideas are appropriate for IS management in their dealings with their customers, both those internal to the firm and external to it.

Yogi Berra, the famous baseball player, once said, "You can see a lot by observing." Similarly, Peters urges employees to learn a lot by listening to others' needs. Because product life cycles are shrinking, companies need to spot new trends earlier. Becoming a listening-intensive organization can help. Peters recounts several instances where people have created informal meetings to break down barriers among people who usually do not talk with one another. These get-togethers are held in a setting that is not charged with tension; participation is voluntary. Their purpose is to offer the opportunity to just chat. For instance, one hospital administrator set aside one early morning each week to offer coffee and rolls in her office, with an open invitation for doctors and administrators to drop by and chat. She had some lonely breakfasts at first, she told Peters, but the chats eventually evolved into the "real staff meeting" of the week. Another hospital administrator held an informal staff meeting at lunchtime every 2 weeks at a local pub and invited some doctors. The doctors felt honored to be invited, and their attendance helped break down stereotypes on both sides and improve communications.

Partner with a line executive.   The Society for Information Management presents a Partners in Leadership Award each year to honor an IS–business executive team who, through their alliance, have achieved significant business results. This award has been well received and is highly sought. It recognizes the partnering needed to successfully guide and deploy IT these days.

Through these approaches, CIOs and their staff can learn the businesses of the organization. Unless these or similar specific steps or mechanisms are implemented and become commonplace, the job of learning the business will be displaced by urgent, but less important, day-to-day work. With this knowledge, CIOs are in a better position to foster a vision of their firm's use of IT.

Creating a Vision of the Future and Selling It.   CIOs used to be seen as followers because IT supported the business. Today, it still does, but as noted earlier, business and technology now coevolve because technology breakthroughs allow companies to operate in new ways. Thus, CIOs have become the technical leaders of their enterprises. As such, they are not only involved in defining their enterprise's IT architecture and establishing its enterprisewide technical standards, but they also must ensure that the enterprise buys into those plans. The reality in many enterprises is that top-down command only goes so far and often hits roadblocks. CIOs and their direct reports often have to sell the vision.

What is a vision?   A *vision* is a statement of how someone wants the future to be or believes it will be. It is used to set the direction of an organization. Beath and Ives[10] present several corporate visions:

- Otis Elevator: Any salesperson can order an elevator in a day.
- USAA, an insurance company for current and retired military officers: Policy holders can accomplish their objective in a single phone call or Web site visit.

- Rittenhouse Homes: Customers can get a house designed and built from a retail store.
- Fidelity Investments: Mutual funds can be repriced on an hourly, rather than daily, basis.

Once a vision is in hand, then a strategy can be formulated on how to bring the vision into being. For instance, a vision might be to become the leading manufacturer of a certain kind of pump. The strategy could be to assign salespeople to specific large customer firms rather than to a geographic area. Once the strategy is decided, planning comes into play to map out the steps for carrying out that strategy. In this case, plans are needed for when and how to make the new assignments, who will make the selections, how smaller customers will be handled, by whom, and so on.

Why develop a vision?   A vision of a desirable future can provide stability when it sets direction for an organization. In the past, long-term strategies were created. They told *how* companies were going to get somewhere. Such multiyear plans are fine as long as the future is relatively predictable. However, in today's environment, people cannot predict important future events because those events are likely to appear random, not linear or rational. In such times, direction setting and short-term explorations within that space are most appropriate. Today, most corporate visions have an IT underpinning— leveraging the Internet for business purposes. That vision sets their direction.

To illustrate how one CIO is leading his enterprise via his vision and how he has structured his organization to sell that vision to the very independent-thinking business units, consider John Leggate, Group Vice President and Chief Information Officer at BP. His approach is described in the Gartner EXP report entitled *Glocalizing Your IS* (meaning, simultaneously globalizing and localizing an IS organization).[4b]

CASE EXAMPLE

BP

BP's main business activities are the exploration and production of crude oil and natural gas; the refining, marketing, supply, and transportation of these resources; and the manufacturing and marketing of petrochemicals. As of November 2002, BP was a $140-billion business (by market capitalization), with more than 100,000 employees serving 20 million customers daily through almost 29,000 service stations. An intense period of merger and acquisition activity has seen the absorption of Amoco, ARCO, Castrol, and Veba Aral in Germany.

The Business Is in the Business Units

BP's business units drive the business. There are 150 business units operating in over 100 countries. Ten years ago there were eight levels of organization

(Case Continued)

separating executive management from business unit management. Today, this separation has been, and continues to be, radically simplified.

Business units have their own balance sheet and are held accountable via a performance contract, which is negotiated with the executive committee of their business stream. In exchange for delivering on their contracts, the business units have the freedom to operate independently.

Headquarters must convince the business units of the wisdom of BP-wide practices. Many decisions are made by peer groups—networks of business units in a business stream. They resemble federations and are a vehicle for sharing knowledge among peers. They are also where the businesses must justify the resources they seek.

Overarching this distribution of power is a set of groupwide policies based on shared core values. At the center is learning and sharing, which drive collegial behavior and enable peer-group decision making. The glues for BP's decentralized business approach are operational excellence and strong core values.

Digital Business Underpins Transformation

In 1999, John Leggate's organization issued a rare companywide mandate for a common operating environment (COE). All Amoco employees were moved to BP's operating environment. Then, in 2000, all BP desktops and laptops were moved to Windows 2000 and Office 2000. COE 3, the latest generation, bridges time and distance by providing the hardware and software needed for employees to live and work on the Web.

In early 2000, Leggate formed Digital Business (DB). This moved IT out of the beleaguered role of technology provider into a strategy-creation role. DB comprises four central groups, which deliver overarching strategy, enterprise infrastructure and projects, and policies and standards while supporting differentiated service offerings driven by the business streams:

- *DB Strategy and Chief of Staff*: Aligns DB's strategic intent with the corporation and business objectives while developing clear business plans and objectives that move the agenda forward. BP's underpinning performance-management processes are used to ensure delivery of the strategy.

- *DB Chief Technology Office (CTO)*: Explores the external market to bring research and development (R&D) technology into BP to move its strategic direction forward, transforming BP into a digital corporation. The CTO group ensures that BP stays in tune with the external market through deployment of appropriate technological advancements.

- *DB Projects*: Undertakes the enterprisewide projects necessary to move its strategic infrastructure architecture forward.

- *DB Operations*: Provides overarching operational policies and standards across the globe to ensure a secure and reliable enterprise infrastructure as well as deliver some operations for the business streams. This is accomplished through an operations peer group

(Case Continued)

to ensure connectivity, alignment, and compliance among the business streams.

Living on the Web

To make "living on the Web" a reality, DB is moving processes and systems to the Web and simplifying both at the same time. BP is handing processes to service providers to consolidate, simplify, and then operate. For example, BP has externalized its human resource (HR) processes through the use of an external provider, Exult. Exult, which is located in California, has integrated the numerous HR databases and is managing the processes via the Web.

The paradox of business simplification is deciding where to seek commonality and standards and where to seek flexibility and innovation.

Socializing Technical Directions

DB's visionary role is to provide thought leadership. Its implementation role is to socialize the idea of a new common good to the point where people accept it. Corporate edicts are not commonly used in BP's culture.

Socialization can take quite some time, especially when a common approach costs more than a local solution. It requires face-to-face enrollment and starts with conversations with the business leaders. From there, local governance boards decide how to implement the general principle locally.

BP's chief technology officer has established a powerful network of architects to help create consensus and drive choices that benefit BP as a whole. All of the architects on the various network teams work in the businesses. The role of each team is to create "the framework for conversation" with the business units about architecture for a specific area, such as wireless, Web Services, and so on. They use a template method to define an area of interest and drive toward consensus.

To educate communities of interest, DB reveals data, such as showing waste so a community will seek ways to reduce it. For example, BP had 36 systems reporting health and safety in 1999. Once the health and safety community knew this fact, it decided how to decrease the number. The rationalization was not centrally managed. The same is happening with the 100 maintenance management systems.

Technical choices are now made through business-based networks of experts. Similar communities handle major system upgrades. They define the global direction, evolve standards collegially, and then look to service providers to supply the components. These communities know they should not permit divergent local actions; thus, they must make difficult choices between corporate fit and local need.

Going Forward: Foster Learning and Focus on Exploitation

A major challenge is fostering learning. Today, too much prompting is needed to get BP employees to look at what others within BP are doing elsewhere in the world. Becoming a connected corporation helps, but the key is behavioral and cultural change.

Within the IT realm, the major question is, "How do we get 100,000 people to fully utilize BP's resources to change our underlying business?" The real leverage comes from the new value a new system opens up. Therefore, adoption and

---

(Case Continued)

exploitation of the new technology and systems become a major challenge but a necessary component to realizing the value of the business transformation. This involves much effort in change management to train and influence employees to accept and use the new technology.

Bright people have been attracted to DB because it is involved in the most important conversation: where BP is going, digitally. Leggate's executive team has a broad portfolio of skills, which is critical when a leadership team is not only creating the future but is also responsible for selling it. Some have deep technical knowledge. Others are more commercially oriented people who want to use digital technology as a transformational tool. They all signed up because the agenda is vast and enthralling. ∎

Encouraging champions of IT projects.   As the rate of change in the IT field has increased, we have heard CIOs say they need to encourage IT experimentation, especially by people in the operating units, to advance company IT experience and evolve the IT vision. Here are the ideas of two researchers and one user company on how to do that—by supporting IT champions.

A *champion* is someone with a vision who gets it implemented by obtaining the funding, pushing the project over hurdles, putting his or her reputation on the line, and taking on the risk of the project, state Professors Cynthia Beath and Blake Ives.[10]

The first step in encouraging champions is to be able to recognize these people. They are likely to be people you already know about, and they may be doing things that make you uncomfortable, say Beath and Ives. For instance, they are probably already circumventing established project approval processes, they are creating isolated information systems, and they may be using nonstandard equipment. They may already be pursuing a vision of how IT can help their business, whether systems people assist them or not.

These people are opinion leaders, and they have a reputation for creative ideas or being involved with innovations. They also have developed strong ties to others in their organization, and they command respect within the firm. They have the organizational power to get strategic innovations implemented.

According to the authors, IS champions need three things from IS management: information, resources, and support.

They need information.   Championing an IT innovation is an information-intensive activity, note Beath and Ives. Therefore, champions need information, facts, and expertise for persuading others that the technology will work. IS staff can help champions gather and assess information about a technology's capabilities, its costs, risks of operation, and how it might be used in an experiment. IS staff also can help by sharing their expertise and by putting champions in contact with other experts, such as vendors or users of a new technology.

IS staff can assist champions in understanding current applications and data relevant to their project. Finally, they can help champions understand how the company manages change, because systems people are continually involved in implementing system changes throughout the enterprise.

They need resources. The authors cite Rosabeth Kanter, author of *Change Masters*,[11] who says champions most need staff time. Giving champions free staff time is especially helpful during the evaluation and persuasion portions of a project. However, systems management can go even further, by assigning, say, information center consultants to help champions.

In addition to staff time, champions are likely to need material resources, such as hardware and software. These resources can be loaned to them free of charge or provided in some other way.

They need support. Finally, champions need supporters, people who approve of what they are doing and give legitimacy to their project. It is important that IS management corroborate statements made about the technology by the champion. The champion does not need to know how the technology works, only how it might be used. The IS organization should handle the technical aspects. Beath and Ives urge demonstrating the champion's claims about the technology and promoting the technology to build enthusiasm for it and to win support from others.

Finally, IS management can assist a champion win endorsement of upper management by helping to create the plans for introducing the new technology. The IS department can assist by contacting vendors and choosing an appropriate implementation approach. All of these supportive actions will improve the quality of the proposal and strengthen it in the eyes of management.

Beath and Ives encourage IS management to make it easier for IT champions to arise and succeed. One company that supported champions is Aetna Life and Casualty.

CASE EXAMPLE

AETNA LIFE AND CASUALTY

In 2000, ING acquired Aetna Life and Casualty, a financial services company with headquarters in Hartford, Connecticut. ING is headquartered in Amsterdam, The Netherlands. Aetna is now ING Life Insurance and Annuity Company.

Before being acquired by ING, much of Aetna's IT work had been decentralized; therefore, the corporate administration department focused on three functions, which they called "plan, build, and run." The operations group ran data center and telecommunication opera-

tions. The corporate technology services group assisted divisions in selecting, building, and implementing computer systems. The people and technology group also helped divisions build and implement successful systems; they emphasized the human perspective.

The planning function was the responsibility of the corporate technology planning group, which was meant to be a catalyst for introducing new technology. Its charter was to help the insurance company understand and use

(Case Continued)

breakthrough technologies. By *breakthrough*, they meant technologies that would increase performance by at least 100 percent. "We constantly seek to make the future credible by encouraging innovation, experimentation, and evaluation," a member of this group told us. They saw their job as encouraging end users to talk about new technologies and test them out in real-life situations. The corporate technology planning group fostered discussions and experimentation in three ways.

They Sought Out Business Champions

The group tested technologies by cosponsoring business projects, acting as a magnet to attract people who wanted to experiment with a technology. They held workshops on specific technologies, published one-page issue papers describing certain technologies, and talked to people in a wide number of functions.

Their goal was to find business champions who thought a technology might solve their business problem. These champions also needed to be willing to share the funding and direction of a pilot project using that technology. The users agreed to let the planning group study their use and write about it. For a project to be funded, it had to have a business champion and be aimed at solving a business problem.

In several cases, the group found champions who recognized the need to test several technologies, some with expected results and others that might change future work life dramatically. These were *smart champions*, because they saw the value of investing in a portfolio of new technologies.

They Studied Pilot Projects

In one pilot project of a 500-user communication system, the planning group did systematic research during the pilot, using before-and-after questionnaires to measure how attitudes changed. They looked to see whether "telephone tag" increased or decreased. They held focus group discussions. In addition, they had some users keep daily diaries of their activities.

Based on this research, they concluded that the system would benefit a majority of employees. To then promote its use, they created a brochure and videos, which they handed off to the corporate operations group for the marketing and management of the system.

They Established Steering Committees

Steering committees can be surrogate champions to guide and build support for a new technology. When the corporate technology group saw a technology that appeared interesting, they sometimes held a one-day magnet session to find champions. Sometimes they found steering committees rather than individual champions when a topic was really hot. In one case, 200 people volunteered to do pilot projects. Because it made too large a group, a smaller steering committee was formed. It put on four seminars, got end users thinking about how they might use the technology, and oversaw some projects.

Challenges They Encountered

The technology planning group encountered three challenges.

One was simply getting people's attention. When a technology was not

(Case Continued)

immediately available, people did not want to take any action. However, many technologies require a learning curve. Even when a technology is not readily available, people should be experimenting with it so that the company has in-house knowledge when products do begin to appear. Thus, making a future technology credible to people was one hurdle.

Keeping people in an experimental mode was another challenge. Once people were funded for a pilot, they wanted to do it right. They did not want to create a quick-and-dirty system; they wanted to create a production-quality system. It was hard to get people to create only quick, experimental systems.

The third challenge was making sure that the use would really pay off. The planning group did not want small productivity improvements; they wanted orders-of-magnitude improvements—at least two-to-one to three-to-one payoffs. They constantly asked users: How do you know you will get this payback?

The group's goals were education and action. They wanted end users to be comfortable using future technologies and to achieve a good payback at the same time. For more ideas on how to stimulate innovation, see *Managing Organizational Innovation*.[12]

Such an approach puts companies in a better position to spot new opportunities, to experiment with them, and then to put them into widespread use before their competitors. In a fast-changing world, nimbleness—a sign of being open to accepting emerging technologies—is needed. ∎

Governing: Establishing an IS Governance Structure

The term *governance* has become prominent, not only in IT circles, but in business circles as well. IT governance is *"the assignment of decision rights and the accountability framework to encourage desirable behavior in the use of IT,"* state Peter Weill and Richard Woodham of MIT's Sloan School of Management.[13] Governance differs from management in that governance is about deciding who makes decisions, whereas management is about making decisions once decision rights have been assigned.

Governance has become important in the business world because financial scandals have shown that there was not much true governance in place in some very large enterprises. Decisions were made by a few top executives, subordinates did not question their superiors, and boards rubber-stamped decisions. There were no checks and balances.

Governance has become important in the IS world because IT expenditures have become so large and so diverse that management has had to find a way to bring order to all the decision making. However, centralizing all IT decisions is not the solution, because business units and local employees legitimately need a voice in the decisions to tailor their business to the local culture and customers. Striking a balance between global and local needs (glocalizing) is a major emphasis in IS these day. The main discussions are at the governance level, assigning decision rights. Just as the U.S. Constitution assigns rights to the states and powers to the federal government, enterprises now see the need to do the same. Finally, a third reason for the rising importance of governance is the issue of creating an IT portfolio that is in sync with business needs and stays that way.

Assigning Decision Rights. Peter Weill of MIT and Marianne Broadbent, formerly of Gartner EXP and now at Melbourne Business School, have undertaken the most comprehensive study of IT governance, surveying 256 companies in 23 countries and conducting over 20 in-depth interviews.[4c] From their research, they see IT governance as having three components, as shown in Figure 2-9: (1) six governance styles of who makes which decisions (the rows), (2) five key IT decision areas (the columns), and (3) governance mechanisms used to carry out IT governance (the cells). The IT governance arrangements matrix in Figure 2-9 illustrates "a good general-purpose IT governance design that balances decision rights for a multibusiness unit enterprise," state Broadbent and Weill.

Six governance styles (the rows). A governance style defines who has a *decision right* (the right and responsibility to make a decision) and an *input right* (the right to provide input to a decision but not make the decision). The six governance styles are:

1. A *business monarchy* is where C-level executives (increasingly including the CIO) hold the right to make decisions. A mechanism used to carry out this governance style could be an executive committee or perhaps an IT council with executive committee members.

FIGURE 2-9 IT Governance Arrangements Matrix

Decision Domain / Style	IT Principles		IT Infrastructure Strategies		IT Architecture		Business Application Needs		IT Investment and Prioritization	
	Input	Decision	Input	Decision	Input	Decision	Input	Decision	Input	Decision
Business Monarchy										Cap appr comm
IT Monarchy				IT leaders		IT leaders				
Feudal										
Federal	Exec comm Biz leaders		Exec comm Biz leaders		Biz leaders Biz proc own				Exec comm Biz leaders	
Duopoly		Exec comm IT leaders					Biz leaders Biz proc own Biz/IT rel mgs	Biz leaders Biz proc own		
Anarchy										

Governance mechanisms   ☐ Input rights   ■ Decision rights

Exec comm	*Executive committee/C-levels*	Cap appr comm	*Exec comm subgroup includes CIO*
Biz leaders	*Business unit heads/presidents*	Biz proc own	*Business process owner*
IT leaders	*CIO, CIO offices and biz unit CIOs*	Biz IT rel mgs	*Business/IT relationship managers*

© 2003 Gartner, Inc. and MIT Sloan Center for Information Systems Research (Weill), drawing on the framework of Weill and Woodham (2002).

Source: Marianne Broadbent and Peter Weill, *Tailor IT Governance to Your Enterprise*, Gartner EXP Club Report, October 2003.

2. An *IT monarchy* is where IT executives hold the right to make decisions. A mechanism could be an IT leadership council that includes corporate and business unit CIOs.

3. *Feudal* is where business unit leaders (or their delegates) have decision or input rights. Feudal governance might use a business-only committee as a mechanism.

4. *Federal* means that the rights are shared by C-level executives and one other tier of the business hierarchy, such as business-unit presidents. In IT governance, an IT group might also be involved as a third participant. The federal style is akin to the U.S. government structure, with a central nationwide government and dispersed state governments. A mechanism for implementing this IT governance style is committees that draw from several organizational levels.

5. A *duopoly* is where one IT group and one business group share a right. A mechanism might be an IT–business-unit committee that draws up a service-level agreement for IT to provide services to the business unit.

6. *Anarchy* is where individual process owners or end users hold a right. The anarchy governance style is rare in the five main IT decision areas, note Weill and Broadbent, because it is not effective in guiding IT in a large enterprise.

Five decision areas (the columns).   There are five key decision areas in IT.

1. *IT principles* are high-level statements about how IT will be used to create business value. Three examples of IT principles follow:
   - Corporate IT is responsible for infrastructure; business units are responsible for business-unit applications.
   - Technical reporting relationships must match corporate reporting relationships.
   - IT purchasing from major vendors must be centrally coordinated to minimize costs and ensure consistency.

As shown in Figure 2-9, Weill and Broadbent found that an IT duopoly (with business and IT executives) provides the business–IT collaboration needed to set the principles that support the business. Input often comes from other business groups (federal).

2. *IT infrastructure strategies* state the approach for building shared and standard IT services across the enterprise. This decision area is technical, so it is generally made by an IT monarchy, as shown in Figure 2-9, often with federal input.

3. *IT architecture* states the technical choices that will meet business needs. Again, this is a technical decision area, so it is generally left up to the IT monarchy, with federal input.

4. *Business application needs* is where the business defines its application needs. As shown in Figure 2-9, these decisions, and input to them, are generally federal.

5. *IT investment and prioritization* defines the process for moving IT-based investments through justification, approval, and accountability. Often, the capital appropriation committee (a business monarchy) approves IT and all other capital investments. As in other decision areas, input comes from various sources (federal style).

The arrangement matrix differs, of course, among enterprises. Those seeking synergies among their business units are more likely to enforce top-down decisions. Those with autonomous business units are likely to emphasize local decision making. Enterprises with pulls both for synergy and local autonomy may make extensive use of IT principles to guide faster decision making in their sprawling enterprise. Such is the case with Duke Energy International, as described in the October 2003 Gartner EXP report on IT governance.

CASE EXAMPLE

DUKE ENERGY INTERNATIONAL

Duke Energy, headquartered in Charlotte, North Carolina, manages a dynamic portfolio of natural gas and electric supply, delivery, and trading businesses. Its international division, Duke Energy International (DEI), operates regional energy businesses, primarily in Latin America; however, the company formerly had interests in the Asian Pacific and Europe as well.

DEI CIO Max Kennedy has been accountable for DEI IT performance and governance and reports to the president of DEI, Richard McGee. The regional energy businesses also have CIOs who report to their regional managing director.

DEI Differentiates Itself by Being Nimble

Product and service innovation, combined with speed and flexibility, are the key drivers in DEI's regional businesses. The company can be nimble and capture opportunities because business governance is local. Lines of communication are short, so decisions can be made quickly.

For example, when DEI still owned interests in Australia, a gas plant operated by another firm encountered a maintenance problem and had to be shut down. Within a few hours, a half-million-dollar deal had been signed with Duke Energy to supply replacement gas. Competitors could not get near Duke Energy's speed; it was the mindset under which the region operated and was one of its strengths.

IT Governance Is Based on Principles and Relationships

The regions also have pressures for synergy with Duke Energy International and among themselves. Principles play an important role in achieving synergy while maintaining agility. DEI's Information Management (IM) organization has principles for organizational and personal governance. Kennedy has espoused eight principles in managing IM:

1. Agree on the reason for being
2. Have a vision for IM
3. Put a clear organizational design in place
4. Implement successful IT governance
5. Implement demand management

(Case Continued)

6. Design useful reporting information flows

7. Manage business–IM value relationships

8. Implement global collaborative networks

As an example, part of the "Manage business–IM value relationship" principle is the guideline to establish multilevel relationships between IM and the business at different levels in the hierarchy. Such relationships are strong because more than one set of two people hold them together. This principle also is used to prepare top technical staff for their next job, which involves relationship management.

The regional CIOs follow Kennedy's three-point stewardship and escalation guidelines to help them answer the question, "When am I free to decide on my own versus when should I involve others?" The guidelines are:

- I involve others if the consequences of my actions will come to bear on those others.

- I do not involve others if the consequences of my actions will come to bear just on me.

- I inform others when the consequences of my actions will be of benefit to others.

In general, regional CIOs would prefer to use the U.S. IM solutions, which could be done about 70 percent of the time, to leverage the lower negotiated licensing prices and to tap their technical expertise. They would only differ when the cost was too high or the product did not have adequate support in the region.

In essence, DEI's IM organization aims to foster relationships with the business. Relationships increase nimbleness, help identify opportunities to save costs, and lead to innovation. ■

Investing: Shaping the IT Portfolio

IT investments have become so large and important to company success that the subject of how to make investments properly has gained increased attention. Business executives used to blame CIOs for poor IT investments. That view is becoming less tenable because CIOs can only implement good systems. They are not responsible for changing business practices to take advantage of those systems. That's the job of line executives.

Following are two perspectives on this IT investment topic: one strategic (*what* to invest in) and one tactical (*how* to make investment decisions). Both show the importance of having business and IT thinking behind IT investing.

A Strategic View of Making IT Investments. Diana Farrell, director of the McKinsey Global Institute, conducted a fascinating study of 20 industries (8 in the U.S., 6 in Germany, and 6 in France) to discern the connections (if any) among IT, competition, innovation, and productivity from 1990 to 2000.[14]

The bottom line of the study is that a "new" economy did indeed emerge in the 1990s, *but only in* the six industries she studied where there was intense

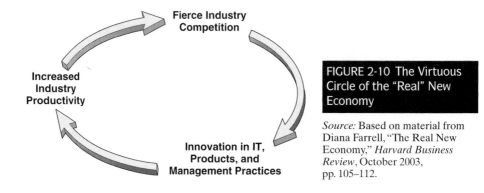

FIGURE 2-10 The Virtuous Circle of the "Real" New Economy

Source: Based on material from Diana Farrell, "The Real New Economy," *Harvard Business Review*, October 2003, pp. 105–112.

competition that was not throttled by government regulation. These six industries were retailing, securities brokerage, wholesaling, semiconductors, computer assembly, and telecommunications.

Farrell found that intense competition forced executives in these industries to innovate—by investing in IT, by improving their business processes, and by offering new products and services. These innovations, in turn, increased productivity. Thus, notes Farrell, the "real" new economy has a virtuous circle: competition leads to innovation, which leads to productivity increases. See Figure 2-10.

As just one of many examples given by Farrell, the mobile telecommunications industry in France and Germany in the 1990s faced little government intervention, so there was intense competition among the national providers. Industry productivity increased 25 percent from 1990 to 2000. In the United States, on the other hand, regulation erected barriers to offering nationwide mobile telecommunications services, and productivity increased only 15 percent.

The McKinsey study also found that all IT investments were not alike. IT investments in industries that depended on information processing (such as large retailers that handled millions of transactions a day) and that faced growing competition had the greatest productivity increases—but only under three conditions:

1. The IT investments targeted the main levers of productivity,

2. The IT investments were made in the right sequence and at the right time, and

3. The IT investments were complemented with innovations in management practices.

Targeting IT investments.   Firms that concentrated their IT spending on "levers that matter" gained the greatest productivity. Because productivity equals outputs divided by inputs, a lever either increases outputs (such as offering new higher-value services) or decreases inputs (such as reducing inventory or working capital). But the "levers that matter" differ among industries.

For example, the applications that mattered most for the big-box retailers, such as Wal-Mart, Kmart, and Target in the United States, that sell high volumes and have low margins were warehousing and transportation systems that more tightly linked them to their suppliers and increased the retailers' inventory turns. On the other hand, for specialty retailers whose items have short shelf lives, the applications that mattered the most dealt with assortment and allocation planning systems that reduced their inventory-holding costs and the amount of out-of-style merchandise in their stores. Concludes Farrell: Smart companies invest heavily in IT applications that increase productivity and seek the least expensive option for all their other IT systems.

Sequencing and timing IT investments.   Companies that reaped the highest productivity generally sequenced their IT investments so that new ones built on existing ones. Wal-Mart and Kmart present contrasting examples, notes Farrell.

CASE EXAMPLE

WAL-MART VERSUS KMART

The sequence of IT investments at Wal-Mart and Kmart offer one example of the effect of getting the sequence right, notes Diana Farrell of McKinsey Global Institute.[14]

In the 1990s, Wal-Mart first installed systems to automate the flow of products in its internal supply chain—from suppliers to its distribution centers and warehouses. Once this internal flow was being well-managed, Wal-Mart turned outward to its suppliers to more closely coordinate its own operations with theirs in hopes of improving effectiveness and reducing costs. With the flow along its supply chain as a base, Wal-Mart again turned to its customers, using IT to better plan its merchandising mix and replenishment.

Last, it built a data warehouse, pulling data from these systems and other sources, to answer complex questions to hone operations. During the 1990s, Wal-Mart's productivity increased.

Kmart, on the other hand, did not get the sequence of IT investments right in the 1990s, says Farrell. As a result, its productivity decreased. Kmart first used IT to better target its marketing promotions rather than investing in supply chain systems to manage fluctuations in product volume. As a result, increases in customer demand from its successful promotions could not be met because Kmart could not get enough of the products into its stores. Demand was higher than supply. Kmart lost potential sales. ∎

Timing is also important, notes Farrell. The question is whether to lead or to follow IT trends. Based on her study, she recommends that companies rush into a new technology only when it advances company goals, builds on company strengths, and cannot be easily replicated by competitors. Jumping on a trend just because "everybody is doing it" signals that the new technology is not likely to provide enough differentiation to increase the company's standing against its competitors.

Complementing IT investments.   IT investments do not reap anticipated results until accompanying management practices change to take advantage of potentially better ways of working. This lesson about the symbiotic relationship between IT and its use has been illustrated time and again for decades. And it's still true.

Farrell again uses Wal-Mart as an example. She notes that Wal-Mart simplified its logistics practices as it automated the flow of products to and from its distribution centers. It also redefined its relationships with suppliers when it was more tightly coordinating its information systems with theirs. The most famous shift was with Procter & Gamble and how it supplied Pampers baby diapers to Wal-Mart stores. The relationship shifted from an arms' length buyer–seller relationship to more of a trusted-partner one. The two shared confidential information, made decisions jointly, and reduced duplicate processes, thereby cutting inventory costs, improving efficiency, and better matching supply and demand.

In conclusion, Farrell believes that the reason the link between productivity and IT investments has not been easy to demonstrate is that it depends on three factors: investing in levers that matter, getting the investment sequence and timing right, and pairing new systems with new processes and work practices that take advantage of the new IT capabilities. Furthermore, IT is not the only contributor to increased productivity.

A Tactical View of Making IT Investments.   In hindsight, it may be easy to see which IT investments were good and which were not so good. However, at the moment of decision, the choice may not be so clear because of the complex and volatile nature of business. The recent approach to making IT investments is to view all company systems as a portfolio and to make investment decisions from that viewpoint, rather than judging each investment only on its own merits. Investment guidelines, such as those provided by Farrell, can then be used in the decision making.

There are numerous approaches for prioritizing projects. Following is one example, as used by AXA Financial.

CASE EXAMPLE

AXA FINANCIAL

The AXA Group is a global financial services organization with 140,000 employees and headquarters in France. Some 10,000 employees work in the United States at AXA Financial. Its retail businesses include AXA Advisors, LLC; The Equitable Life Assurance Society of the U.S.; Alliance Capital Management; and Sanford C. Bernstein & Co. Its wholesale division (AXA Distributors, LLC) works with brokerage houses, large banks, and independent financial planners that sell Equitable Life products through their own channels. As of June 30, 2002, AXA Financial had approximately $441 billion in assets under management, and its IT group employed 650 people.

Paul Bateman leads the enterprise governance process, which resides within the IT organization yet spans AXA

(*Case Continued*)

Financial. He spends about half his time working with the business units. He was hired to manage AXA Financial's IT portfolio. Prior to his hire, senior management believed IT provided competitive differentiation and made so many significant investments in IT infrastructure and applications that the company needed to get more control of its growing portfolio. In 2000, some 200 high-priced, significant projects were in development.

Bateman introduced a governance process to instill more efficient management controls. A key principle of the process is that all projects and investments are *not* created equal. Each one's merit depends on its economics, not on an executive's emotional attachment to it or other nonfinancial factors. This new governance process has brought discipline and a way to value projects.

Introducing a New Methodology

Bateman first undid the level playing field by introducing a methodology to help AXA Financial executives define a hierarchy of importance and prioritize projects against that hierarchy. He called on the people at United Management Technologies (UMT)[15] to demonstrate their portfolio prioritization methodology. He had been exposed to it while at Citigroup and found that UMT had since increased the methodology's functionality, making it best in class. He proposed it to senior management, and they agreed to bring the methodology into AXA Financial.

To begin acquainting the company with the new governance model, Bateman held a series of kick-off meetings with the CFO from each area, including retail and wholesale sales, marketing and prod-

uct development, service delivery, and IT. Needless to say, they were pleased with the financial emphasis of the approach.

Then he introduced it to the executive vice presidents (EVPs)—the business-unit heads—explaining the need to begin managing the portfolio of major IT projects the way fund managers manage their portfolios. Once the EVPs agreed with the concept, Bateman described the UMT tools that could help.

The top-level project review committee is the governance committee, which is cochaired by the company's CEO and CIO. It also includes the CFO and the EVPs. By representing all the lines of business, the committee ensures that approved projects benefit the entire company. This committee helped develop the governance model, which initially was called *IT governance*, but has since become *enterprise governance*, because the process is now used to prioritize more than IT projects.

The Prioritization Process

The process begins each year with the EVPs turning in their wish lists of all projects they would like for the coming year, as if they had an unlimited checkbook. Last year, the lists totaled close to 300 projects.

Winnowing the Wish List. Next, the EVPs are asked to split those projects into three categories: must-have (or else AXA Financial would incur revenue or operational risks), should-have, and nice-to-have. Taking out the nice-to-haves still left over 170 projects.

Selecting Business Objectives. To reduce the 170, AXA used the UMT methodology, which begins by having the enterprise

(Case Continued)

state the objectives upon which the projects will be judged. Although the CEO has set out an AXA Financial-wide vision and goals, the business units are too diverse for a single list of objectives. Therefore, each business unit developed its own objectives with the CEO's strategic goals in mind. Bateman and UMT assisted each business unit to arrive at four to six *measurable* objectives (such as increase customer satisfaction) that could be tracked and that aligned with the CEO's strategic direction.

Prioritizing the Objectives. Each business unit, led by the EVP and including his or her direct reports, then ranked the objectives using UMT's pair-wise methodology. One at a time, the business unit decided how one objective compared with each other objective on a scale of importance. They had seven choices: extremely more important, strongly more important, moderately more important, of equal importance, moderately less important, strongly less important, or extremely less important.

As each decision was made, a color-coded choice was recorded by a facilitator on a matrix displayed on a large screen in front of the group. The side benefit of this ranking exercise was the business discussion it elicited among department members. Executives' assumptions and rationale for their decisions often surfaced when they debated how much more or less important, say, *increasing customer satisfaction* was compared with *increasing market share*. The pairwise comparison approach made it easy to debate two objectives solely on their own merit. The model took care of the final overall ranking among the objectives.

Ranking Projects Using the Objectives. Given this list of prioritized objectives, the committee moved on to ranking each project against how much that project supported each objective—extremely supports, strongly supports, moderately supports, low support, or no support.

There were several keys to performing this step confidently. One key was understanding what, say, *strongly supports* meant. Some business units quantified each level of support beforehand to vote from a level playing field.

Another key to success was each staff member's understanding of each project well enough to make these decisions, which meant having well-defined and consistently defined projects.

A third key was not having too many projects and too many objectives, or else the ranking process would take too long.

As in the objective-ranking meeting, a major benefit of this project-ranking meeting was the personal revelations that surfaced when members explained why they voted that a project *strongly supports* an objective, whereas others voted that the same project provided *low support*. When done well, these discussions yielded both insights and a group consensus. A high comfort level emerged with the results.

Following these two rankings, each EVP had a prioritized list to present to the enterprise governance committee. By this time, the total number of projects had been culled from the over 170 to approximately 70. One by one, the EVPs defended their own list, explaining why each project was included. The committee then decided which ones would advance to the funding phase.

(Case Continued)

Funding the Projects. To help the governance committee decide which projects would be funded, a business case application was then filled out for each one. The application asked for financial projections for the current year plus 5 more. Financial calculations for net present value, rate of return, cash flow, and payback period were then determined using the business case application.

Of course, not all projects are alike. For those that aim to produce income, the committee focuses on payback period. For those that will implement infrastructure improvements, the committee looks at operational efficiencies to be gained or extenuating circumstances (such as the vendor no longer supporting a system).

Thus, the process uses four filters: the EVP's wish list filter, the must-have/should-have filter, the UMT prioritization filter, and the business case filter. The result is a list of projects that *can* be funded.

Throughout the year, the governance committee meets two to three times a month for 2 hours. It reviews the launch dates for new products and works backward to determine when the support mechanisms, such as the underlying IT system, need to be in place.

Projects costing over $250,000 require the full 5-year analysis and approval of the governance committee. Projects requiring less funding need a mini-business case; these are reviewed monthly by the governance committee to ensure that they are strategically linked to company goals. The EVPs have learned to do their own filtering of projects, only taking the ones they know will pass muster at the governance committee meetings.

AXA Financial then uses ProSight portfolio management software to manage its portfolio of ongoing projects. The plan is for the governance committee to begin reviewing this data to keep tabs on the progress of projects, as well as their budgets.

Benefits of the Project Prioritization Process

The UMT-based process provides the enterprise governance committee with a panoramic view of the business, thus discussions of IT projects no long center around budgets. Rather, they center around business strategy, such as looking at the cross-functional nature of a product and how it fits on the road map laid out by the CEO. The attendees benefit from these discussions because they have both a view and a say in that future. Knowing the pending projects in the other areas has significantly increased cross-functional communications. Bateman acts as the secretary for the meeting, recording what has been approved and listing follow-up items. "It is a disciplined way of helping AXA Financial manage its future," he notes.

Another benefit is that approved projects are no longer questioned because they have the blessing of the CEO. The group discussions that precede the approvals also create a powerful group-concurrence effect.

Now that AXA Financial has been using the UMT methodology and the ProSight monitoring software for 2 years, it is turning its attention to comparing planned benefits to actual benefits because it is beginning to receive actual performance numbers. Bateman is working to refine the estimation techniques so

(*Case Continued*)

that they are more accurate. Furthermore, once a project has been implemented, its projected savings are being taken out of the appropriate budgets by the CFOs.

This enterprise governance structure is now seen as a best practice throughout the AXA Group. It is now being introduced to and adapted by some of AXA's European and Canadian operations.

Future Plans

Due to the success of the enterprise governance process in funding and tracking new projects, Bateman is always looking at ways to expand the use of governance tools to other areas of the business. The ongoing goal is to continually search for ways to increase the value of money spent. AXA Financial has started a zero-based budgeting process (based on activity-based costing) where each business looks at the activities it performs each day and calculates the number of people and the time spent on each activity.

As an example, they could then potentially integrate the discipline of a zero-based budgeting process with the UMT prioritization tool. This approach would give the company a new way to see options to further increase the value of investments.

Another way to improve value throughout the IT organization is to ensure that project proposals list, say, two or three options. For instance, one option could be to deliver 80 percent of the functionality the first year for $1 million; the other option could be to deliver 100 percent in 1 year for $2 million. Options would yield better business cases and save the company money. In the past 2 years, the enterprise governance process has deferred approximately $20 million in expenses. The business cases showed the money would have been poorly spent. Bateman and his team are looking at ways to improve the governance process further, to help ensure that the governance committee is making informed investment decisions in support of future growth. ■

Sy Aslan[16] has helped numerous clients in strategic planning, decision making, and IT project prioritization—including clients of UMT. When people talk about prioritizing IT projects, Aslan says the process is really about team decision making; prioritization is just one aspect. He offers the following lessons he has learned over the years in this area.

Realize That the Benefits Come More from the Discussions Than the Prioritizations.
A team-based approach to prioritizing projects offers numerous benefits. The foremost benefit is the business-based discussions that take place as people describe their needs and their projects, debate how projects support the business and the extent of that support, and explain the rationale behind their votes.

When the discussions are structured, focused, and well moderated, the participants better understand the business goals, better support others and other business units, and are more committed to the selected portfolio of projects, says Aslan.

Discussions during prioritization lead to healthier teamwork and better decision processes, both of which reduce political maneuvering and simplify future project reviews. The discussions also generate new ideas, surface incorrect assumptions, and create an environment for in-depth discussions of the organization's mission and goals.

Discussions also lead to better definitions of projects (and even company strategies) and to deeper understanding of the insides of projects. They bring to light what is not needed and crystallize how each project supports specific business needs, if indeed they do.

After a prioritization discussion, the participants can identify which projects can be delayed and how dependent projects are on one another. Discussion also saves time and reduces the amount of noise in prioritization. Low-value and questionable projects are no longer submitted to the group for approval because people know others will scrutinize the submissions.

Put Projects into Categories Where They Are Comparable. Once projects have been defined, it becomes clear that they belong in different categories and thus require different treatment, says Aslan. One category is *R&D*. These projects cannot produce immediate tangible benefits. Furthermore, there is no certainty they will yield any value in the future. These projects should only compete with each other for some percent of the IT budget.

On the other end of the scale is the *volume* category. Volume projects are sure things. For example, when a business unit experiences increased demand, it may need to invest in more IT volume to capture the revenue from that demand. Because these projects support sure growth and have a secure return on investment (ROI), they should not compete with any other project. All that is needed is the assurance of the capacity planning people that the underlying computer system has indeed reached its capacity limit and the investment and action plan are sound.

Finally, it is also wise to have a minimum consideration level, for example, $25,000. Managers should be able to finance projects below that threshold from their discretionary budget. However, these projects should be reviewed by a higher-level sponsor and project outcomes should be part of the manager's performance evaluation.

Address Project Risks. Project managers should address three types of risk in their proposals:

- Risk that the project will fail
- Risk of not doing the project
- Risk that it is the wrong project for what is trying to be achieved

Every project carries with it a *risk of failure*. This risk can range from total failure to failure to yield some of the expected benefits. To properly prioritize projects, they all need to be at the same risk level and have the same probability of success. To evaluate risk of failure, project managers should be able to document answers to at least these four questions:

1. What is the probability the project will be completed on time?
2. Will it be completed within budget?

3. Could it be impacted by an internal issue (over which the company has control)?

4. Could it be impacted by an external issue (over which the company has little or no control)?

When a project has a higher risk than is defined as acceptable by the selection process, the project manager should identify mitigation methods, calculate the cost of the risk, and add that cost to the project, says Aslan.

The second type of risk is *not doing the project*. Here, people need to consider the reason for the project and the problems it will prevent once it is up and running, says Aslan. For example, a project that will introduce virus protection across the network will prevent virus damage. Consider the project as insurance against this damage and use simple actuarial methods to calculate the value of such insurance (probability of the damaging event multiplied by the cost if the event does occur). The calculated insurance value should be added to the project benefits.

The third risk is *doing the wrong thing*. Three examples are introducing a technology that will be quickly replaced by a superior one, supporting a temporary market trend, and developing a system for a process that is not effective or efficient. These projects may be successful, but they will be deemed useless very quickly.

The best mitigation approach for this risk goes back to the basic tenet of project prioritization: team discussion. The team needs to surface the assumptions that support the project and then play scenario games: Create three scenarios about the business and the project's future. Make one scenario a disaster, the second rosy, and the third an extension of the team's pessimism or optimism by a few degrees. Then have the team ask itself, "What effect will this project have in each scenario?" The ensuing discussion will expose holes in thinking and offer mending approaches. The project may be cancelled, divided into phases, consolidated with another, or recreated in a different version.

The prioritization process takes into consideration costs and benefits. In essence, reviewing the risk is the response to the financial manager saying, "I need proof that this project will achieve its benefits within the stated budget."

Prioritize Quarterly and Apportion Your Budget Accordingly. In our constantly changing business world, it is not wise to close the list of approved projects for a long period of time. New project requirements arise frequently, and some of these projects may be more important than others already approved. Also, in most cases, the constraints for undertaking projects are not only budgetary, but also people resources and possibly dependencies and timing. If a prioritization team starts the year allocating its entire annual budget, it may find little leeway for change during the year. People will hold onto their budget allocation as if it were an entitlement.

A quarterly prioritization provides more agility. The first option is to allocate part of the budget as reserve to be allocated at a later time. For example, allocate two-thirds of the budget in the first quarter and save the remainder for the following quarters. Another option is to state that any project that gains approval but does not start in the quarter automatically goes into the next quarter's evaluation—and so does its allocation. People are happy with this approach, says Aslan, because they know they always have a chance to introduce a new project or reexamine a rejected one. The options are not exclusive. Any combination or variation that allows the team to be flexible in the face of change is a good process.

Once a project starts, it should be tracked by the project life cycle monitoring system. If costs change, say, more than 10 percent, that increase should trigger a reconsideration of the project's cost, risks, and benefits. In doing so, the team should only consider the benefits against what is yet to be spent, even if lots of money has already been poured into the project, because the value of the entire project rests on that unspent portion.

Be Consistent.   The main hindrance to team decision making is lack of consistency. To an individual team member, a group decision-making process seems cumbersome. Individuals have a tendency to find shortcuts and change the process on the run. When a new prioritization process is introduced, people become disenchanted. They do not want to learn the new approach; they secretly revolt and revert to their own old method, which contributes to even more inconsistency.

It is important to have a consistent process and an agreed-upon method for changing the prioritization process. Surprisingly, one of the hardest things to keep consistent is the project definition, says Aslan. Without such consistency, it is difficult to compare projects. To achieve consistency, it is important to introduce principles, such as, "a project should be completed within 18 months." Such rules should not be hindrances, but breaking them should require a valid reason.

Consistency comes from understanding the team decision-making process. People need to realize that the process is a balancing act. There is no black and white. For example, they need to see they can either move quickly or scrutinize the details, but not both. If people do not understand how to balance the two, they act as a pendulum. They opt for speed, but fail, so they revert to scrutiny, even when it is not necessary. When they fail again, they go back to speed. The team needs to learn how to balance speed and scrutiny, says Aslan.

Consistency requires patience. Avoid shortcuts. Ensure that the details are well thought-out, recommends Aslan. Some team members will become impatient with the discussion of small, but important points, such as possible future resource conflicts. They need to realize that the value of prioritization comes in such discussions. A well-facilitated session will maximize the team's patience and the discussion value.

Managing: Establishing Credibility and Fostering Change

CIOs are in the change business. Information systems bring about change. But before a CIO and the IS organization will be heard as a voice for change, they must be viewed as being successful and reliable. To foster change, a CIO must establish and then maintain the credibility of the IS organization.

Establishing Credibility.   Management consultant Joseph Izzo[17] believes that IS organizations have two missions: to maintain today's systems and to work on tomorrow's systems. These two missions have distinctly different goals and therefore need to be managed separately and specifically. The "today" operation should concentrate on providing service, says Izzo, whereas the "tomorrow" operation needs to focus on helping the business operate better. The first job of IS management is to get the "today" operation in shape. Until that task is accomplished, CIOs will have little credibility with top management.

Managing the "today" organization better.   The "today" organization includes computer operations, technical support (including network support), the help desk, and the maintenance and enhancement of existing applications. Because their main mission is service, the service levels of these various operations need to be measured and used to manage them.

To run the "today" operation, Izzo suggests hiring managers for each of these functions who are like supervisors—that is, they are delivery-oriented and demand a high level of service from their people.

An increasing number of companies outsource these IT support functions to companies that specialize in this work. This outsourcing releases in-house staff for higher-value work, generally reduces costs, and should result in gradually increasing levels of service. But reaping these benefits requires negotiating good contracts and managing the suppliers. Chapter 8 discusses running "today" operations further.

Once the "today" organization is in shape, then IS management has the credibility to be heard when talks about the need to change business practices to take advantage of a potential new system.

Fostering Change.   IS staff members are often so enthralled with the technical aspects of a new system that they presume a technically elegant system is a successful system. Not so. Many technically sound systems have turned into implementation failures because the people side of the system was not handled correctly. In essence, IT is all about managing change. New systems require changing how work is done. Focusing only on the technical aspects is only half the job. The other job is change management.

Change management is the process of assisting people to make major changes in their working environment. In this case, the change is caused by the introduction of a new computer system. Management of change has not always been handled methodically; thus, choosing a change management methodology and using it is a step toward successfully introducing new computer systems.

Change disrupts peoples' frame of reference if it presents a future where past experiences do not hold true, says ODR, a change management firm in Atlanta, Georgia.[18] People resist change, especially technological change, when they view it as a crisis. They cope by trying to maintain control. In the case of an impending new computer system, which they do not understand fully or are not prepared to handle, they may react in several ways. They may deny the change; they may distort information they hear about it; or they may try to convince themselves, and others, that the new system really will not change the status quo. These reactions are forms of resistance.

ODR offers a methodology to help companies manage technological change. They use specific terms from the field of organizational development to describe the types of people involved in a change project.

- The *sponsor* is the person or group that legitimizes the change. In most cases, this group must contain someone in top management who is highly respected by the business unit because change must be driven from the business unit.

- The *change agent* is the person or group who causes the change to happen. Change agents are often the IS staff. They can introduce the change, but they cannot enforce its use.

- The *target* is the person or group who is being expected to change and at whom the change is aimed.

Using surveys completed by a project's sponsors, change agents, and targets, ODR aims to:

- Describe the *scope* of the change
- Assess the *sponsors'* commitment to the project
- Assess the *change agents'* skills
- Evaluate the support or resistance of the *targets*

By evaluating each area, the change agents can determine (1) whether the scope of the project is doable, or whether the organization is trying to change too much at one time, (2) whether the sponsors are committed enough to push the change through, or whether they are sitting back expecting the organization to change on its own, (3) whether the change agents have the skills to implement the change, or whether they are not adept at rallying support, and (4) which groups are receptive to the change and which are resistant. Once these assessments have been made, ODR assists IS project teams to understand the risks their projects face and identify what they can do to mitigate those risks.

Working Across Organizational Lines. CIOs now find that the systems they implement affect people outside their firm. The interconnectedness permitted by the Internet, and the desire of supply-chain members to increase their supply-chain efficiency, is pulling some CIOs to working as much with these external members of their supply chain as with their own internal people.

On the supplier side, companies and IS organizations alike are rationalizing their supplier base, depending on fewer, deeper relationships. This trend is causing CIOs to work more closely with suppliers' executives to whom they outsource their help desk, PC acquisition–maintenance–disposal, data center, network management, and other functions. The result is more disclosure of future plans, more joint planning, more joint working, and so forth. Some suppliers are treated more as partners than suppliers. This trend has opened up the need for vendor relationship management techniques. In Chapter 8, we describe what Eastman Kodak has done to develop working procedures with its main outsourcers.

On the customer side, CIOs are being increasingly called upon to describe the company's IT-enabled vision to customer executives to get their buy-in to building interbusiness systems. When dealing with suppliers and customers, CIOs and others on the executive team all become involved in fostering change. Here is an example of a CIO who is working with his peers on his firm's executive team to manage change not only in their own company, but at customer companies as well. It is based on the Gartner EXP report, *Managing Your Stakeholders*,[4d] written by Andrew Rowsell-Jones, et al.

CASE EXAMPLE

REXAM

Rexam PLC is one of the world's top five consumer packaging companies and the world's top beverage can maker. Rexam Beverage Can Americas, which covers all the Americas, has sales of $1.6 billion and only 2,500 employees. Globally, Rexam has sales of $4.5 billion and only 20,000 employees.

The beverage can business is over 100 years old, and the business processes in the industry have been mostly based on lowest cost. To invest in new business processes takes a strong business case. Some processes have been automated, yet many remain manual.

Rethinking Interactions with Customers

Three years ago, Paul Martin joined Rexam as CIO of Rexam Beverage Can Americas. When he visited the plants to see how the company did business, he found that most orders were received by phone or fax, keyed into spreadsheets, held for days in anticipation of changes, and then faxed to a plant near the customer, where they were rekeyed into back-office systems. The result: multiple chances for errors and shipments of the wrong products to customers.

"There's a way to leverage the Internet here," Martin told others. Their response, "Our customers will never interact with us via the Internet, or place an order online. You will hit a brick wall." Martin's reply, "If we can demonstrate the value to them, they will." He set about proving his point.

Phase 1: CRM Made Simple

"Our goal is to entangle our customers with e-technology, which means, we will deliver incredible value by creating an environment that delivers such exceptional service that our customers will think twice about leaving Rexam for a lower price," said Martin.

Rather than invest in a large customer relationship management (CRM) system, Martin's staff and some consultants built a platform and some applications based on feedback from Rexam's sales group and customers. The system includes online ordering via the Internet and captures customer feedback about quality problems. It also provides customers with a range of reports and business intelligence tools to slice and dice the data in many ways. The system also introduced invoice reporting and put accounts receivable online to reduce billing errors and to expedite payment to Rexam. Every day Rexam can reduce Days Sales Outstanding, its cash flow improves by $4 million. That is a big impact.

The system benefits customers as well. They can inquire about invoice information online—the bill of lading number, filling location, plant making the cans, and so forth. They no longer need to call Rexam's accounts receivable group for this information. Furthermore, when an online order is changed, the system automatically notifies the customer about the change, so both parties stay more in sync. The parties interact more, but the complexity of these interactions

(Case Continued)

is hidden in the system, offloading it from the employees on both sides.

Testing the System with Customers

To test the value of the system to customers, Rexam approached its largest beverage can customer. The director of procurement saw the potential value, so he said, "Let's test it in one bottling location that rarely changes its orders."

After the 3-month test, the bottler's response was highly positive. The system did indeed eliminate faxes and phone calls to Rexam, which was a huge plus, and the bottler could get needed information in real time.

The customer wanted more. In an e-mail, the procurement officer wrote, "I've got some feedback for you. We see benefits, . . . and we'd like some additional features. We'd like to see shipment history for 3 months because that will help our internal forecasting."

In response, Rexam gave them 12 months of shipping history to use in reviewing orders and pull patterns. The customer rolled out the system to 27 U.S. bottling locations the first year, standardizing the ordering system. Rexam has entangled this customer with e-technology in both interactions between the two firms and in assisting the customer with its internal operations.

Phase 2: Knock Customers' Socks Off

The goal in phase 2 is: Knock their socks off, meaning, impress customers so much that they will not leave Rexam. This phase involves redefining "world-class" for the beverage can industry. In part, it involves implementing SAP, reengineering Rexam processes, and using mySAP to create customer portals to leverage the ordering system and permit collaborative online forecasting. This prospect excites customers, because they have learned that Rexam knows more about some aspects of their business than they do. As a service for its customers, Rexam keeps customers' packaging inventory. Rexam's goal is to reduce these inventories through the collaborative forecasting and scheduling system.

Rexam also plans to design new can labels online so that customers can see the artwork in 3D—a significant advance from the digital pictures they now receive via e-mail.

Finally, the CRM system contains pictures and contact information of its employees. In the future, Martin's group will ask customers if they would like PC-based video conferencing. If so, it will install a small video camera on their PCS. By clicking on a Rexam employee's picture, the system dials that person to initiate video conferencing—all part of Rexam's goal to "knock their socks off."

The CIO's Role

Complexity in Martin's job now comes from Rexam's suppliers and customers more than from its employees. Martin spends as much time giving presentations to these stakeholders as he does to Rexam employees. The key to gaining their buy-in is the value Rexam brings to them. He demonstrates the value of online ordering using the Internet and interlinking systems.

He is able to spend this much time externally because his IS director has taken over management of key development efforts. "This frees me up to do what the CEO wants me to focus on: strategy and getting our external relationships under control," says Martin.

(Case Continued)

The beverage can market has flat growth, just 1 to 2 percent a year. Generally, the only way to improve margins is to cut costs. However, last year prices increased for the first time in 25 years. In renegotiating contracts this year, the vice president of sales is adding a new clause to the contracts to leverage the firm's innovative e-business and SAP work. In essence, the clause states, "if we (Rexam) deliver exceptional value in innovation, Six Sigma, and e-business, we can come back to you to collect additional fees."

Obviously, customers have been asking what this new clause means. In response, Martin visits these customers and gives them a presentation about what Rexam is doing in these areas and the potential benefits to them. "The CEO sees me as a business person. These are not IT projects; these are company projects. It's my job to translate our systems solutions to their business problems," says Martin.

The Steering Committee's Role

When Martin presented the $11-million business case for the SAP and e-business initiatives, the CEO asked, "How long will this take to deliver?" The answer: 3 years. "I need it in 18 months," replied the CEO,

"It's very important to our strategy. We need this foundation in place."

To meet that aggressive schedule, the work has been guided by the executive steering committee, made up of the CEO, CFO, CIO, and heads of operations, supply chain, and sales. It meets every other week for an hour, not to prioritize projects (everyone agreed on those), but to guide implementation, resolve roadblocks, validate new business process designs, and spur progress. None of the members, including the CEO, has missed a meeting.

The committee first defined Rexam's future state so they would all be "reading from the same page." They have since focused on the vision and achieving behavioral change. "We are transforming our internal business processes and the way customers and suppliers interact with us," notes Martin. "Everyone on the executive team understands the impact of these changes on their own organization. So we divvy up the work. We have all put in the plans and procedures to be ready for the new systems." The executive committee's role has been to lay out the game plan. Phase 2 has been simplified tremendously by the committee members agreeing on the agenda. ■

The Rexam case illustrates a number of points about CIOs' current role. One, CIOs are working outside as much as inside these days. Two, they are working in concert with their peers in the company in selling and implementing their visions. Three, to stay ahead, CIOs need to keep their staffs experimenting with new technologies. Four, selling the vision occurs one customer, supplier, or executive at a time. This means CIOs, and others, need to assess how IT-ready a customer, supplier, executive, department, or group is.

The Office of the CIO?

Darwin John, former CIO of the U.S. Federal Bureau of Investigation, Scott Paper, and the Mormon Church, believes that the work of CIOs has become so broad and complex that it should by handled by a team—an office of the CIO—rather than an individual.[19]

When he was CIO, John says he divided his time into thirds: one-third managing the IS organization, one-third working with peers to manage the enterprise, and one-third networking with people outside the enterprise. Today, he says, there are just not enough thirds to go around, because every function has become dependent on IT. Furthermore, CIOs must bring in and integrate new technologies and be highly involved in business planning, because they are part of top management.

One way to divide the job, notes John, is to have an office of the CIO with four positions:

- **Chief information officer (CIO).** This executive heads IS and works with top management, customers, and suppliers.
- **Chief technology officer (CTO).** This executive heads IT planning, which involves architecture and exploration of new technologies.
- **Chief operations officer (COO).** This executive heads day-to-day IS operations.
- **Chief project officer (CPO).** This executive oversees all projects and project managers.

An alternative two-way split is to have co-CIOs, with one focusing on all things external to the IS organization (such as planning and relationships with the business, customers, and suppliers) and the other focusing on all things internal (such as operations and projects).

With IT so crucial to enterprise success, and the know-how needed to run it so deep and so wide, management needs to become a team effort. A few firms have created such an office of the CIO; others have created such a team without designating it as "the office of the CIO."

Whither CIOs?

Neil Fligstein,[20] a sociologist at the University of California at Berkeley, makes an interesting observation about the possible future importance of CIOs by looking at history. He notes that different periods of recent history have seen executives with different backgrounds "running the show," depending on the corporate growth driver at the time:

- *Manufacturing:* In the early 1900s, manufacturing was the growth driver, thus manufacturing executives often rose to became CEO.
- *Sales and marketing:* In the 1930s through the 1950s, growth came through sales. By 1959, nearly 25 percent of the top American corporations had former sales and marketing executives as CEOs, notes Fligstein.
- *Finance:* In the 1970s and 1980s, the large corporations consisted of portfolios of businesses and were best managed by executives who knew how to manage portfolios: chief financial officers (CFOs). They bought and sold businesses like you would buy and sell stock, to get the highest return.

- *Information technology?:* The financial scandals in the late 1990s and early 2000s, though, have hurt CFOs' reputations. Furthermore, given the revolutionary effects IT is having on the world, perhaps CIOs now have the most appropriate background to be future CEOs, says Fligstein. It's an open question at the moment.

CONCLUSION

The transformation IS organizations are grappling with these days, says Dick Dooley,[21] is learning how to create organizations where IT decision making is shared. The main responsibility for managing the use of IT needs to pass to the line, whereas the management of the IT infrastructure should be retained by the IS group. This transformation is reflected in the following, says Dooley:

- "We used to do it to them"—meaning, IS required end users to obey strict rules for getting changes made to systems, submitting job requests, and so on.
- "Next, we did it for them"—meaning, IS moved to taking a service orientation.
- "Now, we do it with them,"—reflecting partnering.
- "We are moving toward teaching them how to do it themselves."

To achieve this transformation, CIOs must play a leadership role in their enterprise and develop partnerships with the senior management team, external customers, and suppliers.

QUESTIONS AND EXERCISES

Review Questions

1. Describe the five waves of innovation from Primozic and colleagues.
2. Describe the three ways American Airlines is reaching the consumer.
3. According to Cox, what are the four areas that make up the overall responsibility of the IS function?
4. What are the two major roles IS departments are likely to play in the future, according to Cox?
5. What is IS Lite?
6. What are the three IT eras and what has been the CIO's job in each, according to Ross and Feeny? (See Figure 2-7.)
7. What are seven ways to understand the business?
8. How is John Leggate selling his Digital Business vision within BP?
9. Describe the needs of champions.
10. How does the corporate technology planning group foster experimentation within Aetna?
11. What is IT governance and why has it become important?
12. What is an IT principle? Give an example.
13. According to Farrell, what three conditions of IT investments yielded the greatest productivity increases in industries dependent on IT and that faced growing competition?

14. What are five lessons Sy Aslan has learned from his work on portfolio prioritization?
15. Describe the three kinds of people involved in change management, as described by ODR.
16. What is CIO Martin's role these days at Rexam Beverage Can Americas with respect to customers?

Discussion Questions

1. A vision is not the responsibility of the CIO. It is the responsibility of the CEO or the top management team. Do you agree or disagree? Why?
2. Present both sides of the argument that business-process owners will/will not take over management of IT.
3. What is going to happen to organizations whose senior executives do not appreciate the strategic value of IT?

Exercises

1. There is considerable discussion of the evolving role of the CIO. At one time, the term *CIO* was defined as "career is over." Find at least two articles on the role of CIOs that make conflicting arguments; summarize the differences.
2. There is also much discussion about partnering between IS and line organizations. Find at least two articles that discuss such partnering and summarize the factors they mention that contribute to successful partnering.
3. Contact the CIO in an organization. What is his or her title? How does he or she perceive the leadership role of the job? How do these characteristics relate to those in the text? How is he or she encouraging partnering with business units?
4. Using socialization to win support from other people is too slow a process for our current fast-moving world. Companies really need to either adapt to mandates or have representatives make decisions on others' behalf. Otherwise, a few recalcitrant people could cause the enterprise to move too slowly. Discuss.

REFERENCES

1. Primozic, Kenneth, Edward Primozic, and Joe Leben, *Strategic Choices: Supremacy, Survival, or Sayonara,* McGraw-Hill, New York, 1991.

2. Seybold, Patricia, with Ronni Marshak, *Customers.com,* Times Books, New York, 1998.

3. Cox, George, *Time to Reshape the IS Department?* Wentworth Research Program (now part of Gartner EXP, Stamford, CT), June 1994.

4. Gartner EXP, 56 Top Gallant, Stamford, CT 06904; www.gartner.com.
   a. Woolfe, Roger, *IS Lite,* July 2000.
   b. Broadbent, Marianne, Barbara McNurlin, and Roger Woolfe, *Glocalizing Your IS,* July 2001.
   c. Broadbent, Marianne, and Peter Weill, *Effective IT Governance. By Design,* Gartner EXP Premier Report, January 2003, and *Tailoring IT Governance to Your Enterprise,* Gartner EXP Club

Report, October 2003. Also see: Weill, Peter, "Don't Just Lead, Govern: How Top-Performing Firms Govern IT," *MIS Quarterly Executive,* March 2004, pp. 1–17. Available online at: www.misqe.org/jsp/index.jsp. Retrieved March 2004.

   d. Rowsell-Jones, Andrew, Roger Woolfe, and Richard Hunter, *Managing Your Stakeholders,* October 2002.

5. Yepez, Hugo, Dorothy Cooney, and Barbara McNurlin, "Aligning the Information Management Department with the Business at LifeScan, a Johnson & Johnson Company," Third Place Winner in 1999 paper competition, Society for Information Management, 401 N. Michigan Ave., Chicago, IL 60601.

6. Ross, Jeanne, and David Feeny, "The Evolving Role of the CIO," in Robert W. Zmud (Ed.), *Framing the Domains of IT Management: Projecting the Future Through the Past,* Pinnaflex Educational Resources, Inc., Cincinnati, OH, 2002, pp. 385–402.

7. Gibson, Chuck, MIT Sloan School's Center for Information Systems Research (CISR), personal interview.

8. Parker, Marilyn, Robert Benson with Ed Trainor, *Information Economics: Linking Information Technology and Business Performance,* Prentice Hall, Upper Saddle River, NJ: 1988, European edition 1989; Japanese edition, 1990.

9. Peters, Tom, *Thriving on Chaos: Handbook for a Management Revolution,* Alfred A. Knopf Inc., New York, 1987.

10. Beath, Cynthia, and Blake Ives, "The Information Technology Champion: Aiding and Abetting, Care and Feeding,"

Proceedings of the Twenty-First Annual Hawaii International Conference on System Sciences, Vol. IV, pp. 115–123. Available from the IEEE Computer Society, Los Alamitos, CA.

11. Kanter, Rosabeth, *ChangeMasters,* Simon & Schuster, New York, 1983.

12. Johnson, Bonnie, and Ron Rice, *Managing Organizational Innovation,* Columbia University Press, New York, June 1987.

13. Weill, Peter, and Richard Woodham, "Don't Just Lead, Govern: Implementing Effective IT Governance," MIT Sloan CISR Working Paper 326, April 2002.

14. Farrell, Diana, "The *Real* New Economy," *Harvard Business Review,* October 2003, pp. 105–112.

15. United Management Technologies (UMT), 500 5th St., Suite 430, New York, NY 10110; www.umt.com.

16. Interview with Sy Aslan, Aslander Strategic Corporation, New York; www.aslander.com.

17. Joseph Izzo, The Teton Group, 13428 Maxella Ave., #414, Marina del Rey, CA 90292, personal interview.

18. From communications with Conner Partners 1349 West Peachtree St., NW, Suite 1910, Atlanta, GA 30309; www.connerpartners.com.

19. John, Darwin, "Mindshare: Team CIO," *CIO Insight,* January 1, 2004. Available online at: www.cioinsight.com/article2/0,1397, 1457532,00.asp. Retrieved March 2004.

20. Varon, Elana, "The Rise of the CIO," *CIO Magazine,* December 15, 2003. Available online at: www.cio.com/archive/121503/ ciofuture.html. Retrieved March 2004.

21. The Dooley Group, 41 Babbling Brook Road, Centerville, MA 02632.

STRATEGIC USES OF INFORMATION TECHNOLOGY

INTRODUCTION

It should come as no surprise that use of the Internet by businesses in the mid-to-late 1990s set off a revolution in the use of IT. Utilizing the Internet to conduct business became *the* strategic use of IT, where *strategic* means having a significant, long-term impact on a firm's growth rate, industry, and revenue. The question is: What now? Has the revolution ended with the dot-com crash? Does an even larger revolution loom? Does IT still matter? If so, what sorts of strategic uses are companies making of IT (especially the Internet)? That is the subject of this chapter.

History of Strategic Uses of IT

For the past three editions of this book, we have seen three strategic uses of IT in business, as shown in Figure 3-1:

- Working inward: Business-to-employee
- Working outward: Business-to-customer
- Working across: Business-to-business

We believe these types of uses continue today; thus, they form the structure for this chapter. To set the stage, we briefly review strategic uses of IT over the past 20 years by noting the changing emphasis in the strategic use of IT over the lifetime of this book.

In the mid-1980s, the hot topic in the first edition was end user computing (working *inward*). IS departments established end user computing departments to help employees learn about PCs and how to use end user computing languages, such as Basic and Focus, to write their own computer programs.

Then, during the second edition, strategic use focused *outward* on using IT to gain competitive advantage. A prime example was Merrill Lynch's cash management account (CMA), which combined a stock account with checking and savings. It was developed in the late 1980s, even through the bleak times following the Black Monday stock market crash in October 1987. When CMA was introduced to the market, it gave

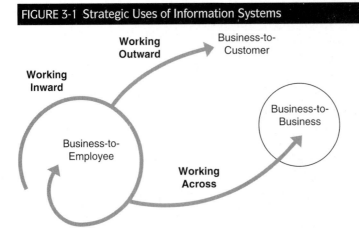

FIGURE 3-1 Strategic Uses of Information Systems

Merrill a huge marketshare boost that other brokerage houses found difficult to take away. This IT-based offering gave Merrill a competitive edge.

In the 1990s, during the third and fourth editions, strategic use turned *inward* to reengineering business processes. The intent was not to automate existing processes, but to totally redesign how the enterprise operated. The notion had merit, but many efforts failed because they were seen as thinly disguised efforts to lay off staff. The introduction of ERP systems was also aimed at improving internal operations, specifically, providing single sources of data enterprisewide.

In the mid-1990s, when the Internet's potential started to become evident, dot-coms looked at its *outward* use to gain a competitive edge. However, most established firms initially used the Internet technology internally, building intranets to improve company processes. Often, the first uses were publishing e-forms on the intranet with accompanying automated workflow processes.

By the late 1990s, the fifth edition showed that use of the Internet for business—e-business—was underway, as established enterprises countered their new, Internet-only dot-com competitors. Then came the bursting of the dot-com bubble, and with it the fervor of e-business slowed down. E-business has become more reality based. Not as many harebrained ideas are being funded. However, the integration of the Internet into how companies work has proceeded.

In the sixth edition, the inward and outward strategic uses continued, but the strategic use emphasis turned to *across*, with efforts focused on linking to suppliers, customers, and other parties in one's value chain or business ecosystem. The innovation unleashed by the dot-coms, and the competitive challenges they presented brick-and-mortar firms, initiated a backlash: The Brick-and-Mortar Firms Strike Back (or Return of the Brick-and-Mortars, depending on whose side you are on). That was the theme of the sixth edition: leveraging traditional operations by using the Internet to work more closely with others.

The theme of this seventh edition should perhaps be "Something has changed," especially with regards to the use of IT for competitive advantage. A recent, highly influential article, to be discussed shortly, questions whether IT can be used for competitive advantage at all. It has caused quite a stir. But although some may question IT's ability to give companies a competitive edge, it is absolutely necessary for competitive parity (keeping up with competitors), and more than ever, it is being used strategically—inward, outward, and across. To set the context for discussing these three strategic uses, several opinions follow on just what has changed about the use of IT and where it might be going.

Whither the Internet Revolution?

It appears that the Internet frenzy peaked in 2000, notes Brian Arthur, Citibank Professor at the Santa Fe Institute.[2] Is this information revolution dead? he asks. Not if history is a guide, he answers. In a fascinating description of history, Arthur compares the Internet revolution with the British railway revolution to support his belief that the golden age of the information revolution has just begun. Here is that story, in brief, as he relates it.

The British railway revolution took place roughly between 1825 and 1875, with 1825 marking the start with the first commercial railway—the Stockton and Darlington—with one locomotive. In 1829, a locomotive trial entered by five contestants demonstrated that an engine could pull a train up a hill at 12 mph. That proof unleashed 15 years of technical innovations. Even Queen Victoria took a train ride in 1842.

Entrepreneurs emerged. The "king," George Hudson, had the golden touch. Whenever his name appeared in an ad for railway shares, people snapped them up, reports Arthur. Railway mania raged, and Hudson became very rich. Shares were divided into portions and sold as scrip; people put their life savings into scrip. Some dozen new railway schemes (railway lines connecting two small towns, for instance) appeared every week at the peak. One judge said that the country had become an asylum of railway fanatics.

Everyone was smiling, until October 1845, when shares of established railroads began to fall and scrip no longer commanded a premium. One railroad lost 40 percent of its value between August and October that year. The next year, a disastrous harvest hurt Britain's economy even more. In the middle of October 1847, a week of terror occurred in which some banks were forced to close. By the time the panic was over, railway stocks had lost 85 percent of their peak value; several hundred failed altogether.

What is interesting about this story, notes Arthur, is what happened after 1847. In 1845, Britain had 2,148 miles of track. In 1910—65 years later—the country had 21,000 miles, a 10-fold increase, most of which was built after the 1847 crash. Before 1847, there was great excitement and small companies flourished. After 1847, the glamour was gone. The railway business became serious and full of hard work—building out the tracks rather than innovating. The industry became orderly and profits began to reflect real returns. Railroad income multiplied and the industry contributed to economic growth. In fact, after 1850, the railroads *were* Britain's economic engine, says Arthur.

Interestingly, a similar revolution had occurred 50 years earlier with Britain's canals. That revolution essentially began in 1761. A speculative mania occurred in 1792 and a crash took place in 1793. At that time, there were 1,000 miles of canals; decades later there were 2,000 miles.

Not all technologies exhibit manias and crashes, of course, but what causes Arthur to correlate the railway and canal revolutions with today's Internet revolution is that all three are *connection technologies*. As connectors, they are natural monopolies, he points out. Only one railway line or canal can profitably connect two cities. Thus, there is a "race for space" in such technologies. That is why there is an investment frenzy: to get there first.

When thinking about the Internet, Arthur believes its cycle is currently about where the British railroads were in the 1840s, when the initial frenzy had ended in a crash. If this history is any guide, the golden age of the Internet is just starting. Even though it could be a lot less glamorous, it will contribute to economic growth. Arthur believes it already has. Productivity gains have not slackened during the economic slump because organizations are adapting to the Internet.

Arthur believes it is not until organizations structure their activities (essentially rearchitect themselves) around the new cluster of technologies that the revolution really arises. For the British railroads, the buildout period began after 1847. Steel rails arrived in the 1860s, after which safety systems, more powerful engines, switching systems to control rail traffic, double rails, air brakes, and Pullman sleeping cars appeared. All of these can be viewed as technologies that adapt railways to human use. Furthermore, businesses located their factories near railway lines.

We are now in a period where organizations are rearchitecting themselves around Internet technologies, tearing down their old structures as they go. Hence, we have seen unexpected productivity gains during the recent economic downturn. The real gains will come, believes Arthur, when Internet technology adapts to organizations and people. That is when the technology disappears and becomes part of life. We are not there yet. We still notice the technology because it is still uncomfortable.

Arthur predicts the buildout of the Internet revolution will last 10 to 20 years, and the developments that will matter most will be "arrangements of use," that is, innovations that adapt the Internet to people and their use of it. The interconnection of business will be the revolution. It will be quiet compared to the frenzy of 1999 and 2000, but Arthur predicts it will be a giant revolution.

The Cheap Revolution

For the past several years, Rich Karlgaard,[1] publisher of *Forbes* magazine, has been talking about what he calls "the cheap revolution." Karlgaard believes we are in an inflection point in the IT industry where CIOs are shifting from buying *expensive proprietary* products to buying *cheap generic* products. He calls it "cheap tech," and he sees the phenomenon occurring in more and more sectors of the IT industry.

For example, he notes that E*TRADE, the online trading firm, replaced 50 Unix servers running Sun's proprietary operating system (and costing $220,000 each) with many cheap generic servers from IBM (costing $4,000 each). Other CIOs are doing the same because the cost savings are so compelling. Karlgaard's favorite example, though, is Google, which he says is the epitome of cheap, because its famous search engine (the fourth most-viewed Web site) runs on 100,000 cheap servers. Furthermore, when one breaks, Google discards it, thereby bypassing expensive service contracts and in-house fix-it staff. By going cheap, Google saves 90 cents of the dollar most IT shops spend, Karlgaard notes.

In fact, he wonders how long some IT vendors that sell proprietary systems can forestall this cheap revolution. Others call this effect "Dellification"; Dell sells generic versions of products at significantly lower prices because its direct-to-customers business model has lower costs. Dell has moved from selling PCs to also selling servers, printers, storage devices, handhelds, and LCD televisions.

Besides computers, "cheap" is occurring elsewhere, notes Karlgaard, in labor (outsourcing to India and China, for example), film production (camcorders and PCs versus expensive video production equipment), software (Linux versus Microsoft), and telecommunications (offerings using unlicensed versus licensed spectrum, Voice-over-IP), to name just four. Being on the wrong side of this cheap revolution, in any industry, is not the place to be, Karlgaard states.

Episode Two: Profitability Strikes Back

The fourth and fifth editions of this text were published during times of "irrational exuberance" (to use Alan Greenspan's famous term) for the Internet, the sixth at a time when people more realistically reviewed its potential. The wild schemes of dot-coms, which became dot-bombs because they could not generate profits, have significantly tempered views.

We would characterize the dot-com euphoria as the Internet's Episode One: The Dot-Com Menace. We would characterize today's leveraging of the Internet as Episode Two: Profitability Strikes Back. Unlike Episode One, which starred companies that only had an Internet presence, the sequel has starred those with a dual physical and Internet presence (initially called bricks-and-clicks firms) and that are profitable. While it took these so-called "old-economy firms" longer to utilize the Web, they realized they had to do so in a profit-making manner. Interlinking the two worlds properly can increase their value proposition to customers.

But, says Michael Porter[3] of Harvard Business School, the only way to sustain advantage through the Internet is to create a distinct value chain that offers unique value. This chain must be highly integrated, so that potential competitors must replicate the entire system to duplicate the value proposition. Porter recommends: Use the Internet to complement your strategy, not replace your past way of serving customers nor disintermediate your channels. Grainger has taken this approach, he notes.

CASE EXAMPLE

GRAINGER

Grainger distributes nonproduction products to companies through stocking locations all over the United States. Its Internet strategy builds on this physical presence, tightly integrating the two, states Porter.[3] Grainger has found that customers who purchase on its Web site also purchase through its traditional channels, and these customers purchase 9 percent more than those who do not use its Web site.

Grainger has also discovered that its physical sites make its online presence more valuable, especially for customers who want fast delivery. They order online and pick up their order themselves at their nearby Grainger site. This combination cuts Grainger's costs in two ways: online ordering is less expensive than over-the-phone ordering and shipping in bulk to its stocking locations is cheaper than small shipments to individuals.

Grainger also chose to continue publishing its paper catalog after putting its catalog on its Web site. It is pleased to find that it receives a surge of online orders every time it issues its paper catalog. The two are synergistic, it turns out. ■

Porter cautions that companies must not only take into account the synergistic effects of conducting business online and off-line, but also realize that there are secondary effects to having an online presence. For example, although order-taking costs may fall, costs in other areas may increase. For instance, online ordering often results in more requests for quotes and information.

That and other issues revolving around conducting a bricks-and-*clicks* business are now being debated and tested as old-economy firms e-enable themselves inside, outside, and across. E-enablement means digitizing where possible. The *e* comes from *electronic*, and it has been attached to all kinds of terms. For example, take the terms *e-business* and *e-commerce.* We see *e-business* as meaning conducting business using telecommunications networks, particularly the Internet. Thus it involves more than buying and selling electronically, which is *e-commerce.* Not all people agree with these distinctions.

At first, the rapid growth of e-business during Episode One (from 1994 to 2000) seems astounding. However, a closer look reveals some clear reasons for the rapid growth. The Internet provided three key components that accelerated online business:

1. Wide access to a public network
2. Standard communication protocol
3. Standard user interface

Earlier systems that linked firms with their customers or business partners required private networks with proprietary applications. Indeed, the private, proprietary nature of the systems was key to their strategic value. The high cost of implementation, training, and use of these systems locked in customers and created barriers to competitors building similar systems. However, the high cost also limited access to the systems, thus restricting their widespread use; only large firms could afford to build such systems. For example, pre-Internet data estimated that 95 percent of *Fortune* 500 companies in the United States used EDI, whereas only 2 percent of all U.S. companies used EDI. EDI was the main technology for transacting commerce electronically.

Because e-business applications run over a public network, the Internet, access and communications costs are drastically reduced. Furthermore, with standardized communication protocols and user interfaces, implementation and training costs are far lower. As a result, a much broader set of users and firms has access to the systems, allowing for rapid growth. Indeed, in just a few years, use of the Internet for e-mail and company Web sites became standard business practice in most companies, large and small.

Does IT Still Matter?

Porter's downbeat view of the Internet's value to individual firms (which is explored further in Chapter 4) got attention, and arguments. But it did not generate nearly as much controversy as "IT Doesn't Matter," the provocative article in the May 2003 *Harvard Business Review* by its former editor Nicholas Carr.[4a] His article generated a firestorm of protest. Carr's point is that IT doesn't matter anymore, at least not *strategically.* He has since expanded his argument into a book.[4b]

According to Carr, IT is an infrastructure technology, like railroads, electricity, and the telephone. Such a technology can create a strategic advantage for an individual firm only at the beginning of its life cycle, when its technology is expensive and risky. That is the only time a firm can create something proprietary that competitors cannot easily copy.

Carr contends that once an infrastructure technology reaches the end of its buildout—that is, when it is neither proprietary nor expensive—it becomes a commodity, available to anyone, and therefore will not yield competitive advantage to any single firm. According to Carr, an investment must provide differentiation to give competitive advantage. Investments in commodity technologies cannot provide (nor sustain) such differentiation, he contends.

It appears that IT has reached the end of its buildout, says Carr, for five reasons. One, the power of IT now outstrips the needs of businesses. Two, IT prices have dropped; it's affordable. Three, the capacity of the Internet has caught up with demand. In fact, there's more fiber than can be used. Four, many computer vendors want to be seen as utilities (somewhat akin to an electric utility). And five, the investment bubble has burst.

When an infrastructure technology reachs the end of its buildout, it becomes a cost of doing business. That is when people should care most about mitigating the business risks it poses (phones, electricity, or computer systems not working), rather than pursuing the innovations it makes possible. First-mover advantages cannot last when everyone has access to the same technologies at affordable prices.

Although IT is necessary for competitiveness, it's not sufficient, he states. Competitive advantage comes from a firm's business model, not its use of IT.

IT has become part of the business infrastructure; therefore, its management needs to change, states Carr. Success hinges on defense, not offense. Management of IT should become "boring" and focus on three areas:

1. *Manage the risks.* Focus on vulnerabilities rather than opportunities. There will be plenty of risks because open systems are more risky than proprietary systems.

2. *Keep costs down.* The greatest risk is overspending, so only pay for use and limit upgrading (do not upgrade PCs when it's not needed, for example).

3. *Stay behind the technology leaders,* but not too far behind, because experimentation is expensive. Delay investments until there are standards and best practices and prices drop. Only innovate when risks are low.

Carr's negative view of IT's value deals with its innovative use by individual firms. Although they lose the possibility of gaining individual competitive advantage, Carr contends, the infrastructure technology brings its greatest economic and social benefits to all once it has become a shared infrastructure. That is what IT is becoming, he believes.

The Debate Is On.   Following are just three of the many insightful pieces that have been written about IT's strategic value that refute Carr's article.[4c] John Seely Brown and John Hagel,[5] two well-known figures in the IT field, state that IT *alone* has not been a strategic differentiator, but it is "inherently strategic because of its indirect effects." It enables firms to do things they could not do before. Firms that see these possibilities first, and act on them, can differentiate themselves. Although computers are becoming ubiquitous, the insight on how to use them is not, they contend. That's what provides strategic uses of IT.

In fact, Brown and Hagel believe the past has taught three lessons about how to use IT strategically:

1. Value comes from IT only when it is paired with concurrent innovations in business practices. Too many companies do not change their business practices when they implement IT. That is why studies have shown no correlation between IT spending and superior financial results, note Brown and Hagel. Executives who think of IT as a commodity have not explored the innovative business practices it makes possible, especially across enterprises.

2. IT's economic impact comes from incremental improvements, not a "big bang" IT project, note Brown and Hagel. Waves of short-term IT projects, built on each other and tied to business changes and specific performance metrics, yield value.

3. Strategic differentiation emerges over time. It does not come from specific innovations in business practices. According to Brown and Hagel, it comes from "the ability to

continually innovate around IT's evolving capabilities." The other infrastructure technologies noted by Carr did not sustain continued business-practice innovation as long as IT has. Furthermore, they reached a dominant design fairly quickly (such as standard railway gauges), state Brown and Hagel. In IT, innovations in one area (such as storage or bandwidth) combine with innovations in another, unleashing new capabilities and new generations of architectures. New skills are needed for these new architectures. IT does not yet have a dominant design, so there is still potential for individual firms to differentiate themselves using IT—if their short-term initiatives support their long-term goals.

Robert Hof[6] states that although Carr may be right in the long run, he is not right about the current state of IT. In fact, like Brian Arthur,[2] he believes that we are now in the golden age of IT, where innovation is accelerating. IT might not matter strategically in 20 years or so, but now, it is still in flux and can provide differentiation. Witness the new developments in wireless technologies, miniaturization, and IP telephony, to name just three. Carr has jumped the gun in saying that IT has no strategic value, says Hof. And he's wrong in his follow-the-leader advice, because delaying the offering of a technology can lead to losing customers. He notes that hotels that offer wireless Internet access now differentiate themselves. Although that differentiation may not last long, at the moment, these hotels are getting his business, and he might stick with them. Hof believes that firms should both manage IT risks and look for opportunities.

Michael Schrage,[7] codirector of MIT Media Lab's e-Markets Initiative, disputes Carr's underlying premise that scarcity is a resource's attribute that yields sustained competitive advantage. Not so, he says. There is no correlation between scarcity and strategic value. Capital is a commodity, but returns on capital vary significantly. Does capital matter? Of course it does.

It is not a resource's commodity status that matters; it is the way the commodity is managed that determines its impact. Capital matters, talent matters, IT matters, and management matters. In fact, argues Schrage, the management matters more as IT becomes ubiquitous. IT's ubiquity does not override management quality.

Rather than compare running IT to running an electric utility, Carr should compare running IT to running a factory, suggests Schrage. But that comparison would undermine his premise because the way a factory is designed and run in the future will affect a manufacturer's competitiveness. "What Carr fails to recognize is that IT can profoundly transform the economics of innovation, segmentation, and differentiation for most businesses. And in that recognition lies the CIO's ultimate opportunity," says Schrage.

Is Carr right? Some think so, some think not. Either way, his views have hopefully prompted important discussions in board rooms, because executives need to understand the underpinnings of IT to know how to guide it. IT is one of their strategic resources, besides money and people, for working inward, outward, and across.

WORKING INWARD: BUSINESS-TO-EMPLOYEE

The essence of using IT strategically inside the enterprise has been, and continues to be, focused on improving business processes. Use of the Internet internally is no exception. It has revolved around building intranets.

Building an Intranet

An intranet is a private company network that uses Internet technologies and protocols, and possibly the Internet itself. The network is intended for employees only, and departments have used them to disseminate information and policies, provide needed forms, and even permit online transactions of former paper-based processes (such as filling out an expense requisition or changing a benefit). Applications use the Web interface and are accessed through browsers; communications use several protocols, including Hypertext Transfer Protocol (HTTP) for addressing Web sites, Hypertext Markup Language (HTML) for Web content structuring, and Transmission Control Protocol/Internet Protocol (TCP/IP) for network routing. The result is open systems using nonproprietary technologies.

The benefits of intranets have been significant: wider access to company information, more efficient and less expensive system development, and decreased training costs. By using an intranet's open-system architecture, companies can significantly decrease the cost of providing companywide information and connectivity. One of the most important attributes of intranets is that they support any make or brand of user device—from high-end workstation to PC, to laptop, to handheld device—as well as existing databases and software applications. Such interconnectivity has been the promise of open systems for many years. The Internet provides the connecting protocols to make the open-system promise a reality.

Furthermore, investments in a companywide electronic infrastructure are significantly less than building a proprietary network. Companies only need the servers, browsers, and a TCP/IP network to build an intranet. If, in addition, the company wishes to use the infrastructure of the Internet to geographically extend its intranet, the only additional components needed are firewalls, which keep the public from accessing the intranet, and local access to the Internet. Figure 3-2 shows the basic architecture of an intranet. The link to the Internet allows the company to expand its intranet worldwide easily and inexpensively—a significant benefit that was unthinkable before the Internet.

Finally, because an intranet uses the browser interface, users do not need extensive training on different products. In addition, due to the HTML standard and the availability of easy-to-use Web page authoring tools, employees can easily create their own Web pages for whatever purpose they need. As a result, all employees are potential site creators, reducing the IS department's programming bottleneck, while adhering to companywide standards. An additional benefit is that companies only need to record information in one place, where it can be kept up-to-date for access by all employees no matter where in the world they are located.

Due to the ease with which Web sites can be created, many employees have built their own, leading to a proliferation of sites with company information. To control the situation, IS departments have created corporate portals that act as gateways to firms' internal resources, information, and Internet services. This solution brings access to company data and applications together in a single site. Employees simply need a browser. At the same time, the portal provides IS management with a way to monitor and control the growth of internal Web sites, and the portal provides a link to Internet resources external to the company, such as sites for industry news, customers, and business partners. GE Power Systems is a case in point.

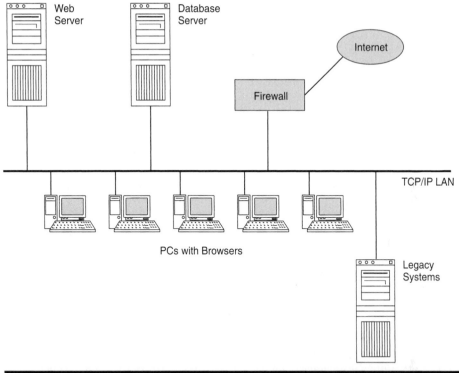

FIGURE 3-2 Intranet Architecture

GE POWER SYSTEMS

Being a marketing man, when Jeff Immelt became chairman of General Electric (GE) in September 2001, he surveyed the sales force. He found that they were spending more time in the office searching for information they needed to sell GE products than out with their customers. He challenged all the business units to reverse the ratio, notes Anthes.[8]

One business unit, GE Power Systems, sells multimillion-dollar turbines and tur-

bine parts and services to energy companies. It answered the challenge by building a Web-based sales portal for its salespeople. In essence, the portal is meant to be their main source of information by linking them to numerous information sources—some inside GE, some outside—without requiring changes to the underlying systems.

The main data feeds into the portal are from the existing Oracle and Siebel

(Case Continued)

databases on sales, parts, pricing, inventory, customers, and such. The portal also has a news feed from the outside. The coordination of all the information is handled by portal software from Vignette. The software assembles dynamic *portlets* that present salespeople with personalized, up-to-date data views. The portlet might show, for instance, the status of the salesperson's customers' orders, recent news stories that mention the salesperson's customers, price changes, sales performance for the month, and so on.

Vignette's system manages the content and its presentation to the salespeople; a special Oracle data mart for the portal pulls the appropriate data from the other systems at the appropriate intervals. Some data, such as customer master file updates, is pulled in real time (when the update takes place), whereas other data, such as turbine installations, is updated weekly, notes Anthes.

The Web server aspects of the system are handled by BEA System's WebLogic Server, and SiteMinder from Netegrity

handles security and user sign-ons. When a salesperson wants to access an application through the portal, SiteMinder uses an authorization table that has access permissions to determine whether to grant the user access to the system. Formerly, salespeople had to enter a different password for each application. Now, they only enter one password to get into the portal.

Power Systems' IT organization was able to build this portal in just 6 months' time by following GE's rigorous project management methodology and by using rapid prototyping ("launch and learn," they call it), building incomplete versions of the portal for salespeople to test out and critique at the annual sales conference and elsewhere.

The portal's architecture is flexible enough to be extended to include more types of information and to permit access to more applications. In short, the portal has greatly enhanced the usefulness of GE Power Systems' existing systems to its salespeople by giving them a single port of entry to them all. ■

Fostering a Sense of Belonging

Intranets are evolving into very important enterprise structures. In fact, in some enterprises, the intranet is seen as the enterprise. It houses videos of executives explaining the enterprise's vision and mission. It includes all the internal forms, rules, and processes. Need to file an expense report? Go to the intranet. Need to make travel reservations? Use the intranet. In short, the intranet embodies the company's processes and culture and can be accessed anywhere an employee has a connection to the Web.

Although this convenience can ease the life of employees, it can also feel colder and more impersonal than the traditional office setting. Frances Cairncross,[9] author of *The Company of the Future*, believes the challenge for corporate management of widely dispersed enterprises today is maintaining cohesion, which takes a lot more effort than when employees are colocated. With so many employees working out of their home, car, hotel room, airport, or customer site, she believes it is important to create a sense of belonging.

An intranet can provide the foundation for creating a sense of belonging by giving a means of communicating and creating communities. Whether enterprises use intranets to help employees feel part of the culture is up to them. Whether they are successful is yet another issue. Cairncross believes this goal should be a major use of intranets because the care of employees is one of the most important things enterprises do. Here is an example of one intranet used for that purpose.

CASE EXAMPLE

WIRE NOVA SCOTIA

Industry Canada has a Community Access Program (CAP) that provides a one-time grant to 10,000 Canadian communities to set up a CAP site, which is a public Internet access site for use by a rural community to stimulate its economic development, note Professors Bruce Dienes and Michael Gurstein.[10] The CAP grant also pays for a summer field worker (age 16 to 30) to set up the site and encourage local businesses, government, and community groups to use the CAP site and the Internet.

Cape Breton, a region in Canada's Nova Scotia province, has become quite impoverished. Its main livelihoods—fishing, coal, and steel—have dried up, and many residents have moved away. University College of Cape Breton opened a center to research and incubate ways to use IT to stimulate Nova Scotia's economy, especially Cape Breton's. The center is not funded, thus its operation depends on funding from the projects it gains.

The Challenge

The center was most interested in the CAP opportunity, but Drs. Gurstein and

Dienes knew that success required the CAP sites to be coordinated and work together. Acting alone, these rural sites would fail. The center could serve as a coordinating site, providing access to government and industry services, such as job listings, health information, and online banking. It could also help with marketing locally created products and services.

The goal of a CAP initiative for Nova Scotia would be to help site staff strategize with rural groups—school boards, corporate sponsors, libraries, regional development agencies, and others—to form collaborative networks to increase economic activity via "rural informatics," enabling rural enterprises to offer their goods and services globally.

The challenge was how to remotely coordinate and manage CAP sites spread across the province's wide geographic area given the limited finances.

The Solution

The initiative to address this challenge was called Wire Nova Scotia (WiNS). It would coordinate the youth workers at

(Case Continued)

67 CAP and other community access sites scattered throughout Nova Scotia. Six regional coordinators would have notebook computers and cell phones to supervise the youth workers. The Cape Breton center would house the main server. The heart of this community would be a password-protected intranet for use by the youth field workers, supervisors, and central staff.

One face-to-face orientation and training session was held for the youth workers and their supervisors so that they knew each other before going off to establish their Internet access site in a small community. Supervisors also held a few training sessions in the field. It turns out that those who attended these sessions had an easier time integrating into the WiNS community. Those who did not attend a session had a much harder time gaining the sense of belonging.

Building an Online Community

From then on, WiNS was managed almost totally online. The intranet supported e-mail, e-mail lists, real-time chat, and online conferences. E-mail gave the dispersed field workers an outlet for peer interaction, which greatly increased morale. Being remote, many of them worked alone most of the time. E-mail gave them peers to talk with and a community to belong to.

The heart of the system was the WebBoard that provided a means for online group discussions. The formal organizational structure occurred online, using various online conferences.

General Conferences. All WiNS staff used the WebBoard to hold general conferences for

- WiNS-wide announcements
- Business development: Staff generated and shared ideas on ways to help local businesses increase their income stream
- Technical support: Participants helped each other on the technical aspects of running their Internet access site. Conferences fostered field workers' dependence on one another rather than just on the central technical staff.

Personal Conferences. Each field worker had a personal conference area where he or she filed weekly reports and site usage statistics. Only the worker and his or her regional coordinator could access this site. Coordinators could review the logs and sometimes head-off problems before they grew too large.

Regional Conferences. Each region also held regional conferences via the intranet to plan joint ventures among nearby sites or to coordinate regional promotions. Regions also held real-time online chat meetings to foster informal socializing amongst their field workers. These sessions not only helped build a sense of community, but they often spread innovations among the sites quickly.

Coordinator Conferences. Finally, the WiNS coordinator held a weekly online staff conference with his six regional coordinators, which helped them learn from and support one another. Each coordinator supervised 10 to 25 sites across Nova Scotia, and each had different expertise. The weekly conferences gave them a way to meet and tap each other's expertise.

(Case Continued)

In all, Dienes and Gurstein believe the only way the 67 sites in WiNS could have operated successfully that summer was via an intranet. It permitted remote management and created a sense of belonging among far-flung remote sites that could not otherwise have been attained at a cost the initiative could afford. ■

WORKING OUTWARD: BUSINESS-TO-CUSTOMER

In most industries, companies need sophisticated computer systems to compete. For airlines, hotels, and rental car companies, a computer reservation system—either their own or someone else's—is a must. In the drug and hospital wholesaling industries, those that had automated order entry and distribution systems gobbled up those that did not have such systems. In financial markets, computerized trading and settlement systems are replacing open-outcry systems. And the list goes on.

As industry leaders increase the sophistication of their systems to concurrently address the four hallmarks of competitiveness—quality, service, innovation, and speed—their competitors must do the same or find themselves at a disadvantage. Using IT (or any technology) as the basis for a product or a service can, in some cases, be viewed as moving up a series of experience curves.

Jumping to a New Experience Curve

The traditional view of an experience curve is that the cost of using a new technology decreases as the firm gains more experience with it. However, in *Strategic Choices*[11] Kenneth Primozic, Edward Primozic, and Joe Leben present the view that more experience leads to a set of connected curves, rather than one continuous learning curve, as shown in Figure 3-3.

Each curve represents a different technology or a new combination of technologies in a product or service as well as in the product's manufacturing or the service's support. Moving to a new curve requires substantial investment in a new technology, and the company often must choose from among competing technologies, none of which is yet the clear winner. A firm that correctly identifies a new market and the technologies to exploit it can shift to the new experience curve and successfully open up a new industry segment. However, management sometimes has such an emotional attachment to the current experience curve that it fails to see the next one and thus loses its market share to swifter competitors. This has repeatedly happened in the computer field. Mainframe manufacturers ignored minicomputer firms. Then minicomputer firms ignored PC manufacturers (considering PCs to be toys). Then PC manufacturers ignored operating system firms, that is, Microsoft. And they, in turn, initially ignored the Internet.

To demonstrate this principle of experience curves and the need to keep up or lose out, consider the authors' example of the shipping industry.

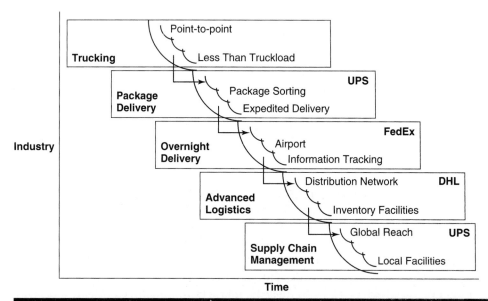

FIGURE 3-3 The Shipping Industry

Source: Based on Kenneth Primozic, Edward Primozic, and Joe Leben, *Strategic Choices: Supremacy, Survival, or Sayonara* (New York: McGraw-Hill, 1991).

CASE EXAMPLE

THE SHIPPING INDUSTRY

Primozic et al.[11] present an intriguing discussion of the shipping industry (which we have extended) to illustrate their concept of experience curves.

The Original Industry: Trucking.

The trucking industry initially shipped two types of truckloads of goods: full point-to-point truckloads and less than truckloads (LTLs), as shown in the upper left of Figure 3-3.

New Industry 1: Package Delivery. Once United Parcel Service (UPS) based its entire business on LTL shipping, a new industry segment was born: package delivery. As a result of this new experience curve, the shipping industry changed, and UPS actually became much larger than the trucking companies because it served a market with far more customers. The new technology that was key to UPS' success — and thus represented this particular

(Case Continued)

experience curve—was the efficient sorting of packages at distribution centers in order to maximize use of its trucks.

New Industry 2: Overnight Delivery. UPS, however, did not guarantee a delivery time nor did it track packages. FedEx capitalized on these two missing functions, jumped to a new experience curve, and started yet another new industry segment: overnight delivery. FedEx became larger than UPS because it tapped an even larger market. And for UPS and other package carriers to compete, they, too, had to invest in the technologies to guarantee delivery and track packages.

Needless to say, IT played a crucial role in this experience curve. In fact, the Internet began playing a role when UPS allowed customers to order package pickup online and when FedEx created a Web page that enabled customers to query the whereabouts of a package directly from its package-tracking database. That Web site, which went live in November 1994, had 12,000 customers a day doing their own package tracking, saving FedEx $2 million just that first year.

New Industry 3: Advanced Logistics. In the late 1990s, a third industry emerged: advanced logistics. Due to their distri-

bution networks and inventory facilities, overnight delivery services could handle inventory for large corporate clients and guarantee overnight delivery of these inventoried items. On this experience curve, client companies outsource not only their inventory, but also distribution to FedEx, Airborne Express, UPS, and other carriers. Clients include computer manufacturers, auto parts suppliers (to handle after-sales service), health-care diagnostic labs, retailers, even movie studios (to ship film to and from theaters). IT continues to play an integral role in the offered services.

New Industry 4: Supply Chain Management. Most recently, the industry has morphed again. Major players are becoming clients' supply chain partners, providing all the services needed to get a client's product from the loading dock to the customer's premises. These companies have extended beyond advanced logistics by having the global reach and local presence (in far-flung locations) that their clients need to move their goods. In essence, these players become their client's distribution function, which requires all of the parties involved to work even more closely with each other. ∎

The following case example of Cisco and UPS illustrates this latest industry. Notice how Cisco taps UPS's global reach and experience with European carriers to complete its supply chain. Also notice how closely linked the companies are becoming, with UPS employees responsible for some of Cisco's inventory and for some of the data in Cisco's ERP system, thereby giving Cisco more visibility into its downstream supply chain.

CASE EXAMPLE

CISCO SYSTEMS AND UPS SUPPLY CHAIN SOLUTIONS

In the late 1990s, Cisco committed itself to manufacturing products within 2 weeks of receiving an order, but it could not guarantee delivery. Customers were responsible for getting their products shipped from Cisco, located in San Jose, California, to their own premises. Shipping to Europe was especially taxing on customers.

To improve the situation, Cisco turned over its European supply chain to UPS Supply Chain Solutions (UPS SCS), a division of UPS, for reengineering and management.[12]

Some 90 percent of Cisco's products are configured and ordered over the Web. Within 24 hours of receiving an order, Cisco sends the customer an e-mail that states that the order has been accepted and that indicates when it will be produced.

When the product for a European customer is ready, Cisco notifies UPS SCS. Within 24 hours, UPS SCS picks up the order and books cargo space to move it to its European distribution center in the Netherlands, where it arrives 2 to 3 days later. In this shipping process, SCS handles customs clearance, documentation, billing, and carrier selection.

Once at the European distribution center, the order is shipped to the customer in one of two ways. If it is a complete order or if the customer chooses to receive the order in several shipments,

UPS SCS ships the product directly using its cross-docking facility. If the product is only part of an order, it is held until the rest of the order is received, then shipped. In some cases, fast-moving products are inventoried at the Netherlands site. UPS SCS personnel manage the site's inventory levels (meeting Cisco's specifications) and handle the last bill-of-material update in Cisco's ERP system once a product has been ordered for dispatch.

UPS SCS uses its own system to find the best shipper to move the package from the Netherlands center to the customer site. In essence, the system issues an electronic request for quote to all approved shippers in the system. The system uses the information they supply to calculate the price, transit time, and service level for the shipment and then places a shipping order. The UPS SCS system also updates Cisco's system so that customers can find out their order status via Cisco's Web site. Until an order is filled, customers can even make changes, such as changing the delivery address.

The systems of the two companies have become increasingly linked. Each movement of a product is recorded in both systems.

UPS now handles over 1 million boxes a year for Cisco through its Netherlands distribution center. Because UPS can ensure reliable transit times, Cisco is able to

(*Case Continued*)

now promise delivery times for its European customers. In addition, these customers have only one point of contact for their shipments: the UPS SCS distribution center. And Cisco has online visibility into its downstream supply chain—to customer delivery in Europe—which it did not have before. ∎

The Emergence of Electronic Tenders

An important development is occurring in the working-outward arena. Initially, IT was embedded in products and services because of its computational capabilities. For example, cars and elevators have computers that make them operate more efficiently. Toys have computers to make them more fun. Now, due to the Internet and wireless networks, the communication capabilities of computers are being extended and emphasized, often in these same products and services. These additions are literally transforming these goods. In essence, we would characterize these additions as adding *electronic tenders*.

An electronic tender is an electronic communication capability in a product or service that allows that product or service to be tended; that is, cared for, attended to, or kept track of by another computer. Electronic tenders open a seemingly unlimited set of possibilities for using IT in the working-outward arena. For example, consider a vehicle and its computers. Those computers can be programmed to perform diagnostics while the vehicle is running. Those diagnostics could be monitored by the car dealer (or an intermediary service provider), in real time, as a service to the owner. If something seems out of kilter, the owner could be notified, perhaps in real time. Likewise, packages and luggage with bar codes or other forms of identification can be tracked and found (if lost). The list of the uses of electronic tenders is endless.

Electronic tenders are occurring with services as well. A growing number of enterprises keep track of their customer interactions, culling them to understand clusters of customers and their buying patterns. Again, the options are endless. The goal is to get closer to the customer.

Getting Closer to Customers

The first wave of using the Internet in the working-outward arena involved the use of Web sites to sell products and services and manage customer relations. Many types of products can now be purchased online, from books, CDs, and flowers to automobiles, legal services, and wine. The advantages of selling online are numerous and seem obvious. Figure 3-4 lists some of these advantages. Indeed, it is not difficult to find success stories, such as Dell, E*TRADE, and Cheap Tickets. However, the potential problems are also numerous and have become more obvious since the dot-com bust. Figure 3-5 lists some of the potential problems faced in creating a B2C system.

Use of the Internet has now become much more sophisticated. CRM systems are used to learn more about customers (and perhaps noncustomers). Whether you visit

Global accessibility: The Internet eliminates geographic boundaries.

Reduced order processing: Automated order processing improves efficiency.

Greater availability: The company is available online 24 hours a day, 7 days a week.

Closer customer relationships: With a direct link to customers, the company can quickly address concerns and customize responses.

Increased customer loyalty: With improved customer service and personalized attention comes greater customer loyalty.

New products and services: With direct links to customers, the company can provide information-based products and services.

Direct marketing: Manufacturers can bypass retailers and distributors, selling directly to customers.

FIGURE 3-4 Advantages of B2C E-Business

a firm's Web site, call it from your home, office, or cell phone, or buy something from it, the firm is keeping track and combining that information to create a profile of you. CRM systems for managing these profiles are the next wave of enterprise systems, following on the heels of ERP. ERP focused on internal data. CRM focuses on customer data.

Examples of CRM are scattered throughout this text. CRM systems are both a boon and a bane, depending on how intrusive you think they are. You may be pleased when companies e-mail you offers that you want to take advantage of, such as a reduced-fare flight to a city you want to visit on the weekend. Or, you may see them as invading your privacy. In response to privacy concerns, some countries have passed privacy-protection laws to require companies to inform customers of whether and under what circumstances customer information is shared with others.

On the other side of the coin, IT and the Internet have changed what customers value. They now expect service to be fast; the key term is *on-demand*. Online business enables firms to respond quickly by drastically reducing the time needed to respond to customer requests for company, product, and price information, to process an order, and to get products to customers.

Customers also now expect convenience. They want more than one-stop shopping; they want a single point of contact in the company. CRM allows the gathering and

FIGURE 3-5 Potential B2C Problems

Technical: The information systems are not always reliable or may be poorly designed.

Logistics: Getting products to customers around the world in a timely manner brings physical barriers to the virtual business.

Personnel: Few people have expertise in dealing with the new environment, both in technical and business arenas.

Legal: Doing business across geographic boundaries means dealing with multiple legal systems.

Competitive response: The ease of creating a Web presence brings low barriers to entry for competitors.

Transparent prices: Customers can easily compare prices across Web sites, reducing profit margins.

Greater competition: The elimination of geographic boundaries means a firm must compete with competitors from around the world.

managing of customer information so that whoever interacts with the customer has all the relevant customer information at hand.

Customers further expect personalization of service. Online business allows direct, ongoing communication with customers; thus, preferences and buying patterns can be tracked and analyzed to provide individual service. By reducing the time to process orders, online business allows firms to customize products to individual customers. Thus, products from music CDs to PCs to bicycles to automobiles can be made to order online.

Online business forces companies to rethink their pricing of products and services. Customers now have access to a wide range of competitive prices and sellers for products, driving down profit margins and the price of products. Some observers have speculated that online business will drive profit margins to miniscule levels. Although some initial studies have confirmed the lower prices for goods purchased online, the highest volume sellers do not always have the lowest prices. Prices are offset by branding, awareness, and customer trust.

The Internet is not used only to sell to customers online. It is also used to provide services to customers. In fact, sometimes it can be difficult to know which is more valuable, the product or the service. For instance, what is more valuable, a piece of machinery or the ongoing monitoring of that machinery and receiving an alert before it malfunctions?

The current focus is on staying in closer contact with customers, understanding them better, and eventually, becoming customer driven by delivering personalized products and services. As Frances Cairncross[9] notes, the shift taking place is from running a company to keeping customers happy. This shift is having a profound effect on company structure and offerings. Here is an example of a Brazilian company that has taken the implications of the Internet to heart in its organization and offerings, moving from manufacturing, to services, to online services: Semco.

CASE EXAMPLE

SEMCO, S. A.

In a *Harvard Business Review* article, Ricardo Semler[13a] describes his company's progress into the digital economy. In a recent book, *The Seven-Day Weekend*, he further explains his unusual company. Semco is a Brazilian manufacturer of heavy equipment, such as industrial grade mixers. Semco's transformation is just as unconventional as the company's history would predict (see case example on page 578). He notes that his company has grown to $160 million in revenue, but he has

resisted defining what businesses Semco is in because that would limit his employees' thinking. He prefers for the employees to choose the work they want to do.

Since 1990, the number of employees at Semco has increased from 450 to 3,000. More importantly, it has moved significantly beyond being a manufacturer. First it expanded into services, which have higher profit margins, and more recently into the marketspace of online business services over the Internet.

(Case Continued)

In 1999, almost 75 percent of Semco's revenues came from services. The shift from manufacturing to services was actually quite natural, states Semler; the employees led the march by listening to what customers wanted, not by following directives from the top of the company. Semler[13b] believes that by giving his employees freedom, they simultaneously act in their own best interest and in the best interest of Semco and lead to change naturally. On the other hand, when management defines the limits of the business, change becomes forced and frustrating.

As an example of natural change, Semler notes that they made cooling towers for commercial buildings in the early 1990s. Over time, though, the owners of these high-rises complained to Semco salespeople about the hassles of maintaining these towers. Some of the salespeople proposed starting a service business to maintain these systems. They would charge the customers 20 percent of the savings they generated (thus letting the customers keep 80 percent), and they would give Semco 80 percent of that revenue and keep 20 percent as their pay in the form of commissions. The business proved successful, saving customers money, reducing their hassles, and moving Semco into the service business.

In fact, the property owners were so pleased that they asked Semco to manage other parts of their buildings: the air conditioning compressors, cleaning, security, general maintenance, and so on. As the business grew, Semco teamed up with Cushman & Wakefield, a major property manager, to launch 50-50 ventures in Brazil. The result is a $30-million property management business.

Semler expects 15 percent of revenues to come from Internet-based services—another major shift that is occurring naturally at Semco. Most of the online business initiatives to date have grown out of the firm's expansion into services. For example, in a joint venture with Johnson Controls, Semco manages retail facilities. In making their rounds and talking to store managers, Semco's employees noticed how much money retailers were losing from lost inventories. One employee asked for a 1-year paid sabbatical to study the possibilities of offering online business services to these retailers. His sabbatical was approved, and he later proposed a joint venture with the largest inventory tracking company, RGIS. Within 2 years, Semco had become the largest inventory manager in South America.

In addition, Semco's property management work showed the inefficiency of the construction industry, so it teamed up with Johnson Controls and Cushman & Wakefield to create an online exchange for the commercial construction industry. Now, all the parties in a project, from architects and engineers to banks and project managers, use this exchange to hold multiparty online real-time chats, issue proposals, send bids, share drawings and documents, and even hire people.

Semco has expanded into the e-world even further, teaming with a virtual trade show company to host virtual trade fairs associated with the exchange so that companies too small to exhibit their products in trade shows can exhibit them online. Semco and its partners held eight such shows the first year.

(Case Continued)

All of this change has occurred by following the employees. When they have a good idea, Semco management is likely to provide the funding to test it out. The company has had more winners than losers taking this self-organizing approach, and it has led Semco naturally into marketspace. ∎

Semco is an unusual company, being employee-driven as it is. However, its forays into using the Internet to expand its business provide lessons for others. This text contains numerous examples of how companies have leveraged the Internet and the electronic tenders IT provides to get closer to customers, sell them complementary goods, or provide them with auxiliary services.

To demonstrate a completely different side of the working-outward arena, we turn to the other side of the coin, from being a seller to being a buyer.

Being an Online Customer

Companies large and small are transacting business via the Internet. Some use it as their main means of business, even after the dot-com crash. Here is an example of one entrepreneur—Terence Channon, CEO of TerenceNet—who is a heavy user of the Internet as both a buyer and seller of services. The story comes from Gartner EXP.[14a]

CASE EXAMPLE

A DAY IN THE LIFE OF AN E-LANCER

TerenceNet is an online consulting, development, and research firm that delivers solutions to small- and medium-sized businesses. A fair amount of its work is procured from Elance (www.elance.com), a Web site that puts freelancers in touch with firms seeking bids for projects. Elance charges a commission of 10 percent of the value of jobs set up through the service. The following is a typical day's journal for Channon's use of Elance.

8:15 A.M. My working day starts with e-mail and checking Elance. I signed up with Elance a few years ago to see what kinds of online work were being offered for freelancers. I think I was one of Elance's first customers. The site's first postings were mainly for

(Case Continued)

online work—Web development and the like—just what my firm does. Recently, I have noticed engineers advertising for AutoCAD drawings, so the site seems to be broadening.

There are lots of freelance Web sites and online marketplaces, but I like Elance because it's where I got my first paid job. I won a job through another site—but never got paid. Elance is a very active site, with 30 to 40 new postings a day; others only have three to four.

This morning I bid on 10 projects.

11:05 A.M. I check Elance several times a day or when I get an e-mail notification that I have received a message, like right now. I've logged onto My-Elance—my own personal Elance Web page—that shows all the work I have bid on, which bids are open and which are closed, and all the projects where my bids have been declined or accepted. It also shows all the projects I have offered, the number of bids I have received, and so on.

A company is considering me for a job I bid on, so its new message to me is flagged. This company tells me it has set up a private message board on Elance for us to talk privately about the work.

At first, I used Elance to supplement my company's income. Now I can pretty much count on the site as a revenue source. It may not be steady revenue, but there are enough postings on it, and I win enough of my bids that I can rely on it for work.

I put considerable thought into the bids I make. Some people just cut-and-paste a generic statement of what they do. I don't do that; I respond to a request by setting out exactly what we can do and pointing to examples of similar work. I think this shows commitment and knowledge.

3:00 P.M. When you sign up on Elance, it's like joining a community. Everything is very open. I can see who is bidding on a job, read their experience, look at the work they have done (such as Web sites they have developed), and see how they have responded to a posting. I can also see who has won a bid.

There's a lot of trust involved on both sides because we don't have contracts. I have to trust that the client will pay me. The client has to trust I will do the work. Elance has a feedback board where I can see that I have a top rating from the companies I have worked for and from the people who have worked for me. Everyone can see these ratings.

I have found everyone to be very professional on Elance, cordial in fact. The bidders all feel as if we are in this together; we don't feel or act like competitors. Naturally, we promote ourselves and our work—but we do not talk down others. I've made some wonderful contacts on Elance. Some short jobs have turned into relationships. TerenceNet is now on retainer with one company because it liked our initial work.

Another company liked our development work and wanted more functionality on its Web site. We were busy at the time so I put a posting on Elance. I got 30 bids in 5 days. When I whittled them down to the bid with the best example of the kind of work I wanted, it

(Case Continued)

was from a company in Bulgaria. This company did the work at a fair price and delivered on time, and I have since given it other work. I had to pay via Western Union, but Elance has a payment system where you can transfer funds between bank accounts.

7:30 P.M. One last check on Elance. Usually, there are not many new job postings in the evening, but I want to make sure I have responded to all my messages. There are 10 new postings tonight—one for designing a business card, two for com-

pany logos, one for 1 million Web site addresses, one for writing a press release, and one for programming in Dreamweaver. None of them interests me.

I put out a posting for some Palm work a few days ago and gave it a 5-day bid period. I'm surprised I have received nine bids so far. I did not know there were so many wireless developers out there.

There are not many job postings on the weekends, so I'm taking this weekend off to spend with my family. ■

A major point of the Semco and TerenceNet case examples is that both are very customer-centric. They keep themselves attuned to the market by continually asking what customers need. This customer-centricity is also changing the strategic use of IT in the working-across arena.

WORKING ACROSS: BUSINESS-TO-BUSINESS

Streamlining processes that cross company boundaries is the next big management challenge, notes Michael Hammer,[15] a well-known consultant in the IT field. Companies have spent a lot of time and effort streamlining their internal processes, but their efficiencies generally stop at their corporate walls. The winners will be those that change their processes to mesh with others they deal with so that they have chains of activities performed by different organizations, notes Hammer. This is not a technical challenge, as most have viewed supply chain management (SCM), but a process and management challenge, he believes.

Working across businesses takes numerous forms. Here are three. One involves working with cosuppliers, a second is working with customers in a close mutually dependent relationship, and the third is building a virtual enterprise, in fact, one that might evolve into an e-marketplace.

Coordinating with Cosuppliers

Collaborating with noncompetitors is a type of working across. For example, two food manufacturers might have the same customers (supermarkets and other retailers) but not compete with each other. Hammer calls such companies "cosuppliers." Their form of working across is illustrated in this example.

CASE EXAMPLE

GENERAL MILLS AND LAND O' LAKES

The seven largest U.S. food manufacturers have about 40 percent of the supermarket shelf space for dry goods. That volume is high enough to support their own fleet of delivery trucks, notes Michael Hammer.[15] However, they have only 15 percent of the refrigerated goods business, which is not enough volume to fill up their refrigerated trucks for one supermarket. Thus, they use one truck to deliver to several supermarkets, which is less efficient because of traffic delays.

To address this problem, General Mills (maker of Yoplait yogurt) teamed up with Land O' Lakes to combine their deliveries on General Mills trucks. The result is better use of the trucks and higher supermarket satisfaction (due to fewer late shipments). Land O' Lakes ships its butter to General Mills' warehouse, either for delivery on the same truck or for pick up by the customer. In fact, notes Hammer, the coordination has been so beneficial that the two are looking into integrating their order-taking and billing processes, again, because they have duplicate processes where they might be able to only have one. To fill their trucks even further, they are creating joint initiatives for customers to order more from both companies at the same time. ■

What has deterred cosuppliers from working together has been the lack of convenient ways to share information quickly and easily, notes Hammer. The Internet takes away that deterrent. In fact, companies can reduce costs through sharing anywhere they use similar resources, such as warehouse space in the same city or shipping between the same two cities.

Hammer recommends companies begin working with cosuppliers by first making their own processes efficient, then collaborating on new joint processes (which is new territory for many companies). Eliminate duplicate activities, focus on customer needs, and let the work be done by the company in the best position, he suggests.

Deciding what type of relationship two enterprises want with each other in many ways determines many factors regarding their relationship. Do they want a loose, close, or tight relationship?

Establishing Close and Tight Relationships

As noted earlier, the action in strategic use of IT and the Internet has moved to the most difficult area, working *across* companies. This means having relationships with various players in one's business ecosystem—investment banks, advertising agencies, specialist providers, suppliers, distributors, retailers, even competitors. Such relationships often have accompanying linking information systems. As Marcus Blosch and Roger Woolfe point out in the Gartner EXP report *Linking Chains: Emerging Interbusiness Processes*,[14b] companies need to determine what level of system integration they want in each case: loose, close, or tight.

- In *loose integration*, one party provides another party with ad hoc access to its internal information. The information may or may not be confidential, and it is accessed when it is needed. An example might be a builder of small power units that lets suppliers and customers check specifications on its Web site, note Blosch and Woolfe. The business processes remain distinct. Such limited integration requires little risk or cost.

- In *close integration*, two parties exchange information in a formal manner. Some of that information is probably confidential, and although the two parties' processes are distinct, they do handle some tasks jointly. For instance, they jointly manage the sharing. An example is airlines sharing pricing data with each other so that they can provide more seamless service to customers using several airlines on one trip. This level of integration leads to greater benefits, so there is greater impetus to make the relationship succeed. However, risks do increase because confidentialities are shared. Costs of integration are also higher than in loose integration.

- In *tight integration*, two parties share at least one business process, as partners, in a business area that is important to them. Generally, high volumes of data are exchanged, the data can be highly confidential, and the data includes key events, such as price changes. An example could be a supplier and retailer sharing a common inventory process. The intent is to synchronize operations to reduce costs and speed response time. Tight integration is the most risky because it is business critical and the most costly to integrate. In some cases, it may be difficult to identify where one organizational boundary ends and the other begins because the two become so intermeshed.

The point to note, state Blosch and Woolfe, is that due to the high costs and risks, companies can only have a few tight relationships. Those would be where the benefits outweigh the costs and risks. That implies that tight relationships are the ones that encompass genuinely critical processes and where working tightly with another party adds significant value. Blosch and Woolfe thus see companies having a pyramid of interbusiness relationships, as shown in Figure 3-6: a few tight ones, some close ones, and many loose ones. The loose ones have basic conformance to integration requirements (such as a negotiated agreement and shared information). Tight ones have advanced conformance as well as significant detail and ongoing maintenance in their agreements.

To illustrate a close relationship that is becoming a tight one, consider the case of The Sara Lee Bakery Group, one of the first food manufacturers to use a specific information technology to establish close relationships with supermarket chains. Based on that experience, it has more recently moved to establish some tight relationships. The case comes from Blosch and Woolfe.

	Numbers of Relationships	Potential Benefit	Cost of Integration	Risk
Tight	Few	•••	•••	•••
Close	Some	••	••	••
Loose	Many	•	•	•

• Basic conformance	•• Intermediate conformance with significant detail	••• Advanced conformance with significant detail and ongoing maintenance

FIGURE 3-6 The Integration Pyramid

Source: Marcus Blosch and Roger Woolfe, *Linking Chains: Emerging Interbusiness Processes*, Gartner EXP, August 2001.

CASE EXAMPLE

SARA LEE BAKERY GROUP

Sara Lee Bakery Group (SLBG), formerly Earthgrains, with headquarters in St. Louis, Missouri, is the second-largest bakery in North America. It specializes in fresh-baked branded goods and private-label refrigerated dough and toaster pastries. Worldwide, SLBG has 26,000 employees.

Fresh-baked goods are delivered to retailers by direct store delivery. Delivery people stand in line at the retailer's back door to have their deliveries counted. To reduce labor costs, retailers have reduced the number of hours their back door is open. SLBG requires more trucks to accommodate the reduced hours. The lines become longer and more time is wasted.

Dealing with the Backdoor Bottleneck

SLBG was one of the first food manufacturers to introduce scan-based trading (SBT), selling bread on consignment. On the first day of the new arrangement, SLBG buys back the bread on the retailer's shelf, which moves the inventory value to the bakery group's balance sheet.

At the end of each day, the store sends the scan data from its point-of-sale checkout system for all SLBG products sold that day to its retail headquarters, which then transmits the data to SLBG via EDI or the Internet. The retailer also uses that scan data to post sales to its accounts payable system, and SLBG posts to its accounts receivable system. The retailer pays SLBG electronically based on the scan data.

More recently, SLBG has established a shared database with 100 stores, hosted by a third party, viaLink. This database facilitates price and item synchronization. Once SLBG has created an electronic

(Case Continued)

connection to viaLink, it can easily exp-and to other trading relationships beca-use viaLink handles translations between trading partners' systems.

Benefits of SBT

SLBG now has 2,143 stores at seven retailers across the United States on SBT. The retailers like SBT because they no longer have money tied up in inven-tory and they pay for bread after it is sold. SLBG likes the arrangement beca-use it receives the scan data, which it uses to improve its merchandizing. SBT also saves time. Delivery people no longer line up at the back door nor deliver only during the backdoor hours. They stock the shelves themselves.

SLBG uses the saved time to improve the quality of work for its delivery peo-ple (less stress in making deliveries), to reduce the number of delivery routes, and to reinvest the time in callbacks in the afternoon to restock the shelves to make the store look better for the before-dinner rush of shoppers.

The shared database eliminates "cha-sing deductions," which is a huge non-value-added activity in the industry.

Seven Prerequisites for SBT

Over the years, SLBG has learned seven prerequisites for creating SBT relationships.

The first is to deal with the major point of contention—shrinkage—right up front. Shrinkage is the amount of product "lost" at the retail store due to theft, misplacement, or other reasons. SLBG deals with shrinkage by agreeing to split the loss 50-50 up to a maximum amount; thus, accountability is shared with the retailer.

Second, SLBG requires the retailer to have an SBT executive sponsor—an executive from headquarters who makes SBT a priority for the retailer. Individual stores cannot initiate SBT on their own because they do not have the authority or the money to create the necessary sys-tems or interfaces.

Third, SLBG requires the retailer to assign a point person. SBT projects touch many people on both sides. SLBG has a project manager as its point per-son for the retailer. It only wants to have to contact one person at the retailer as well.

Fourth, to plan the relationship, SLBG asks the retailer to create a cross-functional group—the executive spon-sor along with people from purchasing (mer-chandising), finance, accounting, security, operations, and IS. IS is involved because converting existing systems costs a retailer between $50,000 and $100,000. One required change is the creation of a path between scan data and accounts payable, which is not a natural path. If the retailer has not been using EDI, SLBG provides a package for transmitting data securely over the Internet.

Fifth, SLBG asks the retailer to cre-ate an as-is process map of how its process currently works and a to-be process map of how it will work in the future. The two processes are vastly dif-ferent. The data and money move on different paths, and in-store processes need to change. For example, the vice president of operations needs to allow SLBG staff in the retail store after noon.

Sixth, SLBG only works with retailers that have invested in achieving almost 100 percent accuracy in their point-of-sale

(Case Continued)

system, because that system determines how much money SLBG is paid. A system that is only 95 percent accurate gives SLBG a 5-percent shrinkage from the outset, which SLBG will not accept.

Seventh, SLBG does not initiate SBT until prices have been synchronized with the retailer.

Managing SBT Relationships

SBT is managed by a 10-person team that is headed by a vice president. The group includes EDI coordinators who handle the technical aspects of receiving SBT data. Project managers integrate customer-driven projects, such as SBT. An analysis group monitors SBT data to ensure that each store is staying within its agreed shrink limits. The analysis group also sends out quarterly invoices to reconcile shrink differences.

Rolling out SBT to a retailer's stores requires lots of coordination. Store employees need to know, "Next Monday everything is going to change." The SBT team works with SLBG's account manager for the retailer to make sure store employees understand the new routine. Store receivers need to understand that SLBG will no longer be standing in line. Store management needs to know delivery people may be tending shelves in the afternoon. SLBG delivery people need to be much more careful about their record keeping—SLBG's income depends on those records.

SLBG's ordering process, in which counting items every day is an integral part, allowed it to move fairly easily to SBT. Manufacturers that do not count individual items, such as soft drink and snack food companies, have a more difficult time making the switch. This is one reason that SBT has not spread more quickly in the industry; it has not yet touched the 85 percent of the grocery items stocked from retailer warehouses. ■

Becoming a Customer-Centric Value Chain

A company's value chain consists of its upstream *supply chain* (i.e., working with its suppliers of raw materials and parts) and its downstream *demand chain* (i.e., working with its distributors and retailers to sell its products and services to end customers). Traditionally, most companies make-to-stock. They build vehicles or package mutual funds and then push them to customers. This is the supply-push world.

Today, we are seeing the rise of the reverse—a demand-pull world—where a customer's order triggers creation of the customized product or service the customer has defined. The chain of events is reversed from supply-push to demand-pull, from running a company to keeping customers happy. Dell is a prime example of this customer-centric, demand-pull business model. In fact, it has become the model that many companies admire and would like to emulate. The case also illustrates the benefits of having a tightly integrated value chain.

CASE EXAMPLE

DELL

Dell, headquartered in Austin, Texas, sells PCs, servers, handhelds, and other equipment directly to customers, either individuals or organizations. It is the largest seller of PCs in the world mainly because of its prices, which are a direct result of its customer-centric business model.

When a customer custom configures a PC online on Dell's Web site, the order information is fed into Dell's production schedule and an e-mail is sent to the customer stating when the computer will be shipped.

However, Dell does not make its computers; its suppliers do. Some 30 of its 200 suppliers get close to 80 percent of Dell's business. That is very few suppliers, notes Cairncross;[9] most PC manufacturers have thousands of suppliers. Dell created an extranet for its suppliers so that they can see order information and Dell's production schedule. In fact, they can grab this information and feed it into their own production systems.

In essence, says Cairncross, Dell's extranet is moving toward becoming a private marketplace, where orders arrive from customers and are distributed to suppliers. In fact, Dell is working toward making the information available to suppliers of its suppliers—two tiers down. Its goal, says Cairncross, is transparency, giving the entire industry a clearer view of supply and demand so that they can see what is selling, and perhaps what buyers are paying, all the while maintaining the privacy of suppliers.

Because suppliers can see through this demand chain and find out which of their components are being ordered and for what kinds of computers closer to real time, they can forecast better. The result is less inventory in the supply chain. Reduced inventory is *very* important in the PC business, notes Cairncross, because some 80 percent of the cost of a PC is in its components. Prices have dropped quickly in the industry; 1 percent every 2 weeks is not uncommon. So the longer they keep inventory, the more money they lose. The fewer days they need to keep inventory, the less money they tie up in it, and the less money they lose.

Dell has a reverse physical value chain from other PC manufacturers. They have supply-push; Dell has demand-pull. Dell also has a demand-pull financial value chain. In the supply-push model, the manufacturer borrows money from a bank to build-to-stock. It then repays the bank, with interest, after the stock has been sold. In Dell's demand-pull financial model, customers pay for their PC when they place their order. Thus, Dell gets paid before it builds the computers. Hence, it borrows less money and pays less interest, lowering its costs and its prices. ■

Pros and Cons of Demand-Pull.   Value chain transparency is a much-talked-about concept. It should, for instance, reduce the number of duplicate orders. During the late 1990s, for instance, when a component was in short supply, manufacturers sometimes duplicated an order for the component with several suppliers just to ensure a steady supply. An order for 10,000 memory chips might appear as 30,000, greatly exaggerating the true demand. In late 2000, when both the dot-com and telecommunications bubbles burst, large amounts of back orders disappeared just about overnight, partly because of this duplicate ordering phenomenon, catching manufacturers unaware. Transparency about orders might prevent such drastic downswings.

Creating private exchanges, such as Dell is doing, changes the level of cooperation among firms as well. Information passes through the chain in a burst and is available to all parties at the same time, rather than sequentially over time. The result, notes Cairncross, is that suppliers and even customers become collaborators in improving efficiency throughout the process. Working closely also introduces technological changes more rapidly. Suppliers would be hard-pressed to keep up without a close working relationship and electronic ties. In fact, some have implemented software that automatically notifies every relevant supplier when a change is made so that they are working from the latest specifications.

One con to demand-pull is the infrastructure. The manufacturer's infrastructure becomes its suppliers' infrastructure as well, binding them more tightly together. If the infrastructure is not robust, crashes can affect the entire ecosystem dependent on the exchange. Another drawback is that such close working requires trust, notes Cairncross. Divulging confidential information to suppliers, such as canceled orders, could hurt the company if it is passed to competitors or Wall Street (perhaps causing the stock price to fall). Furthermore, suppliers that provide parts to competing PC manufacturers must ensure that information from one does not leak to another. This containment of information within a company is often referred to as building "Chinese walls" between the groups that work for competing customers. However, no such containment can be absolute, notes Cairncross. Innovations that employees learn from one customer can naturally seep to another.

Becoming customer-centric is not easy, especially for supply-push companies. Their computer systems, processes, and people follow that model, essentially casting the organization in electronic concrete. That is why the promise of CRM is so alluring. It helps companies shift their attention from managing their operations to satisfying their customers.

Getting Back-End Systems in Shape

To have a hope of working across, internal back-end systems need to be in shape. Most, if not all, B2B systems must integrate with these existing back-end systems, which has proven particularly challenging. Back-end systems cover a wide range of applications, including accounting, finance, sales, marketing, manufacturing, planning, and logistics. Most of these systems have been around for years, operate on a variety of platforms, and were not designed to integrate with other systems. Modifying these systems entails many risks, particularly when the integration must cross organizations. Luckily, most organizations have a head start on interorganizational integration because they have been working for a number of years on internally integrating their systems.

Understanding the need for internal integration, many companies replaced, or are currently replacing, their old back-end systems with newer ones using database management systems (DBMS) and ERP systems. The benefits of DBMS and ERP systems have always stemmed from their ability to provide integration. Recognizing the importance of online business, DBMS and ERP vendors have modified their products to integrate with Internet-based applications. In doing so, the vendors provide platforms for building B2B systems.

Another approach to establishing B2B integration is to create an extranet, as Dell has done. An extranet is a private network that uses Internet protocols and the public telecommunication system to share part of a business' information or operations with suppliers, vendors, partners, customers, or other businesses in a secure manner. An extranet is created by extending the company's intranet to users outside the company. The same benefits that Internet technologies have brought to corporate intranets have accelerated business between businesses.

Whatever the approach, the goal is to extend the company's back-end systems to reengineer business processes external to the company. Example activities include sharing product catalogs, exchanging news with trading partners, collaborating with other companies on joint development efforts, jointly developing and using training programs, and sharing software applications between companies. Initially, the benefits come in the form of greater cost and time efficiencies. Ultimately, the systems will change the structure of industries.

CONCLUSION

Over the years, a few innovative companies have achieved strategic advantage using IT. These firms served as models of what could be done, but most companies did not have the resources or skills to follow their example. With the growth of the Internet and the development of online business, IT has become a strategic tool in every industry.

As their employees become dispersed, enterprises are looking for ways to bring cohesion. Intranets and portals are ways to use IT strategically inside the firm. In working outward, enterprises are creating electronic tenders to provide services that make their products more valuable and help them better know their customers and develop more personal relationships with them. This customer-centric view, now so prevalent in the business world, is affecting the strategic use of IT in working across. Value chains are looking to shift from supply-push to demand-pull. As IT continues to evolve, so do its strategic uses.

QUESTIONS AND EXERCISES

Review Questions

1. According to Karlgaard, what is the "cheap revolution"?
2. Why does Brian Arthur compare the British railway and canal revolutions with today's information revolution?
3. According to Michael Porter, what is the only way to sustain advantage through the Internet?
4. According to Carr, why does use of IT no longer matter strategically? How should the management of IT change?

5. According to Cairncross, what is the challenge for corporate management of widely dispersed enterprises?
6. How did Wire Nova Scotia build an online community?
7. What is an experience curve? Give examples.
8. How has the Internet changed consumer expectations?
9. According to Cairncross, what is the shift taking place today in running a company?
10. According to Terence Channon, why does Elance feel like a community?
11. What is the next big management challenge, according to Michael Hammer? Who will be the winners?
12. How do General Mills and Land O' Lakes cooperate?
13. Explain loose, close, and tight relationships.
14. According to SLBG, what are the prerequisites for it to implement SBT with a retailer?
15. What is a demand-pull value chain? How does Dell exemplify this concept?

Discussion Questions

1. The British railway and canal revolutions are nothing like today's Internet revolution. For one thing, those were just machines that only augmented muscle power. Computers augment brain power. Brian Arthur is wrong in his predictions about the future. Argue both sides of this issue.
2. There have been so few instances of companies gaining competitive advantage from IT that Carr must be right; IT really does not matter strategically any more. Carr is not right, and will not be right, because IT is not one technology (like electricity or railroading); it is many different technologies. New ones are constantly appearing. Choose a side and defend it.
3. Companies are using online applications to build profiles of customers. Privacy advocates consider this practice to be dangerous. Do you agree? Where do you draw the line? Discuss.
4. The prospect of electronic tenders is promising. The prospect of electronic tenders is frightening. Discuss both statements and state where you draw the line and why.

Exercises

1. Learn more about the debate Nicholas Carr has unleashed by finding seven arguments not in the text that convincingly argue that "IT does matter." Present these to the class.
2. Visit a local company and talk to a manager about the firm's intranet. What sorts of functions do they currently have on it? What do they plan for the future? Is it creating a sense of belonging among dispersed employees? If so, give some examples.
3. Describe your personal use of a product or service that has an electronic tender. What do you think of the electronic tender? How valuable is it to you? How could the vendor extend the tender in a way that would help you? How has the vendor stepped over the line in invading your privacy, if you think it has?
4. Visit a local company and talk to a manager about an interbusiness system. Is it loose, close, or tight? Why was it built, what challenges did it present, and what benefits is it producing?

REFERENCES

1. Karlgaard, Rich, "The Cheap Decade," *Forbes*, May 31, 2003. Available at www.forbes.com/global/2003/0331/035_print. html. Accessed June 2004. "The Big Cheap Chance," *Forbes*, April 28, 2003. Available at www.forbes.com/2003/0428/037_print.html. Accessed June 2004 "Cheap-Tech Guru," *Forbes*, May 26, 2004. story.news.yahoo.com/ news?tmpl=story&cid=64&e=4&u=/fo/4629 ecee00981d708cd0932fd19414bc. Accessed June 2004.

2. Arthur, Brian, "Is the Information Revolution Dead?" *Business 2.0*, March 2002, pp. 65–72.

3. Porter, Michael, "Strategy and the Internet," *Harvard Business Review*, March 2001, pp. 63–78.

4. Carr, Nicholas:
   a. "IT Doesn't Matter," *Harvard Business Review*, May 2003, pp. 41–49.
   b. *Does IT Matter? Information Technology and the Corrosion of Competitive Advantage*, Harvard Business School Press, Boston 2004.
   c. Carr's Web site, www.nicholasgcarr.com, has links to articles that debate his premise.

5. Brown, John Seely, and John Hagel III, "Letter to the Editor: Does IT Matter?" *Harvard Business Review*, July 2003, pp. 109–112.

6. Hof, Robert, "Is Info Tech All Washed Up?" *Business Week*, May 24, 2004, p. 24.

7. Schrage, Michael, "Why IT Really Does Matter," *CIO Magazine*, August 1, 2003. Available at www.cio.com/archive/080103/ work.html?printversion=yes. Accessed June 2004.

8. Anthes, Gary, "Portal Powers GE Sales," *Darwin Magazine*, June 2003. Available at www.darwinmag.com/read/060103/gesales. html. Accessed October 2003.

9. Cairncross, Frances, *The Company of the Future: How the Communication Revolution Is Changing Management*, Harvard Business School Press, Boston, 2002.

10. Dienes, Bruce, and Michael Gurstein, "Remote Management of a Province-Wide Youth Employment Program Using Internet Technologies," *Annals of Cases on Technology Applications and Management in Organizations*, Idea Group Publishing, Hershey, PA 1999.

11. Primozic, Kenneth, Edward Primozic, and Joe Leben, *Strategic Choices: Supremacy, Survival, or Sayonara*, McGraw-Hill, New York, 1991.

12. UPS Supply Chain Solutions, "UPS Supply Chain Solutions Builds European Supply Chain Model for Cisco Systems." Available at www.upsscs.com/solutions/ case_studies/cs_cisco.pdf. Accessed February 2004.

13. Semler, Ricardo:
    a. "How We Went Digital Without a Strategy," *Harvard Business Review*, September/October 2000.
    b. *The Seven-Day Weekend: A Better Way to Work in the 21st Century*, Random House, London, 2003; *The Seven-Day Weekend: Changing the Way Work Works*, Portfolio, New York, 2004.

14. Gartner EXP, Stamford, CT 306904; www.gartner.com:
    a. Broadbent, Marianne, and Roger Woolfe, *2001: A Marketspace Odyssey*, January 2001.
    b. Blosch, Marcus, and Roger Woolfe, *Linking Chains: Emerging Interbusiness Processes,* August 2001.

15. Hammer, Michael, "The Super-Efficient Company," *Harvard Business Review*, September 2001, pp. 82–91.

4

INFORMATION SYSTEMS PLANNING

INTRODUCTION

We noted in Chapter 1 that IS management is becoming both more difficult and more important, especially in strategic systems planning. On the one hand, the technology is changing so fast that it is tempting to say, "Why bother?" On the other hand, most organizations' survival depends on IT, so planning its effective use is a matter of organizational life and death.

How can this apparent paradox be resolved? The good news is that a variety of approaches and tools have been developed to assist in systems planning. The bad news is that no best way has been devised. Thus, most organizations use more than one approach or tool.

It is important to establish the appropriate mindset for planning. Although some managers believe planning means determining what decisions to make in the future, this view is untenable today because the business environment is so turbulent, making the future unpredictable. A better view is that *planning* is

>   *developing a view of the future that guides decision making today.*

This seemingly subtle difference significantly changes how managers approach and execute planning. In turbulent times, some executives think in terms of strategy making rather than planning. Our definition of *strategy* is

>   *stating the direction you want to go and how you intend to get there.*

The result of strategy making is a plan.

This chapter first describes the traditional view of planning, and then offers a current version of strategic systems planning, that is, strategy making, which is intended to synchronize with today's faster-paced business world. Finally, some approaches that are used in strategic systems planning are presented.

Why Planning Is So Difficult

Planning is usually defined in three forms—strategic, tactical, and operational—which correspond to three planning horizons. Figure 4-1 summarizes these three planning types and some of their characteristics. This chapter emphasizes strategic planning—the top row. In Chapter 3, strategic was defined as "having a significant, long-term impact on the growth rate, industry, and revenue" of an organization. Strategic systems planning deals with planning for the use of IT for strategic purposes. It attempts to form a view of the future 3 to 5 years out to help determine what should be done now.

Some fundamental reasons explain why systems planning is so difficult. Here are a few of them.

Business Goals and Systems Plans Need to Align.   Strategic systems plans need to align with business goals and support them. Unfortunately, if top management believes the firm's business goals are extremely sensitive, and the CIO is not a member of the top

---

FIGURE 4-1 .Three Types of Planning

Horizon	Focus	Issues	Primary Responsibility
3–5 years	Strategic	Vision, architecture, business goals	Senior management CIO
1–2 years	Tactical	Resource allocation, project selection	Middle managers IS line partners Steering committee
6 months–1 year	Operational	Project management, meeting time, and budget targets	IS professionals Line managers Partners

management team, the IS department can be left out of the inner circle that develops these plans. Fortunately, more and more CIOs are being made part of senior management. In addition, systems planning is becoming a shared responsibility among the CIO, CTO, and other members of senior management. The emergence of e-commerce and globalization caused CEOs and CFOs to realize they need to be involved in systems planning.

Technologies Are Rapidly Changing. How can executives plan when IT is changing so rapidly? One answer is continuous planning. Gone are the days of an annual planning cycle done the last few months of the year and then put aside until the following year. Rather, the planning process first needs to form a best-available vision of the future on which to base current decisions. Then the technology needs to be monitored to see whether that future vision needs alteration. When it does, adjustments in current decisions are made. Some organizations have an advanced technology group charged with watching and evaluating new technologies.

Companies Need Portfolios Rather Than Projects. Another planning issue is the shift in emphasis from project selection to portfolio development. This move requires a more sophisticated form of planning because projects must be evaluated on more than their individual merits. How they fit with other projects and how they balance the portfolio of projects become important. The Internet Value Matrix described later is an example of this approach.

Infrastructure Development Is Difficult to Fund. People understand intuitively that developing an infrastructure is crucial. However, it is extremely difficult to get funding just to develop or improve infrastructure. Often, such funding must be done under the auspices of large application projects. The challenge then is to develop improved applications over time so that the infrastructure improves over time.

Since the mid-1980s, companies have faced a continual succession of large infrastructure investments. First they needed to convert from a mainframe to a client-server architecture to share corporate and desktop computing. Then they implemented ERP to centralize and standardize data so that everyone had the same information. Then they needed to create a Web presence and give users access to back-end systems. Now they are under pressure to implement Web Services–oriented architectures to work intercompany and draw on best-of-breed processes. Boards of directors have realized that they have to bite the bullet and fund these huge multiyear projects just to remain competitive. Making these large-stakes bets increases the difficulty of systems planning.

Responsibility Needs to Be Joint. It used to be easier to do something yourself than gather a coalition to do it. This is no longer the case. Systems planning initiated by and driven by the CIO has not proven as effective as systems planning done by a full partnership among C-level officers (CEO, CFO, CIO, COO) and other top executives. Systems planning has become business planning; it is no longer just a technology issue.

Other Planning Issues. Several other characteristics of planning make strategic systems planning difficult. There is always tension between top-down and bottom-up approaches, thus the planning process must strike a balance between radical change and continuous improvement. Furthermore, systems planning does not exist in a vacuum. Most organizations have a planning culture into which systems planning must fit. This sampling of issues illustrates why systems planning is a difficult but crucial task.

THE CHANGING WORLD OF PLANNING

"The Internet changes everything" was a familiar phrase in the late 1990s until the dot-com crash. It is heard less often today, but it is still relevant. Planning is one of those areas affected by the Internet. The Internet has changed how people think about time and how much time they have to plan and react to competitors' moves. The pace may seem slower than a few years ago, but speed is still an issue. This section discusses those changes.

Traditional Strategy Making

In its *Tactical Strategies*[1a] report, Gartner EXP states that traditional strategy making followed the progression shown in Figure 4-2:

1. Business executives created a strategic business plan that described where the business wanted to go.

2. From that plan, IS executives created an IS strategic plan to describe how IT would support that business plan.

3. An IT implementation plan was created to describe exactly how the IS strategic plan would be implemented.

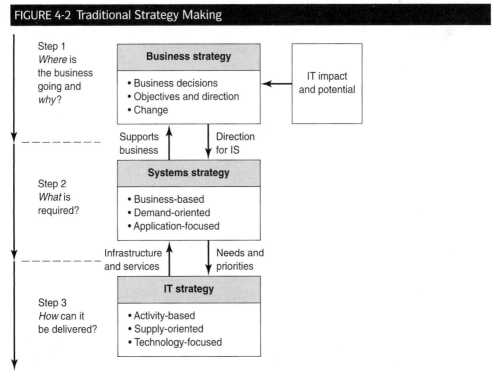

FIGURE 4-2 Traditional Strategy Making

Source: Reprinted with permission from Roger Woolfe, Barbara McNurlin, and Phil Taylor, *Tactical Strategy*, Wentworth Research Program (now part of Gartner EXP, 56 Top Gallant, Stamford, CT 06904), November 1999.

Companies felt comfortable spending quite a bit of time, often a full year, creating a single strategic plan that they would implement over, say, the coming 5 years. That plan was created by top management. If the CIO was part of that group, then IS was involved in the planning; otherwise, IT considerations may or may not have been taken into account.

From the corporate strategy, IS staff developed the systems strategy, which described what was required to support the business plan. Finally, from that systems strategy, IS staff developed the technology-based IT strategy, which described how the company could deliver the needed capabilities.

This traditional planning stance was based on the following assumptions:

- The future can be predicted.
- Time is available to progress through this three-part sequence.
- IS supports and follows the business.
- Top management knows best, because they have the broadest view of the firm.
- The company can be viewed as an army: Leaders issue the orders and the troops follow.

Today, due to the Internet, these assumptions no longer hold true.

The Future Cannot Be Predicted.　The Internet has caused *discontinuous change*, that is, change that can occur in unexpected ways. Industry leaders may not be able to use the same strategies they used in the past to maintain their superior market position. Unexpected and powerful competitors can emerge out of nowhere. For example, in the mid-1990s, how many booksellers predicted Amazon.com's business model of selling only on the Web or the success it would have? Not very many. Likewise, how many top executives seriously considered eBay's online auction model as one that could transform the way they would buy and sell? Not very many. As firms incorporate the Internet into their business, even newer Internet-based business models will appear. Industry after industry is encountering discontinuous changes to the way they have traditionally operated.

Time Is Not Available for the Sequence.　Due to the Internet, time is of the essence. Companies no longer have the luxury of taking a year to plan and several years to implement. Worse yet, the most time-consuming phase of the sequence—IT implementation—is at the end, which means the IS department is late in supporting the business' strategic plan from the outset. To move quickly, IT implementation planning actually needs to be ahead of business strategizing. Furthermore, it needs to be faster than it has been in the past.

IS Does Not Just Support the Business Anymore.　IT has become the platform of business; it makes e-business possible. Bob Benson, Marilyn Parker, and Ed Trainor[2] have pointed out that IT can serve lines of business in two ways. As shown in Figure 2-8 on page 66, one is by supporting current or planned operations, which they call "alignment." The second is by using systems to influence future ways of working, which they call "impact." To fulfill this second role, IS needs to get ahead of the business to demonstrate IT-based possibilities. At the very least, IS and the business need to strategize together, not follow the old model of business first, IS second.

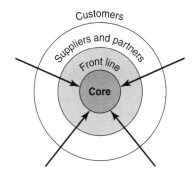

FIGURE 4-3 Outside-In Strategy Development

Source: Reprinted with permission from Roger Woolfe, Barbara McNurlin, and Phil Taylor, *Tactical Strategy*, Wentworth Research Program (now part of Gartner EXP, 56 Top Gallant, Stamford, CT 06904), November 1999.

Top Management May Not Know Best. When change occurs rapidly and when top management is distant from the front lines of the business (i.e., those interacting with customers, partners, and suppliers), having strategy formulated by top management limits it to what these few members of the firm can distill. Today's trend of customizing products and services to smaller and smaller niche markets, even to markets of one, requires diversity in strategy making. It may be best performed by those closest to customers—if not customers themselves—because they know their local environment. Hence, the former inside-out approach to strategy making needs to be shifted to be outside-in, as illustrated in Figure 4-3.

An Organization Is Not Like an Army. Industrial-era planning implicitly viewed companies as an army: Top management edicts rippled down through the organization to be implemented by the troops on the front line who dealt with customers. This metaphor is not holding true. Take, for example, the business process reengineering failures of the early 1990s. Executives learned that their mandates to institute major changes in business processes, imposed from the top, often ended in disaster. Not only did the projects fail; but they ate up resources, burned out employees, created animosity, and even destroyed valuable company knowledge assets because experienced employees left.

A new and controversial view is to see organizations as living entities that evolve. They are not commanded; they can only be nurtured or tended, like a garden. This new approach, if believed, obviously requires a different form of leadership.

Today's Sense-and-Respond Approach

If yesterday's assumptions no longer hold true, thus making yesterday's approach to strategy making less effective, what is appearing to take its place? The answer is a kind of sense-and-respond strategy making, as reported in Gartner EXP's *Tactical Strategy Report*.[1a]

Let Strategies Unfold Rather Than Plan Them. In the past, top management took the time to articulate one enterprisewide strategy. In times of rapid change and uncertainty about the future, such as we are now experiencing, this approach is risky. If a bet proves wrong, it could be disastrous.

When predictions are risky, the way to move into the future is step-by-step, using a sense-and-respond approach. It means sensing a new opportunity or possibility and quickly responding by testing it via an experiment. The result is a myriad of small experiments going on in parallel, each testing its own hypothesis of the future, as illustrated in Figure 4-4.

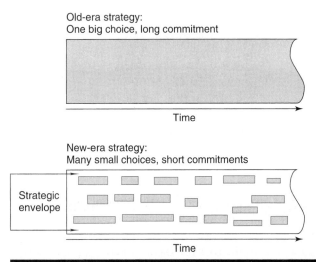

Old-era strategy:
One big choice, long commitment

Time

New-era strategy:
Many small choices, short commitments

Strategic
envelope

Time

FIGURE 4-4 Sense-and-Respond Strategy-Making

Source: Reprinted with permission from Roger Woolfe, Barbara McNurlin, and Phil Taylor, *Tactical Strategy,* Wentworth Research Program (now part of Gartner EXP, 56 Top Gallant, Stamford, CT 06904), November 1999.

A company that illustrates this sense-and-respond approach to developing strategy in the Internet space is Microsoft, say Shona Brown and Kathy Eisenhardt in their book *Competing on the Edge: Strategy as Structured Chaos.*[3]

CASE EXAMPLE

MICROSOFT

Microsoft, the software giant in Redmond, Washington, has taken a sense-and-respond approach to creating its Internet strategy. The company began by building a proprietary version of a network, Microsoft Network, as an alternative to AOL's proprietary network and the Internet. They gave up this stance, even though it had cost a lot of money, when it did not capture enough customers.

Microsoft moved on to buying Internet companies, aligning with Sun to promote Java (and create a proprietary version of Java), and even forging an alliance with AOL.

Over time, they moved into a variety of technologies:

- Explorer browser to compete with Netscape
- Web-only magazine, *Slate*
- Web news site, with NBC
- Cable news channel, with NBC
- Digital movie production, via Dreamworks

(Case Continued)

- Cable modems
- Operating system for handhelds, WindowsCE
- Video servers
- Online music standard to compete with MP3
- Xbox and the multiplayer broadband gaming service, Xbox *Live*
- Smartphone software for cell phones
- .NET platform for Web Services
- Search engine to compete with Google

Bill Gates has made defining announcements, to be sure, focusing the company on the Internet, security, and Web Services. Each announcement has fostered even more explorations. However, the strategies have not always come from top management. The company's first server came from a rebel working on an unofficial project. In addition, management mistakenly passed up some cheap acquisitions that later cost them much more via licensing agreements. Some of these moves could have been predicted, but others are surprising. In short, Microsoft has been sensing and responding to the moves in several industries, getting its fingers into every pie that might become important. ∎

Formulate Strategy Closest to the Action.   The major change introduced by the Internet is faster communication, not only within organizations but, more importantly, with others—customers, suppliers, and partners. Aligning corporate strategy with the marketplace in fast-paced times requires staying in close contact with that marketplace. Hence, strategy development needs to take place at these organizational edges, with the people who interact daily with outsiders.

Furthermore, employees who are closest to the future should become prime strategizers as well. Today, this means including younger employees because they have grown up in an era of the Internet, PDAs, and cell phones. They take all three for granted; they wear them like clothing. One company that is taking this premise of downside-up strategizing to heart is Skandia Future Centers.[1a]

CASE EXAMPLE

SKANDIA FUTURE CENTERS

Skandia Future Centers, located in Stockholm, Sweden, is an incubator for testing ideas on IT, social relationships, and networking for Skandia, the large Swedish insurance company. The center acts as an inspirer and advisor to those who do the strategy making within Skandia.

(Case Continued)

The center was created in 1996 by Leif Edvinsson to give Skandia a laboratory to break out of its current ways of thinking and to provide a place where different generations can collaborate on on-the-edge projects.

3G Teams

One of the first concepts used at the center was 3G teams, getting three generations (25+, 35+, 45+) to work together. The teams were part-time and cross-cultural; coming from Venezuela, Germany, Sweden, and the United States. The participants were chosen by peers as well as nominated from different parts of the company.

To get the generations to actually talk to each other, their mandate was to focus on questions rather than answers. "When you ask for answers, you get a debate. When you focus on questions, you get a dialog," says Edvinsson. The five initial teams were to develop strategic questions on five subjects: the insurance industry in Europe, technology, world economics, demographics, and leadership and organization.

Based on their questions, they arrived at a number of interesting contexts for the questions, such as the evolution of the financial community around the world and the evolution of IT. These contexts were presented to 150 Skandia senior managers, not through a report, but through scenarios of these five future environments performed by professional actors in a theater play.

Knowledge Café

The play led to the first knowledge café among the 150 executives. The café was created by one of the 3G teams and a few of the executives. At the café, the 150 gathered for 1 hour around stand-up tables at different Skandia sites. Each table had coffee and a laptop loaded with groupware software from Ventana Software. In all, 20 laptops were interconnected forming a virtual community of the 150 executives. During the hour, they discussed the questions presented in the play through anonymous entries. The discussion was spiked by the drama they had seen, then nourished and cultivated through the exchange. The result was the collective intelligence of the 150.

The entire project was videotaped and sent to a larger community, along with the questions and a video of the play and the café. The goal of this project was to show the power of collective intelligence. The knowledge cafe accelerated innovation at Skandia, transforming it into an innovation company. The effect has been demonstrated by Skandia's growth, the shift in its organizational design, and the shift in its office design.

Nurturing the Project Portfolio

Edvinsson thinks of the center as a garden, where some of the projects are growing and some are not. He tends them by looking at the level of interest surrounding each one and at the progress each has made, which he equates with gardening.

To peer into the future of IT, Edvinsson believed the center needed ideas from four generations—the current generation of leaders (50+), the second generation of leaders (40+), the third (30+), and the fourth (20+). He formed groups that included young people between the ages of 15 and 25 because they have a much different relationship with IT than older people

(Case Continued)

do. These young people integrate them-selves with the technology. They walk into it and do something with it.

In building the multigenerational teams, the center has learned that 35- to- 45-year-olds have the lowest risk propensity or drive for change. Innovative

behavior occurs amongst young people and seniors. In fact, the more senior, the more risk-prepared they have become, because they see themselves as bullet-proof. Combining senior wisdom with young people's entrepreneurship leads to a real powerhouse. ■

Guide Strategy Making with a Strategic Envelope. Having a myriad of potential corporate strategies being tested in parallel could lead to anarchy without a central guiding mechanism. That mechanism is a *strategic envelope*, as shown in Figure 4-4. Creating and maintaining this envelope is the job of top management. Rather than devise strategy, they define its context by setting the parameters for the experiments (the strategic envelope) and then continually manage that context. Thus, they need to meet often to discuss the shifts in the marketplace, how well each of the experiments is proceeding, and whether one is gaining followership or showing waning interest.

They may perform this work by defining a territory, as Microsoft did. Or they may hold strategic conversations, as espoused by Brown and Eisenhardt.[3] A *strategic conversation* is a regular, frequent meeting at which executives share the workload of monitoring the business environment and responding to it. Perhaps the vice president of operations might be charged with reporting on "today," such as the size of the company's mobile workforce. The emerging technologies director might be charged with reporting on "tomorrow," such as recent developments in Web Services or mobile or fixed wireless services. The HR vice president might be the team's eyes and ears on outsourcing. The purposes of each meeting are to stay in tempo with the marketplace (which may mean setting new priorities), spot trends in their infancy, launch new projects, add resources to promising ones, cut funding for others, and so forth.

Another way to create a strategic envelope is to meet regularly with the experi-menters, as in the case of Shell Oil, described by Richard Pascale in an issue of *Sloan Management Review*.[4]

CASE EXAMPLE

SHELL OIL

Steve Miller, incoming general manager of oil products at Royal Dutch/Shell Group, believed change would only occur

if he went directly to his front lines— employees at Shell gas stations around the world. He felt he had to reach around

(Case Continued)

the middle of the company to tap the ingenuity of employees at the gas stations, encouraging them to devise strategies best for their local market.

He set aside 50 percent of his own time for this work and required his direct reports to do the same. His goal was not to drive strategy from corporate, as had been tried and failed, but to interact directly with the grass roots and support their new initiatives, thus overwhelming the old order in the middle of the company.

Action Labs

His technique was to use action labs. He invited six teams, each with six to eight people from gas stations in one country, to a week-long "retailing boot camp" at which they learned how to identify local opportunities and capitalize on them. The teams were then sent home for 60 days, each to develop a proposal of how to double their net income or triple their market share.

The following week, a fresh set of six teams came to headquarters.

After 60 days, the first six teams returned for a "peer challenge" at which they critiqued each other's plans. They then returned home for another 60 days to hone their plans for the third action lab: approval or disapproval.

At this third lab, each team took turns sitting in "the hot seat" facing Miller and his direct reports, who grilled them for 3 hours on their plan. The teams, in turn, described what they needed from Miller as the other teams watched. The plans were approved, denied, or modified. If funded, the promised results were factored into an operating company's goals. The teams then had 60 days to implement their plan, after which they

would return for a fourth session with Miller and his reports.

The Results

These action labs had a powerful effect. They caused stress on Shell's way of doing business, in effect, unfreezing the status quo. The corporate middle, which had not formerly seen good results from corporate efforts, saw solid plans and energized subordinates. In turn, they became energized. In addition, the labs led to much more informal communications up, down, and across Shell. The teams, for instance, felt comfortable calling up Miller and his staff—a significant departure from the past.

The labs also affected the way Miller and his staff made decisions. In the labs, these executives had to make on-the-spot decisions in front of the front-line teams rather than behind closed doors. They found they had to be consistent and straight with the teams. It was a difficult and trying experience for all, but humanizing for the teams.

In the various countries, "guerilla leaders" emerged and initiated innovative experiments. One, for example, was "the soft drink challenge." Whenever a customer was not offered the full gamut of services at a Malaysian gas station, they received a free soft drink. The result: a 15 percent increase in business.

The projects spawned many more projects, and Miller learned that small local projects can have large effects. The focus was to tap the intelligence at the front lines, with controls and rewards supporting that goal.

Formerly, top management had the illusion of being in control via their directives. Through the action labs, they learned

(Case Continued)

as their staff learned, they received much more feedback, and they knew far more about their customers and the marketplace. Guidance and nurturing came from the top, so there was not complete chaos.

In fact, Miller believes the key is to get the right tension between chaos (at the team level) and order (at the managing director level). He sees it as treating the company as if it were a living system. ∎

Be at the Table.   As noted earlier, IS executives have not always been involved in business strategizing. That situation is untenable today because IT is intrinsic to business. However, to have a rightful place in the strategizing process, the IS function needs to be strategy oriented. Many have been tactical and operational, reacting to strategies formulated by the business. To become strategy oriented, CIOs must first make their departments credible, and second, outsource most operational work to release remaining staff to help their business partners strategize and experiment.

Test the Future.   To get a running start, as well as contribute ideas about the future, IS departments need to test potential futures before the business is ready for them. One mechanism for testing the future is to provide funding for experiments. Another is to work with research organizations. Yet another is to have an emerging technologies group.

Put the Infrastructure in Place.   Internet commerce requires having the right IT infrastructure in place. Hence, the most critical IT decisions are infrastructure decisions. Roger Woolfe and his colleagues[1a] recommend that IT experiments include those that test painful infrastructure issues, such as how to create and maintain common, consistent data definitions; how to create and instill mobile commerce standards among handheld devices; how to implement e-commerce security and privacy measures; and how to determine operational platforms, such as ERP and SCM.

Experimentation is the new sense-and-respond approach to IS strategy making. It differs markedly from the traditional planning described at the outset of this chapter. In fact, it represents a revolution in planning. The following section describes some tools and approaches that can be used to both focus and broaden thinking during planning and strategy making.

SEVEN PLANNING TECHNIQUES

Due to the importance and the difficulty of systems planning, it is valuable to use a framework or methodology. Over the years, a number of techniques have been proposed to help IS executives do a better job of planning. The seven presented here take different views of IS planning, including looking at the assimilation of IT in organizations, defining information needs, understanding the competitive market, categorizing applications into a portfolio, mapping relationships, and surmising about the future. The seven planning techniques discussed are:

1. Stages of growth
2. Critical success factors
3. Competitive forces model
4. Value chain analysis
5. Internet value matrix
6. Linkage analysis planning
7. Scenario planning

Stages of Growth

Richard Nolan and Chuck Gibson published a landmark paper in 1974 entitled "Managing the Four Stages of EDP Growth."[5] They observed that many organizations go through four stages in the introduction and assimilation of a new technology.

- *Stage 1: Early Successes*. The first stage is the beginning use of a new technology. Although stumbling occurs, early successes lead to increased interest and experimentation.
- *Stage 2: Contagion*. Based on the early successes, interest grows rapidly as new products and/or services based on the technology come to the marketplace. They are tried out in a variety of applications; growth is uncontrolled and therefore rises rapidly. This proliferation stage is the learning period for the field, both for uses and for new products and services.
- *Stage 3: Control*. Eventually it becomes apparent that the proliferation must be controlled. Management begins to believe the costs of using the new technology are too high and the variety of approaches generates waste. The integration of systems is attempted but proves difficult, and suppliers begin efforts toward standardization.
- *Stage 4: Integration*. At this stage, the use of the particular new technology might be considered mature. The dominant design of the technology has been mastered, setting the stage for newer technologies, wherein the pattern is repeated. An organization can be in several stages simultaneously for different technologies.

Nolan has since used the Stages of Growth theory to describe three eras, as shown in Figure 4-5.[6] Underlying the three organizational learning curves pictured is the dominant design of each era. The DP (Data Processing) Era's dominant design was the mainframe, the Micro Era's design was the PC, and the Network Era's is the Internet. The eras overlap each other slightly at points of "technological discontinuity," states Nolan, which occur when proponents of the proven old dominant design struggle with the proponents of alternative new and unproven designs. Inevitably, one new dominant design wins out.

The importance of the theory to IS management is in understanding where a technology or a company currently resides on the organizational learning curve. If, for example, use of Web Services is in the trial-and-error Stage 2, where experimentation and learning

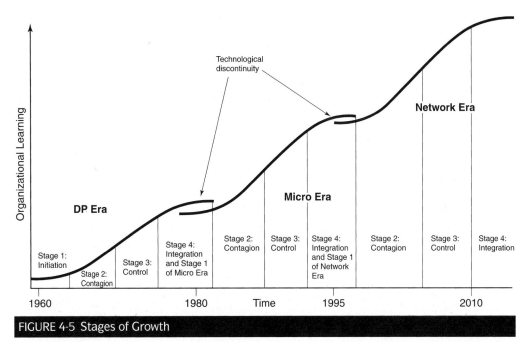

FIGURE 4-5 Stages of Growth

Source: Reprinted with permission from R. L. Nolan, "Information Technology Management from 1960–2000," in *A Nation Transformed by Information,* Alfred D. Chandler and James W. Cortad (Eds.), Oxford, 2000.

take place, then exerting too much control too soon can kill off important new uses of the technology. Management needs to tolerate, even encourage, experimentation.

Because the management principles differ from one stage to another, and because different technologies are in different stages at any point in time, the Stages of Growth model continues to be an important aid to the systems planning process.

Critical Success Factors

In 1977, Jack Rockart[7] and his colleagues at the Center for Information Systems Research (CISR), Sloan School of Management, at the Massachusetts Institute of Technology (MIT), began developing a method for defining executive information needs. The result of their work is the Critical Success Factors (CSF) method. It focuses on individual managers and their current information needs, whether factual or opinion information. The CSF method has become a popular planning approach and can be used to help companies identify information systems they need to develop.

For each executive, critical success factors (CSFs) are the few key areas of the job where things must go right for the organization to flourish. Executives usually have fewer than 10 of these factors that they each should monitor. Furthermore, CSFs are both time sensitive and time dependent, so they should be reexamined as often as necessary to keep abreast of the current business climate. These key areas should receive constant attention from executives, yet CISR research found that most managers had not explicitly identified these crucial factors.

Rockart finds four sources for these factors. One source is the *industry* that the business is in. Each industry has CSFs relevant to any company in it. A second source is the *company itself* and its situation within the industry. Actions by a few large, dominant companies in an industry most likely provide one or more CSFs for small companies in that industry. Furthermore, several companies may have the same CSFs but, at the same time, have different priorities for those factors.

A third source of CSFs is the *environment*, such as consumer trends, the economy, and political factors of the country (or countries) in which the company operates. A prime example is that prior to, say, 1998, few chief executives would have listed "leveraging the Internet" as a CSF. Today, most do.

The fourth source is *temporal organizational factors*, or areas of company activity that normally do not warrant concern but are currently unacceptable and need attention. A case of far too much or far too little inventory might qualify as a CSF for a short time.

In addition to these four sources, Rockart has found two types of CSFs. One he calls *monitoring*, or keeping abreast of ongoing operations. The second he calls *building*, which involves tracking the progress of "programs for change" initiated by the executive. The higher an executive is in the organization, the more *building* CSFs are usually on his or her list. Rockart sees CSFs varying from organization to organization, from time period to time period, and from executive to executive.

One way to use the CSF method is to use current corporate objectives and goals to determine which factors are critical for accomplishing the objectives, along with two or three prime measures for each factor. Discovering the measures is the most time-consuming portion, says Rockart. Some measures use hard, factual data; they are the ones most quickly identified. Others use softer measures, such as opinions, perceptions, and hunches; these measures take more analysis to uncover their appropriate sources. IS plans can then be developed based on these CSFs.

Competitive Forces Model

The most widely quoted framework for thinking about the strategic use of IT is the competitive forces model proposed by Michael Porter[8] of the Harvard Business School in his book *Competitive Strategy*. Porter believes companies must contend with five competitive forces, as shown in Figure 4-6.

One force is the *threat of new entrants* into one's industry. For instance, the Internet has opened up a new channel of marketing and distribution, which, in turn, has allowed all kinds of unexpected new entrants into numerous markets. Travel Web sites, for example, are threats to travel agencies.

The second force is the *bargaining power of buyers*. Buyers seek lower prices and bargain for higher quality. Web-based auction sites, shopping bots, and intelligent agents are all giving buyers more shopping options and more information about potential suppliers, thus increasing their bargaining power. In fact, much of the power of the Internet has to do with this force.

A third force is the *bargaining power of suppliers*. For example, the Internet enables small companies to compete against large ones in uncovering requests for bids and bidding on them—leveling the playing field.

The fourth force is *substitute products or services*. The Internet provides a myriad of examples here. E-mail is a substitute for paper mail. Music downloads are substitutes for CDs. Book and music Web sites are substitutes for book and music stores.

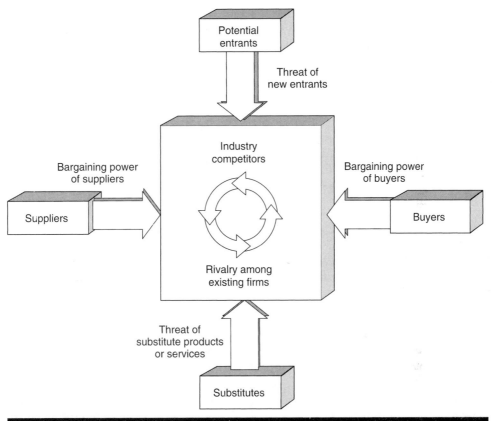

FIGURE 4-6 Michael Porter's Competitive Analysis Model

Source: Michael E. Porter, *Competitive Strategy* (New York: The Free Press, 1980).

The fifth force is the *intensity of rivalry among competitors*. IT-based alliances can change rivalries by, for instance, extending them into value-chain-versus-value-chain competition rather than just company-versus-company competition.

Porter presents three strategies for dealing with these competitive forces. His first is to *differentiate products and services*. By making them different—that is, better in the eyes of customers—firms may be able to charge higher prices or perhaps deter customers from moving to another product, lower the bargaining power of buyers, and so on. It is probably the most popular of his three strategies.

Porter's second strategy is to be the *lowest-cost producer*. He warns that simply being one of the low-cost producers is not enough. Not being the lowest causes a company to be stuck in the middle, with no real competitive advantage.

His third strategy is to find a *niche*, such as focusing on a segment of a product line or a geographical market. Companies that use this strategy can often serve their target market effectively and efficiently, at times being both the low-cost producer and having a highly differentiated product as well.

This framework guides IS planning because all five forces and all three strategies can be enabled by or implemented by technology. Once management analyzes the forces and determines company strategy, the necessary information systems can be included in the plan. In a widely referenced 2001 article in the *Harvard Business Review*, Porter[9] analyzes the Internet using this framework. Here are his main points.

FRAMEWORK EXAMPLE

FIVE FORCES ANALYSIS OF THE INTERNET

In the main, the Internet tends to dampen the profitability of industries and reduce firms' ability to create sustainable operational advantages, argues Michael Porter, because it has "a leveling effect on business practices." He reaches this sobering conclusion by looking at the effect the Internet can have on industry profitability using his five forces framework, described in his 1980 book *Competitive Strategy*.[8] Here are his points.

The Bargaining Power of Buyers Increases.   On the demand side of the value chain, the Internet opens up new channels for companies to deal directly with customers, rather than through intermediaries. Thus, the Internet can decrease the bargaining power of the other channels and their intermediaries, thereby potentially increasing profitability.

However, the Internet gives buyers more information, both about competitors and products, strengthening their bargaining power and lowering industry profitability. The Internet can also decrease switching costs—the cost a buyer pays to switch from buying from one firm to buying from someone else. This also increases buyer bargaining power. In total, the increase in buyer bargaining power decreases industry profitability.

Barriers to Entry Decrease.   Due to the Internet's new channel to buyers, industries may not be so reliant on building up sales forces to sell their goods, making it easier for others to enter the industry because they can compete without having these high fixed costs. Furthermore, location need not be as much of a limiting factor. Small companies can sell to the world via a Web site.

On the other hand, network effects, which increase barriers to entry, are difficult to garner, argues Porter. A *network effect* occurs when the value of a product or service increases as the number of users increases. eBay illustrates this effect: the more buyers, the more eBay is a desirable marketplace for sellers. And the more sellers, the more eBay attracts buyers.

It is a virtuous circle. However, Porter argues that a self-limiting mechanism is at work. A company first attracts customers whose needs it meets well. The needs of later customers may be less well met—presenting an opening for other competitors. Thus, the network effect limits itself.

(Case Continued)

Yet, where it exists, it presents a formidable barrier to entry.

The Bargaining Power of Suppliers Increases.

On the supply side, the Internet can make it far easier for a company to purchase goods and services, which reduces the bargaining power of suppliers. This trend would seem to increase industry profitability. But, at the same time, suppliers can more easily expand their market, finding new customers, thereby increasing supplier bargaining power. Lower barriers to entry also erode the former advantage of a company over its suppliers.

Electronic exchanges, which expand marketplaces, can benefit both buyers and suppliers. However, they can reduce the leverage of former intermediaries between suppliers and end users. This decrease gives companies new competitors (their former suppliers), which can reduce industry profitability.

Finally, in giving equal access to all suppliers, the Internet tends to diminish differentiation among competitors—again reducing industry profitability.

The Threat of Substitute Products and Services Increases.

An industry can increase its efficiency by using the Internet, thereby expanding its market and improving its position over substitutes. For example, online auctions can decrease the power of classified ads and physical marketplaces because the online auctions may be more convenient to buyers. Online exchanges, especially those with many buyers and sellers, can thus discourage substitutes.

On the other hand, the Internet has opened up entirely new ways to meet customer needs. Thus, the threat of substitutes can increase significantly, probably greater than its ability to ward them off through increased efficiencies.

Rivalry Among Competitors Intensifies.

Proprietary offerings are more difficult to sustain in the Internet's open-system environment, states Porter, because products and services are easier to duplicate. Hence, there can be more intense rivalry among competitors. Furthermore, due to the Internet's global nature, companies can extend their range of competition, so there can be more competitors in a marketspace.

Also, the Internet can change the cost structure, emphasizing fixed costs (Web sites rather than call centers, for example) and reducing variable costs (serving one more customer can be much less expensive via a Web site rather than a call center). This change in cost structure can lead companies to compete on price (which hurts industry profitability) rather than on convenience, customization, specialization, quality, and service (all of which can increase industry profitability).

Even partnering with complementary products and services, while seeming to increase a market, may instead decrease profitability if it leads to standardized offerings. Microsoft's operating systems has had that effect on the PC industry. The industry now competes on price; its profitability has decreased.

Outsourcing, another form of partnering, can also depress industry profitability if the companies outsource to the same providers and their products thereby become more alike.

Overall, states Porter, the Internet tends to decrease industry profitability. But not all industries need to see this

(Case Continued)

happen to them. It depends on how their companies react. They can react destructively by competing on price or compete constructively by competing on differentiating factors. However, it will be harder to distinguish themselves on operational efficiencies alone, says Porter, because the Internet can make duplication easier. Instead, firms should focus on their strategic position in an industry and how they will maintain profitability (not growth, market share, or revenue). Success depends on offering distinct value. ■

Value Chain Analysis

Five years after proposing the five forces model in 1980, Porter presented the value chain in *Competitive Advantage* in 1985[8]; it, too, became a popular strategic planning tool. As shown in Figure 4-7, a value chain for a product or service consists of major activities that add value during its creation, development, sale, and after-sale service. According to Porter, primary activities and support activities take place in every value chain.

The five primary activities deal with creating a product or service, getting it to buyers, and servicing it afterward. These activities form the sequence of the value chain:

1. *Inbound logistics:* Receive and handle inputs
2. *Operations:* Convert inputs to the product or service
3. *Outbound logistics:* Collect, store, and distribute the product or service to buyers

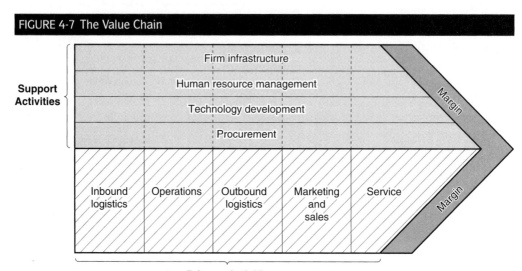

FIGURE 4-7 The Value Chain

Primary Activities

Source: Michael E. Porter, *Competitive Advantage* (New York: The Free Press, 1985).

4. *Marketing and sales:* Provide incentive to buyers to buy the product or service

5. *Service:* Enhance or maintain the value of the product or service

The four supporting activities underlie the entire value chain:

1. Organizational infrastructure
2. HR management
3. Technology development
4. Procurement

By studying how a firm performs the primary and support activities for a product or service, a firm can explore how it might add more value at every activity. Alternatively, it could determine where another company could add more value, and team up with that firm, outsourcing that activity to that partner.

Virtual Value Chains.   Jeff Rayport and John Sviokla[10] distinguish between market-*places*, where physical products and physical location are important, and market*spaces*, where information substitutes for physical products and physical location. In the world of Internet commerce, they ask, "How can companies create value in marketspace?" or "How can they create value in marketspace and marketplace concurrently, leveraging off each other?" They draw on Porter's value chain in their answer.

In the traditional value chain, note Rayport and Sviokla, companies treat information as a support element, not as a source of value itself. To compete in marketspace, companies need to use information to create new value for customers (such as FedEx and UPS did in opening up their tracking systems to consumers via their Web sites). Creating value in marketspace also involves a value chain, but it is a virtual value chain, because the steps are performed with information and through information. At every step, value via information can be added in five ways: gather it, organize it, select it, synthesize it, or distribute it. The IS organization should therefore play a major role in marketspace.

Rayport and Sviokla have observed that companies seem to follow an evolution in using information to add value: first by making operations visible, then by putting in place mirroring capabilities, and finally by creating space-based customer relationships.

Making operations visible.   Companies first create ways to see their physical operations through information. That is, they foster visibility of operations, generally through their production systems, allowing employees to coordinate activities across the physical value chain, sometimes in ways that lead to competitive advantage. Frito-Lay's field employees input information on store-by-store sales as well as information about competitors' promotions and new competitive products. With all this field data, managers can better schedule production to match demand, route trucks most efficiently, and tailor promotions to suit local buying patterns. Frito-Lay can more quickly react to marketplace changes. This sort of visibility, say Rayport and Sviokla, lays the foundation for a virtual value chain.

Mirroring capabilities.   Second, companies begin to substitute virtual activities for physical ones. Here is a case in point from a report by Roger Woolfe.[1b]

CASE EXAMPLE

AN AUTOMOBILE MANUFACTURER

This auto manufacturer has dealerships around the United States. Many of the dealerships have a satellite dish, as does headquarters. In addition to other uses, these dishes are used by the manufacturer's rental car subsidiary to auction off good, clean used vehicles (with fewer than 10,000 miles) to dealers to sell.

For 30 minutes at a specified time, an auctioneer is able to sell 60 vehicles online. As a car comes up for bid, the dealers view it on a monitor at their premises. They can see it from several directions, read its ratings (on cleanliness and condition), and use a mouse to bid against the other dealers online. Headquarters staff monitor the progress of the auction and advise the auctioneer on, say, lowering minimum bids to ensure that every vehicle is sold. The auctions are held once or twice a month.

The dealers have been extremely satisfied with this system because it saves them from having to travel to auctions, and they can get good-quality used cars without much effort. In addition, the manufacturer guarantees satisfaction. If, after taking delivery of a vehicle, the dealer decides he does not want it, he can send it back. ∎

Another example is virtual worldwide teams, such as design teams in the United States, Europe, and Asia that work on designs and prototypes in a virtual information space. Time and space are no longer limitations. The teams can be located anywhere, work can progress 24 hours a day, and many more virtual designs can be created and tested in a shorter time and for less cost than in the physical world. This mirroring of capabilities, note Rayport and Sviokla, marks the beginning of creating a parallel virtual value chain.

Space-based customer relationships.   Third, companies draw on their flow of information to deliver value to customers in new ways. In essence, they create new space-based customer relationships. USAA, the insurance company for military officers, exemplifies this third step, note Rayport and Sviokla. For many years, USAA collected information about customers and made it available companywide so that employees could provide advice and answer questions anytime a customer called (visibility). The company then discovered it could create customer risk profiles and customize policies. From that point, it created new product lines, such as insurance for boat owners (mirroring capabilities). From there, USAA expanded to new areas, such as offering financing to boat purchasers. In fact, it even offers to replace stolen items in a theft claim, rather than send the insured a check, a service many seem to prefer. USAA is managing its information to create new value for customers.

When searching for strategic uses of information, Rayport and Sviokla point out that many of the rules differ from those of the physical marketplace. Digital assets are not used up in consumption; therefore, information can be reused in many forms at a low cost. New economies of scale are present, so small companies can effectively compete against large ones, due to lower overhead, while still covering large geographic areas. New economies of scope allow insurance companies to offer financing and even discount buying programs to policyholders, as USAA is doing, for example. Finally, transaction costs are lower in marketspace; thus companies can capture information that they were not able to capture in the past, as Frito-Lay is doing.

To take advantage of these four changes, though, a significant mindshift is required from supply-side thinking to demand-side thinking, say Rayport and Sviokla. That is, companies need to sense and respond to needs rather than make and sell products and services. That shift appears to be a significant strategic opportunity for companies, and IS should play a role in identifying and helping the company take advantage of it.

E-Business Value Matrix

At a Networld+Interop conference, Peter Alexander of Cisco Systems[11] described a portfolio planning technique used at Cisco to ensure it develops a well-rounded portfolio of IT projects. The approach is further described in Hartman et al.'s *Net Ready*.[12] These days, that portfolio revolves around the Internet.

It can be difficult for executives to prioritize projects, said Alexander, because of the wealth of opportunities. A portfolio management approach is therefore of great value to senior and functional executives to ensure that they are working on a broad front that will lead to success in the Internet economy.

The portfolio management approach Cisco uses is called the e-business value matrix, and every IT project is meant to be placed in one of four categories to assess its value to the company. As shown in Figure 4-8, the value of each project is assessed as high or low in two categories: criticality to the business and newness of the idea (newness not just to the company, but to the world). The result is four categories of projects: new fundamentals, operational excellence, rational experimentation, and breakthrough strategy.

New Fundamentals.   These projects provide a fundamentally new way of working in overhead areas, not business-critical areas. They are low risk and focus on increasing productivity. They can provide significant cost savings by measurably improving operations. An example is Web-based expense reporting, described in the Cisco case example on pages 157–158.

FIGURE 4-8 E-Business Value Matrix

	Criticality to Business	*Newness of Idea*
New fundamentals	Low	Low
Operational excellence	High	Low
Rational experimentation	Low	High
Breakthrough strategy	High	High

Source: Adapted from a speech by Peter Alexander and *Net Ready: Strategies for Success in the E-conomy* by Amir Hartman, John Sifonis, and John Kador (New York: McGraw-Hill, 2000).

These projects should be managed as quick hits: Implement a project to increase productivity in finance within 3 to 6 months, said Alexander, then move on to another area. Often, such projects can be implemented by IS with little user involvement during development. However, an important point to remember is that these systems aim at the grass roots of the company. Thus, they can lead to a cultural shift, such as shifting to working via an intranet.

Operational Excellence.   These projects are of medium risk because they may involve reengineering work processes. They do not aim for immediate returns, but rather intend to increase such areas as customer satisfaction and corporate agility. In essence, they revolve around providing faster access to information. These projects can be important in improving IS credibility because of their high visibility. An example is an executive dashboard for quickly viewing operational metrics. Such a system is highly visible to executives.

These projects have about a 12-month horizon. They should involve cross-functional teams (to ensure that the reengineering does indeed take place), and they should use tested technology.

Rational Experimentation.   These projects test new technologies and new ideas. Hence, they are risky. However, every company needs some of these projects to hope to move ahead of competitors. When described as experiments, they set the realistic expectation that they may fail. The goal is to prove the concept in, say, several months' time or less. One example could be Web Services; another could be desktop video conferencing. When treated as experiments, these projects will not hurt the company if they fail. If they do pan out, however, they could prove a new business or IT model and thus become one of the other three types.

These incubator-type projects should be managed as experiments with short time frames and incremental funding. The team may be full-time, but it does not need to move out of IT. Participants should not be penalized if one of these projects fails.

Breakthrough Strategy.   These projects potentially have a huge impact on the company, and perhaps even on the industry, if they succeed. They capture the imagination, but they are high risk. The typical response, once someone sees the potential is, "If this works, it would change. . . ." An example of a breakthrough strategy is eBay. Its auction business model altered people's thinking about global buying and selling. Another example is extranets for customers. When successful, they move to the operational excellence cell.

Breakthrough strategy projects require strong functional buy-in. One way to get this commitment is to brainstorm with functional partners on the possibilities. Because they are generally bet-the-farm types of projects, they need to be managed like start-ups. They need venture-capital-like funding, not month-to-month milestones. For example, the project may request $10 million with the possibility of failure, but also offer the possibility of huge upside returns.

These IT-based projects need dedicated staff from numerous functions. To attract top talent and foster the intense communication and collaboration needed among the team members, they probably need to be housed in a "skunk works" setting by being set apart organizationally and reporting to the CEO or CFO, who protects them from corporate politics and from the "but this is the way we've always done it" mindset. Finally, the skunk works team needs to be given financial incentives if the project succeeds.

In conclusion, Alexander stated that IS departments can get functional buy-in if they create such a portfolio of IT projects and then manage that portfolio properly. A key to success is leadership. All the C-level executives need to evangelize and empower others to make these projects happen. They need to encourage risk and accept failure of the right kind. Because C- level involvement is key, executives may need to be educated on their role.

To illustrate this portfolio approach, here are examples of Cisco IT projects.

CASE EXAMPLE

CISCO SYSTEMS

Cisco Systems manufactures computers that provide the infrastructure for the Internet. Cisco uses the e-business value matrix described by Alexander[11] to manage its portfolio of IT projects, placing a value on each project based on the newness of the idea it employs and the criticality of the system to the company.

Here are examples of systems in each of the four cells in the matrix: new fundamentals, operational excellence, rational experimentation, and breakthrough strategies.

New Fundamentals

Cisco's expense reporting system, Metro, is a fundamentally new way of handling expense reporting. Its goal is to reduce costs in this overhead area.

To submit an expense report, an employee goes to a Web page to build the report online. As the report is filled in, the system checks to see whether the employee has adhered to company policy.

When submitted, the system routes the report to the employee's manager and explains the purpose of the expense report, the total expenses, and whether any policies were violated. If the manager does nothing, the employee's credit card account and personal account are credited in 2 days' time.

This system quickly delivered major cost savings, because Cisco now only needs three people to manage expense reports for all 31,000 employees. Although abuse is possible, the cost of potential losses from questionable charges is a fraction of the cost of having a larger administrative staff.

Operational Excellence

Cisco's executive dashboards for each functional area are seen as operationally differentiating the company from its competitors. In fact, Cisco executives have said, "I cannot live without this system because . . . it allows me to model sales programs, . . . it allows me to manage the supply chain, . . . it allows me to do trend analysis on component availability, and so on."

Each dashboard is a Web front end to the company's data warehouse. In essence, it is an executive information system that allows executives to drill down into the

(Case Continued)

data to pull up a snapshot of, say, the company's revenues, bookings, or margins (the fundamentals of the company) at a point in time by business unit, region, entire enterprise, product line, and so on. For example, executives can see how well a division is progressing in meeting its forecasts.

Furthermore, the system allows the CFO to close the company's books within 1 day of the end of each quarter, and the company expects to reduce this lag to just 2 to 3 hours.

Such a system is not excellence in product, it is excellence in IT; and it is operational excellence, said Alexander.

Rational Experimentation

Cisco has a continual stream of such experiments going on in IT. One experiment has been multicast streaming video. Executives are watching to see the business value of this new technology to the various functional areas. For example, they have made all-company meetings available online to employees through IP TV. If this technology proves useful, it could be used for new product training.

Breakthrough Strategy

Cisco views its development of a virtual supply chain as a breakthrough strategy. Of the 26 factories that build Cisco products, only 5 are owned by Cisco. Thus, the company's ability to sense and respond is not tied to capital assets. It is a function of their building an effective supply chain. Although not easy, they believe it is critical to their business. If their gamble on virtual manufacturing goes awry, it would present an enormous problem. However, they see it as worth the effort because the returns will be extremely high if they succeed.

Cisco takes its portfolio of IT projects and Internet initiatives so seriously that CEO John Chambers holds a review of leading Internet capabilities each quarter. At these reviews, each functional area describes how it is implementing Internet capabilities that are ahead of its peers in the industry. Most company CEOs do not make this effort, said Alexander. If they did, they would see spectacular returns, he believes. ∎

Linkage Analysis Planning

Linkage analysis planning examines the links organizations have with one another with the goal of creating a strategy for utilizing electronic channels. This approach to strategic systems planning is espoused by Kenneth Primozic, Edward Primozic, and Joe Leben in their book *Strategic Choices*.[13] The methodology includes the following three steps:

1. Define power relationships among the various players and stakeholders.
2. Map out the extended enterprise to include suppliers, buyers, and strategic partners.
3. Plan electronic channels to deliver the information component of products and services.

Define Power Relationships.   To create a strategy for building electronic links among enterprises, Primozic's team believes that management must first understand the power relationships that currently exist among these various players. For this analysis, they begin with Michael Porter's[8] classic model of competitive forces. To this model, they add technology, demographics, global competition, government regulations, and "whatever is important in your environment." The goals of this step are to identify who has the power and determine future threats and opportunities for the company.

The analysis begins by identifying linkages, which are relationships the organization has with other entities. Figure 4-10 on page 162 is a good illustration. The links are represented by lines between organizations (shown in boxes). Once identified, management needs to determine who is managing each link. Oftentimes, no one is, which should be of concern. From here, the team picks the most important link and decides how the firm can control that link. The authors believe that successful organizations will be those that control the electronic channels or the electronic linkages among enterprises.

The discussion of how to gain power within one's world of linkages brings up a host of questions. Two important ones are: How might alliances with other firms across industries or even with competitors help us? How do we need to restructure ourselves to seize an opportunity or ward off a threat?

Map Out Your Extended Enterprise. These questions lead to the second step in this approach to planning—mapping the extended enterprise. An extended enterprise includes all of one's own organization plus those organizations with which one interacts, such as suppliers, buyers, government agencies, and so forth (see Figure 4-9).

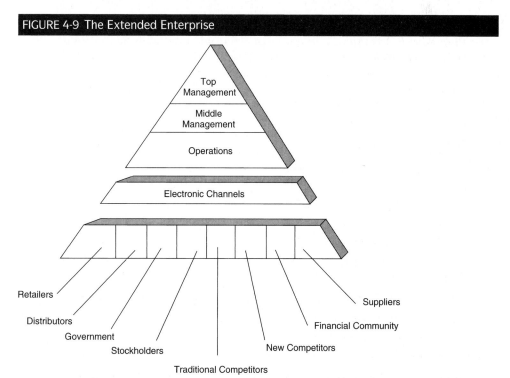

FIGURE 4-9 The Extended Enterprise

Source: K. I. Primozic, E. A. Primozic, and J. F. Leben, *Strategic Choices: Supremacy, Survival, or Sayonara* (New York: McGraw-Hill, 1991).

The purpose of this step is to get management to recognize the existence of this extended enterprise and then begin to manage the relationships in it. Primozic and colleagues believe successful managers will focus on extended enterprises. They see two fundamental principles to managing these relationships:

1. The enterprise's success depends on the relationships among everyone involved, which includes employees, managers, suppliers, alliances, distribution channels, and so forth.

2. Managing information as a strategic tool is crucial because some 70 percent of the final cost of goods and services is in their information content.

An extended enterprise diagram might deal only with external players, such as the government, stockholders, traditional competitors, the financial community, and so forth. Such a chart includes everyone whose decisions affect the organization or who are affected by its decisions. The analysis then moves to discussing how the links might change and how each link should be managed.

In the extended enterprise, each relationship will prosper only when it is win-win, say the authors. For example, in return for maintaining a buyer's parts inventory and providing just-in-time delivery, a supplier should be paid electronically upon delivery of goods. Such an arrangement profits both parties.

Competitive advantage will depend increasingly on being able to exploit the collective resources of one's extended enterprise, say Primozic and colleagues. Such enterprises often require electronic channels to execute business transactions, which leads to the third step in their planning approach — planning the electronic channels.

Plan Your Electronic Channels.   An electronic channel is an electronic link used to create, distribute, and present information and knowledge as part of a product or service or as an ancillary good. These channels focus on the information component of products. The authors believe that those who control the electronic channels will be the winners because they will be able to address new niche markets as they arise. Furthermore, as use of IT leads to a faster-paced world, organizations with the longest electronic reach into their extended enterprise will have the advantage.

The authors use linkage analysis charts to help executives conceptualize the key issues they face in an extended enterprise and focus on the factors that are critical to their future success. This methodology has been used by the Electric Power Research Institute, whose story is told next.

CASE EXAMPLE

ELECTRIC POWER RESEARCH INSTITUTE

The Electric Power Research Institute (EPRI), with headquarters in Palo Alto, California, is a large private research firm serving more than 700 electric member utilities. EPRI's 350 staff scientists and engineers manage some 1,600 R&D

(Case Continued)

projects at any one time. The projects, which study such subjects as power generation, superconductivity, electronic and magnetic fields, and acid rain, are conducted by more than 400 utility, university, commercial, government, and other R&D contractors on behalf of the members.

The Challenge

EPRI's mission is to deliver the information and knowledge from its research projects to the 400,000 employees in the 768 member utilities to help them be more competitive. Management realized EPRI had to compress the "information float," the elapsed time from the availability of research findings to the use of those results in industry.

The institute was suffering from "info-sclerosis," the hardening and clogging of its information arteries. Due to the volume of research findings—gigabytes of information—moving information in and out of EPRI was extremely difficult. In addition, because of the documentation and publishing process, the results often were unavailable for up to 24 months, so the reports were not as timely as they could be. Nor were the results accessible, because they were in massive reports. Solving this information delivery challenge was critical to EPRI's survival.

The Vision

The vision was to assist members in exploiting EPRI's product—knowledge—as a strategic business resource, whenever and from wherever they choose. To accomplish this vision, EPRI built an electronic information and communication service.

As described by Marina Mann and her colleagues,[14] their delivery vehicle is EPRINET, an online channel that includes

- A natural-language front end for accessing online information
- Expert system-based products that contain the knowledge of their energy experts
- E-mail facilities for person-to-person communications
- Video conferencing to foster small-group communications

Using Linkage Analysis Planning

To focus the EPRINET effort and to identify the services and products that would offer strategic business advantages to members, EPRI used linkage analysis in a 3-day workshop led by Kenneth Primozic. The workshop began with management stating that (1) EPRI was both an R&D organization and a knowledge provider and (2) the goal was to leverage knowledge as a strategic asset.

From this starting point, Primozic asked, "Who is linked to EPRI in creating and distributing knowledge?" The participants identified the cocreators as contractors, research firms, universities, the government, and technology firms. They identified the recipients as the utility industry, universities, research labs, government policies, and knowledge as capital—as shown in Figure 4-10. Each represented a link to EPRI; therefore, the group then studied the present and future power relationships in each buyer–seller link. During these discussions, they saw how some current customers, such as universities or research labs, could become future competitors and change the power relationship in a link.

Management's goal was to leverage knowledge, so the group listed all the ways leverage could be achieved. Then

(Case Continued)

they focused on the most important way, which turned out to be treating knowledge as capital. During this analysis, management defined the following CSFs for giving EPRINET a sustainable competitive advantage:

- Establish the right mix of product offerings, a mix that allows people to pick, choose, and combine at the lowest possible cost.
- Keep all customers in mind, including utility executives, research engineers, and operations people.
- Use IT—specifically expert systems and natural language—to make the system easy to use and access.
- Create a range of "knowledge packages" targeted to specific audiences.
- Establish a timely, reliable, secure global distribution channel.

Once EPRINET was made available, a marketing campaign began. The number of users has climbed steadily since. Frequent users report that the system is indeed broadening the number of people they can stay in contact with and allowing them to uncover EPRI research findings that they would not have found otherwise. ■

FIGURE 4-10 EPRI'S Linkage Analysis

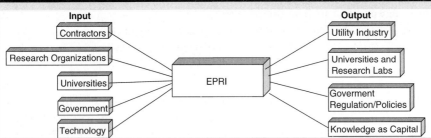

Source: M. M. Mann et al., "EPRINET: Leveraging Knowledge in the Electric Utility Industry," *MIS Quarterly*, September 1991, pp. 403–421.

Scenario Planning

The final strategic planning approach is scenario planning. Peter Schwartz, who has written the definitive book on scenario planning, *The Art of the Long View*,[15] states that *scenarios*, which get their name from the theatrical term for a script or a play, are stories about the way the world might be in the future. Such stories can help people spot and adapt to aspects of their lives that are actually changing today. They help people find appropriate paths to each of the plausible futures described in the scenarios

The goal of scenario planning is not to predict the future (because that is hard to do) but to explore the forces that could cause different futures to take place and then decide on actions to take if those forces begin to materialize.

M. Lynne Markus,[16] of Bentley College, points out that long-term planning has traditionally extrapolated from the past and has not factored in low-probability events that could significantly alter trends. Thus, these straight-line projections have provided little help.

Markus identifies four steps in scenario planning:

1. *Define a decision problem and time frame to bound the analysis.* In thinking about the future of IS, for instance, IS management might ask, "How will IS be managed 10 years from now?" An individual IS employee might then ask, "What skills would I need to succeed in that organization, and what do I need to do to get those skills?"

2. *Identify the major known trends that will affect the decision problem.* Generally, scenario planners think about trends in categories: the business environment, government and regulations, societies and their concerns, technologies, financial considerations, the global environment, and such. Each trend is then judged by asking, "What impacts will this trend have on the decision problem?" "What are the directions of each impact?" Trends with unknown impacts or contradictory impacts are classified as "uncertain."

3. *Identify just a few driving uncertainties.* Driving uncertainties are those around which others tend to cluster. Often scenario analysts choose just two, with two possible states for each, leading to four scenarios. The goal is to explore quite different futures, not the most likely future, notes Markus.

4. *Construct the scenarios.* Each scenario, based on a driving uncertainty, needs to be plausible. To create this plausibility, scenario writers include a "triggering event," something that redirects the future into the desired space. For example, a triggering event could be a world event (the September 11, 2001, tragedy certainly qualifies), an action by a group (a major court decision), or a business event (the collapse of a large company). The scenarios depict the end state (at the selected point in time) and how that path got taken.

With these scenarios in hand, executives and planners then decide how well their current strategies would fare in each case. Then they ask, "Is there a better strategy, perhaps one that would cover more bases?" Also, they should determine what factors they should monitor closely to quickly spot changes in trends.

To give a brief glimpse of a scenario effort, here are four scenarios Markus created around the question, "What will in-house IS management look like in 10 years?"

CASE EXAMPLE

SCENARIOS ON THE FUTURE OF IS MANAGEMENT

The question M. Lynne Markus[16] of Bentley College pondered in developing her scenarios was, "What will IS management look like in 10 years?" In studying IT and IT industry trends, business management trends, and societal

(Case Continued)

trends, she noted that a straight-line extrapolation of the trends would have all organizations acquiring their IT-enabled products and services from external providers through a variety of arrangements, including partnerships, long-term contracts, and spot transactions. To explore the future of IS management, she settled on two driving uncertainties:

- How will companies coordinate IT? Will they use traditional hierarchical coordination mechanisms or pooled organizational forms?
- How will companies manage their data, or content? Will they benefit from managing their own proprietary data or will content be managed by fee-charging external service providers?

These lead to four possible scenarios, as shown in Figure 4-11.

Scenario 1: The Firewall Scenario— Locking the Barn Door After the Horse Got Loose. In this scenario, organizations maintain traditional arm's length relationships with suppliers and customers, and they believe data is proprietary. After a defining event, in which several companies go out of business

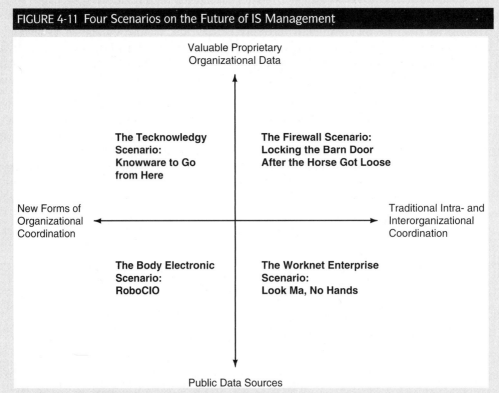

FIGURE 4-11 Four Scenarios on the Future of IS Management

Valuable Proprietary Organizational Data

The Tecknowledgy Scenario: Knowware to Go from Here

The Firewall Scenario: Locking the Barn Door After the Horse Got Loose

New Forms of Organizational Coordination

Traditional Intra- and Interorganizational Coordination

The Body Electronic Scenario: RoboCIO

The Worknet Enterprise Scenario: Look Ma, No Hands

Public Data Sources

Source: M. Lynne Markus, "The Futures of IT Management," *The Data Base for Advances in Information Systems*, Vol. 27, No. 4, 1996, pp. 68–84.

(Case Continued)

from crashes in their computer systems that bring their business to a standstill, corporate managements take a concerned look at their IT operations. Many take on a bunker mentality; their main concerns are security and control. If they outsource their infrastructure to highly regarded outsourcers, they retain tight control over the vendors. All software is off-the-shelf and integrated by professional services firms. All data is housed in virtual bomb shelters. In essence, IS staff become general contractors and enforcement agencies.

Scenario 2: The Worknet Enterprise Scenario—Look Ma, No Hands.

In this scenario, tough privacy legislation is enacted following highly publicized information leaks. Most companies then outsource data management to specialist service providers who comply with the new laws. However, the promised global network does not materialize, so companies cannot turn over their entire IT infrastructures to providers.

Companies continue their traditional arm's length relationships with other firms, but they use IT to mediate workflows between organizations. The result is that competition shifts to networked value chains, called *worknets*. Within these worknets, data is shared, generally through service providers that run interenterprise software packages for the worknet. Thus most IS organizations have handed over their IT work to their worknet's technology consortium, significantly reducing the costs of interworking with these partners. These consortia, themselves, are like self-managing virtual IS depart-

ments, so the IS staff in the contracting firms are mainly either change agents or information brokers tasked with helping the business uncover new uses of IT and implementing them.

Scenario 3: The Body Electric Scenario—RoboCIO.

The triggering events in this scenario are availability of cheap, integrated networking services, plug-and-play computing devices, and portable health and pension plans (due to new legislation). As a result, new forms of organizations flower and data is more likely shared than guarded. In general, people own parts of the small, independent work units (cells) in which they work. Some work under a corporate umbrella; but many are autonomous, combining to deliver goods or services and then disbanding.

The standards for the global IT infrastructure that allow this interworking were created by a global consortium, and vendors adhere to the recommendations. The result is a highly flexible plug-and-play network of interconnected service providers and their services, called Technoos. Cells do virtually no IT work themselves, but they do need to find appropriate IT products and services. This searching is fairly automated and is called "value questing." The other piece of IT work is "IT facilitation," which involves helping cells change how they work when they either form a new alliance or adapt to a new type of software that changes their processes. Specialists can offer both services or they can be handled in-house as part of other jobs.

(Case Continued)

***Scenario 4: The Tecknowledgy Scenario—
Knowware to Go from Here.***   In this
scenario, the growth of the Internet and the
Web lead to an open information society.
Any kind of information is available, for
a price. People specialize in having (or
knowing how to get) certain kinds of
knowledge. Various kinds of intellectual
capital have different, well-publicized
value. Companies organize themselves to
best develop and share knowledge. Those
that learn fastest and share best are the
most successful.

Knowware (advanced groupware)
flourishes because it helps people and
organizations share knowledge. In fact,
knowware is the information technology
most people use. It is part of organizational processes; it is how they work.
Vendors maintain knowware, which handles administrative work as well, so few
companies have IS departments. They rely
fully on external providers. The downside
is that changing knowware packages is
unthinkable because the one a company
adopts forms the foundation of its business. Many jobs even require prior knowledge of the knowware product in use in a
company. Thus, the main IS job within
companies is facilitation, ensuring that
knowledge processes are maintained and
employees understand them. ∎

CONCLUSION

Based on the successes and failures of past IS planning efforts, we see two necessary ingredients for good strategic planning efforts. One is that the plans must look
toward the future. This point may seem obvious, but in turbulent times, the future is
not likely to be an extrapolation of the past. Therefore, a successful planning effort
needs to support "peering into an unknown future"—most likely in a sense-and-
respond fashion.

A second necessary ingredient is that IS planning must be intrinsic to business planning. This point may also seem obvious, but, again, unless the planning
process specifically requires joint development, the systems plans may not be
relevant because they do not align with corporate strategy. A misalignment is not so
likely with the advent of Internet commerce, but it is also not yet natural in many
companies.

In this chapter, we have described a new approach to strategic systems planning
and a number of the most popular techniques. No single technique is best, and no single one is the most widely used in business. In fact, many companies use a combination
of tools because each deals with different aspects of planning. The main goal these days
is to meld speed with flexibility. That goal can best be achieved by creating an overall
strategic envelope and conducting short experiments within that envelope, moving
quickly to broaden an experiment that proves successful. Sense-and-respond is the
new strategy-making mode.

QUESTIONS AND EXERCISES

Review Questions

1. What are the primary differences between operational planning, tactical planning, and strategic planning?
2. Identify and describe several reasons why strategic systems planning is so difficult.
3. What assumptions in traditional strategy making no longer hold true?
4. What is a sense-and-respond approach to planning?
5. Describe Skandia Future Centers' 3G teams.
6. What is a strategic envelope?
7. Describe Shell Oil's action labs.
8. What is the main contribution of the stages of growth theory to IS planning?
9. What are critical success factors (CSFs)? How do they contribute to the systems planning process?
10. Describe Porter's five competitive forces.
11. Describe the components of Porter's value chain.
12. What is the evolution of ways companies use information to add value, according to Rayport and Sviokla?
13. Describe the four types of applications in the e-business value matrix.
14. Briefly describe the goal of linkage analysis planning. List the three steps involved in conducting such an analysis.
15. Briefly describe the four steps in scenario planning, as described by Markus.

Discussion Questions

1. Which of the frameworks for systems planning seem most useful to you? Why?
2. If you were in charge of systems planning for a small firm, what questions would you ask company officers to determine which planning approach(es) would be most appropriate?
3. In Chapter 2, we stated that strategies are out and visioning is in because no one can plan in turbulent times. This chapter states that planning is crucial. How would you reconcile these two viewpoints?

Exercises

1. Survey the current literature on systems planning. What other approaches or frameworks are not mentioned in this text? What automated products are available on the market to assist IS executives in the planning process?
2. Visit the CIO of a local organization. What planning process is used? What is the planning horizon? To what degree do the systems plans and the business plans relate to each other?
3. Create a simple information linkage analysis chart of your current personal relationships. Put yourself in the middle box and each relationship in its own box around you, with a line from you to each of them. Who has the power in each link? How might that power shift in the future? Which is the most important relationship to you? How could you make it more win-win?
4. Ask the CIO of a nearby company what electronic channels his or her firm has in place. Ask about the benefits both parties receive in each link.

REFERENCES

1. Gartner EXP, 56 Top Gallant, Stamford, CT 06904; gartner.com:
   a. Woolfe, Roger, Barbara McNurlin, and Phil Taylor, *Tactical Strategy*, November 1999.
   b. Woolfe, Roger, *Supporting Inter-Business Collaboration*, September 1995.

2. Parker, Marilyn, Robert Benson, with Ed Trainor, *Information Economics: Linking Information Technology and Business Performance*, Prentice Hall, 1988. European edition 1989. Japanese edition, 1990.

3. Brown, Shona, and Kathleen Eisenhardt, *Competing on the Edge: Strategy as Structured Chaos*, Harvard Business School Press, Boston, 1998.

4. Pascale, Richard, "Surfing the Edge of Chaos," *Sloan Management Review*, Spring 1999, pp. 83–94.

5. Nolan, R. L., and C. F. Gibson, "Managing the Four Stages of EDP Growth," *Harvard Business Review*, January/February 1974, p. 76ff.

6. Nolan, R. L., "Information Technology Management from 1960–2000," Chapter 7 in *A Nation Transformed by Information*, Alfred D. Chandler and James W. Cortad (Ed.), Oxford, Cambridge, 2000.

7. Rockart, John, "Chief Executives Define Their Own Data Needs," *Harvard Business Review*, March/April 1979, pp. 81–92.

8. Porter, Michael E., *Competitive Strategy*, The Free Press, New York, 1980; *Competitive Advantage*, The Free Press, 1985.

9. Porter, Michael E., "Strategy and the Internet," *Harvard Business Review*, March 2001, pp. 63–78.

10. Rayport, Jeffrey, and John Sviokla, "Managing in the Marketspace," *Harvard Business Review*, November/December 1994, pp. 141–150; "Exploiting the Virtual Value Chain," *Harvard Business Review*, November/December 1995, pp. 75–85.

11. Alexander, Peter, "Aligning the IT Organization with Business Goals" (presentation at Networld+Interop 2000, Las Vegas, NV, May 8, 2000).

12. Hartman, Amir, John Sifonis, with John Kador, *Net Ready: Strategies for Success in the E-conomy*, McGraw-Hill, New York, 2000.

13. Primozic, K. I., E. A. Primozic, and J. Leben, *Strategic Choices: Supremacy, Survival, or Sayanara*, McGraw-Hill, New York, 1991.

14. Mann, M. M., R. L. Ludman, T. A. Jenckes, and B. C. McNurlin, "EPRINET: Leveraging Knowledge in the Electric Utility Industry," *MIS Quarterly*, September 1991, pp. 403–421.

15. Schwartz, Peter, *The Art of the Long View, Paths for Strategic Insight for Yourself and Your Company*, Currency/Doubleday, New York, 1991.

16. Markus, M. Lynne, "The Futures of IT Management," *The Data Base for Advances in Information Systems*, Vol. 27, No. 4, 1996, pp. 68–84.

PART I
DISCUSSION CASE

WHAT IT STRATEGY WOULD YOU RECOMMEND BASED ON ROYAL DUTCH/SHELL GROUP'S SCENARIOS?

Royal Dutch/Shell Group, a global energy company, was formed in 1907 by the merger of the British import-export company Shell Group and its Dutch oil export competitor, Royal Dutch. Today, the Group still has two headquarters, one in England and one in the Netherlands.

World War I caused loss of business in Europe but growth in North America. Shell expanded its oil business in the 1920s and 1930s, propelled by the mass production of cars, and it moved into aviation fuel and chemicals. During World War II, it supplied the Allied troops with fuel, and after the war Shell began rebuilding its facilities. In the 1950s and 1960s, it expanded to become the seventh-largest oil company, and it led the way in developing natural gas as an alternative fuel. In the 1970s, the oil crisis hit, abruptly increasing oil prices. In Europe, use of natural gas jumped to 15 percent of energy consumption, and Shell had one-half that business. In the 1980s, Shell began selling unleaded gasoline in response to environmental concerns and gained a competitive edge in doing so. In the 1990s, with oil prices much lower, Shell focused on its core oil, gas, and chemical businesses, and started asking itself about the role of energy companies in the future. It began focusing on the environment and sustainable development.

Today, Shell management appears to give much credit for its success since the 1970s to its use of scenarios. As Ged Davis,[1] head of Shell's Scenario Team, noted, Shell's first real use of scenarios was in 1972. It was a particularly notable beginning because one scenario explored the possibility of a sharp rise in oil prices. In that scenario, an accident in Saudi Arabia severed an oil pipeline that decreased supplies, thus increasing prices, noted Ian Wylie.[2] At that time, no one in the industry was thinking about such a possibility because oil supplies had been continually expanding for decades and oil prices had thus remained stable.

One year later, though, prices did rise, dramatically, because OPEC (Oil Producing and Exporting Countries) decreased oil shipments in order to earn more money per barrel. Shell was far more prepared to respond to the oil crisis than its competitors because it had thought about how to respond. Its response, (such as spurring on development and sale of natural gas) differed from that of other companies, and in so doing, Shell gained competitive edge. Shell moved from being the world's seventh-largest to second-largest oil company, noted Wylie.

At Shell, scenarios are described as "coherent and credible alternative stories about the future, incorporating

(Case Continued)

a spectrum of ideas and focusing on issues that are important for our business decisions today," states Davis. They are not projections, predictions, or preferences. Their intent is to get Shell employees to challenge their assumptions, their strategies, and test their plans. The scenarios also give the company a common language for exploring future possibilities. And, as Davis notes, it is not the scenarios themselves, but the process of creating and using them, that yields value. In fact, the most important aspect of scenarios is not that they give answers, but that they spur asking questions about the future.

Shell's Eight Most Recent Scenarios

Shell has gotten into the pattern of creating two scenarios every 3 years. Each looks some 20 years into the future. To illustrate Shell's progression of thinking over the past 13 years, here are those scenarios, in their public form. The scenarios take at least 1 year to write, so they are major efforts. The following brief descriptions are based on Shell's public synopses of the scenarios, which are found on its Web site.[3]

1992 — Three Main Forces. In 1992, the world was being influenced by three major forces:

- *Globalization:* McDonalds and Hollywood movies are around the world.

- *Liberalization:* The "footloose" parts of businesses can be located anywhere, but countries or cities competing to house these parts are subject to global financial markets.

- *Technology:* IT is a revolutionary force. In particular, (1) IT informs by allowing buyers and sellers to find each other; (2) IT disinterme-

diates by allowing customers to talk directly to each other about products and by allowing companies to unbundle themselves and distribute their parts; and (3) IT enables by handling mundane work (often in innovative ways) and by making information ubiquitous, thereby expanding choices and transparency.

The question underlying the 1992 scenarios was, "Will these three forces be embraced?" In the *New Frontiers* scenario, they were; in *Barricades*, they were resisted. *New Frontiers* described rapid growth of developing countries with good relations between rich and poor countries. Interdependence, in essence, raised all fortunes. *Barricades* pitted rich nations against poor, so both missed opportunities for growth. National interests weakened everyone.

Two themes arose from Shell's exploration of these two scenarios. One was that businesses would have to learn how to learn and adapt in open markets, said Davis, and the other theme was that companies would be expected to assume societal responsibilities as their market freedom increased.

1995 — TINA (There Is No Alternative). Formerly, Shell had not chosen a preference between its scenarios. However, by 1995, it decided that the only viable scenario was *New Frontiers*. So it adopted the acronym TINA (There Is No Alternative), meaning, companies and countries have no alternative; they must embrace the forces of globalization, liberalization, and technology.

Thus, the underlying question in 1995 became, "What's the most successful way to embrace TINA?" Shell surmised two possibilities, *Just Do It*, which draws on

(Case Continued)

U.S.-style individualism and sees hyper-competition, and *Da Wo* (meaning Big Me), which uses government-led cohesion to compete globally, as has happened in some parts of Europe and Asia. This scenario's name comes from the Chinese proverb that talks about sacrificing "the small me" (the individual) to benefit "the Big Me" (the welfare of the family, company, or country).

In *Just Do It*, success comes from quickly seizing opportunities because the world is hypercompetitive and people are self-reliant and want customized goods. Groups form to do work, then disband. Individual creativity is rewarded. People in these societies feel more in control of their lives, and they value freedom and autonomy. In this scenario, the United States is the leader because its norms fit this economic style.

Businesses are seen to be more effective than governments, so governments shrink. Acts of violence occur as disillusioned and disaffected people band together in ad hoc groups to protest against the forces they see as being in control, either governments or businesses.

IT's effect in this scenario is "demassification," shifting work from moving things (made of atoms) to moving information (made of bits) over networks. The result is more telecommuting, more intelligent devices, less demand on energy, and increased competition.

In *Da Wo*, on the other hand, companies and countries strive for competitive advantage by taking a holistic, long-term view and building relationships that increase trust and are enabled by governments. They believe societies and businesses are healthiest when they work together holistically, rather than individually. Asian societies have the advantage in this scenario because their citizens

accept the *Da Wo* premise of sacrificing self for a greater good.

In this scenario, networks of trust are more efficient, and thus more successful, than networks based on legal contracts. People in these societies feel secure and included. Governments matter because they provide infrastructure, education, and research. They make longer-term commitments to develop technology than do short-term, individualistic *Just Do It* adherents. *Da Wo* managers also pay more attention to society's needs.

The drawback for businesses used to operating in a *Just Do It* society is breaking into *Da Wo* cultures to serve their markets. Such moves require developing deep relationships, which takes a long time.

1998—TINA's Driving Forces. In this round of scenarios, Shell extended the *Just Do It* scenario, as shown in Figure PC1-1. Shell asked, "What kinds of forces are being exerted on businesses in the *Just Do It* TINA world?" *The New Game* scenario explores *TINA Above*—forces exerted from the world of financial systems, markets, and governments. *People Power* explores *TINA Below*—forces from the world of people who have increased education, wealth, and choice.

Businesses, governments, NGOs (nongovernmental organizations), and even football clubs will be squeezed between the two, Shell believed, but which will dominate? Will institutions cope mainly with a strong *TINA Above* by designing new global rules and strengthening international institutions? Or will consumers and grassroots movements be stronger and cause new kinds of economic activity?

The New Game scenario has the world adapting to the *TINA Above* forces

(*Case Continued*)

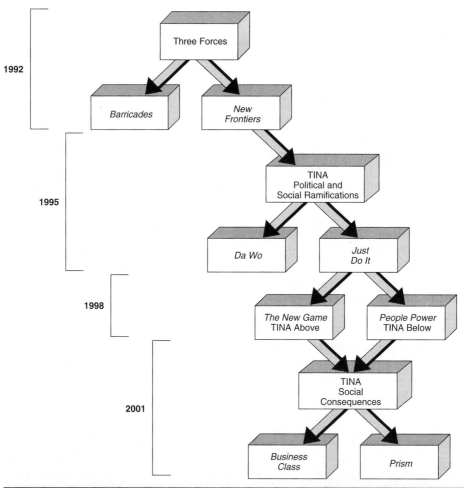

FIGURE PC1-1 Shell Oil's Scenario Development Over Time

by bringing into being new global rules to guide global economic health and new global institutions to help people, groups, and governments work together.

To effectively compete globally, businesses adopt the promulgated best practices, and IT and transparency allow others to watch their corporate behavior. The fast global pace rewards fast learning from experience and short feedback loops, which use experience to quickly improve

goods and services. Organizations that fare the best continually reinvent themselves by becoming learning systems. They aim to stay one step ahead of competitors and regulators who seek to break up monopolies. Companies succeed by adding value; that is, by allocating capital better than others.

However, *The New Game* punishes financial weakness of economies and companies alike, and these financial

(Case Continued)

weaknesses can reverberate around the world, making us all vulnerable. Hence, in this scenario, a global macrostructure emerges, states Shell, supported by public opinion, to provide global accounting rules and be the lender-of-last-resort. New types of institutions arise; some are global. The role of states changes from concern for citizens' welfare to providing safety nets and establishing level playing fields. Global competition occurs within well-defined frameworks.

In the *People Power* scenario, on the other hand, large numbers of people become, for the first time, free to express their values, which they do, often in spontaneous, unpredictable ways. Formerly, people were too poor to express their values. Their increased education and wealth, as well as TINA (globalization, liberalization, and technology), increase their power. *TINA Below* becomes a dominant business driver. The values people have always held are given voice, and the numerous multimedia outlets give those voices listeners and cohorts. As a result, past norms are disregarded, conformity is shattered, creativity is rampant, and diversity reigns.

It is an exciting world to live in, volatile and unpredictable. Divergent voices fragment political parties, making coalitions difficult to cobble together. Governments do not act as swiftly as citizens need them to. Public problems, such as pensions and medical care, remain unsolved. People resort to private solutions or become active locally.

For businesses, brand and reputation matter the most. Their goal is to mirror consumer values, which often means customizing products and services to cultures, niches, and even individuals. Likewise, people look to work for a company that reflects their personal values.

When they find one, they work hard for it. Companies need a diverse workforce to understand the confusing and unpredictable signals they receive from the marketplace. Businesses that succeed understand diversity and leverage it. Diversity is the key descriptor in the *People Power* world.

2001 — TINA's Social Consequences.

Shell's two scenarios from 2001 delve deeper into TINA by asking the question, "Which connections between people will have the greatest influence on globalization, liberalization, and technology?" Stated another way, "What rules will shape globalization, what regulations will shape liberalization, and what restraints will shape technology?" Prior scenarios looked at political and economic ramifications of TINA; the 2001 scenarios explore the societal dimension.

Shell finished the scenarios just before September 11, 2001, and that horrific event brought home the reality of globalization and the wrath it can engender among disaffected people. Protests against globalization have been going on for a number of years; global communication makes them all the more possible because protestors can stay in real-time contact with one another, globally. What they protest is the inequality they see globalization causing. Real or not (and some studies say inequality is not increasing), perception leads to protests, which are reality.

Liberalization and technology are likewise encountering societal backlashes. Liberalization in China and Russia are bringing different results. The bursting of the tech bubble causes some to doubt technology's power, notes Shell.

(Case Continued)

With this backdrop, the current two scenarios focus on people and how they connect. The *Business Class* scenario sees a businesslike world that is shaped by all peoples' global commonalities. The *Prism* scenario sees a world shaped by the interplay of peoples' differences.

Business Class describes a world that rewards efficiency and individual choice; it is businesslike. This world is shaped by global elites, who are highly connected and move around the globe promulgating global commonalities. The United States shapes economic policy because its ideals are the best fit; the global elites form its "Washington consensus," agreeing on the need for property rights, privatization, foreign investment, and such. The centers of this world are the interconnected megacities, and governments seek to support striving companies because the global economy knits the world together more effectively than the governments can. Individual choice is key, and people use it to support NGOs, local and global interest groups, local clubs, and governments.

Global companies help set global policy, thus they become global targets as well. They also face a host of regulatory restraints when they seek to operate in a foreign country—from country laws to local laws. Capitalism, the adopted system, leads to high economic volatility with many short-term crises. The agile gain large rewards, the slow suffer. Communication technologies increase interconnectedness and transparency, but they also increase volatility. A herd mentality occurs, with huge numbers of investors shifting their money from one company or country to another based on news stories. These huge swings could lead to economic shock.

Divisions within countries also appear. Heartlanders, who live in the center of their country, are more conservative and often resent the edge dwellers, who are more cutting-edge and react faster to new circumstances.

To compete, businesses in *Business Class* aim to be global. They organize globally; they form global alliances to spread risk and operate worldwide. They attempt to be exemplars of best practices, such as in service and product quality, because consumers are smart and use the Internet to compare products and services. Such transparency requires clear markers of performance. When companies find they are not best in an area, they outsource that area to someone who is. They end up focusing on core parts of their business at which they are best because attracting the best people is the most difficult job of all. Free agents do well in this environment.

Governments, in general, let the market rule; they only rescue those that are "too big to fail," notes Shell, if they can. NGOs arise that keep track of how well companies are living up to the mark in numerous areas, including social responsibility. Executives pay attention to these ratings because reputation is key; consumer boycotts are an important, and noticed, form of calls for action by consumers.

The most successful products and services in the *Business Class* world are customized, save consumers time, include an "experience," or have meaning. The result is a world of microvariations of products and services offering unlimited choice.

The *Prism* scenario, on the other hand, describes a world of differences—nationalities, cultures, language groups, geographies, and such. A monochromatic

(Case Continued)

globalization is not possible. The protests against globalization demonstrated that, says Shell. People did not like unaccountable global bureaucrats taking control. The alternative is *Prism*: many alternatives at once.

People prefer to look to their past, their roots, and their family as the source of value around which they organize their life. The people connections that matter are those that last over time. As a result, the world has multiple modernities. Western modernity is just one; Buddhist and Islamic are two others.

People are interested in the health of their community, their religion, and their nation. *Prism* is the scenario of the heartland, not the cutting edge. The theme of *Prism* is "our way," as in, "together we will. . . ." Telecommunication supports this emphasis. Interconnected secondary cities emerge in the heartlands and draw people away from crowded coastal metropolises. New kinds of communities also emerge, fostered by the Internet and based on interests (such as soccer or child-rearing). Physical proximity no longer inhibits their growth. They grow and spread because they deal with real and important problems.

However, this sense of identity and belonging can have a dark side, with people getting into boundary disputes or fostering prejudices against other races or religions. In addition, technology allows governments to spy on their people more easily, perhaps in the name of protecting them against "foreigners."

Government's role is to nurture social cohesion, notes Shell, so that societies prosper. Thus, governments provide safety nets for those who fall. However, they tackle issues regionally, not globally.

Arrangements with neighbors turn out to be more powerful than global ones because they are based on long-term relationships and are thus more enforceable. Global alignment, where needed, comes from overlapping areas of agreement. Regions run their economies "their way" based on their regional consensus, which can be quite difficult to reach. Interconnecting networks of groups continually negotiate to reach agreement. This governance model ends up being more flexible and effective than the global alternative.

The *Prism* world is international rather than global; national identities matter. Governments are important, so protesters target them when they do not deliver. The fear caused by globalization subsides, so people focus more on pride than prejudice in their countries.

Conducting business in different countries is difficult because there is mistrust of outsiders; people prefer dealing with local people. Each community, area, or region also has its own culture, values, and government rules. Religious practices may rule some business environments. Interest communities may guide some corporate and government research. Groups with deeply felt concerns can protest and affect product offerings. To work across them, companies need to pay attention to the communities. Communities do make sure they are heard, including through the Internet. One main approach to gaining access to a locale is to establish partnerships with the locals. In fact, companies can act as driving forces for partnerships that enrich a community. The key ingredient is trust. It is crucial for holding these partnerships together. ■

(Case Continued)

CASE QUESTION

The last two scenarios, *Business Class* and *Prism*, are the bases for the following case question. Longer discussions of both scenarios are on Shell's Web site.

1. Choose one of the two scenarios—*Business Class* or *Prism*—and answer the following:
    a. What is the world situation?
    b. What are some appropriate IT provider strategies?
    c. What business strategies would be most successful?
    d. What IS goals would be most appropriate?
    e. What IT strategies would make the most sense?

REFERENCES

1. Davis, Ged, "Questioning Assumptions—Exploring Alternative Business Futures" (speech, Swedbank Conference, Stockholm, March 13, 2002. Available at www.shell.com/scenarios).

2. Wylie, Ian, "There Is No Alternative to…," *Fast Company*, July 2002, pp. 106–110.

3. Shell, "Global Scenarios 1995–2020," "Global Scenarios 1998–2020," and "People and Connections: Global Scenarios to 2020." Available at www.shell.com/scenarios. Accessed February 2004.

II

MANAGING THE ESSENTIAL TECHNOLOGIES

Part II—Chapters 5 through 8—focuses on infrastructure management, as shown in Figure P2-1. The purpose of this part is to present the technological underpinnings of a corporate IS operation and point out the major issues that must be addressed for it to be well managed.

Chapter 5 looks at various kinds of distributed systems architectures and discusses the important concepts of IT architecture and infrastructure.

Chapter 6 discusses telecommunications, including the new infrastructure being built, how the telecommunications industry is transforming itself, the underpinnings of today's networks, the Internet, and the new frontier of wireless Internet access.

Whereas Chapters 5 and 6 deal with the structure of distributed systems, Chapter 7 deals with the content, or the information resources. These resources have been referred to as *data*. Increasingly, this content has context (making it *information*), intelligence, and actionability (making it *knowledge*), and is housed on the Web (*content*). Chapter 7 deals with three of these areas: data, information, and content. Knowledge is discussed in Chapter 13.

Finally, Chapter 8 explores operations, the day-to-day concerns of keeping elaborate, far-flung corporate distributed systems up and running. Back in the old mainframe days, operations were pretty much taken for granted and housed in "the glass room." Today, corporate executives have major operational concerns around their IT infrastructure, including outsourcing, security, and business continuity.

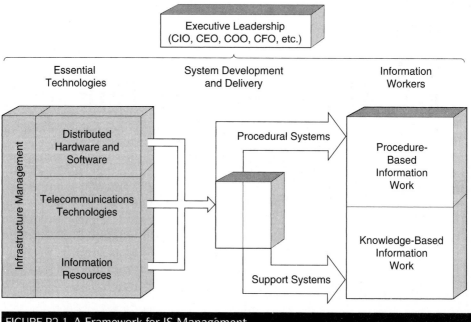

FIGURE P2-1 A Framework for IS Management

CHAPTER 5

DISTRIBUTED SYSTEMS: THE OVERALL ARCHITECTURE

INTRODUCTION

Way back in 1964, Paul Baran at the Rand Corporation wrote a paper about distributed systems. At the time, computing meant mainframes and hardwired terminals; distributed systems were just theory. Today, distributed systems are the architecture of choice. Thus, we begin this part—Part II, which deals with the essential technologies of computing—with a discussion of this important computing framework.

Definitions.   To start, we need to point out that the two terms *architecture* and *infrastructure* are often used interchangeably, which can make discussions of distributed systems confusing. In this book, we make the following distinction:

> *An IT* architecture *is a blueprint. A blueprint shows how a system, house, vehicle, or product will look and how the parts interrelate. The more complex an item, the more important its architecture, so that the interrelationships among the components are well defined.*
>
> *An IT* infrastructure *is the implementation of an architecture. In a city, the infrastructure includes its streets and street lighting, hospitals and schools, utilities, police and fire departments, and so on. In a corporation, the IT infrastructure includes the processors, software, databases, electronic links, and data centers, as well as the standards that ensure that the components work together, the skills for managing the operation, and even some of the electronic processes themselves.*

The term *infrastructure* has become important in computing. Rather than talk about hardware, software, data, and communications as the components of computing, people now often refer to applications and infrastructure. The infrastructure provides the electronic highways, processing, and storage sites, whereas the applications use these facilities to produce value for the organization. Suffice it to say, when you hear *infrastructure*, think of city streets or electronic highways. At the end of this chapter, we delve into both architecture and infrastructure in a bit more depth after looking at the various kinds of distributed systems.

The Evolution of Distributed Systems.   In the first IT architecture—mainframes doing batch processing—some input came from "dumb" terminals and some output went to "dumb" terminals. These "slave" user devices had no processing capabilities. All the processing was done by the "master" (the mainframe), and most was for corporate needs, such as payroll and billing. With the advent of minicomputers, computers moved into departments, but the master–slave model persisted. Processing was centralized; although gradually distribution or sharing of processing among mainframes and minicomputers began to occur.

With the microcomputer, though, the model changed significantly because processing power moved first onto desktops, then into briefcases, and now into handhelds, game consoles, MP3 players, and so on. In the 1990s, this distribution of processing led to processing being thought of as being split between a *client* that requests services and a *server* that provides those services. This concept of requesting services continues today and will be more important in the future as Web Services continues to develop (as discussed later in this chapter).

Throughout this evolution, stand-alone processors (or processors with dedicated terminals) appeared first and then were gradually linked to other computers. As that happened, the notion of a distributed architecture developed. Today, we have the Internet, an example of a global distributed system. Devices and computers of all sizes from any vendor that uses the appropriate standards use the Internet to send messages and files to each other, perform processing for each other, and house data for each other. The Internet has become the center of a worldwide distributed system. It is because of this global electronic infrastructure that the e-business revolution is taking place.

To get a grounding in this important notion in computing, we now delve into distributed system thinking.

Four Attributes of Distributed Systems

The degree to which a system is distributed can be determined by answering four questions:

1. Where is the processing done?
2. How are the processors and other devices interconnected?
3. Where is the information stored?
4. What rules or standards are used?

Distributed Processing. This is the ability for more than one interconnected processor to be operating at the same time, typically for processing an application on more than one computer. The goal in distributed processing is to move the appropriate processing as close to the user as possible and to let other machines handle the work they do best (such as house and manage video databases or process airline reservations).

An advanced form of distributed processing permits *interoperability*, which is the capability for different machines using different operating systems on different networks to work together on tasks. They exchange information in standard ways without requiring changes in functionality or physical intervention.

Charlie Bachman, a pioneer in the database and distributed systems fields, pointed out that only two forms of interoperability are possible. One is the transparent communication between systems using system protocols. In this form, the *systems* decide when to interoperate. To use the Internet, companies have developed protocols for standard file and job transfers to permit this form of interoperability. The second form of interoperability is the interactive or two-way flow of messages between *user applications*. In this form, user applications can be activated by receiving messages; this activity, of course, is supported on the Internet. Both kinds of interoperability are important, says Bachman.

Connectivity Among Processors. This type of connectivity means that each processor in a distributed system can send data and messages to any other processor through electronic communication links. A desirable structure for reliable distributed systems has at least two independent paths between any two nodes, enabling automatic alternate routing in case one node goes down. Planned redundancy of this type is critical for reliable operation. Such redundancy has not been implemented in most LANs, which is one reason they have been so fragile. It is, however, a major feature of the Internet as well as most corporate WANs.

Distributed Databases.   These are being defined in at least two ways. One divides a database and distributes its portions throughout a system without duplicating the data. Any portion is accessible from any node, subject to access authorization. Users do not need to know where a piece of data is located to access it, because the system knows where all data is stored.

The second type of distributed database stores the same data at several locations with one site containing the master file. Synchronization of data is a significant problem in this approach, which is why it has not been the preferred way to distribute data.

An interesting development in this area is edge servers on the Web. An *edge server* is defined as being on the edge of the Internet, which means it is close to a set of users (such as a city). It holds a copy of an organization's Web site. Many edge servers, located strategically around the world, hold the same information. The edge server concept arose to accelerate Web page downloads to site visitors so they would not leave the site because they had to wait too long to see a page appear on their screen. Edge servers—essentially distributed databases—have become an integral part of the Internet.

Systemwide Rules.   These rules mean that an operating discipline for the distributed system has been developed and is enforced at all times. These rules govern communication between nodes, security, data accessibility, program and file transfers, and common operating procedures. Since the 1990s, these systemwide rules have been increasingly based on the *open system* concept. Products using open standards can operate together in one or more distributed systems, such as the Internet. One goal of users is to avoid being locked into the proprietary products of one vendor. Interestingly, the meaning of open systems has expanded over time as open systems have become a reality.

In the 1980s, open systems referred mainly to telecommunication and meant that a company intended to implement products that followed the OSI (Open Systems Interconnection) Reference Model whenever they became available. At that time, OSI implementation was not a reality, just a target.

About 1990, the definition of open systems expanded to include operating systems, specifically UNIX, because it runs on more platforms than any other operating system and is not owned by any one company. At that time, UNIX was tentatively seen as appropriate for mainline business computing. Today, it is an important operating system for servers on the Internet. In business computing, it has gained a foothold, but it has not displaced proprietary operating systems, such as Microsoft's Windows.

At the same time, in the data world, *open* meant structured query language (SQL), the standard intermediary language for accessing relational databases. SQL remains the standard today.

In the early 1990s, the definition shifted to the interfaces between applications. *Open* meant standardized interfaces that would allow products to interoperate across multi-vendor networks, operating systems, and databases. Application program interfaces (APIs) came into being. They define the way data is presented to another component of a system—a machine, a database, even an e-mail system. APIs allow individual products to be innovative, yet connectable, and they have made writing distributed systems far easier.

Today, the term *open* includes the already mentioned definitions and stresses interconnectivity. In this realm, the OSI reference model remains the definition of *open*.

Most people, however, are only familiar with its widest implementation: the network protocol used in the Internet, TCP/IP. Corporate networks, both LANs and WANs, now use TCP/IP to ease interconnection to the Internet.

An interesting twist on the term *open* hit critical mass not long ago. When the Internet first arrived, it allowed programmers to offer software for free (or for a small donation), which many did. This freeware has come to be called *open source*, which means the source code can be downloaded by anyone and can be modified. (In purchased software, you only receive the compiled code, which is undecipherable.) The open source movement led to developers taking some freeware, improving it, and reposting it to the Internet. In the 1990s, Linus Torvalds offered his operating system, Linux, as open source; he has since gained a huge following. Developers around the world have contributed to it, improved it, and extended it. Because it is free, it is being used in a growing number of companies.

The term *open systems* keeps expanding because it truly is the crux of distributed systems, allowing products from multiple vendors to work together.

Although some people see the main reason for distributing systems as improving the use of computer resources, that is just a technical reason. The organizational impetus behind distributed systems is to move responsibility for computing resources to those who use them. The next section briefly addresses the business reasons for distributing applications and the responsibilities that go with them.

When to Distribute Computing Responsibilities

IS management needs a corporate policy for deciding when the development, operation, and maintenance of an application should be distributed. Individual end users and departments should not be left on their own to make these decisions, especially when enterprise connectivity and interenterprise connectivity are important. Although technical considerations are critical, they should not be the determining factors behind a system architecture. Rather, the major reason for choosing a particular distributed system architecture hinges on: *Who should make the key management operating decisions?*

Decision-making responsibilities are being pushed down and out in organizations, with local sites and teams being given more autonomy and responsibility for the resources they use. One such resource is IT. People who make the decisions about how their portion of the business operates also should be making the decisions about how they use IT. Teamwork between IS management and business management is important in designing a distributed processing architecture that supports the business's goals.

Francis Wagner, a computing pioneer, once said he believes people perform best when they are responsible for their own mistakes. If they have no one to blame but themselves, then the quality of their performance increases. The result is a more effective use of corporate resources.

Therefore, a driving force behind distributed processing is the desire to give more people more control over their work. This autonomy can happen at any of seven levels: ecosystem, company, division, site, department, team, or individual.

Professor James Wetherbe[1] suggested asking the following three business questions before distributing IT functions and the responsibilities that go with them. Systems responsibilities can be distributed *unless* the following are true.

Are the Operations Interdependent?   When it is important for one operation to know what another is doing, those operations are interdependent; thus, their planning, software development, machine resources, and operations need to be centrally coordinated to synchronize their operation. Two industries in which interdependency is important are manufacturing and airlines, which is why they have continued to have large centralized systems even in this era of distributed systems.

Are the Businesses Really Homogeneous?   If the operations do not need to know what the other is doing, then many systems functions can be decentralized, unless the operations truly have a lot in common.

For example, in the fast food business, each franchise has the same information processing needs, which makes them homogeneous. But they do not need to know what the other is doing; thus, they are not interdependent. Under these circumstances, processing may be distributed, but planning, software development, and hardware selection should be centralized, to keep processing costs down and to more easily migrate to new systems.

Deciding whether the information processing in two parts of a business is truly homogeneous is not always obvious, says Wetherbe. For instance, not all retail chains are the same. One major retailer found that it needed to create two information systems for handling credit charges—one for its upscale stores and one for its discount stores. The needs of the two types of stores were so different that a single system would not suffice. However, corporate IS does control planning, which gives the retailer the ability to seize marketing opportunities quickly when it can reuse systems built by either operation. He says that centralized planning is important whether processing is distributed or not.

Does the Corporate Culture Support Decentralization?   Even if the business units do quite different things and do not need to know what the other is doing, corporate culture might dictate that some functions be centralized.

Wetherbe cites the example of a large company with 60 widely diverse business units. Although it might appear logical for this company to distribute all functions, management chose to centralize finance, HR, and systems planning. They want to offer corporatewide career opportunities with as little retraining as possible. With central staff doing systems planning and coordination, the company can more easily move people and reuse systems.

If none of these three criteria—interdependency, homogeneity, or corporate culture—forces centralization, each business unit can direct its own IT activity, with the central organization coordinating the plans.

Two Guiding Frameworks

Now that we have briefly addressed why to distribute systems, we now look at how to distribute systems via two guiding frameworks: one from an organizational perspective and the other from a technical perspective.

An Organizational Framework.   One possible distributed system structure looks at serving seven organizational levels. Figure 5-1 illustrates the seven levels.

1. Business ecosystem or value chain (interenterprise)
2. Enterprise
3. Country or region
4. Site (plants, warehouses, branch offices)

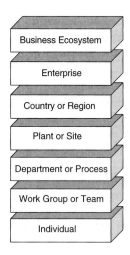

Business Ecosystem

Enterprise

Country or Region

Plant or Site

Department or Process

Work Group or Team

Individual

FIGURE 5-1 A Seven-Level
Organizational Framework

5. Department or process

6. Work group or team

7. Individuals

The top level deals with organizations that work closely together, such as buyers and sellers or partners in a business ecosystem. The other six exist within a single organization; they may or may not link to other organizations. The current hot levels are one (interenterprise computing) and five, where companies are changing from a functional orientation to a process orientation. In the area of SCM, for example, companies want to electronically share information about customer orders and the status of internal operations with suppliers so that those suppliers can have the specific parts on hand when needed. Interenterprise and process thinking require linking disparate systems in different organizations. This linkage can be made firm-to-firm or through intermediaries, such as electronic exchanges, which act as matchmakers over the Internet. The Internet is playing an important role in creating interenterprise electronic links for processes.

Work groups and teams have also become tremendously important as companies change how they work. We see two types of work groups at level 6. One type of work group is people who do essentially the same work. Anyone in the group can substitute for any other, if necessary. Such groups are found in the customer service centers of small ISPs, where the reps need to be able to answer questions on every facet of linking to the Internet. In large ISPs, reps often specialize in answering questions on specific operating systems. Both groups need systems to support their work with customers.

The second type of group or team is self-managed work teams. They contain all the people who serve a particular set of customers or offer a particular product. These people represent all the necessary functions, such as manufacturing, marketing, customer service, and so forth. The intent is to give them more autonomy and decision-making power to serve their customers better. By allowing them to manage themselves, it is hoped they will provide more personalized and faster service. They need their own systems. However, these systems will be far different from the ones needed by the ISP reps.

In all, systems are needed for each of the seven organizational levels. Inter-organizational links can occur at all six internal levels as well.

A Technical Framework.   Way back in 1982, Einar Stefferud, David Farber, and Ralph Dement developed a conceptual framework for distributed systems.[2] It uses the acronym SUMURU, meaning "single user, multiple user, remote utility." Surprisingly, SUMURU is as appropriate today as it was in 1982, perhaps even more so because distributed systems are today's architecture. Their framework includes four components: processors, networks, services, and standards. Figure 5-2 summarizes the SUMURU components, and Figure 5-3 illustrates the architecture.

Processors.   The authors see three levels of processors, usually with associated information storage. The name of their architecture, SUMURU, comes from these three levels of processors. *Single-user systems* (SUs) can operate in a stand-alone mode but also will be connected to local networks. Today, SUs are the clients in distributed systems. *Multiple-user systems* (MUs) serve local groups of users. Today, they are work group servers in corporate LANs. These MUs also provide (1) backup facilities for other MUs, (2) heavier-duty processing for SUs, (3) program libraries for themselves and SUs, and (4) database management for central files. Ideally, say the authors, SUs are scaled-down versions of the MUs, able to run the same software (to reduce software development and maintenance) but without all the features needed for shared operation on an MU.

Remote utility systems (RUs) provide heavy-duty computing, corporate database management, remote processing, and backup for MUs. For most organizations, RUs are the corporate hosts, although they are increasingly becoming external service providers (ESPs) that run corporate data centers or corporate applications. They may house and operate a company's Web site operation, its extranet, and even its intranet. Or they may handle the HR functions for a firm. In addition, Web sites on the Internet can be considered RUs, especially if they provide subscription services to firms.

Networks.   The authors see a network architecture consisting of two levels. *Local networks* (LNs) provide high-speed information transfer as well as close coupling between several SUs and a local MU. Today, these are LANs. MUs may provide personal files, shared files, and program libraries for SUs, and they can be the gateway between the LNs and remote networks.

FIGURE 5-2 Components of the SUMURU Distributed System Architecture

Processors	*Services*
Single-user systems (SU)	Terminal access
Multiple-user systems (MU)	File transfer
Remote utility systems (RU)	Computer mail
Networks	*Standards*
Local networks (LN)	Operating systems
Remote networks (RN)	Communications protocols
	Database systems

Source: E. Stefferud, D. Farber, and R. Dement, "SUMURU: A Network Configuration for the Future," *Mini-Micro Systems*, May 1982, pp. 311–312.

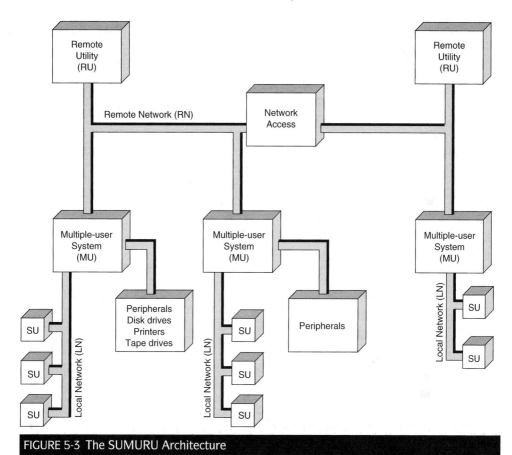

FIGURE 5-3 The SUMURU Architecture

Source: E. Stefferud, D. Farber, and R. Dement, "SUMURU: A Network Configuration for the Future," *Mini-Micro Systems*, May 1982, pp. 311–312.

Remote networks (RNs) provide connections among MUs and connections to both in-house and commercial RUs. RNs, which today include metropolitan area networks (MANs), WANs, cell phone and satellite networks, and the Internet, generally have lower transfer speeds than LNs, but they still should have enough bandwidth to provide downloads within reasonable time limits.

Services. The authors see three main types of services in this network architecture. One service is *access* to any SU, MU, or RU, subject only to management constraints, not technical barriers. Users must also have *file transfer* capabilities to send and receive files, which means having both read and write privileges at both ends of the transfer. Finally, the system must provide an *e-mail* service. Note that all three are available to PCs via the Internet. The challenge today is providing the same capabilities to handheld devices via wireless computing.

Standards. Standards are needed in three areas: operating systems, communication protocols, and DBMSs. Operating system standards are designed to minimize barriers to transferring and using programs and data. Ideally, the selected operating systems should run on more than one vendor's equipment. Standard communication protocols are needed for access, file transfers, and e-mail. In the communication area, TCP/IP (which is used in the Internet) has become the de facto standard. In the database arena, no distributed DBMS has become a standard, although SQL has become the language of choice for accessing different databases.

We believe this distributed system framework has stood the test of time; it is still an appropriate design guide for distributed system architects. Although not often used these days, it provides a clear conceptual framework for understanding the various components of a distributed system.

Now we turn to some specifics: seven system structures that have been called distributed.

SEVEN TYPES OF DISTRIBUTED SYSTEMS

As noted earlier, the distributed systems field has been continually evolving. The seven forms of distributed systems basically developed as follows.

Host-Based Hierarchy

A hierarchy of processors was the first distributed system structure. It was favored by mainframe vendors because the large host computer at the top controlled the terminals below. It is a master–slave relationship. More than one level of processors can be part of this hierarchy, as shown in Figure 5-4, with the total workload shared among them. The important characteristic of this structure is that the host computer is the central and controlling component. The other important characteristic is that the

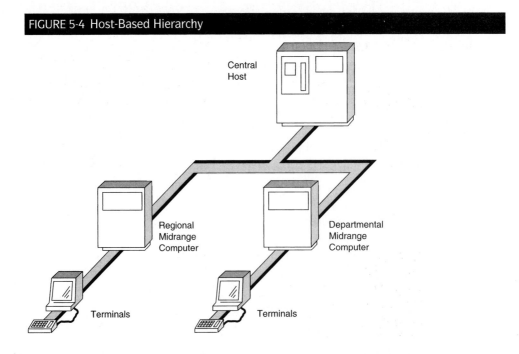

FIGURE 5-4 Host-Based Hierarchy

Central Host

Regional Midrange Computer

Departmental Midrange Computer

Terminals

Terminals

processing is done on the computers. The terminals are simply access devices; they have no processor or hard disk.

It is not always clear just where to store the data in such a system. One view is to store all data at the top. Another is to have the master records at the top but selected subsets at intermediate levels; the master records are then updated periodically and revised records are sent to the intermediate files. Still another view is to store master records where they are most used and periodically provide updated records to the top for backup purposes. In any of these views, though, it is assumed that any processor can access any data record in the hierarchy, as long as it is authorized to do so.

Thin clients are diskless computers meant to obtain their applications from a server (perhaps on the Internet). They are an intriguing flashback to this form of distributed computing, but they have two important distinctions from the terminals of old. One, they initiate requests; terminals of old did not. Two, they can do local processing; terminals could not. It is not the same master–slave relationship as with mainframes and terminals. Thin-client thinking is being used for handhelds requesting tasks over the Internet.

Decentralized Stand-Alone Systems

Decentralized stand-alone systems do not really form a distributed system at all. They are basically a holdover from the 1960s, when departments put in their own mini-computers with no intention of connecting them to the corporate host or to other departmental systems. Hence, they are decentralized, not distributed (see Figure 5-5).

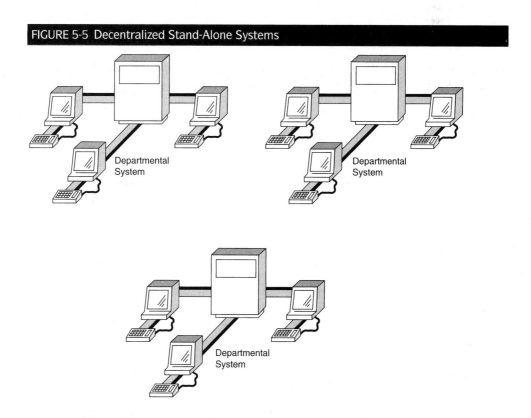

FIGURE 5-5 Decentralized Stand-Alone Systems

Departmental System

Departmental System

Departmental System

Over the years, many such "islands of computing" have appeared and still exist. They have been connected to allow a little data to flow, but this flow has been mostly upward to the corporate host.

A major goal in introducing ERP systems was to replace such disparate systems—in finance, manufacturing, administration—with a single platform of interconnectable modules to serve these various functions.

Peer-to-Peer LAN-Based Systems

LANs have been the basis for distributed systems of desktop machines since the 1980s. This approach began in the office system arena with LANs providing the links between PCs, print servers, and gateways to other networks. As shown in Figure 5-6, this structure has no hierarchy. No computer is more superior than another. Communications among the components are *peer to peer* rather than through a hierarchy using a central hub. It is the key characteristic of this structure. A new development in this area is peer-to-peer wireless LANs, as discussed in the next chapter.

Hybrid Enterprisewide Systems

The typical structure of distributed systems today draws on these three forms of distributed systems linking them via three kinds of networks: MANs, WANs, and the Internet. This system is illustrated in Figure 5-7. Today's distributed systems mix and match hierarchical host-based processing favored for corporate and Web site computing with departmental processing favored by departments such as manufacturing and engineering and the LAN-based systems used in offices. This hybrid structure is likely to be the structure of choice for many years as companies link their various islands of automation and increasingly link to systems in other organizations.

One important point is that this hybrid approach does not necessarily put all the machines under the aegis of a host mainframe computer. In fact, a number of companies have gotten rid of their mainframe(s) altogether, dispersing applications to departmental machines and servers. A host computer is shown in Figure 5-7, but it is not the central control. For some applications, it could be the host; for others, it could be merely just another server, perhaps a "compute server."

FIGURE 5-6 Peer-to-Peer LAN-Based System

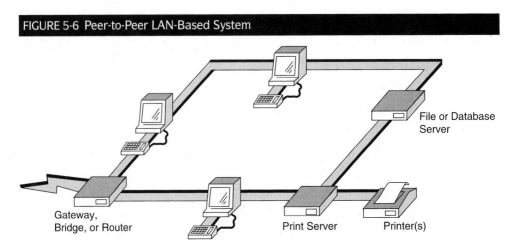

File or Database Server

Gateway, Bridge, or Router

Print Server

Printer(s)

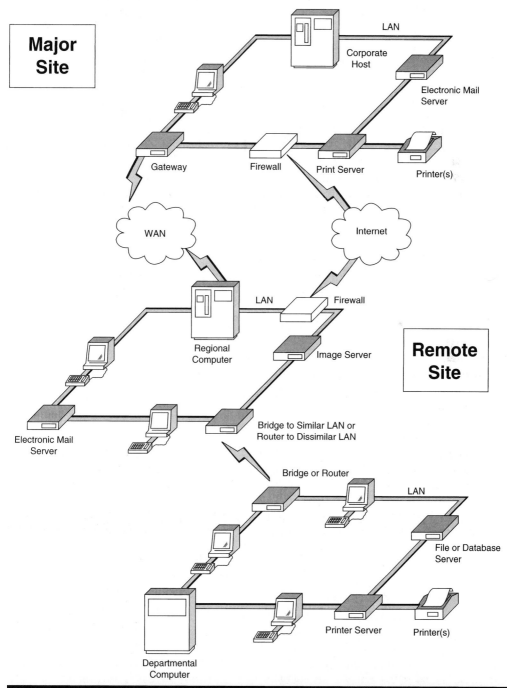

FIGURE 5-7 Hybrid Enterprisewide System

A second important point is that this structure allows companies to automate business processes that span several functions within the organization or work cooperatively with systems in other enterprises. Interenterprise computing is the tenet of e-business. For example, to obtain sporting event tickets, once you enter your order on a ticketing Web site, the system needs to verify that the seats are available (probably on another system), it needs to verify that your credit is good (on another system), and if both are satisfied, it processes the order. Currently, tickets are mailed to you, but if your printer had an IP address (which is possible), your tickets could be electronically sent to a ticket broker (yet another system) who then sends them to your printer where they are printed out.

Such cooperating processes allow companies to take advantage of specialized computer programs, while at the same time extending the usefulness of some legacy systems. The process of pulling together such individual applications or components is called *system integration*. Following is an example of a mainstream application that uses these distributed processing principles and was built via system integration.

CASE EXAMPLE

NORTHWEST AIRLINES

When Northwest Airlines, with headquarters in St. Paul, Minnesota, merged with Republic Airlines, it doubled its business and became a major national carrier. To compete as a world-class carrier, management realized they had to revamp a number of core systems. One system calculates revenue from passengers.

At the time, Northwest sampled a small percentage of its passenger tickets to estimate revenue, but this approach did not yield accurate passenger or revenue data. To improve accuracy, it needed to audit all redeemed tickets—something few major airlines did at the time.

With the help of Accenture, the large consulting firm, Northwest built a system that integrates products from 11 vendors and just about as many different technologies, including expert systems, imaging, relational databases, high-resolution workstations, servers, and LANs.

Management's Goals

Management established six major goals for the passenger revenue accounting (PRA) system:

1. Enforce pricing and commission rules to ensure services are properly priced and travel agencies sell them at correct fares.

2. Calculate corporate earned income and track and reconcile air transport liability accounting.

3. Cope with the volume explosion and the rapid pace of change in the airline industry.

4. Unhook volume growth from staff increases so the department could handle more work without equivalent staff increases. The department had grown 700 percent to 600 people. At that projected

(Case Continued)

growth rate, the department would soon need its own building unless it changed the way it worked.

5. Gather, organize, and disseminate marketing information for making decisions on pricing and flight scheduling and responding to competitors' moves.

6. Provide the flexibility to audit and report on special deals with travel agents and corporate purchasers.

The Distributed Architecture

Data communication is an integral part of this distributed system, which uses both LANs and a MAN among three buildings. The host IBM 3090 is linked to the backbone Ethernet LAN via an SNA-TCP/IP gateway.

The Ethernet backbone acts as a MAN, linking numerous Ethernet subnetworks. Ten of the subnetworks connect a Sun application server to about 40 diskless Sun workstations, which run UNIX. Northwest minimizes traffic across the backbone by designing the network to keep most client-to-server traffic on each subnet. Northwest also has an image server for storing images of redeemed ticket coupons. Several specialized servers perform the ticket auditing each night using expert system technology.

The workstations provide the PRA auditors with windows to the data stored on the various systems: the mainframe that stores the ticket database, external computer reservation systems, the application servers that store tickets with discrepancies, and the image database. The system accommodates large file transfers between these workstations and the mainframe because part of the processing is done on the IBM host and part is done on the workstations. For these file transfers, Northwest created a standard way for COBOL applications (on the mainframe) to talk to C applications (on the workstations). The workstations also draw on the host applications via 3270-terminal emulation on the Suns.

Image processing is also a key element. Each day, Northwest receives some 50,000 auditor coupons from travel agents and 100,000 lift coupons (redeemed ticket stubs) from passengers. Formerly, Northwest employed 20 to 40 people full-time just to retrieve these coupons from their huge storage basement. Now, Northwest scans both types of coupons, creating a photograph-like image and an index for each one. The images are stored on optical disks in jukeboxes, which store the platter-like disks in a jukebox fashion.

The Revenue Accounting Process

Each day, Northwest receives data from three sources: (1) magnetic tapes of ticket sales taken from computer reservation systems and consolidated by regional clearinghouses, (2) audit coupons from travel agents, and (3) lift coupons redeemed from passengers as they board a plane.

The sales data is stored in a DB2 relational database and processed on the IBM mainframe. If all the information is not provided, the sales data is queued to an auditor, who adds the missing information by viewing the appropriate auditor coupon image. Then, the sales data for performing the nighttime audits is downloaded to Sun servers, and a C program retrieves all the travel agency rules that apply to each ticket.

At night, the sales data is run through expert systems, which apply the appropriate rules to recalculate the lowest fare,

(Case Continued)

commission, and taxes. If the recalculation does not match the travel agency's auditor coupon data, the recalculation and corresponding coupon image are made available to an auditor for review.

The next morning, Northwest auditors view the various pieces of data in different windows on their workstations and they decide how to handle the discrepancies. Because all the coupon images are available electronically, handling one box of coupons takes 2 to 3 hours rather than 2 to 3 days.

When passengers' redeemed flight coupons are received by the department, the verified sales data is credited as earned income. Monthly books now close on the seventh of the month, which is one-half the time previously required. Thus, earned revenue can be recognized 50 percent faster.

Lessons Learned

Northwest learned the following four major lessons about developing complex distributed systems such as PRA.

1. *Benchmark and prototype new technologies to verify vendors' claims*. Do not let vendors run the benchmarks by themselves. In image processing, for instance, have the vendors scan most of the kinds of documents in the application, especially if different kinds of paper and different colors of ink are common.

2. *An open architecture works on mission-critical applications*. PRA integrated a variety of technologies. By using an open architecture, Northwest reduced its risk in building such a system. Risk was further controlled by creating an interface to these systems that shielded the developers from the technicalities of the new technologies. Finally, integration was demonstrated early through a small test project.

3. *Large distributed system projects need vendor coordinator*. Due to the complexity of PRA, a clean design for creating a stable set of specifications for the vendors was unlikely; therefore, a big challenge was keeping the right people on the Northwest, Accenture, and vendor teams informed of current status. To fill this role, a full-time coordinator made sure all the various project teams stayed in close contact with each other. Otherwise, the various components would not have worked together.

4. *Use of a computer-based development methodology was mandatory*. Management believes that Northwest could not have done a project of this size without the tools and approaches of a computer-based methodology. For one thing, it allowed developers to work on different components in parallel. Without it, they could not have supported the team of up to 170 developers. Furthermore, it allowed users to play a larger role in development; even to the point of using the design tool to document user procedures, design reports, and supply the text in the help system. Finally, it allows them to use the data definitions from PRA in other systems, which will substantially shorten development time and improve system quality.

The huge system, which took 65,000 workdays to complete, has become a model for airline revenue accounting systems. Managers from more than a dozen airlines around the world have visited Northwest to study it. ■

Client-Server Systems

The 1990s version of distributed systems was client-server systems. This system architecture arose to take advantage of the processing capabilities of both host machines and PCs in the same system. Even though the host could handle huge databases and order processing, the PCs, laptops, and smaller devices could handle graphics, sound, and even video, which were important in some applications.

Client-server computing splits the computing workload between a *client*, which is a computer that makes a request, and a *server*, which answers the request. A request might be to print a document (handled by the print server on the LAN) or it could be a request for the gate number of one's soon-to-leave flight—a request sent by an Internet-enabled cell phone from a taxi and handled by the airline's Web site.

The most famous depiction of client-server computing comes from Gartner EXP.[3] It shows the possibilities for splitting work between clients and servers, as illustrated in Figure 5-8.

As shown in Figure 5-8, the network presents the dividing line between what is housed on a client and what is housed on a server. The three components being split are the presentation software (what the user sees on the screen), the application itself, and the data management software. Briefly, from left to right, the spectrum is as follows:

- ***Distributed presentation*** puts all the data, all the application software, and some of the presentation software on a server. Only part of the presentation is on the client. This approach is one way to leave a mainframe-based legacy

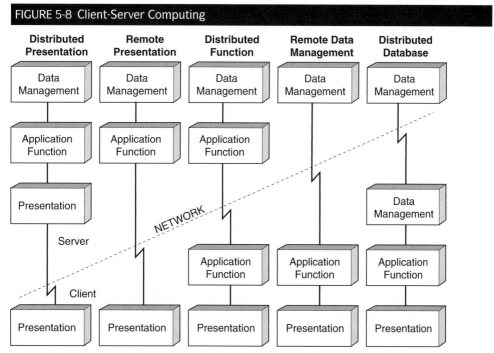

FIGURE 5-8 Client-Server Computing

Source: Roger Woolfe, *Managing the Move to Client-Server*, Wentworth Research Program (now part of Gartner EXP, 56 Top Gallant, Stamford, CT 06904), January 1995.

system in place while updating user screens, making them graphical rather than character based, for example. This approach is also likely for wireless Web-based computing.

- ***Remote presentation*** puts all the presentation software on the client machine but leaves the applications and data on the remote server. This approach also is a way to preserve a legacy system and simply update the face it shows users. It has been used to put transaction processing behind Web sites.

- ***Distributed function*** places all the presentation software on the client, all the data on the server, and splits the application software between the client and the server. This option is quite complex, because splitting application processing between two machines requires coordination. However, it might be the most appropriate option for applications that run packaged software, such as spreadsheets or word processing, on a client in combination with corporate applications on a mainframe. It can also be appropriate for wireless computing and for major front-end applications, such as order entry, inventory inquiry, and so on. E-mail systems use this alternative: part of the processing on the client, part on the servers.

- ***Remote data management*** places all presentation and application software on the client, leaving only data and data management software on the server. This option is popular because it keeps all application software in one place (on a *fat client*) and takes advantage of the huge processing capacity of today's PCs. Although this solution is less complex, it has the disadvantage of requiring all the machines to be updated at the same time with a new release of the software. This level of coordination can be difficult unless all the machines are under a rigorous systems management system that routinely updates them when they connect to the corporate network.

- ***Distributed database*** places all presentation and application software as well as some of the data on the client. The remaining data is on the server. It is a complex solution, especially if the numerous databases are intended to remain in sync. Even so, it is an important option used in mobile computing, where, for instance, each salesperson needs some data locally (probably the less dynamic data). Up-to-the-second data can be stored on the master database and accessed only when needed. This option also leads to fat client machines.

Another way to look at client-server systems is to view their architecture. The preferred architecture has been three tiered, notes Roger Woolfe.[3a] As Figure 5-9 shows, tier 3 is the superserver, perhaps a mainframe or a cluster of Web site servers. It can be connected directly to an in-house client-server network or it may be routed through tier 2 servers to the network. Companies have chosen this latter option to extend the life of their still-good-but-old legacy applications. Short-lived and fast-changing data, as well as corresponding integrity rules, are also stored at this superserver level so that the data can be shared.

Tier 2 is specialized servers. Data specific to departments or work groups is stored here, as is data that does not change often yet requires rapid retrieval. Tier 2 also houses *middleware*, or software that eases connection between clients and servers. Middleware became an important concept in client-server systems because it performs translations

Tier 3
Superserver, often a mainframe,
connected to the network via one or more
servers, and sometimes directly as well

Tier 2
Multiple specialized servers, some
possibly dedicated to middleware

LANs and WANs

Tier 1
Clients, some of which may be portable

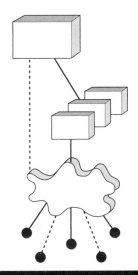

FIGURE 5-9 The Trend to Three-Tier Client-Server Arrangements

Source: Roger Woolfe, *Managing the Move to Client-Server*, Wentworth Research Program
(now part of Gartner EXP, 56 Top Gallant, Stamford, CT 06904), January 1995.

between disparate systems. With middleware, a major application written for UNIX can
later be used to support Windows or Linux without needing to be rewritten. Without
middleware, companies would be hard-pressed to serve a proliferation of new kinds of
computing devices with their existing systems.

Tier 1 is the clients, either desktop or portable, connected via some sort of network.

The alternative architecture is two tier, consisting of only clients and servers or
clients and a mainframe. The three-tiered architecture reduces client complexity by
decreasing the number of interfaces that need to be accommodated by client machines.
The drawback is that clients are more complex and access to tier 3 data is slower than
to tier 2. Woolfe presents a case of a company that uses two of Gartner's client-server
approaches in a three-tier architecture. Here is that story.

CASE EXAMPLE

AN AEROSPACE COMPANY

A corporate enterprise systems group
develops systems for use across the
company. The group's goal is to never
again build monolithic applications.
Instead, it intends to build systems—
even million-dollar systems—from

(Case Continued)

off-the-shelf hardware and software components.

The Software

All the client-server systems use the same structure, with application code on the clients, data on the servers, and communication middleware shared between them. The software is written using object-oriented technology, and most of it comes from an object-oriented component library.

The Data

The heart of the architecture is a repository, which allows reuse of objects. The repository holds *metadata*: information about the data being used. This repository lets developers build sets of common data under the auspices of an enterprise master database, so data elements have common definitions. When in use, data is split between operational data in production systems and data warehouses, which are updated daily via replication software.

The Network

The network is an integral part of this architecture. Each company site has three components: desktop machines, servers, and one or more site hubs. Each of these components uses standard, plug-in equipment; thus, the architecture can be used anywhere in the world. To cope with the increased networking demands of client-server systems, the company is migrating from Ethernet to the higher-speed Asynchronous Transfer Mode (ATM) network. The conversion takes place at each site hub.

The applications communicate to a site hub (a gateway), which plugs into the public telephone network, forming a ring structure of ATM switches. The speed of the ring is 600 mbps. (See Figure 5-10.)

The Architecture

The client-server architecture is *remote data management*, to use the Gartner terminology.[3a] Data resides on servers, and applications reside on clients. The company chose this approach because it discovered that only 5 to 6 percent of the average PC is utilized. The company plans to use the remaining 94 to 95 percent of spare desktop capacity for application code.

The company also uses the *distributed function* approach, but only on a few complex systems, because this approach requires more effort than remote data management.

The *distributed presentation* and *remote presentation* approaches do not take full advantage of the spare PC capacity, so they are not used. The company also does not plan to use the *distributed database* approach, where databases are housed on client machines, because it is just too complex. The client machines must be polled to get the data, which is impractical except for highly structured workflow applications or conversation-oriented applications, such as Lotus Notes.

In short, the company uses the distributed function and remote data management configurations because they minimize total costs. The company's migration strategy has been first to build the architecture and then to build applications using as many reusable components as possible. ■

(Case Continued)

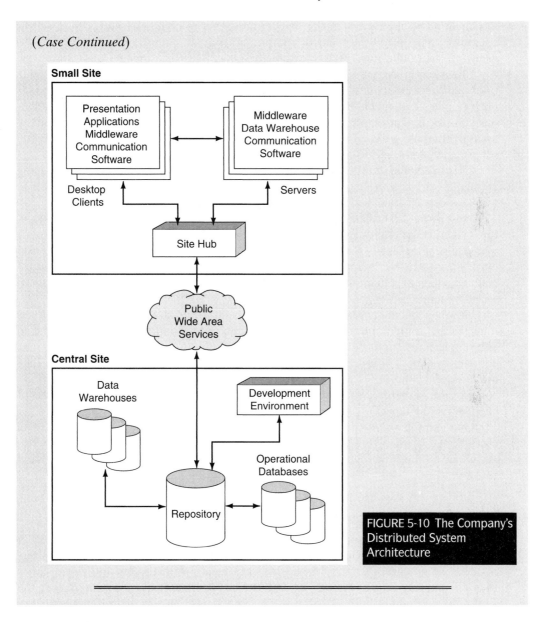

FIGURE 5-10 The Company's Distributed System Architecture

Benefits of Client-Server Computing. Client-server computing promised numerous benefits in the early 1990s. The following ones have held true. The primary benefit of client-server computing was to give people access to data or information when they needed it. This capability was especially pertinent to salespeople, who, for example, wanted to download information about customer orders from a central database using a PC while at the customer's site.

Retail chains have also used client-server systems to look into their stores to see what is selling, what is in inventory, and what is on order. Greater precision helps them keep less stock on hand and replenish inventory more on a just-in-time basis. It also lets them more closely watch the market and react to changes faster. Client-server computing has shifted the focus of computing from keeping track of the business to using information to fulfill strategic objectives.

Client-server computing also blended the autonomy of PCs with the systemwide rules and connectivity of traditional systems. This combination turned traditional computing on its head, reversing the role of the host and PCs. Whereas the host was previously the focus of attention, in client-server computing, PCs are. This change shifted the focus of computing to end users, empowering employees, especially those who directly serve customers.

Client-server systems have also been used to streamline workflows by encouraging people to work together via networks, giving them powerful local processing power as well as access to other people and internal and external information.

Most powerfully of all, client-server computing supports new organizational structures via its connectivity. By providing a platform that supports individuals and groups who are geographically dispersed, it allows companies to experiment with dispersed work groups. In fact, experience with these technologies and their infrastructure enabled companies to more easily take advantage of the Internet. It is like a big client-server system.

However, client-server systems have not been lower in cost than mainframe systems (as first touted), because they entail so much coordination. What initially looked like simple connections between clients and servers has turned into large, often fragile, complex systems. Although client-server systems are easier for end users to use, they are far more complex for IS organizations to manage. Day-to-day management of the complex infrastructure, where servers can be in hundreds of locations, is a costly part of client-server systems.

On the human side, the systems led to organizational turmoil as people dealt with cross-boundary data flow, empowered employees, and cultural differences between people using the same data. The biggest changes were thus often organizational and cultural.

Internet-Based Computing

In the late 1990s, the client-server computing trend was interrupted by the Internet because the Internet provided a ubiquitous communication platform, which was sorely needed by companies wanting to work electronically with the outside world. Since then, the model of a distributed system has come to include the Internet. In fact, the Internet has become the heart of most distributed systems. The main tenet of client-server computing is still the splitting of processing between various kinds of machines. Internet-based computing, a new form of distributed computing, can be depicted as simply a computer and an Internet cloud (Figure 5-11).

Initially, it was expected that network computers—with no hard disk, just a browser, memory, keyboard, and a modem—would access the Internet. When a network computer needed to perform a function, it would get it from the Internet. The concept of *desktop* network computers has not taken off, but the concept of utilizing programs on the Internet has taken hold in the handheld world. The computer field distinguishes between *fat clients* (typical PCs loaded with all the programs) and *thin clients* (devices that utilize remote programs). The thin-client concept often applies to

FIGURE 5-11 Internet-Based System

the retrieval of small programs (applets) off the Web that are written in Java, a programming language created specifically for the Internet.

To illustrate the versatility of Java-based computing, following are two case studies from IBM's Web site.[4] IBM, like most vendors, has wholeheartedly embraced the integration of the Internet into business computing, using the Java language to do so.

CASE EXAMPLE

CHUBB & SON INSURANCE COMPANY

Chubb is a multinational property and casualty insurance company. Management decided to take advantage of the Internet by converting legacy systems to Java-based systems. For example, they converted their cargo certificate issuance system into an extranet application. The application is used to insure ocean shipments and has proven especially important for customers outside the United States. Importers, exporters, freight forwarders, and banks can draw on this application to round out the services they offer shippers.

Likewise, Chubb has put its builder's risk application on its extranet. This application is used to provide insurance policies to builders of small inland marinas. The application is like "an underwriter in a box" so that agents can rate, quote, and book a policy immediately, making Chubb easy to do business with.

Similarly, Chubb launched a self-service accident benefit life application on the Internet so that consumers can obtain travel insurance at various travel sites at the same time they purchase tickets online.

All three applications feed into Chubb's mainframe but have a Java-based Web front end so that client machines only need access to the Web to perform the application. Users do not need special application software on their machines.

Chubb has used a number of IBM technologies to convert these applications, including VisualAge for Java and WebSphere Application Server. Chubb's

(Case Continued)

goal is not only to make the applications Web-centric, but also to deliver them in record time. Chubb believes that by moving to thin-client delivery, where Java applets are delivered to client machines on demand, they can reduce their total cost of ownership by 30 to 40 percent.

Previously, Chubb developed applications in the client-server world using IBM's VisualAge Smalltalk, which is an object-oriented language. When Visual-Age for Java became available, Chubb decided to try it out to move client-server applications to the Web. Much to Chubb's pleasure, IS management discovered developers could reuse some 15 percent of their code (even some of the most difficult-to-write portions), so the migration to Web-centricity was not as difficult as they had anticipated. ∎

CASE EXAMPLE

THE SABRE GROUP

IBM has worked with the SABRE Group (the airline reservation company) and Nokia (the cell phone manufacturer) to create a real-time, interactive service delivered via cell phone.

The service allows business travelers to not only receive updates from airlines (anytime, anyplace) but to even initiate changes. For example, if a meeting runs significantly over and the travelers realize they are going to miss their flight, they can request flight details using their Internet-enabled Nokia phone and make new travel arrangements. Travelers can also make or change hotel reservations, rental car reservations, and so forth. Likewise, if a flight is delayed or cancelled, the service notifies travelers so they can adjust their itineraries.

The service draws on SABRE's online corporate travel purchasing system and Nokia's server, which transmits the travel information to a wireless network and to its Internet- enabled phones. The service utilizes XML (eXtended Markup Language), a language that allows objects to be identified by type, which is important for constructing a user's Web site screen on-the-fly, custom-tailored to that user. It also uses Java, a language for writing small applets used to deliver applications over the Internet. In this case, SABRE is using Java to translate its travel information into XML. Finally, it is using Wireless Markup Language (WML), a language for presenting XML information to Internet-enabled devices. ∎

Server-based Computing. With more and more employees carrying their offices with them on laptop computers, security and operational concerns have increased. Laptops do not have strong security features, updating them en masse is not easy, and even individual downloads can require help-desk support.

The solution companies are turning to is *server-based computing*, where applications reside on corporate servers rather than on the laptops. With server-based computing, applications can be securely accessed by any device, they can be updated directly on the server, and they do not have to be tailored to run on specific machines.[5]

Server-based computing is also replacing the need to install servers at remote offices. Small offices, with, say, 10 workstations, can be handled just as well by a remote server, which IS staff at the headquarters can maintain more easily. In some cases, all that is needed at the remote offices is thin clients.

The following example illustrates server-based computing.

CASE EXAMPLE

3I

3i, which stands for "Investors In Industry," is a U.K.-based venture capital firm. To expand beyond England to Southeast Asia and the United States, the company needed to give its investment professionals anytime-anywhere access to its systems. With this access, staff members could conduct business and complete a deal on the spot with just a laptop and a modem. To permit such location-independent remote and mobile working with up-to-date information in users' laptops, 3i turned to server-based computing.

3i called on Specialist Computer Centre in England to create new data centers in the United Kingdom and elsewhere. These centers consist of Citrix application server software installed on Hewlett-Packard servers.

Remote employees dial in to one of the centers through a secure modem service, which uses both authentication to verify their identify and encryption to jumble the messages. Using Microsoft Windows terminal server software and Citrix software, the staff create their own virtual offices. They have secure access to 120 in-house applications, all of which are housed on a variety of devices. The sessions are managed by the Citrix software.

From the IS department's point of view, the applications are much easier to manage because the software is housed in one place. Thus, updates are made once and remote employees always use the latest version. If employees had the software on their machines, all laptops would need to be updated at once, which is a difficult task.

The arrangement has allowed 3i to expand globally and let its employees work wherever they happen to be. ∎

Peer-to-Peer Computing.   One of the most intriguing forms of Internet-based computing is peer-to-peer (P2P) computing. With P2P, tasks are distributed over a wide number of computers (peers) connected to the Internet. It is a grassroots movement, much like the open source movement, but some corporations now take it seriously.

The most infamous example of P2P was Napster, a central directory of music, and the PCs on which the music was located. Using Napster software, people could find music titles at the Napster site and then download that music from the listed PCs. Everyone swapped with everyone. Napster was infamous because the music industry contended it infringed on copyright laws by encouraging music piracy. It eventually closed down.

Author Jeremy Rifkin[6] says that the Napster dispute goes to the heart of two economies: the old economy that is made up of buyers and sellers and the e-economy that has clients and servers. He believes the Napster model will eventually win out because it allows worldwide distribution of intangibles (even an entire music collection) faster than ringing up the sale of a single CD. Furthermore, Web distribution reduces traditional production costs—including distribution, packaging, inventory, and merchandising. At the same time that sales of hard goods aim to maximize production, distribution via Web sites aims to pool risks and share savings.

The issue has been how to make money in the P2P environment. Rifkin believes subscriptions will replace sales. People will pay for access rather than for ownership. Why buy one CD when you can have unlimited access to a continually growing gigantic music collection for a month? he asks. In physical markets, physical property is purchased. In networks, access to experiences is purchased. When hyperspeed and continuous change are the norm, it makes less sense to own and more sense to subscribe. Furthermore, continual connection provides other benefits, such as a steady stream of new music or other intangibles. Thus, says Rifkin, Napster is just the tip of the iceberg.

Web Services

The forms of Internet-based computing just described could be considered first-generation Internet-based distributed systems. Web Services are said to be the second generation. The term refers to software modules that have a URL, that is, an Internet address, so that they can be called upon to perform their function (as a service) via the Internet. Today, we use the Web for people-to-computer communication. We access a Web page by typing in its URL. Gottschalk and his colleagues[7] call this the *eyeball Web*.

Web Services, on the other hand, is computer-to-computer use of the Internet. One computer program or Web Service makes a request of another Web Service to perform its task (or set of tasks) and pass back the answer. Gottschalk et al. call this the *transactional Web*, and they believe it will be dominated by program-to-program, business-to-business interactions. In essence, many Web Services calling upon each other form a highly distributed system.

Web Services is a very hot topic for many reasons. For one, people see it as the next generation of distributed services because it allows the building of large, complex systems by linking together any number of modules that each perform one or a few tasks. Two, it makes the Internet the hub of computing, which aims to ease interenterprise computing (something many enterprises want). Three, it permits flexible systems not possible in the past, because a Web Service can choose which other Web Service(s) to utilize at the time it needs one. Traditionally, sequences of steps have had to be hard wired (preprogrammed) ahead of time. With the dynamic binding of Web Services, this decision can be made at execution time, making systems far more flexible. Four, Web Services can possibly release companies from having to build and maintain so much software in-house. The promise is that they can rent functionality via Web Services either on a subscription basis or as needed. Five, Web Services will draw on existing systems. Web Services can be used as a *wrappering* technology, state Gottschalk et al. Companies can *wrap* (encapsulate) some functionality from an existing application in an XML envelope and *expose* it for use by others by publishing its existence in a special directory. (Two new terms used in the Web Services world are *wrapping* and *exposing*.) Thus, a bank with a credit authorization system can publish it as a Web Service that others can use, for a fee. Or a company that allows customers to configure their own product online (a computer, a bicycle, a car) may actually be using a Web Service (built in-house or obtained from a third party) to offer that functionality on their Web site to people or to the computers of, say, their largest customers.

The promises go on. Needless to say, vendors are now vying to be the providers of the platforms on which Web Services run. Companies are experimenting with Web Services, either to test out this loosely coupled, service-oriented architecture in-house or with a trusted trading partner. This architecture is different from the tightly coupled structure of most computer programs where one program calls another program. Drawing on object-oriented tenets, in Web Services, one module (a Web Service) sends a message to another Web Service, provides it some data, asks it to perform its specialized function on that data, and then expects an answer. Such message-based systems will allow systems in one company to work with systems in many other companies without first having to hard code the links between each other. The firms can use software standards and communications protocols to make the interconnections.

Web Services Standards.   The world of Web Services will be possible because of three software standards (XML, WSDL, and UDDI) and three communication protocols (SOAP, HTTP, and TCP/IP), note John Hagel and John Seely Brown of 12 Entrepreneuring.[8]

- ***XML (eXtended Markup Language).*** XML is a language for describing data in a standardized way so that different applications can use the same data. Web Services are created by wrapping XML around a piece of software that performs a function. The XML wrapper describes the services its bundle provides.

- ***WSDL (Web Services Definition Language).*** Web Services make themselves known by publishing their description in an XML document using WSDL. This *service description* describes the service, how to make a request to it, the data it needs to perform its work, and the results it will deliver. WSDL provides the standard language for creating these descriptions so that they can be understood by Web Services requestors.

- ***UDDI (Universal Discovery, Description, and Integration).*** The descriptions are stored in a UDDI registry, a "yellow pages" of Web Services. An application or a Web Service can find another Web Service by either knowing its URL or by searching UDDI repositories for services that meet the parameters it seeks.

- ***SOAP (Simple Object Access Protocol).*** Web Services communicate using SOAP, an XML-based communication protocol that works over any network and with any equipment. A Web Service interacts with another by sending a request for service to that other Web Service, "directly binding to it and invoking it," state Gottschalk et al.[7] The two do not have to be preprogrammed to work together. Web Services can be combined in any pattern of use.

- *HTTP (Hypertext Transfer Protocol).* Web sites have addresses that use the HTTP protocol. Web Services draw on this same protocol to indicate the address where they can be located.

- *TCP/IP (Transmission Control Protocol/Internet Protocol).* The Internet is true to its name; it is a network of networks because it uses a protocol that permits transmitting messages across networks. This protocol is TCP/IP, and it is the protocol used by Web Services as well.

The Significance of Web Services.   Hagel and Brown,[8] two leading thinkers in the IT field, believe Web Services offers the computing architecture of the future, and thus will significantly change the job of CIOs. Rather than own and maintain their own systems, companies will buy their IT as services over the Internet, state Hagel and Brown. Thus, within the next few years, old assumptions about managing IT will be overturned.

Today, after some four decades of viewing IT as proprietary and running systems in-house, enterprises have a "mishmash of disparate systems," which they have most recently tried to replace enterprisewide via ERP systems, state Hagel and Brown. In so doing, they have created rigid business processes, making it difficult for them to respond to market changes or restructure themselves.

Web Services offers a completely new IT architecture, one based on the Web and openness. Rather than build proprietary systems, companies can obtain the functionality they need from the Internet. Some Web Services will be proprietary, some public; some will be subscription based and others on demand.

Hagel and Brown see a three-tier Web Services architecture:

1. *Application services* are the top tier. These perform specific business activities, such as credit card processing, shipment scheduling, or loan risk analysis.

2. The *service grid* is the middle tier. It provides utilities used by the application services. One type of utility is *shared utilities*, such as security utilities (to authenticate requestors and authorize access), and billing and payment utilities (to handle charges for using a Web Service). Another type of utility is *service management utilities*, which handle the management and billing of Web Services. *Resource knowledge management utilities*, a third type, provide directories and registrars for requestors and services to find one another and interact. *Transport management utilities*, a fourth type, handle messaging and transportation of files. Until this service grid is robust, though, companies will not use Web Services for their critical business activities, say Hagel and Brown, because they will not have a trusted environment for running important systems.

3. *Software standards* and *communication protocols* (the six listed earlier) reside in the bottom tier. They provide the foundation for the utilities and the application services. Without these standards and protocols, Web Services cannot speak the same language nor connect.

The difference between the past and this future is stark, the two authors note. Consider a loan application. Rather than have one large, integrated, in-house application that handles all the steps in the loan approval and funding process, each step in a Web Services environment will be performed by a different Web Service. In fact, the Web Services will be so specialized that the most appropriate one can be chosen at each processing step. Hence, the application data from a hospital will be sent to a Web Service specializing in risk analysis of hospital loans, whereas the data from a restaurant will be sent to the service that specializes in restaurant risk analysis. Each of these Web Services may draw on other specialized services to do even more specialized processing, depending on the data in the application and the amount of the desired loan.

This modularity of Web Services permits the handling of a huge variety of possibilities by mixing and matching. In addition, it will allow easier cross-company system linking. As a result, companies only pay for the functionality they use when they use it, which reduces the number of IT assets companies need to house and maintain in-house. The providers handle the maintenance of their own services and are forced to stay abreast by the competitive nature of the Web Services marketplace.

Moving to Web Services will require organizational changes in IS. It will require the outsourcing of IT activities to providers (as they emerge) and the designing of their own Web Services offerings based on their enterprise's business acumen. Following is an example of what one enterprise is doing.

CASE EXAMPLE

GENERAL MOTORS

General Motors formed eGM in 1999 to explore how it should interact with car buyers using the Internet. For 3 years, eGM was run by Mark Hogan, who gave innumerable speeches describing the progress his business unit was making. eGM was then folded into GM's IT organization and Hogan was promoted. Hagel and Brown point out that during his tenure at eGM, Hogan became a strong advocate of the Web Services architecture, going so far as to believe it could be used to move GM from its supply-driven, build-to-stock business model to a demand-driven, build-to-order business model. That change would be an enormous (some say impossible) feat.

eGM began modestly, note Hagel and Brown, building Web sites to connect GM to both consumers and dealers. Moving to a demand-driven business model (where every vehicle is built for a specific customer after the customer orders it) would require GM and its 8,000 dealers to collaborate electronically and quite differently. There would be no way to shift the business this dramatically using conventional IT architectures because that would require standardizing the systems used by the dealers, which was too costly a task for GM and its dealers to consider.

However, Web Services provides a way to create such a new business platform without replacing the disparate systems the dealers use or trying to get them all to agree to standard new systems. By exposing existing (and new) functionality in both GM and dealer systems using the

(Case Continued)

Web Services standards, GM can roll out new business processes incrementally at a reasonable cost.

GM began the evolution by first enhancing its existing supply-driven model, state Hagel and Brown, offering new functions via a Web Services architecture. For example, it offers a locate-to-order Web Service to dealers, which allows them to easily find a specific car a customer might want in the inventory of other GM dealers. Another Web Service is order-to-delivery, which shortens the time to deliver a custom-ordered vehicle. Through such incremental steps, GM "paves the way," state Hagel and Brown, to eventually convert to a make-to-order business model.

By taking this incremental route on this new platform, GM can achieve payback with each new Web Service, hopefully avoiding the huge disruption that an abrupt traditional system change would cause, and evolve as the Web Services model evolves. Economically, achieving this goal brings enormous paybacks, note the two authors. GM could cut its $25-billion inventory and working capital in half and potentially shave $1,000 off the cost of each vehicle. Furthermore, by gradually evolving new processes and adopting shared terminologies and meanings, GM and its dealers can influence their parts suppliers as well, fostering industrywide change. ∎

The seven systems discussed in this section are the different types of distributed systems that have emerged. To conclude this chapter, we come back around to the beginning of the chapter and discuss the subjects of architecture and infrastructure.

DEFINING THE OVERALL IT ARCHITECTURE

An architecture is a blueprint. It shows how the overall system, house, vehicle, or other product will look and how the parts interrelate. As Roger Woolfe and Marcus Blosch note in their Gartner EXP report *IT Architecture Matters*,[3b] the intent of an IT architecture is to bring order to the otherwise chaotic world of IS by defining a set of guidelines and standards and then adhering to them. Designing a system architecture used to be considered strictly a technical issue. More and more, though, because the architecture needs to support how the company operates, it reflects the business strategy. Furthermore, as the business changes, the architecture needs to keep pace.

The Job of Chief Technology Officer.   Due to the increased importance of IT architectures, the job title of chief technology officer (CTO) or chief architect has appeared. The CTO is generally the chief architect and reports to the CIO, who is in charge of the use of IT. In a few cases, CIOs have changed their title to CTO to emphasize their role as the technical head within their firm.

In the dot-com world, the title CTO was far more prevalent than CIO because these CTOs viewed CIOs as the executives who ran traditional IT organizations, including operations and maintenance. These CTOs preferred the title CTO to reflect their more strategic role as chief architect of the company's Web presence. Furthermore, most dot-coms began life outsourcing all or most of their IT operations, so the CTO title appeared more appropriate. The dot-coms that have survived, though, now have CIOs at the helm because the job has broadened beyond the architectural aspects of IT.

An Enterprise Architecture Framework

For more than 25 years, John Zachman,[9] an independent consultant, has been preaching the value of enterprise architecture and the modeling of data, processes, and networks. He offers the most comprehensive view of this subject we have seen, so we briefly describe it here.

The real world (an airplane, an enterprise, or a skyscraper) is so complicated that we cannot get our brain around it at one time, says Zachman, so we abstract out single variables. To completely describe an IS architecture, we need to look at the roles people play and the components they deal with. Together, these create the rows and columns of a framework.

The Rows: Planner, Owner, Designer, Builder, Subcontractor, and Consumer or User.
No single architectural representation is available for an information system, says Zachman, because building complex products requires six roles: planner, owner, designer, builder, subcontractor, and consumer. Six perspectives, six models. For instance, an airframe manufacturer needs a statement of the objectives for the planner, an architect's drawings for the owner, an architect's plans for the designer, a contractor's plans for the builder, and detailed representations for the subcontractors. The completed airplane is the consumer's view. The same is true in IT. An information system needs a scope statement, a model of the enterprise, a model of the information system, a technology model, and a description of the components to produce the finished functioning system. These components make up the rows in Zachman's enterprise architecture framework, shown in Figure 5-12.

Each role has its own constraints. For instance, the owner is constrained by the use of the end product. The designer is constrained by physical laws. The builder is constrained by the state-of-the-art and the technology available. For these reasons, six models, rather than one, are needed, and they need to be kept in sync through configuration management.

The Columns: Data, Function, Network. Another significant factor is the lack of a single graphical representation for the components of a complex information system. As in engineering, systems need three components: data models (What is it made of?), functional models (How does it work?), and network models (Where are the components located?). These represent the physical manifestations of the system.

In addition, systems need a who (people), a when (time), and a why (motivation), says Zachman. These three elements represent the soft side of systems. Together, the six are all we need to know to build a complex system. So, the good news is that defining an enterprise architecture is not an infinite problem. The bad news is that no one

	Data (What)	Function (How)	Network (Where)
Scope Planner			
Enterprise Model Owner			
Information System Model Designer			
Technology Model Builder			
Components Subcontractor			
Functioning System Consumer or User			

FIGURE 5-12 An Architectural Framework

Source: Adapted from John Zachman, Zachman International, 2222 Foothill Blvd., Suite 337, LaCanada, CA 91011.

has done it yet. But a few are making progress. The entire enterprise architecture framework is shown in Figure 5-13.

Using the Framework. The cells in the framework contain models that can be used to describe any complex thing—an enterprise, an airplane, even a bicycle. All of these models exist, the question is whether an enterprise spends the time to make them explicit.

For instance, your organization has a data model, whether it has been explicitly defined or whether it just grew haphazardly without an underlying design. That model is intended to work as your enterprise works. A problem occurs, though, when IT or users bring in a package that follows a different data model. If the rules in that model are inconsistent with the rules in your company, you will either spend a lot fixing the package, says Zachman, or you will require people to change how they work to be consistent with the package. Models are important because they allow people to properly evaluate packages. They also help builders align with what owners want. And they can help companies realize what changes need to be made when they move to a new business model, such as deciding to reorganize around customer groups rather than around products.

FIGURE 5-13 Enterprise Architecture—A Framework

	Data **What**	Function **How**	Network **Where**	People **Who**	Time **When**	Motivation **Why**
Objectives/ Scope (Contextual)	List of things important to the business	List of processes the business performs	List of locations in which the business operates	List of Organizations/agents important to the business	List of events significant to the business	List of business goals/ strategies
Planner	Entity = Class of business thing	Function = Class of business process	Node = Major business location	Agent = Class of agent	Time = Major business event	Ends/Means = Major bus goal/ critical success factor
Enterprise Model (Conceptual)	e.g., Semantic model	e.g., Business process model	e.g., Logistics network	e.g., Organization chart	e.g., Master schedule	e.g., Business plan
Owner	Ent = Business entity Reln = Business relationship	Proc = Business process I/O = Business resources	Node = Business location Link = Business linkage	Agent = Organization unit Work = Work product	Time = Business event Cycle = Business cycle	End = Business objective Means = Business strategy
System Model (Logical)	e.g., Data model	e.g., "Application architecture"	e.g., Distributed system architecture	e.g., Human interface architecture	e.g., Processing structure	e.g., Knowledge architecture
Designer	Ent = Data entity Reln = Data relationship	Proc = Application function I/O = User views	Node = I/S function (processor, storage, etc.) Link = Line characteristics	Agent = Role Work = Deliverable	Time = System event Cycle = Processing cycle	Ends = Criterion Means = Business rules
Technology Model (Physical)	e.g., Data design	e.g., System design	e.g., System architecture	e.g., Human/technology Interface	e.g., Control structure	e.g., Knowledge design
Builder	Ent = Segment/Row/etc Reln = Pointer/Key/etc	Proc = Computer function I/O =Screen/Device formats	Node = Hardware/System software Link = Line specifications	Agent = User Work = Job	Time = Execute Cycle = Component cycle	Ends = Condition Means = Action
Detailed Representations (out-of-context)	e.g., Data definition	e.g., Program	e.g., Network architecture	e.g., Security architecture	e.g., Timing definition	e.g., Knowledge definition
Sub-Contractor	Ent = Field Reln = Address	Proc = Language stmt I/O = Control block	Node = Addresses Link = Protocols	Agent = Identity Work = "Transaction"	Time = Interrupt Cycle = Machine cycle	End = Subcondition Means = Step
Functioning System	e.g., Data	e.g., Function	e.g., Network	e.g., Organization	e.g., Schedule	e.g., Strategy

Source: Adapted from John Zachman, Zachman International, 2222 Foothill Blvd., Suite 337, LaCanada, CA 91011.

211

The most important reason to make a firm's enterprise system architecture explicit is to be able to make changes to the enterprise and not disintegrate as those changes are made, says Zachman.

To better understand IT architecture development, consider the case of FMC, noted in Woolfe and Blosch's Gartner EXP report.[3b]

CASE EXAMPLE

FMC CORPORATION

FMC, with headquarters in Philadelphia, Pennsylvania, is a global $2-billion chemical manufacturer with 6,000 employees focusing on three areas: agricultural, industrial, and specialty chemicals. It is first or second in the areas in which it competes, and half its sales come from outside the United States.

In 2000, FMC was a $4-billion conglomerate. In 2001, it split into two equal halves, FMC (to focus purely on chemicals) and FMC Technologies. IS spent all of 2001 pulling the IT architecture apart. The deadline for establishing separate IS operations was January 1, 2002.

Designing Two New IT Architectures

FMC outsources its telecommunications, data networking, voice mail, Web hosting, virtual private networks, remote access, and some data center operations. It worked with its outsourcers to pull the infrastructure apart and architect two new IT infrastructures. Headquarters was moved from Chicago to Philadelphia, yet no IS staff moved; FMC now has 130 IS headquarters staff.

The CIO, Ed Flynn, created a new position to report directly to him: Architecture and Technology Director. During 2001, this director had a virtual organization. He led five subteams—data, applications, integration, desktop, and platform—each with five to six team members from FMC and FMC Technology IS staffs. In addition, he supervised an emerging technologies subteam to look out into the future. None of the team members was full-time on a team; they also had their day-to-day jobs.

The five teams' tasks were to

- Describe the "today architecture" (inventory their area)
- Define the "tomorrow architecture" (how their area would look on January 1, 2002)
- Detail the "next-minute steps" (how to get from today to tomorrow)

They accomplished their task in 2001 with only a few transition service agreements on January 1 (where FMC and FMC Technologies would buy services from one another).

Lessons from the Work

"The split taught us we could get workable solutions by having subteams with subject matter experts define the technical architecture, and overlay them with an architecture steering team to add the

(Case Continued)

enterprise and business viewpoints," says Flynn. The top team consisted of Flynn and some of his direct reports. They implemented some of the recommendations from the subteams and took those requiring corporate action to senior management.

Another lesson from the effort was that the "today architecture" can be created by IS staff. However, it then needs to be put into a framework the business folks can understand, because they need to help define the "tomorrow architecture." Then the work continues as a joint effort to define the "next-minute steps."

"Before the split, we had already standardized on SAP as our transaction backbone and on Windows for our desktops and laptops. But getting those standards was a brutal fight—probably because we were our own worst enemy. We had not defined 'tomorrow,' so everyone's 'today' answer would work," says Flynn.

"When we have a tomorrow architecture, and everyone agrees on it, we have fewer next-minute battles because the architecture limits the choices. We saw this happen in the corporate split. Once we agreed on the tomorrow architecture, we were no longer the people who said 'no.' Being a purely chemical company now also helps us with standardization," says Flynn.

Because the chemical business is so cost competitive, FMC wants low-cost IT; therefore, the operating policy is to use common tools, common processes, and replicable solutions. "You have to architect to be able to do that," says Flynn.

Designing a New "Tomorrow" IT Architecture

Flynn's organization is now using the same approach, starting with a clean slate, to architect a new tomorrow IT architecture. If they can pull the corporate architecture apart in 1 year, they believe they should be able to lay out a new tomorrow architecture in a year, even though the scope is broader. The new architecture will include applications in the operating units. "Tomorrow" means 2004–2005, which is when Flynn expects Voice-over-IP and Web Services to kick in.

The organization for the current architecture effort is the same as the one used for the split—the same subteams, the same steering committee. In fact, some of the business folks who helped support SAP after implementation in the mid-1990s stayed in IS and have been on the architecture efforts, bringing their business knowledge with them.

Once the new architecture is defined and bought off by senior management, it will be communicated and implemented via FMC's capital planning process. The expenditures must track the defined next-minute steps, some of which could have timeframes attached to them. "We may even get to the level where we talk about standards, and all purchases will have to adhere to these standards," says Flynn.

Flynn envisions this rearchitecting process as being ongoing. Each new effort will start with today as its reference point, draw on the work of the emerging technologies group to peer into the future, and create a new "tomorrow" architecture. ∎

In e-commerce, IT architecture is a crucial component of business planning. To give a second example of an architecture, consider the one underlying American Airlines' Web site and the business rationale used in creating it.

CASE EXAMPLE

THE SABRE SYSTEM

The architecture underlying American Airlines' Web site is modular. The existing SABRE computer reservation system serves as the reservation service module. Other modules perform the functions related to the Web. They include an input-output module for turning browser-entered data into data that can be processed by SABRE, and vice versa; an authentication module to verify users' identity; a session management module to manage each Web user's interaction with the system; and so on.

Due to this component-based architecture, it was fairly easy to add new functions, states Patricia Seybold.[10] Electronic ticketing, for example, was housed in its own module using appropriate components.

However, as so often happens, when American looked at the underlying databases, it found customer profiles in one database, AAdvantage member profiles in another, and NetSAAver subscriber profiles in a third. In a huge redesign, American consolidated and linked these databases to have just one profile for each flyer.

Another challenge was figuring out how to present a personalized Web site to each flyer. It required creating a data archi-

tecture, which, in turn, required tagging all the content shown on the Web site so that different pieces could be presented to different groups of flyers for different purposes. The decision was made to create an object database that would contain the tagged pieces of information. Tagging took much longer than anyone projected. To use this database to present personalized Web sites, American used Broadvision's One-on-One software and worked with two system integrators and design firms, says Seybold.

Finally, to do electronic booking, which required a more flexible database than the existing fares database, American created a separate fares database that contains tags such as "skiing" and "golf" attached to appropriate destinations. This database is accessed by business rules created by the system based on the choices customers make in their profiles. With this database, the system can make appropriate recommendations of places to travel based on the preferences stored in the profiles.

American's Web site architecture has numerous pieces, including links between systems, components, modules, databases, data elements, and business rules. ■

The Coming Architecture: Service-Oriented Architecture

As noted, the importance of an architecture is that it spells out the relationships among the components of an airplane, bicycle, building, system, and such. In information systems, the architecture spells out how the software components interact with each other. In the past, these interactions have been hard coded point-to-point (one to another); this is efficient, but costly to maintain. Changing one component might require changing the others that interact with it.

A relatively new system architecture has caught the attention of the field because it moves these interactions away from being hard coded and point-to-point. This new architecture is called Service Oriented Architecture (SOA). Its emergence parallels that of Web Services because it uses the same architectural concept and it can be implemented with Web Services.[11]

Rather than think about how to get information out of one system and into another, this architecture thinks about how to expose the data and functions in a way that other systems can easily use—as a service in a wrapper with a well-defined interface that performs a business process. The wrapping hides the technical complexities developers have had to incorporate in their point-to-point interfaces. Ideally, one service would open a new account, another would update a customer account, a third would close an account, and so on. Applications that needed to provide one of these services would use the existing one, rather than their own version.

The current thinking is that an SOA provides this holy grail of how to attain reusable code, which has long eluded IS organizations. An additional benefit of this architecture is that CIOs can leverage their past systems investments, because functions in legacy systems can be exposed as services and then used in new applications. Thus, SOA supports the integration of heterogeneous systems, which has bedeviled IS organizations for years. SOAs also can help CIOs converse with their business peers because the services are essentially business processes, rather than IT services. Discussions about systems are about the business, rather than the technology.

SOA also addresses the need for IS organizations to be more agile, that is, able to more quickly build systems to address new business needs. Each service can be upgraded to use a new technology without affecting the other services. Companies can build on the systems they already have and continually upgrade either technologies or the use of SOA piecemeal, rather than in one fell swoop. In short, SOA is evolutionary, not revolutionary. That is why it is attracting so much attention.

To briefly delve into the jargon, to achieve the much-desired code reusability an SOA must support *loosely-coupled, coarse-grained, standards-based* interactions. This means, first, that a requestor of a service must simply know where to find it (loose coupling) rather than have a preprogrammed link to it (tight coupling). Second, the interactions must be at the business-service level (coarse grained), rather than at the technical-function level (fine grained). And third, the interactions must use interfaces based on industry standards that have been adopted by vendors so that they work across proprietary platforms (standards based).

An SOA can achieve loose coupling between services in several ways. The most recent is to create the services using Web Services protocols (discussed earlier). Although CIOs may eventually migrate to this option, Web Services is so new that the pioneers have generally not taken this route. A second alternative is to use a publish-and-subscribe approach, which is what Delta Air Lines has done (see Chapter 11). A third is to implement messaging-and-integration middleware. Credit Suisse has used the concept of an "information bus" to build its SOA.

CASE EXAMPLE

CREDIT SUISSE

Credit Suisse, with headquarters in Zurich, Switzerland, is a global financial services company with 60,000 employees operating in 50 countries. Credit Suisse is pioneering the implementation of enterprisewide SOAs. Its former architecture depended on proprietary middleware. Maintenance had become increasingly expensive, because as the number of computing platforms and technologies grew, so did the number of interfaces and the amount of time needed to change the interfaces when applications changed.

To address this maintenance problem, Credit Suisse revamped its IT infrastructure to be a service-oriented architecture by implementing two "information buses"—a service bus and an event bus.

The Service Bus

The front-end bus, that is, the bus that integrates front-end and back-end applications, is the service bus, shown in Figure 5-14. The architecture uses Orbix from Iona Technologies, which is a set of tools for integrating applications that run on mainframes, Unix, and Windows platforms.[12] Through Orbix, Credit Suisse is reusing business procedures, business logic, and data formerly locked up in its applications.

The service bus takes a request–reply approach. Through Orbix, each business service is exposed by being stored in a central repository. When a front-end application has a request, it triggers a call to Orbix, which sends the request to the appropriate business service and waits for a reply (from a backend application), which it then forwards to the requesting application. Thus, the bus uses a demand-pull model—the request from one application pulls the reply from another.

Credit Suisse took this approach so that it could integrate the software functions housed in the multiple generations of technology it has in-house, by presenting its core business applications as a collection of reusable business services. The SOA gives it a way to design new applications that draw on these business services using a documented interface. Because of the interface, developers do not need to worry about the software or database underlying each business service.

The Event Bus

The event bus integrates the back-end systems. It also uses a service-oriented architecture, but it uses a supply-push mode of operation, implemented using publish-and-subscribe. When an event occurs in one system, it is "published." All of the systems that need to know about that event are "subscribed" and are notified of the event that has taken place (the update is pushed to them). An *event* is a

(Case Continued)

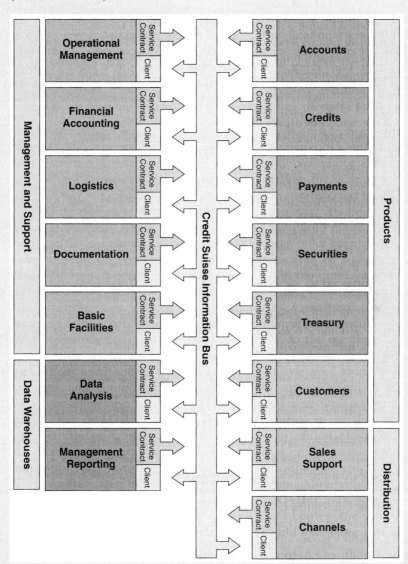

FIGURE 5-14 Credit Suisse's Service-Oriented Architecture

Source: Courtesy of Credit Suisse

change in the state of an object, such as a customer. Credit Suisse has developed specific message types to run over the event bus; each is for a different type of event. The purpose of the event bus is to ensure that all systems are using the same up-to-date data. It connects all back-end systems: host applications, ERP systems, new nonhost applications, databases, data warehouses, and external data feeds.

(Case Continued)

A typical use of the event bus is to replicate the data in Credit Suisse's customer information file from its legacy application (developed in-house) and to copy it to a trading application that stores its own copy of this data. The event bus also allows Credit Suisse to transform the data between applications (that is, convert it from the format used in one system to that used in another) and to route data based on its content. The event bus was built using IBM technologies (Websphere MQ/Integration Broker).

Benefits

The SOA effort began in 1999. By December 1999, Credit Suisse had five SOA-based applications drawing on 35 business services that were being used by 800 users. The numbers have grown since then. Two years later it had 50 applications running on the information bus, drawing on 500 business services and being used by 15,000 internal users. In addition, customers using Credit Suisse's online trading and Web-based e-banking applications generated some 15 million invocations of the SOA-based business services each week.

Today, well over 100 applications use 800 services, invoking 800 million transactions per year on the service bus. Actually, it is no longer quite clear what an application is, but these figures give a feel for the high volumes. The event bus, implemented in 2003, integrates over 32 back-end systems and handles over 1 million messages a day.

Credit Suisse was able to implement the architecture without disrupting applications. The effort was a major investment, but the company can now implement new applications much faster. In fact, it has found that some 80 percent of the business services needed in new applications are already in existing applications. Credit Suisse believes its development speed allows it to respond to customers' requests for new financial services faster than its competition. ■

THE IMPORTANCE OF THE IT INFRASTRUCTURE

In the arena of IT infrastructure, the best work to date has been performed by Peter Weill, director of the Center for Information Systems Research at MIT, and Marianne Broadbent, Associate Dean, Executive MBA Program, Melbourne Business School.[13] They describe the structure of the IT infrastructure, how local, firmwide, and public infrastructures mesh, and the different ways companies justify infrastructure investments. Such investments are a vital part of corporate IT portfolios, yet they are the most difficult to cost-justify beforehand and to measure benefits of afterwards.

The Structure of the IT Infrastructure

Weill and Broadbent define *IT infrastructure* as "the shared and reliable services that provide the foundation for the enterprise IT portfolio." The shared characteristic differentiates an IT infrastructure from IT investments used by just one function. On top of this infrastructure sit applications that perform the business's processes. Thus, infrastructure does not provide direct business performance benefits. Rather, it enables other systems that do yield business benefits, which is what makes infrastructure so difficult to cost-justify.

Weill and Broadbent divide the IT infrastructure into four layers, as shown in Figure 5-15, underlying local applications. Local applications are fast changing. They include such applications as an insurance claims system, a bank loan system, or a customer service support system. Due to their fast-changing nature, they are not part of the infrastructure, but they do draw on it.

It is easiest to understand their view of infrastructure reading from bottom to top because that order describes it from the technologists' point of view to the business users' point of view. Weill and Michael Vitale,[14] of the Australian Graduate School of Management, present the following description of the infrastructure layers, from bottom to top, in their article in the *MIS Quarterly Executive,* which discusses the infrastructure capabilities needed by e-business models:

- *IT Components.* This layer is the foundation of a firm's IT infrastructure. It consists of technology components, such as computers, printers, DBMS packages, operating systems, and such. Whereas technologists understand the capabilities of these components, business people do not. That is why IT and business people have had such

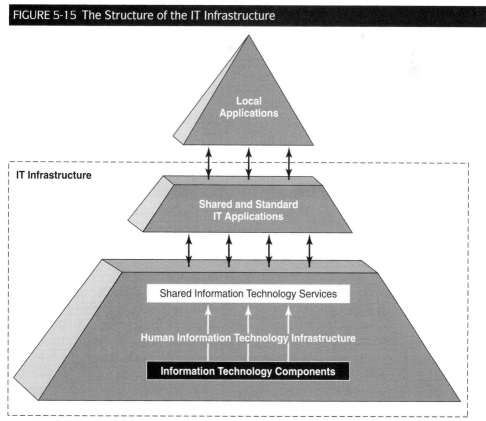

FIGURE 5-15 The Structure of the IT Infrastructure

Source: Adapted from Peter Weill and Marianne Broadbent, *Leveraging the New Infrastructure: How Market Leaders Capitalize on IT* (Boston: Harvard Business School Press, 1998).

a difficult time talking about infrastructure at this level. They are not speaking a common language, note Weill and Vitale.

- *Human IT Infrastructure.* The translation of the IT component layer into business terms occurs at this layer and is handled by humans. This layer consists of experts' knowledge, skills, experience, and standards to bind IT components into services that business people can understand.

- *Shared IT Services.* This layer is the business view of the IT infrastructure, and it presents the infrastructure as a set of services that users can draw upon and share to conduct business. Weill and Broadbent's recent refinement, working with Mani Subramani of the University of Minnesota,[3c] identifies 70 infrastructure services grouped into 10 clusters. Examples of services are Web sites, wireless applications, firewalls on secure gateways, and large-scale data processing facilities.

- *Shared and Standard IT Applications.* These applications, which are at the top of the IT infrastructure, change less regularly than the fast-changing local applications above the infrastructure. They include such stable applications as accounting, budgeting, and HR.

Again, the importance of this four-level description of IT infrastructure is that it gives technologists and business users a common language. Business users can discuss where they need specific services, and technologists can translate those services into the technical components that underlie them.

To take this infrastructure discussion a bit further, Weill and Broadbent note that it sits on top of the public infrastructure, as shown in Figure 5-16, that is, the Internet, industry networks, vendors, and telecommunications companies. Also note in this figure that in some cases the firmwide infrastructure provides corporatewide services. In other cases, it provide infrastructure for individual business units.

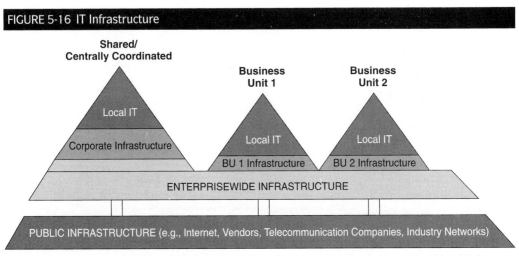

FIGURE 5-16 IT Infrastructure

Source: Adapted from Peter Weill and Marianne Broadbent, *Leveraging the New Infrastructure: How Market Leaders Capitalize on IT* (Boston: Harvard Business School Press 1998).

Similar to Public Infrastructure.   IT infrastructure is strikingly similar to public infrastructure, such as roads, hospitals, sewers, and schools, note Weill and Broadbent.

- Both are provided by a central agency and funded by some form of taxation.
- Both are long-term and require large investments.
- A central agency provides an essential service that users are not motivated or able to provide.
- Both enable business activity by users that would otherwise not be economically feasible.
- Flexibility is valued in both because they must be in place before the precise business activity is known.
- Both are difficult to cost-justify in advance as well as to show benefits in hindsight.
- Both require a delicate investment balance: Too little investment leads to duplication, incompatibility, and suboptimal use, whereas too much discourages user investment and involvement and may result in unused capacity.

Three Views of Infrastructure

The benefits a firm actually realizes from its infrastructure investments depend on its objectives for the infrastructure. A firm might invest in infrastructure for the following three reasons, note Weill and Broadbent:

1. Economies of scale (utility)
2. Support for business programs (dependent)
3. Flexibility to meet changes in the marketplace (enabling)

Utility.   Companies that view their infrastructure as a utility see it as a necessary and unavoidable service that must be provided by IS. Expected benefits are cost savings achieved through economies of scale. Normally, firms with this perspective treat infrastructure costs as an administrative expense, and they act to minimize these expenses. Therefore, they offer the fewest infrastructure services. For instance, they might promote use of networks for messaging but not as part of inter- or intraorganizational business processes. This objective requires the lowest investment, but it also only results in lowering costs (not in reengineering the business). Outsourcing may be viewed favorably because the IT infrastructure is not seen as strategic.

Dependent.   A business that ties its infrastructure investments to specific, known business programs, takes the dependent view. The infrastructure is treated as a business expense because investments are tied to business plans, and its value is measured by short-term business benefits. Firms with this view include infrastructure planning in current business planning. They also see the network as critical. Furthermore, this view of infrastructure appears to smooth the way for simplifying business processes. In fact, Weill and Broadbent surmise that this view is a minimum requirement for successfully implementing business process reengineering.

Enabling.   A firm that develops and continually modifies its infrastructure in *coalign-ment* with its business strategy—where infrastructure influences strategy and vice versa—takes the enabling view of infrastructure. The primary benefit is long-term flexibility, thus the firm does not limit infrastructure investments to current strategy. The infrastructure is intended to provide the foundation for changing direction in the future, if need be. Thus, infrastructure costs are seen as business investments. For example, the firm might use networks extensively in business processes, both within the firm and with customers and suppliers.

Needless to say, the appropriate viewpoint is not a technical decision; it is a top management decision. It is IS management's job to make this clear to senior management and show them the options. Again, as we pointed out in Chapter 2, teamwork among the various levels of management is absolutely necessary to align technical investments with business strategy.

No view is superior, though; different views are appropriate for different strate-gies. Moving from utility to dependent to enabling increases up-front investments and the number of IT infrastructure services provided.

To see how one organization has approached investing in infrastructure, consider the city of Sunnyvale, California.[3d]

CASE EXAMPLE

CITY OF SUNNYVALE, CALIFORNIA

The city of Sunnyvale, California, in the heart of Silicon Valley, is rated as one of the best-run cities in the United States. Its performance-based budgeting sys-tem, which has been honed over the past 25 years, has fostered citywide fiscal soundness and day-to-day accountability by city administrators. This budgeting process, along with the city's 20-year planning horizon, is aiding the IS depart-ment in creating and financing the city's information infrastructure.

Sunnyvale's director of information technology was hired to move the city into the future. He thus concentrated on building the city's information infrastruc-ture because the city sees infrastructure as its foundation for the future. Says the director,

If the city of Sunnyvale is to succeed in leveraging technological resources to deal with increasing customer demands, as well as improve efficiency and customer service, the IS depart-ment must first take responsibility for capturing accurate information and delivering that information in a timely manner.

This statement is the driving force behind the city's IS department. The dri-ver for investing in infrastructure is qual-ity of service. To provide high-quality ser-

(Case Continued)

vice to customers, the infrastructure users (city departments) must have timely and accurate information to do their jobs. For this to happen, the IS department must have the right pieces of information at the right place at the right time. The IS director believes the city needs to develop an expandable infrastructure to leverage technology and capitalize on opportunities.

The infrastructure provides connectivity between the city's traditional mainframes with attached terminals/PCs, numerous stand-alone LANs, and the outside world. It is based on a fiber-optic backbone, Internet-based computing, and relational database technology. A three-level distributed architecture is used, with enterprise servers, midtier servers, and desk-top clients. The architecture encompasses more than traditional computing equipment, though. For example, the 401 copiers throughout the city will someday be replaced by laser printers so that employees can send a request for 50 copies of a report from their desktop rather than ask a secretary or clerk to make the copies.

The information infrastructure is like the foundation for a home, says the director. It needs to withstand all the weight, all the noise, and all the things you want to plug into it. Because IT is changing so rapidly, the city must think long-term about its infrastructure to ensure that it can be easily expanded and upgraded. Unfortunately, traditional fiber-optic vendors have not been able to support upgradability. As a result, the city laid a new type of fiber-optic conduit. From the end, it looks like a honeycomb with 19 cells, only 2 of which were used initially. New fiber bundles can easily be blown through the spare cells in the future using a special gas, thus making it easy to upgrade the fiber backbone to accommodate new services such as video teleconferencing or combined voice and data transmission.

Infrastructure investments are paid through chargeback. When the IS department places equipment on someone's desk, installs a software package on a computer, or hooks up a PC to a LAN, that equipment, software, or communication link immediately begins generating its own replacement funds. Sunnyvale charges back everything on rental rates, because it knows everything will eventually need to be replaced.

"Super" rules guide technology investments. One such rule is that the city will standardize on products to make effective use of resources. Another unwritten super rule is that a person using a computer at, say, the senior center will have the same access and response time as someone working next to the mainframe. Another IT super rule is that all projects are subject to review by an executive body that represents all city departments. Thus, continuous buy-in, support, and fine-tuning of demands forms an improvement cycle. An outcome of this super rule is a more participative executive body— one that understands departmental priority and guides the city's IT goals as a high-performance team. A joint environment is established for a consistent framework from which all departments can benefit. ∎

CONCLUSION

Distributed systems dominate the computing landscape, with the Internet now at the heart. Distributing processing, databases, and communications allow companies to move more quickly because they can more easily snap in new products and services into their existing systems. The advent of Web Services is fueling the use of the Internet to extend the tenets of distributed systems even further.

Although the concepts behind distributed systems were conceived more than 40 years ago, the use of distributed systems moved into a new era with the Internet. Before the Internet, the bulk of distributed systems were in-house, only linking systems within an enterprise. The Internet turned attention outward because it provides the infrastructure for global distributed systems. IS management can turn its attention outward toward customers, suppliers, and its business ecosystem. With IT providing the foundation for electronic collaboration within such an ecosystem, CIOs are also working closely with top management to ensure that the firm's IT infrastructure not only meshes with corporate strategy but is also flexible enough to support changes in strategy. Building a comprehensive infrastructure is the challenge facing CIOs and CTOs. Many of them got caught flat-footed with the Internet. It crept up behind them in the mid-1990s. They now realize how important infrastructure is to corporate success. Even though they might outsource the operation of their infrastructure, they and their top management peers must do the strategic thinking behind selecting infrastructure elements.

With the overall technical framework for systems provided, we now turn to the essential technologies used in distributed systems—telecommunications, information resources, and operations.

QUESTIONS AND EXERCISES

Review Questions

1. What is the difference between an architecture and an infrastructure?
2. What are the four attributes of a distributed system?
3. What does *open source* mean?
4. List and briefly explain the questions that should be asked when deciding whether to distribute computing responsibilities.
5. What are the components of the guiding framework for distributed systems as provided by Stefferud, Farber, and Dement?
6. Give seven examples of system structures that can be called *distributed*.
7. What four lessons did Northwest learn about building their PRA systems?
8. What are Gartner's five types of client-server systems? Which two did the aerospace company choose and why?
9. What are server-based computing and peer-to-peer computing?
10. According to Rifkin, what is the Napster dispute really about?
11. What are the six standards underlying Web Services?
12. Describe the rows and columns in Figure 5-13.
13. What benefits has FMC received from having defined a "tomorrow" architecture?
14. What are the four layers of IT infrastructure, according to Weill and Broadbent?
15. In what three ways can companies view an IT infrastructure?

Discussion Questions

1. Some people want all their programs and data stored locally on a PC. Others would be willing to get everything from a corporate portal. Which would you prefer? Why?
2. Web Services sounds way too complex to be viable. How are little chunks of code from many organizations really going to work together and provide a reliable and secure computing environment? Discuss.
3. Although it seems like a useful, albeit expensive, exercise to create an enterprisewide IT architecture, computing has been going on too long for management to rein in legacy systems. Discuss the pros and cons of this argument.

Exercises

1. Find a recent article in the literature that describes a distributed system.
   a. Describe it using the four attributes given in this chapter.
   b. Does it relate to the SUMURU architecture? If so, how?
   c. What benefits are claimed for the system?
   d. Describe its infrastructure.
2. Identify a company in your community that is using what it calls a distributed system. What was top management's or the business unit management's involvement in justifying the system? How do the system's characteristics compare with those given in this chapter? What challenges has the IS organization encountered in building the system, and how has it dealt with these challenges?
3. Identify a company in your local community that has an IT infrastructure. Does management see it as utility, dependent, or enabling? Explain their rationale.
4. Find a description of a Web Service. Why was this approach taken? What benefits are being received or expected?

REFERENCES

1. Wetherbe, J. C., "IS: To Centralize or to Decentralize," *SIM Network*, Society for Information Management, Chicago, IL, January 1987.
2. Stefferud, E., D. Farber, and R. Dement, "SUMURU: A Network Configuration for the Future," *Mini-Micro Systems*, May 1982, pp. 311–312.
3. Gartner EXP, 56 Top Gallant, Stamford, CT 06904; www.gartner.com:
   a. Woolfe, Roger, *Managing the Move to Client-Server*, January 1995 (from Wentworth Management Research, now part of Gartner EXP).
   b. Woolfe, Roger, and Marcus Blosch, *IT Architecture Matters*, July 2002.
   c. Weill, Peter, Mani Subramani, and Marianne Broadbent, *Reality Bites: Matching IT Infrastructure with Business Initiatives*, November 2001. Also see Weill, Peter, Mani Subramani, and Marianne Broadbent, "Building IT Infrastructure for Strategic Agility," *Sloan Management Review*, Fall 2002, Vol. 44, No. 1, pp. 57–65.
   d. Varney, Cornelia, *Justifying Infrastructure Investments*, Wentworth Management Research (now part of Gartner EXP), May 1995.
4. IBM, "IBM Java Success Stories," IBM Corporation, Armonk, NY. Available at www.ibm.com. Accessed 1999.

5. Datz, Todd, "Remote Possibilities," *CIO Magazine*, November 15, 2003. Available at www.cio.com/archive/111503/et_article.html. Accessed April 2004.

6. Rifkin, Jeremy, "Where Napster Has Gone, Others Will Follow," *Los Angeles Times*, August 21, 2000, p. A13.

7. Gottschalk, Karl, Stephen Graham, Heather Kreger, and James Snell, "Introduction to Web Services Architecture," *IBM Systems Journal*, Vol 41, No. 2, 2002, pp. 170–177.

8. Hagel, John III, and John Seely Brown, "Your Next IT Strategy," *Harvard Business Review*, October 2001, pp. 105–113.

9. Zachman, John, Personal Communication, Zachman International, 2222 Foothill Blvd., Suite 337, La Canada, CA 91011.

10. Seybold, Patricia, with Ronni Marshak, *Customers.com*, Times Books, New York, 1998.

11. This discussion of SOAs is based on three sources: (a) Schmelzer, Ronald, "Solving Today's Integration Challenges While Providing for Tomorrow's Flexibility and Agility Needs," ZapThink White Paper, November 2003. Available at www.iona.com. Accessed April 2004. (b) Datz, Todd, "What You Need to Know About Service-Oriented Architecture," *CIO Magazine*, January 15, 2004. Available at www.cio.com/archive/011504/soa.html. Accessed April 2004. (c) Cousins, Peter, and Ivan Casanova, "Service-Oriented Integration: A Strategy Brief," Iona Technologies, January 2004. Available at www.iona.com. Accessed April 2004.

12. Iona, "Credit Suisse: Business Integration Through Service-Oriented Architecture." Available at www.iona.com/info/aboutus/customers/casestudies/CreditSuisseCS.pdf. Accessed May 2004. Also see M. Pezzini, "Credit Suisse Powers Integration by Including Events," Gartner EXP Research Note, August 26, 2003.

13. Weill, Peter, and Marianne Broadbent, *Leveraging the New Infrastructure: How Market Leaders Capitalize on Information Technology*, Harvard Business School Press, Boston, 1998.

14. Weill, Peter, and Michael Vitale, "What IT Infrastructure Capabilities Are Needed to Implement E-Business Models?" *MIS Quarterly Executive*, Vol. 1, No. 1, 2002, pp. 17–34.

CHAPTER

6

MANAGING TELECOMMUNICATIONS

INTRODUCTION

This chapter examines telecommunications in the broadest sense: electronically sending data in any form from one place to another between people, machines, or objects. In this view, the telecommunications system is an electronic highway system. Generally, IS departments have been responsible for designing, building, and maintaining that information highway in the same way that governments are responsible for building and maintaining streets, roads, and freeways.

Once built, the network, with its nodes and links, provides the infrastructure for the flow of data, information, and messages. This flow is managed not by IS professionals, but by users, just as users manage the flow of vehicles on physical highways. Government agencies provide standards and laws for the flow of highway traffic that are enforced by the police and highway patrol. In the same way, IS departments select and enforce telecommunications standards for information traffic while governments divvy up the spectrum for different wireless uses. This analogy could be pursued in more detail, but the point is clear: Telecommunications is the basis for the way people and companies work today. It provides the infrastructure for moving information, just as a transportation system, such as shipping lanes, railroad right of ways, and the airspace, provides the infrastructure for the movement of people and goods.

This analogy presents telecommunications as a linking mechanism, which it is. However, the Internet has also opened up a different view of telecommunications, that of providing a *cyberspace*, a place where people can "exist" in a virtual world, where organizations can conduct business, and in fact, a place where organizational processes exist. It is an online world, a sort of cybercity. This view, too, is providing the foundation for the online economy.

However, even more is happening. Just about everything about telecommunications is shifting, from the industry itself to the protocols (the languages networks use to communicate with each other).

THE EVOLVING TELECOMMUNICATIONS SCENE

Telecommunications is exciting, perhaps too exciting for many people given the plethora of bankruptcies and plummeting prices of telecommunications stocks. The early 2000s can be viewed as a respite from and a correction of the excesses of the late 1990s when telecommunications expectations separated from reality. Even with the downturn, though, changes occurred, and the rate of change is accelerating. To give an inkling of what is happening, here are some of the major changes that are taking place.

A New Telecommunications Infrastructure Is Being Built

The oldest part of the telecommunications infrastructure is the telephone network, commonly called the public switched telephone network (PSTN), or affectionately called POTS (plain old telephone service). This global network was built on twisted-pair copper wires and was intended for voice communications. It uses analog technology (signals sent as sine waves) and circuit switching, which means a virtual (temporary) circuit is created between caller and receiver and that circuit is theirs alone to use; no other parties can share it during the duration of their telephone call. Although appropriate for delivering high-quality voice, circuit switching is inefficient because of all the unused space in the circuits when no sound is being transmitted.

The overhead of establishing a circuit was tolerable for voice calls because they lasted several minutes, notes an in-depth telecommunications study by PricewaterhouseCoopers (PwC),[1] before it became part of IBM Global Services. However, data traffic is sent in bursts that last less than a second. Opening and closing circuits at this rate is not economical, so the basic traffic-handling mechanism for data had to change.

PSTNs were also built on the premise of dumb voice telephones; therefore, they needed intelligent switches in the network to perform all the functions. Telephone company central offices house the intelligent switches that implement all the services, including call waiting, caller ID, call forwarding, conference calling, and so on.

The new telecommunications infrastructure being built around the world is aimed at transmitting data. The wired portion consists of fiber-optic links (glass fiber rather than copper wire) sending digital signals (ones and zeros instead of sine waves). The wireless portion consists of radio signals. Both use packet switching; messages are divided into packets, each with an address header, and each packet is sent separately. No circuit is created; each packet may take a different path through the network. Packets from any number of senders and of any type, whether e-mails, music downloads, voice conversations, or video clips, can be intermixed on a network segment. These networks are able to handle much more and a greater variety of traffic. Packet nets also can handle voice. The analog voice signals are translated into ones and zeros, compressed, and packetized.

Unlike voice-centric networks, data-centric networks assume intelligent user devices that provide the addressing information; therefore, the network only needs store-and-forward routers to route the packets. This architecture allows new kinds of services to be deployed much more rapidly, notes the PwC study, because the basic functions of the network need not be changed. Thus, for example, it was easy to add the World Wide Web as a new kind of layer on the Internet infrastructure. Other such layers are multiplayer gaming, e-mail, and file transfer. This infrastructure would not have been possible with PSTN. Witness the promise of videophone, which was announced at the 1939 World's Fair in New York. It still has not arrived, except over the Internet.

The Internet can handle new kinds of intelligent user devices, including Voice-over-IP (VoIP) phones, personal digital assistants (PDAs), gaming consoles, and all manner of wireless devices. It can allow these devices to handle different kinds of services, such as voice, e-mail, graphics, gaming, and so forth. Thus, the global telecommunications infrastructure is changing from a focus on voice to a focus on data.

THE TELECOMMUNICATIONS INDUSTRY IS BEING TRANSFORMED

The telecommunications infrastructure of old was originally provided by monopolies such as AT&T in the United States and government-owned postal, telephone, and telegraph agencies (PTTs) in other countries, such as Nippon Telephone and Telegraph (NTT) in Japan, Telefónica de España in Spain, and so on. Gradually, the telecommunications industry has been deregulated, country by country, although in many countries the PTT has simply become the private monopoly. Even so, competition in the industry has increased.

The telecommunications industry is becoming like the computing industry, says Rich Karlgaard, publisher of *Forbes* magazine,[2] in that each year brings predictable improvements. In fact, he believes the industry is now more competitive than the computer industry. Computer processing power has followed Moore's Law of doubling every 18 months since 1959; and it appears likely to continue at that rate for 10 more years, yielding processors with speeds of a trillion bits per second. Bandwidth on fiber, on the other hand, is now doubling capacity every 4 months.

The telecommunications industry basically has two kinds of carriers: long-distance carriers, known as interexchange carriers (IXCs), and local exchange carriers (LECs). In the United States, the deregulation of AT&T in 1984 left AT&T in the IXC business and spun off seven LECs called Regional Bell Operating Companies (RBOCs): USWest, Bell South, Ameritech, Bell Atlantic, Northwest Bell, Southwestern Bell (now SBC), and Pacific Bell. Today, only four remain; they have bought up the others.

These RBOCs provided local access to the long-distance carriers and had a monopoly on this local loop. In short, they handled *the last mile*: the connection between a subscriber and the telephone company's central office (neighborhood switch) where the network switching equipment resides. This last mile has proven to be the bottleneck in telecommunications.

Visualize the world's networks as huge fire hoses, transmitting at the whopping speed of a terabit (10^{12} bits per second) over fiber-optic cable. Then visualize the twisted-pair phone line coming into your home or business as a straw, only operating at speeds of 56 kbps (104 bits for second) for a modem or 1.2 mpbs (10^6 bits per second) for a digital subscriber line (DSL). DSL runs over the same copper wire but has improved electronics that boost the speed, allows simultaneous voice and data, and is always on, eliminating the need to dial in. The *last mile problem* is the bridging of this fire-hose-to-straw gap. See Figure 6-1.

In the 1990s, the RBOCs began encountering competition for this last mile. So the jargon expanded. RBOCs became known as incumbent local exchange carriers (ILECs) and the new competitors became competitive LECs (CLECs). The importance of CLECs is the new kinds of connection options they have brought to businesses and homes, such as cable modems, optical fiber, wireless, satellite, and faster wire lines.

FIGURE 6-1 Telecommunication Technologies and Their Speeds

Bits Per Second	Notation	Abbreviation	Amount	Term	Technologies
1,000,000,000,000	10^{12}	1 tbps	Trillion	Terabits	Optical fiber potential (and higher)
100,000,000,000	10^{11}	100 gbps			
10,000,000,000	10^{10}	10 gbps			Optical wireless local loop (20G), OC-768 (40G), WMAN (100G)
1,000,000,000	10^9	1 gbps	Billion	Gigabits	Microwave LANs (1.5G–2.0G), OC-48 (2.5G), ATM (2.5G), Gigabit Ethernet (1G), WMAN (24G)
100,000,000	10^8	100 mbps			OC-12 (622M), ATM (155M to 622M), T4 (274.176M), OC-3 (155.52M), Faster Ethernet (100M), infrared (100M), WMB (100–400M)
10,000,000	10^7	10 mbps			T3 (44.736M), E3 (34.318M), frame relay (10M), Ethernet (10M), WLANs (10M), cable modem (10M), Wi-Fi (11–54M)

Bits Per Second	Notation	Abbreviation	Amount	Term	Technologies
1,000,000	10^6	1 mbps	Million	Megabits	T2 (6.132M), infrared LAN (4M), stationary 3G wireless (2M), E1 (2.048M), DSL (1.544M to 7M), T1 (1.544M), Wi Max (1.5–10M)
100,000	10^5	100 kbps			Wireless local loop (428K), mobile 3G wireless (384K), ISDN (128K), 2G wireless (128K)
10,000	10^4	10 kbps			Modems (56K), 2.5G wireless (57K)
1,000	10^3	1 kbps	Thousand	Kilobits	2G wireless (9.6K to 14.4), infrared LAN (9.6K)
100	10^2	100 bps			
10	10^1	10 bps			

FIGURE 6-1 Continued

In response, ILECs have bundled local phone access with Internet access, and ISPs use their brand name recognition to expand into the local carrier market, becoming CLECs. You really need a scorecard to see who's who.

To illustrate these twists and turns in the telecommunications industry in the United States over the past 20 years, consider the following case of ICG,[3] whose history has mirrored these changes.

CASE EXAMPLE

ICG COMMUNICATIONS

ICG Communications is a facilities-based CLEC providing voice and data services in 25 metropolitan areas in the United States. ICG serves approximately 6,000 customers, including ISPs, IXCs, and corporate customers with medium to large businesses.

It all began in the mid-1980s in Denver, Colorado. Teleport Denver, Ltd. (TDL), built a satellite teleport with eight earth stations so it could transmit voice around the world. It could reach five continents in a single satellite hop.

In 1984, when AT&T was forced to divest itself of its local telephone companies, TDL management looked into the possibilities of offering local telephone service to Denver. They originally planned to lease circuits from the local RBOC, but the costs were too high, so they decided to install their own private fiber-optic links to connect to

(Case Continued)

the international exchange carriers that carried long-distance voice calls.

Then, in the late 1980s, when a new breed of telecommunications provider arose—the CLECs—TDL management again extended their view, this time to providing long-distance as well as private-line services to businesses.

Once the Denver network was in place in the early 1990s, its new parent, IntelCom Group, expanded its geographic presence by buying other companies that provided fiber telecommunications services. In the mid-1990s, management signed fiber lease agreements with electric utilities—an innovative strategy at the time—that allowed them to more quickly and cost-effectively expand ICG's services.

Then ICG expanded its offerings beyond fiber-based transport to offering switched services by installing switches in its key markets. In 1995, ICG also formed a strategic alliance with Southern New England Telephone through which it could offer an SS7-switched network across the United States.

The Telecom Act of 1996 allowed ICG to enter the local telephone market, so it began aggressively building staff and regional networks in California, Colorado, the Southeast United States, and the Ohio Valley. It also signed a 7-year agreement with Lucent Technologies to purchase switching systems and technical services. It entered the local telephone market in 1997, offering local, long-distance, and calling-card services to small- and medium-sized businesses. By the end of the year, ICG was serving 141,000 lines in several markets.

In 1998 and 1999, ICG moved into the Internet services arena. It merged with Netcom On-Line Communications Services, a major ISP. Hence, it could also offer data services.

In 1999, it sold the Netcom U.S. consumer customer base to MindSpring, another major ISP, to focus on Netcom's backbone network, which has 227 points of presence serving some 700 U.S. cities. ICG also entered into an agreement with MindSpring whereby MindSpring would use ICG's data network and network management capabilities. This agreement moved ICG into becoming an "Internet enabler" for ISPs.

During the first half of 1999, ICG signed a number of multiyear agreements with ISPs to provide them with access, transport, and network management services. In late 1999, it sold off its fiber-optic division and its satellite division because management decided to focus on providing (1) access and transport to ISPs, (2) telecommunications services to businesses across the United States, and (3) direct connectivity to IXCs.

When the dot-com bubble burst, ICG was not immune. The company filed for Chapter 11 bankruptcy to gain protection from its creditors, and the Bankruptcy Court of Delaware accepted its plan for reorganization. After gaining financing to reemerge, ICG moved out of bankruptcy in late 2002.

Its focus is providing broadband, dial-up Internet access, dedicated Internet access, voice and Internet Protocol (IP) solutions, and fiber-optic transport services. Its latest offerings are voice and Web conferencing and a bundled offering of voice, data, long-distance and telecom—thereby combining analog and digital communications. ■

As this case shows, ICG has moved from providing traditional voice telephone service via satellite to becoming an Internet infrastructure provider to seeking shelter in bankruptcy and reemerging as an Internet provider. It is an interesting story that mirrors the fate of the strongest CLECs and shows that all roads are indeed leading to the Internet and its IP protocol.

The Internet Is the Network of Choice

Although it may feel like old news now, the biggest telecommunications story of the past 10 years has been the Internet, the global packet-switching network that is the epitome of next-generation networks. What has surprised most people was the Internet's surprisingly fast uptake for business uses and then the fast plummet of the dot-com and telecommunications industries. However, in both arenas, the crashes were needed reactions to the excesses of the late 1990s. In the mid-1990s, the Internet caught most IS departments by surprise, not to mention the hardware and software vendors that serve the corporate IS community. Many executives are relieved that the Internet pace of the late 1990s has now slowed down so that they can plan their online business strategies rather than feel the need to react quickly to dot-com invasions in their industry.

The Internet actually began in the 1960s; it was funded by the U.S. Department of Defense's Advanced Research Projects Agency and was called ARPANET. The network was intended for electronic shipment of large scientific and research files. It was built as a distributed network, without a controlling node, so that it could continue to function if some of its nodes got knocked out in a nuclear war. Much to the surprise of its creators, it was mainly used for electronic mail among government contractors, academics, researchers, and scientists.

In 1993, the Internet was still mainly a worldwide network for researchers, scientists, academics, and individuals who participated in news groups. It was all text, no graphics. It had e-mail for sending messages, maintaining e-mail lists, and interacting with news groups. It had file transfer protocol (FTP) for sending files, Telnet for logging onto another computer, and Gopher for searching and downloading files from databases.

That all changed in 1994 when the World Wide Web was invented by Tim Berners-Lee at CERN in Geneva. This graphical layer of the Internet made it much more user-friendly. Web sites had addresses specified by their URL. Its multimedia Web pages were formatted using HTML. The Web sites could be accessed via an easy-to-use browser on a PC. Hyperlinks hidden behind highlighted words on a Web page, when clicked, would jump to the linked page. Following the links became known as "Web surfing." This graphical electronic world was first populated by homepages of computer geeks and young people. The Web's use by businesses began skyrocketing a few years later, in the late 1990s.

The Internet has done for telecommunications what the IBM PC did for computing: It brought it to the masses. In 1981, when the IBM PC was introduced, its architecture was open; all the design specifications were published. This openness led to thousands of peripheral manufacturers, component makers, and clone makers producing compatible products. An entire industry developed around this open architecture. The same has happened with the Internet because it provides the same kind of openness, this time in the telecommunications arena. Vendors have a standard set of protocols to work with so that products can work with each other. Businesses do not need to commit to a proprietary architecture. Like the PC, this openness yields the most innovative solutions and the most competitive prices.

The Internet has three attributes that make it important to corporations: ubiquity, reliability, and scalability. It is global, thus it is ubiquitous. Enterprises, both large and small, potentially have global reach with a browser and global presence with a Web site. As noted earlier, the Internet was designed to survive computer crashes by allowing alternate routing. This capability makes it highly reliable. People might not be able to access a crashed server, but they can still access all other nodes that are operating. The Internet has also been able to sustain incredible growth since its beginning. Specific Web sites can handle tremendous amounts of traffic, in the tens of millions of hits a day, if they have been properly designed. That is scalability!

Today, the protocols underlying the Internet have become the protocols of choice in corporate networks for internal communications as well as communications with the outside world. The norm is now end-to-end IP networks.

To illustrate how a company might build a corporate network from scratch utilizing the Internet, here is the fictitious example of XYZ Company.

CASE EXAMPLE

XYZ COMPANY

XYZ Company, which makes and sells widgets, is in the process of installing a corporate network. The CTO has a myriad of decisions to make. Of course he wants employees to be able to access each other, corporate data, and the Internet, so he will create an IP network using the Internet's standard protocol, TCP/IP, which packages data into packets, each with a header that tells where it is to be delivered.

The Internet will be the heart of XYZ's corporate operation. Hence the CTO will create an intranet for use by employees, an extranet for use by suppliers and some large customers, and of course, the Internet as the all-important central public network.

The CTO has a basic way of thinking about all the computer-based devices in his company: He sees them as either clients or servers. Computers, handhelds, cell phones, and wired phones used by the employees are clients; they make requests of other computers. Computers that respond to these requests are servers. They can act as storage devices for shared files for teams or departments or even customers. They may house shared applications or shared peripherals or they can connect the client devices to a network, including the Internet. Now that IP phones offer good voice quality, he may opt for them as well.

Serving Remote Users

Every PC will be outfitted with a Network Interface Card (NIC) that lets it talk to the network. XYZ has four choices of communication wiring: twisted pair (the standard telephone line), coaxial cable (like cable TV), fiber-optic (glass fiber that carries

(Case Continued)

signals via light pulses), and wireless. Fiber carries tremendous amounts of traffic and is expensive; therefore, it is mainly used in backbone networks. Each NIC will support the medium the company will be using.

Each computer also needs a network operating system. These days, it is part of the computer's operating system. Furthermore, some of the machines need a modem to convert (modulate) the digital signal from the computer to an analog signal for the telephone or cable system, and vice versa.

For employees working from computers in their homes, who need to transmit larger and larger files such as PowerPoint presentations, the CTO could choose DSL modems, which communicate at 1.2 mbps (10^6). Or he could choose cable modems, which communicate at a whopping 10 mbps. Like DSL, cable modems are not available everywhere. Also, like DSL, they are always on; no dial-up is needed. However, this convenience can present security problems because the session code does not change as it does with dial-up sessions.

The CTO needs to decide how to connect these remote users to the corporate network and provide the speed and security they need. The salespeople, for instance, no longer have company-supplied offices; their offices are in their homes. They have company-supplied laptops and PDAs; they dial in from hotels, client sites, or their homes or use an always-on personal communication service (PCS) for e-mail.

Serving Local Users

In the office, all the computers and telephones will be connected directly to an always-on LAN.

The various LANs in XYZ's offices will use three types of computers to route traffic.

- *Hubs* are repeaters; they forward packets of data from one machine to another. When a number of computers share a hub, data sent from one goes to all the others. This configuration can get congested with many computers, so hubs will only be used within a work group.

- *Switches* are smarter; they only forward packets to the port of the intended computer using the addressing information in each packet's header. Switches will be used to connect work groups.

- *Routers* are smarter still; they use a routing table to pass along a packet to the next appropriate router on a network. Thus, they can direct packets via the most efficient route or relay packets around a failed network component. Routers also link network segments that use different protocols, such as linking an Apple-Talk network with an Ethernet network. Routers also can connect to WANs. XYZ will use routers to connect its LANs to a WAN.

The CTO will likely choose the Fast Ethernet Protocol for his IP-based LANs. It has a speed of 100 mpbs (10^8) to accommodate employees' multimedia and video needs. Using Ethernet, when a computer has a message to send, it broadcasts the stream of packets and then listens for an acknowledgment of receipt. If it does not receive a reply within a specified time, it rebroadcasts, presuming

(Case Continued)

the packets collided with packets from other computers and did not reach their destination.

The LAN will give in-office employees an always-on connection to the company's intranet, its employee-only Web site that is protected from the outside world by a firewall. The firewall is a server that lets in e-mail but does not permit access to applications or executable code. The intranet will essentially be "the office" for XYZ, because it will house all the firm's forms, processes, and documents. It will also be accessible by remote employees.

Communicating Between Offices

XYZ employees need to communicate between sites, so they need some sort of WAN. As expected, the CTO has choices here as well. Asynchronous transfer mode (ATM) is high speed—up to 622 mpbs (10^8). ATM is used by telephone companies for their network backbones; they then offer ATM services to companies like XYZ for their WANs. However, due to the high cost of ATM long-distance bandwidth, the CTO might not be able to afford it.

A fairly new option to link several offices in a city or to link floors within a building is Gigabit Ethernet, which operates at speeds of 1 gbps (10^9 bits per second). One hundred gigabit Ethernet (10^{11}) is on the horizon. Gigabit Ethernet has been outselling ATM because it is less costly. It is definitely the option the CTO would prefer.

These issues are some of the major considerations for the CTO. He is definitely going to base all his decisions on being IP-centric. ■

Extranets. Not long after creating intranets for employees, businesses realized they could extend the concept into extranets—a special part of the intranet for use by trading partners, customers, and suppliers for online commerce. The following case of National Semiconductor illustrates the use of an extranet and shows how the company tackled the challenge of conducting business online globally.

CASE EXAMPLE

NATIONAL SEMICONDUCTOR

National Semiconductor, with headquarters in Santa Clara, California, designs and manufactures semiconductor products used in personal computers, consumer electronics products (cars, cameras, cell phones, and so on), and telecommunications systems. National is focusing on its key competency—advanced analog and mixed analog/digital signal technologies—for use in the newest breed of electronic

(Case Continued)

devices, information appliances, which are low-cost, easy-to-use, wireless devices that interact with the Internet without the use of a PC. National has sales of $2 billion and employs some 11,000 people around the globe.

To gain market share and move into new markets in Europe, South America, and Asia, National looked to the Web. It created an intranet that the sales force could access to keep up-to-date on products and place orders. It created the "National Advisor" using Internet-based push technology to electronically send news, sales reports, and customer information to the sales force and its management.

National also created an extranet for distributors and channel partners and a Web site for design engineers who use its components in electronic and telecommunications products. This Web site contains descriptions of more than 30,000 products in the form of PDF databooks. Design engineers can view these databooks and order samples either via the Web or through distributors.

To give far-flung engineers decent download times of these 10k-to-200k-size files, National initially installed mirrored servers in Germany and Hong Kong and planned for eight more sites. However, management discovered that the logistics of maintaining 10 such sites would be a nightmare as well as cost prohibitive at approximately $4 million a year.

They thus turned to outsourcing to a company with data centers around the globe that offers hosting and other Internet infrastructure services. It replicates Web sites on edge servers, which are servers close to users (on the edge of the Internet), so that download speed is fast. Some servers even perform language translation so that when a request is made, the closest edge server detects the type of user device, type of network, and country (and its regulations) and adapts the content to those conditions.

The cost would be $400,000 a year, or one-tenth the in-house cost. More importantly, performance was so much better that National could reach markets in Asia, Eastern Europe, Indonesia, and Latin America, where Internet service was generally slow. In addition, the company could distribute daily customer data and market information within 24 hours, which would speed product development and responses to design engineers' queries.

National's Web site now supports 1 million design engineers around the globe who download more than 10,000 databooks a day, in about 2 seconds each. The company only needs to replicate its site once; the hosting company takes care of the global coverage. Finally, National receives reports on which pages are being accessed in each part of the world, which is important information to the sales and marketing staff. ∎

Digital Convergence Has Become a Reality

Digital convergence is the intertwining of various forms of media—voice, data, and video. Convergence is now occurring because, as just noted, IP has become the networking protocol of choice. When all forms of media can be digitized, put into packets, and sent over an IP network, they can be managed and manipulated digitally and integrated in highly imaginative ways. IP telephony and video telephony have been the last frontiers of convergence—and now they are a reality.

IP Telephony.   Recently, enterprises have been investigating the use of the Internet to transmit voice to replace their telephone systems. This new Internet use is called Voice-over-IP (VoIP), Internet telephony, or IP telephony. According to James Cope,[4] it works in the following manner: A special IP phone with an Ethernet jack in the back instead of the standard telephone jack is attached to a company LAN, perhaps through a PC. Rather than the analog signals sent by traditional phones, the IP phone generates a digital signal. That signal is routed over the LAN just like any other data in packets either (1) to another IP phone on the LAN, (2) through the company's WAN to a distant IP phone on another of the company's LANs, or (3) through an IP voice gateway to the PSTN to a standard telephone.

Few companies have yet given up their telephone networks for a VoIP network, but as the cost differential continues, more will switch. Like other devices on a network, IP phones have an IP address, so they can be easily moved to another location and still be located.

IP telephony became the hot telecommunications technology in 2004. Until that time, voice quality over the Internet was poor, so people were not interested in switching to digital IP phones. But by 2003, voice quality was sufficient for early adopters, and surprisingly, Cisco became the largest IP telephone company, shipping over 3 million IP phones by mid-2004 and purportedly shipping over 2 million in the third quarter of 2004 alone. (As the primary supplier of Internet routers, Cisco also expects to sell lots of its routers to telecommunications companies as they switch their networks from analog to digital networks.)

Voice has become another digital media that can be managed electronically, from one's PC, for example. One new possibility this digitization presents is ad hoc conferencing (or just-in-time collaboration, as it is also called). For instance, with the appropriate VoIP infrastructure, two people instant messaging with each other via their computers could seamlessly switch to a voice conversation, talking rather than typing. Furthermore, because each person's telephone, instant messaging, and e-mail share one address book, they can instant message, phone, or e-mail others to join their call just by clicking on their names. Anyone in the conference can pull up a PowerPoint slide or a spreadsheet to discuss a point on it—or even scribble on it—or view a new video clip. They can even archive the call and send it to other people.

Video Telephony.   The same is happening with video telephony, which is not video conferencing via a PBX, but rather video over IP. With the appropriate IP infrastructure, video telephony can be, say, launched from an instant-messaging conversation. IP phones with cameras also facilitate it, phone to phone.

Oodles of new converged products are flooding the marketplace now that high-quality voice has become IP based. In fact, when VoIP is mentioned these days, it is done so in the context of collaboration. The point is not so much that VoIP offers essentially free voice calling worldwide over IP networks. The point is that VoIP now permits cost-effective, full-media collaboration worldwide. That is a new paradigm, which can change how businesses work. One early effect has been the boom in offshore outsourcing.

In addition, some new converged offerings add *presence*, by indicating how someone can be reached at a particular moment, often through a green indicator beside the appropriate contact option in the converged address book. Such a system then automatically dials that option. Presence will likely become a major feature of converged IP systems.

The Toronto Pearson International Airport illustrates the reality of digital convergence via IP.

CASE EXAMPLE

TORONTO PEARSON INTERNATIONAL AIRPORT

Toronto Pearson International Airport is Canada's busiest airport, with 3 terminals serving 65 airlines and 24.5 million passengers in 2003. In April 2004, a new terminal opened that Cisco touts as a next-generation showcase because its infrastructure is a single, common-use IP network.[5]

The network is *common use* because its infrastructure is shared by all the airport tenants. Its backbone is two independent high-speed rings for reliability and growth, with over 100 network switches, 1,000 IP phones, and 1,000 wireless access points. There is no separate telephone network, just one IP network that combines 14 communications systems and that supports integrated voice, data, and video.

Each tenant has a private LAN for its own voice, data, and video applications. The LAN is accessed via virtual private networking (VPN) technology so that it is private and secure. Yet each network can be accessed from anywhere in the terminal with the appropriate authorization by just plugging in, either via a wired or a wireless access point. The wireless network is highly restricted and tightly controlled so that the data traveling over it is also private and secure.

In essence, the airport authority acts as a service provider to the airlines, tenants, and passengers. The network is used for all applications. For passenger check-in, for instance, the gates have IP phones as well as data connections. Each gate can be used by any airline; the gate crew just plugs in to access the airline's voice and data services. Passengers can also check in at any kiosk for any flight for any airline, which has reduced congestion.

Baggage tracking is integrated with passenger reconciliation via the network, improving security. The network also supports security systems, emergency responses, video surveillance, and network security.

The network and the interlinked applications it permits have reduced network operations costs, consolidated network support (because there is only one network), increased operational efficiency in the terminal (in baggage handling and check-in), enhanced security and made it consistent, and increased capacity (handling 15 percent more passengers soon after the terminal opened). ∎

Digital convergence is setting up a collision among three massive industries, state Stephen Baker and Heather Green.[6] The first is the $1.1 trillion computer industry, led by the United States. The second is the $225 billion consumer electronics industry, which has Asian roots and new aggressive Chinese companies. The third is the $2.2 trillion telecommunications industry, with leading wireless players in Europe and Asia and data networking leaders in Silicon Valley. These industries need each other to offer converged services. Innovative offerings and services are now being released by large and small companies alike. It is not yet clear which business models or offerings will emerge as the big winners. It is only clear that this is a disruptive time for all three industries, note Baker and Green, as it likely is for a host of other industries as well, such as the music, television, gaming, and movie industries, to name just four.

The Internet and its protocols are taking over. To understand the complexity of telecommunications, we now look at the underlying framework for the Internet: the OSI Reference Model.

The OSI Reference Model Underlies Today's Networks

The worldwide telephone system has been so effective in connecting people because it is based on common standards. Today's packet-switching networks are also following some standards. The underpinning of these standards is the OSI Reference Model.

Closed Versus Open Networks.   The first concept that is important to understand is the difference between closed and open networks. A *closed network* is one that is offered by one supplier and to which only the products of that supplier can be attached. Mainframe and minicomputer manufacturers used this approach for years to lock in their customers. Closed networks were originally adopted for the corporate, regional, and site levels of computing described in Chapter 5. Companies generally used the proprietary network offered by their minicomputer or mainframe manufacturer. In the Internet world, the first commercial offerings (CompuServe, Prodigy, America Online, and Microsoft Network) also used proprietary software initially. However, as direct connection to the Internet spread, these firms all finally embraced the Internet's open network approach.

An *open network* is based on national or international standards so that the products of many manufacturers can attach to it. Open networks have been favored by suppliers serving the ecosystem, department, work group, and individual levels of computing described in Chapter 5. Today, proprietary networks are out and open networks are in because no provider is large enough to serve all of a firm's telecommunications needs — to say nothing of connecting the firm to other enterprises and people.

We now live in an open systems world, and the most important telecommunications architecture is the OSI Reference Model.

Why It Is Called a Reference Model.   The International Standards Organization (ISO) and other standards bodies have adopted the seven-level OSI Reference Model to guide the development of international standards for networks of computers. It is called a *reference model* because it only recommends the functions to be performed in each of the seven layers; it does not specify detailed standards for each layer. Those details are left up to the standards bodies in the adopting countries. OSI is used by suppliers to make their products interconnectable. Understanding the

OSI Reference Model is a step toward understanding how telecommunications systems actually work.

An Analogy: Mailing a Letter. In the model's layered architecture, control information is used to route messages to their destination. The following is a four-level analogy of an executive mailing a paper document to another executive (Figure 6-2). Although mailing letters is old-fashioned, this example makes the intricacies of message passing understandable. Notice that control information—the address and type of delivery—is on the envelope or mailbag. This control information determines the services to be provided by the next lower layer, and it contains addressing information for the corresponding

FIGURE 6-2 How Control Information Is Used to Route Messages

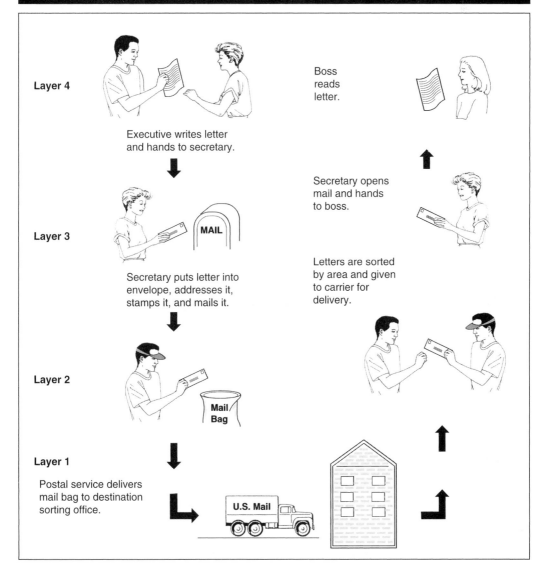

layer on the receiving end. It defines the interfaces between the layers as well as the dialog within a layer.

- At layer 4, the business executive writes a letter and gives it to a secretary.
- At layer 3, the secretary puts the letter into an envelope, addresses the envelope, puts the return address on the envelope, stamps it, and then mails it.
- At layer 2, the mail carrier takes the letter to the postal sorting office where all mail for the same postal district is put into one bag with the destination postal office name on it. Mail of different types—express mail, first-class mail, third-class mail—have their own bags.
- At layer 1, the postal service delivers the mail bag to the destination sorting office.
- At layer 2, the sorting office checks that the bag has been delivered to the right office. Then the letters are sorted by area and passed on to the individual carriers who deliver them.
- At layer 3, the recipient's secretary rejects any mail delivered to the wrong address, opens the letter, and passes it to the recipient, saying, "Here's a letter from . . . "
- At layer 4, the recipient takes the letter and reads it.

When a layer receives a message from the next higher layer, it performs the requested services and then wraps that message in its own layer of control information for use by the corresponding layer at the receiving end. It then passes this bundle to the layer directly below it. On the receiving end, a layer receiving a bundle from a lower layer unwraps the outermost layer of control information, interprets that information, and acts on it. Then it discards that layer of wrapping and passes the bundle to the next higher layer.

The Model's Seven Layers. In a similar way, the OSI Reference Model describes the types of control data produced by each layer. See Figure 6-3.

FIGURE 6-3 The OSI Reference Model

Layer	Name	Job	Protocol Examples
7	Application Layer	Interface to application	HTTP, X.500, X.400, ODA, Internet key exchange (IKE), Postscript
6	Presentation Layer	Translates data to and from language in Layer 7	NetBIOS
5	Session Layer	Controls dialog, acts as moderator for a session	Secure Sockets Layer (SSL)
4	Transport Layer	Controls flow, ensures reliable packet delivery	TCP
3	Network Layer	Addresses and routes packets	IP, X.25, Packet-level Protocol
2	Logical Link Layer	Makes sure no data are lost or garbled	Ethernet, Token Ring, FDDI, ISDN, ATM, Frame relay
1	Physical Layer	Defines physical connection to network	Ethernet 50 ohm coaxial cable, 10BaseT, twisted pair, fiber-optic cable

Starting at the top of the model, or the layer closest to users, here are the layers and what they basically do.

- *Layer 7 is the Application Layer.* This layer contains the protocols embedded in the applications we use. One familiar protocol at this level is HTTP, which anyone who has surfed the Web has used to locate a Web site. Other TCP/IP protocols at this level are FTP, for transferring files on the Internet, and Telnet, for logging onto and using a remote computer on the Internet. Other protocols at this level permit worldwide communication in various ways. For instance ISO's X.500 directory services protocol is for creating distinct Internet (or other) mailing addresses. OSI's X.400 mail handling service is for permitting e-mail systems to handle e-mail created and sent from dissimilar systems.

- *Layer 6 is the Presentation Layer.* The telecommunications protocols in this layer translate data to and from the language and format used in Layer 7. This layer does not have many familiar protocols.

- *Layer 5 is the Session Layer.* Telecommunications protocols in this layer control the dialog for a session and act as a moderator, seeing that messages are sent as directed and interrupted if necessary. An important protocol in this layer is Secure Sockets Layer (SSL), which provides Internet security. It uses a combination of public key and other cryptography to provide confidentiality, data integrity, and authentication.

- *Layer 4 is the Transport Layer.* This layer ensures reliable packet delivery. Protocols in this layer handle flow control and ensure the integrity of each message, resequencing portions if necessary. A main protocol at this level is Transmission Control Protocol (TCP), which is the TCP found in TCP/IP. TCP manages the connections made by IP in the next lower layer, Layer 3.

- *Layer 3 is the Network Layer.* Protocols in this layer address and route packets to their destination. Here resides the all-important IP, which allows packets to traverse an *internet* — that is, a network of networks.

- *Layer 2 is the Logical Link Layer.* Protocols at this layer mainly do error correction, making sure that no data is lost or garbled. LAN protocols, such as Ethernet and Token Ring, work here.

- *Layer 1 is the Physical Layer.* Protocols at this level are responsible for defining the physical connection of devices to a network. This level is the most basic and actually defines the electrical and mechanical characteristics of connections. Thus, these protocols describe modem standards as well as the characteristics of transmission wires, such as Ethernet 50-ohm coaxial cable, 10BaseT twisted-pair wire, and so on.

These layers define the OSI model, which has provided the world with a map for implementing today's telecommunications architecture.

The Rate of Change Is Accelerating

Although no one seems to know for sure, many people speculate that data traffic surpassed voice traffic either in 1999 or 2000. Changes are still moving at a fast clip, even with the retrenching in the telecommunications industry. Author George Gilder[7] explains why he believes the pace of IT change is picking up, and even more importantly, why it will increase faster still.

Gilder notes that the technologies of sand (silicon chips), glass (fiber optics), and air (wireless telecommunications) are governed by exponential rules. *Mead's Law*, named after Carver Mead of California Institute of Technology, says that N transistors on a sliver of silicon yield N^2 performance and value. It is the rule of semiconductors, which is why this technology has been so powerful. This law of semiconductors now is joined by the *law of the telecosm*—networking N computers yields N^2 performance and value. Combining the two laws leads to the compounding force of exponentials that have been sweeping through the world economy.

To get a sense of the power of exponents and why it is inexorable, consider the story of the emperor of China and the inventor of chess, says Gilder. The emperor was so exultant with the invention of chess that he told the inventor he could have anything he wanted in his kingdom. The inventor thought for a moment and then said, "Just one grain of rice, your majesty, on the first square, two on the second, four grains of rice on the third, and so on through the 64 squares of the chess board."

Of the two possible outcomes to this story, one is that the emperor goes bankrupt, because at 10 grains per square inch, 2^{64} grains of rice would cover the entire surface of the earth with rice fields two times over, oceans included. The other possibility, which is even more alarming, is that the inventor loses his head. Confronted with exponential technologies, emperors often decapitate. One rule of this story is "Keep an eye on the emperor," says Gilder, because they can suppress the spread of technology quite effectively. The governments of many countries have done just that in stifling IT through their PTTs.

It is also worth noticing, says Gilder, that at the halfway point (the 32nd square), the emperor only needs to give 2^{32} grains of rice (4 billion), which he could easily do from his rice fields. Therefore, nothing much happens during the first 32 squares. But after that, look out.

To relate this story to the present day, Gilder presents the following astounding facts: In 1995, exactly 32 doublings of computer power had occurred since the invention of the digital computer after World War II. Therefore, since 1995, we have been on "the second half of the chess board," and a stream of profound developments has taken place. E-mail outnumbered postal mail for the first time in 1995—95 billion external e-mails to 85 billion postal mails. The number of PC sales overtook the number of TV sales in late 1995. And on and on. Such changes will only accelerate, he predicts. For this reason, everyone in business must become comfortable with technology to cope with a world of ever-increasing technological change.

The Optical Era Will Provide Bandwidth Abundance

Gilder also predicts an abundance of bandwidth around the world. He notes that an economic era is defined by the plummeting price of the key factor of production. During the industrial era, that key factor was horsepower, as defined in kilowatt hours, which dropped from many dollars to 7.5 cents. Since the 1960s, the driving force of economic growth has been the plummeting price of transistors, translated into MIPS and bits of semiconductor memory. The latter has fallen 68 percent a year, from $7 some 35 years ago to a millionth of a cent today.

We are now at another historic cliff of cost in a new factor of production: bandwidth. "If you thought the price of computing dropped rapidly in the last decade, just wait until you see what happens with communication bandwidth," says Gilder, referencing a remark by Andy Grove, CEO of Intel. Up to this point, we have used MIPS and bits to compensate for the limited availability of bandwidth, says Gilder, but now we are moving into an era of bandwidth abundance.

Fiber-optic technology is just as important as microchip technology. Currently, 40 million miles of fiber-optic cable have been laid around the world. However, half of it is dark; that is, it is not used. The other half is used to just one-millionth of its potential, because every 25 miles it must be converted to electronic pulses to amplify and regenerate the signal. The bandwidth of the optical fiber has been limited by the switching speed of transistors, 2.5 to 10 billion cycles per second.

The intrinsic capacity of each thread is much greater. There is 10 times more capacity in the frequencies used in the air for communication, from AM radio to KU-band satellite. The capacity of each thread is 1,000 times the switching speed of transistors—25 terahertz. As a result, using all-optical amplifiers (recently invented), we could send all the telephone calls in the United States on the peak moment of Mother's Day on one fiber thread. Putting thousands of fiber threads in a sheath creates an era of bandwidth abundance that will dwarf the era of MIPS and bits. Or to give a more personal example from *Business Week*,[8] downloading a digital movie, such as *The Matrix*, takes more than 7 hours using a cable modem and 1 hour over Ethernet; it would take 4 seconds on an optical connection.

Over the next decade, bandwidth will expand 10 times as fast as computer power and completely transform the economy, predicts Gilder.

The Wireless Century Begins

The goal of wireless is to do everything we can do on wired networks, but without the wire, says Craig Mathias of Farpoint Group, an expert on wireless telecommunications.[9a] A better term than *wireless* would be *radio*, because most wireless is over-the-air radio signals—for nationwide networks as well as LANS.

Einstein defined a wired telegraph as being a very long cat with its head in Los Angeles and its tail in New York. When you pull its tail, it meows in Los Angeles Wireless is the same, but there is no cat, says Mathias. Wireless actually goes back to Benjamin Franklin, who believed energy could move through the air. Then Guglielmo Marconi created the first radio in an 1895 broadcast.

The problem with wireless is that radio waves are nondeterministic; that is, you cannot tell if a transmission will reach its intended antenna. Furthermore, as people move around, the relationship between the transmitter and the receiver changes. That's how calls get dropped. Wireless networks also experience interference, echoes, fading, and power limitations.

Wireless communications have been with us for some time in the form of cell phones, very small aperture terminals (VSATs), pagers, building-to-building microwave links, infrared networks, and wireless LANs in warehouses. Tomorrow's uses span a vast spectrum. We are on the cusp of an uptick in wireless use, says Mathias.

Frank Dzubeck, a long-time telecommunications consultant,[10] agrees, stating that whereas the twentieth century was the Wireline Century, the twenty-first century will be the Wireless Century. The motivation for laying copper wire, cable, and fiber throughout the twentieth century was voice communications. The motivation for wireless is data. Dzubeck sees wireless equivalents arriving that rival today's wireline technologies. But before delving into these alternatives, it's important to understand the distinction between licensed and unlicensed radio frequencies.

Licensed Versus Unlicensed Frequencies. Some frequencies of the radio spectrum are licensed by governments for specific purposes; others are not. The distinction has become very important in the wireless arena because it has led to the rapid innovation, and resulting tumult, the telecommunications industry is currently experiencing.

Anyone can create a wireless device to operate in unlicensed frequencies without first getting a license from the government, notes Heather Green.[11] Wi-Fi and other technologies mentioned here use unlicensed frequencies. This has led to greater competition, more innovation, and faster changes in unlicensed technologies than in those using licensed frequencies. The licensed portions of the spectrum are owned by large companies that can afford government licenses that give them a monopolistic hold on specific frequencies. In the absence of competition, these companies have tended to be more plodding in introducing new innovations. But now they face more fleet unlicensed competitors.

The devices that tap unlicensed frequencies are cheaper than their licensed counterparts because they do not need to absorb the huge billion-dollar licensing fees. This discrepancy has caused major pricing disparities, which is good for consumers, but not for licensees.

The downside of the unlicensed frequencies, though, is the possibility of collisions between signals in these parts of the radio spectrum. That is why, notes Green, there is so much lobbying in the United States for the U.S. Federal Communications Commission to take away frequencies from the major TV broadcasters and open it up for unlicensed uses.

This section discusses wireless technologies for networks that cover different distances, from a few feet to thousands of miles, as shown in Figure 6-4:

- ***Wireless Personal Area Networks (WPANs).*** Networks that provide high-speed connections between devices that are up to 30 feet apart.

- ***Wireless Local Area Networks (WLANs).*** Networks that provide access to corporate computers in office buildings, retail stores, and hospitals, or access to Internet "hot spots" where people congregate.

- ***Wireless Metropolitan Area Networks (WMANs).*** Networks that provide connections in cities and campuses at distances up to 30 miles.

- ***Wireless Wide Area Networks (WWANs).*** Networks that provide broadband wireless connections over thousands of miles

WPANs. For distances of a few feet, the high-bandwidth wireline technology is USB—the ubiquitous port on PCs for fast connections to printers, monitors, DVD drives, and the like. The equivalent wireless technology, notes Dzubeck, is IEEE 802.15, which is also known as ultrawideband (UWB) and 802.15.3 (WiMedia). It can transmit from 100 to 400 Mbps (or higher), and it uses unlicensed bandwidth. Green foresees UWB being

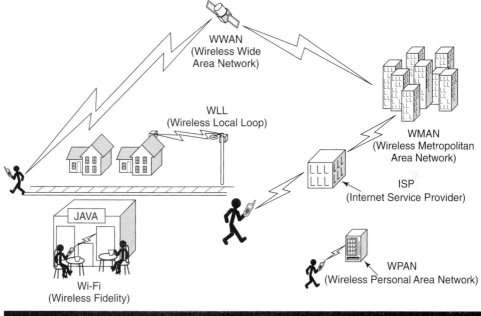

FIGURE 6-4 The Span of Wireless

used to transmit huge files from a laptop sitting in the trunk of a salesperson's car to the PDA being held in the front seat. However, standards are not yet in place.

WLANs.   For distances greater than several hundred feet, the high-speed wireline technology has been Ethernet, transmitting at 4 to 10 Mbps. Its wireless counterpart is IEEE 802.11, also known as Wi-Fi. Some people call Wi-Fi the wireless technology for the last 100 feet. Using a wireless modem card, which is essentially a radio transmitter, a laptop or PDA can transmit at 11 Mbps. Newer 802.11 standards are increasing speed and distance.

Wi-Fi is replacing wired LANs in offices and creating wireless LANs where none previously existed—hot spots. A *hot spot* is an area around a Wi-Fi relay antenna that transmits the wireless signal from a laptop or PDA to a nearby computer or to an ISP to link to the Internet. Some hot spots are public; some are private; some are free; others charge by use or subscription. They are now found wherever people congregate—in restaurants, airports, hotel lobbies, parks, convention centers, and so on.

One private use of Wi-Fi is in cash registers, notes Green, so that salespeople can check inventory and prices at the register rather than having to check the racks. Such uses will grow, she believes, especially for people who must be on the move in an area, such as a hospital, a construction site, a warehouse, an airport terminal, and such.

The following example is a fairly typical use of a WLAN in manufacturing. The importance of this example is that the LAN is used to provide visibility into manufacturing operations, which is a crucial first step that companies need to make internally to take advantage of online commerce.

CASE EXAMPLE

BMW

BMW builds more than 1 million vehicles a year in Germany and the United States. It opened a facility in South Carolina, and more than 30 suppliers have built facilities nearby to work with BMW. When this plant was slated to take on the manufacture of the company's sport utility vehicle, BMW wanted to implement the new assembly line quickly, which meant helping its suppliers scale up quickly as well.

Real-time delivery of data to the suppliers was one key to moving quickly. Suppliers needed accurate inventory data on the components they were supplying to BMW so that they knew when to make just-in-time deliveries to the plant. BMW uses SAP's ERP system to track parts inventory. To gather the inventory data that needed to be fed into the ERP, BMW decided to place bar codes on each part. The bar codes could then be scanned as the parts moved through the assembly process so that BMW's planners, operations personnel, and suppliers would know the current status of all parts.

Originally, BMW used Intermec bar code scanners attached to hard-wired data terminals at different locations on the plant floor. But more recently, it upgraded to Intermec's wireless scanning system. The scanner terminals transmit the data from the bar code readers to the SAP ERP via a wireless network that covers the entire 2-million-square-foot plant. The system uses radio frequency (RF) technology. The move to wireless allows BMW to more quickly reconfigure or expand the data collection system. Stations are simply moved; they do not need to be rewired.

A number of BMW's suppliers have followed suit and have implemented wireless data collection networks in their operations. As a result, the supply chain—from supplier to supplier warehouse to BMW's production line to shipment to a dealer—is supported by a flow of data that travels over interconnected wireless and wired networks. ∎

WMANs. For distances of 10 to 30 miles, three wireline technologies have been used for local-loop connections and access to cable networks: T-1, cable modem, and DSL.

The wireless equivalent to these wireline technologies is 802.16, which can deliver speeds of 5 to 10 Mbps over these distances. The stationary version is called WiMax (Worldwide Interoperability for Microwave Access). Like Wi-Fi, WiMax creates a hot spot around its radio antenna. It is perfect for aggregating 802.11 hot spots, notes Dzubeck, giving them access to a long-distance carrier network. Proprietary broadband microwave transmission capabilities have been around for years, notes Green, connecting buildings on a campus, for example. What is new with WiMax is that it is attempting to standardize the technology. Once it no longer uses proprietary technology, equipment costs will plummet.

The mobile version of 802.16 (also called WiMax) could replace cellular technologies, such as GSM, which is used in cell phones, notes Dzubeck. As yet, though, there are no standards for mobile WiMax. It also has a competitor in the licensed spectrum, notes Green, called Mobile-Fi. It, too, lacks standards. Green envisions both technologies eventually providing high-speed (1.5 Mbps) connections to devices being used in moving vehicles and trains.

Cellular companies offer a third option called 3G (third generation), which also uses licensed spectra. The new 3G networks are slower (.3 to .5 Mbps), notes Green, but they are reliable and widely available, unlike Mobile-Fi or WiMax. Some cities already have wireless broadband Internet access via a 3G mobile phone network.

Wireless local loop.   Within the WMAN category is the local loop, or "the last mile," where individual homes and offices are connected to a telephone company's central office a few miles away. Eventually, high-speed wireless will be available for the last mile, notes Dzubeck. Newly released spectra (71 to 76 GHz, 81 to 86 GHz, and 92 to 95 GHz) will enable high-speed connections of 2.48 Gbps and 100 Gbps (in its next generation) for up to 1 mile. This speed is carrier-grade quality, so it will be used to replace fiber in the last mile.

WWANs.   Whether the subject is wireless WANs or LANs, the only two wireless technologies are infrared light and radio airwaves (sine waves at specific frequencies) up into the microwave range. Figure 6-5 shows the electromagnetic spectrum and the broadcast frequencies where the different technologies lie.

The most familiar wide area mobile wireless technology is cell phones, where *cell* refers to a geographic area with a radio transmitter and receiver. The range of a cell explains why a cell phone used in a moving car fades in and out: As the call is passed from one cell to another it fades out of one range and into another. In essence, a cell phone is like a miniature radio station, says Roth, broadcasting on a certain bandwidth. With the cellular structure, a phone only needs to compete for bandwidth with other phones in the cell. Cell phones operate in the upper radio waves in the microwave frequency band of 2.4 to 5 GHz.

1G cellular.   First-generation (1G) cell phones used analog technology and circuit switching. Callers were charged for the amount of time they used the circuit, not for the amount of information transmitted. And, like a telephone or modem, users dialed in.

In the early 1980s, Europe had nine cell phone standards. But seeing the need for one standard to allow continent-wide communication, the European countries developed a digital standard called Global System for Mobile Communications (GSM). GSM operates at a slow 9.6 kbps, but it has encryption to prevent eavesdropping. GSM has become the mobile telephony standard, even in the United States. Unlike the computing industry, a number of the leading global telecom manufacturers are outside the United States. NTT is in Japan, Ericsson is in Sweden and Nokia is in Finland.

Frequency	Frequency Name	Technologies	Spectrum Uses
3,000 EHz		Gamma rays	
300 EHz			
30 EHz			
3 EHz		X-rays	
300 PHz			
30 PHz		Ultraviolet radiation	
3 PHz			
		Visible light	
300 THz		Infrared radiation	
30 THz			
3 THz			
300 GHz			
	Extra high frequency	Microwave	Wireless Local Loop (71–95 GHz) Terrestrial microwave
30 GHz			
3 GHz	Super high frequency		Satellites (0.5–51.4GHz)
	Ultra high frequency	Radio waves	Wireless LANs (2.4–5.0 GHz) 3G wireless (1,800–2,200 Mhz) 1G cellular (800–900 MHz) UHF TV (500–800 Mhz)
300 MHz			
	Very high frequency		VHF TV (175–216 MHz) FM radio (88–108 MHz)
30 MHz			
3 MHz	High frequency		
	Medium frequency		Wireless local loop (1.25 MHz) AM radio (540–1800 KHz)
300 KHz			
	Low frequency		GSM 2G wireless (200 KHz)
30 KHz			
3 KHz	Very low frequency		
300 HZ			
30 HZ			
7.5 HZ	Earth		

FIGURE 6-5 The Electromagnetic Spectrum and Broadcast Frequencies

2G cellular. Second-generation (2G) cellular, which predominates today, uses digital technology, but is still circuit switched. Although not developed to provide data transmission, 2G phones can carry data. Anyone who has used a laptop computer with a wireless modem to communicate is familiar with 2G data transmission. The Louisville Metro Sewer District provides an example.

CASE EXAMPLE

LOUISVILLE METRO SEWER DISTRICT

In 1997, Jefferson County, Kentucky, received 13 inches of rainfall in 4 hours. Sewers and drains overflowed, causing 40,000 homes to be flooded. The damage was $200 million, notes Owen Thomas.[12] At the time, the repair workers had cell phones and walkie-talkies, but they had to return to headquarters to get assignment details and look up customer records—a process that slowed their response to the flooding.

In July 2001, the county again experienced heavy rains. Three storms in one weekend left 12 inches of rain. The pressure in the drainage system was so high that manhole covers blew off. But this time, the repair crews had laptops that could connect to district databases by wireless modems, so they could view maps of neighborhoods, locate broken water mains and pipes, and check out the most likely areas of damage—the downtown brick sewers built before the Civil War in the 1850s.

As customers called in for emergency repairs, the operators at the sewer district's headquarters entered the orders into a database, which the work crews could immediately access from the field. Thus, they were able to quickly install auxiliary pumps, for example, which prevented neighborhoods from flooding. In fact, Jefferson County cleaned up its storm damage in a few days, whereas the rest of the state took weeks, notes Thomas.

The wireless network uses off-the-shelf network software and a CRM database. The system has not only saved the sewer district millions of dollars by preventing damage, but the district also can operate with fewer people. Each field technician can now do the work of two, and the IT staff has been cut, even though the call center has been expanded to 24-hour service. The field technicians cannot imagine doing their job without their laptops, states Thomas. ■

2G also can carry messages using short messaging service (SMS). SMS is packet based and is used for paging and short messages, often from one cell phone to another. SMS is a large driver of wireless data services. It has been hugely popular with Scandinavian teens who use it for instant messaging. And in Japan, NTT DoCoMo introduced i-mode phones for Internet services and e-mail in 1999. Within a year, NTT had 6 million subscribers and some 12,000 i-mode sites. Many were for consumer uses, such as banking, ticketing, weather reports, paying bills, and so on.

3G cellular.   The goals of third-generation (3G) technologies are to provide WANs for PCs and multimedia devices to access the Internet or to tap other wireless services at data rates of 384 kbps for mobile and 2 mbps fixed. These speeds are orders of magnitude greater than 2G wireless services. They could support multimedia and video. Some believe that low-bandwidth wireless services, such as the BlackBerry e-mail pager and SMS, are still the true killer applications.

It is too early to tell what the killer apps of wireless will be, because the promise of 3G networks is alluring. As Peter Howe notes, "Coming soon to your cell phone: Everything!"[13] Cell phones have gone from just being telephones to being cameras, camcorders, televisions, messaging and gaming devices, Etch-A-Sketch art screens, flash cards, small computers, and digital wallets. They may become whatever consumers want in the future, he notes. The uses truly are exploding. South Korea's SK Telecom even claims to have ring tones that are silent mosquito repellents. Another claims to be a smoke detector. Phones that can send signals to devices remotely, such as starting the home air conditioner so the house is cool when the owner arrives, are being called smart phones.

Of course, one mitigating factor with cell phones is battery life. Companies are investing lots of resources to resolve this issue. Another mitigating factor is input, due to the tiny keyboards found on most cell phones. Speech recognition has long been hailed as the solution to the input problem. Time will tell whether that's what consumers will want, notes Howe. It's part of the digital convergence noted earlier.

Cell phones are also becoming multimodal, supporting 802.11 as well as cellular technology. With this development, notes Mathias,[9b] the cell phone can become the relay point between the Internet (via Wi-Fi) and other devices, such as a notebook computer, PDA, camera, or some other device. In fact, Mathias believes cell phones with Wi-Fi will act as a type of router, because it is a far cheaper solution than installing a WAN radio in every device, each with its own WAN service (and monthly fee).

Wireless mesh networks.   Mathias[9c] goes so far as to say that wireless mesh networks will become very important. A *mesh network* is a type of network in which many nodes are both end points and relay points. That is, each node can generate traffic, receive traffic, or pass traffic along to a nearby node.

What's important about a wireless mesh network, notes Mathias, is that it is far more flexible than a wired mesh network because its links are radio signals, not wires. Paths through a wireless mesh can change, depending on traffic loads, transmission conditions, and such. He believes they are the most flexible network structure ever created. Furthermore, the more users, the more capacity. The downside, though, is that it uses a lot of battery power (a precious commodity these days). Even so, he believes they will influence the future of wireless.

VSAT (Very Small Aperture Terminal).   Stationary *wireless* broadband is best provided today by VSAT, which is why this technology has taken off, notes Mathias. Just look on the roofs of gas stations and chain stores. They all have small VSAT dishes. The speed is 0.5 mbps. Hughes, for instance, provides two-way satellite at hundreds of bits per second—better than dial-up. Numerous wideband VSAT-based services will come online in the next couple of years, he predicts.

Obviously, companies use the Internet to sell their products and services. One company that was an early Internet user has also become an early wireless user, extending its Internet presence to cell phones. That company is American Greetings. Here is the history of its use of the Web.

CASE EXAMPLE

AMERICAN GREETINGS

American Greetings, a $2.2-billion greeting card company, was a pioneer in utilizing the Web. It launched its Web site in 1996, featuring paper greeting cards, electronic greeting cards, flowers, and gifts.

At Business OnLine97, a conference sponsored by Giga Information Group,[14] the director of electronic marketing for American Greetings described how his firm decided to take advantage of the Web to sell its greeting cards.

The First Web Site

The director noted that his team began its thinking by asking, "Who is our biggest competitor?" The answer was not the other paper-and-ink greeting card competitors. The answer was "forgetfulness." People forget to buy greeting cards. The people who forget the most are those who are on the Internet—men. Although the team could not address forgetfulness at the retail store level, they could address it via the Web—to a potentially huge market—on a self-serve basis.

The company created a Web-based reminder service whereby a consumer can sit down for one-half hour and enter 6 months' worth of upcoming events that require greeting cards, such as birthdays and anniversaries. Once American Greetings has this list, it will send the consumer an e-mail reminder to buy a card shortly before each event. Or, the consumer can select a card on the Web site, and American Greetings will address and mail it and send a follow-up e-mail to the consumer stating when the card was mailed.

The electronic marketing group then realized that being able to talk directly to consumers could be used as a value-added service. As a promotion, they sent 50,000 e-mail messages to people who had asked to be reminded of Mother's Day. But rather than simply send the reminder, they offered free postage for any Mother's Day card bought online. The response was overwhelming. In fact, it was far more successful than the group expected. An even more recent Mother's Day promotion swamped the site.

To build brand loyalty, the electronic marketing group went further by taking advantage of a unique attribute of the Web—personalized marketing. American Greetings has some 35 licenses with well-known brands. One, for instance, is with the National Football League. The electronic marketing group has leveraged these 35 licenses using the profile each consumer fills out for the reminder service. For instance, if a consumer notes in his profile that he is a football fan, he may receive a special promotion to buy a specific NFL card when he visits AmericanGreetings.com.

The manager's goal for all of these services—reminder service, electronic cards, and personalized online marketing—has been to build brand loyalty and establish switching costs so that customers will purchase all of their greeting cards from his company.

Not only is he targeting the consumer market, but he is also aiming at the enterprise market, especially salespeople

(Case Continued)

and bosses. These people are likely to see greeting cards as a nice gesture, which will help them maintain and improve relationships with customers or subordinates.

Forming an Online Alliance

The demographics of card buying have changed over the past 20 years. Twenty years ago, 65 percent of greeting cards were bought in specialty card shops. Today, 66 percent are bought in mass retail chains, where the buyers are younger. American Greetings is the leader in this mass retailing channel. To continue as a leader, the company had to find new ways to offer greeting cards. The Internet is one possible channel.

To tap that channel, the electronic marketing group extended American Greetings' alliance with Wal-Mart to the Web. When consumers visit Wal-Mart's online greeting card section, they are actually sent to American Greetings' Web site through a special side-door Wal-Mart entrance. American Greetings then gives Wal-Mart a percentage of sales from these consumers' online purchases.

By using the side-door approach to link the two sites, American Greetings can track the origin of the purchaser and thereby pay Wal-Mart the agreed-on percentage. In addition, American Greetings can make its site appear to be part of Wal-Mart, strengthening Wal-Mart's brand. In reinforcing Wal-Mart's Web-based distribution channel, American Greetings also becomes a value-added partner, which is important if Wal-Mart decides to consolidate greeting-card suppliers.

In addition, to spur purchasing on the Web as well as at Wal-Mart's stores, American Greetings has given online

purchasers of greeting cards a money-off coupon that they can print out on their printer and take to a Wal-Mart store. Thus, each partner hopes to increase the traffic of the other. In so doing, they tighten their alliance, both in the marketplace and the Web marketspace.

Consolidating Its Online Presence

AmericanGreetings.com is the online greeting and personal expression subsidiary of American Greetings. Its network of sites in early 2002 was one of the world's top 15 Web sites, with more than 16 million unique monthly visitors. The company says it offers the largest selection of online greetings. To achieve that status, the company has acquired BlueMountain.com, Egreetings.com, BeatGreets.com (featuring musical greetings from over 200 artists), and Gibson Greetings.

American Greetings sees its mission as helping "people everywhere express their innermost thoughts and feelings, enhance meaningful relationships, and celebrate life's milestones and special occasions."

Moving to Wireless

Today, members of American Greetings' online card club, who pay $14 a year for membership, receive a choice of thousands of greeting cards, and they can create and print paper cards, invitations, package decorations, business cards, newsletters, stickers, and more on their color printers. Their personalized site contains their profile, favorites list, address book, list of cards sent and to whom, and a reminder list.

To extend the usefulness of membership, American Greetings teamed up with Nokia in 2002 to create a wireless Web presence. Using the WAP browser built into a Nokia phone, members can access American Greetings' WAP-based Web site to send an electronic greeting, either to another phone or to a computer. The company reasons that when people have idle time, besides checking e-mail or playing a game using their cell phone, they also might want to send a funny animated card to someone. ∎

Is Wireless Secure?   Security is a major issue today, notes Mathias.[9a] When both wireline and wireless use the IP protocol, both will rely on the same kinds of security. Until that happens, though, different approaches are needed. Wireless security is not really a major additional concern, notes Mathias, because signals fade fast when they travel through the air. Eavesdroppers need special equipment to pick up radio signals from far away. Radio scrambling and spread-spectrum technologies add security, encryption protects data, and eventually, 802.11i will provide a framework for security.

However, the network is often not the main problem, notes Mathias. Security leaks happen at the end, in the notebook computers; therefore, the data need to be encrypted on the equipment. Security issues are gradually being addressed; the area requires eternal vigilance

Is Wireless Safe?   Although a lot of attention is focused on wireless services, a troubling question has not yet been answered: Are these transmissions safe for humans? The higher-frequency services are in the microwave range. They use almost the same frequency as microwave ovens. Microwave frequencies are more dangerous than lower-frequency radio waves because they cause molecules to vibrate faster, causing heat as the molecules rub against each other. This is how microwave ovens cook food. The power limits on cell phones, wireless modems, and WLANs (3 watts) aim to protect people from this short-term microwave heating phenomenon, says Roth.[15] Microwaves operate at 500 watts. Long-term effects from low-level vibrations that do not raise body temperature are still possible, though. Some studies on rats showed damage to DNA, which can cause diseases such as cancer.[16]

Although such health concerns have been dismissed by many scientists and scientific studies, their confidence has not settled the issue. Many have long believed that electromagnetic radiation from power lines, electrical appliances, and computers can interfere with the body's bioelectromagnetic field, causing an imbalance.[16] These imbalances leave people feeling drained, fatigued, and stressed out. Although it is likely that our bodies can rebalance disruptions caused by occasional exposure to electromagnetic radiation (EMR), frequent bombardment likely has an effect. It is probably difficult to directly link exposure to disease; it is more likely that exposure will gradually lower a body's immunity.

The amount of radiation emitted by cell phones is limited by governments, but these limits are averages. Spikes are possible, and these are known to kill cells; therefore, holding a cell phone next to one's head for prolonged periods of time is not wise. Voice use of cell phones by young people is especially disturbing. Thus, it is quite possible that there could soon be a backlash against wireless devices similar to the protests against genetically modified organisms.[16] Objective research is needed and protection could become a hot topic. Anyone care for metal-lined hats?

In conclusion, the success of wireless is guaranteed, Mathias says, because people will not give up being mobile. There is no substitute technology, but we advise prudent use.

Messaging Is a Killer App

What has proven true with data communication technologies over and over again is that the killer application is messaging. As noted earlier, the original inventors of the Internet expected it to be used by researchers to send files back and forth. Instead, researchers used it mainly for e-mail. And e-mail has remained a major use. In the wireless arena, the BlackBerry messaging service is indispensable to many people, and the driving force for wireless data services using 2G phones in Scandinavia and Japan has been SMS.

Likewise, instant messaging (IM) has become an important mode of communication. Importantly, it appears to be the current preferred mode of communication among young people. In his 2004 keynote address at Networld + Interop, Andy Mattes,[17] president and CEO of Siemens Information and Communications Networks, USA, included two brief video clips of five children, ages 8 to 11, talking about how they communicate with their friends. Behind several of them was a computer screen, often showing a couple of rows of open IM chat boxes, lined up side by side. As the children explained, they use IM to chat with all of their friends at the same time. One boy only uses the phone once a day, to call his Mom (who works in the computer industry). Another girl says that she does not use the phone because then she can only talk to one friend at a time. And she does not use e-mail because it is like regular mail—slow. In short, they prefer to chat with many friends at once. IM gives them this capability.

Many see IM as the killer app of wireless as well, not just for teenagers, but for businesses. Steven Cherry[18] points out that the U.S. Navy's Office of the Chief of Naval Operations turned to IM to communicate with its displaced employees who could not use the secure telecommunications system following the September 11, 2001, terrorist attacks. Top naval officers now use this specially designed and secured IM system routinely to communicate with each other and with their staffs. In addition, the U.S. Navy has connected 300 ships at sea with IM. Whereas teenagers use IM to chat, corporations and other enterprises are using it to quickly ask a question of someone, to share documents, and to exchange notes, says Cherry.

Newer technologies will allow messaging to become even more personal. This is one reason why camera phones have become so popular: a picture is often more personal than a voice description. Photo messaging will add to voice and text messaging. Video messaging is more personal still. Video phones will allow others to be there—a sick grandparent will be able to attend a graduation, a traveling mom will be at a grade school play, and a far-off relative can help celebrate a birthday party.

The key attribute of IM is that it provides *presence*, which means that a person on your buddy list can see when you are using a computer or device (if it has the appropriate IM software and service) and therefore knows that you are present and available to receive an instant message. Presence is being built into collaboration software, Webcasts, and online games as well. The downside of presence, of course, is that people with large buddy lists can be deluged with instant messages whenever they have their phone or computer on.

Always on is the communication mode of the future because it allows instant notification. For example, a sales team may ask to receive news releases and intranet entries about their specific clients or their main competitors, so they are always up-to-date. If the team's devices support a team calendar, team members might be able to schedule a quick telephone conference call if they receive important news, such as a competitor trying to snag an important customer or information about a market test. Or, they might just collaborate asynchronously via SMS. On-the-go multiparty collaboration is an important use of low-bandwidth wireless devices, and it could become the same with high-bandwidth devices. Or, a collector might ask for instant notification when specific items within specific price ranges come up for auction. The service might give the collector one-click transaction capabilities so the collector can bid on an item once he or she receives notification.

Mei Chuah, a researcher at Accenture Labs,[19] foresees cell phones, their IM capabilities, and online commerce commingling physical and virtual worlds. She believes the cell phone will become a person's portal to other people, physical things, and virtual entities as well. All will be part of a person's social network. Personal devices (including our cars) will be "socialized" by having communication capabilities and will potentially communicate wirelessly with each other. Phones will have sensing and even control capabilities. For example, a software robot in the phone will "sense" what friends are doing, and connect those who are, say, watching the same TV program or downloading the same song. Once companies realize they can sell more products and services to consumers by creating social activities (including virtual ones) around their products or services, even more types of things will be given communication capabilities, Chuah believes.

Furthermore, she sees the physical and virtual worlds interconnecting, with social networks in one moving to the other. People in virtual worlds already hold parties over the Internet. Such socializing in one world will flow to socializing in the other. Furthermore, items in one world will move to the other. Chuah cites the example of the virtual sword won by an advanced player in the online game Everquest being sold on eBay. Wireless communications will eventually link both worlds, she believes, and the nexus will be the cell phone.

A current-day example of using IM to sell products is Keebler's RecipeBuddie.

CASE EXAMPLE

KEEBLER

In September 2002, Keebler, the cookie and cracker company, launched Recipe-Buddie on it's Web site, notes Gordon Bass.[20] "She" is an instant-messenger bot that converses with people who IM her. But she only talks about recipes, using her database of 700 recipes to, say, help someone figure out what to cook for dinner.

(Case Continued)

Keebler's goal, of course, is for her to get people to buy more Keebler products. She has been given the personality of a humor-filled suburban housewife, which seems to best fit the demographics of Keebler's audience: suburban women ages 25 to 54.

Her origin is ActiveBuddy, a company founded by Timothy Kay that builds interactive agents (bots) to run on IM networks, private networks, and wireless networks. RecipeBuddie, for example, sits on someone's AOL IM buddy list and can answer natural-language questions about recipes. She can be accessed at www.keebler.com.

Emedia, the developer of Keebler's Web site, built RecipeBuddie using the scripting language BuddyScript (from ActiveBuddy). Development entailed writing scripts to reply to user questions. For RecipeBuddie, each natural-language response acknowledges the other party, repeats the request, and makes a suggestion, which is often one or more recipes. Scripting entailed making the link between what people might ask about (cooking dinner for the kids, a picnic lunch, no onions, feeling sad, etc.) and recipes in the database. Emedia initially wrote 2,000 pieces of dialog for RecipeBuddie, notes Bass.

Once developed, Emedia had to get permission to launch RecipeBuddie on the three major IM networks: AOL, MSN, and Yahoo! ActiveBuddy receives a fee every time RecipeBuddie is accessed. Keebler tracks the number of people who put RecipeBuddie on their buddy list, the number of messages exchanged with RecipeBuddie, and the number of recipes viewed and printed.

RecipeBuddie has been very successful, exceeding Keebler's expectations. The main developer, Anna Murray of Emedia, notes three lessons she learned from building the bot. One, users really like to converse with bots, so a lot more can be done with them. Two, scripting is like writing a novel, so it needs to be done by just a couple of people, and they need to work together very closely. And three, others, besides the original scripters, should be able to add their own content, such as answers to frequently asked questions. ∎

Coming: An Internet of Things

Wireless communications are not just for people, of course. A machine-to-machine Internet is coming, note Andy Reinhardt[21] and Heather Green.[11] Machines will likely use Wi-Fi as one wireless communication protocol. Another protocol is ZigBee, a radio-based communication standard used by tiny sensors. Such sensors might monitor the main systems in a vehicle; the inventory of ice cream in vending machines; a building's HVAC system; or the soil moisture, nutrients, and temperature in a field as well as a myriad of other uses.

The sensors are designed to send specific bits of information, be long lasting, require little energy, and communicate efficiently. With ZigBee, the sensors pass their information on to the next sensor in a sort of bucket-brigade fashion, with the last one passing the data to a computer for analysis or communication, notes Green.

Yet another protocol that involves communication among things is radio-frequency identification (RFID), which is discussed in Chapter 11. Like the bar code, it is a technology that involves small tags affixed to objects that provide information about the object. For example, an RFID tag on a package could tell a scanner where it is going, where it has been, the temperature range it has experienced (if that is important to the contents), and so on.

The problem CIOs face is tying such new sensor-based systems into their corporate databases. It is likely that the communication systems will use a mix of wired and wireless technologies, as appropriate. That is just one challenge.

THE ROLE OF THE IS DEPARTMENT

This long discussion of telecommunications gives just a glimpse into its complexity as well as its increasing importance. Given this central role of telecommunications networks, what is the IS department's role? We believe IS has three roles: create the telecommunications architecture for the enterprise, run it, and stay close to the forefront of the field.

A network architecture needs to contain a set of company policies and rules that, when followed, lead to the desired network environment. The key challenge in network design is connectivity. *Connectivity* means allowing users to communicate up, down, across, and out of an organization. The goal is not a single coherent network, but rather finding the means to interface many dissimilar networks. One guiding principle is to build systems that are coherent at the interfaces so that users think they are only dealing with one network.

The second key concept in architecture design is *interoperability*, which means the capability for different computers, using different operating systems and on different networks, to work together on tasks—exchanging information in standard ways without any changes in functionality and without physical intervention. A truly interoperable network would allow PCs, laptops, handhelds, devices, and objects to interoperate, even while running different operating systems and communicating over IP networks. This interoperability is the goal of architecture and is the main job of the IS department.

The second job of the IS department is to operate the network. This subject is discussed in Chapter 8, "Managing Operations." Suffice it to say here that many companies are outsourcing this work to companies that specialize in network management because the area is so complex, there are too few network specialists to go around, and network infrastructures are costly investments.

The third job of IS is to stay current with the technology. In this day and age, if an IS department is not already experimenting with how handheld devices can interact with its Web site, they are behind competitors who are. Keeping abreast of telecommunications requires continually peering into the future and testing out new ideas. It is a crucial job of IS departments, even when budgets are tight.

CONCLUSION

The telecommunications world is big, and getting bigger by the day. It is complex, and becoming more complex. Some see it as a global electronic highway system where the goal is to establish links and interoperability. Others see it as a cyberspace where commerce is conducted and businesses operate.

The business world of old depended on communications, of course, but not to the extent of online commerce. The Internet unleashed e-mail, then Web sites for getting noticed globally, and now it is used for transactions and business. Although worldwide communication over the Internet enables global business, it also has the opposite effect: customized personal service to individuals anywhere, anytime.

The first generation of the Internet economy was wired. The second could be unwired. This untethering could change how we live our lives and do our work. You only need to sit in an airport for a short time to realize how those with cell phones are doing different things than those without phones. Today, telecommunications is all about connecting. The number of possible connections is exploding worldwide.

QUESTIONS AND EXERCISES

Review Questions

1. What are the two ways to view telecommunications?
2. What is the Internet? What three attributes make it important to businesses?
3. Describe the functions of hubs, switches, and routers.
4. What is digital convergence and why is it important?
5. Briefly describe each layer of the OSI Reference Model.
6. Why are unlicensed frequencies important?
7. What are four types of wireless area networks?
8. How is American Greetings moving into wireless?
9. Why might wireless devices not be safe for humans?
10. What was Andy Mattes' point in his speech at the 2004 Networld+Interop conference?
11. What is presence and why is it important?
12. Why is always on important?
13. What is RecipeBuddie and what does she do?
14. What is ZigBee?
15. What are the three roles of the IS department with respect to telecommunications?

Discussion Questions

1. The chapter implies that a company should stay at the forefront of telecommunications technology lest it fall seriously behind. On the other hand, it might be better to let others go first and then learn from their mistakes. When is each approach most appropriate? Why?
2. None of us needs a phone at home and a phone at the office. All we need is one phone that we always carry around. Such a practice would relieve the pressures on the telephone system for so many additional phone numbers and area codes.

Better yet, each phone should have an IP address. Discuss the pros and cons of these ideas.

3. Although having a wireless device is handy, it is also an intrusion. People need some privacy. They should not always be reachable. Discuss.

Exercises

1. Read five articles on telecommunications. What developments not discussed in this chapter do they see as important and why? Present a short briefing on these issues to the class.
2. Contact the CIO of a company in your community. What is the company's telecommunications architecture? What telecommunications standards does it use? How is it using the Internet? What is it doing about wireless?
3. Find one article that discusses senior management's or line management's role in either telecommunications, the use of the Internet, or online commerce. What role do they play? Are they in partnership with IS? Discuss.

REFERENCES

1. PricewaterhouseCoopers, "Technology Forecast: 2000; From Atoms to Systems: A Perspective on Technology," PricewaterhouseCoopers Technology Center, 68 Willow Road, Menlo Park, CA 94025, April 2000, p. 774. PwC Consulting has since become part of IBM Global Services.

2. Kaarlgard, Rich, keynote address at Comdex, Las Vegas, NV, November 1999.

3. Bean, Bill, keynote address at Networld+Interop 2000, Las Vegas, NV, updated from IGC's Web site. Available at www.icgcomm.com.

4. Cope, James, "Vendors Tout Voice Over IP," *Computerworld*, February 21, 2000, p. 64.

5. Cisco Systems, Inc., "New Terminal 1 at Toronto Pearson International Airport Showcases Cisco Intelligent Airport Solutions," March 30, 2004. Available at newsroom.cisco.com/dlls/2004/prod_033004d. html. Accessed May 2004. Waltner, Charles, "Potential of IP Communications Takes Off at Toronto Pearson International Airport," March 30, 2004. Available at newsroom.cisco.com/dlls/partners/news/ 2004/f_hd_03–30.html?CMP=AF17154. Accessed May 2004. "Toronto Pearson International Airport Deploys a Common-Use Network for Tenants, Travelers, and

Employees," March 2004. Available at business.cisco.com/servletwl3/FileDownloade r/iqprod/106917/106917_kbns.pdf. Accessed June 2004.

6. Baker, Stephen, and Heather Green, "The Info Tech 100: The Big Bang," *Business Week*, June 21, 2004, pp. 68–76.

7. Gilder, George, *Telecosm: How Infinite Bandwidth Will Revolutionize Our World*. The Free Press, New York, 2000, and in a speech at the Aspen Institute, Aspen, CO, July 18, 1996.

8. Shinal, John, and Timothy Mullaney, "At the Speed of Light," *Business Week*, October 9, 2000, pp. 145–152.

9. Mathias, Craig, Farpoint Group, Ashland, MA; www.farpointgroup.com:
   a. Speech, Networld+Interop 2002, Las Vegas, NV, May 2002.
   b. "The Relay Point Model," ITWorld.com, May 3, 2004. Available at wireless.itworld.com/4267/040504 relaypoint/pfindex.html. Accessed June 2004.
   c. "The Importance of Wireless Mesh Networks," ITWorld.com, February 3, 2004. Available at wireless.itworld. com/4285/040202/wirelessmess_fpg/ pfindex.html. Accessed June 2004.

10. Dzubeck, Frank, "The Dawn of a Wireless Century," *Network World*, May 10, 2004, p. 53.

11. Green, Heather, "No Wires, No Rules," *Business Week*, April 26, 2004, pp. 94–102.

12. Thomas, Owen, "The Sewers of Jefferson Country" *Business 2.0*, October 2001, pp. 116–117.

13. Howe, Peter, "Coming Soon to Your Cellphone: Everything!" Boston.com, February 2, 2004.

14. Giga Information Group, One Kendall Square, Cambridge, MA 02139, www.gigaweb.com.

15. Roth, Cliff, *Mobile Computing for Dummies*, IDG Books, Danville, CA, 1997.

16. McNurlin, Barbara, "The Wireless Backlash," *Business Recreation AD 2000*, Gartner EXP, Stamford, CT 06904, January 2000.

17. Mattes, Andy, keynote speech, Networld+ Interop, Las Vegas, NV, November 2004.

18. Cherry, Steven, "IM Means Business," *IEEE Spectrum*, November 2002, pp. 28–32.

19. Hardy, Quentin, "E-Gang: Going Virtual," *Forbes*, September 1, 2003. Available at www.forbes.com/forbes/2003/0901/106_print.html. Accessed June 2004.

20. Bass, Gordon, "Virtual Elves," *New Architect*, March 2003, Available at www.newarchitectmag.com. Accessed June 2004.

21. Reinhardt, Andy, "A Machine-to-Machine 'Internet of Things,'" *Business Week*, April 26, 2004, p. 102.

7

MANAGING INFORMATION RESOURCES

INTRODUCTION

Managing information resources initially meant managing data, first in files, then in corporate databases that were well structured, carefully defined, and generally under the jurisdiction of the IS department. Next, the term expanded to include information; that is, data that has meaning. There also has been much talk of managing knowledge. With the emergence of the Internet, talk has turned to managing content, which includes text, graphics, sound, video, and animation. Managing them all is now included in our discussion of *information resources* in this chapter and in Chapter 13.

To begin, a few definitions are in order:

- *Data* consists of facts devoid of meaning or intent, where meaning and intent are supplied by a particular use.
- *Information* is data in context, which means the data has been given an explicit meaning in a specific context. In this book, we will often use the term *content* to refer to information. This term arose with the emergence of the World Wide Web. Content includes information presented electronically in a variety of media: charts, text, voice, sound, graphics, animation, photographs, diagrams, and video.
- *Knowledge* is information with direction or intent, where intent is derived from strategies or objectives.

As the breadth of the kinds of information resources has expanded, so has the job of managing them. Oftentimes, that job ends up in the IS organization, even though it may not have started there. For example, when PCs came on the scene, people created their own personal files to do their work. They depended on these files, but no one else did until they were shared. Then, when shared files were destroyed and had no backup, all of a sudden a department might not be able to function. Therefore, users asked IS to back up the file or house it on a computer that was regularly backed up. Thus, IS became involved. The same has occurred with Web content. When departments and field offices initially created their own Web sites, IS often was not in the picture. However, as the need for recovery, version control, corporate consistency, and such appeared, people again looked to IS to put in the necessary management procedures. Thus, IS has been continually managing new forms of information resources in addition to the ones it has already been managing.

- Corporate databases are still a major responsibility of IS organizations, and management of data has gotten increasingly complex as it has become distributed. Not only is data now global in some cases, but the data is housed in a variety of *database models*, such as hierarchical, relational, and object-oriented ones. Production databases support transaction processing of airline reservations, customer orders, and such. Data warehouses house gigantic amounts of historic data to be analyzed with data mining techniques to support decision making for such applications as CRM.
- Information, in the form of documents (electronic or paper) and Web content, has exploded the size of the databases that organizations now manage. Furthermore, with the digitization of sound files, photographs, video, and 3D models, file sizes are growing at a fast clip. Unlike structured data, these unstructured forms of information are not easy to index for retrieval purposes.
- Knowledge management is becoming a key to exploiting the intellectual assets of organizations. The types of knowledge organizations are attempting to manage include explicit knowledge (know-what), which can be housed in a file or a process, as well as tacit knowledge (know-how), which is generally in people's heads and is difficult to make explicit.

This text deals with all three areas. Data and information (in the form of documents and content) are discussed in this chapter. Knowledge and related intellectual capital topics are discussed in Chapter 13. We begin by discussing managing data.

MANAGING DATA

As noted, data is facts devoid of meaning or intent. Data is primarily facts about entities, such as individual employees, customers, parts, or transactions. Well-structured data records hold a set of attributes that describe each entity. Database management systems (DBMSs) are the main tools for managing these entities in the business world. DBMSs have been around since the 1960s and are based on two major principles: a three-level conceptual model and several alternative data models for organizing the data.

The Three-Level Database Model

One of the easiest-to-understand discussions of database technology is by James Bradley[1] in his description of the three-level database model. The concept is still an underpinning of the DBMS field. The following discussion is based on Bradley, Martin,[2] and Atre.[3] It begins with the level that the application developer sees.

- *Level 1* is called the external, conceptual, or local level. As Figure 7-1 illustrates, this level contains the various user views of the corporate data. Each application program has its own view. This level is not concerned with how the data is physically stored or what data is used by other applications.

- *Level 2* is called the logical or enterprise data level. It encompasses all an organization's relevant data under the control of the data administrators. Data and relationships are represented at this level by the DBMS. This level contains the same data as Level 3, but with the implementation data removed.

- *Level 3* is called the physical or storage level. It specifies the way the data is physically stored. A data record consists of its data fields plus some implementation data, generally pointers and flag fields. The end user, of course, need not be concerned with these pointers and flags; they are for use by the DBMS only.

The advantage of this three-level model is that Level 2 absorbs changes made at Level 3, such as using a new physical storage method, so that individual application programs in Level 1 do not need to be changed when the physical layer changes. Furthermore, data only needs to be stored once in Level 2, and different programs can draw on it and vary the relationships among the data.

Four Data Models

The second major concept in database management is alternative ways of defining relationships among types of data. Data models are methods to structure data to represent the real world and the way data is accessed. Four main data models are in use today: hierarchical, network, relational, and object.

Hierarchical Model.   In this model, each data element is subordinate to another in a strict hierarchical manner, like the boxes on an organization chart. This model uses the terminology *parent* and *child* to represent these relationships, and each data item can have only one parent.

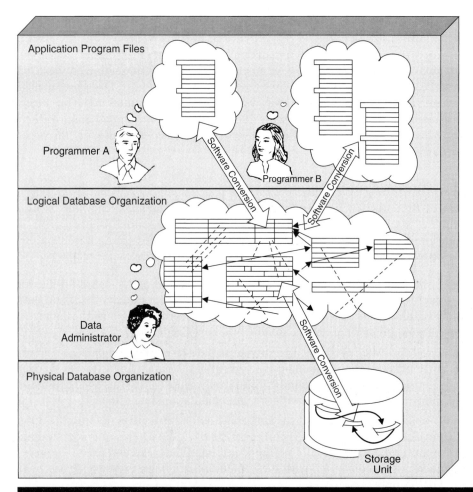

FIGURE 7-1 The Three-Level Database

Source: James Martin, *Principles of Database Management* (Upper Saddle River, NJ: Prentice Hall, 1976).

Network Model. In this model, each data item can have more than one parent. Assembly parts lists illustrate this structure; the same part can be used in more than one assembly. In both the hierarchical and network models, the data relationships are stated explicitly, generally by pointers stored with the data. These pointers provide the means by which programs access the desired data records.

Relational Model. Edgar F. Codd of IBM[4] proposed the relational model in 1970. In it, relationships among data items are not expressly stated by pointers. Instead, it is up to the DBMS to find the related items based on the values of specified data fields. Thus, all employees of a certain department are found by searching for the department number in each employee record.

Relational databases store data in tables. Each row of the table, called a *tuple*, represents an individual entity (person, part, account). Each column represents an attribute of the entities. Various kinds of operations can be performed on the data, such as selecting one or more columns, projecting one or more rows, joining rows from several tables by matching column values, and such.

Relational systems are not as efficient as hierarchical or networked database systems, where navigational maps through the data are predefined. However, because relational systems allow people to create relationships among data on the fly, they are much more flexible. Thus, they were first used to handle end user queries and they are now widely used in high-volume transaction systems with huge files. Relational has become the database technology of choice.

Object Model.   As the newest data model, the object-oriented approach expands the view of data by storing and managing *objects*, each of which consists of the following:

- A piece of data
- Methods, or procedures that can perform work on that data
- Attributes describing the data
- Relationships between this object and others

Objects are important because they can be used with any type of data, whether a traditional name or address, an entire spreadsheet, a video clip, a voice annotation, a photograph, or a segment of music. A collection of objects is called an *object database*.

Object data management techniques draw from the past. They retain traditional DBMS features, including end user tools, high-level query languages, concurrency control, recovery, and the ability to efficiently handle huge amounts of data. They include two other important concepts as well. One is object management, which is the management of complex kinds of data, such as multimedia and procedures. The other concept is rule management, that is, managing large numbers of complex rules for reasoning and maintaining integrity constraints between data.

Stonebraker and Kemnitz[5a] provide an example of an application that requires object management as well as data management and rule management. It is a newspaper application that needs to store text and graphics and be integrated with subscription and classified ad data. In this application, customer billing requires traditional data management, whereas storage of text, pictures, and the newspaper's banner require object management. Finally, it needs the rules that control the newspaper's layout. One rule might be, "Ads for competing retailers cannot be on facing pages." Stonebraker and Kemnitz believe that most data management problems in the future will require all three dimensions: data, object, and rule management.

The tenets of objects become even more important in the world of Web Services because the XML modules utilize object principles. You can think of objects as little black boxes. They tell you what data they need to perform their function and what output they will give you. However, they will not tell you how they perform their function. If they need help performing their work, they send a request to another module. So, in addition to handling all varieties of data, objects provide a programming discipline to Web Services.

Silberschatz, Stonebraker, and Ullman[5b] give the following examples of typical, yet complex, database applications that may require objects.

- CAD data for a large office building must maintain and integrate information from the viewpoints of hundreds of subcontractors. For example, when an electrician drills a hole in a beam to run an electrical wire, the system should, ideally, recalculate the stresses on the beam to ensure that its load-bearing capabilities have not been compromised.

- Large retail chains record every product code scanned by every cashier in every store. Corporate buyers explore this data using ad hoc queries to uncover buying patterns. This procedure, called *data mining*, is growing, not only in retailing, but also in medicine, science, and many other fields.

- Databases of insurance policies now store photographs of damaged property, handwritten claim forms, audio transcripts of appraisals, images of insured objects, and even video walk-throughs of houses. These images contain so much data that these databases are enormous.

Just as there is essentially one worldwide telephone system and one worldwide computer network, some believe there will eventually be one worldwide file system. Achieving this vision requires collaboration among nations, which is actually happening in some areas. The Human Genome Project is one example. Defense contractors want a single project database that spans all subcontractors and all portions of a project. Auto companies want to give their suppliers access to new car designs. Both of these applications require inter-company databases. The challenge is making these databases behave as though they are part of a single database. This interoperability is the main challenge of distributed systems, as noted in Chapter 5.

Finally, security is of major importance in today's DBMSs. Distributed, heterogeneous Internet-linked databases exacerbate the problem. Companies may want to permit access to some portions of their databases while restricting other portions. This selective accessibility requires reliably authenticating inquirers. Unless security and integrity are strictly enforced, users will not be able to trust the systems.

Getting Corporate Data into Shape

Attempts to get corporate data under control began in the late 1960s and early 1970s with DBMSs. Not long after that, the *database administration* function appeared to manage DBMSs and their use. Then, in the 1970s, the broader role of *data administration* was created to manage all the computerized data resources of an organization. These two functions have remained important.

The Problem: Inconsistent Data Definitions.   In a nutshell, the problem has been incompatible data definitions from application to application, department to department, site to site, and division to division. How has this inconsistency happened? Blame expediency. To get application systems up and running quickly, system designers have sought the necessary data either from the cheapest source or from a politically expedient source, that is, using data from existing files and adding other new data. In effect, data has been dribbled from application to application. The result has been data showing up in different files, with different names, or the same name for different data items, or the same data in different files with different update cycles.

Use of such data may be acceptable for routine information processing, but it is far from acceptable for management uses. Management cannot get consistent views across the enterprise with such variations. Also, changes in data and programs are hard to make because a change can affect files anywhere in the organization. Furthermore, such inconsistency makes it difficult to change the tracking and reporting of the organization's products, markets, control structure, and other elements needed to meet changing business conditions.

If a major role of the IS organization had been managing data rather than getting applications running as quickly as possible, then a quite different scenario would have occurred. All the types of data of interest would first be identified. Then the single source of each data type would be identified, along with the business function that creates that data. Finally, a transaction system would be built to collect and store that data, after which all authorized users and applications would have access to it.

This data-driven approach does not result in one huge database to serve the entire enterprise, but it does require administrative control over the data as well as designing databases to support users from the outset. It starts out by describing the data the enterprise needs. Then the approach is selected that provides the data that gives a good balance between short-term, application-oriented goals and long-term, data-oriented goals.

The Role of Data Administration. The use of DBMS reduced, to some extent, the problems of inconsistent and redundant data in organizations. However, installing a DBMS is not sufficient to manage data as a corporate resource. Therefore, two additional thrusts have moved organizations in this direction: broader definition of the data administration role and effective use of data dictionaries.

Database administration concentrates on administering databases and the software that manages them. Data administration is broader. One of its main purposes is determining what data is being used outside the organizational unit that creates it. Whenever data crosses organizational boundaries, its definition and format need to be standardized under the data administration function.

The data dictionary is the main tool by which data administrators control standard data definitions. All definitions are entered into the dictionary, and data administrators monitor all new definitions and all requests for changes in definitions to make sure that corporate policy is being followed.

ERP. To bring order to the data mess, data administration has four main functions: clean up the data definitions, control shared data, manage data distribution, and maintain data quality. Interestingly, many companies did not take these four jobs seriously until the mid-1990s when they needed consistent data to either install a companywide ERP package, such as SAP; support a data warehouse effort; or, in some instances, consolidate country-based databases on an intranet so that everyone in the company, worldwide, could draw from the same data pool.

ERP, in particular, has been the main driving force for getting some data into shape in many companies. It provided the means to consolidate data to give management a corporate-wide view of operations. MeadWestvaco, in Chapter 1, provided one example of implementing ERP. Here is another: Monsanto.[6a]

CASE EXAMPLE

MONSANTO

Monsanto, based in St. Louis, Missouri, is a $9-billion provider of agricultural products, pharmaceuticals, food ingredients, and chemicals. It is heavily international, with some 50 percent of revenues outside the United States. It has always had a tradition of being decentralized. The CEO's vision includes five global themes.

1. Being responsive and efficient in meeting customer needs

2. Thinking and acting from a global perspective

3. Taking some risks to enter new markets

4. Treating the earth as a closed system where consumption and contamination of finite resources cannot be sustained

5. Creating an environment of trust, honesty, openness, and initiative where people can thrive

To accomplish these (and other) goals, Monsanto established three large enterprise-wide IT projects. One is to redevelop operational and financial transaction systems using SAP. The second is to develop a knowledge-management architecture, including data warehousing. The third is to link transaction and decision support systems via common master data, known as enterprise reference data (ERD), as shown in Figure 7-2. Monsanto wants to be "small but connected" to benefit from both global integration and local flexibility. ERD is a key to achieving both simultaneously. The Center of Technical Expertise is implementing all three initiatives.

Transaction Systems. The worldwide operations and finance project is dominated by SAP, an ERP product that covers all core business transactions, including finance, order processing, inventory

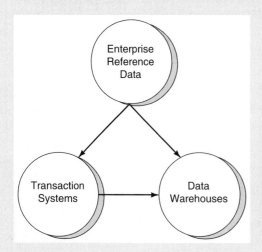

FIGURE 7-2 The Role of Enterprise Reference Data

Source: Courtesy of the Monsanto Corporation

(Case Continued)

management, product planning, and manufacturing resource planning. SAP is international and handles multiple languages and multiple currencies.

Monsanto is too large and complex to operate SAP as a single installation. Hence, they have created a distributed SAP architecture with separate instances of SAP for reference data, finance, and operations in each business unit. The master reference data integrates these distributed components.

Knowledge Management. To convert SAP data to knowledge, Monsanto uses data warehouses, which are targeted at mid- to upper-level management. These warehouses focus on the big picture of the company and contain data from internal and external sources that can be sliced and diced with drill-down capability from summary data to supporting details. Again, the reference data allows the warehouses to compare and leverage information across Monsanto.

ERD. ERD, a separate use of SAP, is the repository for most master table information in the company. The information includes vendors, customers, suppliers, materials, finance, and control tables. Each table has multiple views. For instance, materials has separate views for purchasing, engineering, accounting, and safety, among others. The beauty of using a system such as SAP is that it can ensure referential integrity (adherence to complex relationship rules) of the data.

The sole source of master data is ERD, but the data can be distributed wherever it is needed in transactional SAP systems as well as in the data warehouses. However, as comprehensive as SAP is, it still does not contain all the reference data. Monsanto stores external data, such as crop statistics and economic trends, outside SAP.

The purpose of ERD is to enable integration. Vertical integration enables closer coordination with suppliers, which will reduce Monsanto's working capital and improve customer service. Horizontal integration across Monsanto's business units enables team marketing, leveraged purchasing, and interplant manufacturing. For example, common vendor and material tables enable Monsanto to leverage purchasing across the company. With total purchases of about $5.5 billion a year, even a few percentage points of leverage can yield significant savings. Without ERD, Monsanto had to rely on limited polls of many purchasing functions—a process that could not be sustained.

Getting Corporate Data into Shape

Turning data into a corporate resource is not easy for a large company with a history of decentralization. To accomplish its task, Monsanto has had to change its entire data management process. To start, it created a formal department known as ERD Stewardship. This department is independent of MIS or any other function and its job is to set data standards and enforce quality—hence its nickname, "the data police."

Another new function in ERD management is entity specialists. These key managers have the greatest stake in the quality of the data. For example, the specialist for vendor data is the vice president of purchasing. In cases of no obvious specialists, a steward has been appointed.

The third part of ERD management is the analysts who manage the data. In many cases, they are the same people

(Case Continued)

who maintain systems, but they must now adhere to the new ERD rules. This requirement has led to a large cultural change because these folks formerly only maintained local data. Now they maintain a global resource that the entire company uses. The idea of tweaking a system to fix a local discrepancy, which was formerly a common occurrence, can now cause a major disruption in operations or a bad decision based on faulty data.

Getting the data right in the first place is a large undertaking, one that can easily take several work years per table to extract the data, put it in a common format, eliminate the duplicates, add miss-

ing data, and load into the ERD. Even with tools, it is labor intensive. Where possible, Monsanto is using standard external codes, such as Dun & Bradstreet numbers, universal product codes, or European article numbers, so that the company's trading partners can recognize the reference data for electronic commerce purposes. Unfortunately, none of these number schemes is truly universal, so the need to build, maintain, and cross-reference reference data appears to be unavoidable. Monsanto is working through this process and is already reaping bottom-line benefits from better integration (horizontally and vertically) and greater flexibility. ■

One of the benefits of ERP is that it gives companies a ready-made IT architecture. But, as John Langenbahn of Mead Corporation wondered (in Chapter 1), does it reduce flexibility because divisions of a company need to move in concert with each other? McGrane of MeadWestvaco, Langenbahn's successor, thinks not, because once a decision is made it can be implemented quickly and across the entire corporation. However, the question of flexibility of ERP still remains.

Once enterprises get their data in shape, that data can more easily be turned into information. That is the next subject in this chapter.

MANAGING INFORMATION

As noted earlier, information is data in context, which means the data has been given an explicit meaning in a specific context. We often hear such statements as "Information is power" or "We are in the information age." These and similar statements would lead you to believe that managing information is a key corporate activity. Indeed it is, and it is becoming increasingly so. In fact, some believe that information management, rather than technology management, is the main job of the IS department. We believe both are important. The technology can be viewed as the infrastructure and the information as the asset that runs on that infrastructure. Yet, information is just an intermediary—an intermediary for action. In this important intermediary position, the management of information is important. We begin this discussion by discerning four types of information.

Four Types of Information

One view of information resources is shown in the 2 × 2 matrix in Figure 7-3. The rows depict two *structures* of information—record based and document based—and the columns depict two *sources* of information—internal and external. Record-based data contains mainly facts about entities, such as patients, vehicles, and parts, and is housed in data records. The discussion up to this point in this chapter has dealt with record-based data. Document-based information, on the other hand, deals with concepts, such as ideas, thoughts, and opinions, and is housed in documents, messages, and video and audio clips. Figure 7-4 lists various differences between the two.

Internal record-based information was the original focus of IS organizations, because it is the type of information that computer applications generate and manage easily. External record-based information can now be accessed over the Internet or through other electronic means via public databases. End users themselves have generally handled the procurement of this kind of data by subscribing to database services.

However, internal and external document-based information have received little attention from IS organizations until recently, because it has been so difficult to manipulate in computers. Intranets changed that. Documents are now an integral part of information on these sites. Even in companies where the administrative vice president or the corporate librarian believe documents are their realm, after a short time, they gladly turn over responsibility for the technical issues to IS.

In short, in the past, these four realms of information have been the responsibility of different functions, as shown in Figure 7-5. Today, the IS organization is likely to be involved in some way in each area. In fact, because the two types of information have such different characteristics, they are being managed in quite different ways. The following discussion notes that division. Managing record-based information is illustrated by the use of one technology: data warehouses. Managing document-based information is illustrated by two technologies: document management and Web content management.

Data Warehouses

Data warehouses appeared in the early 1990s, a bit before ERP systems. Like ERP systems, they, too, spurred getting record-based data into shape. Data warehouses house data used to make decisions. The data is generally obtained periodically from transaction databases—five times a day, once a week, or maybe just once a month. The warehouse thus presents a snapshot at a point in time.

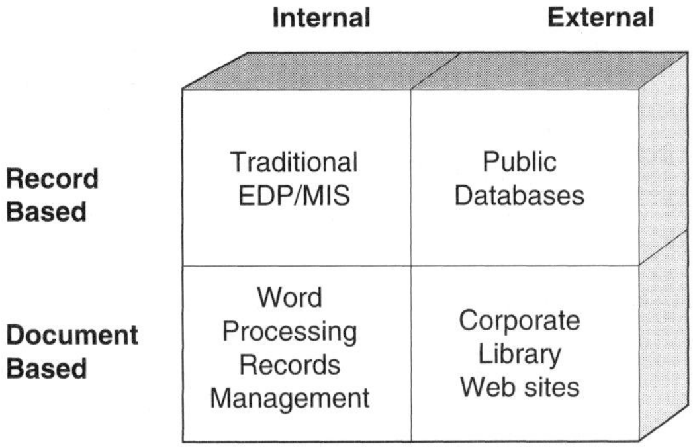

	Internal	External
Record Based	Traditional EDP/MIS	Public Databases
Document Based	Word Processing Records Management	Corporate Library Web sites

FIGURE 7-3 Four Types of Information

	Data Records	*Documents*
Item of interest	Entity	Concept or idea
Attribute of item	Field	Set of symbols
All attributes for item	Record	Logical paragraph
All related items	File	Document
A group of related files	Database	File cabinet
A collection of databases	Application system	Library, records center
Data models (representational approaches)	Hierarchical, relational, etc.	Keywords, hypertext

FIGURE 7-4 Structure of Information

Data warehouses differ from operational databases in that they do not house data used to process daily transactions. Operational databases are meant to be updated to hold the latest data on, say, a customer's flight reservation, the amount of product in inventory, or the status of a customer's order. Data warehouses are not. They are not updated as events occur, only at specific points in time. In addition, unlike transaction databases, data warehouses are used with tools for exploring the data. The simplest tools generate preformatted reports or permit ad hoc queries. Yet warehouses are reaching beyond reporting on internal data. They are being combined with purchased data, such

FIGURE 7-5 The Scope of Information Management

	Typical Corporate Authority	*Information Sources*	*Technologies Used*
Internal record-based information	Information systems department	Transaction processing Organizational units	DBMS Data dictionaries Enterprise data analysis techniques
Internal document-based information	Administrative vice president Word processing center Records management	Corporate memos, letters, reports, forms, e-mail	Word processing Micrographics Reprographics Text-retrieval products
External record-based information	End users Corporate planning Financial analysis Marketing	Public databases	Internet-based services Public networks Analysis packages
External document-based information	Corporate library	Public literature News services Catalogs and indexes Subscriptions Purchased reports	Bibliographic services Environmental scanning Public networks

as demographic data, late-breaking news, and even weather reports, to uncover trends or correlations that can give a company a competitive edge. For example, a retailer might put the umbrellas and raincoats by the front door because a surprise storm is moving in.

The most common type of data in a warehouse is customer data, which is used to discover how to more effectively market to current customers as well as non-customers with the same characteristics. As a result, the marketing department has, in large part, been the driving force behind warehouses. They want to use customer data—from billing and invoicing systems, for example—to identify customer clusters and see the effect different marketing programs have on these clusters.

Data warehouses are seen as strategic assets that can yield new insights into customer behavior, internal operations, product mixes, and the like. However, to gain the benefits, companies must take the often-delayed step of reconciling data from numerous legacy systems. When the perceived benefits appear to outweigh the costs, companies tackle the tremendous task.

Due to the strategic nature of such uses of data, warehousing projects need sponsorship from top management, not only to provide funding and guide the project in truly strategic uses, but also to ensure that departments cooperate and yield up their data for cross-correlations.

Key Concepts in Data Warehousing.   As with all other areas of IT, data warehousing has its own set of terms and concepts. Here are few of them.

Metadata: Defining the data.   One of the most important elements in a data warehouse is its metadata; that is, the part of the warehouse that defines the data. Metadata means "data about data." Metadata explains the meaning of each data element, how each element relates to other elements, who owns each element, the source of each element, who can access each element, and so on.

Metadata sets the standard. Without it, data from different legacy systems cannot be reconciled, so the data will not be clean; that is, comparable. Without comparable data, the warehouse is not of much use. So an important aspect of data warehousing is creating and then enforcing common data definitions via metadata definitions.

Because the world continues to change, so, too, does the metadata. Thus, a metadata librarian is needed to keep it up-to-date, to enforce the standards, and even to educate users about metadata features of the warehouse. Metadata can be used not only to understand the data in the warehouse, but also to navigate through the warehouse.

Quality data: The biggest challenge.   Once metadata definitions have been established, the largest job of data warehousing teams is cleaning the data to adhere to those standards. This cleaning process is onerous, lament warehousing teams, because legacy data often has definitions that have changed over time, gaps, missing fields, and so on. Sometimes, the source data was not even validated properly, for instance, to ensure that the postal code field contained the right number and type of characters.

The older the data, the more suspect its quality. However, because users want to track items over time, even with poor quality, data warehousing teams cannot discard the old, poor-quality data. They must find ways to align it with the more recent data, generally by estimating the data that should be in the missing fields, realigning figures based on the newer formulas, and so forth. This grueling manual task is one of the largest the warehousing team must perform.

Data marts: Subsets of data warehouses.   When data warehousing was first espoused, the ideal was to build one huge, all-encompassing warehouse. However, that goal has not always proved feasible or practical. For one thing, search times can be excruciatingly long in huge warehouses. For another, the cost may be too high.

Thus, the concept of data marts became popular. A *data mart* is a subset of data pulled off the warehouse for a specific group of users. A data mart is less expensive to build and easier to search. For these reasons, some companies have started their data warehouse work by first building data marts. Then they populate the data warehouse by drawing from these marts. This approach is the reverse of what was espoused just a few years ago when purists believed that data should go from a data warehouse to data marts.

The main challenge in following this mart-to-warehouse approach is that the company must have unifying metadata, so that the data in all the marts uses the same definitions. Otherwise, the data cannot be meaningfully correlated in the warehouse.

Steps in a Data Warehousing Project.   A typical data warehousing project has five main steps.

1. ***Define the business uses of the data.*** Warehousing projects that are run solely by IS departments without a sponsoring user department are generally unsuccessful. The data needs a business use to demonstrate payback.

2. ***Create the data model for the warehouse.*** This means defining the relationships among the data elements. This process can be quite a challenge, especially when commingling data from a number of systems.

3. ***Cleanse the data.*** This notorious step requires moving the data out of the operational systems and then transforming it into the desired standardized format. Specific tools can help cleanse standard kinds of data, such as names and addresses, but defining the transformations is often manual, as is filling in gaps.

4. ***Select the user tools.*** Consider the users' point of view and then select the tools they will use and train them to use them.

5. ***Monitor usage and system performance.*** Warehouse teams need to be particularly alert to changes in use. In many cases, usage begins slowly. But when it catches on, performance can degrade seriously as the system and the team are swamped with requests. If, however, the team monitors use and creates standard queries that serve groups of users rather than individuals, the team can reduce its workload and speed up system response time as well.

The following lengthy case example illustrates numerous ways one company is using its data for competitive advantage. The case illustrates use of ERP, data warehousing, and the Web, not only for internal use of data, but as the basis for new revenue-generating services to customers and suppliers. It shows how innovative companies can use advanced information management technologies. This case is based on a paper that won one of the awards in the Society for Information Management's[7] annual paper competition. This competition attracts some of the best in-depth descriptions of IS management in practice. The company is Owens & Minor.

CASE EXAMPLE

OWENS & MINOR

Owens & Minor (OM), headquartered in Richmond, Virginia, distributes name-brand medical and surgical supplies from 14,000 suppliers to over 4,000 hospitals, integrated health-care systems, and group purchasing organizations throughout the United States. OM employs 2,700 people and had sales of $3.8 billion in 2001.

As Don Stoller, Director of Information Management,[7] and his co-authors point out, OM is in the middle of its value chain. The supply side begins with raw material suppliers who sell to manufacturers (such as Johnson & Johnson), who sell to OM (the distributor), who then sells to health-care providers (such as hospitals), who sell to patients. In this field, distributors compete for contracts between manufacturers and health-care providers.

In the mid-1990s, OM bought a competitor, doubling OM's size to $3 billion. However, merging the two cultures proved so difficult that OM recorded its first loss. This loss spurred management to implement a new three-part strategy:

1. Achieve operational excellence
2. Follow and support patient care
3. Turn information into knowledge and then into profit

This strategy depended on building a leading-edge IT infrastructure and an IT R&D culture, which it did. In 1999, it won an award for its industry-leading e-business infrastructure. Here is what OM did.

Achieving Operational Excellence

OM augmented its ERP system to automate order forecasting, which improved inventory turns, reduced ordering rates from five times a week to once a week, and improved customer service. OM also installed an activity-based costing system to separate the cost of its products from the cost of delivery. Thus, customers, such as hospitals or purchasing groups, could pay just for the delivery service they wanted. Some wanted delivery to a loading dock; others wanted delivery to an emergency room. Some customers saved large amounts of money with this new option, and OM increased its sales. A new warehouse management system that uses handheld devices also increased OM's operational efficiency.

Following and Supporting Patient Care

OM implemented an Internet-based inventory management system, called OM-Direct, so that customers could order over the Internet, even using handheld devices. For example, when a hospital signs up for this service, it can ask OM to place bar codes on the products and establish replenishment levels. Then, when a hospital employee scans the bar code with, say, a Palm device, enters the on-hand inventory of that product, and uploads the data to OM's system, the system automatically reorders the product, if needed. Some 1,100 customers signed up for OM-Direct during its first 2 years.

(Case Continued)

To serve smaller customers and suppliers, such as physicians' offices, small hospitals, and small specialist suppliers, OM teamed up with trading exchanges to provide online marketplaces for these members to buy and sell products and even use OM-Direct. The exchanges have encouraged these customers to start using the Internet for ordering, even though they only offer 1,700 of OM's 150,000 products.

Turning Information into Knowledge and Profit

Most interestingly, OM initiated a data warehousing and decision-support initiative, building one subject area at a time (sales, inventory, accounts receivable, and so on), and permitting queries across the subject areas. During the first year, much of the work was handled by a system integrator familiar with building data warehouses. After that, it became the responsibility of a 12-person OM team that included a director, a manager, three developers who add new subject areas and load data, one data administrator, and six business analysts, who work with the users.

Initially, the warehouse was for internal use only. Within the first 30 months, some 500 OM employees in sales, marketing, supply chain management, finance, and other departments had learned to use the BusinessObjects tool to make queries or create reports from the warehouse, report Stoller et al.[7]

For several reasons, the warehouse team then investigated offering decision support over the Web. Customers were asking sales reps for more information; some requesting up to 30 reports a month. Why not let the customers serve

themselves? Also, the Web would allow casual users, such as customers or executives who do not want to learn Business-Objects, to access the data in the data warehouse. Furthermore, OM realized that customers and suppliers were asking for information to run their own businesses because they did not have the systems or technology in-house. Delivering this information over the Web could give OM a competitive advantage by strengthening its relationships with trading partners, giving it a market-leading feature to entice new customers, and even turning the data warehouse into a new service; in fact, a new source of revenue.

To assist its trading partners, OM created an extranet and asked a pilot set of customers and suppliers to list the kinds of information they needed to, say, reduce their costs or better manage their inventories. From these lists, the OM warehousing team created queries and let these partners pilot test the system for 4 months. During that time, OM debated whether to offer this service for free or for a fee. It decided to charge money, reasoning that the information would appear more valuable if it had a price. Furthermore, the fees would be reasonable, especially compared with the up-front data warehousing costs partners would be able to avoid.

When the service, called Wisdom, was rolled out, it became the first "e-business intelligence application" in the medical and surgical supply distribution industry, state Stoller et al.

All users have a profile of the information they can access. Every access is checked by the security system. Every

(Case Continued)

query contains the user's account number so that the system knows which information can be used to answer the query. The browser interface is easy to use; people point and click on over 50 predefined queries, or, more recently, make ad hoc queries.

OM has continued to improve the service. Suppliers and customers can now add external data, such as data from other manufacturers, into OM's data warehouse so they can study more relationships and perform more "what if" investigations.

For example, a typical-size hospital spends $30 million a year buying all its medical and surgical supplies. Hospital groups can have a difficult time analyzing purchases across all their hospitals, because each has a disparate system. Rather than invest in consolidating the systems themselves, hospital groups would rather purchase data about their own transactions from, say, a distributor, who is well placed in the value chain to have that information.

OM has thus become an important "infomediary," note Stoller et al., because hospital purchasing staffs may have a much easier time getting the purchasing information they need from OM than from their own hospital. They can then discover, for instance, which purchases were "on contract" with OM, and thus had the lower contract price, and which were not. Oftentimes, up to 40 percent of hospital purchases are off-contract, which costs these hospitals money they need not spend. Furthermore, purchasing managers can see how many suppliers they use for the same

product and negotiate higher-volume discounts from just one or two. They can also see ordering frequency and optimize it by increasing order volumes, perhaps. In addition, they can more easily spot delivery problems.

OM's Wisdom service turns out to be equally valuable to suppliers, such as Johnson & Johnson. Wisdom has over 30 queries and 100 reports for suppliers to watch their products move out to consumers. They can analyze their market-share in specific regions, analyze product shelf life, coordinate shipping from several locations, see on-contract purchasing (and help customers increase the levels), analyze drop shipments (which are more expensive than OM distribution), and so forth.

Wisdom has become a valuable service to both OM suppliers and customers, and it becomes more valuable the more sales or purchases go through OM rather than through other distributors. In fact, Wisdom led to over $60 million in new business in 1 year because it is providing visibility throughout OM's value chain. Because partners pay for its use, there is constant pressure to keep it market leading, note Stoller et al.

The next step is to turn the data warehouse into an industry-wide warehouse by asking suppliers and customers to place all their data there. If this occurs, conceivably, other distributors might become paying customers of Wisdom as well. Or, as OM and three competitors have agreed, they will establish an independent, neutral health care information exchange. ■

Document Management

Now we turn to managing document-based information. Management of *internal* document-based information has traditionally rested with the vice president of administration, who has traditionally overseen records management (document records, not data records). Technologies used to manage documents have included micrographics (microfilm and fiche) and computer output microfilm (COM), generally in stand-alone systems. That is, until the Internet arrived. Now corporate intranets house many former paper-based internal documents.

External document-based information, on the other hand, has generally been the responsibility of corporate librarians. Yet, as the amount of such external information grows and as more of it has become computerized, it is increasingly being included in IS executives' jurisdiction. Again, it has been the Web that has brought these external documents to the attention of CIOs, yet many of them consider documents to be the least manageable form of information.

Even in today's Internet-rich world, paper still plays a major role in most enterprises. And while paper is around, there is a need to move seamlessly between digital and printed versions of documents. Hence, the importance of document management. The field of electronic document management (EDM) uses new technologies to manage information resources that do not fit easily into traditional databases. EDM addresses organizing and managing conceptual, descriptive, and ambiguous multimedia content.

Using IT to manage documents is a challenge for enterprises because most of their valuable information is in documents, such as business forms, reports, letters, memos, policy statements, contracts, agreements, and so on.[8] Moreover, most of their important business processes are based on or driven by document flows. While computer systems have mostly handled facts organized into data records, far more valuable and important are the concepts and ideas contained in documents. Reports drawn from computerized databases fill important roles in status assessment and control. Oftentimes they must be accompanied by a memo or textual report that explains and interprets the report. Meetings, phone conversations, news items, written memos, and non-computerized reports are usually rated more important by managers. Technology applied to handling documents promises to improve these forms of communication.

A document can be described as a unit of "recorded information structured for human consumption."[9] It is recorded and stored; therefore, a speech or conversation for which no transcript is prepared is not a document. This definition accommodates "documents" dating back to cuneiform inscriptions on clay tablets. What has changed are the ways information is represented and the ways documents are processed. Information previously represented primarily by text is now also represented by graphical symbols, images, photographs, audio, video, and animation. Documents previously created and stored on paper are now digitally created, stored, transported, and displayed.

Applying technology to process traditional documents changes what documents can accomplish in organizations. A definition more oriented to technology comes from *Byte* magazine.[10]

A document is a snapshot of some set of information that can

- *incorporate many complex information types;*
- *exist in multiple places across a network;*

- *depend on other documents for information;*
- *change on the fly (as subordinate documents are updated);*
- *have an intricate structure or complex data types such as full-motion video and voice annotations; and*
- *be accessed and modified by many people simultaneously (if they have permission to do so).*

It is hard to think of anything more pervasive and fundamental to an organization than documents. The impact of applying emerging technologies to document management is potentially significant. EDM promises to advance the management of conceptual information, thereby improving the levels of support and productivity for manager and professional. With documents as the primary vehicle for business processes, EDM contributes to business process redesign and quality improvement. Numerous EDM applications generate value. In this section, we will examine three:

1. To improve the publishing process
2. To support organizational processes
3. To support communications among people and groups

The concept of just-in-time (printing, publishing, and forms processing) pervades the design philosophy in all three areas.

Improving the Publishing Process.   Technology enables a major restructuring of the process of publishing and distributing paper documents. For those organizations that produce documents as a product or as support for a product, this change is reengineering their document production processes. The stages of the traditional process, designed primarily for high-volume and high-quality documents, is shown in Figure 7-6. The document is created, generally with the use of electronic tools, and a photographic plate is made for an offset printing press. The offset press requires long print runs to amortize the extensive setup costs. Thus, a large quantity of documents is produced and stored in a warehouse and then documents are shipped to their destination when they are required. R. R. Donnelley & Sons Company, the country's largest publisher, estimates that 60 percent of the total cost of delivering these documents is in storage and transportation.

Figure 7-7 shows the steps in the revised publishing/distribution process using newer technologies. Documents are stored electronically, shipped over a network, and printed when and where they are needed. The major benefits result from reducing obsolescence (revisions are made frequently to the electronically stored version), eliminating warehouse costs, and reducing or eliminating delivery time.

Here is an example of how a traditional printing process has been changed by emerging technologies.

FIGURE 7-6 Traditional Publishing Process

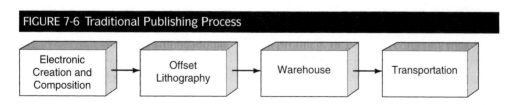

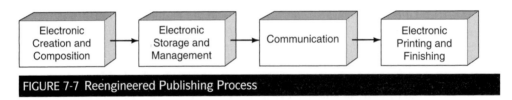

FIGURE 7-7 Reengineered Publishing Process

CASE EXAMPLE

HICSS PERSONAL PROCEEDINGS

The Hawaii International Conference on System Sciences has been held each January since 1967. It brings together academics and professionals to discuss research papers from a wide variety of computer-related subjects.

The conference proceedings have made an important contribution to the literature for many years. But with more than 450 papers averaging 10 pages each in length, the proceedings have grown to 4,500 pages in 9 volumes weighing 25 pounds. As a result, conference management decided to produce a paper book of abstracts with a CD-ROM of the full papers tucked in a sleeve inside the back cover. This publishing approach reduced the paper problem, but many participants wanted to see the full papers during the presentations and discussions. They had

been using the paper versions to take notes and to understand additional details of the presentation.

Conference management then introduced personal proceedings. A month before the conference, participants can use a Web site to choose 20 papers they would like to have in their personal paper proceedings. The papers they choose are printed on a Xerox Docutech machine with their name on the cover and delivered to them at the conference. Additional papers can be printed individually at the conference using the conference print-on-demand service for a nominal fee. This new use of print-on-demand technology has helped the conference meet the participants' needs while cutting costs and reducing paper. ■

Supporting Communications Among People and Groups.   The value of documents is that they transfer information across time and space. Of course, the Internet can handle such communication, but when all members of a group do not have Internet access, or do not use it frequently, companies may need to continue to rely on paper documents. EDM can be used to facilitate such communications among people and groups. In the broadest sense, all EDM applications support this function. The following case illustrates using various technologies to communicate with customers via paper and ensure that each customer gets the right pieces of paper.

CASE EXAMPLE

TAPIOLA INSURANCE GROUP

Tapiola is a group of three insurance companies with headquarters in Espoo, Finland, a suburb of Helsinki. By Finnish law, an insurance company can sell only one type of insurance; therefore, each of Tapiola's three companies sells either life, non-life, or pension insurance. Tapiola calls itself "an insurance department store."

Some 90 percent of insurance in Finland is sold by five insurance groups; Tapiola is the fourth-largest group. It has 14 percent of the market with 1.5 million customers and 3 million policies. Each year its mailroom sends out 4 million letters, so printing is an important and expensive part of its operation.

Formerly, the Tapiola group offered 150 kinds of insurance policies and had 300 different insurance policy forms. Half of the forms were in Swedish and half were in Finnish because both are official languages in Finland. The policy forms were preprinted by an outside print shop, generally on sprocket-fed computer paper. Then the forms were filled in by printers connected to their IBM mainframes.

This mode of operation presented several problems. If a change was made to a form, the inventory of old forms had to be discarded. Reprinting new forms often took weeks. That time represented possible lost revenue. Also, the computer printers could print on only one side of each sheet of paper. Finally, for more complex policies, Tapiola had to use large-size computer paper that was often unwieldy to handle and mail.

Document-Processing Goals

The production manager and the insurance applications development manager looked around for an alternate way to print policies and statements. They had several goals. One was, of course, to reduce costs. A second goal was to stop using preprinted forms. Their third goal was to give Tapiola marketing people new ways to advertise insurance products by making computer-generated letters to customers more flexible. The fourth and most important goal was to make Tapiola "the most personal insurance company in Finland." These two systems managers wanted their computer-generated correspondence to prospective and current policyholders to appear more "human," as if a Tapiola employee had used a typewriter to write a personal reply to an inquiry or request for information.

Centralized Solution

To overcome the computer-generated appearance of their output, they switched to plain paper printers from Rank Xerox, the European subsidiary of Xerox Corporation. Xerox is best known for its photocopiers, but it is increasingly creating products for electronic document processing where a document can include text, data, images, and graphics. Conversion of the output equipment at Tapiola took 15 months, during which time it reduced its 300 preprinted forms to 4.

(Case Continued)

Four New Forms

The four new forms are actually four types of standard European A4-cut paper. (In the United States, the equivalent would be the $8^1/2 \times 11$ sheet of paper.) The first form is a plain white A4 sheet of paper. It is used for internal communications within Tapiola.

The second form is the same blank white paper with four holes punched along the left-hand side to fit in the standard European four-ring binder. (In the United States, the standard is a three-ring binder.) This form is also mainly for internal use.

The third form has the Tapiola logo preprinted in green in the upper left-hand corner, and both sides of the paper have the word "Tapiola" printed in tiny, faint green letters over most of the page. This form is the standard company stationery, and it has become one of Tapiola's standard computer printout forms for communicating with the outside world.

The fourth form is the same as the third except that it has a 4×6-inch (10×15-cm) perforated area in the lower right-hand corner. This form is used for all their insurance policy bills. The tear-off portion can be paid at any bank; the money and information about the payment go directly from the bank to Tapiola.

Programming and Conversion

Reprogramming the IBM applications was extremely easy, because only the output routines needed to be changed. That programming took 2 work years of application programmer time. In addition, one systems programmer spent 6 months working with Xerox on the IBM-to-Xerox system software interfaces. One forms designer spent 15 months redesigning all 300 preprinted forms into 240 printing formats for the application programmers. About 60 forms disappeared altogether because they were found to be unnecessary; the remaining 240 forms are not all different because one-half of them are in Swedish and the other half are in Finnish.

The conversion was done in two stages. First, customer policy statements were printed in a form-like manner on two sides of the new-size paper. These looked somewhat like the old forms so that policyholders could understand the changeover. Then, the terse, table-like data was replaced with text to make the statements look more like personal letters.

Envelope Stuffing

Interestingly, these redesigns of customer documents were the easy part of the conversion. The more difficult and sensitive part was making sure that each envelope contained the correct pieces of paper. Because Tapiola was now using smaller sheets of paper, each envelope often needed to include several sheets, and, of course, Tapiola did not want to put a cover letter for one policyholder into the same envelope as a statement for another policyholder.

To solve this problem, the company found an envelope insertion machine made by PMB Vector in Stockholm, Sweden. This machine contains a microprocessor that can read an eight-dot code printed at the top of each sheet of paper. Thus, the Xerox printer not only prints the correspondence but, at the same time, it prints a code at the top of each sheet of paper—one code for all pages to go in one envelope. The Vector insertion machine makes sure that each envelope only contains pages with the same code.

(Case Continued)

Decentralized Expansion

This document-processing conversion was just one part of the effort to improve and humanize customer correspondence. In the midst of the document redesign, Tapiola also decided to move some printing of customer correspondence to its 62 branch offices.

To illustrate how a remote printer is used, consider the case of a female policyholder who has received medical care. She can mail the medical bills to Tapiola or visit her local office in person. If she visits them and presents her bills to a Tapiola employee, that employee uses a desktop machine to access the policyholder's data from the central database. If she has brought all the proper documents needed for reimbursement, the employee can initiate a direct electronic payment from a Tapiola bank account to her personal bank account, no matter which bank they both use.

Once a day, Tapiola transmits all such electronic transactions to its bank, and those transactions are cleared that same day. (The five major Finnish banks have collaborated and created a sophisticated and fast banking system.) The employee then gives the policyholder a letter verifying the transaction. That letter is generated by the central IBM computer but is printed on the local Xerox printer. If the policyholder is missing some information, the employee can create a personalized letter explaining what is missing by assembling phrases stored in the central database and then printing the letter on-site.

The people at Tapiola Data recommend that other IS organizations become involved in electronic document management by first looking at the output their computers are generating. It was not difficult to mix traditional host computing with document processing technology.

A poll of Finnish citizens showed that Tapiola is seen as a dynamic company, and it has the best reputation among young people of all the insurance groups. The people at Tapiola Data believe their use of document-processing technology is helping to build and reinforce this image. ∎

Supporting Organizational Processes.   Documents are still the vehicle for accomplishing many processes in organizations. Typical examples include processing a claim in an insurance company, hiring a new employee, or making a large expenditure. The documents are primarily forms that flow through the organization carrying information, accumulating input and approval from a sequence of people. Many such workflow systems still rely heavily on the physical circulation of paper forms.

Using IT to support these processes generates significant value in reducing physical space for handling forms, faster routing of forms (especially over geographical distances), and managing and tracking forms flow and workload. Two trends in organizations have increased the importance of workflow systems: total quality management and business process reengineering.

In addition to improving transaction-oriented business processes with EDM, many organizations are improving the management processes of reporting, control, decision making, and problem solving as well. Several EISs now supply documents to supplement the more traditional data-based reports. Organizations with a custom-developed EIS also add so-called *soft information* in the form of documents.[11]

To give an example of how one organization improved a work process via a new document management system, consider the Tennessee Valley Authority.[12]

CASE EXAMPLE

TENNESSEE VALLEY AUTHORITY

The Tennessee Valley Authority (TVA) is the largest supplier of power in the United States, serving some 8 million customers in the eastern United States by generating energy using fossil, hydroelectric, and nuclear fuels. Not long ago, the nuclear division, which has three facilities, revamped its maintenance management system—a system that relies on documents, such as manuals from vendors, drawings, and work instructions, that are regulated by government.

TVA spends more than $48 million a year creating maintenance work orders and then planning and performing the work. One plant alone processes 14,000 work orders a year. Government regulations that oversee the documentation of this work contribute significantly to TVA's high maintenance costs.

The improvement project was handled by a team from various parts of the nuclear operation. They analyzed and charted the existing work processes, determined which improvements were most needed, and investigated how those improvements could be achieved. They spent 350 hours interviewing people and looked at 15 other utilities.

One thing they discovered was that the work orders were inextricably linked to document workflow and the ways procedures were managed. Previously, the three areas—work order management, document workflow, and procedure management—had been viewed as separate, and thus managed separately. Upon investigation, the team realized that every work order included accompanying diagrams, documentation, and procedure instructions. However, the three were not always in sync. For example, a work order might be planned several months in advance, but in the meantime, procedures might be changed, yet those changes were not noted when the work order was about to be performed.

The new process designed by TVA electronically combines maintenance orders in one system with procedural document management in another system and eliminates a number of existing systems that did not talk to one another. Maintenance workers can now access documentation on equipment, parts, and records as well as work instructions from desktop machines. Work orders are generated electronically and then routed for approval with the most current drawings and procedures electronically attached. In addition, the documents are indexed by, say, piece of equipment, and the three

(Case Continued)

plants now use the same systems. Thus, maintenance people can review past activity and better plan for the future.

The system has been successful, but the team underestimated the change management effort needed. They did not realize they had to bring many employees up-to-speed on using computers; some had not used keyboards. In addition, the team realized they should have set expectations differently. Rather than emphasize the benefits of the new systems to each employee (because sometimes the new systems required more work of some employees), the team should have emphasized the benefits of the system to TVA, which were significant.

The average amount of human time spent processing a work order has decreased by almost half, from 39 hours to 23 hours; labor savings are large. More importantly, maintenance workers now have captured data for improving processes. ∎

Content Management

We now turn to the other form of document-based information: Web content. As noted earlier, many corporate intranets now house documents that used to be paper based. In some cases, these documents appear in PDF form on the intranet, which is like taking a photograph of the pages so that the pages cannot be changed.

The question for CIOs has become: How should we manage all the internal and external content on our Web sites? The field that addresses this question is called *content management*. It deals with managing Web-based content of all types, writes Chuck Tucker in the Gartner EXP report entitled *Dealing in Web Currency*.[6b] A major reason content has become important to CIOs, he notes, is because it is a core management discipline underlying online business. Without production-level Web content management processes and technologies, large-scale online-business is not possible. The content on Web sites attracts customers, answers questions, and handles transactions. If the content is not refreshed frequently, perhaps as news occurs, or if it is full of errors, or if it cannot handle transaction volumes, a company's Web channel will stave off rather than attract customers.

Content is no longer static; it is active. It can cause actions to happen. An underlying reason is the adoption of XML. XML is used to put tags on data that give that data meaning. Computers use the meanings to manipulate the data and perform work. In essence, use of XML moves Web content from being in a human-only readable format to being in a computer-readable format. Thus, the content can be passed to back-end transaction processing systems and cause an action to take place, such as ordering a book or configuring a recently ordered computer. XML is an intrinsic part of managing Web content because it is the language for manipulating the content to work with transaction applications, which is the basis for e-commerce.

In the beginning, when Web sites were new, Web content was managed as follows: Someone in a department, usually HR or marketing, decided to use this new communication channel. They designed a format, decided on the sections on the site, and wrote the content or gathered it from written documents. The department then gave all this content to the Webmaster to publish. When new material needed to be added, they gave it to the Webmaster, who turned it into HTML and published it to the Web site. Before long, the Webmaster became the publishing bottleneck; time to publish got longer and longer. This home-grown method was not only inefficient, but it also did not present a good image to Web site visitors.

To create a content management strategy, states Tucker, companies need to understand the three phases of the content management life cycle and the goals for each one. As shown in Figure 7-8, the three phases, which can be viewed as input–process–output, are:

1. Content creation and acquisition
2. Content administration and safeguarding
3. Content deployment and presentation

Managing Content Creation and Acquisition.   Each phase needs a different emphasis to be effective, notes Tucker. Content creation and acquisition, for instance, needs to focus on *creating content quality*. That is why it might be wise to buy some content from specialists, which is called *syndicated content*, rather than create it in-house. For example, why create a stock ticker or a weather report or a news feed? Draw on the ones that already exist.

High-quality in-house content comes from subject matter experts and local employees. Thus, the best organizational structure is to distribute content creation and maintenance to employees in HR, marketing, sales, and field offices. They should be responsible not only for creating their content, but also for keeping it updated and fresh.

To avoid anarchy, though, these dispersed experts should be directed centrally and use centrally created formats and an automated workflow system that moves their work along. The system might even send them reminder e-mails of publishing deadlines. Finally, to improve content quality, it is wise to create a feedback loop so that comments from Web site visitors reach these content creators. Then these creators know what types of content attract visitors and customers.

FIGURE 7-8 The Web Content Management Life Cycle

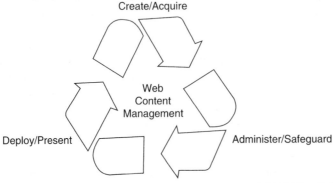

Source: Tueber, Chuck, *Dealing in Web Currency*, Gartner EXP, 56 Top Gallant, Stamford, CT, June 2001.

Content Administration and Safeguarding. The emphasis in this phase, like any operational phase, is *efficiency*, states Tucker. The goal is to achieve the most with the least effort. Content management software tools can help. These tools are used to identify types of content and the business rules that apply to each type. For example, publication of press releases on a Web site should follow business rules that state that each release will first be approved by the manager of corporate communications, each press release will use the standard press release format, and each release will move to the archive file 1 month after being published. Business rules form the heart of content administration. They present the parameters for the automated workflow for each type of content, thus relieving the Webmaster bottleneck.

So, whereas content creation should be distributed, content administration should be centralized, which is the same type of federal structure noted in Chapter 2 for managing IS. This structure permits overall central guidance of distributed creative efforts. However, it does present some vexing challenges. One involves the approval process of foreign-language content. Companies that create an approval process believing that all content will be in, say, English, create translation bottlenecks for themselves if they expect all drafts to be translated into English for approval and then translated back into the original language once the document is approved. Companies need to consider multilanguage issues when creating their workflows, selecting their content management software, and designing their Web sites.

Content Deployment and Presentation. The third phase of the content management life cycle is the output phase, distributing content to Web site visitors. The emphasis in this phase should be on *effectiveness*, that is, presenting the content so that it attracts visitors, allows them to navigate the site easily, and leads them to the desired actions, notes Tucker.

Because this phase can determine the success of a firm's e-commerce efforts, it is best to design a Web site beginning with this phase, then move on to ensuring content quality and processing efficiency. The Eastman Chemical Company example that follows illustrates this outside-in viewpoint; most companies take an inside-out view. Eastman redesigned its site to take its customers' point of view rather than its internal organizational point of view. The change had a major positive impact.

Today, most Web sites need certain features to attract and keep visitors. Two such features are personalization and localization. Personalization means allowing Web site visitors to customize how they view the page. For instance, some visitors to consumer sites may want lots of sports news but little international news. On the other hand, business visitors to corporate sites might want the site to open to the products they buy or recent news pertinent to their industry. Web content software gives site builders the ability to offer site visitors viewing options. Once selected, the choices are stored in the users' profile and referenced every time they visit the site. Companies can also use personalization to offer complementary products, such as corkscrews to wine buyers, notes Tucker, or take into account a customer's past buying record.

Localization, on the other hand, means tailoring a site to a culture, market, or locale. For instance, a site may be designed to present its content in the language of the country or region of the visitor. Likewise, localization may mean making appropriate currency conversions automatically. Localization is crucial for companies involved in global e-commerce.

Finally, a growing issue in deployment is multichannel distribution; that is, being able to display the site in the manner appropriate to each type of device, from PC to cell phone. Ideally, the information comes from a common repository, rather than existing in several places, and is put in the appropriate form when requested, notes Tucker. Otherwise, if the same content is stored in several places, it can get out of sync. Central storage is important to maintain content quality.

In summary, the way to manage content is to understand the goal of each phase of the content life cycle—quality, efficiency, or effectiveness—and design the phase with that goal in mind. In addition, there should be a feedback loop, so that Web site visitors can tell Web site content creators which content is most useful to them. Such a loop can then drive continual improvement in the Web site.

To illustrate how one company is managing its Web content, consider Eastman Chemical, whose story appeared in Tucker's report entitled *Dealing in Web Currency*.

CASE EXAMPLE

EASTMAN CHEMICAL COMPANY

Eastman Chemical Company, which is located in Kingsport, Tennessee, is a global manufacturer of chemicals, fibers, and plastics. Founded in 1920 to make chemicals for Eastman Kodak, it was spun off in 1994. Annual sales were $5.4 billion in 2001.

Management considers the company a leader in using IT. Eastman.com was operational in 1994, several years before most companies had Web sites. Originally the site was used for HR and recruiting. Over time, as more content was added, the site became a hodge-podge of different sections targeted at different audiences, structured like Eastman's organization chart.

Redesigning the Web Site to Take the Customer Viewpoint

In mid-1999, Eastman initiated a companywide effort to become more customer focused and launched a major e-commerce program. This was the catalyst for rethinking the Web site design. The redesign was championed by the vice presidents of e-commerce and corporate communications because their departments jointly managed content.

The e-commerce group provides the tools and processes for employees to create and update Web content. The corporate communications department enforces corporate content policy and approves all Web content for correct use of trademarks, brands, terminology, and so on.

In line with the corporate refocus, the two groups decided to change the Web site structure from presenting an inside-out view based on Eastman's corporate structure to presenting an outside-in view with sections devoted to the markets the company serves.

A packaging customer who bought plastics from two Eastman operations formerly had to search the site to find who

(Case Continued)

supplied plastics. Once found, each section had a different navigational system. In the redesign, a single section on food packaging was created for all Eastman operations dealing with packaging.

Eastman worked with a Web design company on the new site architecture, site map, and layout.

Upgrading the Content Management Software

At the same time, Eastman searched for content management software to replace home-grown software in use since 1994. The flat HTML files created a maintenance bottleneck because each page had to be updated separately and required a programmer to translate the content into HTML.

Eastman selected a content management product to create pre-approved templates for employees to use, then forward the pages to corporate communications for approval. This approach eliminated the programmer bottleneck. The software manages employees' rights to update, add, and publish content. Each user ID has a security level and permissible functions associated with it.

Pulling all the business content together for the new site turned out to be a massive effort. Once the content had been compiled, cataloged, and approved, moving from the old system and server to the new system and new content proved to be a second major undertaking.

Benefits of the Site Redesign

The benefits of the redesign were far greater than expected. Within 6 months, overall traffic doubled, and hits to the new market sections, where Eastman sells its products, increased from 30 percent to 60 percent of total hits. Today, traffic has tripled, and 70 percent of the hits are in the market sectors. Adding new content significantly helped increase traffic, but so, too, did the customer focus.

Eastman underestimated the value of the technical product data sheets published on the site, especially to people outside the United States who previously were unable to get this information easily or quickly. More than 50 percent of the site traffic is from outside the United States. Customers report that the technical data has also significantly accelerated their internal decision-making processes.

To manage the technical data, Eastman uses an internally developed product catalog. Formerly, a data sheet could exist in multiple locations, which led to quality problems, because each had to be updated separately. With the product catalog, the data is stored once and is pulled into a data sheet when needed. Thus, Eastman can ensure that everyone sees the same data on a chemical, even in two different markets.

The site has a public part that anyone can access and a protected part for customers only. Once customers are registered and have a user name and password, they can place orders, look at their order history and status, and browse the product catalog in this protected part. They can also personalize their view of the site to some extent and create their own catalog of the products they normally order.

Since the redesign, Eastman has continued to expand the site. It recently improved search capabilities and added a synonym directory, which has proven important because site visitors often use different names for the same product.

(Case Continued)

Moving Forward: Globalization and Localization

Globalization and localization are major issues. Eastman has a presence in more than 30 countries and sells in all major regions of the world. A significant portion of sales comes from overseas, so the company wants to allow a site visitor to choose one of, say, eight languages and see the relevant content in that language. If it had treated English as a foreign language during the 1999 redesign, it could add other languages easily. Thinking globally in all content management decisions is a necessity.

Another major challenge is finding a workable global approval process. Checking for adherence to content policies by corporate communications is quick today because all content is in English. However, translation into multiple lan-guages and adaptation to local cultures can significantly complicate and lengthen this approval process. Retranslation into English for corporate approval is too expensive to be feasible. The e-commerce and corporate communications depart-ments are currently working on creating a workable translation and approval process for content originating in other languages.

Eastman has learned that it is best to push content management to the source as much as possible so as not to create bottlenecks at central control points. It also learned the value of consistent organization throughout the Web site. This helps present a cohesive image of the company to site visitors. Having the content management system pull infor-mation from the product catalog also ensures data consistency. ■

Managing Blogs.   The term *blog* is short for "*Web log*" or "Weblog." A blog is a Web site where an individual makes intermittent Web postings. It is akin to a personal online journal. People write and post on blogs as a form of self-expression. What do they write about? They write about whatever comes to mind. They may write about their private life or their work life. Most blogs also invite comments from others, which appear on the blog as well. Blogs are a different form of Web content, but they still need to be managed. Enterprises need to establish guidelines for employees who choose to blog.

Blogs are powerful tools for democratizing online expression, notes Dan Farber.[13] According to Farber, "Combine blogs with social networks and presence services (such as instant messaging and global positioning), and you have a new person-to-person, information-sharing connection fabric." In short, individuals can compete with major media via blogs, and they can have major impacts such as influencing politics or com-pany policies. Some forward-thinking companies have recognized the power of this immediate form of publishing and communication. One corporate use of blogs is for crisis management. A blog can be more appropriate than e-mail in managing a crisis (such as a fire or a security breach). All the postings can be on one site, in journaling style, rather than passed as disconnected e-mails, notes Farber.

What readers seem to trust about blogs, that they do not trust about conventional media, is their opinionated and personal nature. These characteristics present both opportunities and challenges to organizations. For example, Farber notes that Microsoft employee Robert Scoble's popular blog about the company's forthcoming version of Windows, Longhorn, is not vetted by Microsoft. It's Scoble's opinions. But he does admit that he talks to the company's public relations department to be sure he does not divulge company-confidential information, notes Farber. Scoble's blog can be found at http://radio.weblogs.com.0001011

Employees who are not careful about the information they blog can find themselves in trouble. A hypothetical case study of a blogger who works for a disposable-glove manufacturer is presented in the September 2003 issue of the *Harvard Business Review*.[14] Known as "Glove Girl," her highly popular blog has increased sales of a company glove, but she has also talked about competitors' products, potential deals, and industry statistics—all from her own point of view, not the company's. This case poses the question, "What should company management do about Glove Girl?" to four experts. It's a question all top management teams should be asking themselves.

One of the experts is Ray Ozzie, Chairman and CEO of Groove Networks, a company that provides software for group collaboration. He notes in his comments that he believes employee blogs are "more often than not" good for companies. But companies need policies to guide employees in expressing themselves via Weblogs or Web sites, while both protecting the company and reflecting positively on it. He notes that in 2002 his company developed such a policy, shown in the following case example, to address four concerns:

1. That readers would see blogs as official company communications rather than personal opinions
2. That confidential information would be disclosed, intentionally or not
3. That a party—the company, an employee, a customer, or other—could be disparaged on a blog
4. That a blog might violate the quiet period imposed by securities regulations, during which time a company cannot discuss an upcoming securities-related event

Ozzie's advice in the case, and to executives in general, is to create a policy for their firm and to become more familiar with blogging—even perhaps write their own blog, as he does at www.ozzie.net, to "communicate convincingly with employees, markets and shareholders."

CASE EXAMPLE

GROOVE NETWORKS

Employee Guidelines for Personal Web site and Weblogs[15]

In general, the company views personal Web sites and Weblogs positively, and it respects the right of employees to use them as a medium of self-expression.

(Case Continued)

If you choose to identify yourself as a company employee or to discuss matters related to the company's technology or business on your Web site or Weblog, please bear in mind that, although you and we view your Web site or Weblog as a personal project and a medium of personal expression, some readers may nonetheless view you as a de facto spokesperson for the company. In light of this possibility, we ask that you observe the following guidelines:

- Please make it clear to your readers that the views you express are yours alone and that they do not necessarily reflect the views of the company. To help reduce the potential for confusion, we would appreciate it if you put the following notice—or something similar—in a reasonably prominent place on your site (e.g., at the bottom of your "about me" page):

  The views expressed on this Web site/Weblog are mine alone and do not necessarily reflect the views of my employer.

If you do put a notice on your site, you needn't put it on every page, but please use reasonable efforts to draw attention to it—if at all possible, from the home page of your site.

- Take care not to disclose any information that is confidential or proprietary to the company or to any third party that has disclosed information to us. Consult the company's confidentiality policy for guidance about what constitutes confidential information.

- Please remember that your employment documents give the company certain rights with respect to concepts and developments you produce that are related to the company's business. Please consult your manager if you have questions about the appropriateness of publishing such concepts or developments on your site.

- Since your site is a public space, we hope you will be as respectful to the company, our employees, our customers, our partners and affiliates, and others (including our competitors) as the company itself endeavors to be.

- You may provide a link from your site to the company's Web site, if you wish. The Web design group has created a graphic for links to the company's site, which you may use for this purpose during the term of your employment (subject to discontinuation in the company's discretion). Contact a member of the Web design group for details. Please do not use other company trademarks on your site or reproduce company material without first obtaining permission.

Finally, the company may request that you temporarily confine your Web site or Weblog commentary to topics unrelated to the company (or, in rare cases, that you temporarily suspend your Web site or Weblog activity altogether) if it believes this is necessary or advisable to ensure compliance with securities regulations or other laws. ∎

CONCLUSION

As can be seen by the wide-ranging discussion in this chapter, the job of managing information resources is widening significantly. Not only must IS departments get corporate data in shape, but they must also create and build an infrastructure for managing the full range of information types. In some ways, the Internet helps because it gives companies an easily accessible place to store information. On the other hand, the Internet contributes mightily to the information glut we all face. We continue this discussion of information resources in Chapter 13 where we discuss supporting knowledge work. That is where we discuss managing knowledge and issues surrounding intellectual capital.

QUESTIONS AND EXERCISES

Review Questions

1. How do data, information, and knowledge differ?
2. Describe the three-level database concept. What are its advantages?
3. What are four database models?
4. What is the main problem in managing data?
5. Why was ERP a driving force in getting data into shape in many companies?
6. What are the four types of information?
7. What is a data warehouse?
8. What is metadata?
9. Why is O&M's Wisdom service valuable to suppliers?
10. What three electronic document management applications generate value?
11. Give the four goals of Tapiola Insurance Group's EDM project.
12. Why is XML important?
13. What are the three phases of the content management life cycle, according to Tucker, and what are the goals of each one?
14. Why did Eastman Chemical Company redesign its Web site?
15. What are the Weblog guidelines Groove Networks gives its employees?

Discussion Questions

1. In this chapter, the assertion is made that IS departments should concentrate on getting data right rather than getting systems up and running quickly. Discuss the pros and cons of this argument.
2. Technology does not change culture. Agree or disagree? Explain your point of view.
3. Do you agree that the IS department should take the lead in developing EDM? Why or why not?
4. If your answer to question 3 was yes, how can IS motivate other departments? If no, who do you think should coordinate the development of the systems and how?

Exercises

1. Find two articles on data management. Present any new ideas in these article to the class.
2. Find an example of each of the four kinds of information presented in Figure 7-3. They may be from company documents, the Web, or public publications. What new ideas on the (a) corporate authority, (b) technologies used, and (c) information sources did you gain from where you found these items? Did you find any evidence of a merging (or a diverging) of the management of these different types of information?
3. Visit a local company with a data administration function. Talk to the data administrator and find out:
   a. What kinds of data does the IS organization control and not control?
   b. What types of data problems is the group trying to solve?
   c. What progress is the group having in bringing data under control?
4. Visit a local company with a Web site and talk to the person who oversees content management and find out:
   a. What information technologies are used to store, catalog, and retrieve content?
   b. What kinds of information sources are used to supply the content?
   c. What is the organizational structure for managing content?
   d. What are the main content management issues today?

REFERENCES

1. Bradley, James, "The Elusive Relation," *Computerworld*, March 8, 1982, pp. 1–16. (This material was based largely on the author's book, *File and Data Base Techniques*, Holt, Rinehart & Winston, New York, 1982.)

2. Martin, James, *Principles of Database Management*, Prentice Hall, Upper Saddle River, NJ, 1976.

3. Atre, Shaku, *Data Base: Structured Techniques for Design, Performance, and Management*, John Wiley & Sons, New York, 1980.

4. Codd, E. F., "Relational Database: A Practical Foundation for Productivity," *Communications of the ACM*, February 1982, pp. 109–117.

5. "Special Sections: Next-Generation Database Systems," *Communications of the ACM*, October 1991, pp. 31–131.
   a. Stonebraker, M., and G. Kemnitz, "The Postgres Multi-Generation Database Management System," pp. 78–92.
   b. Silberschatz, A., M. Stonebraker, and J. Ullman (editors), "Database Systems: Achievements and Opportunities," pp. 110–120.

6. Gartner EXP, 56 Top Gallant, Stamford, CT, 06904; www.gartner.com:
   a. Varney, Cornelia, *Managing the Integrity of Distributed Systems*, Wentworth Research Group (now part of Gartner EXP), January 1996.
   b. Tucker, Chuck, *Dealing in Web Currency*, June 2001.

7. Stoller, Don, Barbara Wixom, and Hugh Watson, "WISDOM Provides Competitive Advantage at Owens & Minor: Competing in the New Economy," Honorable Mention Paper in the Society for Information Management's 2000 Paper Competition.

8. Sprague, Ralph H., Jr., "Electronic Document Management: Challenges and Opportunities for Information Systems Managers," *MIS Quarterly*, March 1995, pp. 29–49.

9. Levien, Roger E., *The Civilizing Currency: Documents and Their Revolutionary Technologies*, Xerox Corporation, Rochester, NY, 1989.

10. Michalski, G. P., "The World of Documents," *Byte*, April 1991, pp. 159–170.

11. Waston, Hugh, Candice Harp, Gigi Kelly, and Margaret O'Hara, "Including Soft Information in EISs," *Information Systems Management*, Summer 1996, pp. 66–77.

12. Hildebrand, Carol, "Knowledge Fusion," *CIO*, June 1, 2000. Available at www.cio.com.

13. Farber, Dan, "What's Up with Blogging, and Why Should You Care?" *Tech Update*, February 22, 2004. Available at techupdate.zdnet.com/techupdate/stories/main/What_is_up_with_blogging.html. Accessed April 2004.

14. Suitt, Halley, "HBR Case Study: A Blogger in Their Midst," *Harvard Business Review*, September 1, 2003, pp. 30–40.

15. Groove Networks Weblog Policy, Employee Guidelines for Personal Web site and Weblogs. Available at www.groove.net/ default.cfm?pagename=WeblogPolicy. Accessed April 2004. Reprinted with permission.

CHAPTER

8

MANAGING OPERATIONS

INTRODUCTION

A discussion of managing the essential information technologies is not complete without describing operational issues facing CIOs. Due to mergers, the Internet, e-commerce, increasing attacks on networks, and the September 11, 2001, terrorist attacks, the subject of computer operations has been receiving a lot of attention. Systems operations are important because if they are not professionally run (and backed up properly), a company could suffer a computer or network crash that could shut down its business for some period of time. It is not a trivial area, especially as companies become increasingly reliant on networks and computers to run their businesses. Furthermore, poorly run IS shops cause IS executives to end up fighting fires instead of setting policy. Or they may find themselves looking for a new job or their operations outsourced. Actually, this last option is often seen as a welcome relief by many IS executives.

As shown in Figure 8-1, the main change in operations is a shift in viewpoint. Traditionally, managing operations meant managing inward; that is, managing one's own operations staff, including those who work in the data center, data administration, network administration, and systems programming. Today, it is just as likely to mean managing outward; that is, managing the company's relationships with IT ESPs who have taken over the day-to-day operational work. That shift was noted in Chapter 2, in IS Lite, where the infrastructure-support function is mainly outsourced.

We begin this chapter by presenting one former IS executive's views on the breadth of the operations job and how it needs to be managed. Then we discuss three major operational issues:

1. Outsourcing IS functions

2. Information security in the Internet age

3. Planning for business continuity

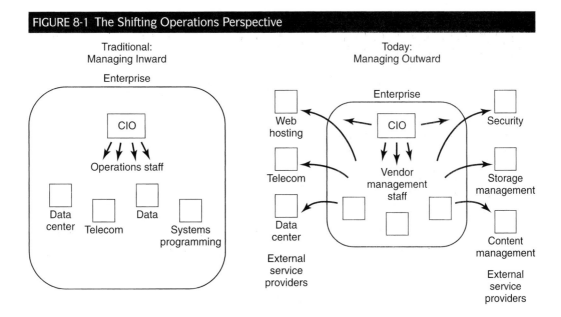

FIGURE 8-1 The Shifting Operations Perspective

WHAT ARE OPERATIONS?

In a lecture at the University of California at Los Angeles (UCLA), William Congleton described the important operational issues he faced in one IS department.

Why Talk About Operations?

Keeping the shop running is getting increasingly difficult, Congleton says. The reasons become apparent at budget time. His total annual IS department budget had the following split:

- 33 percent for systems and programming, of which 70 percent was for maintenance and 30 percent was for new development
- 10 percent for department administration and training
- 57 percent for operations

Thus, one reason operations are important is because they involve more money than any other part of the IS organization.

At his company, operations included computer hardware at 64 locations, including 12 seaports, 12 parts warehouses, and 12 sales offices. Hardware included computers, disk drives, backup drives, printers, and PCs. Operations also included communication lines and equipment and software, such as operating systems, compilers, and networking software. In addition, the budget included data center personnel, such as systems consulting for developers and operators who scheduled and ran production jobs, performed backups, delivered reports, and monitored the machines and network. Operations also included disaster recovery planning and security.

"Putting all these things together sometimes gave me more excitement than I could stand," quips Congleton, "plus they were more expensive than I wanted. Therefore, achieving a 10 percent reduction in operations had a far greater effect than a 10 percent reduction in any other area. That is why operations are important."

Solving Operational Problems

Systems operations problems are obvious to the entire company: Response times are slow, networks are down, data is not available, or data is wrong. What can be done to improve operations? Congleton describes three strategies. One is to buy more equipment. As equipment costs drop, this solution might appear the most cost-effective, unless you run out of room for the equipment. The second approach is to continuously fight fires and rearrange priorities, getting people to solve the problem at hand. This solution really only moves the problem of poor management from one hot spot to another. The third solution is to continually document and measure what you are doing to find out the real problems, not just the apparent ones. Then set standards. This is the solution Congleton prefers. It is needed no matter who runs operations, the in-house staff or an outsourcer, and no matter whether the systems are legacy transaction systems or new Web-based front ends.

Operational Measures

Operational measures are both external and internal. External measures are what customers see: system and network uptime (or downtime), response time, turnaround time, and program failures. These aspects directly relate to customer satisfaction. Internal measures are of interest to IS people: computer utilization as a percentage of capacity, availability of mission-critical systems, disk storage utilization, job queue length, number of jobs run, number of jobs rerun due to problems, age of applications, and number of unresolved problems.

Problems reported by the external measures can generally be explained by deviations in the internal measures. To help uncover problems related to equipment capacity, quality of applications, or improper use of systems by users, numerous vendors sell monitoring software and devices. Other measurement systems log performance of computer and telecommunications equipment, says Congleton. Storage management systems manage space more efficiently. Schedulers schedule jobs. Library management systems keep track of versions and backups of files and programs. Plenty of tools are available to help IS organizations measure how efficiently their equipment is being used.

The Importance of Good Management

Tools are useless, however, unless IS management has created a culture that recognizes and values good operations, says Congleton. It is hard to find good computer operations managers because the absence of prestige (and sometimes pay) does not attract individuals with the proper combination of skills and training. This reality is unfortunate, he says, because in a good environment, an operations job can be particularly rewarding, both financially and professionally.

The skills required of an operations manager are similar to those needed in a factory or oil refinery. The factory manager must schedule work to meet promised delivery dates, monitor performance as work flows through the key pieces of equipment, and respond quickly to production breakdowns. In a well-run factory, the manager can usually recover from one or two individual problems. In a badly-run factory, a manager faces many little problems and often does not know where to start to fix the problems. The same is true in computer and telecommunications centers where the "factory equipment" is the disk drives, database machines, host computers, servers, network gateways, network routers, and the like.

In conclusion, CIOs need to be concerned about operations, says Congleton, by putting the proper operations environment in place. The key to managing operations is the same as in any management job: Set standards and then manage to those standards by finding an outstanding operations manager.

What's New in Operations?

Over the past few years, several changes have taken place in operations.

Companies Have "Cleaned Their Operational House."   Y2K and the Internet forced companies to "clean house" in their data and network center operations, says Rosemary LaChance of Farber/LaChance,[1] a company that provides consulting on automating data center operations.

In the late 1990s, companies were fearful that their old computer applications could not handle processing in the year 2000 because many of the programs left out the digits "19" in, say, "1993." Once the millennium hit, these programs would think the year 2000 was the year 1900, yielding erroneous results.

Y2K forced companies to not only look at their existing software, but also their computer operations, says LaChance; in particular, their standards and policies. Formerly, operations were managed reactively. They upgraded hardware but they rarely updated processes. Companies would not spend the money to improve procedures, thinking, "If it ain't broke, don't fix it."

Y2K, and then the Internet, required management to think about the processes that computer operations supported and ask, "How are we going to do what we say we will do? How will we be able to add services or outsource operations? Will we be able to support e-commerce?" The resulting changes have led to far better operational structures because management took the time to define the rules for operations and put better policies and procedures in place.

"Had they not gone through Y2K, most companies would not have been operationally prepared for the Internet," says LaChance. Although automation provides discipline, the rules must be in place to automate. Y2K forced companies to define such rules as how to gain access to systems. They also got rid of such outdated procedures as transferring data via tapes (moving to more efficient and less costly online data transfers), and distributing reports on paper (moving to making them available via the company intranet).

In short, Y2K gave computer operations the attention it needed but had not gotten. Companies were forced to move from a survival mode ("Let's just get this job run") to a planning mode ("What do we need to support e-enablement?"). However, challenges remain. Computer operators still cannot link identified problems with changes, so they still have integration and change management problems. That piece of the operations structure is still missing.

More Operations Managers Are Managing Outward.   The picture Congleton paints is based on the traditional managing inward view where enterprises manage their own data centers. By and large, that view remains true. However, as the next section on outsourcing points out, a growing number of companies are turning to a third party to run their data centers. Even more are contracting with a network provider to manage their networks. These changes do not mean that CIOs relinquish responsibility for operations. It just means they need to ensure that their people are properly managing the service providers.

Even for companies keeping their own data centers, an increasing number are taking advantage of operational services provided by third parties, especially for Internet-based operations. For example, some host their Web site at a company that specializes in Web hosting. Offloading Web operations allows enterprises to forgo large equipment and facility investments, expensing operational costs instead. Furthermore, they offload the job of finding the needed talent to the specialist. Finding qualified employees can be an acute problem in the IT field. It is easier to attract and retain IT talent when a company's core business is IT because staff can see a career path, the company is more likely to buy the latest tools and equipment, and the culture is more likely to be IT-friendly.

Operations Are Being Simplified.   Another trend is to simplify operations by centralizing applications in one place rather than distribute them on PCs. Programs are then downloaded when requested. This practice is called *server-based computing* and was discussed in Chapter 5.

Certain Operations Are Being Offloaded. Yet another trend in operations is to offload certain kinds of operations or certain aspects of computer and network operations. Often, these relate to the Internet. For example, a relatively new area is Web event management, which means hosting a real-time event on the Web. When successful, such events, called Webcasts, lead to huge spikes in Web site hits. To avoid being swamped and having the Web site crash, companies offload the operational aspects of these events to third parties that specialize in hosting such activities. Here is an example of such a Webcast.

CASE EXAMPLE

MICROSOFT

When Microsoft officially announced a new version of Windows, it did so not only at a major launch event in San Francisco, California, but also via a public Internet broadcast and a private Webcast to 6,000 original equipment manufacturer (OEM) system builders in 83 countries.

This private global Webcast to OEMs was handled by Akamai. Akamai specializes in providing e-business infrastructure through 12,000 edge servers in 66 countries. They are called *edge servers* because they are at the edge of the Internet; that is, close to end users. This approach gives users in far-flung locations fast downloads of Web content, streaming media, and applications from Web sites hosted on these servers. Like the Internet, Akamai's global distributed system has no central control; therefore, if a server, data center, or even a major network link (a backbone) fails, data can be routed around these failures. Having no single point of failure makes the network fail-safe.

Akamai has also gotten into hosting broadcasts of live events via its cus-

tomers' Web sites—Webcasting—which requires high bandwidth capabilities to accommodate streaming media; that is, live audio and video. In addition, Akamai's Netpodium service allows such events to be interactive with dispersed audiences.

The Microsoft Webcast for the system builders was the largest online seminar Microsoft had held. It originated at Microsoft's headquarters in Redmond, Washington, and began with an introduction by Microsoft's OEM team. The Webcast then joined the San Francisco event with an on-site commentator and special presenters.

At their sites, the system builders could use Netpodium to send questions to the presenters. They sent some 1,800 and received real-time responses. In addition, Netpodium was used by the presenters to poll the system builders at several points during the event.

Microsoft was pleased with the private Webcast because it set a record for attendance, global reach, and audience participation. ∎

In conclusion, the focus of CIOs in operations is changing. Their attention used to be focused on ensuring that they had the in-house expertise to keep systems and networks up and running. Their attention now is toward determining where best to perform the various kinds of operations, in-house or with a third party, and then manage accordingly. In an increasing number of cases, the choice is to use an outside specialist; that is, outsourcing IS functions.

OUTSOURCING IS FUNCTIONS

In the IT world, *outsourcing* means turning over a firm's computer operations, network operations, or other IT function to a provider for a specified time; generally, at least a few years. In 1989, outsourcing became a legitimate management strategy by CIOs. Until that time, the only companies that outsourced their IS operations were those that were poorly run. However, in 1989, Kodak outsourced its well-run IS operations to become a more competitive company. That surprising move caused top executives around the world to consider the use of outsourcers. Today, CIOs are expected to investigate outsourcing sufficiently to satisfy executive management that their IS operations are as efficient and effective in-house as they would be if they were outsourced; otherwise, they should outsource what they do not do well.

The Driving Forces Behind Outsourcing

At a meeting of the Chicago Chapter of the Society for Information Management, Mel Bergstein of DiamondCluster Int'l.[2] gave an overview of outsourcing. His main message was that outsourcing is another step in the evolution of the IT field.

Outsourcing descended on IS departments as a follow-on to the merger and acquisition activities in the 1980s, says Bergstein. In the 1960s, only 10 percent of the U.S. economy had global competition. In the 1970s, that rose to 70 percent. In response, companies had to focus on core businesses in the 1980s, which led to the huge amount of merger and acquisition activity. This activity was also driven by a new market for corporate control. High-yield bonds allowed a few people to buy a company and leverage it with debt. Companies were priced based on their shareholder value; that is, their discounted cash flow.

These two drivers—focus and value—are still leading companies to restructure and focus on core businesses by asking themselves, "Where do we really add value?" As examples, some apparel companies no longer cut, sew, manufacture, or distribute goods because they see their core businesses as design and marketing. Likewise, some publishers no longer manufacture books. They manage and finance projects, and outsource everything else.

Thus, outsourcing is part of the drive for focus and value, and it is not solely an IT issue, says Bergstein; it is a business issue. Because top management must stress value, they must consider outsourcing in all their functions.

Changing Customer–Vendor Relationships

IS outsourcers perform the same activities for a company that an IS organization performs in-house. Over time, the amount of work done by outsiders has increased, says Bergstein, as the following expansion in customer–vendor relationships illustrates.

Traditionally, IS organizations bought professional services, such as planning (or consulting), building or maintaining applications, building or maintaining networks, and training. They also bought products, which may or may not have included training. They also bought transactions, such as payroll check processing from a service bureau or credit reports from a credit rating service. Purchasing transactions allows buyers to shift fixed costs to variable costs and gives sellers higher margins because they take on the risks.

With the high use of packages and the need to integrate them to create integrated systems, companies have contracted with systems integrators. They generally handle the entire life cycle—planning, development, maintenance, and training—for major systems projects. Finally, the most bundled approach to contracting for IT services is outsourcing, where the outsourcer contracts to handle all or most of certain IT activities. The main difference between the latter two options is that systems integration is project based, whereas outsourcing is time based.

This five-option continuum, shown in Figure 8-2, demonstrates how the IT field has moved, says Bergstein. As you move from the more traditional professional services category (on the left) to outsourcing (on the right), four changes occur in the vendor–customer relationship:

1. IS management loses an increasing amount of control because more of the activities are turned over to outsiders.

2. Providers take more risks as they offer options on the right.

FIGURE 8-2 Customer–Vendor Relationships

Relationships

Activities	Professional Services	Product	Transactions	Systems Integration	Outsourcing
• Planning/consulting	X				
• Building/maintaining applications	X				
• Building/maintaining networks	X				
• Training users/clients	X	X	X	X	X
• Operating platforms					
• Performing administrative functions					
• Building/using product					

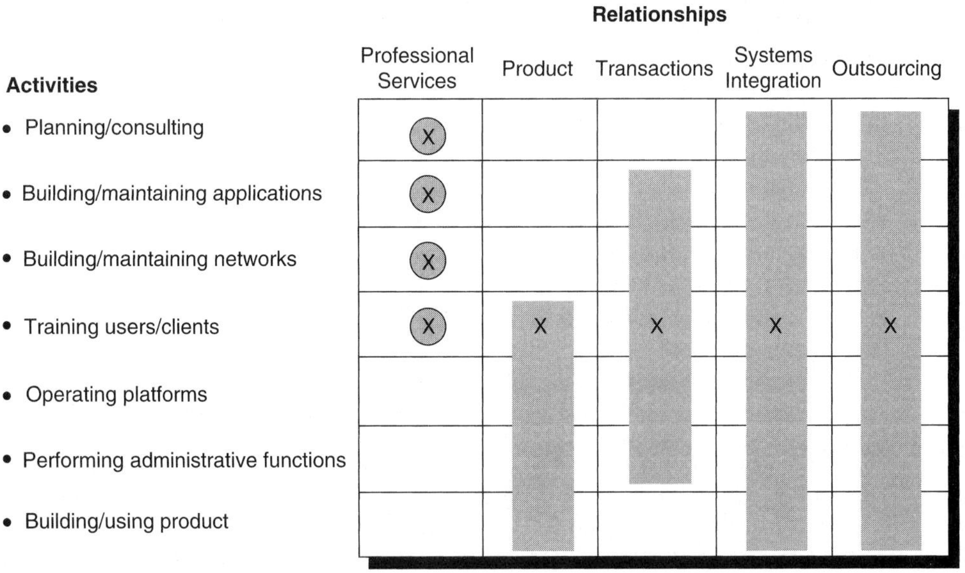

Source: Mel Bergstein, DiamondCluster Int'l., Chicago, IL.

3. Providers' margins improve as they offer services on the right.

4. The importance of choosing the right provider becomes more important to the right, because more is at risk in using an outside source.

Outsourcing's History

In 1989, essentially only one kind of outsourcing involving IT was available. Since then, the field has expanded significantly. Here is a glimpse of its history, based largely on attendance at the semiannual conferences of the Sourcing Interests Group, founded and led by Barry Wiegler since 1991.[3]

IT Outsourcing.   IT outsourcing essentially began with "big bang" deals, or mega-deals, which consisted of outsourcing all of a company's data center operations for up to 10 years. These deals involved selling existing equipment to the outsourcer, transferring all software licenses, moving significant numbers of in-house IS personnel to the outsourcer's payroll, negotiating how the outsourcer would help in the transition and which party would carry which costs, establishing desired service levels and ways to measure performance, and specifying every single service to be provided—because if it was not in the contract, it would be an added cost.

In those early days, the goal of these large data center contracts was purely financial. Companies wanted to remove the huge IT infrastructure investments from their books and shift those fixed costs to variable costs; and they wanted to save money, generally about 15 percent. The deals were front loaded, with the outsourcers losing money or breaking even the first year or two, but then becoming profitable after that as the costs of technology dropped, as they leveraged licenses across clients, as they shared expertise across clients, and as they invested in productivity tools that made them more efficient.

Several problems occurred, though. An "us versus them" mindset often set in because neither the clients nor the outsourcers handled the transition well. A lot of finger-pointing took place as outsourcers tried to charge for services clients thought were included in the contract. In addition, service levels did not always live up to expectations or interpretations of the contract language differed.

Furthermore, cultures clashed. Former employees might have kept their same desk, but once they became an employee of the outsourcer, they became a provider and were treated differently. Users had higher expectations of outsourcers than of their IS organizations. In short, companies learned that managing the relationship was really the tough job. Formerly, they had thought that negotiating the deal was the difficult part, so they had not carefully defined governance structures; that is, how the relationship would be managed.

Today, the IT outsourcing industry has matured. Providers have learned that heavy-handed treatment of clients can backfire. They are much more careful in transition planning. Clients' attorneys have learned what is important in a contract and where the pitfalls lie. Those early contracts have been renegotiated, and although the clients may not have changed providers, they have generally become more adept at renegotiating because they now know what they really need.

Of course, not all outsourcing deals were mega-deals, but even the small deals felt like a big bang to the employees who moved to the outsourcer.

Transitional Outsourcing. In the early 1990s, a new type of computing arose: client-server computing, as noted in Chapter 5. IT outsourcing had been around for a few years, so CIOs with their hands full supporting legacy systems looked into using outsourcing to transition to client-server computing. They chose one of two routes. Either they outsourced maintenance of their legacy systems so their staff could concentrate on building new client-server systems or they outsourced client-server development to specialists and kept maintenance in-house. In either case, once the new systems were brought in, the legacy systems they replaced were shut down.

Then, in the late 1990s, when the immense size of Y2K compliance surfaced—to retrofit old applications so they would work after the year 2000—most companies outsourced as much of their Y2K work as they could. Because of the enormous volume of work, offshore outsourcing to India, Ireland, and other countries grew significantly. Unlike traditional IT outsourcing, however, contracts were generally shorter and did not include operations. This project-based outsourcing has been called *transitional outsourcing.*

Best-of-Breed Outsourcing. All through the 1990s, IS departments outsourced different pieces of their work—mainly infrastructure support, as noted in Chapter 2 and IS Lite. However, CIOs learned that although selecting one outsourcer with broad capabilities might be easiest to manage, no single company was best in class in all areas. Thus, selective outsourcing began, where one outsourcer handled desktop operations, another data center operations, and a third network management. Even though the concept was good for getting best-of-breed providers, coordination among the multiple providers became a nightmare.

A more recent trend has been *collaborative outsourcing*, where one company becomes the prime contractor for numerous facets of IS operations but some of the work is provided by other ESPs. Often an operations partner, a development partner, and a telecommunications partner collaborate to bid on the work, but one is the prime partner. Thus, teams of large ESPs bid against other teams for contracts. In some cases, these contracts take on quite a bit more than simply operations; the work includes development of new systems as well. Best-of-breed outsourcing has perpetuated the tradition of long and complex outsourcing contracts.

Shared Services. When IT outsourcing began to gain credibility, executives wondered, "Can we get the same economies of scale by pulling disparate non-core functions together into one shared services group?" In many cases, they felt they could. So they "insourced" to themselves, creating a shared services organization to handle such functions as IT, legal, facilities management, real estate, mail room, finance, and on and on. The goal was to improve efficiencies and save money. Generally, companies created a center of expertise in each area, with all the centers reporting to one shared services vice president.

IT was not always included, but, as in the case of MeadWestvaco Corporation (see Chapter 1), it was. Some executives believe having IT in shared services gives them the ability to leverage the IT underpinnings of the other services. Shared services also centralize the management of outsourced functions because, in many cases, the functions are centralized and then outsourced. Shared services groups have become adept at negotiating and managing contracts and supplier relationships because these tasks are a main part of their job.

Business Process Outsourcing.   As the IT outsourcing field matured, data center outsourcing, desktop outsourcing, and other standard IT outsourcing areas became so well understood that they became commodity services; hence, profit margins dropped as the number of competitors rose. To move into higher-margin services, ESPs began specializing in specific functional areas, offering to handle specific business processes as well as their IT underpinnings. This *business process outsourcing* (BPO) is defined as outsourcing all or most of a reengineered process that has a large IT component.

Improving a non-core process by tapping the expertise and investments of a provider that focuses solely on that process (rather than cut costs) has been the main goal in BPO. Companies are outsourcing logistics, customer service, and many other essential, yet peripheral, functions to the experts.

Balboa Travel,[3a] a travel agency in San Diego, California, handed over its ticket accounting to Unisys. Each week, travel agencies must report the tickets they have sold to the Airline Reporting Corporation. The process is important, yet burden-some, and the president of Balboa Travel did not want to hire a programmer to maintain such a reporting system, which is what he would have had to do if he had not outsourced the work. Unisys provides him a more sophisticated service than he could afford in-house. It lets him offer his clients—corporate travel departments—reports about their employees' travel habits via an extranet. Balboa is also able to do data mining on its ticket sales to uncover trends that will help it offer new and better travel services.

As is obvious, BPO moves IT-based outsourcing out beyond the IS organization; it involves business units as well. BPO outsourcing is often quite a bit more complex than IT outsourcing because it requires clients to change their business processes to fit with the processes of the service provider. Furthermore, some clients want to retain parts of a process, so complex coordination may be necessary between the two firms as well.

BPO has brought a mindset change to the field. Whereas IT outsourcing moves suppliers and customers closer to one another in terms of working together, the two parties still do not have the same goals. Clients want to save more money, whereas outsourcers want to make more money. In BPO, though, when providers take over an entire process, they can be measured and paid based on outcomes rather than transactions. Outcome-based outsourcing gives the two parties common goals. The client focuses on "what" needs to be done; the provider focuses on "how" to do it.

Rita Terdiman[4a] noted this phenomenon in a speech to the Sourcing Interests Group. As shown in Figure 8-3, BPO deals aim to be more like joint ventures and alliances, moving them to the right side of the chart. Therefore, trust, joint financial investments, and partnering are part of the deal.

As an example of BPO, consider ANZ Banking Group and its outsourcing of its procurement function, as described in a Sourcing Interests Group research report.[3b]

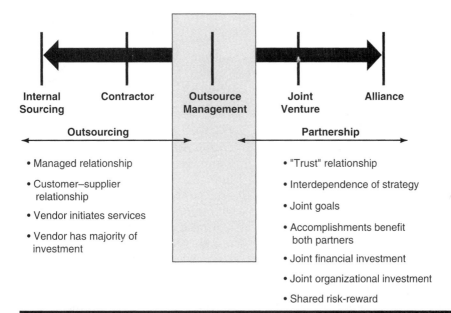

FIGURE 8-3 The Outsourcing Management Spectrum

Source: Courtesy of Gartner EXP, 56 Top Gallant, Stamford, CT.

CASE EXAMPLE

ANZ BANKING GROUP LTD.

ANZ is Australia's third-largest bank, with AU$150 billion in assets; it operates in 28 countries and has 22,000 staff. ANZ's cost-to-income ratio had been 63 percent; it is now at 47 percent, with a target of about 45 percent.

The bank's challenge in outsourcing procurement was not to reduce costs, but to gain greater quality purchases and lower ANZ's annual spend of AU$1.36 billion. ANZ outsourced its entire procurement operation, except strategy, in Australia and New Zealand to PwC, now part of IBM Global Services,

in May 1999 for 5 years, with a 2-year option to continue. ANZ moved fixed asset management and accounts payable into strategic sourcing at the time; neither of them has been outsourced yet. The contract was worth AU$850 million in 1999; as of 2002 it was worth AU$950 million.

The benefit objectives of outsourcing to PwC were to leverage PwC's already global capability, reduce transaction costs (which has occurred), and better manage ANZ's spend information (which was poor at the time).

(Case Continued)

Lessons Learned

Peter Donald, General Manager of Strategic Sourcing at ANZ, recounts a number of lessons he has learned in outsourcing procurement.

Be Prepared to Change the Contract As Your Environment Changes. At ANZ, the total number of contracts managed by procurement has risen from 600 to 900, and could well rise to over 1,000. Furthermore, a new goods and services tax in 2001 has forced new issues into the relationship.

Originally, ANZ and PwC had the stretch goal of saving AU$100 million over the 5 years. That goal changed to save AU$130 million over just 2 years' time—a substantial change. Donald thus recommends reviewing the arrangement regularly and being prepared to change it.

Make Step Changes in Technology and Processes to Save Time and Money. ANZ moved to Web-enabled PeopleSoft; 50 percent of the activity now goes through this e-procurement system. This step change was made easier because ANZ had outsourced to PwC, giving ANZ management the time to concentrate on strategic issues. Formerly, the bank had spend leakage of AU$50 million to AU$100 million a year to maverick buying and such. Over the next 12 months, due to the PeopleSoft front end and PwC's operations, ANZ stopped much of that leakage.

Focus on Having an Effective Transition. The transition should be managed so that there is little or no noise from the business units. Some people look for ways to make noise. ANZ experienced some early problems, but PwC recovered quickly, actually more quickly than Donald expected. The lesson was to understand beforehand how a provider can recover, so they can do so quickly.

Do Your Best to Make the Outsourced Group Appear Seamless to Employees. Some employees look for ways to find fault. Seamlessness can be difficult to achieve if the provider's staff advertise themselves to employees. This is not a good idea. It is always nice to get a pat on the back, like the one Donald received from a line manager who had prepared a requisition for office supplies on his desktop on Friday 4 P.M. and received the supplies Monday morning. His note to Donald: "Congratulations."

Focus Early on What You Want, and Don't Get Sidetracked. Everyday operations are going well, so Donald is pleased with the service delivery. The outsourcing gives him and his staff more time to manage strategically to capture the AU$130 million in savings. Thus, he wants more strategic input from PwC than he has been receiving. He wants PwC to push him and his staff to improve. His advice to others is to be sure global input is reaching you, if that is what you want.

Along the same strategic lines, Donald wants PwC to work closely with ANZ on large projects. Thus, PwC has moved its commodity management people closer to ANZ's business so that they better understand the procurement strategy being developed with the business units on large projects.

Keep Incentive Mechanisms Simple and Transparent. When incentive mechanisms are excessively complex, too much

(Case Continued)

effort is required from both sides. Complex incentives may also promote the wrong behavior. For instance, the provider may focus on the stretch targets rather than the daily bread-and-butter issues.

PwC receives a fixed but declining management fee over the term, so there is an incentive to lower ANZ's cost base. There are other incentives as well, which are working fine, says Donald. For instance, PwC risks 50 percent of its profits when it fails to meet the stated minimum service levels. This has only happened in one quarter of the last 19.

Be Able to Benchmark Performance. Benchmark data is important in evaluating the outsourcing of procurement. Donald uses CAPS, which provides very good data. However, because he reports to the market every 6 months, he needs that data more frequently than once a year or once every 2 years.

Understand, to a Fair Degree of Detail, the Value Chain You Plan to Embrace. Little things can catch you up. For example, information security issues need to be addressed so that third parties in ANZ's supply chain have access through its firewalls. ∎

E-Business Outsourcing.   With the arrival of business use of the Internet, outsourcing enabled companies to quickly get Web sites up and handling business. In large companies, e-business outsourcing started with marketing departments outsourcing the development of their corporate Web site. Once developed, IS took over operations. However, in dot-coms and Internet-based operations, outsourcing all or most of the IS function has been the preferred mode of operation for several reasons. Even with the dot-com crash, this is still a legitimate way to mobilize for e-business.

One, outsourcing allows a company to move fast. When a firm cannot spend a year developing a system, outsourcing the e-business infrastructure can help it get a site up and running within months, perhaps weeks. Two, companies can remain flexible, which can mean staying small and focusing only on a few key functions. Generally, IT has not been seen as a core differentiating area when tailorable off-the-shelf products and services have been available. Three, outsourcing does not tie up a firm's funds in computer and networking equipment, which could become obsolete fairly soon. A company can rent rather than buy. It can draw on best-of-breed as well as change course quickly if need be, swapping out one ESP and swapping in another, to keep pace with the market.

Unlike traditional IT outsourcing, with e-business outsourcing, machines do not need to be purchased from the client, personnel do not have to be moved, and software licenses do not need to be transferred. The outsourcing starts from scratch. Some large companies have followed this route as well to get into e-business, for the same reasons.

Utility computing.   E-business outsourcing and IT outsourcing are combining into a new form of managed services outsourcing that is being referred to by various names: *utility computing, on-demand computing, virtual data centers, autonomic (self-healing) systems,* and *grid computing* (a take-off on the term *electricity grid*). The idea is that computing power can be treated like electricity: You plug in and only pay for what you use.

Numerous vendors, especially IBM, HP, and Sun, are promoting access rather than ownership. By supplying computer processing, network bandwidth, and applications on demand, they are selling the idea of turning clients' fixed IT costs into variable costs. Clients can then scale their IT infrastructure or handle spikes in computing demand without having to buy more IT assets.

To educate themselves and their business on the utility computing concept, CIOs can test it by using an IT outsourcer in a high-need area, such as e-mail, security, or redundancy, notes Thickins.[5] It is important to understand the amount of consulting this form of outsourcing requires, the chargeback mechanism (for only paying for use), the contract terms, where it could provide benefits, and so on. Mobil Travel Guide illustrates the convergence of e-business and IT outsourcing into utility computing in one of its high-need areas: its Web site.

CASE EXAMPLE

MOBIL TRAVEL GUIDE

The Mobil Travel Guide provides travelers in the United States and Canada with information on destinations, route planning, resorts, restaurants, and other travel-related information. Its printed versions have been published for 45 years and sold in bookstores and other retail outlets.[6]

Mobil put the guide online, but the information was static and the site could not handle the spikes in demand that took place around holidays and during the summer. Site visitors endured long response times.

Mobil wanted to upgrade its site (www.mobiltravelguide.com) to provide real-time data, such as custom travel planning, 24-hour service, and rewards at hotels and restaurants. But rather than making the large investment to upgrade its own IT resources, Mobil turned to IBM to host and manage the site, which runs on

Linux-based servers. Mobil signed up for IBM's on-demand utility computing service, so that it only pays for the processing, storage, and networking capacity it uses. IBM ensures that its infrastructure can scale up to handle the demand spikes.

Mobil did not have to make the major upfront investments in IT assets and it does not need to be concerned with having enough capacity to handle peak loads. Furthermore, the Web-based portion of the system is housed on IBM's cache servers around its network, thereby providing users with faster response times and Mobil with lower per-transaction costs than if the site was housed on Mobil's servers.

Mobil believes it is saving 35 percent in maintenance and software costs by outsourcing to IBM—and it is only paying for what it uses of IBM's world-class, highly scalable e-business infrastructure. ∎

Thus, in 15 years' time, IT outsourcing has expanded significantly, from outsourcing data center operations to outsourcing business processes and from domestic outsourcing to offshoring, which is discussed shortly.

Managing Outsourcing

Numerous aspects to managing outsourcing need to be handled well to create a successful working relationship. Here are just four—organizational structure, governance, day-to-day working, and supplier development. All are based on research reports published by the Sourcing Interests Group.[3c, 3d]

Organizational Structure. Managing outsourcing is different from managing internal staff because, for one thing, it is a joint effort between parties that may not have the same goals, as noted earlier. Therefore, during contract negotiations, the two parties need to figure out and negotiate how they are going to jointly manage the contract they sign. In fact, governance needs to be explicitly addressed in the contract.

Typically, parties establish layers of joint teams. A top-level team of a couple of executives from each firm generally has the final word on conflict resolution. An operational team with members from both companies oversees day-to-day functioning. They hold a formal meeting, say, once a week to once a month; but they are generally in daily contact. Also, some joint special-purpose teams may be created from time to time to deal with pressing issues. Some companies have ongoing standing committees, such as a pricing committee or a change management committee, to oversee the use of formal change management procedures.

Although joint committees are a common management structure, each side needs a single executive in charge of their side of the relationship. On the client side, this executive is the relationship manager. This job position has not been prevalent in IS departments, but we believe it is going to become the norm as companies move toward IS Lite. Needless to say, the skills of a relationship manager are far different from those of a data center manager. A relationship manager needs to be good at negotiating, cajoling, and being an effective liaison between end users and service providers.

To illustrate how one company has managed its outsourcing, we look at Eastman Kodak Company because it created a thoughtful and effective governance structure. The following description comes from the Sourcing Interests Group; it focuses on the outsourcing between Eastman Kodak and IBM Global Services.[3e]

CASE EXAMPLE

EASTMAN KODAK COMPANY

Eastman Kodak Company, with headquarters in Rochester, New York, is an international manufacturer of imaging and chemical products. In 1989, the company rocked the IS world by announcing strategic relationships with four suppliers to manage

(Case Continued)

significant portions of its IS organization. Until that time, outsourcing had been viewed as a desperation move to improve poorly-run IS departments. Because Kodak's unit was well run, and benchmarked accordingly, its pioneering stance caused many IS executives—and a few CEOs and CFOs as well—to seriously reconsider outsourcing.

Kodak announced that one ESP would operate its data centers and networks, another would manage its telecommunications, a third would handle PC support, and a fourth would manage voice messaging. Initially the agreement with IBM to manage the data centers was U.S. based; it was later expanded to include Canadian operations, other U.S. divisions, and eventually six international sites. Kodak encourages IBM to leverage its data center for both Kodak and other companies' work for improved efficiencies. Due to efforts on both sides, the Kodak–IBM relationship has worked well. They developed trust and good processes. When issues arise, the relationship has effective processes to deal with them.

Outsourcing Management Structure

Kodak views its outsourcing management role as exercising leadership, staying in control, and managing the high value-added functions for flexibility. Kodak sets the tone for its key IT relationships. The key themes have been collaborative (not adversarial), long-term mutual benefits (not short-term), and making systemic improvements on a global basis (not local). The management structure has six elements: a management board, an advisory council, a supplier and alliance management group, a relationship manager for each relationship, ad hoc working groups, and client surveys.

Management Board.   This board meets twice a year and includes senior management from both companies. It focuses on strategic issues in addition to any policies or practices on either side that are getting in the way of mutual success. It has dealt with international strategies, IT architecture, telecommunications directions, disaster recovery plans, and so forth.

Advisory Council.   This council meets monthly and has 15 members. It handles technical and operational issues by focusing on what Kodak wants, not on how the services currently are delivered. Kodak's trust in IBM has grown; thus it leaves more of the "how" details up to this ESP. The advisory council reviews service levels, usage measurements and forecasts, tactical plans, migration objectives, business recovery plans, and the like.

Supplier and Alliance Management Group.   This group manages the longer-term outsourcing relationships as well as other contracts with large IT suppliers. It works closely with IS management. This group of 10 people includes a manager, the relationship manager for each primary alliance, plus support staff and supplier management for other IT sourcing. Initially, this group managed only the alliances. Contracts with major vendors were handled in other groups. Eventually all these functions were brought together to increase their focus, leverage global agreements, and align the management of alliances and suppliers. About one-half of the staff have IS backgrounds; the other half come from purchasing.

(Case Continued)

Relationship Manager. This manager is key to the success of a strategic relationship, Kodak believes, because this manager is the focal point between the company and its ESP. The job of each of Kodak's four relationship managers is to ensure that Kodak receives more than just delivery on the contract. Thus, they also manage value creation. The relationship managers negotiate, coordinate, and manage agreements and ensure that service level agreements (SLAs) are established. SLAs are very precise descriptions of each service to be delivered, when, by whom, for what price, and such. Relationship managers also assist in pricing and billing strategies.

Working Groups. These groups were not part of Kodak's original outsourcing management structure; they were added to deal with specific technology areas. They are chartered by the advisory council. Their goals are to facilitate changes in processes, promulgate standards, achieve business recovery in case of disruption, and promote effective use of IS services. They have proven to be effective vehicles for talking about important issues, such as the timing and appropriateness of upgrading to new releases of software. The groups are represented mainly by operational staff. For example, database administrators from the major sites are in one working group.

Client Surveys. These surveys are sent out twice a year to nearly 5,000 internal users of the services. Feedback on quality, cycle time, and product and service leadership are assessed and shared with the ESPs. Improvement plans are mutually developed to close perceived performance gaps.

Because Kodak's outsourcing has such a large scope, draws on four main suppliers, and covers a large geographic area, the company has discovered that it needs all of these forms of coordination for effective supplier management. ∎

Governance. The foundations of governing an outsourcing relationship are laid out in the contract, which can be hundreds of pages long (with appendices). A major governance item in the contract is the service level agreements (SLAs) because they are used to gauge supplier performance. For every contracted service, its SLA spells out responsibilities, performance requirements, penalties, bonuses, and so on. Completeness is an important attribute of good SLAs; generally everything should be detailed, perhaps even with times of deliveries, who will deliver what to whom, and so on.

Another important component of SLAs is metrics. An SLA needs to be measurable to be of use. Establishing metrics can be tricky because, in many cases, IS departments have not kept good measures of their own performance. In BPO, the situation is even worse; companies do not know how many people are in the process, departmental costs do not reflect overhead or IT costs, and so on. Measures are needed to establish benchmarks against which vendors want to demonstrate improvements. Clients also need metrics to negotiate better deals. Clients who do not know their own performance levels negotiate from weakness; they know less than the vendor because they have not tracked details, and vendors are not apt to correct mistaken impressions. Furthermore, clients are likely to overlook important details, which will later cost them money.

In addition to SLAs, parties establish governance rules to be used when either party is making a decision so that both are "singing from the same hymnal." Most parties in strong relationships say they put the contract in the drawer after it has been signed and work from trust and agreed-upon rules. It is only when trust in one another breaks down that they turn to the contract. Figure 8-4 lists some governance rules from a number of different enterprises.

Day-to-Day Working.   The Sourcing Interests Group[3] reports provide advice from outsourcing executives on how to manage day-to-day interactions between two parties. Here are a few of those recommendations.

Manage expectations, not staff.   The outsourcer's staff is no longer under the purview of the client, so command-and-control is not a wise option—it only results in an acrimonious relationship. Facilitation becomes the mode of working. Rather than say "do this," the approach becomes "how can we solve this together?" Furthermore, relationship managers have the important role of influencing users' expectations so that delivery meets business objectives.

Realize that informal ways of working may disappear.   More formality is inevitable as outcomes are measured and are more tightly controlled, especially if the relationship is handled strictly by the book, which happens in some cases. This increased formality can be a shock to people who are used to, say, getting a small job done by calling their friend "Joe" in the IS department. Once Joe works for the ESP, he may no longer be able to provide that service; he must follow the work authorization process defined in the contract. This change can cause unhappiness as users see providers as "them," making them the scapegoat. The two parties need to find ways to reduce this tendency.

Loss of informal ways of working can add rigor.   Rigor frequently improves work quality. Users may think twice before requesting changes and prepare better definitions of what they want. Furthermore, better processes can streamline work, improve

---

FIGURE 8-4 Examples of Outsourcing Governance Rules

- Service levels must stay in the top 25 percent as benchmarked against the client's peers.
- Escalation of problems becomes more painful as it goes higher to encourage early resolution.
- The supplier is the grand project manager and is responsible for managing multiple vendors.
- Work style is based on respect and confidence; there should be no personalization of problems.
- Add significant value.
- Aim to operate in an "open book" manner, sharing key operating information with each other.
- New services can be put out for bid.
- No exclusive agreements.
- Meet our standards.
- Let us know about potential problems before they happen.
- Spend our money as if it were your own.

Source: Reprinted with permission of Sourcing Interests Group, Bell Canyon, CA, www.sourcing interests.org.

effectiveness, and potentially reduce unnecessary work. Service providers do introduce new discipline; the client should prepare employees for this change and assist them in adapting because it is generally best to use the provider's processes. This is one reason why transition planning is so important: to help client personnel move to new procedures with the least disruption and disgruntlement.

Integration of the two staffs requires explicit actions. Integration does not happen naturally. Explicit policies are likely to be needed. Some examples are to (1) grant outsourcing staff access to appropriate work areas, not unduly restrict them; (2) hold joint celebrations and social events; (3) invite each other to meetings; and (4) perhaps even have a client executive move to the provider for 2 years to learn how they work internally. However, integration generally can only go so far; the client still needs to remain in control and guide the relationship. Furthermore, the more side-by-side the parties work, the more likely they will experience scope creep in which the provider takes on more work.

The best way to manage day-to-day is to communicate frequently. One executive said he carried around a top-10 list in his shirt pocket, which he revised every week. They were the most important items he had to handle. The list kept him on focus and turned out to be his best informal management technique.

Supplier Development. A topic that is receiving increased attention in the production sourcing arena—that is, buying parts and services that go into one's own products and services—is supplier development. It means assisting one's suppliers to improve their products and services, generally by improving their processes. Although supplier development has not been prevalent in IT outsourcing, we think it will be. It will likely be prevalent in BPO.

Here is an example of supplier development from manufacturing, not IT, from a Sourcing Interests Group research report.[3d]

CASE EXAMPLE

HONDA MOTOR COMPANY

When Dave Nelson was head of purchasing for Honda Motor Company, he became widely known for his pioneering work in supplier development. To him, supplier development means being involved in improving suppliers' capabilities. The benefits include receiving higher quality goods, getting lower prices, tapping suppliers' expertise, and improving one's supply chain. In e-business, where

alliances are so crucial, working together to improve processes will be of major importance.

In manufacturing, Nelson undertakes supplier development by sending two of his supply development engineers to a supplier, for free. They team up with two supplier engineers with the goal of cutting labor hours and inventory of a single part bought by Nelson by 50 percent in

(Case Continued)

13 weeks' time. The team works under two main guidelines: No supplier employees will be laid off. They will all have a job elsewhere in the company, perhaps teaching others how to improve their processes. Two, Nelson splits any savings 50/50 with the supplier.

The team of four starts by cleaning and painting the area where the part is produced. That single act gets everyone's attention. Then they ask for suggestions from the workers on how to improve the process. They map the existing process and try to implement (quickly and in any way possible) every suggestion so that the workers can test it out. Generally, once the workers see they are being heard, the suggestions pour in.

The results can be dramatic. As one small example, one assembly line of 15 women on one shift and 10 on another made 1,500 air conditioning hoses a day using 15 machines. In total, the women walked 13 miles a day and hauled 3 tons of material. After redesign, only five women were needed on one shift to make 1,550 hoses, and they only needed to walk 50 yards and haul 100 pounds.

Nelson says supplier development is like "walking around picking up money off the floor." So why isn't it more prevalent? He believes it is because manufacturing companies still maintain their internal focus. Although they now outsource most parts production—up to 70 percent at Honda—firms have not shifted their resources to managing suppliers. They still treat suppliers as outsiders rather than departments of their own company. Management has to be sold on the idea of investing in supplier management, and sold even more on supplier development. They need proof that supplier management will yield bottom-line benefits. ■

Offshoring

To round out our discussion of outsourcing, we turn to the topic receiving much attention today: sending work offshore. In the late 1990s, when labor markets were especially tight and IS organizations needed to retrofit their systems to make them Y2K compliant, the use of offshore outsourcers to maintain IT applications grew dramatically. Offshore, of course, is relative. For U.S. companies, *near-shore* means outsourcing to Canadian and Mexican companies, whereas *offshore* means Ireland, India, the Philippines, and other countries. For European companies, near-shore is Ireland, Poland, and other Eastern European countries.

Companies turn to offshoring to tap lower labor costs and an ample supply of qualified people. During the recent economic downturn, offshoring gave companies a way to cut costs. The trickle of IT jobs in the late 1990s has turned into a steady stream of white-collar work going offshore. Application maintenance and development, call centers, customer service, back-office processing, BPO, claims processing, and other functions can all be moved offshore.

Now that the U.S. economy is improving, offshoring has become a political issue, because companies are not expanding their domestic labor force as rapidly as some had expected. There's an outcry that offshoring is taking jobs from away domestic workers. Politicians are trying, at the very least, to "shame" companies into not moving domestic work abroad. But as with manufacturing jobs in the 1980s, offshoring is unstoppable because the economics are so strong. Once one company in an industry lowers its costs by moving work to lower-wage countries, its competitors need to reduce their costs as well. That may mean that they, too, need to offshore.

For all the "this is terrible" talk, offshoring might actually be good for developed countries, because increasing the living standards in other countries increases their citizens' demands for consumer products that can, in turn, be supplied by highly efficient companies in developed countries.

Furthermore, white-collar offshoring has been inevitable, argues author Daniel Altman,[7] because service sector productivity in the United States has not kept up with manufacturing sector productivity. In the early 1950s, each service sector employee produced about $39,000 in output (in 2000 dollars), he notes; in manufacturing, the output was $48,000. Now, 50 years later, service productivity has increased to $54,000 (a 47 percent increase), whereas manufacturing productivity is at $207,000 (a 330 percent increase)!

Manufacturers have faced international competition, whereas service firms have not. Manufacturers have been forced to increase their productivity to stay in business—mainly by increasing the quality of their products, notes Altman. It should come as no surprise that service companies are tapping cheaper sources of labor now that they can because of globally available telecommunications technology, he notes. This global competition in services will force American companies to increase the productivity of their workforce in the same way and increase the quality of their services, Altman believes.

Offshore outsourcing differs in some unique ways from domestic outsourcing. In two reports, the Sourcing Interests Group (SIG) explores IT offshoring and the areas CIOs and their staff need to consider.[3f] Here are four points from those reports.

Offshoring Options Are Broadening.   India has become the premier IT and BPO offshoring country because its huge, highly educated workforce speaks English and is hardworking. College graduates in India apply for jobs that only high school graduates will apply for in the United States, such as working in a customer service center. Hence, the quality of work is often higher, while the labor costs are lower. Furthermore, in IS, all of the major IT outsourcers in India have achieved the highest level (Level 5) in the Capability Maturity Matrix, which means their processes produce high-quality software. Most IS organizations in the United States and in other developed countries are not even up to Level 3. So the quality of software from these Indian firms is very high—as long as the specifications for the work are clear and truly what the customer wants.

After having good initial IT experiences in India, client companies are offshoring higher-value white-collar work beyond short-term software maintenance projects to ongoing software maintenance work, new development projects, and even BPO. The types of firms offering offshore options are also broadening. U.S. outsourcers are building their own offshore capabilities or acquiring existing offshore providers, often in India, sometimes in China, to lower their own costs. Client companies not wanting to deal directly with unfamiliar overseas providers can now tap offshore resources through onshore outsourcers. In fact, as noted in the SIG reports, all large IT outsourcing deals will likely have an offshore component. Global sourcing is becoming the norm.

Both Parties Need Cultural Training to Bridge Cultural Differences.   Offshoring does bring cultural differences into sharp relief, which can hinder success unless properly handled. Outsourcers and offshore advisory firms (who advise clients on the offshore marketplace) now realize that both parties need cultural training to overcome management and communication gaps.

For clients, offshorers now routinely put client employees who will deal with the offshore employees through a cultural integration program. Here is a brief description of the program at Syntel, a large U.S.-based IT provider that uses an offshore (India) model, as recounted in one of the SIG reports[3f]:

> *We initially hold a 1.5-day workshop, and then a follow-up orientation a few months later. We find that clients often restructure their operations during the first few months, sometimes bringing in new people. These new people need the orientation, also, which is why we repeat the orientation.*
>
> *In the workshop we talk about how lifestyles and cultures differ between the U.S. and India. In fact, we tailor each workshop to the client's location because Midwest employees differ from New Yorkers, for example. We illustrate, for instance, how the same words have different meanings in the two countries. We point out differences in dress, foods, even eating times. We show a video of these differences, we have people wear the native dress, and we demonstrate how Indians prepare a lunch, which we then serve. We have learned that U.S. employees often have a third-world view of India that is not accurate. Our goal in the orientation is to familiarize them with today's modern India.*

On the provider side, offshorers often put their own employees through an accent neutralization program if they have an accent the client country will find difficult to understand. This practice is especially prevalent for Indian providers with American clients. Providers also teach their employees about the client's company culture (going so far as to hang the same posters on the walls as the client has on its walls) and the client country's culture (going so far as to familiarize employees with holidays and keep them up-to-date on sports teams and major sporting events).

Communication Issues Need to Be Addressed from the Outset.   Different cultures have different communication norms, even when they speak the same language. These differences show up immediately when people from two cultures try to negotiate an offshore contract. The differences need to be addressed, beginning with the negotiations.

Here is just one example. The word "yes" in Asia typically means, "I hear what you are saying," whereas in the United States it means "I can do what you ask" or "I agree with you." When conversing, an Indian might nod his head "yes," which an American might misinterpret as an agreement. The American is then surprised at the next meeting when there has been no agreement after all.

There are substantially more risks in negotiating offshore than onshore contracts because of such communication misunderstandings, notes the global law firm of Mayer, Brown, Rowe & Maw LLP in a SIG report[3f]. The firm uses many mechanisms to mitigate these risks. Here are just five:

- Avoid colloquialisms, such as sports analogies ("we've got to punt on this"), because these statements do not bridge cultures.
- Simplify communications by using short, concise sentences with common words, rather than the typical legal practice of lengthy, convoluted sentences and paragraphs.

- Have the offshore provider write a "statement of work," to gauge their understanding of what they think they are being asked to do.

- Get all commitments in writing.

- Include a person on the client negotiating team who knows the offshore country culture so that he or she can explain the country's norms to the client team as issues arise and prevent the offshorer's team from holding side discussions in their own language at the bargaining table. A "country-wise" member can significantly change negotiating dynamics.

Communication issues continue throughout offshore relationships. This is why migrating the work, which is often fairly quickly defined in onshore contracts, can require lengthy discussions in offshore deals. Common understandings do not exist, so every step in moving work from one country to another, and who pays for what, must be agreed upon. Furthermore, country laws and norms must be taken into account.

Country Laws Need to Be Followed. Offshoring contracts must bridge a myriad of differences between cultures. To preclude dealing with some legal issues, offshore vendors now typically sign their contract in the client's country. For example, as noted earlier, Syntel is a U.S. company. Its contracts with U.S. clients are signed in the United States, and are governed by U.S. law.

Even so, clients need to be aware of data privacy laws, which may not allow customer data to leave its home country or enter certain other countries. The European Union (EU), for instance, does not allow personal data to be moved outside of EU countries. Likewise, clients need to understand the enforceability of intellectual property laws in the outsourced country. Lack of enforceability may preclude moving some IT work to a country, such as China, which does not have enforceable intellectual property laws. Likewise, taxation, employment, immigration, and other laws can significantly affect an offshoring arrangement. All of these must be taken into account.

The list of issues in offshoring can be truly mind-numbing. However, as the trend continues to grow, common practices are arising that make the negotiating task less daunting and the resulting arrangement less risky and more likely to succeed. As an example from the SIG report[3f] of a company using offshoring for its IT maintenance work, consider Exult, which is itself an example of a BPO company. It manages human resources for other firms.

CASE EXAMPLE

EXULT

Exult provides full-service human resources (HR) outsourcing to Global 500 companies. The range of administrative processes Exult provides can be grouped into four main areas. One, Exult maintains and manages employee data

(Case Continued)

and HR records, thereby facilitating various HR functions for clients. Two, Exult manages clients' payroll, compensation, and benefits processes. Three, it provides recruiting and flexible staffing services. Four, Exult provides learning, global mobility, and relocation services to help clients deploy their people most effectively.

Exult is mature in outsourcing relationships because outsourcing is its primary business. Furthermore, most Exult executives were either on the buyer or seller side of outsourcing before joining the company.

In October 2001, Exult signed two contracts with two Indian companies to maintain its core HR computer systems, which include both PeopleSoft and SAP platforms as well as systems built on those two platforms. This was the first time Exult outsourced any IT services.

"We chose to outsource application maintenance to India for three reasons: to garner cost savings, to increase system quality, and to achieve scale (that is, increase our access to resources as we grow our business)," says Steve Unterberger, executive vice president of business model architecture at Exult. He is responsible for Exult's service delivery model.

Exult chose two providers rather than one to ensure that resources could be scaled up as needed. Having only one provider could constrain growth. Management also wanted a fallback position, so that one provider could back up the other if need be. Finally, having two providers would let Exult migrate work offshore faster, moving one client to one provider and another client to the other

provider. There would be no single point-of-capacity limit.

Choosing the Providers

"We led the project, but we called on two advisors: neoIT to do the detailed review and content, and TPI to structure the contract," says Unterberger. He continues, "We contracted with neoIT because of their experience contracting with Indian firms. Our goal was to get the best arrangement for ourselves and our clients. To do that, we needed to understand the Indian market and its practices. NeoIT helped us achieve that."

The Exult internal outsourcing team was composed of Unterberger and Exult's top people in sourcing, IT management, application management, IT connectivity and infrastructure, and IT security and privacy.

Early in the considerations, Exult and neoIT made a 4-day trip to India and visited 9 providers. "Our goal for that first trip was to meet as many companies as we could, to see first-hand how they compared. We knew the only way we could expect to have a clear view of the Indian marketplace was to personally visit India. There are five or six main cities where the major providers are located, so it's easy to see many companies in a short time. We met management, walked around operations, and chose employees at random and talked to them. They showed us real customer service reporting, work processes, and quality measures," says Unterberger.

"We were able to accomplish a lot very quickly because we were clear about what we needed. We knew the specific skills, competencies, and commitments we needed because these are spelled out

(Case Continued)

in our contracts with our clients. So we were able to quickly direct conversations to get to the points we wanted to cover. We looked for a demonstrated ability to scale, a track record for managing people, and good IT maintenance processes," says Unterberger.

"That trip taught us that India has an incredible number of people who are very disciplined and highly motivated. In the end, we came away convinced that many companies could satisfy our needs. I returned from that trip with a real zeal, believing that anyone who is not investigating Indian providers is doing their company a disservice," says Unterberger.

Following the trip, neoIT and Exult ranked the providers and selected two using neoIT's neoQA process. "NeoIT was a very good advisor during this whole process, in two ways. First, they suggested other companies for us to consider—companies not typically on the big list. That was helpful because it kept everyone on their toes. Second, they knew where to push and not push, and they were able to distinguish for us the areas specific to Indian-based firms that we might have overlooked without their guidance," says Unterberger.

Negotiating the Deals

The negotiations were straightforward, and neoIT did help Exult avoid some pitfalls in pricing, taxes, staffing commitments, and telecom. "The providers have standard things they will do, but they do not volunteer them. You have to know to ask," says Unterberger. He states, "Telecom is one of those areas because, while the people costs in India are lower than the U.S., telecommunications costs are on a par with the U.S. We had also

been forewarned that interconnecting would be the pacing factor in getting up and running—and, in fact, it was."

The agreements with the two providers are expected to be for 5 years, but each statement of work aligns with an Exult client and that client's agreement with Exult. These client relationships range from 5 to 10 years in length. The contracts specify service level commitments.

"All the companies have a similar model for training and knowledge transfer, so there is a well-known discipline in migrating the work. Our transition went according to plan," says Unterberger. He states, "We transitioned client by client; some clients went to one provider, some to the other."

"Data privacy was managed through extensive planning and review. We built upon the commitments in our own client contracts. The data is only accessed remotely from India, and the development environments work only with encrypted data. Backup data is stored in the client country, as are business resumption facilities. We spent a lot of time working through these data privacy issues to ensure there were no misunderstandings," says Unterberger.

Migration and Ongoing Management

The current split of IT maintenance work is as follows:

- Seventy percent of the staff members are offshore in India; they handle most of the ongoing maintenance of the HR systems.

- Fifteen percent are provider employees and work onshore at Exult; they handle quick turnaround work and coordinate

(Case Continued)

change control and testing with the offshore staff.

- Fifteen percent are Exult employees who work onshore; they handle client communications and specifying system requirements.

Exult has the ability to influence key positions, and the providers are quick to rotate people when issues arise.

"The offshore companies are very good at engineering discipline. Taking advantage of that capability, though, requires us buyers to work within those highly disciplined Indian maintenance processes rather than try to change them," says Unterberger. According to Unterberger, Exult had to transition its retained IT managers to:

1. Shift from managing people to managing outcomes
2. Take the time to learn how the Indian staff work and think

3. Be open to suggestions from the Indian staff on how to improve the quality of our HR software.

"Transitioning IT managers to manage offshore work requires new skills because they are familiar with having direct control over their people," says Unterberger. He states, "They need to become more general managers and know which levers to pull to obtain results from afar."

According to Unterberger, "Exult also draws on neoIT in managing the relationships day-to-day. NeoIT has a person who acts as our eyes and ears in India because we are not there every day," says Unterberger

Exult is very pleased with the results. From an economic standpoint, the arrangements have exceeded all the goals. From a quality standpoint, Exult has spent time getting the onshore and offshore processes to work harmoniously. ∎

Use Offshoring to Advantage.   A main criticism of offshoring is that it decreases the skills and know-how of the client's IS organization. This need not be so. Kate Kaiser of Marquette University and Stephen Hawk of the University of Wisconsin-Parkside[8] describe an 8-year arrangement between an unnamed financial services firm in the United States and an unnamed IT outsourcer in India. In their recent article in *MIS Quarterly Executive*, the two authors note that the U.S. firm wanted to reduce its system development costs but also increase its in-house IS staff's knowledge—a fairly unusual dual goal. To do so, the two firms have evolved their relationship to "IT cosourcing," which Kaiser and Hawk define as "when the vendor and client collaborate so closely that the vendor can replace or augment the client's IT competencies." In essence, resources from both firms are used to meet the client's needs. Project teams are mixed, and team leadership can come from either firm—both of which require the vendor to have a large onsite presence. Two mechanisms, in particular, have ensured that the U.S. firm's IS staff gain competencies rather than lose them: formalized knowledge transfer between the two firms and a dual project-management hierarchy.

To formalize knowledge transfer from the Indian staff to the U.S. staff, U.S. staff members are sometimes *formally* assigned to projects to learn from an Indian mentor. The two firms initially made such assignments *informally*, but that approach did not improve skills. So the two firms formalized learning-oriented mechanisms, such as mentoring. At the U.S. firm, each IS employee has a development plan, which includes career goals and steps to achieve the needed skills. For the Indian firm, job assignments with the U.S. client include such tasks as mentoring a specific U.S. team member in specific areas. The cost of mentoring is included in the cost of the project.

To create the dual project management hierarchy, the hierarchies of the two firms now mirror each other to improve communication across them. Furthermore, the tiers of leadership in projects can come from either firm, depending on the circumstances. The Indian firm may lead to provide mentoring. The U.S. client may lead for business reasons. Again, the roles of each job are formally agreed upon, and mentoring or other knowledge-transfer skills are part of the cost of the project.

Both mechanisms increase the cost of outsourcing, note Kaiser and Hawk, because, for one thing, dual leadership requires more Indian staff to be located in the United States. But the additional cost improves the in-house staff's technical and application skills, which the firm believes is well worth the added expense, because they highly value their employees' career development.

Redefine Services Using Offshoring, Automation, and Self-Service. Uday Karmarkar,[9] research director of UCLA's Center for Management in the Information Economy, like author Daniel Altman,[7] believes that outsourcing of services is inevitable and that the real concern of service firms should be their loss of competitiveness, not the loss of jobs in their own country. He believes that the service economy is in the midst of restructuring itself, which is terribly painful when it happens in any industry. Offshoring, automation, and self-service are all combining to cause "the industrialization of services," he believes. Like manufacturing firms before them, service firms therefore need to find new ways to add value. He suggests looking in five places for determining new strategies for surviving and using offshoring, automation, and self-service to execute these strategies.

Understand customers. Companies that understand niches of customers, and serve them well, will themselves do well, believes Karmarkar, especially as they move their services to the Web. Edmunds, a company that has published books for car buyers for many years, now focuses on its car-buyer Web site. The site has been so well designed that it has won numerous awards. Edmunds understands its customers and caters to them, states Karmarkar.

Understand demographics. Look for underserved niches, like Wells Fargo Bank has done in offering specific services to the Hispanic population in the western United States. The bank now opens 22,000 Hispanic accounts a month by understanding and catering to this growing group, notes Karmarkar.

Stay in touch with customers. Do not outsource customer service, Karmarkar recommends. Many have done it and found that they lose touch with their customers. Some have realized the effect and brought the function back in-house. A far better strategy is to deliver responsive and error-free service, he believes.

Offer end-to-end service.   Customers are most interested in buying services from firms that offer end-to-end services. For example, Virgin Atlantic Airways provides its business-class passengers with limousine service to the airport and drive-through check-in. People are willing to pay for such pampering to relieve themselves of hassles. This is an important strategy some service firms are delving into by using data mining to understand preferences of customer clusters and then catering to those preferences, notes Karmarkar.

Dominate the screen.   As information moves online, companies are vying to control "the screen," that is, where the information ends up. Service companies have a shot at dominating the screen, because the design of the service and the interface (rather than the technology or the appliance) will determine success, states Karmarkar. For example, NTT DoCoMo, the telecommunications company in Japan, knows how to sell content on cell phones and appliances—from service providers to consumers. Due to this skill, NTT has claimed a disproportionate degree of control over the information chain, notes Karmarkar; it dominates the screen. In short, service companies need to understand what kinds of information various clusters of customer want and cater to them. For many service firms, that catering will be via the Web and mobile devices, using offshoring, self-service, and automation where each can contribute the most value.

In conclusion, outsourcing has become a strategic alternative. With the rapid pace of business change, the best hope of many enterprises is to tap the expertise of companies that are keeping pace rather than trying to do everything themselves. That is why so much inter-company collaboration is taking place. However, outsourcing does not mean relinquishing responsibility. In fact, taken to its extreme, it can mean devoting resources to assist suppliers improve their processes. We believe it is a coming focus in the world of IS Lite.

INFORMATION SECURITY

Whereas information security used to be an arcane, technical topic, even CEOs know about it today due to the importance of electronic information in running their businesses. Actually, all business executives now need to understand Internet-based threats and countermeasures and continually fund security work to protect their businesses.

As one security officer told us:

> *If I were an e-tailer, I might not call the Internet a bad neighborhood, but I would certainly "watch my back." My equivalent brick-and-mortar store would have automatic locks on the doors, cameras watching every aisle, and only $20 in the safe, because I would never know what kinds of thieves might show up or what kinds of attacks they might launch—from anywhere in the world. Furthermore, as an e-tailer, I would need more security than a brick-and-mortar store manager because customers can get a lot closer to the guts of my business.*

The Threats

Since 1996, the Computer Security Institute and the San Francisco Federal Bureau of Investigation Computer Intrusion Squad[10] have conducted an annual survey of

U.S. security managers to uncover the types of computer crimes committed, the counter-measures being taken, and other aspects of cybercrimes. The Spring 2004 survey report (which covers 2003)[10a] contains responses from 494 computer security practitioners from a wide range of enterprises—government and private industry and from those with fewer than 99 employees to those with over 50,000 employees. Two of the report's key findings relate to threats:

- The unauthorized use of computers is declining.
- The most expensive cybercrime was denial of service.

The Unauthorized Use of Computers Is Declining.   As shown in Figure 8-5, attacks on computer systems or detected misuses are declining. The largest declines from the

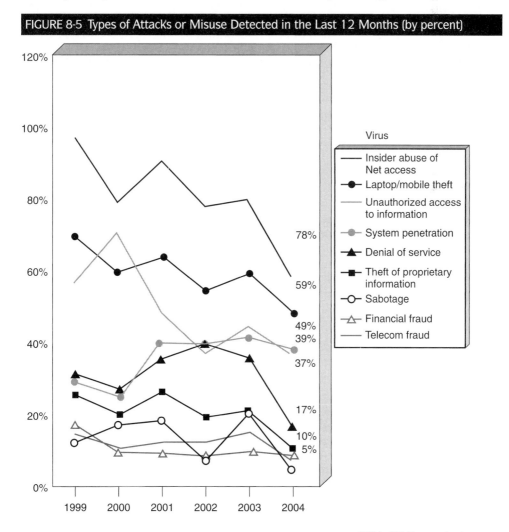

FIGURE 8-5 Types of Attacks or Misuse Detected in the Last 12 Months (by percent)

2004: 481 Respondents

Source: Reprinted with permission of Computer Security Institute, *2004 CSI/FBI Computer Crime and Security Survey*, Computer Security Institute, San Francisco, CA, www.gosci.com, Spring 2004.

2003 to the 2004 report are the 18 percent drop in enterprises reporting insider abuse of Internet access, the 20 percent drop in enterprises reporting denial-of-service attacks, and the 10 percent drop in those reporting theft of proprietary information. For the first time, the survey asked about three new types of cybercrimes: abuse of wireless networks (15 percent reported experiencing this abuse), misuse of public Web applications (10 percent reported this occurring), and defacement of a Web site (7 percent reported occurrences). Every respondent reported experiencing a Web site incident, but 89 percent reported only 1 to 6 occurrences. Only 11 percent had more than 6 incidents.

The Most Expensive Cybercrime Was Denial of Service.   For the 5 previous years, the security breach that caused the greatest financial losses was theft of proprietary information. But in 2003, it was denial of service, resulting in over $26 million in losses (versus $11 million from theft of proprietary information, the second-highest amount), as shown in Figure 8-6. The report authors speculate that this shift may have occurred because of the greater number of viruses in 2003 that unleashed denial-of-service attacks, such as MyDoom.

A related and important finding was that reported losses from security breaches decreased—from $201 million in the 2003 report to $141 million in the 2004 report—whereas the number of respondents reporting loss estimates actually increased from previous years. For the 2004 report, 269 of the 484 respondents provided loss estimates.

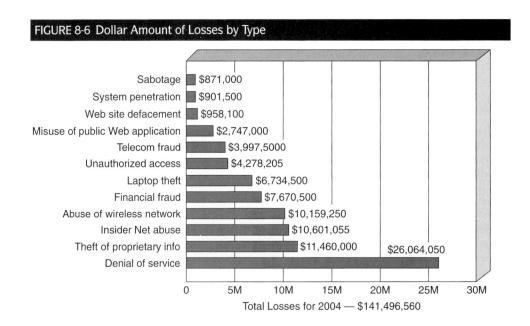

FIGURE 8-6 Dollar Amount of Losses by Type

Type	Amount
Sabotage	$871,000
System penetration	$901,500
Web site defacement	$958,100
Misuse of public Web application	$2,747,000
Telecom fraud	$3,997,5000
Unauthorized access	$4,278,205
Laptop theft	$6,734,500
Financial fraud	$7,670,500
Abuse of wireless network	$10,159,250
Insider Net abuse	$10,601,055
Theft of proprietary info	$11,460,000
Denial of service	$26,064,050

Total Losses for 2004 — $141,496,560

2004: 269 Respondents

Source: Reprinted with permission of Computer Security Institute, *2004 CSI/FBI Computer Crime and Security Survey*, Computer Security Institute, San Francisco, CA, www.gosci.com, Spring 2004.

Although down, financial fraud is still a major threat. The 2002 CSI/FBI report[10b] discussed it in more detail. Credit card information is the single most commonly traded financial instrument for attackers, states the report. This can be sold, used to buy things, or traded. No data of value should be stored on Web servers, recommends the report. Data should be stored in back-end database servers, and communications with front-end Web servers should be restricted and watched very carefully.

CASE EXAMPLE

CREDIT CARD FRAUD

A major problem is the theft of large numbers of credit card records. Here are two examples from the 2002 CSI/FBI report.[10b]

One Bug in a Software Package

In one case, MSNBC reported that a bug in one shopping cart software product used by 4,000 e-commerce sites exposed customer records at those sites. The FBI issued a public warning, but one small e-commerce site did not receive this warning message because it had bought the software through a reseller.

Within days, cybercriminals charged thousands of dollars on the credit cards of users of this small site, buying phone cards, gambling at gambling sites, and buying software off the Web. Instructions on taking advantage of the flaw circulated on the Internet underground, the URLs of other companies that did not obtain the patch were posted on chat rooms, and cybercriminals could even pick up the URLs using search engines.

Two Foreign Cybercriminals

The U.S. Department of Justice has a Web site that describes past cybercrimes. One involves two Russians who committed 20 crimes against two U.S. banks that offer online banking and a U.S. online credit card company. The two stole 56,000 credit card numbers, bank account information, and other personal financial information. Then they tried to extort money from the cardholders and the banks, threatening to publicize the sensitive information they had unearthed.

They also used the stolen credit card numbers to establish fake e-mail accounts, which they used to act as fake sellers and fake winning bidders on online auctions; they paid themselves using the stolen credit card numbers.

They gained access to this information by taking unauthorized control over many computers, including one belonging to a school district. They then used these compromised computers to commit their crimes. The Moscow computer crime unit worked with the FBI to apprehend these cybercriminals. It often takes such international cooperation to fight cybercrime. Power[8b] notes that this one case is just an indication of what is happening. ■

RSA Security Inc.,[11] a prominent, long-time network security firm, notes that it is easier to guard a bank vault than to guard every house in town. That is why many companies are outsourcing their data center operations to data center specialists with vault-like security.

Mobile computing and telecommuting also increase the possibility for cybercrime because the greater number of network openings provides more opportunities for illegal entry. E-commerce sites are also open to everyone, including hackers. And because the Internet does not have intrinsic security protocols, this public space is vulnerable.

In addition, the hacker community has become "a public club," says RSA, with hacker Web sites and newsgroups available to anyone who wants to learn hackers' tricks. Furthermore, hacker tools are becoming increasingly sophisticated and easier to use; and they are continually being revised to outsmart the countermeasures used by companies to protect themselves. It has become a cat-and-mouse game of a continual one-upmanship. Securing an online business is not a one-shot deal; it requires constant vigilance.

RSA describes the following nine approaches hackers use:

1. *Cracking the password:* Guessing someone's password is easier than most people think, says RSA, because some people do not use passwords, others use the word "password," and still others use easy-to-remember words such as their child's name, a sports team, or a meaningful date. Hackers also use software that can test out all combinations, which is called *brute force* password detection.

2. *Tricking someone:* To get users to divulge their passwords, a con artist calls up an employee posing as a network administrator who needs the employee's password to solve an immediate (fictitious) network problem. It happens more than you think, says RSA.

3. *Network sniffing:* Hackers launch software that monitors all traffic looking for passwords or other valuable information. Because most network traffic is in clear text rather than encrypted (appearing as gibberish), sniffing can find information and write it to a file for later use.

4. *Misusing administrative tools:* Helpful tools can be turned against a network. For example, a well-known program written to uncover weak spots in a network, which is important for network administrators, has been used by hackers to find weak spots in target companies' networks. Interestingly, the program's name is Satan.

5. *Playing middleman:* Placing oneself between two communicating parties and either substituting one's own information in place of one of the parties' information or denying one party access to a session, such as denying a competitor access to an important online auction, is another common ploy.

6. *Denial of service:* This tactic floods a party, such as a Web site, with so much useless traffic that the site becomes overwhelmed and freezes. Legitimate messages are locked out, essentially shutting down the business for a period of time.

7. *Trojan horse:* A malicious program can be housed inside an innocent one or, worse yet, one that appears to be helpful.

8. *Viruses:* These pieces of software run without permission. Their most common entry point has been as e-mail attachments. Once such an attachment is opened, the

program is released and performs its task, such as destroying files (a worm) or replicating itself in e-mails sent to everyone in the e-mail directory. Internet-based viruses have attracted lots of attention, not just for PCs, but for wireless devices as well.

9. *Spoofing*: By masquerading as a legitimate IP address, hackers can gain access to a site. A site can masquerade as another Web site and redirect traffic to a fraudulent lookalike site that, for example, allows credit card information to be captured for later use.

Security's Five Pillars

Five pillars make up today's security techniques, says RSA.[11]

1. *Authentication:* Verifying the authenticity of users
2. *Identification:* Identifying users to grant them appropriate access
3. *Privacy:* Protecting information from being seen
4. *Integrity:* Keeping information in its original form
5. *Nonrepudiation:* Preventing parties from denying actions they have taken.

Authentication.   *Authentication* means verifying someone's authenticity: They are who they say they are. People can authenticate themselves to a system in three basic ways, says RSA: by something they know, something they have, and something they are. "Something they know" means "something only they know," generally a password or a mother's maiden name, for example. "Something they have" means "in your possession." In computer security, one possibility is a token that generates a code a user enters into the computer to gain access to, say, an e-mail system. Users just have to remember not to lose the token. Or they may have a digital certificate, which will be discussed shortly. "Something they are" generally means a physical characteristic, such as a fingerprint, retinal scan, or voice print. These characteristics fall under the area called *biometrics*. Each type of user authentication has its strengths and weaknesses. RSA recommends choosing two of the three, which is called *two-factor authentication*.

Identification.   *Identification* is the process of issuing and verifying access privileges, like being issued a driver's license, RSA says. First, you must show proof of identity to get your license. Once you receive your license, it becomes your proof of identity, but it also states your driving privileges (able to drive an automobile but not a truck or a bus). Therefore, identification is like being certified to be able to do certain things.

In the Internet world, identification is moving toward application-level security, says RSA; that is, authentication for each application. It requires users to sign on for each application, which many feel is a large burden. Some companies are taking a single sign-on approach.

Data Privacy and Data Integrity.   These mean keeping information from being seen (*privacy*) or changed (*integrity*). Both are especially important when information travels through the Internet because it is a public space where interception is more possible. The most common method of protecting data is encryption, to be discussed shortly.

Nonrepudiation.   *Nonrepudiation* means that neither party in a sale or communication of sensitive information can later deny that the transaction or information exchange took place. Nonrepudiation services can prove that someone was the actual sender and the other the receiver; no imposter was involved on either side.

Management Countermeasures

The major problem these days, notes RSA, is that enterprises cannot have both access to information and airtight security at the same time. Due to online commerce, companies want unimpeded information flow among a complex set of alliance partners. Thus, it is no longer feasible to define *good* as "inside the network" and *bad* as "outside the network," as in the past. Today, companies must make trade-offs between absolute information security and efficient flow of information. Although they might think technology can solve security loopholes, the human dimension is equally important—making employees cognizant of security threats they may encounter and teaching them how to strengthen the company's security measures. Today, due to the importance of computers in company operations, security decisions are not just technical; they are being influenced by business managers, which affects the bottom line.

The 2004 CSI/FBI Computer Crime and Security Survey[10a] had five key findings that relate to how companies are managing security and the security management policies they have put in place.

- Most organizations evaluate the return on their security expenditures.
- Over 80 percent conduct security audits.
- The percentage of organizations reporting cybercrimes to law enforcement declined.
- Most do not outsource cybersecurity.
- Most respondents view security awareness training as important.

Most Organizations Evaluate the Return on Their Security Expenditures.   For the first time, the CSI/FBI survey asked how managers quantify the costs and benefits of their security expenditures, because the report's authors note that there has been considerable discussion in security circles about how to evaluate these investments. The survey found that 55 percent of the respondents measure value on return on investment, whereas 28 percent use internal rate of return and 25 percent use net present value.

On the subject of budgets, 46 percent of the respondents spend between 1 and 5 percent of their IT budget on security, 16 percent spend less than 1 percent, 12 percent spend more than 5 percent, and 14 percent did not know how much their organization spends on security. Even more interesting is security expenditures per employee. Economies of scale turn out to be significant. For example, on average, firms with less than $10 million in annual revenue spend about $500 a year per employee on security ($163 on capital investments and $334 on operating expenses), whereas firms with over $1 billion in revenue spend only $110 a year ($30 on capital investments and $82 on operating expenses), on average. The smaller firms spend over four times as much!

Over 80 Percent Conduct Security Audits.   As the 2004 CSI/FBI report notes, industry literature has long recommended that firms begin a security program by conducting an audit, but until this survey, no one had surveyed the prevalence of this practice. The survey found that 82 percent of the respondents conduct security audits. However, the report authors were surprised that this figure was not higher. Because it is such a well-known practice, they wonder why the other 18 percent are not conducting audits.

The Percentage of Organizations Reporting Cybercrimes to Law Enforcement Declined.   Although organizations may be willing to estimate cybercrime losses for the CSI/FBI survey and to conduct internal security audits, they apparently are not so willing to make the incidents public. Figure 8-7 shows the four ways organizations respond to a security breach: patch the hole, do not report the breach, report it to law enforcement, report it to legal counsel. As the figure shows, 91 percent patch the hole, 48 percent do not share information about the incident with others (the same percentage as in 1999), and only 20 percent report it to law enforcement—a significant downward trend.

Why not report an incident? The CSI/FBI survey found that 51 percent do not report a cybercrime to law enforcement because the negative publicity would hurt their stock price or their corporate image. Some 35 percent do not report incidents because they believe a competitor will use that information to its advantage. Only 20 percent see a civil remedy as the best course to take (hence, a reason to report a crime). And even though organizations may be aware of law enforcement's interest,

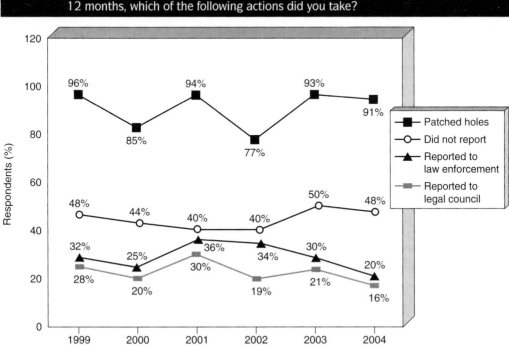

FIGURE 8-7 If your organization has experienced computer intrusion(s) within the last 12 months, which of the following actions did you take?

2004: 320 Respondents

Source: Reprinted with permission of Computer Security Institute, *2004 CSI/FBI Computer Crime and Security Survey*, Computer Security Institute, San Francisco, CA, www.gosci.com, Spring 2004.

they do not see that as sufficient reason to report a security breach. So there is not as much sharing of cybercrime information as some would hope.

Most Do Not Outsource Cybersecurity.   A new question asked on the 2004 CSI/FBI 2004 survey was whether organizations outsource their cybersecurity function. The survey found that 63 percent do not outsource any cybersecurity function, and only 7 percent outsource more than 20 percent of their cybersecurity function. The report authors imply that they expect cybersecurity outsourcing to increase.

A related new question was whether the organizations purchase insurance to manage cybersecurity risks. Such insurance is available, and the survey found that 28 percent have taken it out. The report authors believe that more organizations will purchase such insurance in the future.

Most Respondents View Security Awareness Training As Important.   Even though most organization see training as being important, a high percentage of respondents believe that their organization is not doing enough such training. They believe that employees especially need training with regards to the organization's security policy, network security, access control systems, and security management.

Because airtight security is not possible, companies need to prioritize their risks and work on safeguarding against the greatest threats. To give an example of one company's approach to overall network security, consider this case from a Gartner EXP report.[4b]

CASE EXAMPLE

AN INTERNET SERVICES COMPANY

This firm provides services to Internet professionals and performs security assessments.

Planning and Building for Security

When establishing network connections, the firm's starting point is to deny all access to and from the Internet. From there, it opens portals only where required, and each opening has a firewall and only permits specific functions, such as FTP or e-mail.

In essence, the company has put a perimeter around itself. It determines the worth of the information inside and spends the appropriate level of money to protect those assets. It can be hard to define the perimeter, though. For example, the company does work from client sites and that work needs to be protected as well.

It recognizes that it must also stay vigilant within the perimeter to avoid having a "soft chewy center." It uses a layered approach with numerous ways to protect each layer and some redundancy. For example, it worries about telephone hackers as well as computer hackers.

The IS organization is responsible for all in-house systems and all security. A central authority oversees all servers and workstations. In addition, all machines run the latest virus-detection software. When a system reboots, it

(*Case Continued*)

accesses the central server where its virus definitions are checked. If they are not the latest ones, the newest versions are downloaded.

Finally, the company has disaster recovery plans that include having servers geographically separated. It recommends that clients do the same so that e-business sites can remain operational, at least partially, if some of the servers are hit by an attack or become overloaded.

Monitoring

The company views security on the Internet as a war of escalation. Every few weeks someone finds a clever new way to penetrate software, and a new type of attack is launched. Once the security team has closed one hole, attackers will find and attack another. The best the security team can hope to achieve is to deter attackers by closing more and more holes.

The security team therefore believes it needs to constantly "check the locks," which it does in the following ways:

- The team keeps track of the latest bugs found in systems. The company belongs to suppliers' bug alert communities. When it receives an alert, the team looks to see whether it applies to the company's systems. If so, the team assesses the vulnerability and takes needed action.

- The team keeps up-to-date on the latest security attacks that have taken place around the world by subscribing to security organizations and constantly visiting their Web sites for the latest news.

- The team subscribes to hacker e-mail lists and bulletin boards to see

what the bad guys are doing and talking about. The security team believes it must think like the enemy.

- Team members personally explore some threats by setting up a test system and trying various attacks on it—attacks they have read about on the e-mail lists and bulletin boards. It is fun for the security staff, it provides a break from the normal work, and it presents a welcome technical challenge.

- The team logs and monitors all incoming and outgoing traffic. A dedicated team manages the firewalls.

- A senior security person scans the company's Web sites monthly from a remote site, comparing the services being run on the servers with the official inventory of services that should be running on the servers. Major surprises are investigated. This person also checks to ensure that no servers are running known compromised software.

Education: The Key to Improving Security

The greatest security challenge is employee and customer apathy; they always say, "This cannot happen to us." Hence, the greatest security need is employee and customer education. The company tries to balance education with a taste of what could happen so that its security message is taken seriously without frightening employees and clients so much that they think any countermeasure is useless. Management has learned that fear-mongering becomes counterproductive if it is too scary or used too often.

(Case Continued)

Education is a two-way street, though. Businesspeople need to determine the value of the assets, but they also need input from IS on what is technically feasible to guard specific assets. For example, the company has alerted all its high-profile clients about the possibility of denial-of-service attacks. The bigger and more well known the company and its Web site, the more it needs to be prepared for such attacks by having the technology and plans in place to identify and deal with attacks when they occur. Management warns, "If you have a determined adversary, they are going to keep trying until they get you."

The company has found that businesspeople do understand security when it is related to money. They understand that they, not the technicians, are the ones who need to justify security expenses because only they understand the worth of protecting different kinds of information. For example, they understand that protecting Web servers that contain public information requires keeping the servers from crashing. That type of protection costs less than safeguarding servers that house proprietary company or confidential client information, which must also protect the data from prying eyes; not every one can access it. ■

Technical Countermeasures

The trend in computer security is toward policy-based management: defining security policies and then centrally managing and enforcing those policies via security management products and services. Hence, for example, a user authenticates to a network once, and then a rights-based system gives that user access only to the systems to which the user has been given the rights. A finance employee might have the rights to company finance records, but a manufacturing employee might not.

Figure 8-8 shows the types of security technologies used by the 494 security managers in the 2004 CSI/FBI survey. Some 99 percent use antivirus software, 98 percent use firewalls, and 71 percent use server-based access control lists.

To explain a bit more about countermeasures, following are three techniques used by companies to protect themselves: firewalls, encryption, and virtual private networks (VPNs).

Firewalls. To protect against hacking, companies install *firewalls*, which are hardware or software that controls access between networks. Firewalls are widely used to separate intranets and extranets from the Internet, giving only employees or authorized business partners access to the network. Typically implemented on a router, firewalls perform their job by filtering message packets to block illegal traffic, where "illegal" is defined by the security policy or by a proxy server, which acts as an intermediary server between, say, the Internet and the intranet. Proxy servers can look deeper into traffic than do packet filters, which just look at the header information on each packet. However, proxy servers are slower than packet filters. Some products perform both. Without policy management, says RSA, firewalls may not be effective

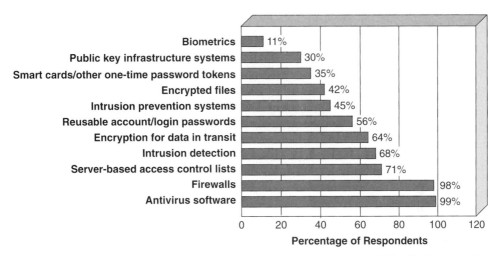

Percentage of Respondents

2004: 483 Respondents

FIGURE 8-8 Security Technologies Used

Source: Reprinted with permission of Computer Security Institute, *2004 CSI/FBI Computer Crime and Security Survey,* Computer Security Institute, San Francisco, CA, www.gosci.com, Spring 2004.

because they may just be treated as stand-alone devices. The most effective security programs create layers of security.

Encryption. To protect against sniffing, messages can be encrypted before being sent over the Internet. Two classes of encryption methods are in use today: secret key encryption and public key encryption. The most common secret key method is the Data Encryption Standard (DES) developed by IBM, the National Security Agency, and the National Bureau of Standards. Using this method, sender and receiver use the same key to code and decode a message. The level of security is a function of the size of the key. DES is widely used and available in many software applications.

The most common public key encryption method is RSA, named for the three developers: Rivest, Shamir, and Adleman. To send an encrypted message using RSA, two keys are necessary: a public key and a private key. As its name implies, the public key is known to many people and is not kept secret. However, the private key must be kept secret. The two keys are used to code and decode messages; a message coded with one can only be decoded with the other.

Figure 8-9 shows how an encrypted message is sent. First the message is encrypted using the receiver's public key. The message is now secure—it can only be decoded using the receiver's private key, which is only known to the receiver. Note that the sender uses the receiver's public key, not a key belonging to the sender. If a secure message is to be sent back to the original sender, then the public key of the original sender would be used. Thus, for two-way secure communications, both parties must have a set of keys.

The RSA method is incorporated into all major Web browsers and is the basis for the Secure Socket Layer (SSL) used in Internet communications. However, full two-way secure communication requires all parties to have a public and private key. Most individuals do not have such keys, so most B2C applications requiring encryption, such

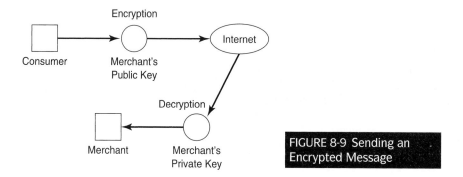

FIGURE 8-9 Sending an Encrypted Message

as for the transmission of credit card numbers, are only secure from the consumer to the merchant, not from the merchant to the consumer.

To protect against spoofing, firms need a way to authenticate the identity of an individual. This verification requires a form of digital ID. The most common form of digital signature uses the RSA encryption method. Because the private key is known only to one person and a message encrypted with that key can only be decoded with the matching public key, the private key provides a way of verifying that the message came from a certain individual. Figure 8-10 shows the basic process.

For digital signatures to work, though, a trusted third party must issue the keys to individuals and firms. These parties are called *certification agencies* and can be government agencies or trusted private companies. The agency issues a digital certificate containing the user's name, the user's public key, and the digital signature of the certification agency. See Figure 8-11. The digital certificate can then be attached to a message to verify the identity of the sender of the message.

Virtual Private Networks (VPNs).   Most offices now have a local ISP, so no matter where they are located in the world, the least costly way to create companywide networking is to utilize the Internet and its TCP/IP protocols. However, the Internet is not secure because, for one thing, none of the TCP/IP protocols authenticate the communicating parties.

One approach to security has been to obtain a VPN from a CLEC or an ISP. A VPN runs over a private IP network, so it is more affordable than leased lines, and it is secure. VPNs use tunneling technology and encryption to keep data secure as it is transmitted.

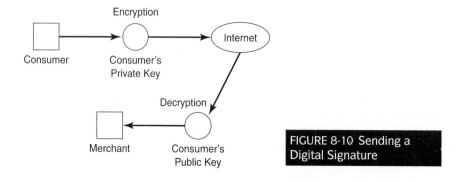

FIGURE 8-10 Sending a Digital Signature

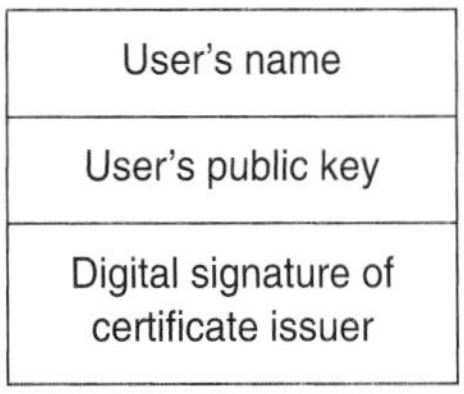

| User's name |
| User's public key |
| Digital signature of certificate issuer |

FIGURE 8-11 A Digital Certificate

Tunneling creates a temporary connection between a remote computer and the CLEC's or ISP's local data center, which blocks access to anyone trying to intercept messages sent over that link. Encryption scrambles the message before it is sent and then decodes it at the receiving end. While in transit, the message cannot be read or changed; hence, it is protected.

VPNs can be used in three ways, according to PwC.[12]

1. *Remote access VPNs* give remote employees a way to access an enterprise's intranet securely by dialing a specific ISP, generally a large one with local telephone numbers in many cities. The ISP establishes a secure tunnel through its network to the corporate network, where the user can access e-mail and the intranet. This option offloads network management to the ISP, something most IS executives want to do.

2. *Remote office VPNs* give enterprises a way to create a secure private network with remote offices. The ISP's VPN equipment encrypts all transmissions.

3. *Extranet VPNs* give enterprises a way to conduct e-business with trading partners, advisers (such as legal firms), suppliers, alliance partners, and customers. These partners dial a specific ISP, which then establishes a secure link to the extranet.

As an example of using a VPN, consider Plymouth Rock Assurance Corporation.[13]

CASE EXAMPLE

PLYMOUTH ROCK ASSURANCE CORPORATION

Plymouth Rock Assurance Corporation (PRAC), with headquarters in Boston, Massachusetts, sells personal automobile insurance through some 165 independent agents throughout the state. The company wanted to create an extranet, Agent Web, where an agent could transact business with PRAC.

The two main issues were ensuring that communications between the agents and the Web site were both secure and fast. Without secure links, the agents said

(Case Continued)

they would not use Agent Web, and PRAC did not want agents to have to wait for page downloads.

PRAC considered using frame relay to get the speed, but that technology turned out to be more expensive than they wanted. So they looked into DSL, which would provide 20 times the speed of a regular dial-up modem. They also looked into creating a VPN from the local sites to the Agent Web site to ensure secure transmission of data back and forth.

They settled on using the services of HarvardNet, a local Massachusetts provider of Internet services, which offers a DSL-based VPN service. PRAC chose HarvardNet because its geographic footprint closely matched the geographic locations of the independent

agents. Furthermore, the cost of providing these agents' offices with DSL was just one-third the cost of frame relay. HarvardNet's RemoteConnect VPN service would also allow PRAC to extend its secure corporate network to all these remote independent agent sites. Creating the DSL-based VPN provides both the sub-second response time and the secure communication links PRAC wanted to provide to the agents to streamline claims processing and reduce paper.

In addition, PRAC decided to turn over all the operations of Agent Web to HarvardNet. HarvardNet now hosts Agent Web and handles the VPN network management so that PRAC's IS department only needs to focus on the applications of Agent Web. ∎

Information security has become an important management topic, yet it has no clear-cut answers. It is too costly to provide all the security a company wants, and performing security checks on packets takes a lot of processor power, which can slow performance. Even with world-class technical security, management needs to make sure that all employees follow security policies, because companies are only as safe as their weakest link. In fact, that weakest link could be a supplier or contractor with secure access to a company's systems, yet poor security of its own. One final thought: Security is as much a human problem as a technical problem.

PLANNING FOR BUSINESS CONTINUITY

Sadly, the terrorist attacks on September 11, 2001, taught a lot of U.S. companies that there is a big difference between disaster recovery and business continuity. In the past, executives expected their IS organization to focus on disaster recovery; that is, getting computers and networks up-and-running after a hurricane, flood, fire, or other disaster. September 11 taught them a broader issue—business continuity—that is, getting the business back up and running. Business continuity involves far more than IT equipment, notes Chuck Tucker in the Gartner EXP report, *September 11: Business Continuity Lessons*.[4c]

Business continuity broadens the discussion to include safeguarding people during a disaster, documenting business procedures (instead of relying on certain employees who may become unavailable), and giving employees the tools and space to handle personal issues first so that they can then concentrate on work. Tucker notes that business continuity includes:

- Alternate workspaces for people with working computers and phone lines
- Backup IT sites that are not too close but not too far away (to be within driving distance but not affected by a regional telecommunication disaster)
- Up-to-date evacuation plans that everyone knows and has practiced
- Backed up laptops and departmental servers, because a lot of corporate information is housed on these machines rather than in the data center
- Helping people cope with a disaster by having easily accessible phone lists, e-mail lists, and even instant messenger lists so that people can communicate with loved ones and colleagues

In short, business continuity is a business issue. IT disaster recovery is just one component of it. Disaster recovery practitioners agree that (1) disaster contingency planning needs to be an integral part of doing business, and (2) commitment of resources to a disaster recovery process must be based on an assessment by top management of cost versus risk. Companies essentially have two options for disaster recovery: use of internal or external resources.

Using Internal Resources

Organizations that rely on internal resources for disaster recovery generally view this planning as a normal part of systems planning and development. They cost-justify backup processing and telecommunications based on company needs during foreseeable emergencies. Companies use the following approaches to backing up their computer systems, data, and communication links with company resources:

- Multiple data centers
- Distributed processing
- Backup telecommunications facilities
- LANs

Multiple Data Centers.   Over the past few years, to save money organizations have consolidated their multiple computer centers or outsourced them to a provider operating mainly from one data center. September 11 caused many executives to rethink the wisdom of having all corporate computing in one location. Multiple centers can provide emergency backup for critical services.

For backing up data, companies create protected disk storage facilities, sometimes called direct access data storage, or DASD farms. These farms are regularly refreshed with current operating data to speed recovery at an alternate data center. They are normally company-owned, unattended sites and remote from the primary data center. They house disk controllers and disk drives that can be accessed either online or in batch mode.

Distributed Processing.   Other organizations use distributed processing to deal with disaster recovery. They perform critical processing locally rather than at a data center so that operations can continue uninterrupted when a disaster hits a data center. Companies that use this approach standardize hardware and applications at remote locations so that each local processing site can provide backup for the others.

Distributed processing solutions to disaster recovery can be quite costly when data redundancy between central and remote sites is required. Therefore, this alternative is most commonly used for applications that must continue to operate, such as order entry and financial transaction systems.

Backup Telecommunications Facilities.   Companies appear to be handling telecommunications backup in two ways: (1) by utilizing duplicate communications facilities and (2) by using alternate technologies that they redeploy in case of an emergency. However, as Tucker notes, in New York City, companies signed up with different telecommunications carriers (without checking their carriers' routing), thinking that they had alternate communication routes. Then they discovered that 30 percent of Manhattan's telecommunications traffic, from many different carriers, went through Verizon's West Street switching office, which was destroyed on September 11.

Some companies turn to alternate communication technologies when their communication links fail, such as when the infamous Hinsdale fire destroyed the Hinsdale Illinois Bell Telephone Company central office switching station. The station handled 118,000 long distance lines, 30,000 data lines, and 35,000 local voice lines, reports Jeff Bozman.[14] It served as a hub for some 30 local exchanges in northeastern Illinois. The fire disrupted telephone service to the area for 4 weeks. Local companies used at least two alternative technologies to handle their telecommunication needs during this emergency.

MONY Financial Services in Syracuse, New York, switched a satellite link from its smaller San Juan, Puerto Rico, office to its large Hinsdale office by installing a VSAT dish on the roof, reports Crockett.[15] It was used to communicate via satellite to a communication hub in New York City and from there via land lines to Syracuse. The San Juan office then instituted its own communication backup plan, using terrestrial lines to communicate to Syracuse.

Zurich Insurance Company, in Schaumburg, Illinois, established a line-of-site microwave link between headquarters and an AT&T switching office located about 2 miles away, reports Crockett. In fact, 38 temporary microwave links were established in the Chicago area.

September 11 taught the importance of restoring or relying on more personal forms of communication—e-mail, handhelds, instant messaging, intranets, and even paging systems. Business no longer relies just on data in data center computers; much of it is now stored in laptops, departmental servers, and e-mail. Before September 11, few IS organizations had disaster recovery plans for these computers and systems.

LANs.   Servers on one LAN can be used to back up servers for other networks. As with mainframe DASD farms, data servers used for such backup need to be refreshed regularly to keep their data up-to-date. Keeping up-to-date is accomplished by linking the networks. Network master control programs permit the designating of alternate devices when primary ones fail.

Using External Resources

In many cases, a cost-versus-risk analysis may not justify committing permanent resources to contingencies; therefore, companies use the services of a disaster recovery firm. These services include:

- Integrated disaster recovery services
- Specialized disaster recovery services
- Online and off-line data storage facilities

Integrated Disaster Recovery Services. In North America, major suppliers of disaster recovery services offer multiple recovery sites interconnected by high-speed telecommunications lines. Services at these locations include fully operational processing facilities that are available on fewer-than-24-hours notice. These suppliers often have environmentally suitable storage facilities for housing special equipment for their clients.

Subscription fees for access to fully operational facilities are charged on a per-month basis. Actual use of the center is charged on a per-day basis. In addition, a fee is often charged each time a disaster is declared. Mobile facilities, with a mobile trailer containing computer equipment, can be moved to a client site and are available at costs similar to fully operational facilities. Empty warehouse space can be rented as well.

Recognizing the importance of telecommunications links, major disaster recovery suppliers have expanded their offerings to include smaller sites that contain specialized telecommunications equipment. These sites allow users to maintain telecommunications services when disaster recovery facilities are in use. They house control equipment and software needed to support communication lines connecting recovery sites with client sites.

Needless to say, companies now in the business of hosting corporate Web sites also handle disaster recovery for those sites.

September 11 pointed out a shortcoming of regional disasters: The backup sites fill up fast. In fact, one firm located in the World Trade Center declared a disaster with its provider 4 minutes after the first plane hit and was told that the closest available workspace facilities were hundreds of miles away. This company resorted to triage instead, notes Tucker, asking some employees to work from home and giving their workspaces at other locations to the displaced employees.

Specialized Disaster Recovery Services. Some suppliers of backup services can accommodate mainframe clients who also need to back up midrange machines. Others provide backup solely for midrange systems. Some will even deliver a trailer with compatible hardware and software to a client location.

Telecommunications firms also offer a type of recovery service, through network reconfiguration, where network administrators at user sites can reroute their circuits around lines with communication problems. Specialized telecommunications backup services also exist. Hughes Network Systems, in Germantown, Maryland, helped a company that had 49 of its pharmacies affected by the Hinsdale telephone switching station fire. Within 72 hours, Hughes installed a temporary network of VSATs at 12 sites. The 37 remaining sites had small satellite dishes installed within 2 weeks. Other firms offer data communications backup programs, where they will store specific telecommunications equipment for customers and deliver that equipment to the customer's recovery site when needed.

Online and Off-Line Data Storage.   Alternate locations for storage of data and other records have long been a part of disaster planning. Services generally consist of fire-resistant vaults with suitable temperature and humidity controls. Several suppliers offer "electronic vaulting" for organizations that need to have current data off-site at the time a disaster occurs. These suppliers use two methods to obtain current data from their clients. One method uses computer-to-computer transmission of data on a scheduled basis. The other uses dedicated equipment to capture and store data at a remote location as it is created on the client's computer. This latter method assures uninterrupted access to data from an operationally ready disaster recovery facility selected by the client.

In summary, when disaster recovery needs do not shape the architecture of an enterprise's computer systems, the cost of reconfiguring the systems to provide the needed redundancy and backup can be prohibitive. In these cases, external backup alternatives may be a more cost-effective form of insurance. For e-business, however, mere backup capability does not suffice. Disaster recovery must be an integral part of system design, because companies need immediate roll-over to backup facilities when operations are interrupted.

To illustrate the use of disaster recovery facilities, consider the case of Household International.

CASE EXAMPLE

HOUSEHOLD INTERNATIONAL

Household International, with headquarters in Prospect Heights, Illinois, is a major provider of consumer lending, banking, insurance, and commercial financial services in the United States. The company also provides similar services in the United Kingdom, Canada, and Australia through subsidiaries.

The core of its consumer finance business is serviced by some 700 consumer lending branches and 60 bank branches throughout the United States. Household is also a large credit card issuer in the United States and operates a major credit card service center in

California. Household's major data center is in its corporate offices. The center is linked to the branch network via leased lines with regional connections to more than 10,000 remote devices and terminals.

Typical of large financial services institutions, Household justified its disaster recovery planning based on legal and regulatory requirements and the need to maintain uninterrupted customer service. The centralized design of its data network simplified recovery planning but made the headquarters data center critical to recovery.

(*Case Continued*)

The company established a full-time staff to prepare, maintain, and exercise (test out) disaster recovery plans. After exploring several alternatives, including adding reserve processing capacity to their network, Household decided to rely on Comdisco Disaster Recovery Services. Comdisco is a major supplier of alternate site data processing services in North America.

Services provided by Comdisco included use of facilities at one or more of its recovery centers throughout North America and hot site equipment and software to provide immediate operational support on request. In addition, Comdisco provided technical assistance in disaster planning, testing, and the use of recovery centers. Household viewed the monthly cost of these services as their most economical recovery alternative.

After 6 months, all critical banking applications had been tested at the alternate site and contingency procedures had been developed for the branch offices. Household had also begun developing contingency plans for the consumer lending operation and testing application programs at the alternate site. In addition, they had begun developing business recovery priorities and operating procedures for end users.

In the midst of this effort, nature intervened. At 9:00 A.M. on a Friday after meeting with key personnel, Household declared a disaster. More than 9 inches of rain had fallen on the Chicago area in 12 hours. Widespread flooding had closed major highways, leaving thousands of homes and businesses without power or telephone service. A retention pond at corporate headquarters had overflowed, causing an overnight runoff into the basement of the headquarters building where the data center was located. By 10:30 A.M. the water had risen to 31 inches— 9 inches above the 22-inch false floor— and it rose even further before the disaster ended.

With telephone lines down and the company PBX out of service, the recovery coordinator relied on plans made early in the year. Computer operations were transferred to the Comdisco alternate site 20 miles away. Fortunately, Household made the call to Comdisco early; other clients who called later were relocated to sites as far as 800 miles (1,300 kilometers) away. Because five Chicago-area businesses declared disasters, Comdisco's hot site resources in Illinois were quickly saturated.

At the backup site, work began on restoring vital bank and check processing systems. Critical processing for most branches resumed within 24 hours. Teller systems at branches used local computers, so they operated without interruption. However, online information on the current status of customer accounts was not available until the following Monday.

After pumping out the flooded data center, the data processing staff found extensive damage to disk drive motors and circuit boards below the high-water mark. However, they were able to quickly restore the communication control units. They were then able to use these units as the links for all communications between the backup site computers and the remote computers in the branches. The local telephone company used a central switch to establish a link between the disaster

(Case Continued)

recovery alternate site and the Household home office.

By the third day, all the important work that had been moved to key Household locations was up and running, and communication links among these locations were working. Communication links to all offices were available by the sixth day.

A few days after the disaster, more than 220 analysts and programmers were assigned to work at the alternate site on a 24-hour schedule. The disaster recovery coordinator arranged for special food service, dressing facilities, and rest areas at the alternate site. Workspaces were created using rented furniture and equipment.

Special meetings were held with senior management to establish recovery priorities for the consumer lending operation. Daily meetings, chaired by the executive vice president of IS, were attended by nearly all managers and vendors affected by the disaster—some 40 to 50 people in all. These meetings became the day-to-day means for reporting status, handling special problems, and developing recovery schedules. The meetings turned out to be the best means for communicating quickly and making decisions using the existing organization. The meetings lasted several hours each day and covered a wide range of topics. Thus, no special organizational structure was used for managing the disaster; however. the disaster recovery manager played a key role in coordinating the recovery.

The company left the backup site on the fifteenth day. Eighteen days after the disaster, normal operations had been fully restored.

Lessons Learned

Household learned six lessons from this disaster, which it offers as recommendations to others.

1. Consider the risks of a natural disaster when selecting a data center location. Areas with high exposure to flooding, heavy rainfall, fire hazards, or earthquakes will be more costly to protect.

2. Create a plan to return to the primary site after the disaster. This plan is just as important as the plan to move to an alternate site.

3. Do not expect damaged equipment to always be replaced in kind or restored to original condition. Therefore, make plans for new configurations, and regularly monitor sources of equipment and supplies to assure early delivery of replacements.

4. Test hot site resources under full workload conditions to ensure that sufficient computer capacity is available to meet high-priority needs.

5. Plan for alternate telecommunications routing for multiple-site operations during a disaster. Household's original telecommunications disaster recovery plan called for key sites around the country to handle the headquarters processing load in case of a home office disaster. The quick recovery of the communication control units at headquarters allowed Household to use an alternate plan: rely mainly on processing at the nearby disaster recovery site. Thus, for 16 days they operated with both the headquarters center and the disaster recovery center. The other key Household centers handled mainly their normal work, but their computers were available if needed.

(Case Continued)

6. Maintain critical data at the alternate site or at another nearby location for fast system recovery.

Household has used its experience to refine and complete the plans started before the rainstorm. In addition, Comdisco services have been extended to other subsidiaries under a corporate-wide contract. In retrospect, key participants believe that early restoration of the headquarters computer center, the existence of computer and telecommunications backup procedures, staff familiar with the backup plans, and use of normal management channels were all important in their rapid recovery. ∎

CONCLUSION

The subject of managing computer operations is, perhaps surprisingly, at an all-time high because of the emergence of e-commerce, the increasing use of outsourcing, news-grabbing computer viruses, attacks on major Web sites, and terrorism. Outsourcing, security, business continuity—all are important operational issues. As enterprises increasingly rely on computing and telecommunications to work closely with others, they open themselves up to more threats by electronic means. As we noted in the security section, one security manager would not call the Internet a bad neighborhood, but he would watch his back. That attitude increasingly means being vigilant to outside threats, just as outsourcing means learning to work with outsiders. In short, the view of operations is shifting from managing inward to managing outward, on all fronts.

QUESTIONS AND EXERCISES

Review Questions

1. What has been the main shift in the operations viewpoint?
2. What are three solutions to operations problems, according to Congleton?
3. How did Microsoft manage its special OEM Webcast?
4. How thoroughly are CIOs expected to investigate outsourcing?
5. What are the driving forces of outsourcing, according to Bergstein?
6. What are IT outsourcing, transitional outsourcing, best-of-breed outsourcing, shared services, business process outsourcing, and e-business outsourcing?
7. What management elements has Kodak put in place to manage its outsourcing relationships?
8. What is supplier development?
9. What are five ways to reduce miscommunications in negotiating an offshore outsourcing contract?
10. What types of cybercrimes result in the greatest financial losses, according to the CSI/FBI study?

11. According to RSA, what approaches do hackers use?
12. Describe the five pillars of information security.
13. How does the Internet services company "check its locks"?
14. How did the terrorist attacks on September 11, 2001, expand the notion of disaster recovery?
15. What lessons did Household International learn from its disaster?

Discussion Questions

1. Outsourcing offloads a burdensome technical responsibility and allows management to focus on its core business. Outsourcing strips a company of an important core competence—IT know-how. Which statement do you agree with? Why?
2. Security is such an important area that every employee should be required to carry around a security token that generates a new password every time they log on. Security threats are overblown; imposing on employees to carry a security token is too much to ask. Discuss both sides of this issue.
3. The Internet provides all the redundant routing and alternate sites an enterprise needs. It need not contract with a backup and recovery firm as Household International did. Present arguments against this belief.
4. September 11 was a one-time event. It is not going to happen again. Executives do not need to plan for such a regional disaster. Discuss whether you agree or disagree with this statement.

Exercises

1. Read a few articles about outsourcing. What did you learn about outsourcing that is not mentioned in this chapter? Relay your findings to the class.
2. Read three articles that describe the negatives of offshore outsourcing and three that present the positives. Present both sides to the class.
3. Read several articles on Internet security. Present any new information to your class.
4. Visit a company in your local community. Learn about its disaster recovery and business continuity plans. Which threats are they aimed at? Which threats are not dealt with? What is it doing about Internet security?

REFERENCES

1. Farber/LaChance Inc., Mechanicsville, VA, 2000; www.farberlachance.com.
2. Bergstein, Mel, DiamondCluster Int'l., Chicago, IL.
3. Sourcing Interests Group, 30 Hackamore Lane, Suite 12, Bell Canyon, CA, 91307, www.sourcinginterests.org.
   a. McNurlin, Barbara, *Business Process Outsourcing Research Report*, 1998.
   b. McNurlin, Barbara, *The Fast-Developing World of Business Process Outsourcing Research Report*, 2002.
   c. McNurlin, Barbara, *Managing Outsourcing Results Research Report*, 1997.
   d. McNurlin, Barbara, *Implementing and Managing High-Impact Strategic Sourcing*, 1999.
   e. McNurlin, Barbara, *Eastman Kodak Company's PC Outsourcing Strategic Alliance*, 1992.
   f. McNurlin, Barbara, *Offshore Outsourcing—Part 1—State of the Industry* and *Offshore Outsourcing—Part 2—Implementation*, 2003.

4. Gartner EXP, 56 Top Gallant Road, Stamford, CT, 06904; www.gartner.com:
   a. Terdiman, Rita, in speech to Sourcing Interests Group.
   b. Flint, David, *Security in an Online World*, Wentworth Research Group (now part of Gartner EXP), May 2000.
   c. Tucker, Chuck, *September 11: Business Continuity Lessons*, May 2002.

5. Thickins, Graeme, "Utility Computing: The Next New IT Model," *Darwin Magazine*, April 2003. Available at www.darwinmag.com/read/040103/utility.html. Accessed April 2004.

6. IBM Global Services, "Mobile Travel Guide Uses IBM E-business on Demand to Help Travelers Get Going," March 24, 2003. Available at www-1.ibm.com/services/US/index.wss/CS/imc/a/001204?cntxtId=a1002810. Accessed April 2004.

7. Altman, Daniel, "A More Productive Outsourcing Debate," *Business 2.0*, May 2004, p. 39.

8. Kaiser, Kate, and Stephen Hawk, "Evolution of Offshore Software Development: From Outsourcing to Cosourcing," *MIS Quarterly Executive*, Vol. 3, No. 2, June 2004, pp. 69–81.

9. Karmarkar, Uday, "Will You Survive the Services Revolution?" *Harvard Business Review*, June 2004, pp. 101–107.

10. Computer Security Institute, *CSI/FBI Computer Crime and Security Survey*, 600 Harrison St., San Francisco, CA, 94107; www.gocsi.com:
    a. Gordon, Lawrence, Martin Loeb, William Lucyshyn, and Robert Richardson, Spring 2004.
    b. Power, Richard, Spring 2002.

11. RSA, "A Guide to Security Technologies," RSA Security Inc., Bedford, MA, 01730, 1999.

12. PwC, *Technology Forecast: 2000, from Atoms to Systems: A Perspective on Technology*, PricewaterhouseCoopers Technology, April 2000.

13. Washburn, Mark, CEO of HarvardNet (speech, Networld+ Interop 2000, Palo Alto, CA).

14. Bozman, J. "Illinois Phone Effort Puts Data Links Last," *Computerworld*, May 23, 1988, p. 101.

15. Crockett, B., "Users Turned to Satellite, Microwave Links after Fire," *Network World*, June 27, 1988, pp. 31–32.

PART II
DISCUSSION CASE

MANAGING INFORMATION SECURITY ON A SHOESTRING BUDGET

Varadharajan Sridhar
Indian Institute of Management, Lucknow, India

Bharat Bhasker
Indian Institute of Management, Lucknow, India

EXECUTIVE SUMMARY

As organizations continue to deploy mission-critical, network-centric information systems, managing the security of such systems has become very critical. Building and managing such security infrastructure can be potentially very expensive, especially for small and medium-sized organizations. The Indian Institute of Management, Lucknow (IIML), the premier teaching and research business school in India, embarked on implementing a robust security management infrastructure with a limited budget on hand. This case examines how IIML successfully implemented the security infrastructure by appropriately developing security policies and selecting a proper combination of freeware and proprietary software components. Since security management is not a one-time activity and uses intensive technology, a careful analysis is required to assess whether the maintenance of the security infrastructure can be done in-house or outsourced. This case illustrates the trade-offs involved and presents experiences of IIML in outsourcing the post-implementation phase to a Security Service Provider. This case also highlights the challenges organizations face while implementing freeware security products and outsourcing security services.

BACKGROUND

IIML is one of the six national level management institutes set up by the Government of India at Lucknow, India, in 1984. The IIML's mission is to help improve the management of the corporate and the noncorporate sectors and also the public systems in the country through pursuit of excellence in management education, research, consultancy, and training. In order to fulfill its objectives, IIML undertakes a diverse range of academic and professional activities.

IIML has a large IT infrastructure and has an annual budget of about 10 million Indian Rupees (INR) (equivalent to about $200,000) allocated in recent years for the development of IT resources. The details of the annual budget allocated for the computer services of IIML for the year 2001–2002 is given in Appendix A. Students, faculty, and staff of IIML use Internet resources quite extensively for teaching, research, consulting, and

(Case Continued)

administrative activities. The IT infrastructure of the Institute is distributed across the sprawling 20-acre campus. There are about 400 client machines and about 10 high-end servers running various operating systems, applications, and services catering to the needs of students, faculty, and staff of the Institute. There are about 600 users on the campus.

The Computer Center (CC) at the Institute is responsible for all IT services on the campus and maintains 24-hour computer labs housing about 200 machines for the students and also hosts the servers and networking equipment. The CC employs one Manager and six systems and programmer analysts who are involved in the maintenance of IT services of the Institute. Most of the CC staff has been with IIML since the Institute started CC operations in 1986. Even though some of the Center's staff do not have academic and professional qualifications in Computer Science or related disciplines, they have acquired expertise in software development and networking through on-the-job training.

The IIML Web site (www.iiml.ac.in) is viewed by prospective students, researchers, and scholars at various institutions and corporations around the world. The Web site also provides information to about 80,000 potential candidates who apply every year for the MBA program offered by the Institute. Apart from the World Wide Web (WWW), e-mail is another Internet application that is widely used by faculty, students, and staff of the Institute. E-mail communication by students and faculty spans geographical boundaries and is one of the mission-critical Internet services of the Institute. The Institute intranet is connected to the Internet via two Internet-access links. There is a plan to network all the student hostel rooms and

faculty residences in the coming academic year to provide campuswide networking. This will further increase the population of client machines by 500. The Institute also has plans to offer distance education programs to corporate executives in the near future.

SETTING THE STAGE

In a recent security survey report released by Internet Security Systems (ISS, 2002), it is reported that Internet risk was, in general, high in 2001 and is getting worse. ISS noted 830 million alarm events and dealt with 2,185 security incidents in 2001 alone. ISS also points out that 70 percent of the security attacks happened through the widely used WWW services. IIML was also one of the thousands of affected organizations. The IIML Web site was defaced a number of times between May and August 2001, and a large number of man-hours was spent restoring the damaged Web pages. A spate of virus attacks caused considerable damage leading to data loss, increased clean-up costs, and a subsequent drop in productivity levels of the users. These attacks impacted the normal function of the users and caused considerable drain of CC resources. IIML had installed simple security services that could not prevent the above-mentioned security intrusions. To address the above-mentioned security threats, a three-member security planning team was formed in August 2001. The team, including Mr. Mohapatra, the CC Manager, set out to prepare a framework for the implementation of a comprehensive information security management system for IIML.

Despite the importance of information security, it is reported in Dinnie

(Case Continued)

(1999) that 45 percent of companies worldwide made no allowance in their budget for information security and 41 percent had no budget for maintenance. It is not surprising that only $20,000, a mere 10 percent of the annual budget of IIML, was allocated for information security management. The challenge was to minimize the security threats by implementing appropriate security components within the allocated budget. Moreover, because security management is an ongoing activity, Mr. Mohapatra also had to decide about the strategies for the continuous maintenance of the deployed infrastructure.

CASE DESCRIPTION

According to von Solms, von Solms, and Caelli (1994),

> The goal of Information Security Management (ISM) is to lessen either the probability that something undesirable will happen (or the frequency with which it is known to be happening) or the severity of the consequences when it does happen, or both. (p. 143)

The operational environment of an organization is the total set of information services needed and responsible for storing, producing, and distributing information throughout the organization (von Solms et al., 1994). ISM is an effort to provide an optimal level of security for the organization's operational environment. The main elements in ISM are given in Figure PC2-1. An optimal security level is determined by the trade-off between cost and complexities of security measures against the risk, vulnerabilities, and the loss the organization faces in the event of security breaches. Security risks

arise because a security attack can exploit vulnerabilities. Countermeasures reduce risk by lowering vulnerabilities, but new ones may appear, hence the feedback loop shown in Figure PC2-1, indicating continuous refinement of security policies and procedures.

Risk Analysis and Security Policy Formulation

Risk analysis, as noted in Figure PC2-1, is the first step in any security deployment exercise. Risk is realized when a threat takes advantage of vulnerability to cause harm to the organizational information resources. There are more than 70 risk analysis methods, including the widely used tool CRAMM (United Kingdom Central Computer and Telecommunications Agency's Risk Analysis and Management Method), available for organizations to conduct security risk analysis (Spinellis, Kokolakis, & Gritzalis, 1999). The security management team did a risk profile analysis based on the risk profile matrix given in Guttman and Bagwill (1997).

Based on the risk analysis, a security policy document had to be formulated that defined the threats and risks of the information resources within IIML and the procedures and mechanisms for preventing or recovering from any such threats. The key trade-offs when formulating the security policy guidelines are: (1) services offered versus security provided, (2) ease of use versus security, and (3) cost of security versus risk of loss (Fraser, 1997). The main purpose of an information security policy is to inform the users and staff of their obligatory requirement to protect the information assets and resources of the organization. As pointed out in Whiteman, Townsend, and Aalberts (2001), a baseline security

(Case Continued)

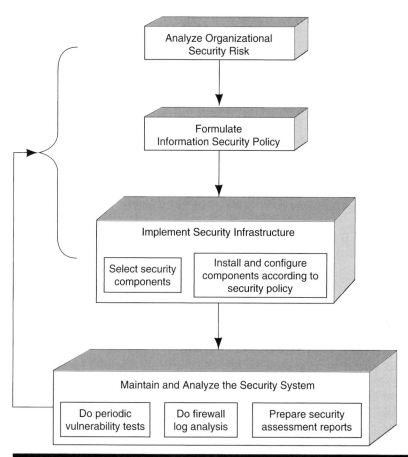

FIGURE PC2-1 The Main Elements in Information Security Management

policy consisting of a minimal set of guidelines was first developed and circulated among the users to get feedback and suggestions. A security policy document covers areas such as identification and authorization control, incident handling, Internet usage, firewall policies and administration, e-mail usage, and WWW usage (refer to Guttman & Bagwill, 1997, for a comprehensive guide on security policy formulation). IIML wanted to provide many different services both for internal users and to the outside, each of which required different levels of access

needs and models of trust. A comprehensive list of services as compiled by the security team as given in Fraser (1997), and the corresponding access-control guidelines were developed. As given in Abrams and Bailey (1995), policy can be expressed in three different forms: natural language statements, mathematical, or nonmathematical formal statements. The security policy document for IIML was prepared using a combination of natural language statements and formal expressions. Mathematical statements, although reducing ambiguity to a

(*Case Continued*)

minimum, are not understood by the heterogeneous user community, and hence were not adopted. To minimize the ambiguity in natural statements, a nonmathematical but constrained and more precise form of the policy construct is also incorporated. A sample policy statement in both forms is given in Appendix B. This methodology helped the security team to effectively disseminate the policies to the user community and define precise benchmarks for the security infrastructure implementation phase.

Selection of the Security Components

There are various components in an information security infrastructure, such as the firewall, intrusion detection system, virus protection system, and content inspection systems (refer to McBride, Patilla, Robinson, Thermos, & Moser, 2000, for a comprehensive description of security components). The firewall is a single network access point between the organization network and the external networks. The organizational information resources are protected by the firewall. Firewall solutions can be as simple as installing the latest version of the operating systems on the public servers of the network and hardening the operating system to reduce vulnerabilities. On the higher end, there is the commercial product by Checkpoint that integrates all security functions, costing about $3,000 for a 25-user license. However, a firewall alone cannot prevent all security threats. Although firewalls remain critical frontline defensive equipment, other security components are also needed to guard against the evolving intrusions (ISS, 2002).

The second most important component in a security infrastructure is an intrusion detection system (IDS), which is extremely effective in identifying intruders (ISS, 2002). An IDS uses techniques such as pattern matching, expression matching, or byte-code matching to detect any intrusions. Once a possible intrusion is discovered, the IDS will take actions ranging from sending an alert to the console of the security administrator to initiating a close to the intruder's network connection. An IDS such as Real Secure from Internet Security Systems costs from $10,000 to $20,000. Freeware products such as Snort are also available.

With the ever-increasing virus attacks, an active virus protection system that detects virus patterns and cleans the files and e-mail messages before they enter the internal network servers is very much essential. A content management system scans the messages for obnoxious and offensive content and filters the messages and sends notifications to the senders. The content management system also improves network and server performance by filtering unsolicited mail messages and blocking spamming. Virus protection systems and content management systems are available, such as the Trend Micro Interscan eManager, which is priced at about $6,000 for a 300-user license.

Additionally, there may be upgrades required for the network devices such as switches and routers to incorporate network security features. In effect, the bill for setting up the security infrastructure could run as high as $60,000 to $200,000, depending upon the size of the IT infrastructure of the organization. Apart from the hardware and software, trained manpower is needed to install, configure, and manage the security infrastructure. In practical terms, a dynamic proactive defense that combines a firewall, intrusion detection, antivirus, and content

(Case Continued)

management, coupled with strong policies and procedures and a strict regime for software updates and security patching is very much required for an effective security infrastructure. The various security components along with the required characteristics as defined by the security team are enclosed in Appendix C.

Comprehensive information security management is a big budget item, and with the awareness of security management still in the nascent stage in India, organizations think twice before embarking on such a project. With a given budget constraint and other limitations, organizations should choose a suitable combination of the various security components that are compatible with the assessed risk level and the defined security policies of the organization.

One way to reduce the infrastructure cost is to look at open source software (OSS), which is available free or at minimal price. The term *open source* refers to the code that is open to the public (refer to Swift, 2001, for a comprehensive guide on OSS). The open source technologies may not provide a comprehensive security solution, but help to reduce the total cost of ownership, and can fit in to the organization's security infrastructure at a very low price compared to proprietary components. The main disadvantage of OSS is lack of support and scalability. It has been noted that OSS is used mainly in smaller organizations that do not have many mission-critical applications (Gill, 2002). Most of the free software also relies on security experts for installation and configuration. Though OSS provides source code, it is practically impossible for a nonexpert to fix any problems. On the other hand, OSS advocates argue that minimal changes in the requirements are easy to make, as the open source

community consisting of millions of programmers around the world constantly works on patches, bug fixes, and customized modifications of the software (Gill, 2002). Documentation for OSS is minimal, and it is not user friendly. Compared to OSS, the commercial software, such as Checkpoint Firewall, comes with the support of a wide array of hardware and software and has experts trained in the configuration. Under GNU public license (FSF, 2002), freeware comes with no warranty. But Checkpoint gives a warranty for its product.

The alternatives before the security team were (1) select OSS components, (2) select proprietary components, and (3) select a combination of OSS and proprietary components. The selection depends on factors such as functionality, flexibility of the product, robustness, product support, ease of use, and finally, the cost. Based on the desired characteristics outlined in Appendix C and the initial bids received from the vendors, the comparison chart shown in Table PC2-1 was prepared.

Table PC2-1 indicates that the OSS products satisfy all the desired characteristics as outlined by the security team. However, the hardware/ software platform support was limited in the case of OSS products compared to the proprietary products. The cost of the proprietary products is much more than the allocated budget. The decision was clearly in favor of OSS products, especially because of the cost savings, although the security management team was aware of the limitations of OSS products as outlined previously. For virus protection and content management, all the bids were for TrendMicro's Interscan VirusWall and cManager, respectively. These are proprietary

(Case Continued)

TABLE PC2-1 Comparison of OSS and Proprietary Security Products		
Security Component/Metric	**OSS Product**	**Proprietary Product**
Firewall	**Astero**	**Checkpoint NG**
1. Centralized management	Yes	Yes
2. Single-point access (network address translation and masquerading)	Yes	Yes
3. Strong access control and authentication	Yes	Yes
4. Built-in proxy server with authentication	No	Yes
5. Hardware/software platform support	Limited	Comprehensive
6. License	GNU	Proprietary
7. Price	Freeware	$10,000 (INR 5,00,000) for 250 use license
Intrusion Detection System	**Snort**	**ISS Real Secure**
1. Server intrusion monitoring	Yes	Yes
2. Priority based alerts	Yes	Yes
3. Centralized management	Yes	Yes
4. Automatic signature updates	Yes	Yes
5. Network intrusion detection	Yes	Yes
6. Hardware/software platform support	Limited	Comprehensive
7. License	GNU	Proprietary
8. Price	Freeware	$8,000 (INR 4,00,000) for one network sensor plus $2,000 (INR 1,00,000) for software subscription services

products and no equivalent OSS products were available. Because the selected OSS products lack proper documentation and hence require expertise for installation, it was decided to outsource the installation and configuration to Bangalore Labs, a Security Service Provider (SSP). The implementation costs, as given in Table PC2-2, were well within the budget.

Implementation of the Information Security Architecture

Security consultants from Bangalore Labs installed and configured the firewall and IDS components as per the security

(Case Continued)

TABLE PC2-2 Cost of the Security Infrastructure Implementation at IIML	
Activity	*Cost*
1. Trend Micro Interscan VirusWall and eManager @ $18.1 for 300 users	$5,430 (INR 271,500)
2. Installation and configuration of Astero Firewall, Snort IDS, Squid Proxy, Trend Micro Interscan VirusWall, and Trend Micro Interscan eManager	$7,400 (INR 370,000)
Total Cost of the Project	**$12,830 (INR 641,500)**

policy. All the e-mail messages from within and from outside the campus network are first scanned by the Interscan VirusWall before being delivered to the mailboxes. This prevents virus-laden mail messages from ever reaching the user mailboxes and hence reduced the virus threats noticed earlier. The VirusWall was configured to get the updated signature files from the vendor Trend Micro (www.anitivirus.com) site every 24 hours to keep up with new virus and worms. Within minutes after completing the installation, the benefits of the security infrastructure were evident when the IDS alerted the system administrator of Code Red virus intrusions, and the VirusWall filtered them.

There were other complexities when the IIML network connected to two ISPs. IIML wanted to route the traffic through both the links so that load balancing would be achieved. To do this, the SSP implemented a "policy-based routing," so that all Web traffic is directed through a high-capacity Internet access link and e-mail and other traffic is routed through the low-bandwidth access link. These were the additional value-added services that the SSP provided to IIML in addition to installing and configuring the security components. The architecture of the IIML network is given in Figure PC2-2. The whole project took about 3 weeks. The project plan and the

rollout of the different services are shown in Appendix D.

Outsourcing Maintenance of the Security Infrastructure

After the successful implementation of the recommended security control, it is important that operational and administrative procedures are developed to support and enforce the security controls. To enforce the continuous, effective functioning of the security controls, it is very important that the controls are also effectively maintained and monitored (von Solms, 1998). Security management is not a one-time activity, and as new vulnerabilities are exposed through penetration testing, patches, and configuration, changes are required for the security components on a continuous basis, which act as a feedback mechanism, as shown in Figure PC2-1. It has been reported in Weissman (1995) that periodic penetration testing, which is a form of stress testing that exposes security weaknesses, is a must for high-rated security systems. ISS (2002) reports that even though vulnerability assessment is a very important proactive measure, many organizations do not have the staff, resources, or processes to develop institutionalized standards for routine scans and remediation.

Whether to do the maintenance of the security infrastructure using in-house

(*Case Continued*)

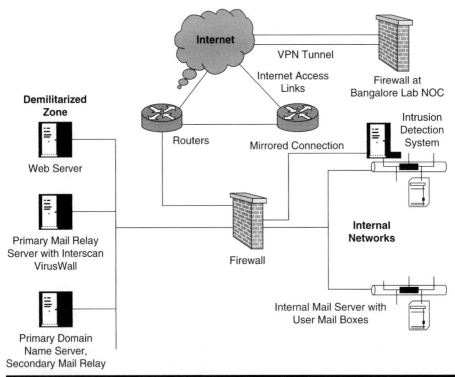

FIGURE PC2-2 Information Security Architecture at IIML

expertise or to outsource it to a service provider is a dilemma that haunts security administrators. The primary motive for considering outsourcing is that long-term outsourcing contracts tend to convert variable costs into fixed costs and thus make technology spending more predictable (Alner, 2001). Security management involves intensive technologies and requires highly skilled and trained security specialists. The organization must recruit, train, and retain employees with unique skills to provide maintenance of the security systems. With little expertise available in this area, businesses can outsource the security management to SSPs (Pereira, 2001). SSPs also have the advanced system and communication monitoring tools and professionals

trained in specific security technologies, and hence can guarantee service and system availability.

The security service provisioning industry is still evolving, even in the United States. In India, Bangalore Labs started this movement, and was followed by others. The parameters that organizations should investigate before outsourcing their security management services include: technology of SSP to support the services, availability of key infrastructure such as Internet connectivity and network operations centers, comprehensiveness of services offered, and finally, the price and value of service offerings. Typical security services provided by SSPs are included in Appendix E (Sridhar & Bhandari, 2002). Most of the maintenance can be done

(Case Continued)

by SSPs remotely from their Network Operations Centers (NOCs).

The IIML security team decided to outsource the maintenance activities because of the reasons just discussed. Service Level Agreements (SLAs) are critical in the outsourcing business (Alner, 2001). The information security SLA should specify the services expected from the outsourcer and indicate what functions will be retained by the client. SLAs and an Annual Maintenance Contract were signed with Bangalore Labs, the cost details of which are given in Table PC2-3. Bangalore Labs has a state-of-the-art NOC at Bangalore. A Virtual Private Network (VPN) tunnel (refer to Stallings, 2000, for VPN technology) was constructed between the IIML firewall and the firewall at Bangalore Labs through which remote monitoring is done (refer to Figure PC2-1). The first successful vulnerability test postimplementation was done at the end of November 2001, and the firewall withstood the rigor of the test.

CURRENT CHALLENGES/ PROBLEMS FACING THE ORGANIZATION

The deployment of IIML's information security infrastructure was completed, and the project completion was signed-off with Bangalore Labs on November 5, 2001. Problems started surfacing at the end of December 2001. Performance of the firewall deteriorated, and there were frequent network disconnects with the firewall server. Because all the internal and external traffic was being routed through the firewall, the users started noticing an increase in the Web traffic response time. Some users who used services such as remote login (Telnet) to outside computer systems were not able to do so because of the policies incorporated in the firewall. Complaints started pouring in at the help desk of the CC. Even though the consultants at Bangalore Labs were in constant touch with the IIML CC and were coming up with some solutions, the problems persisted. At this stage, the following three issues regarding the security infrastructure project raised alarms for IIML:

1. Would the OSS components withstand the rigor of the operational environment? Would OSS really reduce the total cost of ownership?

2. Does outsourcing security management lead to compromises?

3. Has the deployment of the security infrastructure reduced the functionality of the services?

TABLE PC2-3 Cost of the Annual Maintenance Contract	
Activity	*Cost*
Annual Maintenance Contract	
a. Vulnerability scanning at $176 per server, 3 times a year for four servers	$2,112 (INR 105,600)
b. Vulnerability scanning at $526 per network device per year for four devices	$2,104 (INR 105,200)
c. Firewall log analysis every 14 days at $100 for 26 fortnights	$2,600 (INR 130,000)
Total Annual Maintenance Contract Cost	**$6,816 (INR 340,800)**

(*Case Continued*)

Will OSS Meet the Functionality of the Operational Environment?

Repeated attempts by the security consultants at Bangalore Labs and the support team at Astero, Germany, could not provide a permanent solution to the decreasing performance and throughput of the Firewall. In early January 2002, Astero released the new version of its Firewall, which had bug fixes for some of the problems, including the high swap usage problem experienced at the IIML site.

The open source movement believes in producing a product that can be tested by millions around the world. There are user forums, such as those available at www.snort.org, where the worldwide user community shares its experiences and problems. Solutions for trouble-shooting or enabling a new feature, which is not mentioned in the documentation, can be found out through these forums almost instantaneously. However, because these are technology intensive, it is normally impossible for nonexperts to fix problems, as pointed out in Gill (2002). Having the source code did not really help IIML, as the CC staff was unable to make changes to the code and patch up the bugs. They had to depend on SSP, who in turn depended on the vendor and the user community to solve the problems. It took time to find a solution, in contrast to what the advocates of OSS point out.

Even though Bangalore Labs sent the new version of the firewall to IIML under the contract agreement without any additional fees, the trend in the freeware market throws up uncertainties for IIML. The ideological purity of the OSS business is being diluted as start-ups build proprietary products on top of an open source solution. For example, Sistina, which developed an open source file system that multiple computers can share, changed course in August 2001, switching to a closed-source license for the newer versions of its Global File System (Shankland, 2001). Shankland (2001) also points out that many other companies have followed a similar path, becoming increasingly protective of their intellectual property. Astero, which started improving the security features of Linux when it started the product development on Astero Firewall, also has developed additional components that are integrated into the firewall. The firewall code is supported under the GNU public license. However, the Web interface for managing the firewall and other components, such as "Up2Date" services, which provides updates on bug fixes and new releases, is not provided as part of the licensing agreement. Astero charges about $4,000 for commercial use of its Firewall software and an annual renewal fee of $1,000 for 500 active Internet Protocol (IP) addresses. The migration of freeware software to commercial proprietary software will affect the total cost of ownership of the security infrastructure of organizations, especially those in developing countries that have limited budgets for security management.

Outsourcing Security Management: Is it Really Secure?

Because the maintenance of the security infrastructure had been outsourced, IIML had to depend on the SSP for solving any problem that cropped up. The consultants at Bangalore Labs and even in some cases the vendor of the firewall were given access permission to log in to the Firewall through the VPN connection to look at the trouble spots and analyze the system logs. Does this not leave the security infrastructure of IIML completely exposed to SSPs and the vendors?

(Case Continued)

Some are of the opinion that since OSS does not hide the source code, it is inherently vulnerable. But Swift (2001) says, "Security through obscurity is a common misconception" (p. 30). In practice, attackers do not need to know the source code to find vulnerabilities. Hence, the movement on "security through transparency" gained attention leading to the widespread deployment of OSS. Security experts tend to agree that computers are less prone to hacking and viruses when running OSS such as Linux and Apache Web server. However, once the security management is outsourced, even though an OSS solution is implemented, it opens up vulnerabilities and "back doors" for the SSPs who install and configure the security components. While for an educational institution such as IIML, security threats from SSPs may be minimal, for a business organization it is certainly a matter of utmost concern.

Mr. Mohapatra, manager of the CC at IIML, is exploring whether the security and e-mail administrators can be sent for security training programs to develop in-house expertise so that some of the common problems can be solved internally instead of being referred to the SSP. High-profile hacking incidents last year are serving to spur the focus on security

training initiatives by organizations. For example, United States Automobile Association (USAA) plans to spend 10 percent of its IT training budget to enhance its security policy training (Dash, 2002). Although it is possible for USAA to spend a sizable budget for security training, small and medium-sized organizations with limited budgets for security will have to think twice before embarking on such an expensive exercise.

Controlled Security Environment: Does This Mean Less Flexibility?

Even though the IIML security policy developed by the security team was circulated among the user community for comments and suggestions, some services that have multiple vulnerabilities such as video and audio chats (ISS, 2002) had to be stopped. This proved to be a deterrent for some faculty who do collaborative teaching and research with other institutions around the world. Also, IIML students were not able to participate fully in some global virtual team projects because of the nonusability of certain technologies. Thus, the comprehensive information security infrastructure, while protecting IIML, restricts the flexibility of service offerings. ■

QUESTIONS

1. What are the main challenges faced by IIML in the implementation of its security management system?
2. What methodology did IIML use in selecting the various security components?
3. Why did IIML decide to outsource maintenance of the security infrastructure?
4. What are possible solutions for the current problems faced by IIML?
5. What are the specific issues faced by organizations in developing countries, such as India, in implementing information security management practices?
6. What four lessons did you learn from this case?

REFERENCES

Abrams, M. & Bailey, D. (1995). Abstraction and refinement of layered security policy. In M. Abrams, S. Jajodia, & H. Podell (Eds.), *Information Security: An Integrated Collection of Essays*, pp. 126–136. Los Alamitos, CA: IEEE Computer Society Press.

Alner, M. (2001). The effects of outsourcing on information security. *Information Systems Security*, 35–43.

Dash, J. (2002). Training: Spending to rise for business, security skills. *Computer World*, 36(3), 30, January 14.

Dinnie, G. (1999). The second annual global information security survey. *Information Management & Computer Security*, 7(3), 112–120.

Fraser, B. (1997). *RFC 2196: Site Security Handbook*. Available online at: http://www.faqs.org/rfcs/rfc2196.html. Retrieved on April 13, 2002.

Free Software Foundation (FSF). (2002). *Licenses*. Available online at: http://www.gnu.org/licenses/licenses.html. Retrieved on March 30, 2002.

Gill, L. (2002). Does open-source software really work? *News Factor Network*. Available online at: http://www.newsfactor.com. Retrieved on March 28, 2002.

Guttman, B. & Bagwill, R. (1997). *Internet Security Policy: A Technical Guide*. Available online at: http://csrc.nist.gov/isptg/. Retrieved on August 1, 2001.

Internet Security Systems (ISS). (2002). *Internet Risk Impact Survey*. Available online at: http://www.iss.net. Retrieved on April 6, 2002.

Lodin, S. (1999). Intrusion detection product evaluation criteria. *Computer Security Journal*. XV(2), 1–10.

McBride, P., Patilla, J., Robinson, C., Thermos, P., & Moser, E. (2000). *Secure Internet Practices*. Boca Raton, FL: Aurbach Publishers.

Periera, B. (2001). Management services: The next wave in facilities management.

Network Magazine (India Edition), 17–19, October.

Shankland, S. (2001). Open-source approach fades in tough times. *CNET News*. Available online at: http://news.com.com/2100-1001-276056.html. Retrieved on April 1, 2002.

Spinellis, D., Kokolakis, S., & Gritzalis, S. (1999). Security requirements, risks and recommendations for small enterprise and home-office environments. *Information Management & Computer Security*, 7(3), 121–128.

Sridhar, V. & Bhandari, R. (2002). Security solutions: Be holistic, buy best. *Voice & Data*, 8(7) 92–97.

Stallings, W. (2000). *Cryptography and Network Security*. New Delhi: Pearson Education Asia.

Swift, B. (2001). Opening up a discussion on computing: Finding security alternatives and more. *Risk Management*, 26–32.

von Solms, R., van der Haar, H., von Solms, S.H., & Caelli, W.H. (1994). A framework for information security evaluation. *Information & Management*, 26, 143–153.

von Solms, R. (1998). Information security management (2): Guidelines to the management of information technology security. *Information Management & Computer Security*, 6(5), 221–223.

Weissman, C. (1995). Penetration testing. In M. Abrams, S. Jajodia & H. Podell (Eds.), *Information Security: An Integrated Collection of Essays*, pp. 126–136. Los Alamitos, CA: IEEE Computer Society Press.

Whitman, M., Townsend, A., & Aalberts, R. (2000). Information systems security and the need for policy. In G. Dillon (Ed.), *Information Security Management: Global Challenges in the New Millennium*, pp. 9–18. Hershey, PA: Idea Group Publishing.

Zwicky, E., Cooper, S., & Chapman, B. (2000). *Building Internet Firewalls* (2nd ed.). Sebastopol, CA: O Reilly.

Appendix A

ANNUAL BUDGET (2001–2002) FOR THE COMPUTER SERVICES OF IIML

Activity	Budgeted Amount
Planned Expenditure:	
1. Desktop computers for faculty and Computer Labs	$66,000 (INR 3,300,000)
2. Uninterrupted Power Supply (UPS) units for the computers	$10,000 (INR 500,000)
3. Security Infrastructure and Implementation	$20,000 (INR 1,000,000)
4. Campus-wide Networking	$50,000 (INR 2,500,000)
5. Accessories and high-speed printers	$8,000 (INR 400,000)
6. Expenditure carried-over from last year	$16,000 (INR 800,000)
Nonplanned Recurring Expenditure:	
1. Annual Maintenance Contract fees, software license fees, and Internet connectivity charges	$50,000 (INR 2,500,000)
Total Budget	**$220,000 (INR 11,000,000)**

Appendix B

SELECT SET OF STATEMENTS FROM THE INFORMATION SECURITY POLICY DOCUMENT OF IIML

Natural Language Constructs

E-Mail Policies

1. Both primary and secondary mail servers will be inside the firewall. All messages will be scanned for viruses and other maligned content by gateway-based antivirus software.

2. Users will be able retrieve e-mail through Internet Message Access Protocol (IMAP) or Post Office Protocol (POP3) services from inside the network. From outside the network, users will be allowed to access their mail only using "Web mail" service available through IIML Web page. Authentication is enforced for retrieving the messages.

3. E-mail servers will be configured to refuse to relay any e-mail addressed to non-IIML domains.

World Wide Web Policies

1. The Institute Web server (www.iiml. ac.in) will be placed inside the firewall in the Demilitarized Zone (DMZ). All the other Web servers will be hosted in the internal network. All HyperText Transfer Protocol (HTTP) requests from outside to internal Web servers will be processed through the firewall and appropriate reverse proxy servers.

2. All files downloaded over WWW will be scanned for viruses or other malign content using gateway-based antivirus software and content analyzer.

Formal Nonmathematical Constructs

	Policy				
	Inside to Outside		Outside to Inside		
Service	Status	Authenti-cation	Status	Authenti-cation	Policy Statement
HTTP	Y	N	N	—	All WWW servers intended for access will be hosted inside IIML firewall. Restricted inbound HTTP requests will be allowed through the firewall.
Web Mail	Y	Y	Y	Y	Web mail available through the Institute Web page will be accessible even from outside. It will be only through the Web mail interface that users can access their e-mail boxes from outside.

Appendix C

PRINCIPAL COMPONENTS OF AN INFORMATION SECURITY INFRASTRUCTURE

Component	Required Characteristics
Firewall	Provide single-point access from internal to external networks and vice versa; allow only authorized traffic as defined in security policy; authenticate outside users for internal services as defined in the security policy; provide application and cache proxy services (for complete details on Firewall characteristics, refer to Zwicky, Cooper, & Chapman, 2000)
Intrusion Detection System (IDS)	Support security policies of the organization; monitor intrusions on servers; provide priority-based alerts to system administrators; provide centralized management; implement automatic intrusion signature updates (for details on IDS, refer to Lodin, 1999)
Virus Protection System	Provide real-time virus protection for e-mail and other Internet traffic; provide compatibility with deployed firewall products; provide flexible configuration and centralized management; implement automatic virus signature updates
Content Management System	Support content filtering as defined in the security policy; block spam mail messages; provide flexible configuration and centralized management; provide integration with firewall and virus protection systems

Appendix D

INFORMATION SECURITY PROJECT PLAN

Date	Activity
October 12, 2001	Meeting up with IIML system analysts
October 13, 2001	Network study
October 14, 2001	Network architecture planning according to the design
October 15, 2001	Firewall installation pilot testing on the new hardware
October 17, 2001	IDS installation and testing
October 18, 2001	Pilot testing of firewall IDS
October 20, 2001	Hardening
October 21, 2001	Hardening
October 22, 2001	Mail server pilot testing in the firewall environment
October 24, 2001	Interscan pilot rollout
October 26, 2001	Rollout
October 29, 2001	IDS rollout and testing
October 30, 2001	VPN establishment between NoC, Bangalore, and IIML
November 1, 2001	Remote management testing
November 2, 3, & 4, 2001	Postinstallation support
November 5, 2002	Final

Appendix E

LIST OF SERVICES PROVIDED BY SSPS

Service Offering	Description	Deliverables
Assessment Services	Survey of existing security infrastructure and help preparing security policy	Information Security Policy
Advisory Services	Up-to-date information about vulnerabilities on customer infrastructure	Latest vulnerability notification, patch release notification, virus warnings, security solution recommendations
Scanning Services	Scanning of networks, systems, and databases to check for the effectiveness of security measures and to prepare an audit security baseline	Periodic scan reports
Penetration Testing	Simulation of real intruder's attacks in a controlled and safe way to discover any vulnerabilities in the system	Periodic penetration test reports
Online Intrusion Detection	Protecting the network by analyzing the information from a variety of system and network sources for signs of intrusion and responding to containing these intrusions	Incident reports, forensic analysis reports, event summary reports, intrusion trend report
Security Services Implementation	Installation and configuration of firewall, intrusion detection system, content management, and virus wall services	Working security services
Remote Firewall Management	Remote support and management of firewalls, managing and maintaining firewall policies, firewall log analysis and auditing, firewall incident reporting	Remote policy, management reports, and log analysis report

Biographical Sketches

Varadharajan Sridhar *is associate professor in the Information Technology and Systems group at the Indian Institute of Management, Lucknow, India. He received his Ph.D. in Management Information Systems from the University of Iowa. He taught previously at Ohio University (Athens, Ohio), and American University in Washington, D.C. He has also served as a visiting faculty at the University of Auckland Business School, Auckland, New Zealand. His primary research interests are in the area of telecommunications technology and management, information security management, collaborative technologies, and global virtual teams. He has published his research articles in the* European Journal of Operational Research, Journal of Heuristics, IEEE Transaction on Knowledge and Data Engineering, *and* Telecommunication Systems.

Bharat Bhasker *is a professor in the Information Technology and Systems group at the Indian Institute of Management, Lucknow, India. He received his Ph.D. in Computer Science from Virginia Polytechnic Institute and State University. He has worked at Goddard Space Flight Center of NASA and MDL Information Systems and Sybase Inc., California, in leading research and research management positions. Dr. Bhasker was a member of the High Performance Computer and Communications (HPCC) initiative of NASA. He was awarded NASA's Best Research Productivity Award in 1992 in recognition of his research contributions. He has also served as visiting professor in the school of business at the University of Maryland, College Park; University of California; and the University of Texas. Dr. Bhasker also serves as Internet security advisor to the Controller of Certification Authority, Ministry of Information Technology, India.*

PART
III

MANAGING SYSTEM
DEVELOPMENT

art III of this book consists of two chapters that deal with developing enterprise-based systems; that is, system development. As noted in the following figure, system development has traditionally been aimed at procedure-based work. Procedure-based activities are large-volume transactions where each transaction has a relatively low cost or value. These activities, which consist mainly of handling data, are well defined, and the principal measure for gauging their performance is efficiency. Information systems were, in most cases, first built to automate this kind of work, beginning initially with accounting, and then progressing into manufacturing, administration, sales and marketing, and so on. Development of these systems has been handled by IS professionals.

Chapter 9 begins by describing the foundations of system development, which are the technologies and methodologies that form the basis of today's approaches. Then it discusses two areas of current importance: system integration and Internet-based systems. We conclude the chapter by discussing project management—the underpinning of successful IT projects, especially large ones.

Chapter 10 discusses a number of management issues that surround system development: IT staffing, managing the change that surrounds system implementation, what to do about legacy systems, and measuring the benefits of systems.

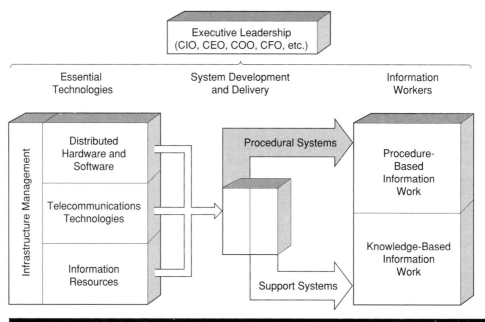

FIGURE P3-1 A Framework for IS Management

TECHNOLOGIES FOR DEVELOPING SYSTEMS

INTRODUCTION

One of the toughest jobs in IS management is developing new systems. It seems to be an area in which Murphy's Law—if anything can go wrong, it will—reigns supreme. In spite of the complexity of system development, the IT field has made significant progress in improving the process of building systems. The traditional approach, with variations, of course, appears in many textbooks and professional books. Two of the first books to describe a life cycle approach for developing systems were published in 1956 and 1957, both written by Richard Canning.[1]

During the 1970s, a relatively well-defined process called the *system development life cycle* emerged. This life cycle improved the development process significantly. However, continued backlogs, cost overruns, and performance shortfalls underscored the difficulty and complexity of the system development process.

The 1980s saw progress in more friendly languages and automation of portions of development, such as code generation. Yet, maintenance continued to eat up 70 to 80 percent of the system development resources in most companies.

The 1990s began with the promise of significantly increasing developer productivity and reducing maintenance by relying more on packages and by building systems by linking together components. The business process reengineering movement spawned the growth of integrated enterprise systems and the widespread adoption of ERP systems. Then, all of a sudden, in the late 1990s, e-business and Internet-based systems appeared.

In the 2000s, the Internet brought the need for faster system development and integrated enterprise systems; that is, systems that pull together various aspects of the enterprise. New tools for rapid development became available; they relied on reusable components and open systems architectures. As a result, application development projects became application integration projects; systems were built by integrating prebuilt components.

These days, you could say that every application is a network application. The network is becoming the system. Web-based applications were the first generation of Internet-centric computing. The new field, Web Services, is touted as the second. In it, as described in Chapter 5, small modules of code perform specific functions and can be called by other modules to perform that work, all via the Internet. The Web Services world is upon us. In addition, the trend toward increasing the interconnectedness of supply chains is leading companies to build inter-organizational systems, which is a far more complex undertaking than single-company systems. This chapter reviews the evolution of system development to provide an understanding of the underlying principles of building applications.

FOUNDATIONS OF SYSTEM DEVELOPMENT

In the early years, system development was considered a "craft." Since then, the goal has been to make it more scientific. In the 1970s, structured system development emerged to make the process more standard and efficient. It was characterized by the following elements:

- Hand coding in a third-generation language (such as COBOL)
- A structured-programming development methodology
- An automated project management system
- A database management system
- A mix of online and batch applications in the same system
- Development of mostly mainframe applications
- Programming by professional programmers only

- Various automated, but not well-integrated, software tools
- A well-defined sign-off process for system delivery
- User participation mainly in requirements definition and installation phases

This development approach supposedly followed the famous "waterfall" approach, shown in Figure 9-1. However, says Bob Glass,[2] a well-known author in software development, this unidirectional waterfall was much touted but rarely used. Development did not proceed in a straight line from requirements through operation; a lot of backtracking and iteration occurred. Developers really always followed the spiral approach, says Glass, which is generally attributed to Barry Boehm and shown in Figure 9-2.

Structured Development

Structured development methodologies accompanied this system development life cycle and were meant to handle the complexities of system design and development by fostering more discipline, higher reliability and fewer errors, and more efficient use of the resources.

More Discipline.   By establishing standards for processes and documentation, the structured methodologies attempted to eliminate personal variations. At first they seemed to threaten programmers' creativity, but their discipline did increase productivity and permit developers to deal with greater complexity. The complexity was handled through successive decomposition of system components, coupled with preferred practices for conducting analysis, design, and construction. The result was a more disciplined system development process.

Higher Reliability and Fewer Errors.   The structured methodologies recognized that mistakes of both omission and commission were likely at all stages of system building. One of the main tools for coping with this tendency was (and still is) inspections, performed at every development stage and at every level of system decomposition. The goal has been to catch errors as early as possible. The methodologies also recognized that iteration would be required to redo parts of a system as mistakes were uncovered.

FIGURE 9-1 The "Waterfall" Development Life Cycle

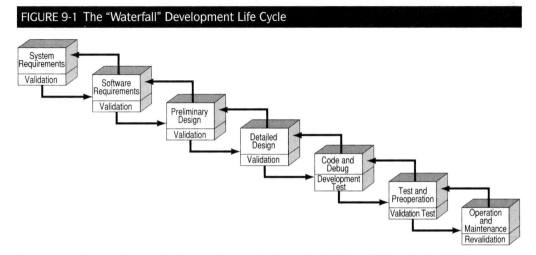

Source: Barry Boehm, *Software Engineering Economics* (Upper Saddle River, NJ: Prentice Hall, 1981).

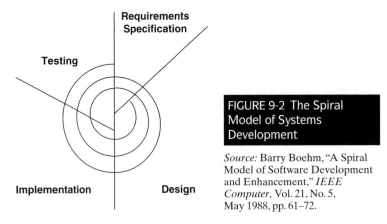

FIGURE 9-2 The Spiral Model of Systems Development

Source: Barry Boehm, "A Spiral Model of Software Development and Enhancement," *IEEE Computer*, Vol. 21, No. 5, May 1988, pp. 61–72.

More Efficient Use of Resources. The project management approaches usually included in the structured methodologies contributed to cost savings, increased productivity, and better allocation of human resources. By imposing a time and cost control system, the classic approach decreased (but did not eliminate) the tendency for system development efforts to incur cost and time overruns.

Fourth-Generation Languages

In the early 1980s, two major developments occurred. One was the availability of fourth-generation languages (4GLs); the second was software prototyping. Fourth-generation languages are really more than computer languages; they are programming environments. Their major components are listed in Figure 9-3.

The heart of a 4GL is its DBMS, which is used for storing formatted data records as well as unformatted text, graphics, voice, and perhaps even video. Almost as important is the data dictionary, which stores the definitions of the various kinds of data.

FIGURE 9-3 Features and Functions of Fourth-Generation Languages

- Database management system (DBMS)
- Data dictionary
- Nonprocedural language
- Interactive query facilities
- Report generator
- Selection and sorting
- Screen formatter
- Word processor and text editor
- Graphics
- Data analysis and modeling tools
- Library of macros
- Programming interface
- Reusable code
- Software development library
- Backup and recovery
- Security and privacy safeguards
- Links to other DBMSs

The language that programmers and users use is nonprocedural, which means that the commands can occur in any order, rather than the sequence required by the computer. The commands can be used interactively to retrieve data from files or a database in an ad hoc manner or to print a report (using a report generator). The screen formatter allows a user or programmer to design a screen by simply typing in the various data input field names and the locations where they are to appear or by choosing graphics from a menu. Some 4GLs include statistical packages for calculating time series, averages, standard deviations, correlation coefficients, and so on.

Previously, developers only had third-generation languages, such as COBOL and PL/1. The advent of 4GLs allowed end users to develop some programs and programmers to use a different development method: prototyping. Formerly, system requirements were fully defined before design and construction began. With prototyping, development could be iterative.

Software Prototyping

"A prototype is a software system that is created quickly—often within hours, days, or weeks—rather than months or years." Franz Edelman, a pioneer in the use of software prototyping, described the process of software prototyping as "a quick and inexpensive process of developing and testing a trial balloon." Its purpose is to test out assumptions about users' requirements, about the design of the application, or perhaps even about the logic of a program.

With only conventional programming languages, such as COBOL, it was much too expensive to create both a prototype and a production version. Therefore, only production systems were developed. With end user tools, people can get prototypes up and running quickly. The prototype is relatively inexpensive to build because the language creates much of the code.

Prototyping is an iterative process. It begins with a simple prototype that performs only a few of the basic functions. Through use of the prototype, system designers or end users discover new requirements and refinements to incorporate in each succeeding version. Each version performs more of the desired functions and in an increasingly efficient manner.

Both 4GLs and prototyping have proven to be important underpinnings for today's application development world.

Computer-Aided Software Engineering

Even though the structured programming and analysis techniques of the 1970s brought more discipline to the process of developing large and complex software applications, they required tedious attention to detail and lots of paperwork. Computer-aided software engineering (CASE) appeared in the 1980s to automate structured techniques and reduce this tediousness.

Definition. CASE, as defined by Carma McClure,[3] a CASE pioneer, is any automated tool that assists in the creation, maintenance, or management of software systems. In general, a CASE environment includes:

- An information repository
- Front-end tools for planning through design

- Back-end tools for generating code
- A development workstation

Often not included, but implied and necessary, are a software development methodology and a project management methodology.

An information repository.   A repository forms the heart of a CASE system and is its most important element, says McClure. It stores and organizes all the information needed to create, modify, and develop a software system. This information includes, for example, data structures, processing logic, business rules, source code, and project management data. Ideally, this information repository should also link to the active data dictionary used during execution so that changes in one are reflected in the other.

Front-end tools.   These tools are used in the phases leading up to coding. One of the key requirements for these tools is good graphics for drawing diagrams of program structures, data entities and their relationships to each other, data flows, screen layouts, and so on. Rather than store pictorial representations, front-end tools generally store the meaning of items depicted in the diagrams. This type of storage allows a change made in one diagram to be reflected automatically in related diagrams. Another important aspect of front-end design tools is automatic design analysis for checking the consistency and completeness of a design, often in accordance with a specific design technique.

Back-end tools.   These tools generally mean code generators for automatically generating source code. A few CASE tools use a 4GL. Successful front-end CASE tools provide interfaces to not just one, but several, code generators.

Development workstation.   The final component of a CASE system is a development workstation, and the more powerful the better, to handle all the graphical manipulations needed in CASE-developed systems.

Timeboxing.   One of the most intriguing approaches to system development in the 1980s was the "timebox," a technique that uses CASE to guarantee delivery of a system within 120 days. Today, IS departments that aim for speed turn to a development technique known as rapid application development (RAD). The following case illustrates the use of timeboxing and RAD.

CASE EXAMPLE

DUPONT CABLE MANAGEMENT SERVICES

DuPont Cable Management Services was formed to manage the telephone and data wiring in DuPont's office buildings in Wilmington, Delaware. AT&T had owned and managed the wiring for DuPont's voice networks, but then responsibility

(Case Continued)

passed to DuPont's corporate telecommunications group. At DuPont's Wilmington headquarters campus, cabling is complex and wiring changes are continual. The average telephone is moved one and a half times a year. Much of the telephone moving cost is labor to find the correct cables and circuit paths.

When the cable management services group was formed, the manager realized he needed a system to maintain an inventory of every wire, telephone, modem, workstation, wiring closet connection, and other pieces of telephone equipment. Technicians could then quickly locate the appropriate equipment and make the change. Although several cable management software packages were available, none could handle the scale or workload required by DuPont. The only option was to build a custom system.

The system had to be flexible, because the company's telecommunications facilities would need to handle new kinds of equipment for data and video. Furthermore, because cable management services were not unique to DuPont, the manager believed he could sell cable management services to other large companies. Therefore, the system needed to be tailorable. So that he did not have to hire programmers, the manager decided to use DuPont Information Engineering Associates (IEA), another DuPont business service unit, to build the system.

DuPont Information Engineering Associates (IEA)

IEA believed it could significantly speed up development by combining a code generator with software prototyping and project management. The resulting methodology was called rapid iterative production prototyping, or RIPP.

Using RIPP, a development project could take as few as 120 days to complete; it had four phases.

- ***Phase 1: Go-Ahead.*** Day 1 is the go-ahead day. IEA accepts a project, and the customer agrees to participate heavily in development.

- ***Phase 2: System Definition.*** Days 2 through 30 are spent defining the components of the system and its acceptance criteria. At the end of this phase, IEA presents the customer with a system definition and a fixed price for creating the application.

- ***Phase 3: The Timebox.*** The following 90 days are the "timebox," during which the IEA–customer team creates design specifications, prototypes the system, and then refines the prototype and its specifications. The final prototype becomes the production system.

- ***Phase 4: Installation.*** On Day 120, the system is installed. The customer has 3 months to verify that the system does what it is supposed to do. If it does not, IEA will refund the customer's money and remove the system.

Cable Management's Use of IEA

The cable management group contracted with IEA to develop the cable tracking system. After spending the first 30 days defining the scope of the project, IEA estimated that the system would require two timeboxes to complete, or about 210 days.

During the first timebox, IEA developed those portions that the cable management group could concisely define. During those 90 days, one cable management engineer worked full-time on the project, another worked part-time, and IEA had a project leader and two developers. The system they developed included display screens, the relational database, basic system processes, and reports.

At the end of the 90 days, IEA delivered a basic functional system, which DuPont began using. The second timebox added features uncovered during this use. Both parties agreed that this phase was ambiguous, which might affect the 90-day limitation. So they extended the project to 110 days. By that time, the development team had entered DuPont's complete

wiring inventory, enhanced the basic system, and delivered a production version.

In all, the system took about 9 months to develop. The department manager realized that was fast, but he did not realize how fast until he talked to other telecommunications executives who told him their firms had spent between 2 and 3 years developing cable management systems.

The cable management group was pleased with its system. It was initially used only to manage voice wiring, but has since been extended to handle data communications wiring. ■

Object-Oriented Development

Just as 4GLs were a revolutionary change in the 1970s, object-oriented (OO) development was a revolutionary change in the 1980s. In fact, companies had a choice. They could choose the evolutionary approach of CASE or the revolutionary approach of OO development. OO development caught on in the early 1980s because of the PC; the graphical user interfaces were developed using objects. Developers just needed to point and click at generic items—menus, dialog boxes, radio buttons, and other graphical components—and then rearrange them to create a screen. This form of programming has come to be known as *visual programming*.

By the end of the 1980s, OO development was beginning to be noticed in IS departments for business applications. That trickle became a tidal wave when client-server systems appeared in the early 1990s, as developers attempted to simplify these extremely complex systems by reusing objects. In the early 1990s, OO system analysis and design techniques began to appear that could be used in conjunction with OO languages such as C++ and Smalltalk.

OO development is not so much a coding technique as a code-packaging technique, notes Brad Cox,[4] an OO development pioneer. An *object* contains some private data (that other objects cannot manipulate) and a small set of operations (called *methods*) that can perform work on that data. When an object receives a request in the form of a message, it chooses the operation that will fulfill that request, it executes the operation on the data supplied by the message, and then it returns the results to the requester.

Combining data and procedures in an object, which is called *encapsulation*, is the foundation of OO development. It restricts the effects of changes by placing a wall of code around each piece of data. Data is accessed through messages that only specify *what* should be done. The object specifies *how* its operations are performed. Thus, a change in one part of a system need not affect the other parts. As you might expect, even though OO development promised significant benefits, it does have costs, especially at the outset. OO projects have gotten stuck in the mire of defining and redefining objects. Once defined, objects can be reused, another of OO's attractions. There are many other aspects of OO development, but this very brief description of objects suffices here. As will be seen later in the chapter, OO is a significant foundation for today's development efforts.

Client-Server Computing

In the 1990s, two developments became the major news: client-server systems and Web-based (or network-centric) development. Underlying these two trends, which continue today, is the increasing use of packages and system integration. As much as possible, companies prefer to buy a package rather than build an application in-house. To develop large applications, they integrate hardware and software components. For example, they buy a ready-made Web browser to become the standard access software for Web-based applications rather than write their own front-end client software. In both realms, the major construction methods are system integration and component-based development.

Client-server systems generated a lot of excitement in the early 1990s because they promised far more flexibility than mainframe-based systems. The desktop and laptop client machines could handle graphics, animation, and video, whereas the servers could handle production updating. It was a clever way to meld the pizzazz of the PC world with the necessary back-end production strengths of the mainframe world, even though mainframes were not always in the picture. The following is a typical example of the allure of client-server systems and how one company—MGM—developed its first client-server system.[5]

CASE EXAMPLE

MGM

Metro-Goldwyn-Mayer (MGM), the movie studio in Hollywood, has an extremely valuable asset: its library of TV shows and movies. The studio's first client-server application was built at the urging of end users to leverage this asset. The vice president of IS knew that the only way to meet the users' expectations for a multimedia, laptop-based system with a graphical interface was to employ client-server technology.

Previously, more than 26 disparate systems on PCs, minicomputers, and the corporate mainframe were used to maintain the rights to show MGM's films. As a result, it was not possible to get a consolidated, world-wide view of which films were being leased. The client-server system—the largest IS project in Hollywood at the time—collected and consolidated all data on the film library so that MGM would know what films it has the rights to license and to whom.

Client-server technology was chosen because it could empower MGM's

(Case Continued)

20 worldwide film-rights salespeople. They could visit the head of a cable TV network anywhere in the world with an SQL database on their laptop and built-in CD-ROM capabilities to play 20- to 30-second clips of their films. They could browse the laptop's inventory database to verify availability of films and then print the licensing deal memo on the spot. Details of the deal could then be transmitted to headquarters when convenient. Only a client-server system would provide this flexibility.

The System's Three-Level Architecture

The system's architecture had three layers. At the core was an AS/400, which acted as the central processor for the database that contains descriptions of 1,700 TV shows and movies, an index, the availability of movies in different regions, license time periods, status of bills, and so forth. MGM deliberately chose a tried-and-tested rights licensing software package to manage the database because it provided the needed processing; however, it did not support graphical interfaces, laptops, or decision support. Therefore, MGM surrounded the package with the most-tested technology possible for the client-server components. In fact, wherever possible, MGM minimized technical risk by using proven products.

The second layer was an HP 9000 server, which contained data and processing, but no presentation software. The Unix front end was built using Power-Builder. In 1 hour with Power-Builder, developers could do 8 to 10 hours of COBOL-equivalent work.

The third layer was the client machines, either desktop or laptop. They contained local processing, local databases,

and presentation software. The laptops also had a database for the salespeople. They could upload and download information from their laptops via dial-up lines.

The premier skill required in this environment was systems integration. The developers needed both hardware and software expertise for Unix and NT, PowerBuilder, and SQL Windows.

The Development Environment

Even though partnering was always possible in the mainframe era, it was mandatory with client-server computing. With tools like PowerBuilder and a development life cycle that relied on prototyping, developers had to constantly interact with users. They could not seclude themselves for months. Moreover, client-server teams had no boss. The users and developers were equal; neither told the other what to do.

The role of IS at MGM changed from system development and delivery to one of cooperating and partnering. This change required a huge cultural shift in the roles and attitudes of the IS staff. Developers who formerly buried themselves in code had to conduct meetings and work side-by-side with users. In short, they had to learn people (interpersonal) skills and the business. Interestingly, the CIO felt that women had an edge because, generally speaking, they had better interpersonal skills.

With client-server systems, the hardware was cheaper than with mainframe systems, development was faster, and software support was cheaper—all by orders of magnitude. Operating costs were more expensive than MGM expected because version control of client-server software and service and systems management were more costly. ■

These technologies—structured development, 4GLs, prototyping, CASE, OO development, and client-server systems—have all proven to be foundations of today's system development environment. We now turn to that environment, beginning first by discussing the main method of building systems: system integration.

SYSTEM INTEGRATION

Integration is by far the biggest software problem CIOs face. That is why offerings that integrate systems generate so much interest. The increasing complexity of IT, with systems from various eras and technologies that must coexist and even work together, makes the integration challenge even more difficult to solve. That is why large integrated enterprise-wide systems have been adopted: to replace the myriad "silo" systems with one interconnected one.

CIOs have long strived to integrate the information systems in their organizations so that they work together. However, integration is complex and expensive, and it can cause systems to crash. But competitive pressures have raised the importance of integrating business processes and, thus, the underlying information systems. The trend away from in-house software development toward the use of off-the-shelf software has furthered the need for integration. Online business requires integrating systems across organizations. Technology vendors have responded with a number of products to facilitate the integration of systems.

Three main approaches to integration are:

- DBMSs
- ERP systems
- Middleware

The DBMS approach takes a data-oriented view to integration. As discussed in Chapter 7, DBMSs allow applications to share data stored in a single or distributed database. The applications can come from a number of sources, but they employ a common DBMS.

The ERP approach, discussed in Chapter 7 and in the next section, takes an application view of integration. All applications come from a single vendor and are specifically designed to communicate with each other.

The middleware approach takes a third-party approach; applications communicate with each other through third-party translation software.

Each of the three approaches has advantages and disadvantages, depending on the conditions in the enterprise. Typically, organizations use a combination of the three. Indeed, a quick look at vendor strategies reveals a mixture of the approaches. Oracle, firmly in the DBMS market, has moved toward offering enterprise applications. SAP, a major ERP vendor and long a competitor of Oracle, has modified its products to use standard DBMSs, including that of Oracle. The three approaches are not mutually exclusive.

ERP Systems

An ERP system aims to integrate corporate systems by providing a single set of applications from a single vendor operating with a single database. The goal is to provide the means to integrate business departments and functions across an organization. ERP vendors offer a complete set of business applications, including order processing, HR management, manufacturing, finance and accounting, and CRM. By automating many of the tasks involved in business processes and standardizing the processes themselves, the ERP system can provide substantial payback to a company if the system is installed properly.

The history of ERP contains both successes and failures, though the failures have been especially notable. Scott Buckhout and his colleagues[6] reported on a study of ERP implementations in companies with more than $500 million in revenues. The average cost overrun was 179 percent, and the average schedule overrun was 230 percent. Despite these overruns, the desired functionally was 59 percent below expectations, on average. Only 10 percent of the implementation projects actually finished on time and within budget; another 35 percent of the projects were canceled. Even IT companies have had problems. Dell canceled its ERP project after 2 years and expenditures of more than $200 million.

Some of the failures can be attributed to factors common to other IS projects, such as the system's large size and complexity. However, ERP systems differ in a significant way from other systems, which is not always recognized. Because they are designed to integrate and streamline numerous business functions, they have significant implications for the way the firm is organized and operates. Many failures result from too much attention being given to the technical aspects of the system and too little attention being given to its organizational impacts.

An ERP system contains a model of the business that reflects assumptions about the way the business operates. The vendor makes these assumptions and designs the system to reflect the vendor's understanding of business processes in general. As a result, the business model embedded in the ERP system may be different from the way the business actually operates. Even though the ERP system can be customized to some degree, configuring the system entails compromises. The company must balance the way it wants to operate with the way the system wants the company to operate.

To realize the benefits of ERP—integrated systems and integrated business processes—a company must therefore change its organizational structure and culture. From his extensive studies of ERP, Thomas Davenport[7] stresses that companies that have derived the greatest benefits have viewed ERP (he prefers the term *enterprise system*, ES) primarily in strategic and organizational terms, not in technical terms; they "stressed the enterprise not the system." The managers have asked: "How might an ES strengthen our competitive advantages? How might it erode them? What will be the system's effect on our organization and culture? Do we need to extend the system across all our functions, or should we implement only certain modules? What other alternatives, if any, for information management might suit us better than an ES?"

As an example of a successful implementation of ERP, consider Colgate-Palmolive.

CASE EXAMPLE

COLGATE-PALMOLIVE

Colgate-Palmolive Company is a 190-year-old consumer products leader. In the mid-1990s, it faced a competitive crisis. Sales of personal care products dropped 12 percent and operating profits dropped 26 percent in North America. Colgate-Palmolive had a decentralized structure, with national or regional control in more than 200 countries. This structure produced independent operations that were expensive to coordinate, slow to respond to market changes, and constrained company growth. Management needed to develop new products, reduce product delivery cycles, and reduce the cost of operations.

Management's vision was to abandon the decentralized structure and become a truly global company with an integrated business environment and standardized business processes. Their first step toward this vision was to integrate their supply chain in 80 countries and distribution to 200 countries. The goal was to reduce the annual cost of the supply chain by $150 million and to standardize business processes. A key element to achieving this integration was a global ERP system.

After setting up a prototype environment in the United States, Colgate was convinced that the SAP R/3 modules for sales and distribution, materials management, finance, and HR would provide the functionality and flexibility it needed worldwide. Management also decided on Oracle's relational DBMS and a Sun hardware platform running the Solaris operating system. The current network has 270 servers, 11 terabits of data storage, and can support 3,000 concurrent users accessing the network from PCs around the world. The global ERP implementation took 5 years and cost $430 million.

The company quickly met its goals, realizing savings of $50 million the first year and $100 million the second. These savings were invested into creating and marketing new products, including the successful Target toothpaste, which allowed Colgate to regain the number one market position for toothpaste in the United States that they had lost 34 years earlier. The company also reduced the product delivery cycle by more than 60 percent. Integration allowed regional cooperation on purchasing, resulting in larger contracts with fewer suppliers, which saved $150 million the first 2 years.

Colgate also accrued substantial savings in IT operations. The old, highly complex, decentralized IT infrastructure, which had many data centers and local applications, was streamlined. Data centers around the world were consolidated from 75 to 2. The complexity of the global data networks was also simplified. SAP's R/3 provides a standard for applications, although the core support for the applications remains with each division.

The success of Colgate's ERP project stems from senior management convincing all employees that the company faced a crisis that only a dramatic change in strategy and organization could solve. The need for global restructuring of strategies and operations drove the need for a

(Case Continued)

global, integrated IT infrastructure. The initial focus on the supply chain led to immediate positive results, validating management's strategy and providing support for the organizational changes. Colgate was also under pressure to integrate its operations from its larger customers, who had already begun to integrate their own operations. The ERP project was actually part of a larger project to rethink and realign Colgate's business strategies, structures, processes, and systems. ■

Middleware

Most organizations have a wide range of applications, new and old, from a variety of vendors, running on numerous platforms. Replacing or rewriting these applications is not feasible. One option is to employ a class of development products known as *middleware.* As its name implies, middleware is software that works between and connects applications, allowing them to share data. Without middleware, applications would have to be modified to communicate with each other, usually by adding code to each application, perhaps causing unintended negative effects. Middleware acts as a translator between the applications so that they do not need to be changed.

As Woolfe[5] points out, middleware simplifies development by acting as the glue that binds the components, allowing them to work together. A plethora of middleware is available, as Figure 9-4 illustrates. Some are for communicating among applications,

FIGURE 9-4 Types of Middleware Used in Client-Server Applications

INTERAPPLICATION COMMUNICATIONS FACILITIES: LINK COMPONENTS

- Application programming interfaces (APIs): provide a standard way of interfacing
- Remote procedure calls (RPCs): enable a dialogue between two geographically dispersed applications
- Object request brokers (ORBs): allow applications or utilities to inter-work in standard ways
- Message-oriented middleware (MOM): uses asynchronous message passing for inter-application communications

TRANSACTION MANAGERS: HANDLE TRANSACTIONS ACROSS MULTIPLE PLATFORMS

- Standard query languages (SQLs): standardize the way in which databases are accessed
- TP monitors (CICS, for example): monitor online transaction processing with a database
- Two-phase commit: a protective mechanism for transactions that fail to complete successfully

UTILITIES: PROVIDE GENERAL SERVICES

- Directory services: resource allocation
- Time services: timing
- Security services: encryption, and so on
- Software distribution: including configuration control

Source: Roger Woolfe, "Managing the Move to Client-Server," Wentworth Research Program (now part of Gartner EXP, Stamford, CT), 1995.

others are for managing transactions across platforms, and still others provide general services, such as security, synchronization, or software distribution.

One type of middleware that has gained popularity is Enterprise Application Integration (EAI) products. EAI tools typically use a message broker to transfer data between applications. They allow users to define business processes and make data integration subject to rules that govern those processes. As an example, a rule might state that data moves automatically from the purchasing application to the accounts receivable application only after the appropriate person has signed off on the purchase. Companies acquire a central module plus the interfaces needed to connect the applications. To handle unique integration needs, EAI vendors provide custom programming to modify the EAI modules to fit the company's requirements. Here is an example of a use of such middleware.

CASE EXAMPLE

A TELECOMMUNICATIONS FIRM

In the highly competitive telecommunications industry, a company must offer a wide range of products and services and be able to rapidly modify them to respond to market changes and new technologies. As a result, processing customer requests for new and updated services is a major source of company cost and customer dissatisfaction. It has been estimated that 65 percent of new and change orders in the telephone industry have errors that must be corrected after the fact. This situation leads to tens of millions of dollars in unnecessary direct costs and a 20 percent annual customer churn. The result: significantly reduced profits.

To improve the process and retain customers, one telecommunications company implemented a CRM system. However, processing requests for new phone lines still was tedious because each request required interacting with three back-office applications before the CRM system could respond to the customer. Most of the connectivity was manual,

not automated, so response to customer requests was still unacceptable. To address the problem, the company looked to EAI so that no new ordering process would be needed; the existing process would simply be automated.

With the new EAI system, processing a customer request begins with the customer calling the call center, which creates a CRM-based order. The customer's name and address are passed to the ERP system, which retrieves the necessary information for the provisioning application to validate the request and ensure that the new service is compatible with the customer's existing services. The telephone service is specified and, if appropriate, a new phone number is allocated. Pricing is retrieved from the packaged accounting system before all the information is returned to the call center for presentation to the customer through the CRM system.

The process is now entirely automated. What used to take days or weeks is now handled in minutes while the customer is on the line, tremendously

(Case Continued)

improving customer responsiveness. Processing costs have been reduced, errors eliminated, and customer churn lowered. No new applications were required and the existing applications remained untouched. ■

INTERORGANIZATIONAL SYSTEM DEVELOPMENT

As noted in Chapter 1, one of the main business trends is the appearance of business ecosystems; that is, groupings of businesses that work closely together. This trend is obviously affecting the kinds of systems being built and how they are built. Systems that integrate supply chains, supply chain management (SCM) systems, are now a major trend, as supply chains compete against one another on their ability to reduce costs and time across their entire chains. Needless to say, development of these inter-organizational systems, which cross organizational lines, requires teams from the different organizations to work together.

Another type of inter-organizational system is a *platform*, which provides the infrastructure for the operation of a business ecosystem, a region, or an industry. In fact, platform development is a major trend in an increasing number of industries. One example, albeit an old one, is American Airlines' development of its SABRE computer reservation system. Originally, American developed SABRE for its own use. But the system was so leading-edge, and so expensive to build, that other airlines paid American to use it. SABRE became a platform for the airline industry. Today, the video game industry has intense competition among platform developers Sony (PlayStation 2), Nintendo (GameCube), and Microsoft (Xbox). Following are two examples of platform developments. The first one, yet to become a platform, is in the form of a Discussion Case. The second is in the form of a Case Example; it points out the types of coordination needed to develop an inter-organizational system for a business ecosystem.

DISCUSSION CASE

HOW SHOULD EXXONMOBIL LEVERAGE ITS IT ASSET?

In 1996, Mobil Corporation created Mobil Speedpass, a system that uses a 1.5-inch-long wand that motorists can attach to their key chain and wave at an electronic reader on a Mobil gas pump to pay for gas. Mobil's goal was to speed motorists in and out of its stations. It calculated that Speedpass would save motorists one-half minute off of a 3.5-minute transaction, states Hammonds.[8]

(Case Continued)

The device caught on. Mobil, now part of $230-billion ExxonMobil, has 5 million Speedpass holders. Furthermore, these customers buy more Mobil gas than non-Speedpass customers, they visit Mobil stations one more time per month, and they spend 2 to 3 percent more money at the stations that have paid $15,000 for the Speedpass scanner, notes Hammonds.

Speedpass is free to motorists. It uses radio frequency identification (RFID) technology from Texas Instruments to store the driver's credit card information and transmit it to the scanner. It is easy to use. No keyboard, no swiping.

ExxonMobil's Dilemma

The RFID technology is easy to replicate, so other gas station chains are testing competitive systems. Mobil has been in this situation before. In the early 1990s, the company invested early in pay-at-the-pump technology so that motorists could just swipe their credit card to buy gas. But competitors quickly caught up, and Mobil's first-mover advantage disappeared.

From that experience, Mobil learned it could lose its competitive advantage by keeping its technology proprietary. So

with Speedpass, management is taking the opposite approach. Mobil now sees the value of Speedpass as being its relationship with its 5 million users—not the Speedpass technology.

How should Mobil leverage this customer relationship? To start, it has changed the name from Mobil Speedpass to simply Speedpass to eliminate the exclusivity aspect. It also has teamed up with McDonalds restaurants in Chicago to test the use of Speedpass to pay for food. Mobil also plans to create similar deals with a United States drugstore chain, a supermarket chain, and other chains, notes Hammond.

The goal is to create a network effect: The more motorists sign up for Speedpass, the more attractive it becomes for retailers. The more retailers Mobil signs up, the more consumers will be attracted to Speedpass. It forms a virtuous circle; see Figure 9-5.

QUESTION

1. Given that ExxonMobil has a head start, what actions should management take to make Speedpass an ecosystem platform? ∎

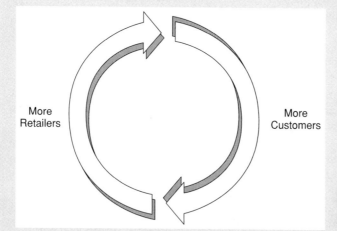

More Retailers

More Customers

FIGURE 9-5 Speedpass's Potential Virtuous Circle

CASE EXAMPLE

HONG KONG EXCHANGES AND CLEARING

Hong Kong Exchanges and Clearing (HKEx) is Asia's second largest, and the world's ninth largest, stock market. Due to the globalization of stock markets, stock exchanges now compete against one another for investors. And investors have become very demanding. They want more features from exchanges, more flexibility in how they trade securities, and faster, cheaper, and more cross-border trading. Furthermore, there has been much talk about exchanges forming global alliances.

Aiming for an Inter-organizational System, AMS/3

To put itself in a stronger competitive position, HKEx decided to embed its business processes in an open trading architecture, note David Lo, vice president of trading and participant services at HKEx, and his coauthors,[9] so that it can extend its market reach beyond Hong Kong, handle greater trading volumes, and more easily interconnect with business partners' systems. This architecture underlies HKEx's third-generation automatic order matching and execution system, called AMS/3, which is the system that handles securities trading at HKEx.

The first-generation system, a closed system, allowed brokers to enter orders, but only from special terminals on HKEx's trading floor. The second-generation system allowed orders from dedicated terminals in brokers' offices. However, it still did not connect to external networks nor to the computer systems of HKEx's 500 brokerage-house members.

In planning for AMS/3, HKEx wanted to improve the efficiency of the exchange, open up the system to individual investors, and lay the foundation to eventually automate the entire trading process so that it could offer "straight-through processing." In short, HKEx's goal is integrated end-to-end computerized trading processes from investors through brokers to markets.

AMS/3 permits brokers to enter orders as they have in the past, using dedicated terminals on and off HKEx's trading floor. Or they can use a new option: accessing AMS/3's trading host through an "open gateway." Thus, data can flow back and forth between a broker's back-office system and AMS/3, which gives those back-office systems the data to perform, say, market analyses not feasible before.

Furthermore, individual investors can make online inquiries or order requests using their mobile phone or the Internet once their broker has registered them with HKEx. Of course, each transaction is safeguarded with an authentication check.

Due to the flexibility of AMS/3, HKEx can now offer members and individual investors customized services, such as bundled products or distinctive trading processes. It has also made the market

(Case Continued)

more transparent by providing more timely information to members and investors. It also gives trading service partners, such as software developers and mobile phone operators, a new market for their services, note Lo et al.

Building AMS/3

The project was daunting, involving both internal and external people—40 staff from different departments, 150 consultants, and 500 brokerage firms. The project had five development teams, for the network, the host and open gateway systems, the multi-workstation system (for brokerages wanting to use HKEx's system instead of their own back-office system), the order routing system (for access via the Internet or mobile phones), and user acceptance testing.

PCCW (formerly Cable & Wireless HKT) built the trading network, the order routing system, and the multiworkstation system. Compaq supplied the host and the open gateway systems. Accenture, the large consulting firm, designed the architecture, managed user acceptance testing, coordinated the 500 critical project activities, managed the interdependencies among the numerous project segments, and oversaw the work of the contractors through a project management office of 10 people.

Each week the project management office reported to the project steering group, which included senior HKEx executives from the various business and IT areas.

Another group, the trading and settlement committee, had members from brokerage firms and other organizations involved in HKEx's market, such as accountants, solicitors, Hong Kong's Monetary Authority (which manages Hong Kong's fiscal policy), the Securities and Futures Commission (which regulates the brokerage industry), and the Financial Services Bureau (which regulates Hong Kong banking). This committee reviewed development of the system, offered opinions on the planned trading mechanisms, and made sure their firms (and the market) were on schedule to be ready to use the new system when it was launched.

Throughout the 2-year development, HKEx maintained a dialog with all interested parties to be sure they accepted the plans, contributed ideas to improve them, put the appropriate regulations in place, and got their own systems and processes ready to use AMS/3. Furthermore, they held open forums and used the media to educate investors about their coming new trading options.

Testing the System

To guard against system failure, HKEx conducted three levels of system testing. The first was single-component testing, where each component was tested on its own until it reached the needed performance level. Then came partial integration tests between components to catch as many interconnection problems as possible. Third was integration testing, which tested end-to-end processes. Overall, testing was 40 percent of the project. One thousand errors were found, mainly during integration testing, because vendors had made different assumptions during development.

Some of the major system specifications were that AMS/3 be able to process 200 orders per second (higher than American and European exchanges),

(Case Continued)

process 150 orders per second on an individual stock (a "hot stock"), handle off-hour orders transmitted all at once from 1,000 systems, accommodate new computers easily, and have a "flood control" mechanism so that no hot-stock activity can destabilize the system. AMS/3 has achieved all these requirements, and HKEx has recovery procedures for all the system-failure scenarios that people could dream up.

About 100 brokerage firms have built their own systems to interface with the open gateway. These could inadvertently interrupt AMS/3's processing and disrupt the market, so HKEx opened up an AMS/3 testing environment every Saturday for 6 months for the brokers to perform end-to-end testing. Some 35 brokers at a time had 5 consecutive weeks to perform their tests. In addition, HKEx inspected brokers' offices, and only allowed those that passed the tests to move into production mode, either when AMS/3 went live or at successive rollout times. Finally, HKEx also held market-wide network tests to test the system fully loaded.

Rolling out AMS/3

Once acceptance testing was complete, HKEx and its many partners followed a detailed, 9-month-long, 3-layer migration plan, state Lo et al. Each change was high risk, so to mitigate the possibility of disrupting Hong Kong's stock market, enough time was given between each layer to stabilize the environment before adding the next layer.

In preparation, applications were moved from their development environment to the production environment, and data was converted from AMS/2 to AMS/3. Then, the infrastructure layer was implemented first: The AMS/2 terminals were migrated in batches to the new AMS/3 trading network. Second came the accessibility layer: The access portions of the system—the new terminals, the multi-workstation system, the broker-supplied systems, and the open gateway—were launched in batches. Third came the functionality layer: New trading functions were introduced one-by-one so that the brokers had enough time to learn each one before being presented with another.

Some 300 of HKEx's broker-members have implemented new trading devices; 60 have even made order routing system connections to allow online trading by investors via mobile phones or the Internet. The 200 smaller brokers continue to use HKEx's traditional terminals to access AMS/3.

AMS/3 came in on time and on budget. It has not gone down, and the number of hotline calls has not increased, which is a real achievement. HKEx appears to have fully prepared its market.

The Results

Due to its new capabilities, HKEx is now open 20 hours a day and allows trading on several markets concurrently (adhering to the trading rules, hours, etc., of each one). It launched a South Korean and a Taiwanese index fund to boost local trading in these funds. Both funds are also traded in the United States, but the U.S. market is not open when these two Asian markets are open, note Lo et al.

With 500 exchange participants, HKEx is the world's largest networked trading system, so it is attracting interest from other countries that want foreign investment. Its 20-hour trading window

(Case Continued)

and its ability to handle online trading allow brokers and investors to access overseas markets directly through AMS/3.

Furthermore, by providing brokers with the infrastructure to offer more services and better security, HKEx enhances their market position. Individual investors also have more online capabilities. They can place, modify, and cancel order requests, check the status of requests, see real-time stock prices, and obtain other information.

HKEx is also adding new kinds of participants, such as financial information service providers, proprietary networks, and the Hongkong Post, the authority that issues and manages public key encryption certificates.

In short, HKEx now has the foundation for its industry ecosystem, with processes built on an open architecture and an inter-organizational system with components from numerous sources and participants of many kinds. ∎

INTERNET-BASED SYSTEMS

HKEx's system is actually a good introduction to Internet-based systems. AMS/3 is not Internet based, but it allows Internet access for online trading as well as other actions. The Internet has opened up the options HKEx can offer. Internet users have become so sophisticated that Internet-based systems must now be scalable, reliable, and integrated both internally and externally with the systems of customers and business partners. In developing such systems, companies have learned they must negotiate programming language differences. For example, a system may have to port old COBOL applications to Java, reconcile interface discrepancies, and interface with back-end legacy applications, often without documentation or past experience with those systems.

Internet-based systems are where the system development action is occurring. This section discusses three aspects of Internet-based systems: a framework, a language, and an environment. We examine these aspects for the following reasons:

- *Application servers* because they appear to provide the preferred framework for developing Internet-based systems
- *Java* because customers are demanding open systems; they do not want to be tied to a single vendor's proprietary technology. Java is a fairly open language that has evolved from client-side programming to being a server-side application development standard.
- *Web Services* because they are touted as the development environment of the future

Application Servers

Originally conceived as a piece of middleware to link a Web server to applications on other company systems, the application server has grown into a framework for developing

Internet-based applications. Figure 9-6 illustrates the basic application server architecture. A set of application servers is connected to create a single virtual application server. This virtual server takes requests from clients and Web servers (on the left), runs the necessary business logic, and provides connectivity to the entire range of back-end systems (on the right).

In addition to providing middleware and integration functions, application servers have become application development platforms, with a wide range of development and automatic code generation tools. They can provide common functions, such as security and database connectivity, notes Radding,[10] they can store business logic components (forming the building blocks for applications), and they provide development capabilities inherited from CASE [now called integrated development environments (IDEs)]. In short, they aim to increase programmer productivity by automating and managing many of the technical tasks in developing and running Internet-based applications. They also provide scalability. As demands on applications grow, a company can increase the power of its virtual application server by either installing more servers or replacing smaller servers with larger ones. The application server also provides automatic load balancing among the multiple servers.

Java

If companies are to develop Internet-based systems quickly, as the e-business environment demands, they need component-based development tools. If, in addition, the systems being developed are to be portable and scalable, then the companies need to employ an open system architecture. For both component-based tools and open systems, industry standards are necessary. Currently, some of the most widely used standards for Internet-based systems development have evolved from Java.

Java was originally developed to provide applets that run on Web clients. However, it quickly evolved into a full programming language with the goal of providing platform

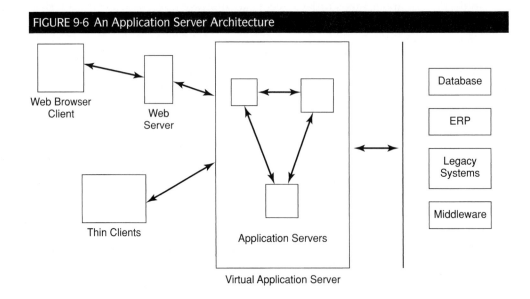

FIGURE 9-6 An Application Server Architecture

independence; that is, Java applications could run on any system through a *Java virtual machine*. This promised application portability was dubbed "write-once, run-anywhere." That promise has not been met, though. Java performed poorly relative to other languages, such as C++. Therefore, companies have not converted their client applications to Java. However, Java has evolved into a standard platform for developing server-side applications.

The two major components in the Java server-side platform are Enterprise JavaBeans (EJBs) and the Java 2 Enterprise Edition (J2EE) software specification. EJBs emerged on the developer scene in 1998 when Sun Microsystems unveiled a specification for creating server-based applications using software components. EJBs are preconfigured pieces of code that IS staff no longer have to build from scratch. They can be as simple as an order entry form or as complicated as a virtual shopping cart that even protects shopper privacy. Use of EJBs can greatly enhance programmer productivity. Microsoft competes with its own version of components called COM (Component Object Model) components. (Note the term *object*. OO programming has become increasingly important in system development.)

J2EE defines a standard for developing Internet-based enterprise applications. It simplifies enterprise application development by basing it on a collection of standard server-side application programming interfaces (APIs), providing a set of services to modular components, and handling many of the core functions for the applications. Components include an API for database access, security modules that protect data in the Internet environment, and modules supporting interactions with existing enterprise applications. J2EE also supports XML.

Together, J2EE and EJBs provide an alternative to building online business systems from scratch or buying packaged online business systems because of their multi-vendor platform capability and pre-built, reusable components.

Web Services

As described in Chapter 5, the vision of Web Services is that modules of code can be assembled into services, which, in turn, can be linked to create a business process at the moment it is needed and run across enterprises, computing platforms, and data models. There are a couple of ways to build a Web Service. One is to wrap an XML wrapper around an existing piece of code that performs a specific function, thus exposing it. Then give that Web Service an Internet address and let others use it, for a fee.

John Hagel III and John Seely Brown[11] point out that this is what Citibank has done. In the late 1990s when online exchanges were popping up like weeds, Citibank noticed that although the purchasing process was handled electronically, the actual exchange of money was generally handled manually or through special banking networks. Citibank had expertise in electronic payments, so it created a payment processing Web Service called CitiConnect.

When a company plans to purchase, say, office supplies through an online exchange, the company can utilize CitiConnect by first registering with CitiConnect the bank accounts to withdraw funds from as well as the purchasing employees and their spending limits. When a purchase is made, the buyer clicks on the CitiConnect icon on the screen. That click automatically assembles an XML-wrapped message that contains the buyer's ID, the amount of the purchase, the supplier's ID, the withdrawal bank account number, the deposit bank account number, and the timing of the payment, note Hagel and Brown. Using predefined rules, that message is then routed to the appropriate settlement network to perform that financial transaction.

The benefits of this Web Service are substantial, note Hagel and Brown. Settlement times are 20 to 40 percent shorter, and settlement costs are half or less. In addition, Citibank has extended its brand into a new market, and the exchanges have happier customers.

This arrangement also illustrates the second way to build a Web Service: use one someone else has already exposed. Commerce One drew on Citibank's Web Service, allowing Commerce One to focus on the other aspects of its business. Hagel and Brown believe companies will couple their own Web Services with those of others to create complex, yet flexible, best-in-class systems. To illustrate the basics of building a Web Service, consider the following simplified example, followed by a case about Bekins.

CASE EXAMPLE

BUILDING A WEB SERVICE

A graphical example of building a Web Service from an existing in-house application is shown in Figure 9-7. Following is a much simplified description of that process.

Step 1: Expose the Code. A currency conversion Web Service is created by *exposing* the currency conversion code of a credit card processor by encapsulating it in an XML wrapper.

Step 2: Write a Service Description. A description of the currency conversion service is written using WSDL (Web Services Definition Language). Housed in an XML document, this description describes the service, how to make a request to it, the data it needs to perform its work, the results it will deliver, and perhaps the cost to use it.

Step 3: Publish the Service. The currency conversion service is then published by registering it in a UDDI (Universal

Discovery, Description, and Integration) registry. Publishing means that its service description, along with its URL (its address), is housed in the registry for others to find. The registry is essentially a Web Services yellow pages.

Step 4: Find a Currency Conversion Web Service. The currency conversion service can now be found by, say, a pricing Web Service. The pricing Web Service sends a request in the form of an XML document in a SOAP (Simple Object Access Protocol) envelope to one or more registries. This special envelope is also based on XML. This particular request of the UDDI registry asks for a listing of currency conversion Web Services. The reply is sent in an XML document in a SOAP envelope back to the requestor.

Step 5: Invoke a Web Service. The pricing service can now bind to and invoke

FIGURE 9-7 Building a Web Service

Step 1: Expose the Code
using an XML wrapper

Credit card
processing
application

XML wrapper

Currency
conversion
service

Step 2: Write a Service Description
using WSDL

Currency
conversion
Web Service
description

URL:.......

Step 3: Publish the Service
in a UDDI Registry

UDDI Registry

Currency
conversion
description

**Step 4: Find a Currency
Conversion Web Service**

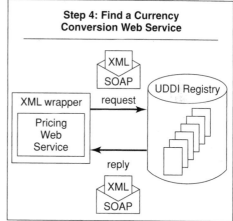

XML
SOAP

XML wrapper

Pricing
Web
Service

request

UDDI Registry

reply

XML
SOAP

Step 5: Invoke a Web Service
using a SOAP envelope

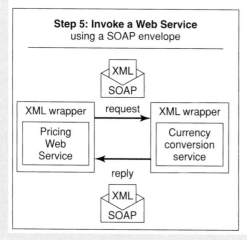

XML
SOAP

XML wrapper

Pricing
Web
Service

request

XML wrapper

Currency
conversion
service

reply

XML
SOAP

(Case Continued)

the selected currency conversion service by sending it an XML message in a SOAP envelope asking it to, say, convert US $1,250.25 into Australian dollars. The currency conversion service performs the task and returns the answer in an XML document in a SOAP envelope and quite likely invokes a payment Web Service to be paid for performing that conversion service. ■

CASE EXAMPLE

BEKINS

Bekins, the moving company, is using Web Services in its HomeDirectUSA business unit, which specializes in the home delivery of household appliances, large-screen televisions, and other large, expensive furniture. Bekins uses some 1,000 independent moving agents across the United States to move furniture when Bekins' own fleet cannot.[12]

Formerly, Bekins faxed or phoned these agents to arrange deliveries, but the process was slow and not equitable to all the agents. To automate the process, Bekins used Web Services technology to create an online brokering system called Tonnage Broadcast Exchange (TBE). When Bekins receives an order to deliver, say, a refrigerator, that its centrally managed fleet cannot handle, it uses TBE to "tender" that job to its agents (and perhaps other shippers). All agents are sent the tender at the same time based on pre-established criteria; so the system is fair. Once an agent accepts a job, it becomes

unavailable to the others. The results have been lower tendering costs, faster customer service, and better utilization of agents' trucks. Furthermore, because the system is so efficient, Bekins can offer lower-margin jobs to the agents, increasing its shipping volume and revenues.

Bekins' E-Commerce Platform

In 1999, Bekins made two key IT decisions about how it would develop future systems. One, it chose Java, rather than Microsoft's NET, as its e-commerce platform. Two, it chose IBM's WebSphere to develop and deploy future applications. TBE uses two systems that initiated Bekins' new e-commerce environment. The first system was the Shipment Tracking System, which lets Bekins' customers (such as manufacturers and retailers) and consumers track shipments via the Web. Retailers like this system because its accuracy lets them bill their customers

(Case Continued)

for home delivery faster. The second Java-based system was the Customer Order Management and Inventory System, which lets customers and shipping agents enter shipping orders via the Web. This system improved order accuracy up to 40 percent and allows customers to see the inventory Bekins is holding.

The TBE system, which is also based on the Java platform and built using WebSphere, advances Bekin's e-commerce platform by adding Web Services technologies. These technologies allow Bekins to link an agent's transportation management system into TBE almost instantly once the agent has readied its system to exchange messages using the Web Services standards: XML, SOAP, WSDL, and UDDI.

TBE runs on Bekins' mainframe. Each business partner has a client-side Java application running on one of its servers. When an agent wants to accept a tender from Bekins, its client-side application accesses the private TBE UDDI registry to find out how to communicate with the SOAP servlets. The SOAP servlet transmits the acceptance message to Bekins, where an XML parser translates it. A Java interface then passes it to Bekins' customer order management system, where it is booked as an order in the DB2 database.

Building TBE

The TBE development team consisted of an XML expert, two Java developers (one senior and one junior), an architect who knew IBM's WebSphere and DB2 database, and two COBOL programmers. They developed TBE in just 5 months' time, partly due to their experience and partly due to WebSphere, which provided the framework and sample code they built upon.

The team followed a formal development methodology with the developers focusing on creating TBE's components and the architect helping put the pieces together. The project was divided into five phases:

1. Code the core of TBE in Java (to be hosted on a Bekins' mainframe)
2. Convert the Java objects to Web Services
3. Deploy the Web Services
4. Code the client side of TBE (to be run on each agent's server)
5. Test the integration of the various parts of TBE

Building TBE required commitments from several moving partners because it was to be an inter-organizational system. Three partners were readying their companies to use Web Services technologies internally to integrate their own systems. Another seven acted as beta test sites for TBE using actual data. The tests gave Bekins confidence that TBE met its partners' requirements. TBE went live with 10 percent of the agents. Agents have been coming online since. Agents not ready to participate in TBE using Web Services technologies can access the system through a Web portal. Involving its partners in the development proved important, but equally important was their comfort with the new Web Services environment. ■

Preparing for On-the-Fly Web Services Development.   Although Web Services can help enterprises develop systems faster, the technology might have other ramifications as well—ramifications that CIOs would do well to prepare for, before they actually happen. One possibility is end user development of Web Services, believes Jonathan Sapir, of InfoPower, a company that offers an SOA-based development platform.[13] He believes that companies are experiencing a crisis in software development because their IS organizations cannot keep up with users' requests for changes to applications. Due to the increasingly volatile business environment, systems need almost continual enhancement. When they do not get it, they do not change as fast as the business environment.

This "crisis" situation has occurred before. When corporate databases first appeared, only programmers had the tools and know-how to generate reports from them. But those reports did not solve individuals' needs. When report writers and query languages appeared, end users eagerly learned them to query the databases on their own, reducing the time needed to answer their questions. Likewise, programmers wrote large financial programs to manage corporate finances, but those programs did not meet the needs of individual accountants. Thus, when spreadsheets arrived in the 1970s, accountants (and others) eagerly used them to write personal applications. In fact, the spreadsheet was the "killer app" that drove the initial growth of the PC industry.

Today, Web Services and service-oriented architectures have set the stage for yet another round of even-more-powerful, on-the-fly end user development, believes Sapir. The need is here; so is the IT savvy. Many people have been using computers for at least 20 years—some, for their whole life. They play games, manage their finances, buy stock, and perform other online tasks that are a form of programming. They would develop their own personal programs if they had the tools. End user tools based on Web Services and SOA are coming, and they will again let users write personal applications. The difference this time is that these applications will use Web Services standards, so they will be packaged as services that others can find, use, and even build upon.

Sapir foresees people computerizing their part of the business on their own with these user-friendly tools, thereby shifting computerization from top-down to bottom-up. To do so, though, people will need to view business needs as a series of small events that are handled throughout the day as they occur, rather than consolidated and addressed after-the-fact in one large development effort by the IS organization.

This bottom-up shift has come before, as noted, with minicomputers, then PCs, as well as with spreadsheets and fourth-generation languages. Each time, most IS organizations were caught unprepared. They had not laid down an infrastructure, provided tools or training, nor established principles for end user development using the new technologies. Companies ended up with "personal silos of data and apps" that were difficult to share and were not maintained nor backed up. IS departments had to catch up to bring order to the chaos. It behooves CIOs to respond to users' current requests for changes to applications by piloting a companywide Web Services platform and tools that users can use to get ahead of the curve.

Most importantly, IS management needs to implement a management system to manage the eventual intertwining of Web Services—before it happens. Without a Web Services management system, it is going to be awfully difficult to know which applications depend on which Web Services. Corporate executives will not want their major business processes to be based on applications that are not well managed. This management aspect of Web Services is a looming issue CIOs need to address, believes Sapir, before users take development into their own hands, as they have done so eagerly in the past.

CONCLUSION

The traditional approach to system development from the 1960s evolved to give the process more discipline, control, and efficiency. It was valuable in moving programming and system analysis from pure free-form "art" to a better defined "craft." Problems remained, though, with long development times, little user involvement, and lack of flexibility in the resulting systems. The tools and methods of the 1970s and 1980s—4GLs, software prototyping, CASE, and OO development—permitted more rapid development and even experimental development; some were seen as revolutionary techniques to conventional developers.

The 1990s brought the need for integrated enterprise systems and Internet-based systems. Both required more flexibility and speedier development with a significant amount of integration, both internal and external to the company. With the integration efforts, companies realized the importance of focusing less on technical issues and more on the impacts of IT on business strategy, organization, and people. Widely reported failures of large ERP projects reinforced this need to concentrate on the business.

Most recently, the IT industry has responded with new tools and approaches. Application servers support integration across a wide range of new and legacy systems, Java supports Internet-based application development, and Web Services promise to make the Internet the heart of systems building. We have indeed entered a new era of application development where the focus is on the Internet, inter-organizational development, and ecosystem applications.

QUESTIONS AND EXERCISES

Review Questions

1. What are the goals of the traditional system development life cycle approach?
2. Refer to the list of features and functions of 4GLs in Figure 9-3. Briefly explain each.
3. What are the main characteristics of the prototyping approach?
4. Define the components of a computer-aided software engineering system.
5. What is unique about DuPont Cable Management Service's use of CASE?
6. What are the basic characteristics of an ERP system?
7. Why have so many ERP implementation projects failed?
8. Describe Colgate-Palmolive's approach to implementing their ERP.
9. What is a platform inter-organizational system? Give a few examples.
10. In a nutshell, what does HKEx's AMS/3 system do?
11. Describe HKEx's testing procedure for AMS/3.
12. What is Java and why is it important?
13. What are five steps in building a Web Service?
14. What does Jonathan Sapir foresee with regards to Web Services?

Discussion Questions

1. IS organizations will no longer need to develop a proprietary infrastructure; they can just rely on the Internet. Therefore, they will again focus mainly on developing applications. Discuss.
2. The field is moving too fast for companies to keep developers abreast of the state-of-the-art. To keep up, they should outsource application development to the experts, providers who specialize in development. Discuss.
3. How do you think ExxonMobil can leverage Speedpass?

Exercises

1. Find a description of an Internet-based application. What features does it have? What approach did the company choose to develop the application?
2. Visit a company in your community with an IS department with at least five professionals. Prepare a short case description to summarize the company's current approach to developing systems. Does it have one standard approach or a combination of several? Is it developing Web Services? If so, describe one or two. Is it participating in inter-organizational system development? If so, describe the development.
3. Visit the Web sites of three vendors of Web Services tools. What are they selling? Relay some client successes to the class.
4. Prepare two scenarios of what ExxonMobil could do with Speedpass. What are the crucial differences in assumptions between the two?

REFERENCES

1. Canning, R. G., *Electronic Data Processing for Business and Industry*, John Wiley & Sons, New York, 1956, and *Installing Electronic Data Processing Systems*, John Wiley & Sons, New York, 1957.
2. Glass, Robert, *Building Quality Software*, Prentice Hall, Upper Saddle River, NJ, 1992.
3. McClure, Carma, Extended Intelligence, Inc., Chicago, IL.
4. Cox, Brad, *Object-Oriented Programming: An Evolutionary Approach*, Addison-Wesley, Reading, MA, 1987.
5. Woolfe, Roger, *Managing the Move to Client-Server*, Wentworth Research Group (now part of Gartner EXP), January 1995.
6. Buckhout, Scott, Edward Frey, and Joseph Nemec, Jr., "Making ERP Succeed: Turning Fear into Promise," *Journal of Strategy & Business*, Issue 15, Second Quarter, 1999, pp. 60–72.
7. Davenport, Thomas, "Putting the Enterprise into the Enterprise System," *Harvard Business Review*, July/August 1998, pp. 121–131.
8. Hammonds, Keith, "Pay as You Go," *Fast Company*, November 2001, pp. 44–46.
9. Lo, David, Ali Farhoomand, and Pauline Ng, "Embedding the Business Landscape in Open System Architectures: The Case of Hong Kong Exchanges and Clearing Ltd.," Second place winner, Society for Information Management 2001 Paper competition.
10. Radding, Alan, "Application Servers Fuel E-Business," *Informationweek.com*, June 19, 2000.
11. Hagel, John III, and John Seely Brown, "Your Next IT Strategy," *Harvard Business Review*, October 2001, pp. 105–113.

12. IBM, "The Bekins Company Moves into the Future with E-Business on Demand," June 13, 2003. Available at www-306.ibm.com/software/success/cssdb.nsf/CS/BEMY-5NG3MR?OpenDocument&Site=default. Accessed March 2004. Also see Bob Sutor and Gardiner Morse, "Plumbing Web Connections," *Harvard Business Review*, September 2003, pp. 18–19.

13. Sapir, Jonathan, "Are You Ready for the IT-Savvy Company?" *Darwin Magazine*, August 2003. Available at www.darwinmag.com/read/080103/performance.html Accessed October 2003.

10

MANAGEMENT ISSUES IN SYSTEM DEVELOPMENT

INTRODUCTION

Chapter 9 dealt with developing systems. This chapter looks at the issues surrounding system development. The context for this discussion is set by the ideas of John Hagel III and Marc Singer while they were at McKinsey & Company.[1] They see companies as being in three businesses:

1. Infrastructure management
2. Customer relationship
3. Product innovation

Traditionally, companies have bundled the three, which leads to compromises because the three have conflicting agendas. The Internet allows companies to unbundle them, say the authors, by specializing in one business and optimizing it.

IS departments can be viewed as being in the same three businesses. Operations are infrastructure management. The help desk is the customer relationship business. System development is product innovation. The three need to be managed differently, state Hagel and Singer.

Infrastructure Management. The goal of infrastructure management is to reduce costs. Providing infrastructure, such as hospitals, roads, wireless networks, and such, involves high fixed costs, so the goal is to build scale. High barriers to entry also mean that only the few largest players will dominate, which explains the huge battle now ensuing among telecommunications companies, handset makers, and others to become wireless service providers. Management focuses on efficiency and standards, which is just what we have been seeing in network and computer operations. Companies outsource their network management and data centers to large ESPs such as IBM, CSC, and EDS to lower costs.

Customer Relationship. The goal of the customer relationship business is service. Here the goal is scope, by having lots of custom offerings to increase the company's "wallet share" of each customer. In this business, the customer is king, and developing relationships with customers requires large investments. Here, again, Hagel and Singer see only a few large players dominating. In the IT arena, PC support and help desks are often outsourced to specialists, especially in Europe, where multilingual support is needed. Outsourcing offshore is also increasing dramatically in the customer service arena.

Product Innovation. The goal of product innovation is speed because it provides nimbleness. Low barriers to entry mean many small players. The key to success is talent. In IT, developers are king, so software companies give them the coolest tools, allow them to work day or night, permit their pets at work, always have a stash of free Jolt Cola on hand, and so on. Software companies are always on the lookout for talent, and they reward stars generously, which is one reason IS departments can have a hard time attracting the talent they need.

One of the most sought-after skills in system development today is project management. This chapter begins with a discussion of project management and then moves on to discussions of how to improve legacy systems and how to measure the benefits of systems.

PROJECT MANAGEMENT

Today, much organizational work is performed via projects. In IS as well as other functions, being able to manage a project to completion, and deliver the expected outcome within the allotted time and budget, has become an increasingly valuable skill. This section explores six aspects of project management:

1. What is project management?
2. The job of a project manager
3. A day in the life of an IT project manager
4. Change management (an area IS teams have not always handled well)
5. Risk management (another area IS teams have not always handled well)
6. Some tips for good IT project management

What Is Project Management?

Project management is simply the management of a project, notes Michael Matthew of Matthew & Matthew consulting firm.[2] This definition may sound simple and self-evident, but that does not make it easy. Many people get confused or concerned about IT project management because it involves the "T" word: *technology*. In reality, IT project management is not much different from other forms of project management, such as those used to construct an office building or a bridge.

A *project* is a collection of related tasks and activities undertaken to achieve a specific goal. Thus, all projects (IT or otherwise) should:

- Have a clearly stated goal
- Be *finite*, that is, have a clearly defined beginning and end

It has been said that IT project management is 10 percent technical and 90 percent common sense or good business practice. Indeed, many of the best IT managers do not have a background in IT at all, but they possess the important skills of communication, organization, and motivation. Perhaps the most difficult component of IT project management is keeping in mind, and under control, all the interdependencies of the numerous tasks being undertaken.

"A *project* is a temporary endeavor undertaken to achieve a particular aim and to which project management can be applied, regardless of the project's size, budget, or timeline," states the Project Management Institute (PMI).[3] *Project management* is "the application of knowledge, skills, tools, and techniques to project activities to meet project requirements," states PMI's 2000 edition of *A Guide to the Project Management Body of Knowledge* (PMBOK, 2000 Edition).

PMI, which was founded in 1969 in Philadelphia, Pennsylvania, has established the standard for project management and is the leading association in educating project managers in all fields, including IT. It has some 125,000 members in 240 countries and over 10,000 Project Management Professionals (PMPs) who have passed its rigorous set of tests and been certified as PMPs. PMI views project management as encompassing five processes (initiating, planning, executing, controlling, and closing) and nine knowledge areas. To become a certified PMP, a person must pass tests covering all nine knowledge areas:

1. *Integration*, which involves ensuring that the various elements of a project are properly coordinated
2. *Scope*, ensuring that the project includes all the work required, and only the work required
3. *Time*, ensuring timely completion of the project
4. *Cost*, ensuring that the project is completed within the approved budget
5. *Quality*, ensuring that the project satisfies the needs for which it was undertaken
6. *Human resources*, making the most effective use of the people involved
7. *Communication*, ensuring timely and appropriate generation, collection, dissemination, storage, and disposition of project information
8. *Risk*, identifying, analyzing, and responding to project risks
9. *Procurement*, acquiring goods and services

To explore project management in a bit more detail, here is one view of the job of a project manager.

The Job of a Project Manager

Project management was once viewed as a specialty, with roots in construction, engineering, and IT, note Craig Anderson, a practice leader in KPMG's Queensland, Australia, office, and Michael Matthew, a partner in Matthew & Matthew in Sydney, Australia.[4] But now, business managers need project management skills to implement change in a disciplined and successful manner. Business project management is evolving from IT project management. Both IT and business project managers are responsible for the following tasks:

- Setting up the project
- Managing the schedule
- Managing the finances
- Managing the benefits
- Managing the risks, opportunities, and issues
- Soliciting independent reviews

Setting Up the Project.   Each project needs a project charter or document to serve as the one source of truth for the project and the first point of call when there are differences of opinion in the project, note Anderson and Matthew. It should spell out the following:

- ***Why.*** A brief background of the project (i.e., the result of a strategic review) and the business objectives to be achieved.

- ***What.*** A description of the non-financial benefits to flow from the project and a list of the key outputs to be produced.
- ***When.*** A list of the milestones and expected timing (a high-level project plan).
- ***Who.*** A definition of the project team and an analysis of the stakeholders of the project and their expectations.
- ***How.*** A definition of the work that needs to be undertaken to achieve the project, its scope, and specific exclusions. This definition also needs to address how much the project is expected to cost (a detailed financial breakdown) and expected benefit.

Risks, opportunities, prerequisites, assumptions, and the communications plan also should be included. Then this document needs to be approved.

Managing the Schedule.   The schedule or project plan is the heart of a project because it communicates the activities that need to be completed to achieve the benefits, when they need to be completed, and who needs to complete them. First develop a high-level plan of the entire project. Next, break down the business objectives into deliverables and then into the pieces of work to produce these deliverables (and the time required). Do not plan the details of the entire project at the outset, recommend Anderson and Matthew, because that is too difficult and the project will change. Instead, plan the details of a stage at its outset based on the work completed and the deliverables yet to be achieved.

Then baseline the schedule, affixing a starting point so that you can gauge progress. Tracking is essential for anticipating completion and taking corrective actions when issues arise. Many automated tools are available to help project managers manage the schedule.

Anderson and Matthew make four recommendations on managing the schedule. One, focus on the date that tasks are completed rather than the percentage of the overall project that has been completed. Two, review progress at least monthly, preferably weekly or fortnightly for shorter projects. Three, focus on tasks to be completed, not those that have been finished. And four, reforecast when new evidence comes to light.

Managing the Finances.   At its most basic level, the financial plan describes the project's costs, who is accountable for them, the expected financial benefits from the project, and the cash flow. These projections flow from the project plan and are determined by the resources committed to the project, when these resources are committed, and external costs, such as contractors or general expenses.

The greatest areas of contention in most projects are project costs and benefits. Whereas outsiders may focus on deliverables, insiders will focus on financials. Just as with the project plan, once authorizations have been obtained, it is a good idea to baseline the costs and track them as you do the project plan, recommend Anderson and Matthew, because the approved figures are only estimates. They will change over time. As the project manager, you will need to know how much has been spent and how much money is left.

Managing the Benefits.   Four benefits can emerge from IT and business projects: profitability, cost reduction, changes to working capital, or adherence to legal or regulatory reform. Benefits are much more difficult to estimate than costs. Anderson and Matthew offer four suggestions for managing benefits. One, be realistic (most people overestimate benefits). Two, make sure the benefits are greater than the estimated costs. Three, base costs and benefits on the same assumptions. And four, forecast for various scenarios.

It also is important to forecast the timing of benefits. Discounted cash flow is one technique to compare the timing of benefits and costs. And again, a project manager should track benefits throughout the life of the project by asking, "Why are we doing this?" The answer might need to change if the business environment changes, as often happens in long-term projects.

Managing Risks, Opportunities, and Issues.   Every project encounters the following:

- ***Risk.*** A potential threat that may prevent the project from achieving its business benefits
- ***Opportunity.*** A project going better than planned
- ***Issue.*** Something that threatens the success of the project

All possible risks and opportunities should be listed at the project outset and then analyzed to determine each one's likelihood and impact. Risk mitigators for high risks need to be built into the project plan. Likewise, major opportunities need to be built into the plan to maximize potential benefits. Both risks and opportunities need to be monitored.

Ongoing monitoring of risks and opportunities is one of the weakest areas of project management, note Anderson and Matthew. A good project manager continuously monitors the risks and opportunities along with the schedule, costs, and benefits. One of the most effective tools for monitoring risks and opportunities is a risk log.

Likewise, issues management is an ongoing task. Once an issue is identified by a project team member, it should follow a standard resolution process, recommend Anderson and Matthew. An issue should be brought to the project manager's attention, its impact assessed, and then it should be assigned to a team member for resolution and its resolution monitored.

Soliciting Independent Reviews.   Reviews help the project manager and project sponsor assess the "health" of a project. As the project progresses, team members often focus on delivering on specific objectives. They lose sight of the overall project benefits. An independent review can identify overlooked risks and opportunities. However, this review is not the same as a progress report. It should look at whether the project is still appropriate, whether its approach is the most effective, whether the deadline will be achieved, and if the costs are as expected.

To give a flavor of what project management work actually entails, here is an example of a day in the life of a project manager, excerpted from a blog on ITToolbox's Web site (www.Ittoolbox.com).[5]

CASE EXAMPLE

A DAY IN THE LIFE OF AN IT PROJECT MANAGER

Larry Cone is an independent IT project management consultant in Pennsylvania. He has managed over 100 IT projects. On January 28, 2004, Cone began a highly informative and entertaining blog about his day-to-day experiences, starting with his managing a project to implement a content management system for a medical publisher.

The blog appears on ITToolbox.com, a Web site for IT professionals, that features blogs from IT professionals, providing site visitors a look at the day-to-day challenges these professionals face and how they address them. The following are brief excerpts from Cone's blog.[5]

January 28, 2004: The Project Manager's Prayer

A few years back I got together with a group of like-minded IT project managers and did a formal review of projects we had done that had run into trouble. We tried to figure out just when the seeds of disaster were sown. In the majority of cases, a project that ran into trouble was in trouble at the beginning. Most often the project had been scoped improperly, but sometimes there were governance issues or management support issues. Another common problem was "missing" project phases, such as a needed trial or pilot phase. The pilot phase may be in the project plan, but without allowance for a substantial revision and test cycle post-pilot. All of these problems were "baked in" at the beginning.

Thus, the Project Manager's Prayer: "Bless our Beginnings". That's where we most need a blessing, and most need vigilance, because all too often the seeds of our later pain are sown well before the project kickoff meeting.

February 3, 2004: Project Benefits— Mapping the Minefield

The client has a number of different publications that have transitioned from paper to electronic over the past 5 years. It has become increasingly clear that customers want the ability to search electronically across several or all of the publications. The goal of the project is to make this not merely possible, but effective, and to turn content access into a competitive advantage.

This is a relatively small project, so I'm where I like to be—in the thick of user and customer interviews, capturing requirements. I think I have a feel for the "real" needs of a business, and I enjoy helping to capture and document those needs. I've done 15+ interviews, with an ear for three things:

- *Use cases*—I ask for details of the "typical" user, their job title, their business situation, the query they would run, and the information they would want to retrieve. I think we are all clear that successful

(*Case Continued*)

systems start with understanding the use cases—whether it's A/R or fly-by-wire.

- *Issues*—a catch-all term for stuff—important or no. Here is where I carefully capture and document everyone's pet peeve, favorite feature, annoyance, or beef. Why? The stakeholders need to feel like they have been heard. That favorite feature may not make it into release 1 or even release 21, but if they look they see it on the Issues list. This gains me credibility and builds trust.

- *Benefits*—I listen for potential benefits at every turn, and carefully capture and collate them. I've got 18 on the list, so far. I've published the benefits list back to the users, and asked them to rank them in order of importance to them.

I use the proposed benefits list to smoke out hot issues as early as possible. Is there a creaky user registration process that frustrates everyone? A high ranking for improving the process tells me this. Who other than the VP of Sales thinks that the real point of the system is to increase cross-sells across publications? How many think that the most important outcome is to reduce training and support costs? How highly does protection of intellectual property rank?

February 7, 2004: Project Benefits— A Trail Through the Swamp

I asked the management team to rank the benefits list, and got a 95 percent response rate, after some cajoling. The results held some relief, and some surprises.

A close inspection of the benefits signposts tells me a lot about what will make the project a success. I can take each of the top-rated benefits, and capture a checklist of three or four features or subsystems necessary for their delivery. Take, for example the highly ranked *cross-sell of subscriptions* benefit. To deliver increased cross-publication sales activity, I'd better make sure that the system logs every subscriber that looks at content in a different publication, and forwards that sales lead information to the sales team in the form of reporting.

February 10, 2004: It's All About the Interface

In my project, as we work through business requirements specification, I'm doing interviews with managers, customers, and users. Not surprisingly, they don't talk about business requirements— they talk about application interface details. They bring up Google, and show me how well it works. They take me to house wares shopping sites, and show me how you can cross-link from a lamp to other lamps with similar attributes. They describe features of search sites that they have used successfully, that allowed them to save their last search, or apply parentheses and Boolean logic to their current search.

Meanwhile, I'm trying to figure out how many "components" there are in the system, the nature of the interfaces between the components, and which ones we will buy, which ones we will build, and which ones we have already. I know that we are going to buy a software package as the core of the solution, and I'm trying to formulate a map of the overall solution, with my eye on the RFP to come,

(Case Continued)

and how we will ask for what we need. I suspect that most of the user interface details will come with the package.

February 15, 2004: Inventories of Content — Part I

This project, like many others, will be successful when a bunch of "stuff" that is now in an old place will be accessible in a new place, and in a new way. In this case the "stuff" is medical content documents.

Thus the need for an inventory of online content. I wasn't surprised when there was no such inventory available, so I went about building one.

I started with the current print catalog, and built a spreadsheet framework containing a row for every area described in the published catalog. For the columns, I created fields for facts of interest. These included how many documents, what format they were in currently, how they were delivered to the Web where the underlying content was stored, the from and to date ranges, who was responsible, and how often the content was updated. I set up the spreadsheet, and logged onto the Web, and went looking for content.

February 20, 2004: Inventory of Content — Part II

I ended up with the first comprehensive inventory of online content — useful to the client in and of itself. For me it is a checklist of how much stuff there is, where it is, and in what format it is. This is the set of stuff that must be searchable and accessible at the end of the project. And if I can deliver that, I will be truly content.

February 24, 2004: Magic Happens

We have been interviewing customers, users and management for about 8 weeks now on the way to defining our content management system requirements. We have inventoried the content areas involved, and created use cases and benefits analyses from the interview contents. We have come to one of the most interesting parts of the project — where "Magic Happens."

I'm talking about the moment when an analyst rereads the requirements, and sits down with a pad of paper, or a white board. She reads and reviews, and starts coalescing the many individual statements like "User clicks on search result link, and if he has access rights to the document, he links through and the document appears" into solution components. There is an aha! moment where the analyst draws a circle on the white board and labels it "Document Access Control."

Then more circles appear, and lines connecting them, and a solution takes shape.

For me, that is a Magical Moment.

March 1, 2004: Structure–Function

We left the analyst in front of the white board, drawing circles and arrows. She was engaged in the primal act — creation. Out of the formless requirements void was emerging the light of a solution, an architecture. Or at least the components of a solution.

Well, we don't need to code this system; we are going to buy it (most of it, anyway). But we need more than a formless functions and features list. Why?

Well — I'm a confirmed believer in structure–function; that is, the critical relationship between a system's structure and its function. We want to buy the solution

(Case Continued)

that supplies most of our needed functionality. We also want to buy the solution that makes sense architecturally—has components that perform the high level functions that map to our high-level needs.

March 4, 2004: Trade Shows, Tom Peters, and Martinis

In the Blog alternate universe, we are wrapping up a requirements/content inventory/high-level components document package for this content management system package. In the real world, we are a few weeks ahead. We have convened a "blue ribbon" RFP evaluation committee, and I'm trying to develop a vendor shortlist to work from.

A great place to do that is a trade show, and I've gotten a bit of luck. The AIIM 2004 Enterprise Content and Document Management Show is in the Javits Center in NYC next week.

I'll be heading up there to see some demos, talk to some vendors, and try to get a general sense for the budget of this project. I need to do some expectation setting with my client's senior management. In an informal setting, I can ask some questions, and formulate some ideas about pricing and budget.

March 18, 2004: Project Management Tools—The Hourglass

I have been running IT projects for quite a while, and I have accumulated a set of tools that I use in my work. I thought you might be interested in a tour through my personal toolbox.

Opening my toolbox, the first tool I see is one of my oldest, the Project Manager's Hourglass.

Like most of my tools, the hourglass is a conceptual tool. Here is how I visualize it: It consists of 2 brushed aluminum plates, 6-inches square, set 12 inches apart by 4 steel rods threaded and bolted through holes in the corners. Inside the cage of the rods is a blown-glass hourglass, containing about 2 cups of black basaltic sand.

It is a precision tool for a precision job—the job of measuring the end of the analysis phase of a software project. Here is how I use it.

When the analysis phase of a project starts, I mentally turn over the hourglass. It could be a user requirements gathering phase, a data analysis phase, or a user interface design phase. As the project goes on, I keep my eye on the Hourglass. At some point, the sand runs out. When it does, I say, "Enough analysis; lets wrap up this phase."

March 23: Project Management Tools—The Scope Axe

Continuing on the theme of project management tools, we are taking a tour of my personal project management toolbox. I open the toolbox and I see one of my favorites and most used tools, the scope axe.

Most projects run into trouble at some point, and as the project continues, the options for the project manager are progressively reduced. As discussed earlier, most problems stem from unanticipated tasks or complexity. The initial reaction is to add budget and resources to handle this, but the wise project manager will get out his scope axe.

Use project creep to have the hard discussions with your users and your sponsors, and chop off some scope. You don't have

(Case Continued)

to amputate it completely, just restructure the phases to push the particular scope area to a later time.

April 20, 2004: If You Measure It, They Will Come (Back)

In my Project Manager's toolbox, I always carry the indispensable measuring tape. It's like the old saw (pun intended): "if you can't measure it, you can't manage it." And, there are lots of things to measure.

Overall, there are three areas of measurement, corresponding to the golden triangle of project management: time, resources, and functionality. The triangle is used because it is a symbol of balance and stability; change any one side without adjusting the others and you get a distortion. Just so in a real project: change the timeline without adjusting the amount of resources or the functionality or both and you are either smarter now than you were before (when you built the triangle) or you are a masochist.

May 25, 2004: Project Management Tools—My Pants are on Fire I

In a Letter to the Editor about a recent *Business 2.0* magazine article, the author used the phrase "Pants on Fire" to describe the state of an IT project manager. It was a thought-provoking phrase, and it got me thinking about how a PM's pants reach the point of ignition, and what PM tools can combat the dreaded "Pants on Fire."

In my view, "Pants on Fire," or POF, refers to the project state in which:

1. Things have gotten out of control
2. They are getting worse fast
3. The project can still be recovered, and

4. The project will fail if you don't do something quickly.

I'm unaware of a generalized project manager's pants extinguisher tool, but here are some thoughts on remedying the POF state.

In situations relating to run-away scope, I would reach for my scope axe, and hack away at the burning part, and try to remove or defer it to a later phase. Or at least reduce the size of the overall fire down to more manageable proportions.

Another POF situation is the technical fire. A recent example occurred in a project "parallel" to one of mine in a client setting. A software product release in Beta was experiencing infrequent but catastrophic database response problems with SQL Server. I didn't get the exact details, but every few hours the Beta system database server would choke and hang with some sort of resource problem. Release schedules were slipping, the Beta client was concerned, the product management leadership team wanted hourly updates—you get the scenario.

The PM, an experienced hand, rang the fire alarm, flew in technical experts, and cashed in a pile of chits in Redmond. His actions were effective on several fronts: Management saw lots of activity and saw that the situation was being strongly addressed. The experts didn't come up with a fix but did help isolate the failure scenario. His coders were able to code around the failure scenario, and keep the Beta moving.

I'm interested in readers' comments about Pants on Fire scenarios, and tools used to combat the POF situation.

(Case Continued)

(In April, Cone's project issued a Request for Proposal to vendors of content management products. By July, the proposals had been received and the decisions on which to accept were being made.) ∎

Change Management

IS staff members are often so enthralled with the technical aspects of a new system that they presume a technically elegant system is a successful system. However, many technically sound systems have turned into implementation failures because the people side of the system was not handled correctly. IT is all about managing change. New systems require changing how work is done. Focusing only on the technical aspects is only half the job. The other job is change management.

Change management is the process of assisting people to make major changes in their working environment. In this case, the change is caused by the introduction of a new computer system. Management of change has not always been handled methodically, so choosing a change management methodology and using it is a step toward successfully introducing new computer systems.

Change disrupts people's frame of reference if it presents a future where past experiences do not hold true, says ODR, a change management firm in Atlanta, Georgia.[6] People resist change, especially technological change, when they view it as a crisis. They cope by trying to maintain control. In the case of an impending new computer system that they do not understand fully or are not prepared to handle, they may react in several ways. They may deny the change; they may distort information they hear about it; or they may try to convince themselves, and others, that the new system really will not change the status quo. These reactions are forms of resistance.

ODR offers a methodology to help companies manage technological change. They use specific terms from the field of organizational development to describe the types of people involved in a change project.

- The *sponsor* is the person or group that legitimizes the change. In most cases, this group must contain someone in top management who is highly respected by the business unit because change must be driven from the business unit.

- The *change agent* is the person or group who causes the change to happen. Change agents are often the IS staff. They can introduce the change but they cannot enforce its use.

- The *target* is the person or group who is being expected to change and at whom the change is aimed.

Using surveys completed by a project's sponsors, change agents, and targets, ODR aims to:

- Describe the scope of the change
- Assess the sponsors' commitment to the project

- Assess the change agents' skills
- Evaluate the support or resistance of the targets

The goal of these initial evaluations is to determine whether the change can be made successfully with the current scope, sponsors, change agents, and targets. By evaluating each area, the change agents can determine (1) whether the scope of the project is doable or whether the organization is trying to change too much at one time, (2) whether the sponsors are committed enough to push the change through or whether they are sitting back expecting the organization to change on its own, (3) whether the change agents have the skills to implement the change or whether they are not adept at rallying support, and (4) which groups are receptive to the change and which are resistant. Once these assessments have been made, ODR assists IS project teams to understand the risks their project faces and what they can do to mitigate those risks.

As an example of an organization that used this approach and successfully implemented nine change management projects, consider BOC Group, as described by Neil Farmer.[7]

CASE EXAMPLE

THE BOC GROUP

The BOC Group is an industrial gas manufacturer with global headquarters in Windlesham, England, and U.S. headquarters in Murray Hill, New Jersey. The company operates in 60 countries and sells industrial gases such as oxygen for steel making, carbon dioxide for food freezing, and so on.

The industry is mature and highly competitive, so companies compete on price and service. To improve the company's competitive position, management committed $35 million to reengineer BOC's core processes. In all, nine reengineering projects were initiated. All succeeded over a 30-month time frame—a significant achievement.

The company established nine full-time teams, each to improve a selected process. Following completion, all team members were guaranteed a return to

their former (or equivalent) job. Each team was co-led by a business and information management (IM) process leader because IT was a major component of most of the projects. Each team also sat together in a bullpen setting.

For the first 6 months, each team studied its chosen business process. The research was not parceled out among team members; every team member studied everything. Thus, IM team members were like all the other members. They studied the existing processes and then had a say in how implementation should be handled; they supplied input into the training plan; and they helped devise the customer communication plan. They were often significant influencers because the other team members respected their opinions and their technical knowledge.

(Case Continued)

Garnering True Executive Sponsorship

Although the president was the executive sponsor for all the teams, he was not intimately involved in each project. Thus, the real executive sponsors were vice presidents and directors. Although they understood the need for the changes and were committed to the concepts behind them, day-to-day operational pressures put a strain on true sponsorship. To address this problem, BOC called on ODR to teach sponsorship to the nine sponsors in a 2-day event.

The sponsors were reticent to go offsite for 2 days to talk about managing change. They believed employees did what they were asked to do. The sponsors did not understand the full impact of the changes on employees nor how employees would be assimilating the changes. They also did not realize their sponsorship job included building sponsorship down through company levels.

During the 2-day event, the ODR facilitator described the sponsorship job in basic here's-what-is-needed terms, and he challenged the nine sponsors to ask the important questions, such as: "What in our culture might make our project not work? What has failed in the past at BOC? Are we asking too much? Is this realistic?" The facilitator pressed the sponsors to question the company's capacity to assimilate change. He got them to be honest and identify obstacles. They were, indeed, challenged. Up to that point, they had not addressed these questions.

The workshop did the job. It opened their eyes to their sponsorship role, which turned out to be crucial to the success of all the projects. They had underestimated the involvement required from the total organization. They had been sitting back expecting their teams to make change happen. But the teams could only put the tools in place; the organization had to make change happen. The workshop taught the sponsors the difference. They left understanding how they needed to drive change through the organization. The facilitator led them into planning their own strategies and examining possible consequences.

One Change Project

One of the reengineering projects changed the way BOC processed the paperwork for delivering gas products and invoicing customers. Previously, drivers received a batch of shipping tickets each morning from a clerk. These tickets described their route for the day. When they dropped off a cylinder of gas or picked up an empty one, they marked it on a full-size sheet of paper and handed it to the customer. They also returned handwritten notes to the clerk for entry into the system.

The solution was to replace the paper with a point-of-delivery handheld device (PODD). Schedules would be made at night and downloaded electronically to the PODDs. Loaders would use this information to load the trucks during the night. In the morning, the drivers would pick up their PODD, which contained their route for the day. When they delivered a cylinder, the PODD would accept the customer's signature and then print out a delivery document the size of a grocery store receipt. At the end of the day, the driver hung the PODD back on the rack and the billing data was automatically transmitted to headquarters.

(Case Continued)

To arrive at this solution, the team, as a whole, studied the process from order to delivery to billing. In working as a unified team, the IM folks began to act as business folks, and vice versa. At the end, the two were indistinguishable because they had absorbed each other's knowledge.

This interaction was a much-appreciated by-product of the process. Once the entire team devised the solution, the IM staff built the technical infrastructure.

Involving Middle Management. To engage middle managers in the nine reengineering projects, BOC established an advisory council for each one. Each advisory council's job was twofold, upward and downward. The upward job was to give feedback on recommended changes, pointing out implementation issues. The downward job was to describe the recommendations to employees and get their buy-in.

The PODD advisory council had 11 members, which included drivers, logistics, IM, field people, and managers. They met several times, and they had more influence than they realized. Their upward feedback significantly affected the PODD team's decisions and their downward communication gave the field people a way to be heard. Through all the advisory councils, BOC created a cascade of influencers, which was a key contributor to their success.

Training the Drivers. The PODD team developed a handheld device that was so logical and intuitive that little training was needed. However, to make the drivers comfortable and ensure success of the project, the team created a 6-hour training program.

The training theme was "A day in a driver's life," and the purpose was to show the truck drivers how to use the PODD to do their job. The lead trainer (a former truck driver) first led the drivers through "A perfect day" scenario where nothing went wrong. With PODD in hand, each driver followed the lead trainer in going through an entire day's use of the PODD, from loading cylinders into the truck to dropping off the PODD at night. This rapid scenario gave them the overall feel of its use. The drivers made mistakes, but as they corrected their own mistakes, they became more and more comfortable with the PODD.

The drivers then worked at their own pace through three successively harder scenarios following a laminated sheet of instructions that included cylinder bar codes and other pertinent information. The drivers who got through all three had no problem with the PODD. Those who got through two might need a little support. Those who struggled would need a trainer to ride with them for a day or two.

To ensure that the drivers were fully comfortable with the PODD, the PODD team offered to ride with any driver for a day. Many accepted, not just to build their confidence, but because they enjoyed the company of another person. Whenever the driver raised a question during that day, the team member usually responded, "What do you think you should do?" Generally the driver's answer was right, which built self-confidence.

Due to all the training, the PODD team encountered little resistance from the drivers. In fact, the drivers were so pleased the company was investing in them that they proudly showed their

PODD to their customers; they were the only drivers in the industry to have them.

The project was successful because the PODD team had assessed its people aspects at the outset and mitigated the identified risks by holding the sponsorship event, involving middle management via the advisory council, and thoroughly training the truck drivers. ■

Risk Management

Not all IT-based projects succeed. In fact, many fail—especially the really large projects, such as those implementing ERP or CRM systems. Thirty to 70 percent of IT projects fail. Why do IT projects fail? Because they do not overcome their risks, either technical or business ones, notes Chuck Gibson, a long-time IT consultant and senior lecturer at the MIT Sloan School of Management, in an *MIS Quarterly Executive* paper on risk management.[8]

Technical risks might be a vendor package not scaling up as expected or the project's scope creeping so much that the project becomes too complex to implement. Although technical risks cannot always be anticipated, they can be contained with the right technical corrections, notes Gibson. *Business risk*, on the other hand, is the risk that the business does not change properly to use the new system. Business change is necessary to achieve business results from IT. Lack of business change can come from the appropriate new work environment not being put in place or people's skills and attitudes not being updated to take advantage of the new environment.

Business risks are not as easily righted as technical risks, notes Gibson. Instilling the right business changes requires using the project management approach that reduces the main risks. When the risks change, the project management approach probably needs to change to keep the project on track. Gibson proposes eight project management approaches, from the *Big Bang* approach (which is appropriate when all the main business risks are low) to the *Mitigate or Kill the Project* approach (which is appropriate when all the main risks are high).

To ascertain which project management approach is most likely to yield the needed business changes, Gibson proposes using a three-step process whenever the main risks in a project change: assess the risk, mitigate the risks, and adjust the project management approach.

Step 1: Assess the Risks. The business case for an IT project should include the business risks. Based on his experience and research, Gibson believes the three predominant risk factors are *leadership* of the business change, *employees' perspective* on the change, and the *scope and urgency* of the change.

To visually see a project's overall risk from these three factors, Gibson creates a decision tree. It shows the eight possible combinations of the three factors (Figure 10-1). A plus sign (+) on a factor means "positive support for the business change"; it increases the likelihood of success by reducing the risk. A minus sign (−) on a factor means "negative support for the business change"; it decreases the likelihood of success by

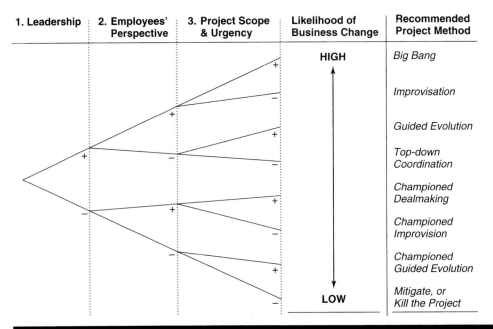

1. Leadership	2. Employees' Perspective	3. Project Scope & Urgency	Likelihood of Business Change	Recommended Project Method
			HIGH	Big Bang
				Improvisation
				Guided Evolution
				Top-down Coordination
				Championed Dealmaking
				Championed Improvision
				Championed Guided Evolution
			LOW	Mitigate, or Kill the Project

FIGURE 10-1   Risk Management Decision Tree

Source: C. Gibson, "IT-Enabled Business Change: An Approach to Understanding and Managing Risk," *MIS Quarterly Executive*, Vol. 2, No. 2, September 2003, pp. 104–115. Used with permission.

increasing the risk. The factor that is the greatest contributor to project success or failure should be placed on the left. In this example, it is leadership, which is often, but not always, the case. On the far right are the eight project management approaches, one for each path through the decision tree.

A project leader is the executive (or executives) responsible for the change. The project leaders should be business executives, not IT executives, notes Gibson, because the business (not IS) is being required to change. To assess whether a project's leadership contributes to success or failure (whether it is a plus or a minus on the decision tree), Gibson recommends asking six questions:

1. Are they committed to the business case?
2. Do they understand the extent of change in work behavior required for the project to succeed?
3. Are they formally motivated to pull off the change, such as built into their performance goals?
4. Are they at the appropriate organizational level and have the formal power to influence the needed changes in work behavior?
5. Do they have experience with a project of similar scope, urgency, and people impact?
6. Do they have informal power, such as respect and credibility?

The answers are likely to be mixed, notes Gibson, so give each a weight to ascertain whether the leadership factor should be a plus or minus on the decision tree.

To assess employees' perspectives, he recommends asking two questions. One, "How will the affected people react?" Will they embrace the change, follow orders, follow others, wait and see, resist, or sabotage the change? Two, "Why are they likely to react this way?" This assessment should also yield a single plus or minus on the decision tree.

To assess the project's scope and urgency, Gibson suggests asking three questions: "Is the scope wide?" (A wide scope is a minus.) "Is the change scope deep and severe?" (A major change in processes is a minus.) "Is there urgency?" (Urgency is a minus because it increases risk.) Overall, the scope and urgency factor on the decision tree gets a plus or a minus. The result of these three analyses yields a path through the decision tree that indicates both the project's level of risk and the appropriate project management approach.

Step 2: Mitigate the Risks.   Mitigation means "thoughtful management action based on anticipation of high change risk," states Gibson. Some examples are provided in the Dow Corning case.

Step 3: Adjust the Project Management Approach.   Gibson divides project management styles into whether they are authoritative or participative and whether the project's budget and time frame are rigid or adjustable; see Figure 10-2. The resulting four project management approaches are appropriate for the least risky projects, he believes, which are the four top paths in the decision tree.

The *Big Bang* approach is authoritative and has a fixed budget and deadline. This approach is only appropriate when all three factors are positive. *Improvisation* is participative and has an adjustable budget and deadline. This is the approach to use when leadership and employee perceptions are positive, but scope or urgency place the project at risk, because the committed workforce can adapt to difficult tasks, states Gibson. The *Guided Evolution* approach is participative, but it has a fixed budget and deadline. This is the project management approach to use when only the employee-perception factor is negative, because that negativity can be overcome by involving the employees through strong leadership, motivating them to accept the change. *Top-down Coordination* is an authoritative approach with an adjustable budget and deadline. This method only works when the leadership factor supports the business change and when the leadership is respected, full time, and highly experienced in leading business change, notes Gibson.

The projects on the bottom half of the decision tree, where the leadership factor is negative, are the riskiest. The only project management approaches that will lead to the success of such projects, believes Gibson, are those that have a champion in the user organization. These champions generally have to be willing to bet their job on the

	Management Style	
Project Budget and Deadlines	**Authoritative**	**Participative**
Fixed	Big Bang	Guided Evolution
Adjustable	Top-down Coordination	Improvisation

FIGURE 10-2 Four Approaches to Project Management

Source: C. Gibson, "IT-Enabled Business Change: An Approach to Understanding and Managing Risk," *MIS Quarterly Executive,* Vol. 2, No. 2, September 2003, pp. 104–115. Used with permission.

project's success. In actuality, these four options "are not in the realm of responsible senior management," notes Gibson, but they do happen. And champions can pull them off, generally by gaining adherents through informal channels—except when all three factors are negative. That's when *Mitigate or Kill the Project* is the only option.

To illustrate effective choices in project management, Gibson presents the successful implementation of ERP at Dow Corning from 1995 to 1999. Each project phase had different business risks. Realizing this, the project executive took a different project management approach in each phase. The project management terms used in the case are Gibson's.

CASE EXAMPLE

DOW CORNING

In 1995, Dow Corning gained a new CEO, Dick Hazelton, who led his operating committee through a strategic review to decide the company's strategy for the next 10 years.[8] They decided to leave the business strategy intact, but use IT to foster business process change.

Phase 0: Get Ready

The operating committee viewed business process change as highly risky, for the following reasons (to use Gibson's framework):

- *Leadership* of business change: High risk, because the IT organization had recently failed to implement a global order-entry system.

- *Employee perception* of business change: High risk, because the company had never experienced a major change and its culture was long employee tenure and adherence to existing practices.

- *Scope and urgency* of business change: High risk, because the scope was wide (company-wide), it was deep and severe (new

processes, new jobs), and it was urgent (which actually was the only positive factor because it got people's attention).

According to Gibson's decision tree, this was the riskiest type of project: *Mitigate or Kill the Project*.

To change the leadership from negative to positive, Hazelton appointed a 30-year Dow Corning veteran, Charlie Lacefield, to be in charge of both IT and the business change. Lacefield would report directly to Hazelton. To mitigate the other two risks, the operating committee followed Lacefield's recommendation of using a package, SAP's R3 ERP suite, and minimizing changes so that the company could focus on the business changes, not the technology changes.

Phase 1: Understand the New System

Use the Improvisation approach of participative management and flexible deadlines. In the first phase, Lacefield was most concerned about employee reticence in the later phases, so he focused this phase

(Case Continued)

on building commitment to the SAP ERP system by getting 40 of the most respected managers in Dow Corning on his implementation team full time and having them work closely with his IT staff. They used the traditional Dow Corning approach of consensus and flexible milestones to understand the SAP ERP system and to redesign work processes to match it.

Phase 2: Redesign the Work Processes

Use the Guided Evolution approach of participative management with fixed deadlines. Although the Improvisation approach worked in phase 1 to get the 40 managers deeply committed, it did little to get the work processes redesigned. As a result, Dow Corning employees were seeing little progress (but hearing that big changes were coming), so their perception turned negative. In response, Lacefield changed his project management approach. He appointed a new project manager, a man who was comfortable with IT and had a highly respected track record in manufacturing at the company. Lacefield also set firm deadlines so that employees would see progress. This *Guided Evolution* approach continued through the pilot—a cutover to the SAP ERP at a newly acquired European business.

Phase 3: Implement the ERP Worldwide

Use Top-down Coordination with its authoritative management style and flexible timelines. The pilot's success demonstrated management's determination and shifted employee perception to positive. But the scope of the rollout in this third phase shifted to negative, because it was company-wide. Lacefield thus changed his project management approach in response, to authoritative, but permitted flexibility in deadlines because the three risk factors at Dow Corning sites varied widely. During this phase, Lacefield traveled extensively for a year, negotiating and cajoling executives at the company sites to stick to their commitment to change to the new ERP-based work processes. He even made project success one of his performance goals for the year.

Phase 4: Complete Implementation

Use the Big Bang approach of authoritative management and firm deadlines. By the end of 1998, most of the company sites had implemented the SAP ERP system, so all the risk factors had turned positive. So Lace-field opted to implement the system in the few remaining pockets of resistance by setting firm deadlines. Initially, site conversion took 18 months. In these remaining sites, though, Lacefield required that it take only 4 months.

In 1999, Dow Corning became the largest successful single-database implementation of SAP's ERP. Gibson attributes the success, in part, to the adroit use of four project management approaches, each fitting the circumstances at hand. ∎

Tips for Good IT Project Management

Most people would agree that a successful project has the following characteristics, notes Michael Matthew:[2]

- It is delivered on time.
- It comes in on or under budget.
- It meets the original objectives.

However, some people do not realize that success also means that the project meets users' and the organization's needs, which may have changed since the original objectives were stated. Projects that do not give users what they want cannot be deemed a success. Following are some tips from Matthew on how to better assure IT project success.

Establish the Ground Rules.   Define the technical and architectural specifications for the systems following four guidelines:

- Adhere to industry standards.
- Use an open architecture.
- Web-enable the system.
- Power with subsystems.

These principles should help ensure no nasty surprises along the way, as well as provide the ready ability to update/switchover systems in the future. The basic tenet is that the systems should be as simple as possible while fulfilling all of the (reasonable) user requirements.

Foster Discipline, Planning, Documentation, and Management.   In many respects, these elements are what project management is really all about. It does not matter how well the requirements have been specified or whether the "perfect" solution has been selected; if the process is not controlled properly, anything can happen or, more realistically, potentially nothing will happen.

A firm timeline for system rollout needs to be formally established and signed off. Once this task has been done, the project team needs to work backward from the critical dates and map out the timing for the intermediate steps and include any interdependencies. Teams should take the critical date and subtract some time to factor in unforeseen contingencies. The project must progress with the target critical date in mind, which requires strong discipline.

The project also needs to follow a sound methodology and have key points planned and documented (and reported on) using a product such as Microsoft Project. All members of the team need to be aware of their responsibilities and timelines. Nothing should be left assumed. In addition, regular meetings and updates of the project plan are needed, along with proper documentation of the system development effort. Senior management needs to be able to see this documentation whenever they want. Management, key users, and even vendor personnel should be included on project steering groups, which should meet regularly to make sure the project continues on track. Such meetings also provide a venue for airing problems and raising issues that might affect others.

In addition, it is desirable to have an overall IT project steering committee. Regular project manager meetings from the various projects are key to keeping each other informed of their progress and for raising issues that might affect other projects.

Obtain and Document the "Final" User Requirements. Documenting user requirements is critical because it is the only way the team can evaluate the project outcome. Scope creep (users asking for more and more functions) causes many system failures. Documenting requirements helps lock in the scope of the work and reduce the possibility of costing problems and time overruns due to additional requests. Documenting user requirements can be done via a variety of methods, including facilitation sessions and one-on-one interviews.

A common mistake is writing user specs in technical jargon, notes Matthew.[8] Some IT consultants make this mistake to "maintain the IT mystique." However, this approach can do harm. Similarly, IT project teams should not accept overly technical sign-off requests from software houses. These developers need to prove they can fulfill the users' requirements.

Obtain Tenders from All Appropriate Potential Vendors. Today, much software is bought rather than built in-house. This option needs to be considered when beginning a project, notes Matthew. In fact, companies that do not have expertise in the area under consideration might want to call in consultants to make a recommendation. Their extensive contacts in the IT community can significantly improve selection of the package or packages. Or consultants may simply help the IT project team create the selection criteria for evaluating bids and selecting a winner.

Include Suppliers in Decision Making. If development is to be handled by an outside firm, then create a joint project team. The supplier, or suppliers, will undoubtedly appoint their own project managers for their respective assignments. They need to be part of the governing team.

Convert Existing Data. Data conversion needs to be properly planned to make sure that the output data is complete and accurate. Although this task might appear quite simple, it is often the area that creates the biggest headaches. Here, perhaps, the oldest maxim in the IT industry applies: garbage in, garbage out.

Follow Through After Implementation. After successfully implementing the systems, project managers need to cross their t's and dot their i's in terms of documentation, future maintenance processes, and so on.

The bottom line is that IT project management is no different from any other form of project management. Success requires good planning, along with good communication, and ensuring active participation of all appropriate parties, says Matthew. These elements, along with some hard work, will better ensure a successful system.

Thus far, this chapter has dealt with managing system development projects. We now shift to an issue that repeatedly comes around: How to improve legacy systems.

IMPROVING LEGACY SYSTEMS

Most IS executives feel trapped by the past. They have thousands of legacy programs and data files they would love to replace. The worst offenders were discarded because they were not Y2K compliant. However, with the onslaught of e-commerce and then the economic downturn, CIOs may not have the resources to replace all the remaining legacy systems. Replacement is not the only option, though. In many cases, it may not even be the wisest option.

To Replace or Not to Replace?

To replace or not to replace? That is the question studied by the Boston Consulting Group (BCG)[9] in 18 manufacturing companies, service firms, and government organizations in North America, Europe, and Japan that had either just replaced or upgraded legacy systems or were in the process of replacing or upgrading. Of the 21 projects compared, 12 were successful in that they worked and had a bottom-line impact. However, the other nine were either unsuccessful or did not deliver the anticipated results.

From these findings, BCG concluded that upgrading (rather than replacing) made more sense in most cases, even if it was difficult and not seen as exciting as a totally new system. They noted that people get seduced by a new technology and want to rush out and replace old systems with it. However, most of the replacement projects that failed could have been upgrade projects. In fact, in some cases, the company reverted to upgrading the old system anyway.

When a system's technology is so obsolete that it does not exist in many places, then replacement is probably the only choice. Otherwise, BCG recommends that companies perform three analyses. The first is to rigorously analyze the costs and benefits of the new system. Most companies underestimate the cost of replacing a system and overestimate the achievable business value, even on the successful projects. Furthermore, they do not factor in the risk of failure. The second is to determine how specialized the new system really is. Sometimes companies think they need a made-to-order system when a purchased solution would do just fine. Their requirements are not as unique as they think. The third is to assess the IS staff's capabilities honestly. Several companies in the study failed to develop replacement systems because management had overrated the staff's skills. In conclusion, BCG recommends that the burden of proof lie with those who advocate replacement of a legacy system rather than with those who advocate an upgrade, especially for mission-critical systems.

Options for Improving a Legacy System

With this insightful study as a backdrop, here are seven choices for creatively dealing with legacy systems from least to most amounts of change (Figure 10-3).

Enterprises use a variety of approaches in these options. In moving to a totally new platform, such as ERP, for example, companies have taken one of two strategies in using outsourcing firms. The first has been to keep the legacy maintenance work in-house, hiring the third party to implement the new system and then phasing out the legacy maintenance work. Others have opted for the opposite. They have outsourced maintenance of the legacy systems so that the in-house staff could focus on developing the ERP system. As the new system has come online, the outsourcer has turned off the legacy

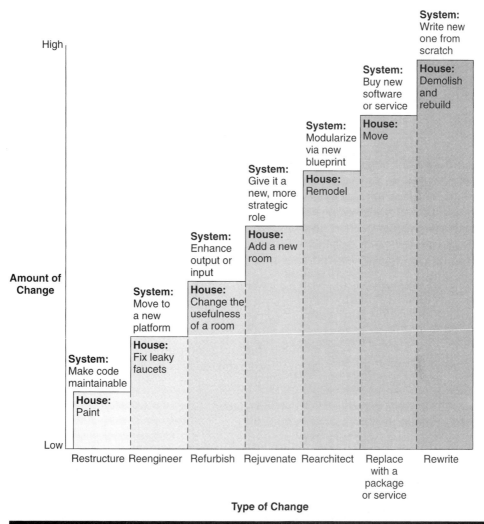

FIGURE 10-3 Options for Improving a Legacy System with Home-Improvement Analogy

systems. Companies take this transitional outsourcing approach when they feel they have (or can get) the in-house expertise required by the new platform. As BCG found in its survey, in-house skill levels can be the main determinant in deciding whether this second approach is even feasible.

Here then, is the spectrum of options for improving legacy systems. As shown in the figure, it may be useful to compare these seven options to fixing up a house.

Restructure the System. In fixing up a house, restructuring is akin to updating the look of a room or the house, perhaps by repainting or getting rid of clutter so that it "feels" better to live in. In IT, if an application program is basically doing its job but it runs inefficiently or is "fragile" or unmaintainable, then it may simply need to be restructured. For years, vendors have offered software products to aid in this process.

The most popular ones use automated restructuring engines to turn "spaghetti code" into more structured code. The process involves the following seven steps.

1. Evaluate the amount of structure in the current system, including the number of layers of nesting, degree of complexity, and so forth. Use the tools to present a trace of the program's control logic. Subjectively evaluate the code to determine whether restructuring is warranted at all or if more extensive change is required; this task can only be performed by people.

2. Compile the program to be sure it is in working order. A code restructuring tool will not make a non-operative program run.

3. Clean up and restructure the code by running the program through a structuring engine. This automated process does not change the logic of the program; it simply replaces poor coding conventions with structured coding conventions, such as reducing the number of GOTOs, removing dead code and alter statements, highlighting looping conditions, and grouping and standardizing input-output statements. It uncovers the structure hidden inside the convoluted code.

4. Reformat the listing, making it easier to understand, by using a formatting package.

5. Ensure that the old and new versions produce the same output by using a file-to-file comparator.

6. Minimize overhead introduced by restructuring by using an optimizer package. After optimization, restructured programs generally require between 5 percent less and 10 percent more run time than the unstructured versions.

7. "Rationalize" the data by giving all uses of the same data one data name. This step is optional.

These seven steps can be used to restructure a functional system or to get it in shape to be reengineered.

Reengineer the System.   In fixing up a house, reengineering is akin to fixing what isn't working, such as replacing broken door handles, repairing leaky bathroom fixtures, adding more insulation in the attic, and even feng shuiing the house to put furniture in more harmonious locations. In IT, a step beyond restructuring is reengineering, which means extracting the data elements from an existing file and the business logic from an existing program and moving them to new hardware platforms. This use of the term *reengineering* should not be confused with the term *business process reengineering*. The term *system* or *application reengineering* is much narrower and refers only to software. The other term refers to redesigning business processes. Like code restructuring, reengineering requires automated tools because the process is too complex to be cost-justifiably done manually. Database reengineering tools began appearing on the market in the late 1980s.

According to Charles Bachman, a pioneer in the database field, the major problem in the computer field is that people consider existing systems as liabilities that must be maintained, taking resources away from developing new and exciting applications. Instead, management needs to see existing systems as assets from which to move forward.

If developers can *reverse engineer* a system, that is, extract the underlying business logic, they can *forward engineer* that business logic to a new system platform. With this

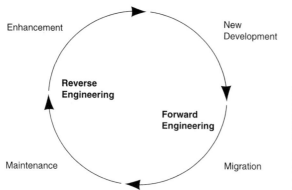

FIGURE 10-4 The Reengineering System Development Life Cycle

Source: Courtesy of Charles Bachman, founder of Bachman Information Systems, Cambridge, MA.

approach, existing systems become assets. Developers can extract the intelligence in them rather than start over from scratch.

Bachman believes a new system development life cycle can use automated products to help perform the reverse engineering. It encompasses all four basic development activities: maintenance, enhancement, new development, and migration. This life cycle is circular rather than linear, as shown in Figure 10-4.

- *Reverse engineering*—where existing programs, along with their file and database descriptions, are converted from their implementation level descriptions that include records, databases, code, and so on, into their equivalent design-level components of entities, attributes, processes, messages, and so on.

- *Forward engineering*—which goes the opposite direction, moves from requirements-level components to operational systems. Design items created by reverse engineering are used to create new applications via forward engineering.

The cycle continues because as new applications go into operation, they become candidates for reverse engineering whenever they need to be changed. Neither people nor automated tools can use this new life cycle by themselves, notes Bachman, but together, it becomes feasible. GTE Directories is an example of a company that used such reengineering tools.

CASE EXAMPLE

GTE DIRECTORIES

GTE Directories produced, marketed, and distributed more than 1,500 different telephone directories in some 14 countries. To accelerate their response to changing markets, GTE Directories began automating its telephone directory publishing business.

(Case Continued)

The directory publishing system had four main databases. The largest supported all of the administrative functions for creating and selling Yellow Page advertising, from sales to photo composition. The second was used by representatives to sell Yellow Page advertising for non–GTE directories. The third database handled billing. The fourth database provided order entry for independent telephone companies for whom GTE produced telephone books.

The databases were originally designed application-by-application. The result was records that contained data elements with no business relationship to each other, making them difficult to reuse, enhance, and change. The data administration group acquired reverse engineering tools to help them improve these databases.

To reverse engineer the database, a designer used a design administrator to display the existing database definitions graphically. The designer made changes by manipulating the graphical icons. The tool helped draw complete and consistent relationship diagrams because it had the intelligence to identify inconsistencies and incomplete structures.

Once the new database design had been created, the designer forward engineered the database design and ran the physical implementation design rules. When the design was satisfactory, the new database statements were automatically generated.

Such database reengineering was used on two projects.

The Blueprint Project

The largest database had not been properly designed, so the data administra-tion group used the toolset to create a blueprint of what the database should look like. They reverse engineered the existing database from its physical to its data model from which they created a new, properly designed data model using entity-relationship modeling techniques. By experimenting with this model, they created a design that was more adaptable to change. It became their blueprint for the future and was used to guide maintenance work. As the database administrators maintained the database, they made changes to align it more closely with this blueprint. Without the reengineering tools, they would not have even attempted this project because they could not have done the "what if" modeling necessary to create the blueprint.

A Reuse Project

The database administrators reused some of the data elements in the largest database for a new production scheduling system. The company had scheduled production of their 1,500 directories among their three printing plants using a 15-year-old system. Some scheduling data was in the system; some was in the new administrative system.

The company created a new scheduling system, drawing some scheduling-related data from the administrative database. Again, they used reengineering tools to create the design models for the new scheduling databases. From these models, they used a tool to generate the necessary database statements. With the new system, salespeople no longer had to interrogate both the 15-year-old publishing system and the

(*Case Continued*)

administrative system—which had different sets of data— to see directory publishing schedules.

Because maintenance was the bulk of the work of the database administra-tion group, the tools became invaluable in helping them redesign old databases, design new databases using portions of existing ones, and create their blueprint for the future. ■

Refurbish the System. In fixing up a house, refurbishing is akin to enhancing the usefulness of the house, perhaps by replacing old furniture in a room, relandscaping the yard to improve its curb appeal, or turning a college graduate's bedroom into an office. In IT, if an old system is maintainable and is causing no major problems, it may be worthwhile to add some extensions. Potential extensions would supply input in a new manner, make new uses of the output, or allow the programs to deal more comprehensively with data.

Refurbishment is actually occurring quite a bit these days because of the Web. Companies are leaving existing systems in place but adding a Web front end, along with accompanying query translation software, so that the system can be accessed directly by employees, suppliers, or even customers. Witness FedEx's Web site, which allows customers to directly access the company's tracking database. In such cases, companies generally follow a "surround" strategy, where they treat the old system as an untouchable black box and surround it with new facilities. This approach has been a popular way to upgrade legacy systems, even before the Web's appearance.

Rejuvenate the System. In fixing up a house, rejuvenating means adding new functions, such as adding a room, a porch, or a swimming pool. In IT, rejuvenating an old system is a step beyond refurbishing the system because it adds enough new functions to a system to make it more valuable to the firm. The first step is to recognize a system's potential. The second is to clean up the system, perhaps using restructuring tools. The third step is to make the system more efficient, perhaps using the reengineering approach mentioned earlier, then port the system to a new operating environment and database structure. The fourth step is to give the system a more strategic role, such as allowing it to feed a data warehouse so that people in field offices can access data far more quickly. Another possibility is to give it a role in a company's e-commerce strategy by using it as a back-end system accessible via the Web.

As an example, consider Amazon.com, the online retailer, which is using Web Services technology to give third-party developers access to its data and content to use in their software, hardware, or services. Amazon's goal is to use its information to increase the company's market share.

CASE EXAMPLE

AMAZON.COM

In 2002, Amazon.com initiated its Web Services program where anyone can receive a license to access Amazon's data and content via XML feeds—for free. The licensees must agree, though, to not use any of the logos on Amazon.com's site nor use any of the restricted or copyrighted material on the site (such as copyrighted reviews).[10]

Over 27,000 people have obtained licenses, some for their personal use, some to offer free software to Amazon.com users, others to build hardware for use with Amazon.com's site, and still others to sell software or services related to the site. Examples of these third-party offerings include:

- Software for people to download their Amazon.com wish list onto their cell phone to use when shopping in stores
- Software to help merchants offer their products on Amazon.com, with the merchant paying a percentage of each sale to the software developer
- A small bar code reader for scanning UPC codes of inventory to be sold via Amazon.com

- Software to add a "real-time scrolling ticker tape" of Amazon.com-based data to a Web site
- Software that links Amazon.com's music offerings to radio play lists so that listeners can buy a song when they hear it

Amazon.com takes the risk of not controlling how others use its information, but in return, others are creating gadgets, links, services, and software that Amazon.com could not build itself, increasing the value of its site to consumers. Amazon.com is using its data to create an online ecosystem of businesses and services that rely on its marketplace and the vast amount of data it collects. In so doing, Amazon.com seeks to transform itself from a retailer into an e-commerce platform where "buy" buttons on many, many Web sites take buyers to Amazon.com. Furthermore, Amazon.com now handles content hosting and order fulfillment for some large retailers and many small ones. In short, it is using Web Services to rejuvenate its data, giving it a strategic role via XML. ■

Rearchitect the System.   In fixing up a house, rearchitecting is akin to rethinking the use of its space by perhaps gutting a major portion of a house and remodeling it by combining the kitchen, dining room, and family room into a great room. In IT, the step beyond rejuvenating a system is the newest option—rearchitecting it. This option involves having a to-be architecture for new systems, and then using that architecture to upgrade legacy systems. As noted in Chapter 5, due to the increasing complexity of enterprise systems, the advent of inter-enterprise systems, and the dependence of interlinked systems in supply chains, CTOs are devising enterprise IT architectures. In the past, IT architectures were not seen as necessary. They now are seen as mandatory because they show how systems are interconnected. Where possible, CTOs work hard to migrate their enterprise to that desired to-be architecture, generally one system at a time. Following is the example of Toyota Motor Sales. As Roger Woolfe and Marcus Blosch[11a] of Gartner EXP point out, a main use of Toyota's IT architecture is to remediate legacy systems.

CASE EXAMPLE

TOYOTA MOTOR SALES

Toyota Motor Sales, headquartered in Torrance, California, handles U.S. sales of Toyota and Lexus vehicles for its parent, Toyota, in Japan. In 1998, Barbra Cooper became CIO and found no IT architecture, no development methodology, no application integration, and no standards. Each part of the business had its own applications, information, and technical architectures. Cooper thus formed an architecture group, drawing from her applications group, headed by her most senior technology manager and reporting directly to her.

The Business Environment

One of the dilemmas Karen Nocket, chief architect, faced as head of the new group was the shrinking business cycle. In the 1970s and 1980s, Toyota's business cycle was 5 to 7 *years*, thus its IT cycle time could be 3 years. In the 1990s, though, Toyota's business cycle time plummeted to 9 to 12 *months*, so IT's had to shrink likewise, to 6 to 9 months. For 2002 to 2010, Nocket sees the business cycle time shrinking to 3 to 6 months, so IT's

plans must be 1 to 3 months. "How do you optimize 3-month plans into an IT plan?" she asks.

Nocket notes that competitors are addressing the shortened business cycle and other changes in the business environment by emphasizing online sales, moving to shorter delivery times, letting customers configure their own vehicles, and moving toward a "no hassle" sales experience.

Another issue facing the architecture group was IT's approach to building systems the old fashioned way: supporting silos (sales and marketing, parts, accessories, warranty, HR, finance, and so on). Costs were higher because functions were duplicated in numerous systems rather than drawing from common systems.

Creating an Architecture

Nocket's group chose six initial projects: create a first iteration of an enterprise IT architecture, review it, then review development tools, look for infrastructure patterns, create an e-commerce architecture, and work on security.

(Case Continued)

In creating the first iteration, the architecture team quickly discovered that Toyota's most immediate need was a standard, integrated application development environment so that all systems would be developed using the same methodology. Nocket's team chose a methodology that includes tools as well as a development process. The process gives Toyota a way to move from business requirements to IT standards and strategies. This link is important because it helps business folks understand how IT supports them and why an enterprise architecture is important to them.

The architecture group then developed a global reference architecture. This architecture defines the current goal: Toyota's to-be IT architecture. It consists of enterprise services and products that support five tiers of services:

1. *Presentation services*: user interface, Web servers
2. *Application services*: logic specific to a business unit
3. *Business services*: reusable enterprise components
4. *Integration services*: access to legacy data sources; mapping to a common XML structure
5. *Resource services*: data resource managers, relational DBMSs

To develop this to-be architecture, Nocket used her budget to have her group describe the as-is architecture of Toyota's six largest systems. From these six, the group defined Toyota's as-is enterprise architecture. From it, they defined the global to-be architecture.

Nocket and her group have also carefully defined their focus (they do not

build systems), understood the true business benefits of having an architecture (discussed later), and promulgated an architecture-first approach to developing systems.

Nocket has learned that a key to success in IT architecture is having a domain architect for each domain to create the plans to migrate their domain to the to-be architecture and then see that everyone follows the plans. "Having domain architects assigns accountability to a single leader," says Nocket. However, having only technical people on the architecture staff has not fully gotten the message out, so she recently hired a project manager whose job is to foster communication among the numerous parties in a project. "He's our communication link to the world. He brings people together," she says.

Benefits of the Architecture

Through the development and use of the architecture, Nocket and her group have come to understand that the architecture can bring the following kinds of value to Toyota.

Rearchitect Legacy Systems. Both the as-is and to-be architectures have proven valuable in remediating legacy systems. Using a system's as-is architecture, Nocket's group can give business units alternatives to totally replacing a system. Her architects can show, for instance, how the user interface tier is separate from the data and application tiers. Pieces of code can be remediated, for example, by being rewritten in Java, to migrate the legacy system toward the new architecture, leaving the rest of the system as is. One business unit recently accepted this approach to

(Case Continued)

upgrading a major legacy system. The architects are now detailing the as-is architecture to determine which code needs to be replaced. They will then write it to fit the new architecture.

Keep System Designs Robust. Using the new architecture-first approach to building systems, integration between the new system and other systems must be demonstrated in the design stage (rather than uncovered in the final system-integration stage). The new approach forces design breaks in the design phase, where errors can be fixed by redesign. When such errors are not caught until system integration testing, after the system has been built, the only solution is patching, which often destroys the system's original design. The architecture-first approach thus results in a much more coherent and maintainable design, and the architecture risk areas are addressed first, which is the only way to keep an architecture relevant.

Deliver Applications Faster. In understanding the patterns of applications to create the architecture, Nocket and her group are using the patterns to develop new applications much faster because they have turned silo infrastructure elements into services that can be reused. The global reference architecture thus addresses a major business pain point—applications not being delivered fast enough—thereby demonstrating the architecture group's value to both business folks and to IT project teams. To shift to a new development approach, the architecture-first approach, both groups must see the value of an architecture. That value has been devilishly difficult to demonstrate in most companies.

Permit Future Flexibility. Nocket's group has successfully architected Toyota's three e-commerce Web sites—Toyota.com, Lexus. com, and Financial.com—using the "UNIX pattern" in its new architecture. Because the three sites share the same infrastructure, Toyota can easily bring the one hosted outside back in-house, if desired. Furthermore, the company will be able to more easily integrate other systems in the future; for instance, allowing vehicle owners to manage their own vehicle warranty from the Web site.

More recently, IT architects from the three Toyota regions (Europe, North America, and Asia) have worked together to develop a second iteration of the architecture as well as review, as a group, the architecture of two Japanese applications. Nocket believes that the move to standardization and architecture on a global basis, which these two recent efforts demonstrate, will give Toyota a real competitive advantage. ∎

Replace with a Package or Service. In fixing up a house, replacement with a package or a service is akin to realizing that the house no longer works for you, so you move to another house. In IT, many old systems built in-house have been replaced by a package developed by a third party. In fact, this alternative has become the norm. One widely chosen use has been to replace many old and disjointed applications with one corporate-wide system, such as SAP. The other popular option is to distribute an application's workload among a host computer, some servers, and many PCs and laptops. An increasing number of commercial packages permit such three-tiered processing. These packages not only support communication among the three types of machines, but they also split the processing job and facilitate downloading and uploading of files.

Another reason to consider replacing an old system with a commercial package is that packages are becoming more versatile. Many offer selectable features that allow purchasers to tailor the package to their work style. The options can be turned on or off using control files, so no programming is necessary. Even end users can specify some of the operating instructions. Even so, replacing one or more applications with a package is not a trivial task, especially for large systems. Just ask people who have installed an ERP system.

Another option, one being touted as "the future," is to replace a system with a service delivered over the Internet. Now that software vendors have a ubiquitous delivery mechanism—the Internet—they can sell a per-seat, per-month service in place of leasing a package. Companies may reap several benefits from choosing this option. One, the software will be available quickly. Two, the cost can be expensed rather than be a capital expenditure. Three, the software is run and maintained by the vendor. Four, it is centralized in that it is handled by the vendor, but it is distributed in that it can be accessed from anywhere. Companies are even considering creating corporate portals where commonly used software is accessed via the Web rather than housed on PCs. That software can be located anywhere. The promise of Web Services fits in to this replacement option. As an example of replacing a system with a service, consider what Wachovia did.

CASE EXAMPLE

WACHOVIA

Wachovia is a large U.S. bank with headquarters in Charlotte, North Carolina.[12] Its capital management group was growing so fast a few years ago that it outgrew Wachovia's contact management system, which had been written in-house when the sales team was one-third the size.

The system was used by the sales reps to support existing clients and identify and pursue new prospects. But the original programmers had left the bank, so the system was being maintained by consultants. The system did not work with newer bank systems, and it was so inflexible that it did not support the bank's newer sales processes. Furthermore, no one could ensure that remote entries actually updated the database, so the data was not seen as reliable. As a result, the sales force only used the system to record basic customer information once they closed a sale. They used their PDAs and other means—not the system—to keep track of prospects. Hence, the system did not give management the data needed to forecast sales or spot trends that could be useful in setting bank strategy.

(Case Continued)

Management decided to replace the contact management system with a full CRM system with a central repository of real-time data so that the sales reps could manage all their customer dealings online. Management looked at various CRM packages, but found them to be very expensive and time-consuming to implement. At the time, the national sales director happened to see an article in a business magazine about Salesforce.com, which offers a Web-based, pay-by-use CRM system. The director realized that the money he was spending on consultants to keep the old system barely alive would almost cover his use of Salesforce.com. So he opted for it. The system was installed in 6 weeks, which included customizing the service to Wachovia's processes and training all the employees who would use it.

Using the system, the sales reps have at least 30 more hours a month to spend on selling—time they used to spend on administrative work. The system also gives management the data it needs to identify the most valuable clients and its own highest yielding work.

The sales director uses Salesforce.com to coach his salespeople. He reviews their notes about their sales calls to see whether they are using the right approach and following up using the correct strategy. He coaches them on how to improve their approach. And when potential clients have a wide geographic spread, the sales reps can now collaborate on their sales calls. Formerly, they were not able to see who was selling what to whom. Now, they can collaborate and present more valuable combined offerings to their potential clients. ■

Rewrite the System. In fixing up a house, rewriting is akin to realizing the house no longer is appropriate for the family but the location is perfect, so the house is demolished and rebuilt with a new one. In IT, in some cases, a legacy system is too far gone to rescue. If the code is convoluted and patched, if the technology is antiquated, and if the design is poor, it may be necessary to start from scratch. Today, few companies write new applications from scratch. It is just too time-consuming and too expensive. Rewriting a system now means system integration; that is, finding packages that do pieces of the work and then using middleware tools to link them together.

Whether a system is new or a replacement, or anything in between, the question that is always asked is, "What is this system worth to us?" It is a question all executives need to be able to answer because investment in IT has become such a large part of corporate expenditures.

MEASURING THE BENEFITS OF SYSTEMS

Measuring the value of information systems is a continuing request. Never mind that the Internet has changed the world or that e-commerce and e-business are impossible without computers. Executives want specific links between new systems and corporate financial measures, such as increases in revenue, stockholder value, or earnings.

Achieving this link is devilishly difficult because IT is only one of the factors contributing to successful use of systems.

The value of decision support systems and data warehouses, for example, is difficult to measure because they are intended to change such unmeasurable actions as improved decisions, better identification of opportunities, more thorough analysis, and enhanced communication among people. E-commerce systems, which aim to improve a firm's competitive edge or protect its marketshare, also elude measurement. It makes no sense to determine their return on investment (ROI) in terms of hours saved when their intent is to increase revenue or help the firm enter a new market. Finally, infrastructure investments upon which future applications will be built cannot be justified on ROI because they have none. Only the subsequent applications will show a ROI, which has caused the measurement conundrum.

In *Uncovering the Information Technology Payoffs*,[13] Walter Carlson offers the following three suggestions, as well as numerous others, on how to deal with these measurement dilemmas.

1. Distinguish between the different roles of systems.

2. Measure what is important to management.

3. Assess investments across organizational levels.

Distinguish Between the Different Roles of Systems

Paul Berger,[14] a management consultant, believes that companies can measure the value of IT investments by using many of the management measures now in place. Information systems can play three roles in a company, Berger told Carlson.

1. They can help other departments do their job better. Berger calls these "support systems." Their goal is to increase organizational efficiency.

2. IS can carry out a business strategy. Examples are CAD systems that customers and suppliers can use together to design custom products. Web-based systems and other such strategic systems need to be measured differently from support systems because they are used directly by customers, suppliers, and clients; support systems are not.

3. Systems can be sold as a product or service or as the basis for a product or service. Many Web-based information services fall into this category.

The benefits of these three kinds of systems are measured in different ways.

Measuring Organizational Performance.   Organizational performance has to do with meeting deadlines and milestones, operating within budget, and doing quality work. Performance measures the efficiency of operations.

A number of years ago, Berger worked on developing a large HR system with decision support capabilities and then tracking its benefits. To measure the value of the system, the development team compared the productivity of people who used it to the productivity of people who did not. Data was collected on the cost of operating the system and the total costs of running the HR departments.

Operating costs did not rise as fast in the HR department where the system was used, the team found. By the fifth year, the using department had a cost of $103 per work unit (up from $82), whereas the non-using department's cost was $128 per work unit (also up from $82). During those 5 years, the unit costs in the department using the system rose about 25 percent; the non-using department's costs rose more than 56 percent.

Measuring Business Value.   Measuring business unit performance deals with internal operational goals, whereas measuring business value deals with marketplace goals. Systems that are part of a business plan can be measured by their contribution to the success or failure of that plan. However, for systems to be measured on their business value, they must have a direct impact on the company's relationships with its customers, clients, or suppliers, says Berger.

Berger's HR system was measured on departmental performance. It could not be measured on business value because its effect on the corporate bottom line was indirect. No direct link to increased revenue could be identified. This distinction is important in measuring the value of IT investments.

In another firm, several information systems were developed to help marketing people analyze their customer base, both current and potential customers. The goal was to improve the quality of their customer base so that sales per customer would increase, while, at the same time, decreasing sales and promotion costs.

After implementing the systems, advertising and customer service costs did decrease. The company also experienced higher customer retention and lower direct sales costs compared to industry standards. By being able to equate the particular information system expenditures to marketing, they could identify a direct correlation between system costs and sales revenue. They could measure business value. The information systems affected their sales directly through the marketing decisions the system supported, thus the value of the investment could be stated in business terms.

Measuring a Product or Service.   An information system can be offered as a product or service or it can contribute to a product or service intended to produce revenue. In these cases, its value is measured as is any other business venture, by its performance in the market. The measures are typical business profitability measures, such as ROI, return on assets, and return on equity.

Measure What Is Important to Management

Charles Gold,[15] an IT consultant, recommends measuring what management thinks is important. Information systems support can only be linked to corporate effectiveness by finding all the indicators management uses, besides the traditional financial ones. Relating proposed benefits to these indicators can make it easier to sell a system at both the individual and aggregate levels.

Gold suggests trying to assess benefits in terms of customer relations, employee morale, and cycle time or how long it takes to accomplish a complete assignment. Each measure goes beyond monetary terms, which few executives deny are vital to a company's success. He gave Carlson two examples.

As a measure of customer satisfaction, one power company kept a log of how many complaint letters customers sent to the Public Utilities Commission each month; this commission regulates the utility companies within its state. The power company installed a computer system for its customer service representatives, giving them online access to the information they needed to answer customers' questions. When the system was in operation, the number of complaint letters decreased; when the system was down, the number of letters increased. Thus, one aspect of the effectiveness of this system was measurable in terms of public opinion.

A second possible measure is cycle time. Faster cycle times can mean much more than saving hours. It can mean higher-quality products, beating competitors to market, winning a bid, and so on. The benefit may have nothing to do with saving money. Rather, it may focus on making money.

So, says Gold, concentrating only on cost and monetary measures may be shortsighted. Other measures can be even more important to management.

Assess Investments Across Organizational Levels

Kathleen Curley at Lotus Development Corporation and John Henderson at Boston University,[16] recommend measuring IT benefits at several organizational levels. They developed the Value Assessment Framework to do just that.

The Value Assessment Framework.   Potential benefits of IT investments differ at various organizational levels. Curley and Henderson believe that companies need a systematic way to separate these benefits by organizational level. They see three organizational levels, or sources of value, as benefiting from IT investments: the individual, the division, and the corporation. Furthermore, the impact focus of an IT investment extends beyond business performance measures to encompass three dimensions:

1. Economic performance payoffs (market measures of performance)
2. Organizational processes impacts (measures of process change)
3. Technology impacts (impacts on key functionality)

Combining the two views creates a 3×3 matrix that can be used to systematically assess the impact of a potential IT investment in nine areas. This framework was used by a trucking company, and its use uncovered benefits that otherwise would have gone unrealized.

CASE EXAMPLE

A TRUCKING COMPANY

A medium-size company in the refrigerated carrier business has been around since the 1920s. When the Motor Carrier Act deregulated trucking companies, competition increased. Midsize truckers like this one were hit the hardest. Even though it had been one of the top five refrigeration trucking firms, its share of shipped tons fell to less than one-half the former level because national and regional carriers took away its business. In response to the crisis, management made two decisions: First, they would manage the company by information, transforming company procedures and tracking success via a large suite of

(*Case Continued*)

measures. Second, management would use IT to differentiate the firm from other refrigeration trucking firms, initially with a $10-million investment in a state-of-the-art satellite system and a computer in every truck cab so that drivers could be in constant voice and data communication with the company and customers.

The results were remarkable. Tons shipped increased from 300,000 tons to 1,100,000 tons, and the trucker became an industry leader in the innovative manipulation of information. It introduced groundbreaking information services that provided superior levels of customer service.

Their Measurement Program

On the measurement front, the company developed world-class goals for each of its three mission statement objectives:

Our mission is to exceed the expectations of our customers, earn a return on investment that is the best in the industry, and provide our employees an opportunity to attain fulfillment through participation.

Overall performance was measured in three ways:

1. *Customer satisfaction*—determined by "moment of truth" questionnaires filled out by customers to rate the company's service performance
2. *Return on investment*—measured by an operating ratio
3. *Employee satisfaction*—from questionnaires that captured employee sentiments and charted them on an index

The company established interim performance improvement goals for the company as a whole and for each department to be achieved by specific dates. These interim measures were to see how fast and how well it was progressing toward its world-class goals. As performance improved, the goals were raised so that performance improvement was built into its measurement system.

After studying its measurement and tracking processes, Curley said, "They have one of the most detailed sets of measures I have ever seen."

Measuring the Value of the Satellite System

Following IBM Consulting's recommendation, the trucker used the Curley and Henderson Value Management Framework to evaluate the satellite investment after-the-fact, with eye-opening results. The trucker began by identifying the specific process improvements made possible by the system, entering them into the framework along with an outcome and outcome measure for each one.

- *At the individual level*, the company estimated that improved communications from the truck cab would increase driver production time by one-half hour a day. The result: a savings of $59.60 a month per driver.

- *At the work group level*, it estimated that improved truck-to-load or vice versa matching would save 1 percent deadhead time: a $49.68 savings per month per truck.

- *At the business unit level*, it estimated that improved customer service would increase marketshare,

(Case Continued)

but it could not pin down a dollar amount for this increase.

Once these figures were calculated, a manager was assigned to assess the savings targets, allowing the company to evaluate whether it was realistically estimating the investment. It intended to manage the value it was receiving from its investment, not just make the investment and hope it paid off.

The most interesting piece of the Value Management Framework analysis, Curley said, was not the identifiable cost savings, but the large, unexpected revenue benefits. Due to the analysis, management discovered that customers were willing to pay a premium price for the ability to call a truck driver directly from their warehouse. Constant communication with drivers was worth a lot—much more than management thought. This discovery gave management even more confidence in their decision to bet on technology and in their ability to sell information-based services. Due to the sophisticated and ingrained measurement system, management was even able to see the effect of pricing on marketshare. ■

Do Investors Value IT Investments?

An even more intriguing question than how business executives value IT investments is how investors value IT investments. As reported in the recent Gartner EXP report *Getting Shareholder Credit for IT* by Andrew Rowsell-Jones and Marcus Blosch,[11b] three researchers recently performed a study to see whether or not a company's stock market valuation correlated with the size of its computer investments and with its organizational practices. Their results show that investors do indeed value IT investments.

Erik Brynjolfsson of MIT's Sloan School of Management, Lorin Hitt of University of Pennsylvania's Wharton School, and Shinkyu Yang of New York University's Stern School[17] found that every $1 of "installed computer capital" yielded up to $17 in stock market value, and no less than $5. Whereas, $1 in property, plant, and equipment (book value) only yielded $1 in stock market value; and $1 in other assets (inventory, liquid assets, and accounts receivables) yielded only 70 cents.

The researchers reason that investors value $1 spent on "installed computer capital" more than the other investments because it leads to organizational changes that create $16 worth of "intangible assets"—know-how, skills, organizational structures, and such.

To reach these conclusions, the three researchers compared 8 years' worth of stock market data for *Fortune* 1000 companies between 1987 and 1994 (importantly, before the dot-com bubble) with these firms' IT investments and organizational practices (from studies in 1995 and 1996). They were able to correlate all three kinds of data for 250 companies, with a total of 1,707 observations.

They found that variations between companies were more important than variations over time in the same company. Firm-specific factors accounted for most of the firms' higher market values.

Past IT investments correlated with higher current market value, but not vice versa. The reasoning is that firms continue to build up complementary intangible assets from these IT investments, say Brynjolfsson, Hitt, and Shinkyu; investors value these additional assets.

Earlier research by Brynjolfsson and Hitt showed that four organizational factors correlate to and complement IT investments: (1) use of teams and related incentives, (2) individual decision-making authority, (3) investments in skills and education, and (4) team-based initiatives. They found that firms making the highest IT investments not only invest in the information systems but also invest in making organizational changes to complement the new systems.

These investments in "organizational capital" generally lead to the adoption of decentralized work practices. The firms (1) use teams more often, (2) give employees broader decision-making authority, and (3) offer more employee training, no matter the size or industry of the firm.

In the latest study, the three researchers found that firms with these three decentralized work practices had a market value 8 percent higher than the mean. They state, "Investors appear to treat organizational capital much like more tangible types of capital by recognizing its contribution to the market value of a firm."

Furthermore, the researchers found that the companies with the highest market valuations; in fact, disproportionately higher than their *Fortune*-1000 peers, had both the largest IT investments *and* decentralized work practices. Investors drove up their stock price more than firms with smaller IT spends and centralized work practices.

They conclude that the market value of investing in IT is "substantially higher" in firms that use these decentralized practices because each dollar of IT investment is associated with more intangible assets because the IT investments complement the work practices. Centralized, low-skill firms do not reap as much increase in intangible assets from their IT investments as team-oriented, high-skilled, decentralized-responsibility firms.

Investors apparently sense that investments in training, organizational structures, and work practices create new assets. Even if intangible, these assets will contribute to higher firm performance in the future, hence higher stock prices today. Yet investors cannot see these intangible assets directly; they can only surmise them through "installed computer capital," hence the link between IT investments and stock price.

CONCLUSION

Managing projects has always been one of the most important, and toughest, jobs in the IS organization. Even with outsourcing and software packages, project management belongs in-house because responsibility for project success remains in-house. In fact, project management skills have grown more important because of the complexity of integrating systems and the need to assess who does and does not support the project, to turn non-supporters into supporters, and to guide the organization in making the needed changes in business processes and work. As shown in this chapter, managing a project requires a plethora of skills. This is one reason CIOs are now emphasizing project management skills in their staff.

Most software is devilishly difficult to keep up-to-date. As a result, at some point in time, management needs to decide what to do with aging software. Among the various options, the most common these days is to replace it with a package. One new alternative is to rearchitect the system to move the company toward a desired to-be architecture.

Another new option is to rent the software from a vendor on a per-seat, per-month basis over the Web. Some contend this option is the wave of the future.

Finally, the question continually asked about applications is, "What is it worth to us?" Because IT is not the only contributor to corporate operational improvements, a direct link can be difficult to establish. However, the process of justifying a new system can uncover what is important to management, and measuring benefits afterward can help companies spot benefits they had not originally planned. Furthermore, even though investors cannot see how well or poorly public companies invest in IT, they do more highly value companies with higher IT investments and more distributed work practices. Thus, the value-of-IT question is gradually being answered.

QUESTIONS AND EXERCISES

Review Questions

1. What three businesses is the IS department in, using Hagel and Singer's framework?
2. According to the Project Management Institute, what are the nine areas of knowledge a project manager needs to know well to successfully manage a project?
3. What are the six things a project manager needs to do, according to Anderson and Matthew?
4. When Cone is interviewing people, what three things does he keep an ear open for?
5. Describe three tools in Cone's project manager's toolbox.
6. Describe the three types of people involved in a change project, according to ODR.
7. How did BOC Group involve middle management?
8. Describe the decision tree that Gibson uses to assess the business risk of a project.
9. Which does the Boston Consulting Group recommend, replacing or upgrading a legacy system?
10. List the seven ways to improve a legacy system.
11. How is Amazon.com promoting third-party Web Services offerings that relate to Amazon.com's Web site?
12. What four benefits does IT architecture bring Toyota Motor Sales?
13. How does Wachovia benefit by replacing a system with a service?
14. What are the three roles of systems, according to Berger?
15. What benefits did the trucking company realize at the individual, group, and business levels?
16. What three decentralized work practices were found at companies with higher market valuation in research by Brynjolfsson, Hitt, and Yang?

Discussion Questions

1. IS staffing should become easier as more people gain experience in e-business or move from failed dot-coms. Do you agree or disagree? Discuss.
2. If companies are moving toward providing corporate portals and Web Services where software is rented from a third party over the Internet, IS departments can get out of the application development business. Do you agree or disagree? Discuss.

3. The strategy of minimum maintenance until a system must be completely redone is still best for challenging and developing the programmer/analyst staff. The few people that like nitty-gritty maintenance activities can take care of the programs that need it, while the majority of the development staff can be challenged by the creativity of new development. The seven options turn most developers into maintenance programmers. Do you agree or disagree? Discuss.

4. Management has no way to estimate the benefit of a system that is intended to generate new revenue, so it must build the system on faith, not estimates. Do you agree or disagree? Discuss.

Exercises

1. In April 2004, Cone's content management project had issued an RFP and was waiting for proposals to arrive. Please visit his blog at blogs.ittoolbox.com/pm/implementation and answer the following four questions: (1) What has happened since then on that project? (2) What problems did Cone encounter? (3) How did he solve them? (4) What did you learn from this blog?

2. Find three articles on IS departments that have established a project management office (PMO). Why did they establish a PMO? How is each staffed? What benefits did the PMO generate? What did you find most interesting about the PMOs?

3. Find a company in your community with more than 20 years' experience using computer systems. Develop a descriptive case study for that company showing how it deals with its legacy systems. Include an inventory of major systems and the company's strategies for maintenance and modernization. How does the company decide which applications to upgrade and which approaches to use? Explain how top management and line management get involved in application portfolio decisions. If they do not, why not?

4. Use the Gibson decision tree to assess the business risks of a project you are involved in or know a great deal about. Present your assessment to the class. What are the three main risk factors in the project? Describe which ones support success and which do not. Based on his decision tree, which project management approach should you use? What have you learned from this analysis?

REFERENCES

1. Hagel, John, III, and Marc Singer, "Unbundling the Corporation," *Harvard Business Review*, March/April 1999, pp. 133–141.

2. Matthew, Michael, "IT Project Management: The Good, the Bad, and the Ugly," Matthew & Matthew, November 2000. Available at www.gacc.mq.edu.au/units/accg812. Accessed May 2004.

3. The Project Management Institute's latest guide for project managers, *Guide to the Project Management Body of Knowledge* (PMBOK, 2000 Edition), can be ordered from its Web site (www.pmi.org).

4. Anderson, Craig, and Michael Matthew, "Project Management—A Way of Life," KPMG and Matthew & Matthew, March 11, 2004. Available at www.gacc.mq.edu.au/units/accg812. Accessed May 2004.

5. Cone, Larry, "A Day in the Life of a Project Manager," ITToolbox. Available at blogs.ittoolbox.com/pm/implementation/. Accessed June 2004. Reprinted with

permission of Information Technology Toolbox, Inc.

6. Communications with ODR, 2900 Chamblee-Tucker Road, Building 16, Atlanta, GA, 30341.

7. Farmer, Neil, *Changes in Our Times*, Wentworth Management Program (now part of Gartner EXP, Stamford, CT), May 1999.

8. Gibson, Cyrus, "IT-Enabled Business Change: An Approach to Understanding and Managing Risk," *MIS Quarterly Executive*, Vol. 2, No. 2, 2003, pp. 104–115.

9. Kiely, Thomas, "Computer Legacy Systems: What Works When They Don't?" *Harvard Business Review*, July/August 1996, pp. 10–12.

10. Salkever, Alex, "How Amazon Opens Up and Cleans Up," *Business Week Online*, June 24, 2003. Available at www.businessweek.com/print/technology/content/jun2003/tc20030624_9735_tc113.htm. Accessed March 2004.

11. Gartner EXP, 56 Top Gallant, Stamford, CT, 06904; www.gartner.com:
    a. Woolfe, Roger, and Marcus Blosch, *Architecture Matters*, July 2002.
    b. Rowsell-Jones, Andrew, and Marcus Blosch, *Getting Shareholder Credit for IT*, July 2002.

12. Salesforce.com, "Case Study: Wachovia." Available at www.salesforce.com/us/customers/casestudy.jsp?customer=wachovia. Accessed March 2004.

13. Carlson, Walter, and Barbara McNurlin, *Uncovering the Information Technology Payoffs*, *I/S Analyzer*, Fall 1992.

14. Correspondence with Paul Berger of Paul Berger Consulting, Inc., Lawrenceville, NJ.

15. Correspondence with Charles Gold of West Cornwall, CT, 1992.

16. Curley, Kathleen, and John Henderson, "Assessing the Value of a Corporatewide Human Resource Information System: A Case Study," *Journal of Management Information Systems*, Special Issue, 1992, pp. 45–60.

17. Brynjolfsson, Erik, Lorin Hitt, and Shinkyu Yang, "Intangible Assets: How the Interaction of Computers and Organizational Structure Affects Stock Market Valuations," 2002. Available at grace.wharton.upenn.edu/~lhitt/itqo.pdf. Accessed March 2003.

PART III
DISCUSSION CASE

A DREAM PROJECT TURNS NIGHTMARE: HOW FLAWLESS SOFTWARE NEVER GOT IMPLEMENTED

Vital Roy
HEC Montreal, Canada

Benoit A. Aubert
HEC Montreal, Canada

EXECUTIVE SUMMARY

It was in 1996 that Integra,[1] a large Canadian life insurance institution, launched its Banking and Loan Insurance Software System (BLISS) development project with the aim of gaining access to the loan insurance market in small credit unions (CUs) across Canada. The company was ready to provide the system free of charge to the CUs on the provision that they commercialize exclusively Integra's loan insurance products. To achieve this goal, Integra entered into a partnership with Intex Consulting, the Canadian subsidiary of a large international information system (IS) integration firm who wanted to gain a foothold in the Canadian banking business. After 1.3 million dollars of investment from each partner and 12 months of intensive efforts, the project came to an abrupt stop. The lessons learned in this case study include: (1) the importance of understanding requirements beyond micro-level user needs, (2) the need to get the enlightened involvement of each interested party in a large complex project, (3) the importance of appraising the specific contribution of each partner in a strategic alliance, and (4) the obstacles faced when entering an unfamiliar market with a new, unproven IS product.

BACKGROUND

The Integra Financial Corporation is a holding company active through its subsidiaries in life insurance, general insurance, trust services, and securities brokerage, as well as asset and portfolio management. Operating mainly in the province of Quebec (Canada), Integra manages assets in the order of 8 billion dollars and a work force of more than 2,200 permanent employees. Integra's life operations rank among the seven largest in Canada in terms of written premium.[2]

(Case Continued)

One of Integra's most successful products (its *'cash cow'* in the words of the CEO) is its Loan and Mortgage Insurance Plan, developed in the early 1980s. With more than 2 million insured loans, this program is one of the largest group insurance plans of its kind in Canada. Commercialized exclusively through financial institutions in the province of Quebec, this product is totally integrated with the banking systems of the participating institutions. Thus, when a loan application is accepted at one of these institutions, the loan officer can offer his client, on the spot, an insurance policy to cover his or her loan. In return, the participating institution receives a percentage of the premium for its efforts.

This capability is available because the banking systems of the institutions are electronically linked to Integra's insurance management systems. These systems automatically determine the risk exposure of the loan and establish the premium to charge for the insurance coverage. Rates are calculated as a function of the balance due on the loan. In other words, the premium declines with each installment applied to the loan. Thus, the client pays an equitable premium for the real financial risk that his loan represents. For example, if the agreed rate of interest charged on the loan is 6.23 percent and the life insurance premium is set at 0.07 percent of the loan, then the actual combined rate will be 6.3 percent of the outstanding debt. Based on a broad experience in the loan insurance market and a huge database accumulating data since 1984, Integra's actuaries have been able to develop a very proficient risk evaluation algorithm. This algorithm enables the institution to offer an insurance product with practically no exclusions (no more than 1 percent of all cases are excluded) applying to any particular field of work or the practice of dangerous sports, thus greatly simplifying the administration and lowering the operating costs of the product. Few, if any, of its competitors had attained this level of sophistication.

According to Integra's management, these hard-to-replicate characteristics gave the firm a persistent competitive advantage over other loan insurance offerings since, as of late 1996, the competition could only offer fixed (and much higher) rates based on the total amount of the loan and had to charge termination penalties when their clients reimbursed their loans ahead of time.

SETTING THE STATE

Although Integra's Loan and Mortgage Insurance product proved to be a huge success in the province of Quebec, the company faced major impediments in its quest to commercialize its leading product in the rest of Canada. One reason for this difficulty is that the Canadian banking sector is fragmented along two basic modes of organization. In the first mode, which comprises the majority of the large financial institutions, banks operate under a federal charter. This charter gives the participating institution the right to operate anywhere in Canada, whereas a provincial charter grants access only to the provincial territory. Most of the small institutions, including the credit unions, operate under provincial jurisdictions. Historically, and for cultural and political reasons, those small financial institutions have tended to structure themselves into very divergent configurations within each province, and the banking infrastructure of each sector differs somewhat. Whereas in the province

(Case Continued)

of Quebec, the credit unions tend to be lightly integrated into large federations and use standardized central banking systems, their counterpart in the other Canadian provinces make do with a bewildering array of banking systems operated at the local or regional levels. As for loan insurance, the CanCoop Life Group, which markets a portfolio of insurance and other non-financial services to Canadian financial cooperatives CUs, and their members, covers most of the loan insurance needs of the CUs. A consortium of companies, including the Credit Union Centrals from each region, a private Canadian insurance company, and one U.S. insurance syndicate, own the CanCoop Group. Thus, because of the diversity of the market in the rest of Canada and the very tightly integrated nature of its own systems in the Quebec market, Integra lacked the means to link the banking systems of those institutions to its loan insurance systems. The company was thus effectively locked out from the loan insurance business in the Canadian market outside the Province of Quebec.

Meanwhile, Intex Consulting, which had developed a widely acknowledged expertise in the U.S. banking industry as an integrator and system developer, had been looking for an efficient channel to penetrate the Canadian banking sector. Informal contacts between Integra's IT executives and Intex Consulting representatives at an IS/IT convention in Las Vegas in December 1995 opened the door for a possible cooperation between the two firms. Indeed, Michael Bricino, Integra's CIO, and Carl Gagnon, a senior project manager, came back from that meeting convinced that Integra had the opportunity for a breakthrough in the Canadian market, provided it could join forces with a competent and resourceful

IT partner. Upon their return to Integra, the two IT managers made a forceful presentation to the First Vice President for Product Development. In essence, their argument was that "We have a good product; we have the best product! Everybody in the Province of Quebec buys it, the Credit Unions will buy it and the consumers will buy it."[3] They believed the loan insurance industry was clearly waiting for such a solution, and that the profitability of the project would far exceed any other project that the organization had ever undertaken.

The First Vice President for Product Development promptly assembled an advisory committee[4] for the project. Apart from the first V.P. for Product Development, this committee was composed of the President, the First V.P. for Finance, the V.P. for Actuarial and Corporate Services, and the CIO.

The pressing issue, according to Bricino, was the development of an appropriate technology solution to interface Integra's loan insurance systems with its prospective clients' banking and loan systems. If the company could effectively develop a compatible solution, then the CUs would most certainly jump on the occasion and join Integra. In fact, as stated in a white paper circulated within the organization at that time, Integra envisioned itself in the role of a commercial software developer. "In the same manner as a producer of high volume commercial software, [with the BLISS project] Integra will become a supplier of a software package specializing in the management and the support of insurance products in Canada and even in all of North America." The ultimate goal was to provide for the insurance needs of the more than 1,200 CUs and other cooperative institutions throughout Canada. Here was an

(Case Continued)

opportunity to easily double Integra's marketshare in the loan insurance market.

For Donald Lapierre, Integra's president, this strategic opportunity proved to be irresistible, and the committee enthusiastically bought into the project. For the members of the new committee, collaborating with Intex Consulting in the venture appeared to be the obvious thing to do, given the complementary nature of each firm's respective competencies and their convergent business interests. On one hand, Integra brought to the table a long and very successful experience in the loan insurance business. Furthermore, it had a winning product to commercialize. Conversely, Intex Consulting had a proven loan system to offer and brought along impeccable credentials as an information systems integrator.

CASE DESCRIPTION

On February 20, 1996, Integra signed a partnership agreement with Intex Consulting for the development and implementation of BLISS. According to this agreement, Intex would assume the development of the loan system and interface it with both the Integra's insurance systems and the CUs' banking systems in a client-server configuration. Furthermore, Intex would have the responsibility to implement the new system in each participating CU and offer technical support thereafter both at the CU level and at Integra's level. For its part, Integra would assume responsibility for developing the client-side loan insurance module (InsurCalc), which would be integrated into Intex's loan system. Integra also had the responsibility to assemble a User Group composed of CUs' representatives and functional managers from Integra.

In forming this group, managers from Integra felt confident that they could avoid misspecifying the system. User participation has been advocated for in the IS literature for a long time (Tait & Vossy, 1988). Finally, the company had the responsibility of testing both the loan and the insurance modules of the application, finding suitable pilot sites, and commercializing the new system in Canada. The business flow diagram depicted in Figure PC3-1 puts into perspective the general architecture of the proposed system.

Once implemented in a CU, the system would permit the origination or the renewal of a loan in the banking system of the institution. Simultaneously, the system would initiate the process of risk evaluation and insurance costing for that particular loan by automatically assessing the client's financial background through the link with the credit bureau, and validating the transaction through the Personal Property Securities Register Service (PPSR). Finally, with the client's consent and under certain actuarial considerations, the system would compute the premium to be charged for this particular insurance coverage, which would then be incorporated in the monthly reimbursement calculations of the loan. In short, the BLISS system would offer the CUs the same functionalities as those already available to the Quebec institutions and which had proved to be such a commercial success.

Roles and Responsibilities of Each Partner

With an annual IT operating budget of nearly 8 million dollars, Integra's IT function has ample experience with IS project management. Over the years, IT management had put into place rigorous project management techniques, which

(Case Continued)

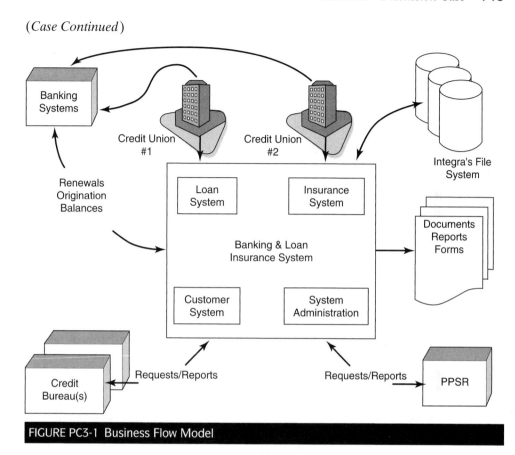

FIGURE PC3-1 Business Flow Model

contributed to the successful realization of large and complex IS projects. The company was also confident that Intex Consulting possessed the know-how to effectively develop and implement the new system in the CU branches. A steering Committee, composed of a very select group of senior executives, was assembled (see Appendix A for an overview of the project organization chart). Because of the high strategic potential of the project, it was felt that the venture had to be managed under very stringent security controls. Thus, apart from the project personnel and a few senior executives, only a handful of people at Integra knew in any detail the content and the scope of the project. For

these same "obvious" reasons, it was decided that project planning could be put on a fast-track mode, thus bypassing the standard risk management and feasibility studies and the political and economic impact studies of the new system for the prospective clients. That decision would eventually prove to be ill-advised, as later events would clearly demonstrate.[5]

For its part, Intex Consulting focused almost exclusively on the technical aspects of the project, relying on Integra's experience and know-how in the loan insurance market for the application design and functionality specifications. The partners laid out everything to ensure the prompt development of an adequate solution:

(Case Continued)

assigning a high priority status to the project; doing a thorough assessment of the integration requirements for the insurance, loan, and banking systems; ensuring a tight coordination of the project by a coordination committee composed of the project director (Carl Gagnon), the business project leader (Stephanie Lemaire), the development team leader (Judith Tremblay), and Intex Consulting's project manager (Tom Delany).[6] The development effort was subdivided between two teams. The first one, headed by Integra's Judith Tremblay, worked on the loan insurance module to be integrated into Intex' loan systems and on diverse interface modules to link up the BLISS system and Integra's back-office insurance systems.

IT managers felt that they were clearly aligned with the organization business strategy and that they had the indefectible support of higher management. They also had a partner with exceptional technical abilities. Even while acknowledging that the project could present a certain level of risk, they assumed they were in what many would consider an ideal situation for successful project development.

The development group worked in close cooperation with the business group. Their task consisted mainly in circumscribing the detailed business requirements for the client side of the insurance module. The definition of the interfaces with outside agencies, such as the PPSR, and with Integra's own internal business systems and data repositories also required extensive efforts. The second team, staffed with Intex's personnel, worked on the adaptation the Canadian CUs' context of the loan and banking systems developed for the U.S. market. Due to the wide variety of circumstances amongst the prospective institutions, the new system had to be flexible, bilingual, modular, and capable of running on multiple platforms such as OS2, Unix, and Windows NT (see Appendix B for a more detailed description of the diverse mix of platforms encountered in the project).

To limit the possibility of competitive intelligence leaks, both partners opted to deal with the implementation details of the project at a later time, when the preliminary tests would be completed and the application would be ready for deployment. To that end, the project plan called for the formation of a User Group composed of seven representatives from local CU branches across Canada. The main responsibilities of this group were to participate in the needs and processes revisions; produce the basic business documents; give feedback on functionalities, screens, forms and reports; validate Integra's added-value components; and participate in the BLISS integration tests.

At the technological level, the targeted institutions were using a rather disparate IT technological infrastructure. The hardware and the applications varied from region to region, from group to group, and often even within a particular institution (see Appendix C). Opportunity studies carried out by Integra revealed that those institutions used at least 10 different technological platforms. In this context, the BLISS project, as conceived originally, consisted in developing a software solution that could be implemented at those institutions with a minimum of personalization while aiming to support the widest variety of existing IT already in place. The total development cost of the project topped 2.5 million dollars. Half of this amount (1.3 million dollars) came from Intex Consulting and the other half came from Integra in the form of wages for Integra's personnel (15 managerial staff,

(Case Continued)

$1^1/2$ years). The project officially started in January 1996 and ended 1 year later, in March 1997. See Table PC3-1.

Roles and Responsibilities of Each Partner in the Implementation Phase

With regard to the eventual deployment and exploitation of the new system, as explained by Integra's CIO, both partners signed an agreement delimiting each other's responsibilities and participation in the future benefits from the project. Under the terms of this contract, Intex Consulting obtained the exclusive rights to commercialize the new system in the U.S. market. It also had the rights to commercialize it in the Canadian market, but only when authorized by Integra on a client-by-client basis. In both cases, Integra would be entitled to royalties on each sale.

We signed an agreement of joint ownership on the software. Roughly speaking, in the end, we kept the ownership of the system. If, for some reason, we decided to give it to a financial institution that bought our products, we could give it for free. Actually, this is what we wanted from the start. If they [Intex Consulting] found to sell the software outside of our territory [in the U.S.], there were also contractual clauses which bind us and which applied. They could approach a customer on their own and sell the software: They were joint owners. That could create enticements for our insurance products in communities outside of our reach.

Unfolding of the Project

In late December 1995, senior management approved the formation of the Steering Committee and allocated the necessary funds to launch the project. Carl Gagnon immediately set out for the task of assembling the coordination committee. He was given license in choosing the best internal resources available in

TABLE PC3-1 Time Line of Project	
Dec. 15, 1995	Possibility of partnering in a joint IS project is broached with Intex representatives
Dec. 21, 1995	Steering committee formed
Jan. 11, 1996	Coordination committee is created
Jan. 29, 1996	Project is presented to selected CU representatives
Feb. 6, 1996	Signature of partnership agreement with Intex
Feb. 29, 1996	Preliminary list of work requirements submitted
March 21, 1996	Prototype level I completed
May 3, 1996	InsurCalc module completed (basic)
July 10, 1996	Needs and processes revision completed
Aug. 23, 1996	A new coordination committee director is nominated
Aug. 29, 1996	Prototype level II completed
Aug. 30, 1996	Banking system modifications completed
Sept. 13, 1996	Start of preliminary activities for BLISS implementation in CUs
Dec. 13, 1996	Added-value development completed
Dec. 13, 1996	Prototype level III completed
Jan. 13, 1997	Project is put on hold indefinitely

(Case Continued)

the persons of Stephanie Lemaire as the business project leader and Judith Tremblay as head of the internal development team. Both managers had extensive experience with Integra's business processes and its supporting information systems and had participated in several highly successful IS projects before.

The project was subdivided into 10 main tasks (Table PC3-2), and the roles and responsibilities for each one of them were apportioned to the concerned parties. One of the first tasks of the project team was to assess the needs and processes revision mandated by the project. The first few weeks were thus spent analyzing the implications of extracting the relevant functionalities of the existing loan insurance module and adapting them to the BLISS context.

Efforts were also spent in the creation of a User Group composed of CU's representatives that would participate in the project. In all, seven CUs from New

Brunswick (1), Ontario (1), Manitoba (1), Saskatchewan (2), and British Columbia (2) accepted to collaborate. Their contribution essentially consisted in individual working sessions at the respondent's premises with representatives of the development team. During those sessions, the development team attempted to assess the functional specifications of the future system from the point of view of each participating institution. By the end of February 1996, a preliminary list of work requirements was compiled and presented to the steering committee for approval. These were approved within the following 2 weeks, allowing the team to start work on a first version of the prototype. In rapid succession, Integra's development team was able to deliver a Prototype level I, and on May 3, the basic functionalities of the InsurCalc module that would eventually be incorporated in the banking module developed by the Intex team.

TABLE PC3-2 Participants' Responsibilities and Major Milestone Schedule			
Task	*Responsibility*	*Participation*	*Milestone Schedule*
Needs and processes revision	Integra	Intex	June 1996
Development of insurance application (InsurCalc Module)	Integra	Intex/CU	May 1996
Development of loan application	Intex	Integra/CU	July 1996
IT infrastructure adaptation			August 1996
• Recommendations	Intex	Integra/CU	
• Acquisitions	CU	Integra/Intex	
• Implementation	CU	Integra/Intex	
Development of value-added components	Integra	Intex/CU	September 1996
Banking system modifications	CU	Intex/Integra	September 1996
Final system tests	Integra/CU	Intex	September 1996
Training	Integra	Intex/CU	October 1996
Implementation	Intex	Integra/CU	November 1996
Support, Help desk	Integra	Intex/CU	November 1996

(Case Continued)

Meanwhile, work on the completion of the needs and processes revision task proceeded rather haltingly. For one thing, it was found that interfacing Integra's file systems was a greater challenge than anticipated. There were actually more than 80 different legacy file systems (hosted on MVS and VSE/ESA platforms) to integrate in the new BLISS system. At least 15 of these systems were in service since the 1980s and were slated for major revisions in light of the Year 2000 deadline. Further complicating the process the business project team insisted in adding what they termed "value-added components" on top of all the standard utilities already implemented in the existing insurance system. From their point of view, the new system imperatively had to offer sophisticated customization and auditing tools, a flexible report generator, and a complete online help file in order to favorably reflect Integra's high standards of excellence and quality. All these requirements had to fit in a system small enough and efficient enough to operate in a microcomputer-based client-server configuration suitable for the smaller CUs.

On the CU side of the project, the collaboration with the CUs' representatives did not unfold exactly as planned either. According to the original plans, each CU was to assign a loan officer for the project duration (approximately a 55 person-days effort for needs and processes revision and a 70 to 90 person-days effort for tests and implementation). Of the seven original CUs who had participated in the first round of meetings in February 1996, only three remained more or less active by the end of June 1996. Even with such a reduced input, the development teams nonetheless managed to complete the requirements and process revision report, which was presented to the coordination committee in time for their bimonthly meeting on July 10, 1996.

Carl Gagnon ascribed the lack of CUs' participation to the fact that he had had little time to spare to cultivate his contacts with the participating CUs. As he explained to the steering committee, most of his efforts were now devoted to coordinating the development teams from each company and to resolving numerous technical and organizational problems stemming from the fusion of two complex systems developed in very different organizational and business contexts. He felt that the business requirements were now clearly circumscribed, and that only the technical issues were left to resolve. Therefore, the reduced participation of the User Group was not to be perceived as a major problem.

Moreover, Gagnon confided that he felt slightly overwhelmed by the task at hand. He suggested that his time could be better spent at the helm of the project rather than being dispersed as both the project director and the head of the coordination committee. The committee members acquiesced to his request and nominated the newly designated V.P. for Product Development, Jim Cochran, to take charge of the coordination committee upon his return from the summer vacations in mid-August.

Cochran was a new player in the project; up to that point, he had not been directly involved in the project.

The BLISS system, when I inherited the project in August 1996, was already on hand and it had been.... Its development program, the contracts with Intex had been negotiated and signed before I arrived at the vice-presidency. My predecessor and the

(Case Continued)

management teams in place before that had been absolutely convinced that, in order to sell the loan-insurance product in the Credit Unions network in Canada, it was imperative to develop this information system tool, that the two were inseparable.

Cochran had long experience in dealing with financial institutions outside the Province of Quebec, having been in charge of the commercialization for Integra of various travel insurance products across Canada. He felt quite comfortable in his new role as an intermediary between Integra and the prospective pool of clients for the new BLISS system. The first clear sign that something was seriously amiss with the project materialized when, in September 1996, the marketing team returned from a field trip empty-handed. Although the CUs' managers generally expressed a genuine interest in the new system, they seemed somewhat reluctant to commit themselves in any meaningful way to the project. This initial disquieting perception crystallized when, a few weeks later, at the end of the development phase, the project managers tried to enlist pilot sites to field test the new system. As reported by Jim Cochran, the project seemed to hit a brick wall: "How many do you think that I [have] sold? I have . . . even when we offered them the system for free, not a single one wanted to become a test site, not even those that had participated in the User Group. They didn't want any part of it!"

Integra's management speedily set up a crisis management group whose primary task was to find what had happened and what corrective actions could be undertaken, if any, to bring the project to completion. Jim Cochran was designated to lead this effort. As explained by Cochran, the first order of the day for the task group was to go back to the CUs and investigate why they had apparently changed their mind on the project.

From then on, I decided we should go up the chain [of the Credit Unions]. I found resistance at the Credit Union level, with all the excuses that came with it. I went up to the regional level, and I still had resistance, but with better excuses. I went all the way up to the National Central where I was squarely laughed at. The CanCoop representative said to me: "Put an ax on this project! Do you want to destroy us? You are asking the Credit Unions to autodestruct themselves. It is plain nonsense!"

To their astonishment, the coordination committee members learned that these high-level executives had never been consulted by the project management group and, therefore, had not had any input on the project. The requirements analysis had been conducted exclusively at the CU level without ever taking into consideration the larger business context of these institutions and their affiliation to regional centrals. Typically, Carl Gagnon and another member of the coordination committee (either Stephanie Lemaire or Judith Tremblay) would meet with some junior executive or a loan officer of the CU branch to discuss the technical aspects of the proposed system. Although the requirements were technically sound and the system design filled the specific needs of the branches, surprises were to be expected when considering the larger institutional picture. At no point in the analysis process did it occur to the project sponsors that both the individual CUs and their Centrals had financial

(Case Continued)

stakes in the CanCoop Group and that a switch to Integra's products might pose some problems.

As was later discovered by Cochran's team, each CU, each Regional Central, and the National Central owned a significant part of this insurance firm, and therefore had good reasons to keep doing business with it.

The problem was that we were asking potential clients to turn their back on a product with which they were comfortable, which generated important incomes for them, which contributed to the development of their insurance company, which generated profits for their provincial Central, which provided them with services, and which generated income for their National Central.

Understandably, the CU Centrals' managers were not very enthusiastic about the idea of having "outsiders" trampling on what they considered as their own territorial business relationships with the CUs.

In hindsight, the task group realized the even if the new system had been offered free of charge, its installation still mandated relatively major investments in network infrastructures and computer equipment for the small CUs, ranging from 100 thousand dollars to more than one million dollars per site. More fundamentally, the Centrals would have considered as treasonous the active participation of any of their institutions in the project. In fact, the adhesion of the CUs to the BLISS project would have meant a gradual weakening of the financial position of their respective Centrals, because a significant part of their financing came from the profits generated by their participation in the CanCoop. Project planning totally overlooked this

aspect and it came as a complete surprise to the project managers.

At the end of the fact-finding mission, in January 1997, Jim Cochran knew the CUs would never implement the BLISS system in its present form, "My boss Donald Lapierre could very well see for himself that this project had been sold quite efficiently by the IT people to marketing. He could also see that senior management hadn't had a clear grasp of the scope of the project, and more importantly, that the whole thing had never been validated by the potential market." Integra's management discreetly shelved the project and negotiated an acceptable settlement with Intex Consulting to put an end to the development effort. Internally, obviously, it was necessary to emerge from the project in an elegant way to avoid the appearance of harassing the intermediate managers who had taken part in that decision.

CURRENT CHALLENGES FACING THE ORGANIZATION

One of the most damaging consequences resulting from this painful episode was the psychological impact on managers regarding future IS development. As reported by Cochran, some of the managers were positively terrorized at the idea of launching large innovative IS projects, "Because, when word passed that the BLISS project was a failure and heads began rolling (even if done discreetly), what was the motivation for a senior manager to venture into a project with a high technological risk? They shut their eyes and put 'X' on it. They said: 'I would rather find another solution,' which of course was not in the best long-term interests of Integra."

(Case Continued)

Eventually, Integra would have to find an acceptable conclusion for this situation and regain confidence in its capability to integrate in an efficient manner promising IT tools to its strategic business plans. On the positive side, the incident prompted the formation of a task committee headed by Cochran, whose objective was the reassessment of the decision process for systems procurement at Integra. As explained by Cochran, the procurement process was found to be ill defined and failed to assign clear responsibilities:

> How were we trapped in this mess in the first place and why did it catch everyone off-guard? I would say that ... the pain is still rather fresh and we pay a little more attention. However, I am not convinced that the lessons are anchored in our [procurement] processes. As long as those who suffered do not make the same errors twice. ... But eventually, there will be a rotation of managers. For those who will take over and who will not have lived through BLISS, there are no guarantees that they will not repeat the same errors. We do have to find a mechanism to anchor these lessons in our decision processes.

Thus, in the early months of 1997, Integra's management was assessing the situation and trying to find an appropriate course of action.

Jim Cochran, V.P. for Product Development, was still trying to figure out a way to gain access to the Canadian market. He was convinced that Integra's loan insurance product was better than the competition's, that the system supporting it was sound and reliable, and that somehow, there had to be a way to overcome the obstacles at hand. How could the millions of dollars that had already been spent on the project be salvaged?

Michael Bricino, the CIO, had a different preoccupation. For him, the IT department had to learn from this experience. What had gone wrong? He had recently read about failed software projects (Glass, 1997; Lyytinen & Hirschheim, 1987) and he was wondering where his project would fit. The system was technically adequate, but somehow it failed to respond to the intended users' goals. The lessons from this project had to be drawn so that the mistakes would not be repeated. It would be too costly for the firm, and much too damaging for the reputation of the IT organization. Meanwhile, he had the disagreeable feeling that his career at Integra was somewhat compromised.

On the other side of the building, the First V.P. of Finance was tapping her fingers on her desk. Clearly, a significant risk had been taken and the company had miscalculated the odds. On the one hand, she felt the need to provide better risk assessment for IT projects to prevent the firm from entering into such costly misadventures. On the other hand, she was worried about the potential damaging effect of the project on the managers' attitude toward risk. If the outcome was that managers, in the future, would avoid all risky projects, the company would indubitably suffer. In her opinion, appropriate risk management did not mean systematic risk avoidance.

For his part, the CEO of the organization was perplexed. Clearly, this was a major dead-end for such a key and promising project. As chairman of the board and chief executive officer of the company, he was accountable for the project to the board of directors and to the shareholders. Mr. Lapierre was trying

(*Case Continued*)

to analyze the unfolding of the project and realized it was very difficult to assign clear responsibility for the outcome. Most players had followed rational routes.

He also felt that the confidence of his management team had been bruised and that morale was severely lowered. What should be the next steps?

QUESTIONS

1. What are the two main problems in this case?
2. What are the factors affecting the problems in this case?
3. Discuss the managerial, organization, and technological issues and resources in this case.
4. What role do different players (decision makers) play in the overall planning, implementation, and management of the IT applications?
5. What are the possible alternatives, and pros and cons of each, for dealing with the problems related to this case?
6. What recommendation would you make to management? Provide your arguments in support of your recommendation.

ENDNOTES

1. In order to maintain confidentiality, the names of the companies described in this case, as well as their geographical location and the names of the participants, have been disguised.
2. For a more detailed financial description of the firm, see Appendix B.
3. This remark is very similar to the title of a paper written by Markus and Keil (1994): "If we build it, they will come: Designing information systems that people want to use," which addresses key issues in IS development and system use.
4. As the project took form, this committee was later transformed into a more formal steering committee.
5. On this subject, see Ewusi-Mensah (1987) and Barki et al. (2001).
6. The Loan Insurance Manager for Canada joined the project coordination committee in the later stages of the development effort.

REFERENCES

Barki, H., Rivard, S. & Talbot, J. (2001). An integrative contingency model of software project risk management. *Journal of Management Information Systems*, 17(4), 37–69.

Ewusi-Mensah, K. (1997, September) Critical issues in abandoned information systems development projects. *Communications of the ACM*, 40(9), 74–80.

Glass, R. L. (1997). *Software Runaways: Lessons Learned from Massive Software Project Failures*. Upper Saddle River, NJ: Prentice Hall.

Lyytinen, K. & Hirschheim, R. (1987). Information systems failures—A survey and classification of the empirical literature. *Oxford Surveys in Information Technology*, (4), 257–309.

Markus, L. & Keil, M. (1994). If we build it, they will come: Designing information systems that people want to use. *Sloan Management Review*, 35(4), 11–25.

Tait, P. & Vessey, I. (1988). The effect of user involvement on system success: A contingency approach. *MIS Quarterly*, 12(1), 91–108.

Appendix A

Project Organization Chart

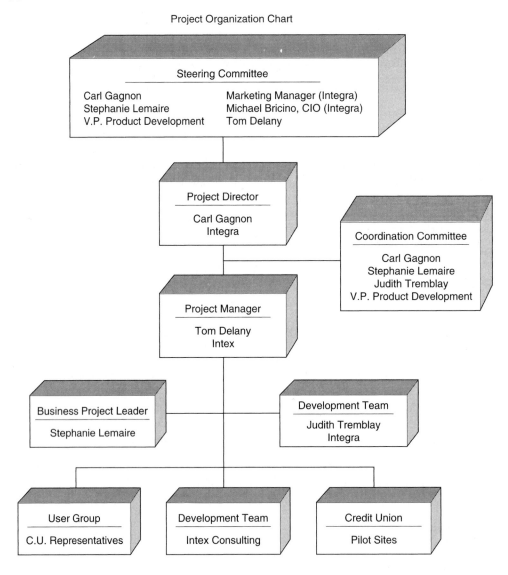

Appendix B

ABSTRACT FROM INTEGRA FINANCIAL CORPORATION REPORT (1997)

Integra Financial Corporation operates principally in the Province of Quebec, Canada. The operations of the company cover the development, marketing, and administration of individual and group insurance products (life, accident, and health), retirement savings products, and investment management. It also offers insurance services developed for the members, employees, and directors of financial institutions and credit unions in Canada.

Total assets under management	$8,555.1 million
Assets (corporate fund)	$5,343.3 million
Insurance premiums and annuities	$1,059.8 million
Net earnings	$73.8 million
Insurance in force	$80.6 billion
Canadian market share	7%
Number of permanent employees	2,200
Number of representatives	1,900

Ratings

DBRS:	**AA (low)**
CBRS:	**AA**
Moody's:	**Aa3**
Standard & Poor's:	**AA**

Appendix C

ABSTRACT FROM THE NEEDS AND PROCESSES REVISION REPORT

"Technologically," the current situation of the CUs is hybrid. It does not represent a uniform data-processing environment. Indeed, each province, each Central, and often each individual CU has its own specific information systems. During the opportunity study, several dozen different technological combinations were identified. In this context, the innovation of this project consists in developing a software application that can be sold and installed at the customer institution with the minimum of adaptation and personalization while at the same time having to support the maximum of data-processing environments already in place. Among the systems that were identified were: Observation, TLA, Loan-Pro II, RBS, Quick Quote, Loan-CalcII, CUIS-Link, Loan Origination System, XY + III, AVD/Credit Unions, InsurCalc, Vision West.

The hardware supporting the banking structures comes from numerous manufacturers. Therefore, the client portion of the software had to be compatible with several combinations of hardware and operating systems. The main hardware suppliers were:

- GEAC
- Unisys
- IBM

The operating systems installed on these computers were MVS, VSE, and VM.

There were also several micros or minis that were used by the CUs. These systems were used to process the loans, and therefore would have to be integrated with the new application. They ran on a wide variety of operating systems, including UNIX, DOS, OS2, Windows NT, and Windows under DOS.

All of these complex combinations of software and hardware would have to interact simultaneously with Integra's mainframes, which were running on MVS and VSE/ESA. ■

Biographical Sketches

Vital Roy *is an assistant professor at HEC Montreal, Canada. He received his BScA from the University of Quebec in Montreal, his MSc in Management from the University of Quebec in Chicoutimi, and his PhD from HEC Montreal. His present research interests are in the following areas: information systems sourcing, organization of the information system function, and the sociopolitical dimension of information technologies.*

Benoit A. Aubert *is an associate professor at HEC Montreal, Canada, and Fellow at the CIRANO (Center for Interuniversity Research and Analysis on Organizations). His main research areas are outsourcing, risk management, and new organization forms. He is currently involved in the development of measures and software tools to support management of outsourcing risk and its integration with other corporate risks.*

PART

IV SYSTEMS FOR SUPPORTING KNOWLEDGE-BASED WORK

This part consists of three chapters that discuss supporting three kinds of work: decision making, collaboration, and knowledge work. As shown in the book's framework diagram in the following figure, we distinguish between procedure-based and knowledge-based information-handling activities. The two previous chapters, in Part III, dealt mainly with building systems aimed at supporting procedure-based work. This part focuses on supporting knowledge-based activities: the systems that support people in performing information-handling activities to solve problems, work together, and share expertise.

Chapter 11 discusses supporting decision making by first presenting four underlying technologies—decision support systems (DSSs), data mining, executive information systems (EISs), and expert systems (ESs)—and some examples of their use. The chapter then discusses the fascinating subject of the real-time enterprise, which has a goal of gaining competitive edge by learning of an event as soon as possible and then responding to that event quickly, if necessary.

Chapter 12 deals with supporting collaboration by first describing various kinds of groups, different systems that support their collaboration, and finally how executives might think about managing virtual organizations, an increasing phenomenon these days.

Chapter 13 discusses supporting knowledge work by presenting a model for thinking about how to manage knowledge. It ends with a discussion of computer ethics and intellectual capital issues in this Internet era.

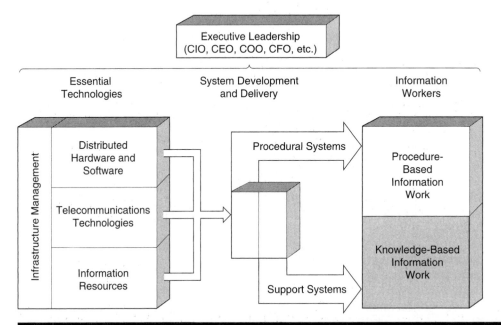

FIGURE P4-1 A Framework for IS Management

CHAPTER

11

SUPPORTING DECISION MAKING

INTRODUCTION

If you think about it, most computer systems support decision making because all software programs involve automating decision steps that people would take. In the mainframe era, the earliest commercial uses of computers aimed to automate such decisions as analyzing sales, updating accounts payable, calculating payroll payments, and recording credit card charges and payments. Since those early days of the 1950s and 1960s, use of computers to support decision making has become increasingly sophisticated, either completely taking over complex decisions or supporting people who make complex decisions. A whole host of technologies has been aimed at this use of computers. This chapter first discusses five of these technologies:

1. Decision support systems (DSSs)
2. Data mining
3. Executive information systems (EISs)
4. Expert systems (ESs)
5. Agent-based modeling

The chapter then concludes with a discussion of the hot topic of moving toward the real-time enterprise; that is, the pros and cons of being able to gauge the current state of affairs and make decisions nearer to when an event occurs.

Decision making is a process that involves a variety of activities, most of which deal with handling information. To illustrate such a process, here is a scenario about a vice president with an ill-structured problem and how he confronts it using a variety of decision-making technologies.

CASE EXAMPLE

A PROBLEM-SOLVING SCENARIO

Using an EIS to compare the budget with actual sales, a vice president of marketing discovers a sales shortfall in one region. Drilling down into the components of the summarized data, he searches for the apparent causes of the shortfall, but can find no answer. He must look further, so he sends an e-mail message to the district sales manager requesting an explanation. The sales manager's response and a follow-up phone call also reveal no obvious single cause, so he must look deeper.

The vice president investigates several possible causes:

• *Economic conditions.* Through the EIS and the Web, he accesses wire services, bank economic news letters, current business and economic publications, and the company's internal economic report on the region in question. These sources, too, reveal no serious downturn in the economic conditions of the region.

• *Competitive analysis.* Using the same sources, he investigates whether competitors have introduced a new product or launched an effective ad campaign or whether new competitors have entered the market.

• *Written sales reports.* He then browses the reports of sales representatives to detect possible problems. A concept-based text retrieval

(*Case Continued*)

system allows him to quickly search on topics, such as poor quality, inadequate product functionality, or obsolescence.

• *A data mining analysis*. He asks for an analysis of the sales data to reveal any previously unknown relationships buried in the customer database and relevant demographic data.

The vice president then accesses the marketing DSS, which includes a set of models to analyze sales patterns by product, sales representative, and major customer. Again, no clear problems are revealed.

He thus decides to hold a meeting with the regional sales managers and several of the key salespeople. They meet in an electronic meeting room supported by group DSS (GDSS) software such as GroupSystems by Ventana Corporation. During this meeting they examine the results of all the previous analyses using the information access and presentation technologies in the room, brainstorm to identify possible solutions, and then develop an action plan.

No discernible singular cause has led to the shortfall in sales, so the group decides that the best solution is to launch a new multimedia sales campaign that sales representatives can show on their laptop computer when they visit customers.

The vice president then enters a revised estimate of sales volume into the financial planning model, taking into account the new sales promotion plan, and distributes it to the sales force in the region.

He holds a sales meeting in the GDSS room and by video conference launches the new campaign and trains sales personnel in the use of the multimedia presentation. ■

This scenario illustrates the wide variety of activities involved in problem solving. Where does the decision making start and stop? Which are the crucial decisions? It really does not matter because all the activities are part of the overall process of solving the problem. The scenario also illustrates the wide variety of technologies that can be used to assist decision makers and problem solvers. They all aim to improve the effectiveness or efficiency of the decision-making or problem-solving process.

TECHNOLOGIES THAT SUPPORT DECISION MAKING

Whereas the purpose of tractors, jackhammers, and steam engines has been to enhance humans' physical capabilities, the purpose of computers has been to enhance our mental capabilities. Hence, a major use of IT is to relieve humans of some decision-making tasks or help us make more informed decisions. At first, IT relieved us of procedure-based decisions—those that involved easily discernible procedures. Software now has progressed to the point where computers can make goal-based decisions. The following are five technologies that support decision making: DSSs, data mining, EISs, ESs, and agent-based modeling.

Decision Support Systems

During the 1970s and 1980s, the concept of decision support systems (DSSs) grew and evolved out of two previous types of computer support for decision making. One was management information systems (MISs), which provided (1) scheduled reports for well-defined information needs, (2) demand reports for ad hoc information requests, and (3) the ability to query a database for specific data. The second contributing discipline was operations research/management science (OR/MS), which used mathematical models to analyze and understand specific problems.

The definition of DSSs that prevails today was described in *Building Effective Decision Support Systems*, by Ralph Sprague and Eric Carlson.[1] They define DSSs as:

- Computer-based systems
- That help decision makers
- Confront ill-structured problems
- Through direct interaction
- With data and analysis models.

The last two items have become the basis of the architecture for DSSs, which Sprague and Carlson call the DDM paradigm: the dialog (D) between the user and the system, the data (D) that supports the system, and the models (M) that provide the analysis capabilities. Sprague and Carlson make the point that a good DSS should have balance among the three capabilities. It should be easy to use to support the interaction with non-technical users; it should have access to a wide variety of data; and it should provide analysis and modeling in numerous ways.

The Architecture for DSSs.   The model in Figure 11-1 shows the relationships among the three components of the DDM model. The software system in the middle of the figure consists of the database management system (DBMS), the model base management system (MBMS), and the dialog generation and management system (DGMS).

The dialog component.   The dialog component links the user to the system. It can take any number of styles. One dialog style uses a mouse to access pull-down menus and move icons on a color screen to get a graphical presentation of analysis results. The Apple Macintosh introduced this style in the 1980s. The current standard is the browser interface.

The data component.   Data is either accessed directly by the user or is an input to the model component. Typically, summarized data, rather than transaction data, is used and put into extract files. Extract files are used for security, ease of access, and data

The DSS

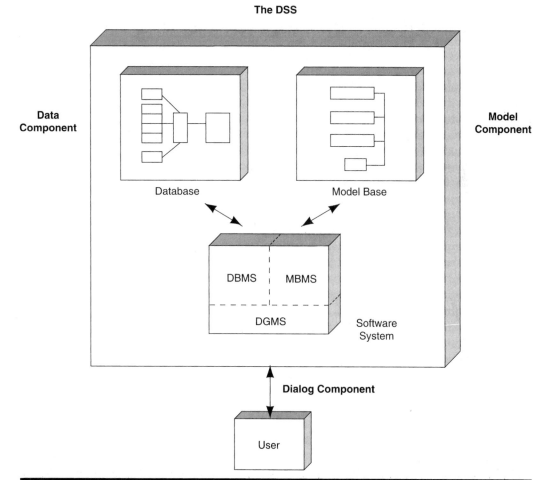

FIGURE 11-1 Components of a Decision Support System (DSS)

integrity reasons. They keep the all-important transaction systems away from end users. Most recently, the data component has taken the form of data warehousing (discussed in Chapter 7) and data mining (discussed shortly).

The model component. Models perform the analysis in a DSS, generally using a mathematical representation of the problem. There are many kinds of models: strategic, tactical, and operational, as well as model-building blocks and subroutines. Together, they can be thought of as the model base. Models need to fit with the data, they need to be kept up-to-date, users need to understand and trust them, and if several models are used, they need to work together.

Basically, there are two kinds of DSSs: institutional and "quick hit." Institutional DSSs are generally built by professionals, often decision support groups. They are intended for organizational support on a continuing basis, and they are generally written using a decision support language. The following case example illustrates an institutional DSS.

CASE EXAMPLE

ORE-IDA FOODS

Ore-Ida Foods, Inc., is the frozen food division of H. J. Heinz and has a major share of the retail frozen potato market. Its marketing DSS must support three main tasks in the decision-making process.

- *Data retrieval*, which helps managers find answers to the question, "What has happened?"

- *Market analysis*, which addresses the question, "Why did it happen?"

- *Modeling*, which helps managers get answers to, "What will happen if . . . ?"

For *data retrieval*, a large amount of internal and external market data is used. External data, such as economic indexes and forecasts, is purchased. However, the company makes limited use of simple data retrieval. Only about 15 to 30 pages of predefined reports are prepared each sales period.

Market analysis is the bulk (some 70 percent) of Ore-Ida's use of DSS and is used to analyze, "Why did such and such happen?" Data from several sources is combined, and relationships are sought. The analysis addresses a question such as, "What was the relationship between our prices and our share of the market for this brand in these markets?"

Modeling for projection purposes offers the greatest potential value to marketing management. The company has found that, for successful use, line managers must take over the ownership of the models and be responsible for keeping them up-to-date. The models must also be frequently updated, as market conditions change and new relationships are perceived. ■

As this example illustrates, an institutional DSS tends to be fairly well defined, it is based on predefined data sources (heavily internal, perhaps with some external data), and it uses well-established models in a prescheduled way. Variations and flexible testing of alternative what-if situations are available, but such tests are seldom done during interaction with the ultimate decision maker.

A "quick-hit" DSS, on the other hand, is developed quickly to help a manager make either a one-time decision or a recurring decision. A quick-hit DSS can be every bit as useful for a small company as for a large one. One type of quick-hit DSS is a reporting DSS, which can be used to select, summarize, and list data from existing data files to meet a manager's specific information needs, such as to monitor inventory in a region, compare actual to planned progress on a project, or follow a trend. A second type of quick-hit DSS is a short analysis program, which can analyze data and print or display the data. These programs can be written by a manager, they generally use only a small amount of data, and they can be surprisingly powerful. Finally, a third type of quick-hit DSS can be created using a DSS generator, which builds a DSS based on the input data. As an example of a powerful short analysis that shows quick-hit DSS in practice, consider the DSS used by the vice chairman of a services company with offices throughout the United States and Europe.

CASE EXAMPLE

A MAJOR SERVICES COMPANY

The vice chairman of the board at a major services firm was considering a new employee benefit program: an employee stock ownership plan (ESOP). He wanted a study made to determine the possible impact of the ESOP on the company and to answer such questions as: How many shares of company stock will be needed in 10, 20, and 30 years to support the ESOP? What level of growth will be needed to meet these stock requirements?

He described what he wanted—the assumptions that should be used and the rules that should be followed for issuing ESOP stock—to the manager of the information services department. The information services manager herself wrote a program of about 40 lines to perform the calculations the vice chairman wanted and then printed out the results. These results showed the impact of the ESOP over a period of 30 years, and the results contained some surprises.

The vice chairman presented the results to the executive committee and, partially based on this information, the ESOP was adopted. Some of the other executives became excited about the results of this analysis and asked if the computer program could be used to project their individual employee stock holdings for 10, 20, and 30 years. The results of these calculations aroused even more attention. At this point, it was decided to implement the system in a more formal fashion. The company treasurer became so interested that he took ownership of the system and gradually expanded it to cover the planning, monitoring, and control of the various employee benefit programs. ■

This example shows that simple programs of 100 lines of code are indeed practical and can be used to support real-life decisions. In this case, a 40-line program was adequate for the initial evaluation of the ESOP. Eventually, of course, the programs for this system became much larger, but the 40-line program started everything. This example also illustrates the concept of iterative development (a form of prototyping), which is a key concept in DSS development. Other examples of DSSs are given by Sprague and Watson in *Decision Support for Management*.[2]

Data Mining

The data component of the DSS architecture has always been a crucial part of the success of DSSs. Recently, however, many of the advances in DSSs have been in the area of data warehousing and data mining. In fact, Hugh Watson of the University of Georgia and Paul Gray of Claremont Graduate School have devoted a book to the subject, *Decision Support in the Data Warehouse*.[3]

As noted in Chapter 7, data warehouses hold gigantic amounts of data for the purpose of analyzing that data to make decisions. The most typical use of data warehouses has been users entering queries to obtain specific answers. However, an even more promising use is to let the computer uncover unknown correlations by searching for interesting patterns, anomalies, or clusters of data that people are unaware exist. Called data mining, its purpose is to give people new insights into data. For example, data mining might uncover unknown similarities within one customer group that differentiates it from other groups. Data mining is an advanced use of data warehouses, and it requires huge amounts of detailed data. The most frequent type of data mined these days is customer data because companies want to know how to serve their customers better. Here is such an example: Harrah's Entertainment.

CASE EXAMPLE

HARRAH'S ENTERTAINMENT

Harrah's Entertainment of Memphis, Tennessee, is owner of 26 casinos around the United States, including the Rio in Las Vegas, Harrah's at Lake Tahoe, and Harrah's North Kansas City on a riverboat on the Missouri River.

To better know its customers, Harrah's encourages them to sign up for its frequent-gambler card, Total Rewards. In return for inserting the card in a gaming machine when they play it, gamblers can receive free hotel rooms, free shows, free meals, and other giveaways.

Some 25 million Harrah's customers have a Total Rewards card, reports Joe Nickell,[4] just by filling out their name, age, address, and driver's license number. When they insert the card in a machine, it tracks what they do. Thus, on

Nickell's 4-hour-and-40-minute visit to the Rio in Las Vegas, Harrah's learned that he placed 637 wagers on nine slot machines, his average bet was 35 cents, and he lost $350.

Until its Total Rewards program began in 1998, Harrah's only knew how much money each of its 40,000 machines made, notes Nickell, not which customers were playing them. Furthermore, each casino operated independently. Customers might receive VIP treatment at one casino, but not at another.

When competition among casino owners increased in the late 1990s due to legalization of gambling on Indian reservations and riverboats, Harrah's realized it needed to reward its best customers to keep them coming back. But first it had to find out

(*Case Continued*)

who they were, which was the rationale behind its Total Rewards program.

Harrah's estimated it was getting 36 percent of its customers' gambling money in 1998. It further calculated that a 1-percent increase would equal $125 million in more revenue, states Nickell. Thus, Harrah's goal has been to increase the gambling "wallet share" of each of its customers. During 2001, Harrah's calculated its share had increased to 42 percent.

Using Data Mining to Understand Its Customers

Harrah's mined its Total Rewards database to uncover patterns and clusters of customers. It has created 90 demographic clusters, each of which is sent different direct mail offers—a free steak dinner, a free hotel room, and such—to induce them to pay another visit to any Harrah's casino.

Harrah's has gotten to know its customers well. From just a person's gender, age, distance from any casino, gaming machines played, and amounts of bets, it can fairly accurately estimate the long-term value of that customer. The company creates a gaming profile of each customer and a personalized marketing campaign, offering giveaways appropriate to that customer's cluster, all with the goal of encouraging customers to spend their gambling time at Harrah's rather than at competitors' casinos.

Over time, Harrah's compiles a profit-and-loss for each customer to calculate how much "return" it is likely to receive for every "investment" it makes in that customer. It also tracks how each customer responds to its direct mail offers, ratcheting up or down its giveaways based on changes in that customer's expected long-term value.

Harrah's goes to this much trouble to know its customers, says Nickell, because it learned from mining its Total Rewards database that much of its $3.7 billion in revenues (and 80 percent of its profit) comes from its slot-machine and electronic-gaming-machine players. It is not the high rollers who are the most profitable. In fact, Harrah's discovered that only 30 percent of those who spend between $100 and $500 on each visit bring in 80 percent of Harrah's revenue and close to all its profits. These slots and gaming players are the locals who gamble often.

Using Data Mining to Improve Its Business

"Harrah's Entertainment has the most devoted clientele in the casino business," writes Gary Loveman, CEO.[5] That loyalty is reflected in its bottom line: Its 26 casinos increased their same-store revenues 16 quarters in a row. Data mining has shown Harrah's the link between revenue and customer satisfaction. Customers who report being "very happy with their experience at Harrah's" have increased their spending by 24 percent, whereas those who report being "disappointed" decreased their spending by 10 percent.

Harrah's strategy is to increase loyalty by treating its best customers well. In so doing, Loveman and his predecessor have followed a decidedly different strategy to the casino business than competitors. Others have built lavish facilities and amenities—dazzling attractions in their buildings, high-end shopping malls, spas, and such—to attract new kinds of customers, not just gamblers.

Harrah's has focused on its most lucrative customers—its local slots players—using what Loveman calls a

(Case Continued)

"data-driven marketing" strategy. Rather than devise a marketing strategy first, Harrah's has let the data suggest the marketing ideas based on its mining of customer satisfaction surveys and reward-card data. The data suggested that Harrah's could increase loyalty by focusing on same-store revenue growth by encouraging locals to visit their nearby Harrah's casino often using *appropriate* incentives. Data mining also showed that most locals prefer $60 in casino chips over a free hotel stay with two free dinners and $30 in chips.

To hone customer service even more, Harrah's has divided its Total Rewards program into three tiers—Gold, Platinum, and Diamond—with Diamond customers receiving the highest level of customer service, because they have the highest value. Through mining its customer satisfaction surveys, Harrah's discovered that these gamblers value fast service and friendliness. So Harrah's does its best to make sure they do not wait in line to park their car, check in at the hotel, or eat in the restaurant. And to encourage non-Diamond card gamblers to aspire to receive these same perks, Harrah's makes the differences in service obvious. Marketing to customer aspiration is working "wonderfully," notes Loveman.

Furthermore, because Harrah's sees customer satisfaction as being so important to increasing revenue, it now links employee rewards to customer-satisfaction scores on the two important metrics: speed and friendliness. When a casino's rating increases 3 percent on customer satisfaction surveys, every employee in that casino receives a bonus. In 2002, during the recession, when gambling revenues only increased by 1 percent in one city, the Harrah's casino increased its customer satisfaction rating by 14 percent.

In addition, the company is using data mining to understand its individual slot machines, such as why customers prefer some machines over others. From what it has learned, Harrah's has reconfigured its casino floor.

In all ways possible—from the parking valets to the telemarketers to the individual slots themselves—Harrah's is using insights from its data-driven strategy to treat its best customers the way they say they want to be treated and thereby gain their loyalty and more of their gambling wallet share.

Within the first 2 years of operation of Total Rewards, revenue from customers who visited more than one Harrah's casino increased by $100 million. Due mainly to this program, Harrah's has become the second largest casino operator in the United States, and has the highest 3-year ROI in its industry, notes Nickell. ∎

Executive Information Systems

As the name implies, executive information systems (EISs) are systems for use by executives. Originally, some people argued that CEOs would not use computers directly and quoted CEOs who agreed with them. But that has not been the case. EISs are used by executives to:

- *Gauge company performance:* sales, production, earnings, budgets, and forecasts
- *Scan the environment:* for news on government regulations, competition, financial and economics developments, and scientific subjects

Using the DDM model described earlier, an EIS can be viewed as a DSS that (1) provides access to (mostly) summary performance data, (2) uses graphics to display the data in an easy-to-use fashion, and (3) has a minimum of analysis for modeling beyond the capability to drill down in summary data to examine components. For example, if sales in a region are denoted as "red" (meaning, below planned targets), the executive can perhaps drill down by country, sales office, and maybe even salesperson to better understand where the shortfall is occurring (as in the opening scenario in this chapter.) The experience at Xerox is an example of the successful development and use of an EIS. In many companies, the EIS is called a *dashboard* and may look like a dashboard of a car.

CASE EXAMPLE

XEROX CORPORATION

Paul Allaire became the executive sponsor of Xerox's EIS project while he was corporate chief of staff. Although he felt that an EIS would be valuable to the executive team, he insisted that it earn its usefulness, not that it be "crammed down their throats." In fact, the system began small and evolved to the point where even skeptical users became avid supporters.

Improved planning was a clear objective from the start. For example, Allaire describes the problem of getting briefing information to executives before regular executive meetings. Due to the time required to prepare the materials and mailing delays to international offices, many exec-

utives ended up reading 100 pages or more the night before a meeting without access to related information or time for discussions with staff. When the materials were put on the EIS, the executives had enough information or preparation time to make the necessary decisions.

The EIS helped make strategic planning more efficient and resulted in better plans, especially across divisions. Instead of each division preparing plans that were simply combined, the EIS allowed the executives to explore interrelationships between plans and activities at several divisions. The EIS played an important role at Xerox during Allaire's tenure. ∎

Stories like the Xerox case appear frequently in the public and trade press. The implication is that computers are finally being used by executives to help them perform their job better. The underlying message is that executive use is just a matter of installing popular software packages, and the only reason more executives are not using computers is their timidity. However, the situation is not that simple. Successful IT support of executive work is fraught with subtle pitfalls and problems. Consider the following description of a failure.

Doing It Wrong.   Hugh Watson, a professor at the University of Georgia, has worked with many corporations in the development of EISs. Watson describes a (hypothetical) company and its well-intentioned effort to develop and install an EIS.[6] The IS director at Genericorp had heard of successful EIS experiences. He thought that such a system would be valuable to his company, so he arranged for a presentation by a DSS vendor, which was well received by the executive team. After some discussion, they decided to purchase the product from the vendor and develop an EIS. The allocated budget was $250,000.

They assembled a qualified team of IS professionals who interviewed executives concerning their information needs (whenever the executives could find the time) and developed an initial version of the system consisting of 50 screens to be used by five executives. The response from these executives was quite good, and in some cases enthusiastic. Several of them seemed proud to finally be able to use a computer, says Watson.

With the system delivered, the development team turned it over to a maintenance team and moved on to new projects. The maintenance team was to add new screens and new users—in short, to evolve the system. Nine months later, little had happened, apparently because other systems maintenance projects had become more urgent. About this time, a downturn in revenue generated cost-cutting pressures on nonessential systems; the EIS was discontinued.

What went wrong? Watson identifies five problems that serve as a guide to the "hidden pitfalls" in developing a successful EIS.

1. ***Lack of executive support.*** Although it has been listed as a potential problem in system development for years, executive support is crucial for EIS for several reasons. Executives must provide the funding, but they are also the principal users so they need to supply the necessary continuity.

2. ***Undefined system objectives.*** The technology, the convenience, and the power of EISs are impressive, maybe even seductive. However, the underlying objectives and business values of an EIS must be carefully thought through.

3. ***Poorly defined information requirements.*** Once the objectives of the system are defined, the required information can be identified. This process is complicated because EISs typically require nontraditional information sources, such as judgments, opinions, and external text-based documents, in addition to traditional financial and operating data.

4. ***Inadequate support staff.*** The support staff must have technical competence of course, but perhaps more important is that they have an understanding of the business and the ability to relate to the varied responsibilities and work patterns of executives. A permanent team must manage the evolution of the system.

5. ***Poorly planned evolution.*** Highly competent systems professionals using the wrong development process will fail with EISs. An EIS is not developed, delivered, and then maintained. It needs to evolve over time under the leadership of a team that includes the executive sponsor, the operating sponsor, executive users, the EIS support staff manager, and IS technical staff.

Although EIS development is difficult, many organizations report that it is worth the effort. Avoiding the pitfalls identified by Watson improves the probability of a successful EIS. Many questions must be answered when considering an EIS. Some of the answers are specific to the organization—who it will serve, where and when it will be developed—so it would serve no purpose to discuss them here. However, the other questions—why, what, and how—have more general answers.

Why Install an EIS? There are a range of reasons for wanting an EIS. The following motivations are listed in the sequence of strongest to weakest, as far as probable project success is concerned.

- *Attack a critical business need.* An EIS can be viewed as an aid to deal with important needs that involve the future health of the organization. In this situation, almost everyone in the organization can clearly see the reason for developing an EIS.

- *A strong personal desire by the executive.* The executive sponsoring the project may want to get information faster or have quicker access to a broader range of information. Or the executive might want the ability to select and display only desired information and then probe for supporting detail. Or the executive might want to see information presented in graphical form. Within divisions, once corporate management begins using an EIS, division management feels at a disadvantage without one.

- *"The thing to do."* An EIS, in this instance, is seen as something that today's management must have to be current in management practices. The rationale given is that the EIS will increase executive performance and reduce time wasted looking for information.

A strong motivation, such as meeting a critical business need, is more likely to assure top management interest in, and support of, the project. At the other extreme, a weak motivation can lead to poor executive sponsorship of the project, which can result in trouble. Thus, motivation for the EIS is fundamental to its success because it helps determine the degree of commitment by the senior executives.

What Should the EIS Do? This question is second only to motivation as a critical success factor. It determines the extent to which executives will make hands-on use of the system. It is important that all the people associated with the project have the same understanding of just what the new system is expected to do and how it will provide executive support.

In general, EIS and dashboards are used to assess status. At their heart, both should filter, extract, and compress a broad range of up-to-date internal and external information. They should call attention to variances from plans and also monitor and highlight the critical success factors of the individual executive user. Both are a structured reporting system for executive management, providing them with the data and information of their choice in the desired form. Both are for monitoring what is going on in the company and in the outside world. With this information at hand, executives can work to resolve any problems they uncover.

An EIS or a dashboard can start small and quickly with this data-and-information approach and still accomplish something useful. For example, EIS developers asked the company president of one large insurance company the 10 things he would look at first after returning from vacation. He gave them this list. Two weeks later, they gave him an EIS "system" with those 10 items listed on the main menu as the first iteration of the EIS. The president was delighted and was soon asking for more!

This data-and-information approach uses information the executives already get or would like to get. But the EIS provides it faster, in more convenient form, pulling information together that previously had to be viewed separately and using graphics to aid comprehension. Here is another example of an EIS in the form of a dashboard.

CASE EXAMPLE

GENERAL ELECTRIC

In Spring 2001, the CIO of General Electric (GE) received the first executive dashboard.[7] Now, most senior GE executives have a real-time view of their portion of GE. Each dashboard compares expected goals (sales, response times, etc.) with actual, alerting the executive when gaps of a certain magnitude appear. The CIO's dashboard, for instance, shows critical GE applications. Green means the system is up and running OK, yellow means there is a problem, and red means the system is down. When systems remain red or yellow for a given time, the CIO can have the dashboard system send an e-mail to the developers in charge. The CIO can also pull up historical data to see whether the event appears to be one-time or recurring.

GE's goal is to gain better visibility into all its operations in real time and give employees a way to monitor corporate operations quickly and easily. The system is based on complex enterprise software that interlinks existing systems.

GE estimates that it saves $1.6 billion a year from the system.

GE's actions are also moving its partners and business ecosystem closer to real-time operation. For example, GE has installed online kiosks at some Home Depot stores. Customers can order an appliance, choose a delivery date and time, and learn, at that moment, whether that delivery can be made.

Likewise, GE has installed sensors on a number of its products—turbines, aircraft engines, and locomotives, to name a few. These sensors record what is happening on its attached object and transmit that data via satellite to a GE remote monitoring center. If, for instance, there is something wrong with a jet engine, GE learns of that event in real time from the sensor, uses its systems and people to determine a probable cause, and notifies the airline. Likewise, GE can tell its customers how efficiently a GE turbine is running, in real time, and work with the customer on improving that efficiency. ∎

Expert Systems

Expert systems (ESs) are a real-world use of artificial intelligence (AI). AI is a group of technologies that attempts to mimic our senses and emulate certain aspects of human behavior, such as reasoning and communicating, says Harvey Newquist[8] a well-known consultant and columnist in the field. AI technologies include ESs, neural networks, fuzzy logic, machine translation, speech recognition, and natural language.

AI has been a promising technology for at least 40 years. In the early 1990s, that promise finally began to unfold, quietly. In particular, ESs, also called knowledge-based systems, became one of several system development methodologies. They have become a prolific application of AI. The auto industry uses them to troubleshoot robots and check cars for noise and vibration. Telecommunications firms use them to diagnose switching circuits. Financial services firms use them to choose financial planning and tax planning alternatives. And the list goes on.

ESs are not new. The first was the Logic Theorist developed in 1956 by Allen Newell and Herbert Simon of Carnegie-Mellon University together with J. C. Shaw of the Rand Corporation. The field changed in the 1970s with the introduction of two AI languages, LISP and Prolog, which made the systems easier to develop. They brought ESs out of the lab and into businesses. The field changed again with the introduction of PC-based tools, called shells, that used conventional languages, such as C.

Definition. An ES is an automated analysis or problem-solving model that deals with a problem the way an expert does. The process involves consulting a base of knowledge or expertise to reason out an answer based on the characteristics of the problem. Clyde Holsapple and Andrew Whinston[9] define an ES as a computer-based system composed of:

- A user interface
- An inference engine
- Stored expertise (in the form of a knowledge base)

Note that this definition looks a lot like the description of a DSS given earlier in the chapter.

The *user interface* is the interface between the ES and the outside world. That outside world could be another computer application or a person. If a person is using the system directly, the user interface contains the means for the user to state the problem and interact with the system. Some systems use multiple-choice graphics, voice, and even animation in the interface. When the system is interacting with another application, though, the interface is the program that presents the facts to the expert system. An example is the Northwest Airlines system described in Chapter 5, where the program that gathers the data about each airline ticket presents those facts to the expert system.

The *inference engine* is that portion of the software that contains the reasoning methods used to search the knowledge base and solve the problem. The expert system generally asks questions of the user to get the information it needs. Then, the inference engine, using the knowledge base, searches for the appropriate knowledge and returns a decision or recommendation to the user. Unlike conventional systems, ESs can deal with uncertainty. Users can answer, "Yes (0.7)," meaning, "The answer is probably yes, but I'm only 70 percent certain." In these cases, the system may produce several possible answers, ranking the most likely one first.

The *knowledge base* contains facts and data relevant to the specific application.

Knowledge Representation.   Knowledge can be represented in a number of ways. Following are three ways: cases, nodes in a network, and rules.

Case-based reasoning (CBR).   One way to represent knowledge is as a case. ESs using this approach draw inferences by comparing a current problem (or case) to hundreds or thousands of similar past cases. CBR is best used when the situation involves too many nuances and variations to be generalized into rules.

Evan Schwartz and James Treece[10] provide an excellent example of a CBR system: the Apache III system used by the intensive care unit at St. Joseph Mercy Hospital in Ypsilanti, Michigan. When 35-year-old Sharon entered the hospital with a potentially fatal respiratory disease, the physicians and nurses in intensive care entered her vital statistics and medical history into a workstation running Apache III. The system drew on records of 17,448 previous intensive care patients to predict whether Sharon would live or die. Its first prediction was that she had a 15 percent chance of dying.

As the statistics were entered daily, the system compared her progress to the base of previous cases. Two weeks later, the prediction of death soared to 90 percent, alerting the physicians and nurses to take immediate corrective action. Then, literally overnight, her chance of dying dropped to 60 percent, and 12 days later to 40 percent. She did recover. The intensive care unit's director credits the system with catching the increased likelihood of death days before his staff would have seen it. The Apache III system is helping the unit respond faster and control costs better.

Neural networks.   A second way to store knowledge is in a neural network. Although they are not seen as expert systems, neural networks are a type of decision-making system. They are organized like the human brain. The brain is a network of neurons—nerve cells—that fire a signal when they are stimulated by smell, sound, sight, and so forth. As Brian O'Reilly[11] explains, scientists believe that our brains learn by strengthening or weakening these signals, gradually creating patterns. A neural network contains links (called synapses) and nodes that also fire signals between each other. Neural networks are more intelligent than the other forms of knowledge representation discussed here because they can learn.

O'Reilly presents a good description of how a neural network learns by describing how a simple one might evaluate credit applications. As shown in Figure 11-2, the first layer of this neural net has six "neurons" that represent the criteria for distinguishing good credit risks from bad credit risks. The six criteria are high salary, medium salary, owns a home, less than 3 years on the current job, prior bankruptcy, and has a dog. (The dog probably does not have an effect, but who knows?) Each of the six is connected to the two neurons in the second layer: profitable customer and deadbeat.

To train the system to distinguish between the two, the network is fed the example of an applicant with a high salary who owns a house and has a dog. Each of these three neurons sends a signal of equal strength to both the profitable customer and deadbeat neurons because it has not been trained.

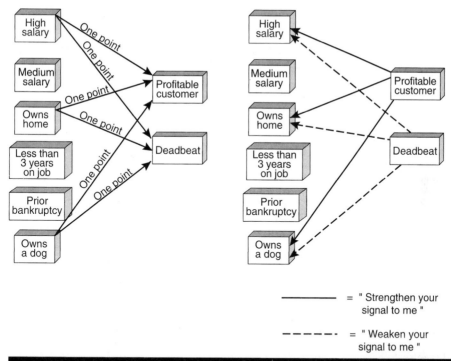

FIGURE 11-2 Training a Neural Network

Source: Brian O'Reilly, "Computers That Think Like People," *Fortune*, February 27, 1989, pp. 90–93.

The network is trained by telling the two second-level neurons the outcome of this previous loan: It was paid back. The profitable neuron sends a signal back to the three saying, in effect, "You are right, send a stronger signal next time." The deadbeat neuron, on the other hand, replies with, "You are wrong, send a weaker signal next time." The network is then given many more examples so that it learns the predictors of profitable customers and deadbeats, readjusting its signal strengths with each new case.

Once the network is trained, the high-salary neuron might send a signal worth 10 points to the profitable neuron, whereas the homeowner neuron might send only 2 points. And the less-than-3-years-on-the-job neuron may send 2 points to the deadbeat neuron and a minus 2 points to the profitable one. Because owning a dog is irrelevant, it will send zero points to both. New applications will be evaluated based on these learned patterns.

Neural networks have been used by an automaker to detect defective motors, by oil drillers to describe the progress of underground rock cracking based on sensor data, by a manufacturer to track manufacturing variations to determine the optimum manufacturing conditions, and by computer manufacturers to recognize hand printing.

Rules-based systems. A third way to store knowledge in an ES knowledge base is through *rules*. In fact, this is the most common form of knowledge representation. The rules are obtained from experts who draw on their own expertise, experience, common sense, ways of doing business, regulations, and laws to state the rules. Rules generally present this knowledge in the form of if-then statements. The number of rules determines the complexity of the system, from 50 to many thousand. Rules are appropriate when knowledge can be generalized into specific statements.

One of the first commercially successful ESs was built by American Express. It is still in use today and is actually a fundamental part of the company's everyday credit card operation. It is a rules-based ES. Here is that story.

CASE EXAMPLE

AMERICAN EXPRESS

In 1988, American Express (AmEx) implemented the Authorizer's Assistant, an ES that approves credit at the point of sale. It started as an R&D project, took 2 years to develop, and was put into production with 800 rules. Today, it has over 2,600 rules and supports all AmEx card products around the world. Its purpose is to minimize credit losses and catch fraud. It saves the company millions of dollars a year and has been a phenomenal success.

Whenever an AmEx card is run through a point-of-sale device, the transaction goes into AmEx's credit authorization system (CAS), which is a very important system for AmEx because, in essence, it gives away money. CAS is implemented worldwide and operates 24×7. It is such a significant system that the company president is notified if it is down for 45 minutes or more.

Coprocessor systems, such as the Authorizer's Assistant, have been added to CAS. The Authorizer's Assistant authorizes credit by looking at whether cardholders are creditworthy, whether they have been paying their bills, and whether a particular purchase is within their normal spending patterns. It also assesses whether the request for credit

could be a potential fraud. Before deploying Authorizer's Assistant, transactions that were not automatically approved by CAS were referred to a person for analysis and a decision. The most difficult credit-authorization decisions are still referred to people, but the Authorizer's Assistant has automated judgment to raise the quality of authorization decisions.

Authorization decisions are driven by the type of credit charge—store, restaurant, and so on. They are also influenced by whether cardholders are in their home city, on vacation, or traveling. A hotel bill or charges in a city other than where they reside would point to the latter. To detect fraud while someone is on vacation, the credit authorizer looks at the number of charges per day. An appropriate question for the system to ask would be, "Is the cardholder's spending velocity 'in pattern' (following his or her typical spending pattern)?" Customer-servicing issues and credit policies are also taken into account in the authorization decision. For example, a restaurant charge needs to be handled differently from a camera store charge, because the restaurant charge happens after the service has been rendered and the

(Case Continued)

purchase, unlike a camera, cannot be resold. AmEx also does not want to embarrass a cardholder in the social setting of a restaurant.

Development of the System

The Authorizer's Assistant is a rules-based expert system, and in creating the rules, AmEx had to refine its company policies. One example was the commonly used phrase "sound credit judgment." Before the system was built, this phrase was often used but never defined. Developing the system forced the company to define the phrase in quantifiable rules.

A rule might be framed in terms of the question, "Does this person shop at this store or often buy this kind of merchandise?" If the answer is "yes," the charge would be "in pattern." If the amount is high, another rule might ask, "Does the cardholder pay his or her bill on time and is his or her 12-month credit history good?"

The rules were generated by interviewing authorizers with various levels of expertise. Five were assigned to work with the developers. Some were the top experts (who made correct decisions at least 90 percent of the time); others had a track record of being right only 80 to 89 percent of the time. Both types of experts were used so that the developers could compare good and not-so-good decisions.

To codify the experts' knowledge, the developers studied individual charge histories in detail, broke down the decision process into its components, and focused on each one to refine it. Sometimes they also proposed cases to the experts and recorded the information they asked for to make a decision.

Two kinds of knowledge are captured in the Authorizer's Assistant: policy knowledge and judgment knowledge. Policy knowledge is like textbook knowledge. Judgment knowledge is applied to bend the rules set down in the policy to benefit the cardholder (and keep his or her business). This type of knowledge is very important because it enhances customer service in the eyes of cardholders. Thus, the rules in the system protect the company against loss and the cardholder from embarrassment.

The seven developers also spent several weeks working in the credit authorization environment so that they could understand what the experts were talking about. The system was designed to mimic how people made credit authorization decisions. The knowledge engineers (developers) thus had to develop expertise in credit and fraud as well as in the analysis of cardholder charge patterns. In essence, they acted as credit authorizers for a short time, talking to real cardholders and making authorization decisions on the telephone on the fly. This experience helped them realize how time-sensitive authorization decisions can be. The cardholder may be waiting at an airline counter to get the charge approved; a delay could cause the cardholder to miss the flight. The system had to be designed to deal with this type of customer-sensitive situation; AmEx does not want to embarrass a cardholder by bringing him or her to a telephone unnecessarily.

The vice president of risk management states that the system can be adapted quickly to meet changing business requirements. For example, if a large manufacturing company falls on

(Case Continued)

hard times, AmEx can change the rules that apply to the cities where that company is a major employer so that it can respond compassionately and quickly to credit issues that inevitably will arise. In all, management reaction to the Authorizer's Assistant has been very positive. ∎

Degree of Expertise.   The degree of expertise in an ES can be characterized by the kind of assistance it might provide to a person. It might function as an assistant, a colleague, or a true expert.

As an *assistant*, the lowest level of expertise, the ES can help a person perform routine analyses and point out those portions of the work where the expertise of the human is required. The Dipmeter Advisor developed by Schlumberger Ltd. falls into this category. It reads charts produced by instruments that have been lowered into an oil well that is being drilled. Reading such charts, looking for a small amount of significant data, is a tedious job for humans. The ES reads the charts and indicates those portions where human experts should concentrate their attention.

As a *colleague*, the second level of expertise, the system and the human can "talk over" the problem until a "joint decision" has been reached. In this use, the human may employ the "why" and "how" features of the ES to understand the system's train of logic. ESs move beyond the capabilities of DSSs because they are not only able to solve a problem but also explain to some extent how they solved the problem and provide a reliable means of solving similar problems. When a colleague system seems to be going down the wrong track, the human can put in more information to get it back on track to reach a joint decision.

As an *expert*, the highest level of expertise, the system gives answers that the user accepts, perhaps without question. This means that the system performs as well as the top 10 to 20 percent of the experts in the field.

Agent-Based Modeling

Agent-based modeling is a simulation technology for studying emergent behavior; that is, behavior (such as a traffic jam) that emerges from the decisions of a large number of distinct individuals (drivers), notes Eric Bonabeau, president of Icosystem, which builds such modeling systems.[12]

The simulation contains computer-generated agents, each making decisions typical of the decisions an individual would make in the real world. Thus, if modeling a day at a theme park, the agent representing a family of four would make different decisions than the agent representing teenagers on a date. Bonabeau believes modeling the confluence of a huge number of individual behaviors underlies understanding the mysteries of why businesses, markets, consumers, and other complex systems behave as they do. In modeling the behavior of highly complex systems via individual agents, agent-based systems often arrive at counterintuitive results. He states that this decision-making technology can be used to predict the unpredictable, and he gives numerous examples of how it has been used. Here are just a few.

- Nasdaq was going to switch its tick size from eighths to decimals, believing that the change would allow stock buyers and sellers to negotiate more precisely and decrease the buy–ask price spread. Using agent-based modeling, with agents representing all the players in its stock market, each making decisions based on real-world strategies, Nasdaq found that the smaller tick size would actually increase the buy–ask price spread because it reduced the market's ability to do price discovery.

- A European retailer wanted to redesign its incentive plan for its country managers. At the time, incentives were based on having the fewest stock-outs (a product running out of stock on the shelves). However, this incentive encouraged hoarding, spoilage, and high-cost rush orders. Agent-based modeling recommended basing incentives both on low stock-outs and on storage costs, because it would connect managers' local behavior with the organization's global performance.

- Southwest Airlines wanted to revamp its cargo operations. The dispatchers loaded cargo onto the flight that would reach the destination soonest. But the result was piles of packages at the end of the day, high security costs, and endless loading and unloading of packages. Agent-based modeling found that costs would be lower and packages would arrive just as quickly by putting them on a plane that would eventually land in the destination city.[13]

- A company planned to change its recruiting practices from hiring college graduates who fit its company culture to hiring experienced people. Agent-based modeling demonstrated that this change would lead to higher staff turnover (which the company had expected) and a decrease in the company's knowledge base (which the company had not expected). Thus, if it was to change recruiting practices, it would need to find ways to capture the knowledge of experienced employees before they left.

These five seemingly competing technologies that support decision making often overlap and combine. For example, some DSS products incorporate tools and techniques from AI. In the form of agents, DSSs are providing the delivery vehicle for ESs, knowledge representation, natural language query, and voice and pattern recognition. The result is intelligent DSSs that can suggest, learn, and understand managerial tasks and problems. Likewise, data mining is often part of a DSS or EIS. In fact, the next section demonstrates how these decision support technologies and other technologies are being mixed and matched to form the foundation for the real-time enterprise.

TOWARD THE REAL-TIME ENTERPRISE

The essence of the phrase *real-time enterprise* is that organizations can know how they are doing at the moment rather than waiting days, weeks, or months for needed information, as has been the case. It is often equated to an airline pilot trying to fly the plane using time-delayed sensors or trying to drive a car without split-second information about what is happening on the highway.

Through IT, organizations have been able to see the status of operations closer and closer to real time. The Internet is giving companies a way to disseminate closer-to-real-time information about events, such as a large customer order or cancellation, a supply chain disruption, weather or governmental disruption, important news, and so forth.

The notion has gotten to the hype point. It is prominent in vendor advertising. That means the notion has some validity, but it is not as easy to achieve as vendors might lead you to believe. This real-time reporting is occurring on a whole host of fronts. Following are just five of those fronts: enterprise nervous systems (to coordinate company operations), straight-through processing (to reduce distortion in supply chains), real-time CRM (to automate decision making relating to customers), communicating objects (to gain real-time data about the physical world), and vigilant information systems (to move to a sense-and-respond culture).

Enterprise Nervous Systems

One approach to the real-time enterprise is to build an enterprise nervous system. In an interesting white paper from Tibco and Gartner,[14] the two companies state that an enterprise nervous system (the technical means to a real-time enterprise) is a kind of network that connects people, applications, and devices. This system differs from many past systems in four ways:

1. It is *message based*, which means that applications, devices, and people communicate with each other via messages. As the Internet has shown, sending messages is a very efficient and effective way of dispersing information among huge numbers of parties.

2. It is *event driven*, which means that when an event occurs—a car arrives at a dealer's lot, a passenger boards a plane, a factory ships a truckload of parts—that event is recorded and made available.

3. It uses a *publish-and-subscribe* approach, which means that the information about the event is "published" to an electronic address and any system, person, or device authorized to see that information can "subscribe" to that address's information feed, which is automatically updated whenever a new event occurs. Portal technology has a similar self-service characteristic. A company posts information on its portal, and if you are authorized to see that information, you can access it when you want, or subscribe to receive it automatically in real time. This approach is one way to inform hundreds, thousands, or millions of people or systems of an event in real time in a format customized to their system or device.

4. It uses *common data formats*, which means the data formats used in disparate systems are reduced to common denominators that can be understood by other systems and shared.

Here is an example of one such nervous system.

CASE EXAMPLE

DELTA AIR LINES

Delta Air Lines has implemented an enterprise nervous system that is, over time, incorporating the disparate systems the airline had in the late 1990s. At that time, Delta had 60 million lines of code, 70 databases, and 30 technology platforms, most of which did not communicate with each other nor share their data, notes Tom Stewart.[15]

Now, Delta has a nervous system that has gotten rid of over 30 of the databases and one-fourth of the code, and the consolidation is continuing. This system manages the airline's gate operations. Delta has 2,200 flights a day, one every 39.3 seconds, says Stewart. Each is managed by the system, in real time. When a flight has a gate change, for example, everyone who needs to know about that change—gate attendants, baggage handlers, caterers, passengers—gets the data in the appropriate way. Passengers, for instance, receive the information on screens above each gate.

The system was installed by the Feld Group, notes Stewart, led by Charlie Feld, the former CIO of Frito-Lay who installed a real-time system at Frito-Lay and has gone on to do the same at a number of other companies. At Frito-Lay, all the sales force had laptops to record every sale in real time; all the executives had PCs to see the sales. As a result, Frito-Lay took back $40 million *less* in stale product each year, sales force paperwork dropped by 40,000 hours a year, and Frito-Lay's revenue increased from $3 billion to $4.2 billion in just 3 years.

At Delta, Feld drew on software from Tibco, which provides the foundation for the enterprise nervous system. Feld believes the best way to get a real-time enterprise is to use a publish-and-subscribe approach using EAI products. Using the Tibco products, which include a type of messaging middleware, disparate applications can talk to each other. The software puts the data in these systems into common forms so it can be understood by the numerous applications.

Generally, to start down this EAI path, a company needs a system that is large enough to affect customers, impress the CEO, and intrigue the IT organization, states Stewart. At Delta, this first system was a new gate-and-boarding system. The system is big, it is used by 60,000 Delta employees and 100 million customers, and it affects everything from maintenance crews to reservation clerks to Delta's frequent flyer program. Formerly, the various functions had their own systems and databases. The new system replaced them all with one set of data. Now, when an event occurs, it ripples to everyone. Delta is now expanding those ripples out to its partners who also serve its passengers: caterers, security companies, and such. ■

Straight-Through Processing

The notion of a real-time enterprise has generated two buzzwords worth knowing. One is *zero latency*, which, according to Gartner EXP, was coined in 1998 and means reacting quickly to new information (with no wait time). The premise is that faster action leads to a competitive edge.

The second term is *straight-through processing*, which means that transaction data is entered just once in a process or a supply chain. The Delta example shows straight-through processing within an enterprise. The notion applies even more in supply chains. In fact, reducing lags and latency in supply chains is a major goal these days.

As the *Economist*[15] points out, supply chains experience a bullwhip effect when they do not have straight-through processing. A customer order can trigger a company to generate an order to its supplier, who, in turn, generates its own orders to its suppliers. But generally, these orders are larger because the supplier wants to compensate for unforeseen events. Those upstream suppliers, in turn, order from their suppliers, and their orders are often larger as well. Moving upstream through the supply chain there is increasingly greater variance from the original order. If the customer then cancels the order, that cancellation ripples through the supply chain with the upstream firms experiencing the *bullwhip effect* (a small change by a customer results in a huge change upstream).

Real-time information through the supply chain would likely reduce that ever-growing discrepancy from reality and thus reduce the bullwhip effect. In short, if this supply chain had straight-through processing, the original customer order would be entered only once and all suppliers at all levels in the chain would see the original order and respond accordingly. This is a tall task, but the approach being used is similar to the enterprise nervous system with events, messaging, and publish-and-subscribe features.

Real-Time CRM

Another view of a real-time response might occur between a company and a potential customer, perhaps via a customer call center or a Web site. Following is an example of real-time automated decision making using some of the technologies discussed in this chapter.

CASE EXAMPLE

A REAL-TIME INTERACTION ON A WEB SITE

As an illustration of a real-time interaction via a Web site, consider an example from E.piphany,[16] a company that sells real-time CRM software as a component of its suite of CRM products. Following is the sequence of events (1 to 11), as noted in Figure 11-3:

1. A potential hotel guest visits the Web site of a hotel chain that uses E.piphany's software.

(Case Continued)

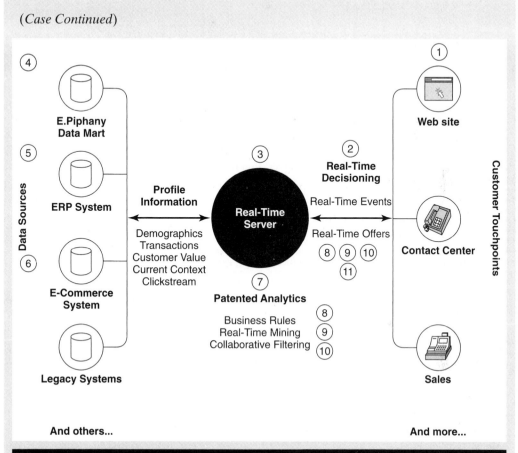

FIGURE 11-3 A Real-Time Interaction on a Web Site

Source: Reprinted with permission of E.piphany, Inc., www.epiphany.com.

2. The site visitor clicks on a hotel in the Orlando area. Information on that real-time event flows to the real-time server powered by E.piphany software.

3. The server initiates a number of requests to create a profile of that customer.

4. It may request past history of interactions with that customer from the E.piphany data mart. Those interactions would include not only

Web site interactions but also call center interactions, hotel stays, and so on.

5. The server may request past billing information from the chain's ERP system.

6. It may want past purchase history from the hotel's e-commerce system.

7. Using all those pieces of information, the server then uses its analytics to make some real-time offers to the Web site visitor.

(Case Continued)

8. If it is off-season in Orlando, hotel management may have created a *business rule* that says, "For any repeat customer considering booking at least a 2-night stay at this hotel in off-season, offer a 20 percent discount." If, indeed, this customer has stayed at the chain before, the server can make that offer on the spot, probably in a very noticeable pop-up box on the Web site.

9. Or the server might use the E.piphany *real-time mining tool* to make an offer based on the customer's past stays at the hotel, having mined that information from the compiled profile. For instance, it might ask if the customer still wants a king-size bed in a nonsmoking quiet room, as in the past.

10. Or, using the E.piphany *collaborative filtering* technology, based on preferences of other hotel guests with a similar profile, the system might offer three special choices: a laptop computer in the room, a bottle of wine, or a half hour massage at the hotel's spa. Generally, the real-time mining and collaborative filtering tools are used together.

11. The Web site visitor's responses to all the offers are recorded and taken into account by the E.piphany software and used when making offers to other Web site or call center visitors.

In a call center, the call center representatives would have the same kinds of technology support for making decisions and verbally making these offers (and recording responses) over the phone.

Besides the real-time nature of this interaction, another feature is that the system learns from each interaction. Thus, it includes the latest responses in its real-time decision making and offers, keeping up with trends and honing its knowledge of clusters of customers and non-customers. ∎

Communicating Objects

The notion of the real-time enterprise is intriguing for yet another reason. The *Economist* articles on the subject mention sensors and tags that provide information about the physical world via real-time data. We take the editorial freedom of calling them *communicating objects*.

A communicating object can tell you what it is attached to, where it is located, where it belongs, and a lot more information about itself. Technically speaking, such an object is a radio frequency identification device (RFID). It is a small chip that contains information about the object it is attached to, such as a jet engine, a hotel uniform, or a package—anything someone wants to keep track of.

As Glover Ferguson[17] of Accenture explains, communicating objects are also called *smart tags*. They can be as small as a match head, and they are implanted on a wafer surrounded by a coil of wire that serves as the tag's antenna. The antenna allows the tag to be polled by a reader that passes within a few feet. The tag can be passive (read only) or active (send out signals). Those that are larger can be read from further away. Any number of tags can be read by a reader at once, so multiple items on a pallet can be read simultaneously, not one at a time, even in harsh weather conditions. Most importantly, these tags can carry far more information than their predecessor, bar codes. They can carry the history of an item, not just its ID code and price.

In 2003, RFID became a hot technology because Wal-Mart announced that by January 2005 it wanted its top suppliers to place RFID tags on all pallets, cases, and high-ticket items. (Wal-Mart's schedule has since been extended.) The U.S. Department of Defense announced its own initiative the same year. Foreseeing the impact of RFID technology in 1997, the Uniform Product Council (UPC) began an initiative called "Sunrise 2005" to encourage retailers to make their systems RFID compliant by that time. The UPC recognized that bar codes have 11 digits, but that the electronic product codes (EPCs) used by RFID have 13 digits. Retrofitting legacy systems to accommodate the two additional digits is akin to the Y2K challenge CIOs faced in the late 1990s. Efforts to retrofit the old bar code system to the new EPCs required for RFID will be mammoth.

RFID presents a number of potentially other large costs to CIOs. The tags can accumulate histories of products. How much more storage and bandwidth will a company need to capture and communicate all this data? Where should the data be stored and for how long? What sorts of new programs will be needed to analyze the data? In short, CIOs need to understand how well their existing architectures and infrastructures can accommodate RFID and the changes that will be needed, notes Levinson.[18] And, as will be noted in Chapter 13, advocates of consumer privacy are concerned about RFID tags placed on individual products.

Ferguson believes smart tags are going to transform industries because one day they will talk to one another, which will change how work is handled. For example, Seagate, the disk drive manufacturer, has a smart tag on each individual disk it manufactures. Each type of disk must go through a specific sequence of processes, depending on its type. The checklist on the tag directs it through the correct sequence and ensures that each step is completed before the next one begins. The tags have allowed Seagate to uncover more sources of production errors than in the past, notes Ferguson. A key is the object's ability to capture new information.

Communicating objects are also major theft-prevention devices because they are cheap enough to affix to often-stolen items, such as cartons of liquor and PC motherboards. In the case of motherboards, when one is illegally taken offsite, it can automatically be disabled by the owner, thereby preventing its use. Tags can even be more effective than a set of keys in safeguarding a location, notes Ferguson. People entering an area may be required to wear an RFID wristband. Likewise, these tags can keep people with Alzheimer's disease in appropriate areas, sending out a warning when they are beyond the bounds of their facility or are near a dangerous area, such as a staircase.

Ferguson notes that this technology gets really interesting when objects begin communicating with each other, which he calls object-to-object communication. Theft prevention is a stand-alone application, and new forms of inventory management (say, by a business partner) are a "four walls" application. At first, PCs were stand-alone and used within companies. But the Internet unleashed entirely new uses of PCs and their successors. The same will happen with smart tags, predicts Ferguson.

With these objects, a whole new "silent commerce" will emerge. "Fresh" fish will be able to tell you if they are really fresh, because their smart tag can tell you whether they have been frozen at any time since being caught. Variable pricing could become more of the norm. In Singapore, for instance, cars carry smart tags, and drivers are charged variable prices for where they drive in the city and when. The prices are set to encourage or discourage driving at different places at different times. It is an example of real-time traffic control.

Vigilant Information Systems

The premise of the real-time enterprise is not only that it can capture data in real time, but also that it has the means to act on that data quickly. One theory for how to act fast was espoused in the 1950s by Colonel John Boyd, a U.S. Air Force fighter pilot.[19] He believed he could win any dogfight in 40 seconds (or less). In fact, he put money on his ability. He challenged any fighter pilot, stating that starting from any position of disadvantage he would have his jet on the challenger's tail within 40 seconds or he would pay the other pilot $40. He is said to have never lost a bet, even to pilots in superior aircraft.

He called his theory the OODA (Observe, Orient, Decide, Act) loop because it consisted of the following four actions:

- *Observe* where the challenger's plane is,
- *Orient* himself and size up his own vulnerabilities and opportunities,
- *Decide* which maneuver to take, and
- *Act* to perform it before the challenger could go through the same four steps.

Boyd's goal was to operate *inside* his challenger's loop, that is, to take the four steps faster. By outthinking other pilots, he could outmaneuver them, which often led to confusing them. An OODA loop is shown in Figure 11-4.

Western Digital has used this type of thinking to move itself closer to operating in real time with a sense-and-respond culture that aims to operate faster than its competitors.

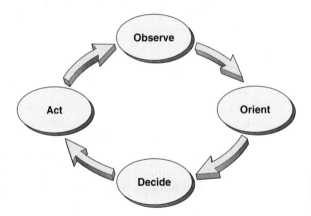

FIGURE 11-4 An OODA Loop

CASE EXAMPLE

WESTERN DIGITAL

Western Digital, with headquarters in Lake Forest, California, manufactures hard drives for PCs, storage systems, and home entertainment systems. It has nearly 17,000 employees, revenues of $3 billion a year, manufacturing plants in Malaysia and Thailand, and customers around the globe.

The industry has short product cycles and experiences intense competition, which keeps product quality high and prices low. Western Digital's main challenge has been to keep up with customers' relentless demands for more storage and faster access while keeping its costs down.

Companies that have not kept up have not survived. Western Digital has survived, even excelled, notes Robert Houghton, Western Digital's CIO, and his coauthors.[20] IT and OODA-loop thinking have been part of this success, providing management with integrated data to manage enterprise-wide and the ability to respond to changes more rapidly.

The Underlying Vigilant Information System

Houghton's IS organization built what they call a *vigilant information system* (VIS), which Houghton et al. define as a system that is "alertly watchful." It is complex, and it builds on the firm's legacy systems. It essentially has four layers, as shown in Figure 11-5:

- **Raw data layer.** The first (bottom) layer consists of raw data from cus-

tomer orders, customer payments, costs of drives, test data on drives, and so on.

- **Functional application layer.** The second layer, the *observe* layer, consists of the transaction systems (ERP, point of sale, logistics, etc.) that Western Digital uses to run its business. Each application performs its specific functions using the raw data form the first layer.

- **Business intelligence layer.** The third layer, the *orient* layer, consists of analysis and reporting systems that use data from the data warehouse (drawn from the second layer systems) to analyze Western Digital's performance—financial, factory, and quality performance.

- **Dashboard layer.** The top layer, the *decide and act* layer, consists of two types of dashboards, one for use in factories (to optimize operations) and one for use by corporate (to plan and forecast). The dashboards display key performance indicators and metrics, they permit drill down, and they issue alerts when data is not within preset boundaries. Western Digital employees use this layer to decide what to do and, in some cases, initiate actions via the dashboard.

The dashboards give factory and corporate management real-time visibility into operations. Houghton et al. define *real-time* as being "sufficiently vigilant for the process being monitored." Thus, for

(Case Continued)

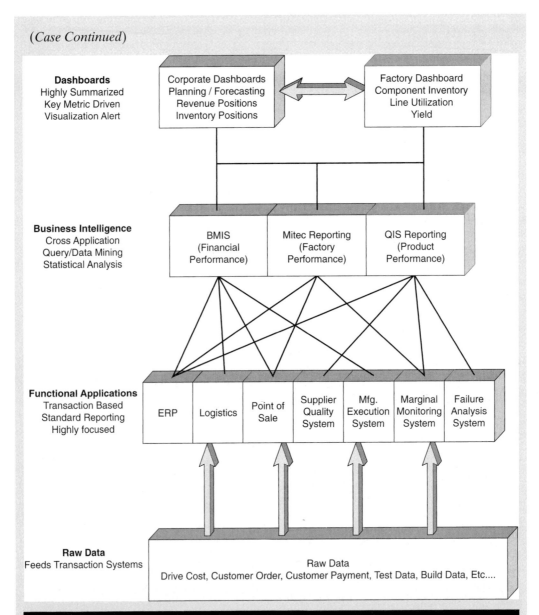

Dashboards
Highly Summarized
Key Metric Driven
Visualization Alert

Corporate Dashboards
Planning / Forecasting
Revenue Positions
Inventory Positions

Factory Dashboard
Component Inventory
Line Utilization
Yield

Business Intelligence
Cross Application
Query/Data Mining
Statistical Analysis

BMIS
(Financial
Performance)

Mitec Reporting
(Factory
Performance)

QIS Reporting
(Product
Performance)

Functional Applications
Transaction Based
Standard Reporting
Highly focused

ERP | Logistics | Point of Sale | Supplier Quality System | Mfg. Execution System | Marginal Monitoring System | Failure Analysis System

Raw Data
Feeds Transaction Systems

Raw Data
Drive Cost, Customer Order, Customer Payment, Test Data, Build Data, Etc....

FIGURE 11-5 Architecture of Western Digital's Vigilant Information System

Source: R. Houghton, O. El Sawy, P. Gray, C. Donegan, A. Joshi, "Vigilant Information Systems for Managing Enterprises in Dynamic Supply Chains: Real-Time Dashboards at Western Digital," *MIS Quarterly Executive*, Vol. 3, No. 1, March 2004, pp. 19–35. Used with permission.

the factory dashboards, real time means "as close as possible to real time." For the corporate dashboards, real time means "after the data has been validated and synchronized among the data feeds so that all the noise has been filtered out." It is the links between these four layers that have turned Western Digital's formerly

(Case Continued)

disparate systems into a coordinated vigilant information system that funnels the appropriate real-time data to the dashboards.

The Changed Business Processes

As important as the underlying VIS is, it had to be complemented by appropriate business processes to give Western Digital a way to operate *inside* its competitors' OODA loops. Management knew that new dashboards on their own would not change the company's decision-making culture. Therefore, three new company policies were drafted to leverage the VIS:

1. The company's strategic enterprise goals must be translated into time-based objectives and aligned across the company so that management has one set of metrics to manage.

2. Key performance indicators (KPIs) must be captured in real time, and be comparable, so that teams can compare operations across groups and business units, thereby improving performance companywide.

3. Decision making should be collaborative, to coordinate actions company-wide. To achieve this new style of working, the dashboards have become the focal point in many regularly scheduled meetings, and teams have worked to ensure that people with different expertise are involved in the meetings, from afar, if necessary. It has taken teams quite a while to figure out what information others need to participate in decision making while being "virtually there" rather than in the room.

Each dashboard contains its appropriate real-time metrics and KPIs, and each metric and KPI has its own target level and a variance setting. When a variance is exceeded, the appropriate executive is alerted.

The Shop-Floor OODA Loop. The shop-floor supervisors in the factories, who manage closest to real time, operate on the tightest OODA loop. They receive a page or a flashing light on their dashboard when one of their variances is violated. The time from alert to action is often minutes, rather than the former hours or days. Sometimes, they can diagnose and resolve the problem using their dashboard because the dashboards can be used to initiate actions.

The Factory OODA Loop. The production managers, who oversee multiple production lines, operate on an OODA loop that is not as tight as the shop-floor OODA loop. They, too, receive alerts, but a more important use of their dashboard is at their daily production meeting, where they assess yesterday's performance and discuss ways to improve operations. The "yesterday problems" already handled by the shop-floor supervisors are filtered out. So the production managers only see the unresolved issues, which reduces their information overload and quickens their OODA loop, note Houghton et al. As a result, their daily production meetings have dropped from 5 hours to 1.5 hours. These meetings involve 15 people, so the dashboard system provides production managers significant time savings in these meetings alone. The system has also reduced micromanagement; there is no longer

(Case Continued)

haggling about who has the right data because they all see the same data.

The production managers also use their dashboard in a learning mode, performing "health checks" of the operational aspects of the factory to see what is and what is not functioning well. Western Digital has learned that the shorter the OODA loop, the more frequent the health checks need to be, state Houghton et al.

The Corporate OODA Loop. Corporate executives receive alerts on their dashboards, and they find they can uncover root causes faster because of the dashboards, note Houghton et al. But they mainly use their dashboards to perform health checks for the enterprise as a whole. Their OODA loop is not as tight as the factory loop, but their decisions often affect the factories. Many decisions require consultation with others, so people routinely send screen shots or references to screens to others so that they all see the same data when discussing an issue.

Benefits of the VIS

The VIS has, indeed, quickened all three OODA loops and helped to link decisions across them. Management's goal is to be able to initiate a change in the factories in the same work shift as the company receives a change request from a customer. When it reaches this speed of responsiveness, it believes it will gain market share, note Houghton et al.

Corporate performance has already improved measurably. Margins have doubled since the dashboards were implemented over 3 years ago. Management attributes the increase, in part, to the dashboards because they have helped improve data visibility, supply chain management, and demand planning.

The VIS is moving Western Digital toward a sense-and-respond culture where it learns and adapts quickly in a coordinated fashion. The sensing (observe and orient) is handled by the VIS, whereas the responding (decide and act) is handled by the people. In this environment, timing is important. There is no point in accelerating sensing if no action can be taken, and there is no point in accelerating responding if there is no fresh information. The two need to be in sync, note Houghton et al., which is how Western Digital's three nested OODA loops now work. ∎

The Dark Side of Real Time

Given the advantages of more real-time activities, what are the disadvantages? Glover Ferguson[17] believes that object-to-object communication could compromise privacy. He asks, "At what point does an object's ability to track, record, and communicate with other objects invade an individual's rights?" There is no cut-and-dried answer; it depends on the circumstances. It is a political issue, not a technical one, and many CEOs are going to face this question in the future, Ferguson believes. Does knowing the exact location of a company truck every minute of the day and night invade a driver's privacy? Can citizens disable their smart cars to drive where they please without being tracked? The answers, notes Ferguson, lie in CEOs understanding the context of the use of smart tags and the sensitivities that can arise in those contexts.

Omar El Sawy[21] of the University of Southern California points out that in the era of speed, a situation can become very bad, very fast—much faster than in a slower economy. He believes that speed must be balanced with caution. People in a high-speed environment need deep visibility into the workings of their environment and must watch constantly for signals that something bad is likely to happen.

It is worth noting that when the New York Stock Exchange allowed programmed trading (stock trading by computers rather than people), the exchange learned after a bad experience that it also had to introduce "circuit breakers" to stop deep dives in the market caused by the systems reacting so quickly to actions by other systems. Enterprises may need to introduce similar kinds of circuit breakers when they depend heavily on systems to make decisions and perform actions for them.

CONCLUSION

It is obvious from this discussion of diverse technologies that use of IT to support decision making covers a broad swath of territory. Some technologies aim to alert people to anomalies, discontinuities, and shortfalls. Others aim to make decisions, either as recommendations to people or to act on behalf of people. Handing over decisions to systems has its pros and cons; thus, their actions need to be monitored. CIOs need to alert their management team to potential social and economic effects of computer-based decision making because errant computer-based decisions have devastated corporate reputations and cost a lot of money. Vendors are pushing toward the real-time enterprise. However, the use of IT for these purposes should give pause so that the ramifications can be explored.

QUESTIONS AND EXERCISES

Review Questions

1. What is a DSS?
2. What is the architecture of a DSS, as suggested by Sprague and Carlson? Summarize the attributes of each component.
3. What is an institutional DSS? Give an example.
4. Explain how Harrah's Total Rewards program works.
5. What is an EIS?
6. What are the pitfalls in EIS development identified by Watson?
7. Describe three kinds of knowledge representation.
8. What does the Authorizer's Assistant do and how does it do it?
9. What is agent-based modeling?
10. What is a real-time enterprise?
11. In what four ways does an enterprise nervous system differ from many past systems?
12. What is a smart tag and how might it be used?
13. Describe the four parts of an OODA loop. What is the goal of OODA-loop thinking?
14. Describe the three OODA loops at Western Digital.
15. Explain the potential dark-side aspects of a real-time enterprise.

Discussion Questions

1. Expert systems are dangerous. People are likely to depend on them rather than think for themselves. If the system contains bad logic, bad decisions will be made and lawsuits will result. Argue for and against this claim.
2. An enterprise cannot be managed from a computer, no matter how slick the executive dashboard. Do you agree or disagree? Discuss.
3. Smart tags intrude into people's lives. There is going to be a revolt against using them to track people's movements. Argue for and against this claim.

Exercises

1. If you have ever used a spreadsheet, an ES, or a DSS, describe one of your uses and what decisions the system helped you make.
2. Find one or more current articles on the real-time enterprise. Present new information in the articles to the class.
3. Visit a local company and find out if and how they use the technologies in this chapter to support decision making: DSS, data mining, ESs, EIS, agent-based modeling enterprise nervous system, straight-through processing, real-time CRM, and communicating objects (RFID).

REFERENCES

1. Sprague, Ralph H., and Eric Carlson, *Building Effective Decision Support Systems*, Prentice Hall, Upper Saddle River, NJ, 1982.
2. Sprague, Ralph H., and Hugh Watson, *Decision Support for Management*, Prentice Hall, Upper Saddle River, NJ, 1996.
3. Watson, Hugh, and Paul Gray, *Decision Support in the Data Warehouse*, Prentice Hall, Upper Saddle River, NJ, 1998.
4. Nickell, Joe, "Welcome to Harrah's," *Business 2.0*, April 2002, available at www.business2.com.b2/web/articles/0,17863,514574,00.html; accessed October 2004.
5. Loveman, Gary, "Diamonds in the Data Mine," *Harvard Business Review*, May 2003, pp. 109–113.
6. Watson, Hugh, "Avoiding Hidden EIS Pitfalls," *Computerworld*, June 25, 1990.
7. "Survey: The Real-Time Economy," *Economist*, January 31, 2002.
8. Newquist, Harvey, "Nearly Everything You Want to Know About AI," *Computerworld*, July 29, 1991, p. 64.
9. Holsapple, Clyde, and Andrew Whinston, *Business Expert Systems*, Richard D. Irwin, New York, 1987.
10. Schwartz, Evan, and James Treece, "Smart Programs Go to Work," *Business Week*, March 2, 1992, pp. 97–105.
11. O'Reilly, Brian, "Computers That Think Like People," *Fortune*, February 27, 1989, pp. 90–93.
12. Bonabeau, Eric, "Predicting the Unpredictable," *Harvard Business Review*, March 2002, pp. 109–116; "Don't Trust Your Gut," *Harvard Business Review*, May 2003, pp. 116–123.
13. Meyer, Christopher, and Stan Davis, *It's Alive: The Coming Convergence of Information, Biology, and Business*, Crown Business, New York, 2003, p. 104. Meyer and Davis also discuss Southwest Airlines' cargo operations.
14. TIBCO, "Business Integration Strategies: The Enterprise Nervous System," 2002.
15. Stewart, Tom, "Tech's Most Valuable Temp," *Business 2.0*, August 2002, pp. 88–91.

16. E.piphany, "E.piphany Real Time," 2002.

17. Ferguson, Glover, "Have Your Objects Call My Objects," *Harvard Business Review*, June 2002, pp. 138–144.

18. Levinson, Meridith, "The RFID Imperative," *CIO Magazine*, December 1, 2003. Available at www.cio.com/archive/120103/retail.html. Accessed May 2004.

19. Hammonds, Keith, "The Strategy of the Fighter Pilot," *Fast Company*, June 2002, p. 98.

Available at www.fastcompany.com/magazine/59/pilot.html.

20. Houghton, Robert, Omar El Sawy, Paul Gray, Craig Donegan, and Ashish Joshi, "Vigilant Information Systems for Managing Enterprises in Dynamic Supply Chains: Real-Time Dashboards at Western Digital," *MIS Quarterly Executive*, March 2004, Vol. 3, No. 1, pp. 19–35.

21. Potterf, Katheryn, "Keep Your Eye on the Prize," *Profit*, May 2002, p. 22.

12 SUPPORTING COLLABORATION

INTRODUCTION

In her book, *The Company of the Future*, France Cairncross[1] states that the company of the future will be a collection of online communities, some internal, some that reach outside the organization's boundaries into its business ecosystem, some that are designed and formed outright, and some that just grow on their own. She believes that a main job of executives and managers is to foster these communities and the collaboration they engender. A major job of CIOs is therefore to provide the technology to support online communities and online collaboration. Cairncross is not alone in her thinking.

Teams: The Basis of Organizations

In the *Harvard Business Review*, Peter Drucker's[2] article, "The Coming of the New Organization," became the most reprinted article in the article's first year. Apparently it struck a responsive chord. In that article, Drucker states that organizations are becoming information based, and that they will be organized not like a manufacturing organization, but more like a symphony orchestra, a hospital, or a university. That is, each organization will be composed mainly of specialists who direct their own performance through feedback from others—colleagues, customers, and headquarters.

This move is being driven by three factors, says Drucker. One, knowledge workers are becoming the dominant portion of labor, and they resist the command-and-control form of organization. Two, all companies, even the largest ones, need to find ways to be more innovative and entrepreneurial. Three, IT is forcing a shift. Once companies use IT to handle information rather than data, their decision processes, management structure, and work patterns change.

For example, spreadsheets allow people to perform capital investment analyses in a few hours. Before this technology was available, these investment analyses generally had to be based on opinion because the calculations are so complex. With computing, the calculations become manageable. More importantly, the assumptions underlying the calculations can be given weights. In so doing, investment analysis changes from being a budgeting question to being a policy question, says Drucker, because the assumptions supporting the business strategy can more easily be discussed.

IT also changes organizational structure when a firm shifts its focus from processing data to producing information, he says. Turning data into information requires knowledge, and knowledge is specialized. The information-based organization needs far more specialists than middle managers who relay information. Thus, organizations are becoming flatter, with fewer headquarters staff and more specialists in operating units. Even departments have different functions. They set standards, provide training, and assign specialists. Work is done mainly in task-focused teams, where specialists from various functions work together as a team for the duration of a project.

Team-based organizations work like hospitals or orchestras, says Drucker. Hospitals have specialty units, each with its own knowledge, training, and language. Most are headed by a working specialist, not a full-time manager. That specialist reports to the top of the hospital, reducing the need for middle management. Work in the units is done by ad hoc teams that are assembled to address a patient's condition and diagnosis. Symphony orchestras are similar. They have one conductor, many high-grade specialists, and other support people.

Drucker believes that we are at the beginning of the third evolution in the structure of organizations. The first, which took place around 1900, separated business ownership from management. The second, in the 1920s, created the command-and-control corporation. The third, happening now, is the organization of knowledge specialists.

Why should IS executives be interested in supporting groups? Robert Johansen,[3] of the Institute for the Future and an author of two books on group working, notes that systems that support groups are important because most people spend 60 to 80 percent of their time working with others. Yet, from informal polls he has taken, people seem to feel they are most productive when they are working alone. Thus, they are not happy about how they work with others. This finding reveals a need for systems that support groups.

Groupware—electronic tools that support teams of collaborators—represents a fundamental change in the way people think about using computers, says Johansen. The things people need to work with others are different from the things they need to work alone. Thus, groupware is different from past software.

Groupware that takes full advantage of IT needs to be just another part of corporate information systems, says Johansen. The products need to be built on existing platforms—e-mail systems, LANs, departmental systems, and public network services, such as the telephone or the Internet. Use of these technologies must advance beyond the "horseless carriage" stage and lead to new organizational structures, he believes.

Given these three opinions on the importance of group working and the need for systems to support such collaboration, we turn to exploring the kinds of groups that exist and the kinds of systems that support their collaboration.

UNDERSTANDING GROUPS

Collaboration is all about getting work done in a group, rather than individually. However, groups differ from one another, and their work styles vary depending on a number of factors. Here are some characteristics of groups.

Characteristics of Groups

Not all groups are the same. Different types emerge for different tasks. Some of the characteristics that differentiate groups include membership, interaction, hierarchy, location, and time.

Membership.   Groups can be open, where almost anyone can join. Or they can be closed, where membership is restricted. Actually, a gray scale between open and closed indicates the degree of difficulty in gaining membership.

Interaction.   The group can be loosely coupled, where the activity of each member is relatively independent of the other members. Salespeople who have their own sales territories often fall into this category. Or the group can be tightly coupled, such as a project team where the work of each member is tied closely to the work of the other members. As in the case of gaining group membership, group couplings range widely from loose to tight.

Hierarchy.   A group can be just one part of a chain of command. Large public events, such at the Olympics or the Rose Parade, for instance, are planned and conducted by a hierarchy of committees. At the top is an ongoing committee that sets the general plans years in advance and selects the site and the top people for putting on each event. The top committee then oversees the work of the various detail committees. In addition, each of the detail committees may have subcommittees working on specific portions of their responsibility. This same hierarchy of committees occurs in large IT projects, such as implementing ERP, or in defining IT policies, such as an enterprise's overall IT architecture.

Location.   Group members may be collocated or dispersed. In the past, location influenced how they collaborated. When collocated, they could meet face-to-face. When dispersed, they either had to travel or use video conferencing to read each other's body language. But IT is making long-distance personal contact easier. More and more, teams and groups can work together effectively while remaining dispersed. In some cases, groups in Asia perform their work on a project and then pass that work on to a European group when their Asian workday ends. The European group progresses the work, then passes it to a group in the Americas when the European workday ends. In this type of group working, location allows round-the-clock work. This work-style is not yet a common phenomenon, but it does happen.

Time.   There are two aspects to the time dimension of group work: duration of the group and time intensity of the work. The work of some groups is short-lived. An ad hoc committee might be formed to uncover the root cause of a recurring problem, for instance, and then disband once that cause has been found. Other groups last for a long time; functions in an organization, such as HR or finance, are examples.

On time intensity, some groups' members work full-time on the group's work. Other groups only require intermittent work by their members. Of course, time intensity usually varies—high intensity at times interspersed with low intensity at other times.

We cite these characteristics to illustrate that providing computer-based support for groups is not uniform because of the many variations. Initially, support was for intra-company groups. However, the Internet has led to the ability to provide world-wide support for global teams that cross organizational lines. The main issues are what types of groups need support and why.

Types of Groups

Here is a list of just a few of the many, many kinds of groups.

- *Authority groups* involve formal authority (and often hierarchy), such as boss and subordinates or team leader and team members. Membership is closed and coupling is tight, but location is irrelevant in more and more cases, and generally these groups work full-time. In matrix management, people may have two bosses, one technical and one administrative.

- *Intra-departmental groups* can have members all doing essentially the same work, full-time, often under the same boss. Membership is closed, seniority generally exists, and interaction can range from tight (only do one job, on their own) to loose coupling (work with their neighbor). Location is generally close, but, as in the case of globally dispersed departments serving different parts of the world, they can be dispersed. These groups generally rely on LANs, departmental computers, and intranets to collaborate.

- *Project teams* generally have members who work full-time to accomplish a goal within a specific schedule. Generally, membership is closed, coupling is tight, and a hierarchy can exist. To obtain the expertise they need, these teams often have dispersed membership. They also have a limited duration: to the end of the project. Some teams bring in experts to fill special needs. For instance, a team creating a document might call on an editor near the end or a graphics person to add diagrams and handle document formatting.

- *Interdepartmental work groups* pass work from department to department (purchasing, receiving, accounts payable) in a chain, forming a super group. Membership is closed, coupling is tight, and hierarchy tends not to be present.

In support areas, such as finance, HR, and even IT, companies have been creating shared services departments that collocate people doing similar work. Formerly, these people were in remote offices, perhaps performing several jobs. Now they work full-time on one job in a center of expertise. In some cases, the function has been outsourced, which generally moves the entire function to the provider's site.

- **Committees and task forces** are formed to deal with a subject area or issue. Generally, neither requires full-time participation. Committees are usually ongoing; task forces just deal with the issue and disband. Membership may not be quite as closed as a project team, and interaction might not be as tightly coupled. Generally, the work is not full-time; although, in the case of a merger, an IT architecture team may need to temporarily work full-time to design the IT architecture of the merged enterprise.

- **Business relationship groups** are relationships with customers, groups of customers, suppliers, and so on. Membership often is closed in that a new organization may have to earn acceptance. Interaction is loosely coupled. A hierarchy is not likely, but favored customers and suppliers can have dominating influences. Generally, these are meant to be long-lived, but that may or may not be true, depending on changes in the business ecosystem.

- **Peer groups** meet to exchange ideas and opinions. Examples are fraternal organizations, repairmen who call on each other for help, and prospects called together for a sales presentation. Membership can range from relatively open to closed, and the interaction tends to be loosely coupled. Hierarchy usually is not much in evidence. Often the group has dispersed members who meet face-to-face rarely but may keep in close contact electronically.

- **Networks** are groups of people who socialize, exchange information, and expand the number of their personal acquaintances.

- **Electronic groups** include chat rooms, multi-user domains, user groups, and virtual worlds, all formed on the Internet to socialize, find information, entertain themselves, gain comfort, or just experiment with the online world. Membership is generally wide open, interaction is loosely coupled, there is usually no hierarchy, and the members are widely dispersed and most likely never meet face-to-face.

- **Communities of practice (CoPs)** is a term coined by the people at the Institute for Research on Learning[4] to refer to a group of people who work or socialize together for so long that they have developed an identifiable way of doing things. Such communities arise naturally at school, at work, in volunteer organizations, and in sports clubs. Some CoPs form as a way to share ideas about a technology they all use (as in the case of some engineers at National Semiconductor; see Chapter 14). Others form as a way to get work done faster and easier; they informally devise shortcuts and practices. Generally, CoPs have open membership. They last as long as their members see them as useful.

- **Network armies** is a term coined by Richard Hunter of Gartner EXP[5] in his book *World Without Secrets: Business, Crime, and Privacy in the Age of Ubiquitous Computing* to mean a widely dispersed group of people that forms to further a cause. Hunter sees the open source movement as a network army. So are most grassroots movements, such as groups opposed to globalization, terrorist organizations, and animal rights activists. Leaders emerge and membership is usually open. Network armies increasingly use electronic means to further their agendas.

These final two types of groups—communities of practice and network armies—are probably unfamiliar because they have only recently been identified. They are likely to increase in the future because they take advantage of IT, they have the flexibility to form and act quickly (which is an advantage in our faster-moving world), and they could increasingly wield power. Thus, we delve into each a bit more.

Communities of Practice

The "father" of CoPs is Etienne Wenger, who identified them and has studied them since authoring the definitive book on CoPs, *Communities of Practice: Learning, Meaning, and Identity*.[6] In an article with William Snyder of Social Capital Group,[7] Wenger and Snyder point out that CoPs are all about managing knowledge (the subject of the next chapter); that is, capturing and spreading know-how, ideas, innovations, and experience. CoPs are an organizational form that complements other means for sharing knowledge. In fact, in some enterprises, CoPs form the foundation of their knowledge management efforts. Wenger and Snyder define them as informal groups that form around a passion for or expertise about something. This "something" can vary from deep-water drilling to check processing, they note. The subject matter really does not matter; the goal in forming a CoP is to share members' experiences, expertise, and problems.

Though informal, some CoPs have had a profound effect on their enterprise by driving strategies, creating new lines of business, spreading best practices, solving seemingly intractable problems, retaining people, and increasing the level of expertise in some areas. To date, few enterprises have formally recognized CoPs or supported them. Without support, CoPs can be difficult to organize and then sustain.

Being informal, CoPs resist being managed. However, some enterprises have seen their value and have learned how to nurture them. Wenger and Snyder believe these enterprises are the forward-thinking ones. They have learned how to provide the infrastructure and climate for these self-organizing entities to form of their own volition, meet and share via numerous channels (face-to-face, e-mail, IM, video conferencing), and even strengthen the organization's formal mechanisms. As an example, consider DaimlerChrysler and its support of CoPs, which began in the Chrysler Corporation in the late 1980s.

CASE EXAMPLE

DAIMLERCHRYSLER

In the late 1980s, when Chrysler Corporation was about to go out of business because of competition from Japanese auto companies, CoPs played a large role in its survival, write Etienne Wenger, Richard McDermott, and William Snyder

(Case Continued)

in their book *Cultivating Communities of Practice*.[8] In the late 1980s, it took Chrysler 5 years to bring a vehicle to market; competitors took as little as 3. To compete, management had to reinvent how the company worked. Its organizational structure at the time was functional, with design units passing vehicle designs to manufacturing units that then passed back the designs after modifying them for manufacturability.

To reduce this iterative process, which added significant time to development, the company reorganized into "car platforms," such as Jeep, minivan, truck, or small car. Engineers and other workers reported to only one platform. This change reduced development time to 2.5 years—a significant improvement. However, it also led to multiple versions of parts, uncoordinated relationships with suppliers, and mistakes repeated among the platform groups, write the authors.

Employees with similar jobs needed to communicate across the platforms, but the new structure did not foster that interchange. So, some began meeting informally. Rather than formalize these cross-platform groups, they became known as Tech Clubs; in essence, CoPs that were supported and sanctioned by top management.

They began to take responsibility for their area of expertise by conducting design reviews. They even revived the old idea of creating "engineering books of knowledge," which are databases that store the information engineers need to do their job, such as compliance standards, lessons learned, and best practices. Such books only succeed when the

users "own" them and naturally keep them up-to-date as part of their everyday work.

Once community members within Chrysler saw the value of their book to their work, ownership took hold. They now spend much of their meeting time debating the items that should be in the chapters, and the wording that should be used, to be sure what they state is correct. The books are intended to deal with the real problems they face. Wenger, McDermott, and Snyder point out that the engineers find these debates and discussions to be just as important as the final documents because they learn a lot from interacting with their peers. Thus, while they are building practice standards they are also building a community. The two go hand-in-hand in successful CoPs, the authors note.

The Chrysler division now has over 100 Tech Clubs, and a team is introducing the concept to its parent, DaimlerChrysler. In fact, this team helps Tech Club coordinators in the United States and Germany launch their clubs, produce useful knowledge resources for members, and keep their clubs vibrant and relevant. The Tech Club support team also helps ensure that the clubs are working on common technology platforms so that they can share knowledge across clubs.

Wenger, McDermott, and Snyder point out that these Tech Clubs provide DaimlerChrysler with the crucial matrix structure they need to have engineers focus on their platform yet share their knowledge across platforms without the administrative headaches that formal matrix structures have required. ∎

Although CoPs cannot be designed, they can be nurtured. Wenger and Snyder[6] believe companies need to perform three nurturing acts to garner benefits from CoPs: identify potential CoPs, provide them with an infrastructure, and measure them appropriately.

Identifying Potential CoPs.   To identify potential CoPs, companies can provide the means and experience for developing them by providing CoP consultants. Thereby, an employee interested in forming a CoP can explore the possibility with someone who understands CoPs and can help the employee interview potential members to see what sorts of problems the community should address to provide real value to members. The employee and consultant can then plan an initial activity to not only address the identified problems, but also link them to the company's agenda. But to even get off the ground, say Wenger and Snyder, the members need to personally "connect" to the group's intent; otherwise, people will not participate.

Providing a CoP Infrastructure.   To provide a CoP infrastructure, executives need to give CoPs legitimacy because they lack resources and formal standing in the enterprise. Sometimes that means extolling the contributions of CoPs and the people who organize them, instituting compensation systems that reward collaboration, and budgeting money to build IT systems that CoPs need. In some instances, membership is not open; an employee must be recognized as an expert to be invited to join. Thus, there is formal recognition of the esteem of belonging. Having executive sponsors also provides a kind of CoP infrastructure, as does linking them to a corporate university, if one exists, or paying for them to participate in CoP activities. Providing support to organize events is also a form of infrastructure.

Measuring CoPs.   To measure CoPs appropriately often means measuring their contributions in nontraditional ways because their effects may not be immediate. Their contributions may only show up in the formal organization (on a team or department's work), not in the community's work. It is not always possible to identify a good idea as originating in a CoP. To assess CoPs, note Wenger and Snyder, listen to the stories members tell about their CoP, such as how a comment at a CoP gathering spurred an idea, solved a major problem, or accelerated a project. Such anecdotes generally do not count in formal measurement programs, but collecting stories systematically can paint a picture of the kinds of contributions specific CoPs are making. In some cases, such collections of stories can even lead to estimates of money saved or revenues generated.

CoPs are emerging first in knowledge-based enterprises. But to flourish, executives need to understand their characteristics and how they work. Wenger and Snyder see CoPs as an emerging business form that will be as familiar in the near future as business units and business teams are today.

Network Armies

As noted earlier, Richard Hunter[5] coined the term *network army*, which he defines as a set of individuals and communities aligned by a cause. They have moral and intellectual influencers as opposed to formal leadership. Major differences may exist among members' overall beliefs. As an example, consider the civil liberties community in the United States, which includes members from both the left and right wings of the dominant political parties. Network armies are as permanent as their common agenda; their cohesive force is their value system. Their communications are in open forums that anyone can join. Modern communication technologies, including the photocopy machine, the fax machine, and most recently the Internet, have dramatically increased the reach of network armies.

Network armies have existed for a long time, but they can now appear suddenly with a lot of power because of three developments: (1) high-speed information flows due to a common language (English) and communication system (Internet), (2) the geometrically expanding power of networks (adding one person geometrically increases the number of interconnections), and (3) the international visibility now afforded just about any cause. Network armies go about their business in the open; anyone can join in or listen in to their discussions. As a result, says Hunter, the network army is the social and political structure that suits a world without secrets.

One of the intriguing observations Hunter makes about network armies is that hierarchies (like traditional businesses, governments, and armies) have a tremendously difficult time fighting network armies because they have no single leader; they are like a hydra with many heads. They are so dispersed and part of the fabric of society that they are difficult to find, let alone fight. Hunter believes network armies are on the rise. Here is an example of a network army.

CASE EXAMPLE

THE OPEN SOURCE MOVEMENT

Richard Hunter[5] of Gartner EXP believes that the open source movement is a prime example of a network army. Open source means that (1) the complete source code must be distributed with any and all distributions, and (2) anyone can modify and redistribute the code to anyone to use. A prime example of open source software is Linux, the operating system whose kernel was written by Linus Torvalds. The opposite of open source is proprietary software, which is sold only in its compiled state (undecipherable by humans) and is not allowed to be changed except by the developer.

Open source is mainly about how software is developed, enhanced, and managed. The open source movement is a community with a shared culture, where people earn their membership by the quality of the code they produce. Members are volunteers; no one is paid. They do it for fun (they love to code), to hang around with other like-minded developers ("fiery brains," says Hunter), and to be part of a worthy cause. Torvalds' goal in developing Linux was to "write software that does not suck." He reasoned that the best way to do that would be to let interested software developers chip in and improve any part that attracted them. Thus, it is a culture of mavericks who want lots of personal autonomy, guided by minimal conformance.

The movement has a massive flat structure with 4 "influencers" (including Torvalds), 6 to 8 distributors who package versions, some 200 project leaders who

(Case Continued)

manage active projects, and some 750,000 volunteer developers (as of late 2001). The number is probably higher now. The developers follow the influencers because they have the same values. This flat structure is possible, says Hunter, because the Internet allows the influencers to communicate directly with the developers, and vice versa. Hence, the influencers know what the volunteers think, which can make it both harder for them to lead as well as to mislead. In addition, all communications are open via bulletin boards, e-mail lists, and other Internet-based channels that anyone can join.

Hunter notes that when he and his Gartner colleagues critiqued the viability of open source software in 1999, they believed it would capture 15 percent of the server operating system market. "We did not realize this was a disruptive technology that could change the software world," he notes. Less than 2 years later, after "getting it," he and his colleagues significantly increased their assessment to predicting that open source would be used in 80 percent of businesses by year-end 2003.

Hunter now believes it is not wise to underestimate the claims of network armies, as Microsoft apparently did. The worst mistake a business can make is to become the nemesis of a network army, and that is what Microsoft did in 1998. Until that time, the open source movement's only goal was to write useful software. However, in August 1998, Microsoft saw the open source movement as a threat and wrote an internal paper that proposed ways to eliminate it. That study, of course, fell into the hands of an open source member, states Hunter, because this is a world without secrets. The open source movement always distrusted

Microsoft, and that distrust hardened into rage once the study was published on the Web under the moniker, *The Halloween Papers*.

Microsoft's past tactics for addressing competitors are not appropriate for dealing with a network army, writes Hunter. There are no open source revenues, so Microsoft cannot undercut prices (as it did in bundling its browser into Windows and destroying Netscape). There is no one to negotiate with, so the movement cannot be bought and then taken apart (as many past competitors have been).

All "negotiations" with a network army must be in public, notes Hunter, and consist of actions, not words, which is what Microsoft is now doing. Its executives are arguing against the movement in public forums, hoping to dissuade executives from using open source software. But when it first denied, and then acknowledged, that it was using such software itself to support Hotmail and other services due to the superiority of the open source software, Microsoft lost credibility. Open source members only believe actions. They want people to do the right thing because they see their cause as a moral one.

Hunter believes Microsoft thought it was up against a rival business and tried to use the tactics it used successfully against other businesses. However, a network army is more like a religion than a business, and you do not fight a religious movement by telling its members that they are worshippers of an evil, false god. Better to find some way to work with them on projects of mutual interest as a means of establishing personal trust. However, Microsoft has not wanted to coexist with anyone, so it has taken

(*Case Continued*)

a different route. It is a dangerous route, Hunter believes. Businesses that face a network army cannot make it go away without addressing the underlying issues. Treating a network army like a business is bound to backfire. ■

Having explored types and characteristics of groups, we turn our attention to systems to support collaboration.

SYSTEMS TO SUPPORT COLLABORATION

The activities of groups can be divided into two generic categories. One is *communication and interaction*. *Communication* means transmitting information from one person to another or to several others; *interaction* means back-and-forth communication over time. Two, groups are involved in *decision making and problem solving*. The members reach a decision or form a consensus. Both types of group activities are needed in collaboration. Historically, systems supporting group work have originated from one or the other of these two major functions. Office systems, and in particular e-mail, support people-to-people communication. Researchers in the area of computer-supported cooperative work generally have emphasized technology to aid communication, such as enhanced computer conferencing and systems to assist two or more people to work on the same project. On the other hand, group DSS work has evolved from the DSS community and focuses on reaching a conclusion, decision, or consensus, even though it includes technology to support communication.

A second way to view the work of groups is the way Geraldine DeSantis of Duke University and Brent Gallupe of the University of Minnesota[9] did in one of the early frameworks. Their matrix, shown in Figure 12-1, has proximity of group members on one dimension (together/dispersed) and duration of interaction on the other (limited/ongoing). The figure gives one technology example per cell. Note that this matrix is relevant for both communication and decision making. For example, decision making has been the intent of decision rooms, whereas LANs are usually perceived mainly as supporting communication.

Groups in close proximity and with a limited decision-making duration might use a decision room where every attendee uses a computer to participate in the group's deliberations. An example of such a room is presented shortly. Groups that are dispersed and have a limited decision-making duration might use decision rooms connected via video conferencing. Or, as at one highly advanced lab with two facilities, they might communicate via video walls. Standing by one wall allowed employees to converse in real time with someone standing by the wall at the other site. People would meet at the wall to make decisions or just to converse (as a person would when happening upon a colleague in a hallway).

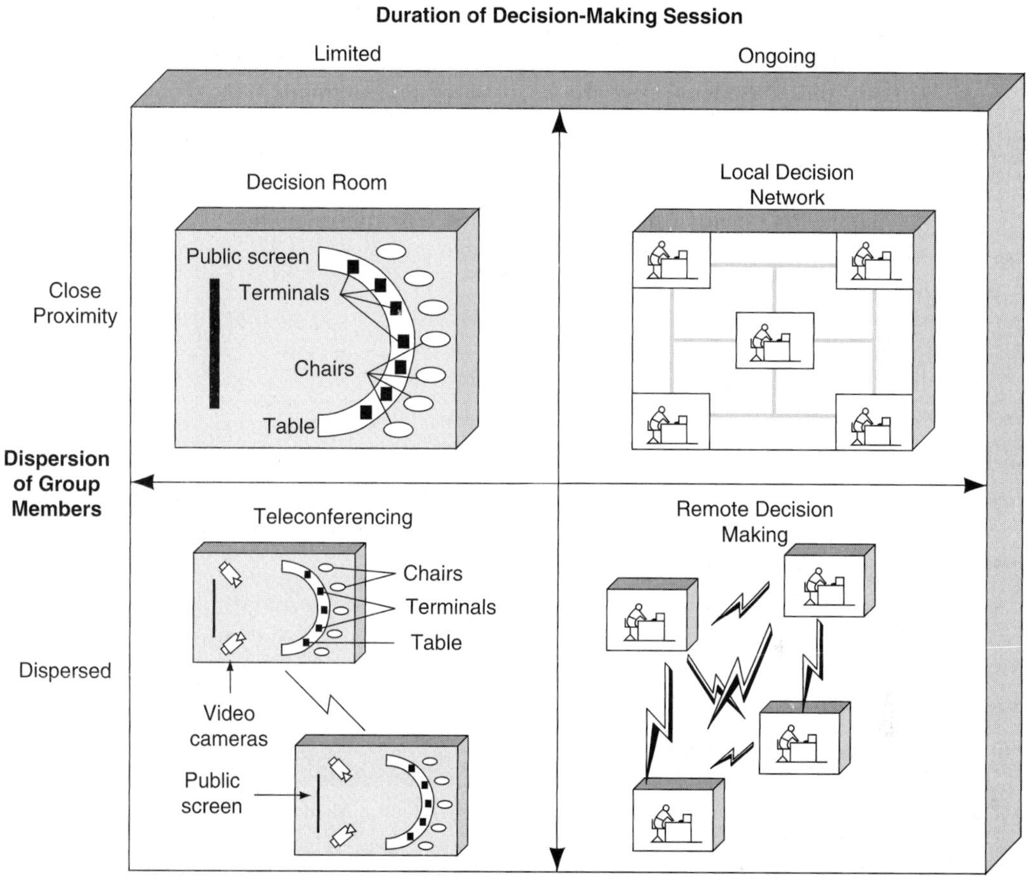

Duration of Decision-Making Session

FIGURE 12-1 Framework for Group Decision Support

Source: G. DeSantis and B. Gallupe, "Group Decision Support Systems: A New Frontier," *Data Base,* Winter 1985, pp. 10–15.

Close-proximity groups with ongoing decisions could use a local decision network, IM, or perhaps a chat room on an intranet. Dispersed groups with ongoing decisions could also use an intranet, if appropriate, or a secure decision system. An example is presented shortly.

Yet a third way to categorize the work of groups uses a variation of the DeSantis-Gallupe matrix by having time on one dimension (same time/different time) and place on the other (same place/different place). This third view has become dominant, so it is used here. Bob Johansen of the Institute for the Future (IFTF) is a leader in the field of groupware. He and his colleagues at IFTF extended the DeSantis-Gallupe matrix to form the time/place framework shown in Figure 12-2.

The two values, either same or different, on each dimension designate whether the group members are communicating and interacting over time and/or distance. The "same time/same place" cell in the upper left, for example, includes electronic meeting support systems. The "different time/different place" cell in the lower right

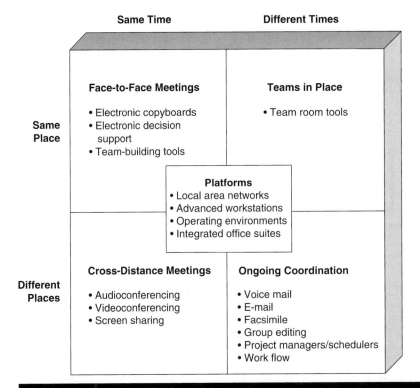

FIGURE 12-2 Groupware Options

Source: Courtesy of Robert Johansen of the Institute for the Future, Menlo Park, CA.

incorporates such communication-oriented systems as e-mail, computer conferencing, and use of Lotus Notes.

Until recently, there has been little integration among the systems in the cells, even though it is clear to researchers and developers that supporting collaboration must aim to permit anytime, anyplace group working. But that is changing. Systems used by individuals are also being used by groups, as demonstrated by Western Digital's use of digital dashboards (Chapter 11). In addition, systems used in meetings are also being used to "extend" those meetings over time after the participants have dispersed. For instance, a Lotus Notes database might be used in a meeting as well as outside of it. Instant messaging is used in both settings, as are the dashboards at Western Digital (Chapter 11). The Internet has aided in extending the use of systems among the cells.

Supporting "Same Time/Same Place" Collaboration

Supporting "same time/same place" collaboration has generally meant supporting meetings, and a lot of work has focused on this area. One study found that the average executive in a U.S. company spends more than 800 hours a year in meetings. Not only does this figure represent a large portion of total work hours (on the order of 30 percent), but even worse, the executives reported that they considered about 240 of those hours to have been wasted in useless meetings.

The Problem with Meetings.   From the many meetings we have attended, many shortcomings have been evident. Meetings often have no agenda or only a superficial one. No problems are clearly spelled out in advance, and no specific action items are proposed to address the problems. If actions (or motions) are proposed, alternatives are not fully considered. If documentation about the issues has been provided before the meeting, some members choose not to study it; they expect to be briefed at the meeting. The chairperson may do little or no follow-up between meetings to see that the members carry out their assignments.

Some meetings are doomed from the start. Key people arrive late or do not attend at all. Necessary information does not arrive. Some group members have forgotten to fulfill their assignments. Then the meeting chairperson may do a poor job of managing the meeting time. Discussion may be allowed to wander from the subject. Time may be spent on briefing attendees or on routine matters—reviewing and correcting minutes of prior meetings, getting committee progress reports, and so on. Such meetings tend to run over their allotted time, with important items receiving poor consideration. Often, too, a few people dominate the discussion; not infrequently, these people are repetitious, saying the same things over and over. Conversely, some people do not speak up and contribute their ideas.

Finally, many meetings are wasteful from a cost standpoint. A meeting involving even a few managers and professionals costs hundreds of dollars per hour in salaries alone; large meetings can easily cost thousands of dollars per hour. If travel is required, costs are even higher. Add to these considerations the fact that the participants are unavailable for other activities while tied up in the meetings.

IT Can Help.   The goals of systems for improving meetings are to (1) eliminate some meetings, (2) encourage better planning and better preparation for those meetings that must be held, and (3) improve the effectiveness of meetings that are held.

Eliminate some meetings.   The most likely candidates for elimination are the meetings that do not call for a group decision or group action but are simply for group updating. Progress report meetings are an example, particularly if progress (actual progress versus planned progress) can be reported frequently by e-mail, the company intranet, or an electronic team meeting place. Meetings where key people cannot attend or where needed information is not yet available can be canceled at the last moment. E-mail, voice mail, and IM systems allow the word to be spread rapidly. Intranets allow progress and status reports to be posted in a form that is easily available to everyone. In short, some of the work done in meetings can be shifted from the "same time/same place" cell to the "different time/different place" cell in the time/place matrix.

Better preparation for meetings.   Computer conferencing can play a significant role in improving preparation for meetings. A computer conferencing system is actually a form of enhanced e-mail. Participants can log on at their convenience, read all entries made by others since they last logged on, and make their contributions. In the planning stage of a meeting, such a system can be used to obtain reactions to the proposed agenda, and those reactions might spur debate and alternatives. Furthermore, routine matters may be handled before the meeting, such as review and approval of minutes, receiving committee progress reports, voting on routine action items, and so on. Group members can give attention to these matters at their convenience, saving valuable synchronous meeting time for more important business. The chairperson can also use the conferencing system for follow-up activities. Finally, the system can provide a written record of pre- and post-meeting communications.

Improve the effectiveness and efficiency of meetings.   One of the major benefits of meeting support systems is improved meeting efficiency and effectiveness. Meetings are more effective when the ideas generated by the group are more creative and everyone in the group is actively involved. Meetings are more effective when group commitment happens quickly. Following is a case in point.

CASE EXAMPLE

BURR-BROWN CORPORATION

Burr-Brown Corporation, with headquarters in Tucson, Arizona, manufactures and sells electronics parts to other electronic manufacturers. It has about 1,500 employees and $180 million in annual sales.

When the University of Arizona, also in Tucson, created a decision room in its IS department, the CEO of Burr-Brown decided to use it for management's 3-day annual strategic planning meeting. He was so pleased with the results that the firm used it again the following year for the same purpose.

The Decision Room

The room has 24 workstations arranged in a semicircle on two tiers. Up to 48 people can use the room, 2 persons per workstation. In an adjacent control room is the file server, and at the front of the room is a facilitator's control station, as well as a rear projection screen for video, slides, and movies, and a white board. All the participants' workstations and the facilitator's workstation are connected by a LAN.

The university has developed a number of decision room software tools, and more than 100 groups have used their decision room. That software is now marketed under the name GroupSystems by GroupSystems.com.

The Electronic Brainstorming System is the most popular of the tools; it is used by more than 70 percent of the groups. Like most of the tools, it allows participants to simultaneously and anonymously key in ideas on a specific question. After an idea is entered and sent to the file server, the participant can see the ideas entered by others.

After the brainstorming portion of a meeting, many groups use the Issue Analyzer to organize the ideas. A Voting Tool ranks ideas and a Topic Commenter attaches comments to ideas already in the system. Finally, the groups can use the Policy Formation software to study alternatives. Most group "discussions" using these tools are done via keyboards rather than by talking. However, some other tools do encourage face-to-face discussions.

Burr-Brown's Use of the Room

Burr-Brown's annual strategic planning meetings had always been held off-site, with some 9 to 10 executives attending. When they used the decision room,

(*Case Continued*)

31 executives attended. The IS department at the university provided a meeting facilitator to help plan the meeting and then facilitate it.

During the meeting, the facilitator explained each tool before it was to be used. The facilitator also kept participants on track and was the neutral leader of the meeting so that Burr-Brown's CEO could attend as a participant. In addition, an assistant facilitator and three other assistants also were present. They helped the participants use the hardware and software, made copies of the documents generated by the system, and so on.

Before the meeting, several planning meetings were held to settle the meeting agenda. Each of the 11 divisions was asked to prepare a document to describe its 1-year action plan and rolling 5-year plan, including objectives and projected budgets. Participants received these plans before the meeting.

The agenda for the 3-day meeting was:

- Day 1: Long-term strategy planning
- Day 2: Short-range action planning
- Day 3: Wrap-up in both areas

The meeting began with the group using the workstations to generate ideas about expected corporate performance in the coming years. They then organized these ideas to create the framework for discussing each division's plans.

For the next day and a half, they entered comments on the 5-year strategic plans and 1-year action plans of each division, one division at a time.

They also spent some time brainstorming ways to accomplish the year's objectives and then ranking the ideas. The group settled on specific actions they would take on the top seven issues.

On the last afternoon, they divided into four groups to discuss important topics face-to-face. The planning meeting ended with the four groups presenting their recommendations.

Executives' Reactions

After the 3-day session, the participants were asked to summarize their reactions to the decision room. They reported the following.

- **It increased involvement.** One senior vice president commented that the decision room allowed them to do in 3 days' time what would have taken months. The CEO noted that the past sessions could not be larger than 10 people to be manageable; and in those sessions, only two or three people really spoke up. With the decision room, 31 people were able to attend without hampering deliberations, and the group's comments were much more open than in the past.

  During one 1-hour electronic brainstorming session, 404 comments were made, with the fewest number of comments from any of the 24 workstations, some of which had two users, being 4 and the highest being 27. Seven workstations contributed more than 20. Thus, contributions were relatively evenly distributed across the group.

  The group had mixed reactions about the efficiency of the system. In a post-session questionnaire answered by 26 participants, 11 stated that it was more efficient than past meetings, 9 said it was not, and 6 were neutral. However, the majority agreed

(Case Continued)

that the facilitator was important in helping them use the room.

- ***The planning process was more effective.*** Several executives mentioned two aspects of the session that enhanced its effectiveness. The main one was anonymity. Due to anonymity, more people asked more questions and made more suggestions than they did in the former meeting format where all discussion was verbal, which identified the contributor.

Second, the planning process itself was extremely educational, said the CEO. "People walked in with narrow perceptions of the company and walked out with a CEO's perception. This is the view that is sought in strategic planning, but is usually not achieved," he commented 3 months after the session. This type of education had not happened at previous planning sessions.

One Year Later

One year later, 25 executives participated in a 2-day session. About 16 had attended the year before. This year, the intent of the meeting was different. It was to critique plans so that their impact on others and the support they needed from others were more explicit.

After the CEO described the firm's objectives and the economic climate, the planning session began with the group critiquing the previous year's results, company-wide. The 2-day session ended with each business unit manager commenting on the ideas received about his or her particular unit

and how those ideas might affect the unit's action plan.

From the previous year's session, they learned that brainstorming is effective if the groups are structured properly. A large group can consider a few issues, such as corporate objectives, and present ideas on those topics. But a large group cannot "converse" because of the large number of ideas to consider.

For "dialogs," Burr-Brown found it best to form several small groups, with each group addressing a few issues. One person puts in a statement, another person comments on it, then someone else comments, and so on. In the second year, they conducted small group dialogs and found them effective.

The company also learned that the discussion room is not a substitute for a planning process. It is excellent for generating many ideas in a short time. However, because face-to-face interaction is reduced, people are less likely to make commitments and agree on courses of action than in a face-to-face setting. Therefore, Burr-Brown does not use the room to reach consensus.

The communications manager recommends that others planning to use such a room tell the participants about the room beforehand. Just send them an e-mail that describes the room and includes a photograph, he suggests. Also, explain to participants how their comments will be used because the use probably will affect how they answer questions.

In all, Burr-Brown participants were pleased with the candor and objectivity the decision room elicited. They believe its use has enhanced their annual planning meetings. ■

Supporting "Same Time/Same Place" Presentations and Discussions

A second "same time/same place" situation that can benefit from group support tools is traditional presentation-discussion sessions found in classrooms, conference sessions, and business meetings. In an article in the *Communications of the ACM,* Robert Davison and Robert Briggs[10] explored the advantages of using a Group Support System (GSS) in a presentation-discussion session held in a workshop setting. The system was similar to the one used by Burr-Brown. Each member of the audience had a workstation, all interconnected by a LAN, with a public screen to show the group's interactions. The presenter had a separate screen for audiovisuals used in the presentation.

To begin their exploration, Davison and Briggs made the following seven hypotheses about the potential advantages and disadvantages of attendees using a GSS at the workshops:

- *More opportunities for discussion.* Using a GSS would eliminate the need to divide available airtime among potential speakers because participants could contribute simultaneously. The parallel, non-oral communication channels would multiply the time available to the audience. In addition, because they would be communicating online, the participants could interact with each other during the actual presentation, which further multiplied available airtime.

- *More equal participation.* Because the GSS provides many parallel communication channels, loud or strong personalities probably would not dominate the discussion. Unlike oral discussions, the amount contributed by one person was expected to be independent of the amount contributed by others. This expectation was more likely to lead to a more equal distribution of discussion among the attendees.

- *Permanent record of discussion.* The GSS would capture a permanent electronic transcript of the online discussion. Thus, both participants and presenters could access the details long after the discussion was over.

- *Improved feedback to presenters.* With unrestricted airtime for audience members and a permanent record of their discussion, presenters anticipated more comments as well as more detail in those comments. Furthermore, the anonymity allowed by the GSS would reduce some participants' concerns about negative repercussions if they contributed unpopular, critical, or new ideas. Thus, the presenters could receive more unfiltered critical analysis of their work using the GSS.

- *Improved learning.* The GSS was also expected to reduce attention blocking; that is, the loss of attentiveness caused by people trying to remember what they want to say during the presentation. Working in parallel, participants could record ideas when they occurred, then return their attention to the presentation. With more discussion time, reduced attention blocking, increased participation, improved feedback, and a permanent record, GSS users would retain more knowledge from a presentation than when they used conventional methods.

- *Remote and asynchronous participation.* In addition, people who do not attend a presentation could still benefit by reading and contributing after the event. However, this opportunity does not mean replacing all face-to-face conferences and presentations with distributed online interaction. Many people find casual conversations in hallways and over meals to be as valuable as formal presentations.

- ***Potential negative effects.*** Despite such benefits, Davison and Briggs were concerned that online discussions during presentations might be a mixed blessing. Human attention is limited, so online discussions might distract participants to the point where they lose the thread of the presentation. Such distractions could outweigh other benefits. Furthermore, the online discussions could digress from the concepts in the presentation or even devolve into flaming. In addition, the anonymity of online discussion could hinder the evolution of a social community among the participants

To explore these hypotheses, Davison and Briggs conducted some experiments at a conference known for its interactive workshop-like sessions.

CASE EXAMPLE

HICSS

As part of the Hawaii International Conference on System Sciences (HICSS), 43 participants attended a 3-hour tutorial on business process reengineering. The workshop had 24 laptops placed around two sets of tables, along with two large screens—one to show the PowerPoint slides for the presentation and the other to show the contents of the electronic discussion. To overcome concerns about politeness, the presenter encouraged the participants to use the equipment by saying that he considered typing while he was talking to be both polite and desirable. However, only eight comments were submitted during the 3 hours. Similarly low levels of participation occurred in two later 9-minute paper presentation sessions. Again, informal interviews revealed a widespread fear of rudeness.

Davison and Briggs hypothesized that because the attendees had not used a GSS during a presentation, they might

not imagine how non-intrusive it could be. They also hypothesized that participants might not realize how easy the software was to use. Therefore, the following day, they used the GSS for three 90-minute sessions. Each session had three paper presentations.

As each session began, the moderator asked participants to use the GSS to respond to the question, "What are the most pressing research issues facing the technology-supported learning research community?" Everyone contributed an idea and then responded online to an idea contributed by someone else.

The first presenter told the group that the oral discussion following the presentations would draw from the online discussion. Two subsequent speakers asked for online responses to specific questions. All others asked for critical feedback about their presentations. As soon as the first speaker began, members of the audience

(Case Continued)

started typing. Participants contributed 275 comments during the three sessions, ranging from 20 to 54 per presentation. About 94 percent of comments were presentation related, with no instances of flaming. Furthermore, during other sessions with no GSS, oral contributions to the post-presentation discussions came from no more than four people. Observations in the GSS-supported sessions showed that contributions came from all over the audience.

One Year Later

During the following year, Davison and Briggs refined both their GSS methods and their questionnaire. They then conducted a more rigorous follow-up study at the next HICSS conference. The study addressed three primary research questions: What effect would GSS have on participation and perceived learning? Would the GSS be perceived as a detrimental distraction? What effect would GSS use have on the perceived value of the presentations and discussions?

At this conference, 34 laptops in a workshop setting let participants have a clearer view of the large public screen. All GSS-supported sessions began with a brief hands-on activity related to the session topic. A moderator invited online participation at the beginning of each presentation, and most presenters added their encouragement. Participants were urged to raise key issues from the online discussions during the post-presentation discussions. After the sessions, Davison and Briggs administered their survey questionnaire. They received data from 173 participants. Of those, 73 reported having used GSS, whereas 70 reported they had not.

Results of the Survey

From the survey, Davison and Briggs learned that GSS users were significantly more willing to participate in the discussions than non-GSS users, and they reported doing so at significantly higher levels. The participants in both the GSS-supported and standard presentations had equal opportunity to contribute to oral discussion and did so at approximately equal rates. However, the participants who used the GSS also contributed hundreds of comments to the online discussions, so their overall participation was substantially higher. Furthermore, a much higher percentage of the audience got involved in the GSS discussion than in the oral discussion. Thus, it appears that the GSS may have accomplished its primary purpose: to increase participation and learning. But at what cost?

Overall, participants were comfortable with the amount of distraction and digression in the sessions. Only three GSS users and four non-GSS users reported negative reactions—too few for meaningful statistical analysis. Thus, the GSS did not appear to create widespread perceptions of undue distraction or digression.

No online flaming occurred, and nearly all the online contributions were relevant to the presentations. Content analysis of the online transcripts suggested that participants grasped the key concepts of the presentations, which is further evidence the GSS did not distract them from the oral delivery of information.

Overall, the respondents also reported receiving positive value from the conference sessions and the GSS. This response suggests that the GSS enabled the groups to increase the

(*Case Continued*)

quantity of something they valued — the discussions and feedback — without reducing its quality. Many participants chose to take electronic transcripts with them at the end of each session, whereas others downloaded transcripts from the Internet. Thus, the value derived from the discussion was extended beyond the walls of the presentation hall. ■

Supporting "Different-Place" Collaboration

One of the most promising uses of groupware is ongoing coordination by groups who work in different places, and perhaps at different times. With the increasing marketplace emphasis on cycle-time reduction, companies can use the globe and its three main regions (Europe, Asia, and the Americas) to extend their workday to round-the-clock by passing work from groups in one region to the next at the end of each one's workday, as the following personal example attests.

> *I had that experience for the first time a few years ago. On one of my first writing projects, the author of the report, who worked in England, e-mailed me his thoughts and questions on the topic at the end of his workday. During my workday, while he was sleeping, I did some thinking and research on the topic, and e-mailed my thoughts and findings back to him at the end of my day. While I slept, he worked. He and I worked this way, swapped long e-mails, for about 1 week. But we got at least 2 weeks' worth of work done. It was tremendously exhilarating and productive without either of us having to work long hours.*

One of the results of using IT to support collaboration is the formation of virtual teams; they exist in space, but not in one place. Some never meet face-to-face. These teams often form to handle a project, then disband after the project is complete. They tend to operate in three cells of Johansen's matrix.

- *Same time/same place:* Typically, the team meets face-to-face initially to develop the basic plan and objectives.
- *Different time/different place:* They then communicate by e-mail and do data gathering and analysis separately.
- *Same time/different place:* If their technology is strong enough, they may have audio or video conferences to discuss developments and progress toward goals.

Following is a case example of a successful virtual team, as described in the award-winning paper to the Society for Information Management by Carman et al.[11]

CASE EXAMPLE

BOEING-ROCKETDYNE

Boeing-Rocketdyne is the major U.S. manufacturer of liquid-fueled rocket engines, which are used to launch communication satellites. When the company faced significant competition and price pressures from Eastern European companies, it initiated a project called SLICE (Simple Low-Cost Innovative Engine). SLICE's business objectives were dramatic: Reduce the cost of the rocket engine to one-tenth, get the engine to market 10 times faster than the Space Shuttle's main engine, and increase the useful life of the rocket engine by 300 percent. In short, it was a breakthrough project. So much so that none of the senior technical managers thought the goals were possible, and these managers, as a group, had hundreds of years of experience designing rocket engines. Only one advanced program manager was willing to give the project a try.

The team faced many challenges. The first was work style. To get the best people on the project, they needed to come from different disciplines and different organizations. Management would not allow them to be taken off their regular work, so they could not be collocated. They had to work virtually, using electronic collaboration technology, without holding face-to-face meetings. Furthermore, the members had not worked together as a team, so they had different product experiences and used different design processes. Finally, they had to submit only one design, a design that Rocketdyne's conservative senior management would accept.

Despite these challenges, the project was a tremendous success. It lasted 10 months, during which time the team held 89 online meetings using a collaborative technology called the Internet Notebook. The members created and critiqued 20 designs and submitted more than 650 entries into the notebook. The seven senior technical managers who reviewed the project at its conclusion stated that it had surpassed its objectives. The design was approved for the next phase: testing the assumptions about how the liquid would flow through the components.

The design accomplished the following:

- The engine's thrust changer had only 6 parts, down from more than 450.

- The manufacturing cost was estimated to be $1.5 million, down from $20 million.

- Quality was predicted to be Nine Sigma, up from the industry standard of Six Sigma, which meant one failure in 10 billion.

- Development cost was $47,000, down from $4.5 million.

The team was awarded the Department of Defense's Advanced Research Program for "validating a process for virtual collocation teams."

In addition, none of the team members spent more than 15 percent of his or her time on the project, the team stayed within its budget (even though the project

(Case Continued)

took longer than expected), and the total engineering hours were one-half normal using the collaborative technology.

Lessons Learned

Why was the team so successful? Carman and his colleagues studied the life of this project and suggested the following success factors.

A Prior Formal Agreement on Sharing Intellectual Property Was Crucial.
Boeing-Rocketdyne anticipated the need for close cooperation on some significant projects well before the SLICE team was formed. Therefore, they began developing a partnership agreement to govern such teams. It turns out that the legal aspects of intellectual property are complicated, so they need time to be defined. Because this agreement was in place when the SLICE team began its work, the team members could move ahead quickly without being concerned about who was able to know what.

The Technology Had to Fit the Team's Virtual Meetings.
The team's collaborative technology—the Internet Notebook—was developed by a third party based on the list of requirements drawn up by several of the team members. The technology allowed the team members to

- Access the notebook from anywhere.
- Create, comment on, reference-link, search, and sort entries that could consist of sketches, snapshots, hotlinks to desktop applications, texts, or templates.
- Use an electronic white board for near-instantaneous access to entries.

Thus, from the outset, the team had a technology suited to its needs, at least as the team initially defined them. The team focused its early discussions on creating a coordination protocol for facilitating its collaborative use. Figure 12-3 shows how the team members rated these features.

The team adapted ways of working that required it to change the fundamental way the members were used to collaborating: from face-to-face discussions to complete reliance on technology, from sharing information sparingly (only when someone needed to know the information) to sharing all information with everyone all the time, and from using personal collaborative tools (such as company-specific e-mail systems) to using a single system. Initially, the team believed that all information would be captured and shared among all members all the time. The result would be a much greater emphasis on knowledge management and retrieval, beyond just communication.

Being Creative Required New Rules of Engagement.
The team learned that its ability to be creative required meeting three requirements:

1. Jointly understand problems, possible solutions, analysis methods, and language
2. Interact frequently as a team, with all members "present," to share work-in-progress, brainstorm ideas, and test out solutions
3. Be able to create new information quickly based on a particular conversation or problem, and then equally quickly discard information that was no longer needed.

(Case Continued)

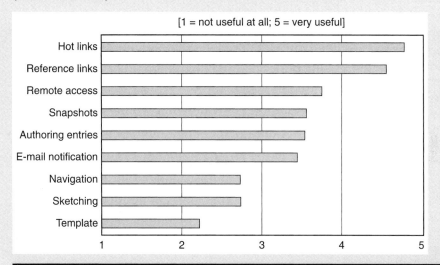

[1 = not useful at all; 5 = very useful]

FIGURE 12-3 Ratings of Notebook Features for Information Retrieval

Source: Reprinted with permission of R. Carman et al., "Virtual Cross-Supply Chain Concept Development Collaborative Teams: Spurring Radical Innovations at Boeing-Rocketdyne," first place winner of 2000 paper competition of the Society for Information Management.

The team members discovered they needed to adapt the traditional work practices of a collocated team to function as a creative body. Figure 12-4 shows how the need to be creative is accommodated in collocated teams, and what the SLICE team members learned they would need to do to adapt these needs to their non-collocated situation.

The Focus of the Team's Effort Changed over Time. As the project evolved, the team learned that it had to shift its thinking among three components, from thinking about strategy (how to fulfill the partnership agreement), to implementing a technology that would support collaboration of the dispersed team structure, to actual work practices that would leverage the technology. It learned that the strategy practices needed to be in place before the work or technology

practices so that members did not have to be concerned with both doing the work and negotiating information-sharing arrangements at the same time.

Furthermore, the team discovered it needed the technology in place before it could think about work practices because the work style depended on the support technology. Along the way, members also learned that the technology had to be flexible enough to be adapted to different ways of working because some of their initial work practices did not work as well as hoped. So, over the course of the project, they evolved their practices, and the tool had to support this evolution.

Figure 12-5 shows the allocation of effort over the course of the project among these three components of the project: strategy, technology, and work practices. As can be seen, the team needed to

(Case Continued)

Core Needs of Creative Teams	Practices of Colocated Teams	Practices Adapted by Virtual Teams
Development of shared understanding	• Lead engineer is "spoke-in-the-wheel" for coordinating information and consolidating ideas into new design proposals, which constitute the shared understandings of the team.	• From spoke-in-the-wheel coordination (with lead manager/engineer in center) to democratic coordination • Encourage development and use of common-language metaphors
Frequent opportunities for interaction with team members	• Colocation allows for frequent and spontaneous interaction.	• Coupling use of knowledge repository with frequent teleconferences • Allowing one-on-one discussions when need arises but documenting results for everyone
Rapid creation and sharing of context-specific transient information	• Most discussion is verbal and undocumented, and it is hard to capture the context.	• Promote only minimal cataloging of new information, even to the extent of restricting it to "touchstones" and "placeholders" • Timely and frequent discussions of new entries in knowledge repository to enable members to learn the context

FIGURE 12-4 Structuring Core Processes for Virtual Teams

Source: Reprinted with permission of R. Carman et al., "Virtual Cross-Supply Chain Concept Development Collaborative Teams: Spurring Radical Innovations at Boeing-Rocketdyne," first place winner of 2000 paper competition of the Society for Information Management.

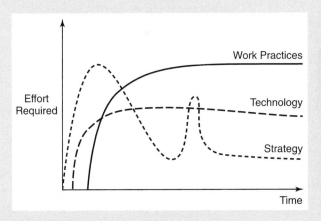

FIGURE 12-5 Effort Distribution over the Team's Life Cycle

Source: Reprinted with permission of R. Carman et al., "Virtual Cross-Supply Chain Concept Development Collaborative Teams: Spurring Radical Innovations at Boeing-Rocketdyne," first place winner of 2000 paper competition of the Society for Information Management.

(Case Continued)

focus on both the technology and its own work practices over the entire span of the project. For example, a technology facilitator was required to attend all teleconferences so that problems could be fixed immediately. Members never knew when someone would not understand how to perform a particular operation or a server would go down and communications would need to be rerouted. In addition, throughout the project, as the team found work practices not working, members devoted some effort to decide on

better ways of working. In the end, this attention paid off.

As noted, the SLICE team at Boeing-Rocketdyne was immensely successful, in large part due to the advanced collaboration technology it used. As usual, though, the technology was necessary but not sufficient. The team also needed a carefully developed partnership agreement in place before work began and work practices to leverage the technology, which needed to evolve as the team members discovered a technology's usefulness. ■

As this discussion of systems to support collaboration has shown, there is a spectrum of group working situations and many types of IT-based support. Furthermore, use of collaboration software can change structure within one enterprise, working relationships between enterprises, and working relationships between people in different parts of the world. To conclude the chapter, we look at research findings about using the lessons from managing one type of dispersed group to managing other types.

MANAGING COLLABORATION IN VIRTUAL ORGANIZATIONS

This chapter on collaboration has presented some intriguing glimpses into the dramatic changes occurring in organizational structures. Frances Cairncross, Peter Drucker, Etienne Wenger, and others believe that the organization of the future will be much more like networks of communities and teams than the hierarchical bureaucracies of the past. The question is: With CoPs, network armies, and global virtual teams becoming more predominant, how are such nontraditional collaborative structures to be managed?

Professor M. Lynne Markus of Bentley College, Brook Manville of Saba Software, and the late Carole Agres of Claremont Graduate School[12] explored this question by looking to the open source movement. Here is their thinking, which appeared in a *Sloan Management Review* article.

They, too, cite Drucker,[13] who stated that the job of executives in managing knowledge workers is not to tell them what to do (manage them), but rather to tell them where the organization is going (lead them). It is akin to leading volunteers who, though unpaid, labor for a cause out of commitment and the expectation of having a voice in the operation. Markus et al. note that CoPs, self-employed freelancers, and industries experiencing the emergence of networked organizational forms all point to a workforce with a more volunteer-like mindset—in spirit if not in fact. The authors researched the open source movement to help the managers of one knowledge-based organization that was having governance troubles. The traditional forms of governance were causing employees to feel distant and leave. The authors' research led them to two conclusions:

1. Executives of increasingly virtual organizations should think about expanding the kinds of motivators they use. The open source movement demonstrates that while money is a motivator for volunteers, gaining a high reputation among peers, taking pride in contributions, and being able to improve and use high-quality software are strong motivators as well.

2. Executives of increasingly virtual organizations should consider adopting a governance structure that fosters self-governance by employees. Although the open source movement appears to have all the trappings of chaos waiting to happen, it is actually very well disciplined because its governance mechanisms foster self-governance.

Here is some of their thinking in these two areas.

Motivating a Virtual Workforce

Markus, Manville, and Agres[12] suggest that managers in virtual organizations put in place motivators that reinforce each other. Open source contributors volunteer for many often-interlocking reasons. They love to build software. That is pure joy for them, states Eric Raymond,[14] who wrote "The Cathedral and the Bazaar," an online paper that has been influential in touting the benefits of open source development of software. They take pride in helping others and giving something back to society. They often believe that software should be given away, as it is in university computer science labs where open source flourishes. In addition, they receive the personal benefit of having better software for their own use. One obligation in this culture is to send software enhancements to the author to be checked. Another is to make the enhancements widely available.

Like academia, open source is a "reputation culture," note Markus et al. Reputation is the measure of success. Gaining a reputation for uncovering bugs and making good fixes spreads because open source contributions are highly visible. Every project includes a credit list of the people who have contributed, note Markus et al. This culture is also a gift type of culture. Reputation is gained by what the contributors give away, rather than what they control (as in the exchange culture found in traditional business). In a gift culture, there is abundance. In open source, there is plenty of computing power, network bandwidth, storage space, and such. A good reputation can lead to a job or venture capital. Although money cannot be earned from the software, it can be earned by selling support or education.

Markus, Manville, and Agres thus recommend that reputation may be the symbol of success in other kinds of knowledge work. Managers should use this "coin of the realm" to motivate employees in their virtual organization.

Governing Virtual Organizations

Managing open source appears to be an impossible task because there are at least 750,000 developers, all of whom signed up on their own volition and can stop volunteering at any time. Yet, note Markus et al., many open source projects work well because they employ three governance principles: managed membership, rules and institutions, and social pressures.

Managed Membership. Open source work has a well-defined leadership, with the originator often maintaining a lead role in development and distribution. Or a lead team might rule, dividing the work, refereeing coordination across teams, and so on. Leaders are rarely elected. Although anyone can be involved in searching for bugs and fixes (in most open source work), project authority only comes from being given it by, say, the project's core team based on the quality of one's work on the project. In some cases, even working on a project may require being voted in. Thus, membership is limited, making it manageable.

Rules and Institutions. One rule is the open source license — how the software can be used. The license may, for instance, permit any form of commercial use or not allow commercial versions at all. Other rules relate to how members and leaders are chosen or how voting and discussions are conducted. All communications are generally done over the Internet and occur in phases for a specific length of time. For instance, there can be a request-for-discussion phase, a call-for-votes phase, and a results phase, note Markus et al. Each phase has its own rules. Most voting is democratic, but some is not.

Social Pressures. To have teeth, rules need means to enforce compliance and resolve disputes. To bring continual non-compliers into line, open source groups generally use social pressures. For example, a group may *flame* someone, which means sending the disobeyer angry e-mail. Or members may *spam* the person, that is, overwhelm the person with e-mail. Or members may simply shun the person by not responding to that person's e-mail. Generally, after such treatment, the disobeyer learns the rules of the community and falls into line. Such pressures can even be turned on leaders who act inappropriately, note Markus et al.

Conflicts that end badly can cause volunteers to simply leave an open source group because it kills their motivation to contribute. Generally, open source groups use escalated sanctions to resolve conflict and bring non-compliers into line. They also monitor work, which represents another type of social pressure.

These social pressures work because reputation is so important, and because the work is so visible to everyone. Also underlying all the governance mechanisms are the shared values of the culture, which place emphasis on self-control (to maintain one's reputation) and social control (monitoring each other's behavior). Needless to say, IT is a key enabler for all these governing mechanisms, permitting the distributed software development, coordination among the participants, and group-wide enforcement of the rules via the various social controls.

Markus, Manville, and Agres recommend that managers in virtual organizations consider adopting these practices from the open source movement because intrinsic motivation and self-management are as important in virtual organizations as they are in open source. Furthermore, managers should consider rewarding collective results (as happens when an open source product gains commercial success) along with individual benefits. They should also foster development of reputation through the assignment of project lead roles and other mechanisms.

However, adopting the tenets of open source to managing in a virtual organization needs to take into account that a strong shared culture is a precondition for the governance mechanisms to work. A virtual organization without such a culture may not have the same results. Furthermore, Markus et al. question whether the mechanisms for governing programmers performing challenging work can apply equally well to employees performing routine activities. In short, self-governance is at the heart of managing virtual organizations. Without self-governance and strong reinforcing conditions, such social governance mechanisms might not work.

CONCLUSION

IT-based tools for supporting collaboration have been around for at least 30 years, becoming increasingly sophisticated over that time. Some are meant to support people attending a planning meeting. These tools permit more discussion, more evenly spread participation, more high-level companywide discussion, and involvement by more people than a traditional planning meeting would allow. Other tools allow real-time collaboration among distributed team members who not only need to hear each other's voices, but also need to simultaneously see their hand-drawn changes to an engineering drawing in real time. Still other collaboration tools help team members located around the globe "converse," not in real time, but at different times of the day.

In all three cases, and others, use of IT-based collaboration tools changes the collaboration process, who can participate, how they participate, and even the kinds of work they do. Collaboration is at the heart of the business world. No single organization can hope to be successful going it alone. The business world is moving too fast to stay abreast on all fronts at once. Partnering with others has become the standard style of work. For this reason, this area of IT-based collaboration support is likely to grow and mature quickly in the years ahead.

QUESTIONS AND EXERCISES

Review Questions

1. According to Drucker, why are team-based organizations like hospitals or orchestras?
2. Explain five characteristics of groups.
3. Name several types of groups and briefly describe each.
4. Explain the three ways Communities of Practice can be nurtured.
5. What are the characteristics of the open source movement?
6. Describe the four cells of the time/place matrix. Give an example of a technology used in each.
7. What are some of the ways IT can help improve meetings?
8. What benefits did Burr-Brown get from its use of a group decision room?
9. List some of the ways GSSs can improve the traditional presentation-discussion session? What are some potential disadvantages?
10. What were the four success factors for the SLICE team at Boeing-Rocketdyne?
11. What sorts of motivators should managers of virtual organizations adapt from the open source movement, according to Markus et al.?
12. What sorts of governance practices might managers of virtual organizations find useful, according to Markus et al.?

Discussion Questions

1. Support for communication and coordination is quite different from support for group decision making. The technologies also should be different. Do you agree or disagree? Explain your reasoning.
2. The lessons from the open source movement cannot be applied to virtual teams because the open source developers are truly volunteers and they have passion for their work. The same is not true of virtual teams getting paid to work. Do you agree or disagree? Explain your reasoning.
3. Network armies hold valuable lessons for the way some organizations should think about reorganizing themselves. Do you agree or disagree? If you agree, describe some organizations you are familiar with and what they could learn from network armies. If you disagree, describe several organizations you are familiar with and why they have nothing to learn from network armies.

Exercises

1. Find an article that describes an IT-based collaborative tool. What is its major purpose? What technology is used?
2. Conduct a survey of products available in the marketplace for supporting collaboration. What kinds of support do the systems provide? How do they compare with the systems described in this chapter?
3. Visit a local company that is using technology to support group work. Map its activities onto the time/place matrix. What infrastructures has the company developed?

REFERENCES

1. Cairncross, Frances, *The Company of the Future: How the Communications Revolution Is Changing Management*, Harvard Business School Press, Boston, 2002.

2. Drucker, Peter F., "The Coming of the New Organization," *Harvard Business Review*, January/February 1988, pp. 45–53.

3. Johansen, Robert, Institute for the Future, Menlo Park, CA.

4. Institute for Research on Learning, Menlo Park, CA.

5. Hunter, Richard, *World Without Secrets: Business, Crime, and Privacy in the Age of Ubiquitous Computing*, John Wiley & Sons, Hoboken, NJ, 2002.

6. Wenger, Etienne, *Communities of Practice: Learning, Meaning, and Identity*, Cambridge University Press, Cambridge, U.K., 1998.

7. Wenger, Etienne, and William Snyder, "Communities of Practice: The Organizational Frontier," *Harvard Business Review*, January/February 2000, pp. 139–145.

8. Wenger, Etienne, Richard McDermott, and William Snyder, *Cultivating Communities of Practice*, Harvard Business School Press, Boston, 2002.

9. DeSantis, G., and B. Gallupe, "Group Decision Support Systems: A New Frontier," *Data Base*, Winter 1985, pp. 10–15.

10. Davison, Robert, and Robert Briggs, "GSS for Presentation Support," *Communications of the ACM*, September 2000, pp. 91–97.

11. Carman, Robert, Vern Lott, Arvind Malhotra, and Ann Majchrzak, "Virtual Cross-Supply Chain Concept

Development Collaborative Teams: Spurring Radical Innovations at Boeing-Rocketdyne," first place winner of 2000 paper competition of the Society for Information Management.

12. Markus, M. Lynne, Brook Manville, and Carole Agres, "What Makes a Virtual Organization Work?" *Sloan Management Review*, Fall 2000, pp. 13–26.

13. Drucker, Peter F., "Management's New Paradigms," *Forbes*, October 5, 1998, pp. 152–177.

14. Raymond, Eric, *The Cathedral and the Bazaar*, O'Reilly & Associates, in Sebastopol, CA, 2001 (Revised).

SUPPORTING KNOWLEDGE WORK

INTRODUCTION

Now that we are reaching the end of this textbook, we deal with two of the most illusive, yet important, topics that relate to supporting knowledge work. One is the subject of managing knowledge. That means not only encouraging people to share knowledge personally, but also to put their knowledge in a form that others can easily access. Because knowledge can come from inside as well as outside the firm, the final sections on knowledge management deal with customer knowledge and researchers' knowledge and how to embed this outside knowledge in a real-time system. Under this topic are the intellectual capital issues of valuing intellectual property, usage, and sharing knowledge.

The second topic is the vast arena of computer ethics, which deals with such areas as information privacy, intellectual property rights, and other legal and ethical issues relating to information and knowledge. Many laws and regulations written before the computer age and the Internet explosion are being applied to today's software, databases that house personally identifiable information, and networks that connect different cultures. The entire realm of intellectual capital challenges the applicability of these laws and norms.

Companies Want to Manage Knowledge

One of the enduring subjects in the IT field since the mid-1990s has been knowledge management. Top corporate executives realize that their greatest corporate assets walk out the door every evening, taking with them another crucial asset, knowledge. Attempts to capture knowledge in computer systems continue. But for some experts and researchers in the field, knowledge is not something that can be captured in a machine; it only exists inside a person's head. Information can be captured in computers, knowledge cannot. Many feel that the term *knowledge management* creates the wrong impression. The term *management* often brings forth the "we can control it" mindset. Knowledge cannot be controlled or engineered, so the mechanical metaphor is wrong. It can only be leveraged through processes and culture. The biological or ecological metaphor is much better. The more people are connected, and the more they exchange ideas, the more their knowledge spreads and can thus be leveraged. This view, of course, is still being debated, and it has raised the question, "If we cannot disembody knowledge, how do we better manage the knowledge within people to leverage this asset?"

Tony Brewer[1a] researched this topic and notes that as we move from a service economy to a knowledge economy, companies move toward managing their intellectual capital in a more formal and deliberate way. In essence, knowledge exists in two states, tacit and explicit. *Tacit knowledge* exists within a person's mind and is private and unique to each person. *Explicit knowledge* has been articulated, codified, and made public. Western management practices have concentrated on managing explicit knowledge; but cultivating and leveraging tacit knowledge is just as important. Effective knowledge management requires transferring knowledge between these two states.

How is that done? Well, says Brewer, because knowledge is not a physical asset, it is not effectively described in terms of manufacturing analogies, such as storing it in inventory. Rather, it needs to be thought of in ecological terms, such as nurturing it, cultivating it, and harvesting it. Furthermore, ways to transfer knowledge back and forth between its tacit and explicit states are crucial and are generally a result of encouraging the free flow of ideas and information, something that organizational norms, departmental boundaries, and national differences can inhibit.

The process of transferring tacit knowledge to others is a key part of managing knowledge. To emphasize this idea, some companies have stopped talking about knowledge management and use only the term *knowledge sharing.* In this regard, IT is seen as one enabler, but not the main one. The key to knowledge sharing seems to be getting people together face-to-face to explain how they do things. Once people sit down and talk about what they do and why, barriers fall, knowledge flows, and sharing increases. Unfortunately, people are not given the time nor the space these days for this kind of interaction; free time for sharing is not seen as important.

A MODEL FOR MANAGING KNOWLEDGE

Due to the increasing emphasis on knowledge, some now call it *intellectual capital* to distinguish it from the other kinds of capital that firms possess. Giga Information Group,[2] a research firm, has published a model for managing intellectual capital. As shown in Figure 13-1, the model is circular and has four stages, which represent what people generally do with knowledge. First they create it or capture it from a source. Next, they organize it and put it into categories for easy retrieval. Then they distribute it (push) or access it (pull). Finally, they absorb another's knowledge for their own use or to create more new knowledge. Thus, the cycle begins again.

The four stages create three types of capital: human, structural, and customer.

- ***Human capital.*** This form of intellectual capital consists of knowledge, skills, and innovativeness of employees as well as company values, culture, and philosophy.

FIGURE 13-1 A Knowledge Management Framework

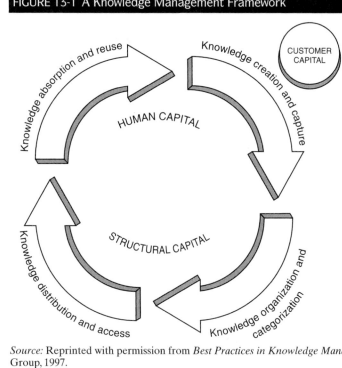

Source: Reprinted with permission from *Best Practices in Knowledge Management*, Giga Information Group, 1997.

It is created during the knowledge creation–capture and knowledge absorption–reuse stages because these two stages focus on getting people together to share knowledge. They deal with the *people* aspects of knowledge management. Their main question is, "How do we get people to have more knowledge in their heads?"

- *Structural capital.* This is the capabilities embedded in hardware, software, databases, organizational structure, patents, and trademarks that support employees as well as relationships with customers. Structural capital is formed in the knowledge organization–categorization and knowledge distribution–access stages because these stages focus on moving knowledge from people's heads to a tangible company asset. These stages deal with the *technology* issues surrounding knowledge management and sharing. Their main question is, "How do we get knowledge out of people's heads and into a computer, a process, a document, or another organizational asset?"

- *Customer capital.* This form of intellectual capital is the strength of a company's franchise with its customers and is concerned with its relationships and networks of associates. Furthermore, when customers are familiar with a company's products or services, the company can call that familiarity customer capital. This form of capital may be either human (relationships with the company) or structural (products used from the company).

Based on a series of case studies, Giga discovered that the human capital stages and the structural capital stages require different mindsets. Hence, companies have had to use different approaches to grow each one; and the techniques for one do not work for the other. The companies that focused on human capital used touchy-feely people-centric approaches. In some cases, no technology was used at all. The companies that focused on structural capital took a typical IS approach: using technology to solve a problem. Little talk addressed individuals, communities, and work practices; talk mainly centered on yellow pages of experts, knowledge bases, and such. However, to succeed in leveraging intellectual capital, companies need to do both.

Now we turn to specifics of what companies have done to build human capital, structural capital, and customer capital.

Building Human Capital

The emphasis in building human capital, notes Giga, is to answer the question, "How do we get people to have more knowledge in their heads?" Giga sees four ways: create it, capture it, absorb it, and reuse it.

Knowledge Creation and Capture.   This phase deals with generating knowledge, either by nurturing employees to create it or by acquiring it from outside. Hence, it deals with both human capital and customer capital. As noted earlier, the Giga cases that emphasized this phase of managing knowledge have used high-touch approaches, such as creating a sharing culture, urging people to meet either in person or electronically, and encouraging innovation.

As another example of what a company can do to promote knowledge sharing globally, consider the approach that Buckman Laboratories has taken. This description is based on Brewer's[1a] work.

CASE EXAMPLE

BUCKMAN LABORATORIES

Buckman Laboratories, an industrial chemical company based in Memphis, Tennessee, has some 1,200 employees around the world. The concept of sharing knowledge and best practices has been around in Buckman for more than 15 years. In fact, the company's code of ethics reinforces the sharing culture. Buckman believes that successfully transferring knowledge depends 90 percent on having the right culture and 10 percent on technology.

To bring the knowledge of all Buckman's employees to bear on a customer problem anywhere in the world—whether in Europe, South Africa, Australia/New Zealand, or Japan—Buckman established a knowledge transfer system called K'Netix, the Buckman Knowledge Network. The goal of K'Netix was to get people who had not met each other, but belonged to the same business, to communicate with each other and develop trust in each other: trust that one person was interested in the other's success, trust that what one person received from others was valid and sincere, and enough trust in the culture to help someone else.

Ten years ago sharing was accomplished mainly by people traveling all over the world to see each other, with lots of face-to-face conversations and meetings. Today, such meetings still occur, but the technology helps people stay in touch between these meetings, making communications more continuous.

When employees need information or help, they ask via forums, which are Buckman-only online forums over the Internet. In all, seven forums in TechForum are organized by industry and are open to all employees.

One particularly influential conversation, which set the tone for companywide sharing, took place over TechForum and concerned Buckman's global sales awards. A large cash award was split among the top three salespeople worldwide; the top 20 got plaques. It was based on a formula that took many factors into account. The salespeople, however, were unhappy with the formula. When this discussion appeared on the companywide forum, then-CEO Bob Buckman jumped into the fray and decided that the entire company should iron out the problems in front of all employees. Hundreds of messages were recorded, and the entire award structure was restructured online in front of everyone. It was a rare opportunity to allow everyone to share in an important, yet sensitive, company subject. Moreover, top management did not dictate the results. This conversation reinforced the sharing culture.

The conversations are the basis for transferring knowledge around the company. So the important ones are captured. Volunteer experts identify conversations that contain valuable information and, more importantly, valuable streams of reasoning. This information is then edited to remove extraneous material, given key words, and stored in the forum library.

(Case Continued)

In essence, Buckman is capturing the artifacts of its virtual teams in action. In so doing, it is creating a self-building knowledge base, which can be used for what-if analyses and can be mined to create new knowledge.

The prime benefit is timely, high-quality responses to customer needs. For example, a new employee in Brazil was scheduled to visit a customer who had a particular problem. The salesperson posted both the problem and a suggested solution in a forum and sought advice from anyone with more experience. A response came quickly: "I've faced this problem and your pH is too high; it will cause odors and ruin the paper. Bring the pH down by two points. That won't hurt the process, and it will clear up the problem." As a result, this new employee, who had only modest experience, was able to present a proposal with the experience of a 25-year veteran, and make the sale. ∎

Knowledge Absorption and Reuse.   This phase of building human capital addresses the notion of getting knowledge into people's heads where it can be enhanced and reused. Irrespective of whether people believe that knowledge only exists in minds or can exist in computers, the Giga cases that emphasized this phase of managing knowledge used high-touch approaches. They too focused on nurturing interactions among people, recognizing the knowledge brokers who exist in companies, and supporting communities of practice.

Recognizing knowledge brokers: "The Rudy problem."   Simply discovering who has what knowledge is a step in the right direction to fostering knowledge sharing. Yet when possessing knowledge is not rewarded by management, neither is sharing, as the following story illustrates.

At a knowledge management conference, Dr. Patricia Seemann,[3] who headed up a knowledge management project at a pharmaceutical company, told the story of Serge and Rudy (fictitious names but real people). Serge, she said, was a "real" manager. He had a three-window office, a big desk, and a title. If you asked him what he did the past year, he would say, "I registered 600 products in 30 countries." Rudy, on the other hand, is a headache, his manager says, because he does not work. He just stands around and talks all day. Whenever you see him, he is talking to someone. When you ask him what he did the past year, he says, "I sort of helped out."

The company downsized and guess who got laid off? Rudy. And then what happened? His department fell apart because there was no one to help, to provide guidance. When they fired Rudy, they fired their organizational memory, said Seemann. He was a crucial, yet unrecognized asset, because he was willing to share his knowledge.

While at this company, Seemann and her team created a yellow pages guide of company knowledge brokers. Guess who was in the book and who was not? Rudy, of course, was in the book. Serge was not, and neither was top management. How can companies fix what she calls "the Rudy problem"? One way is to create a technical career track and promote knowledge brokers. Giving Rudy a title would have made an enormous difference, Seemann said, because it would have sent a signal that knowledge sharing was recognized in the company. Companies cannot appoint knowledge brokers. They just emerge. And when they do emerge, they need support.

One approach to fostering knowledge sharing: T-shaped managers.   If not understanding Rudy's role in the organization is how *not* to foster knowledge sharing, what is a way to nurture it? Morton Hansen of Harvard Business School and Bolko von Oetinger of Boston Consulting Group[4] propose what they call *T-shaped managers*. These are executives who have both a vertical role (such as running a business unit) and a horizontal role (such as sharing knowledge with their peers in other business units).

The goal of this structure is to circumvent the limitations of knowledge management systems: They can only house explicit knowledge (not implicit know-how), they cannot foster collaboration by just making documents available, and their directories of experts can get out-of-date quickly. T-shaped management is especially important in organizations with autonomous business units because it helps counterbalance their tendency to compete with each other and hoard expertise.

Whereas the value of T-managers' vertical work is measured by traditional bottom-line financial performance, the value of their horizontal work is measured in five ways, note Hansen and von Oetinger:

1. Increased company efficiency from transferring best practices among business units
2. Better decisions by soliciting peer advice
3. Increased revenue by sharing expertise, again, among peers who are experts in areas in question
4. Development of new business ventures by cross-pollinating ideas
5. Moving strategically through well-coordinated efforts among peers

However, success in these five areas does not just happen. Knowledge sharing requires clear incentives. The company needs to reward sharing. Furthermore, sharing needs to go both ways—give and take. Benchmarking across business units can encourage underperformers to ask for help. Success also requires formalizing cross-unit interactions, state Hansen and von Oetinger. It does not mean creating bureaucracy, but rather creating peer-level collegial support (and confrontation). It also means picking and choosing which cross-unit requests to fulfill based on expected business results and how much someone can really contribute.

BP is exemplary in its use of the T-manager concept, state Hansen and von Oetinger. The insight Hansen and von Oetinger learned from studying BP is that mechanisms must be put in place to both foster and guide managers' knowledge-sharing activities; otherwise, they start to take up too much time and produce few results.

CASE EXAMPLE

BP

BP is in the energy business. It merged with Amoco in 1998, with ARCO in 2000, and Castrol and Veba Aral in Germany in 2002; it now has 100,000 employees in 100 countries. BP's approach to T-shaped management began in the early 1990s in BPX, its oil and gas exploration division. To cut layers and increase accountability, John Browne, then head of BPX and now head of BP, divided the division into 50 autonomous business units. Unfortunately, each business unit head focused only on his or her unit, not on BPX.

To get the business unit heads working together, Browne instituted peer groups in 1993, each with about 12 business unit leaders in similar businesses. No bosses were allowed in these peer groups, so the discussions would be candid and not consist of political posturing. Sharing did increase, but it was not until 1994 when these groups were made responsible for allocating capital within their group and for setting their performance levels that their sharing started to truly impact BPX's performance. The peer group members finally saw the financial value of sharing expertise. When Browne became CEO in 1995, he instituted peer groups BP-wide.

BP has also created cross-unit networks around areas of shared interest. However, BP found, unfortunately, that these several hundred networks cost a lot of time and money (with people flying all over the globe) without resulting in better results. Thus, the number and use have been limited.

BP has also instituted the practice of identifying a limited number of "human portals" who connect people, so that everyone is not trying to network with everyone else. Typically these people are not the top executives, note Hansen and von Oetinger, and typically they have been at BP a long time and in many jobs and locations.

IT plays a role in these various knowledge-sharing activities. An electronic yellow pages identifies experts, and multimedia e-mail and desktop video conferencing permit easier virtual team meetings, report Hansen and von Oetinger.

Since the mergers, BP has reorganized its business units into new peer groups that are more strategically focused. As Hansen and von Oetinger note, the evolution continues.

One T-Shaped Manager's Experiences

One BP T-shaped executive, who heads BP's gas business unit in Egypt, illustrates this new mode of operation. Formerly, whenever his business unit needed help, he would call headquarters. Now, he looks to his peers in other gas units.

His job essentially has two roles, one vertical and one horizontal. He is CEO of the business unit, so he is responsible for its profit-and-loss statement, capital investment decisions, and such. He is also expected to participate in cross-unit activities, which take up some 20 percent of his time. These activities can undermine his vertical role, so he and the seven gas-production peers in the Mediterranean and Atlantic region in his peer group limit

(*Case Continued*)

their meetings to business purposes. Knowledge sharing is not enough of a reason to meet. Instead, they meet to decide how to allocate capital amongst themselves and how to meet production targets set by their division's executive committee.

In his knowledge-sharing role, in addition to collaborating, he also connects people, acting in some ways like a "human portal," suggesting who might help solve a problem, for example. He also gives advice to peer business units when asked and when he feels he can contribute. He was personally involved in 3 of 20 of his business unit's "peer assists" one year, report Hansen and von Oetinger. In addition, he also requests peer assists, receiving 10 assists one year from BP business units around the world.

Due to all BP's networking, people know where expertise lies, so they go directly to the expertise rather than through headquarters. And because sharing is rewarded, bosses know who is sharing (and requesting assistance) and who is not. In its knowledge-sharing efforts, BP has aimed to change management activities, not corporate structure, to gain the benefits of knowledge sharing while preserving the autonomy of its business units so that they can more quickly and effectively serve their local markets. ∎

Building Structural Capital

The Rudy story also fits with this second subject, building structural capital, because that is what Seemann and her team aimed to do in creating the online yellow pages of knowledge brokers. Her goal was to increase their value. Those yellow pages are a form of structural capital. As noted earlier, companies that emphasize building structural capital generally use high-tech approaches.

Knowledge Organization and Categorization. This phase is often handled by creating best practices knowledge bases or metadata indexes for documents. A few have even tried to measure intellectual capital. Following are two examples, one that focused on improving a knowledge-support process and one that looked into valuing intellectual capital.

CASE EXAMPLE

A PHARMACEUTICAL COMPANY

A project at a major pharmaceutical company was aimed at improving the process of developing new drugs and getting them approved by the U.S. Food and Drug Administration (FDA), a process that takes 5 to 10 years, costs $250 million, and can yield revenues of $1 million a day per drug once it reaches the market.

(Case Continued)

This project, described at the Knowledge Imperative Conference,[3] revolved around creating a "knowledge infrastructure," one that manages information, enables understanding, and supports learning. The crux of the matter was to understand the customer's needs. In this case, the FDA is the primary customer; however, insurance companies, doctors, and consumers are also customers. The company sells all of them knowledge about disease, treatment, and how a drug will work in particular scenarios. When employees understand the type of knowledge they need to create for these customers and their role in its creation, they will identify better ways to work.

The project began by studying and codifying 60,000 pages of documents filed with the FDA to discern how the teams developing drugs and filing their results were sharing knowledge. These regulatory files explain to the FDA what the company knows about a drug, how it learned those things, and what conclusions it has reached.

The knowledge-infrastructure project team found the files lacking. Each file should have four parts: purpose, content, logic, and context. Only one of the files had a statement of purpose, which stated the problem to be solved. A file without a statement of purpose shows that the author does not know the reason for the document. Many files had contradictions, which told the team that the authors had not talked to each other. For instance, they disagreed on whether the drug should be taken once or twice a day.

To rectify the situation, the study team created a generic knowledge tree of the questions the FDA asks when deciding whether to approve a drug. The top of the tree has their three main questions: Is it safe? Does it work? Does it have sufficient quality? The tree lays out the supporting questions for these three main questions, in layers, which shows the teams which questions they need to answer to the FDA's satisfaction. It also shows people why others need specific information, thus giving them a context (beyond trust) for sharing.

In a pilot project, the knowledge-infrastructure team used a different process with one team: writing as a tool for thinking. They got the team to write up their 10-year drug study before they did it, so that the team members were clear about the data they needed to gather and present to the FDA. Furthermore, they wrote the report template publicly as a team. To create the template, they wrote critical points that had to be in the report on Post-It notes. Next, they prioritized the points on huge sheets of paper on the meeting-room wall. Then they designed studies to prove the points that had to be proven. In creating this virtual prototype of the knowledge to be presented to the FDA, publicly, on the wall, they could physically see what knowledge was needed. They created a common mental model of the results. It was a powerful technique.

They have seen tangible progress in filling in the report sections on content, logic, context, and purpose. In another case, where an existing drug was to be registered for use with a new disease, the team had not made much progress in 2 years' time. After they were shown the knowledge tree over a 2-day period, they were able to submit the file to the FDA in 3 months (they had previously estimated 18 months), and the FDA approved it in 18 months (the team had estimated 3 years). ■

Skandia Future Centers,[1b] discussed in Chapter 4, provides an example of delving into the world of valuing knowledge. Few firms have ventured into this realm, but because Skandia deals in knowledge and wants to experiment with the future, this is one area it has explored.

CASE EXAMPLE

SKANDIA FUTURE CENTERS

The charter for Skandia Future Centers is organizational prototyping. One project, the knowledge exchange, has addressed the question of putting a value on intangibles, such as knowledge.

Today, some 70 percent of investments in the United States are for intangibles; in Sweden it is 90 percent. However, no common mechanism for establishing their value nor trading that value is yet available. A knowledge exchange increases the accessibility of hidden knowledge and will act as a multiplier for wealth creators, both people and organizations.

Skandia's knowledge exchange began as a network for exchanging knowledge using software akin to Lotus Notes. Over time, it has evolved into a Web-based trading arena where people can buy and sell knowledge assets. It is now based on Nonet, a Notes-like product from Metaphor, a Spanish company.

It has two test sites called ICuniverse.com (IC stands for intellectual capital) and Futurizing.com. On ICuniverse.com, for example, before responding to an e-mail message, the recipient and the sender first agree on a price to be paid to the responder, perhaps via an auction. Thus, people are paid for the knowledge they provide. Ideas and writings can be housed on ICuniverse.com and resold, which gives high yield to currently unvalued intellectual assets.

The two sites run on an infrastructure (IQport) owned by NatWest in the United Kingdom and were built over several years' time. IQport includes software and a financial clearing mechanism so that information that is generally thrown away can be wrapped into a package and given a price tag. The sites are linked to two accounts at NatWest; one is in financial currency (traditional money), the other is in digital currency, which can be used to purchase other knowledge. Skandia is testing this concept because it could become a new global currency. It is part of the new digital economy.

The knowledge exchange project has been self-organizing from the start. The center simply provides the arena for "knowledge entrepreneurs" or "knowledge nomads"—people who go from arena to arena working on their latest ideas. Thus, the center supports a nontraditional working model.

To illustrate its migration, the project began with IT people from the United Kingdom who were then joined by IT people from Sweden and the United States. Later, students and the professor from Venezuela who developed Nonet for oil companies were the mainstay. The students collaborated

(Case Continued)

with the professor at the center and with Metaphor, the Spanish company that bought Nonet. Today, the knowledge exchange team has people from Sweden and Denmark.

The question that Skandia Future Centers is now asking itself is: How can we reward knowledge nomads? They do not want a career; they want a journey and freedom. Their lifestyle does not fit into traditional organizational models, yet working with them helps speed up accounting and organizational remodeling because they act like bees, moving among research centers pollinating companies with ideas. ■

Knowledge Distribution and Access.   This phase emphasizes both pushing knowledge out to users (distribution) and accommodating users who pull information to themselves (access). The Giga cases that emphasized this phase also used high-tech approaches. They focused on implementing networks and networking tools to access human and structural capital. Intranets and groupware were important IT-based tools. To illustrate one enterprise's approach, we turn to a U.S. energy company discussed in the Giga report.[2]

CASE EXAMPLE

A U.S. ENERGY COMPANY

In this highly autonomous energy company, the 15 business units each focused on their own performance. To instill sharing in this culture, these units would have to see the benefits themselves. In addition, many of the employees were concerned they would not get credit for their good ideas. To overcome both issues, management decided to focus on promulgating best practices across the business units. A *best practice* was defined as a practice, know-how, or experience that had proven effective or valuable in one organization and might be applicable to another, notes Giga.

With management encouragement, a number of programs to collect best practices arose. For example, 13 groups in the refining division documented best practices using Lotus Notes. They documented "hard" practices (such as distilling techniques) and "soft" practices (such as training) and recorded metrics, where possible. The division estimated it saved $130 million a year utilizing each other's best practices, notes Giga. Similar programs appeared in other divisions.

Yet, these efforts were disparate, so an enterprising manager within IS gathered all the statistics together and presented them to top management to demonstrate how the company could be nurtured to become a learning company. With top

(Case Continued)

management support, an important booklet was created to align the various divisions. It explained the company's mission, vision, values, total quality management (TQM), and environmental policies. It became the guide for sharing best practices.

In fact, the TQM principles of focusing on processes, measuring processes, and continuously improving them, which the company's employees understood and used, played an important role in espousing knowledge distribution and reuse.

One example was in its capital projects management process. This process is used to manage some $4 billion worth of projects a year. In benchmarking this process, management discovered it had some gaps. Therefore, the process was redesigned, and management of capital projects improved. Seeing the benefits of this process orientation, the corporate office funded other cross-business-unit initiatives that fostered sharing.

However, there was still no central responsibility for knowledge distribution and reuse, and such centralization would not fit the culture well. To solve this problem, certain people were designated "technical knowledge experts" because they knew about best practices across the company. Their job was to disseminate tacit knowledge. To do that, they looked for technical ways to turn tacit knowledge into explicit knowledge. Lotus Notes, as noted earlier, was commonly used to

house best practices. It links best practice databases across the 15 operating companies. Employees are encouraged to use Notes to describe best practices, search for a mentor on a subject they need to know about, and find best practices. Notes has also been used to support processes. For example, it is used to coordinate the around-the-clock work of 100 employees in the refining company. In creating this workflow system, the employees reengineered the work so coordination worked more smoothly.

The company has also created online discussion databases, some 50 of them, to encourage sharing and reduce travel. Some of the networks have attracted hundreds of employees, leading to a more networked culture. In turn, some of these networks have led to face-to-face get-togethers, which have further spurred sharing on common topics, such as how to reduce energy costs, improve quality, and hone public relations in different cultures.

In short, this company has spurred best practice sharing wherever it makes sense, mainly guided by the interests of the employees. The results have not only been cost savings, but also a change in employee perception, based on the results of employee satisfaction surveys. Employees responded that there was increased emphasis on processes and more sharing of best practices across the company. ■

Building Customer Capital

As noted earlier, customer capital is the strength of a company's franchise with its customers, the percentage of customer "mindshare" in its industry. Brand recognition is part of customer capital. Familiarity with one's products is another. One of the most fascinating case studies in the Giga knowledge management report,[2] all of which are anonymous, is the one about the vice president who derived the notion of customer capital. Here is that story, based on that report.

CASE EXAMPLE

A NORTH AMERICAN BANK

After the U.S. savings and loan debacle and the devaluation of real estate in the 1980s, the vice president of organizational learning and leadership development at a North American bank asked, "Why have banks become so exposed to risk in their lending practices?" The answer he arrived at was, "Because they do not understand the new information age and its underpinning collateral." At the time, and still today, banks lent money against hard assets, such as a shopping mall. However, the value of such assets can dissipate almost overnight, making them risky collateral. "Perhaps there is less risk in lending against soft assets, such as a group's knowledge of a programming language or a patented process," he reasoned. Knowledge in a person's head does not disappear overnight. However, the vice president had no way of valuing such intangibles. He continued to work on the problem of knowledge valuation. Over time, his thinking changed the way the bank evaluated new hires and reshaped some of its operations.

To begin his quest on how to value knowledge, or intellectual capital, he drew on the ideas of human capital and structural capital, and then added his own: customer capital.

Human capital was the know-how to meet customer needs; he asked bank managers to measure it by assessing how fast their teams learned. To increase human capital, he shifted emphasis at the bank from training (pushing instruction to people) to learning (getting people to pull the instruction they needed to them), because he believed the crux of increasing human capital was increasing the pace at which an organization learns. He believed people learned when they "owned" their learning and took responsibility for applying it to improve their performance. He developed a list of skills needed to serve customers and gave employees numerous ways to learn these skills, from reading specific books to choosing a mentor.

Structural capital was the organizational capabilities needed by the marketplace. The vice president measured structural capital by uncovering the percentage of bank revenue that came from new services and similar metrics. He believed that although it takes human capital to build structural capital, the better the bank's structural capital, the higher its human capital; one feeds the other. Thus, he generated structural capital from human capital by creating a competitive intelligence "library" about the industry that the bank considers a valuable "intellectual capital repository." Rather than being a library of documents, however, it was a map that showed the kinds of knowledge the bank held and where it

(Case Continued)

existed, whether in an employee's head or a database.

Customer capital was the intellectual assets in the minds of customers related to the bank. The vice president's team measured three aspects: depth of knowledge about the bank in a customer organization, breadth of knowledge by a customer, and loyalty to the bank. To strengthen these aspects, the vice president believed the bank needed to assist its customers' employees in learning. Some of that learning pertained to learning more about the bank, which required making the bank's

values and strategies congruent with those of its customers. The vice president therefore helped senior bank officials determine customer needs, establish a common language for communicating with customers, develop a sense of purpose for the relationship, and, most importantly, make learning within the customer organization an important part of the bank's services. The vice president believes that assisting customers will increase his bank's customer capital: depth, breadth, and loyalty. Thus, his knowledge management efforts focused outwardly as well as inwardly. ■

To recap, Figure 13-2 shows the key activities in each of the four stages, the form of capital each supports, the skills required of people, and the tools and techniques that are proving valuable for that stage.

The Cultural Side of Knowledge Management

Success in managing knowledge comes as much from changing organizational behavior as it does from implementing new technology, notes Cyril Brooks.[5] His company, Grapevine, offers a product for managing information and knowledge. He notes that besides the platitude of "create a culture that rewards sharing," few people recommend specifics on how to reduce the cultural roadblocks that can hinder knowledge management projects. He describes some cultural barriers, which he calls "red flags."

Watch Out for Cultural Red Flags. Cultural barriers can shut down knowledge management efforts because knowledge management is really about cooperation and sharing. To reach these lofty goals, efforts need to turn the tacit knowledge in people's heads into explicit knowledge in a process, product, or other organizational artifact. Thus, knowledge-management work must tap people's motivations to share and cooperate. Without the motivation, knowledge databases, for example, are not updated or errors are ignored. Or people avoid contributing to a knowledge-sharing network for fear they will give away their best ideas and lose their "competitive advantage" against their peers in the company. Such red flags are not obvious; they are often subtle, yet harmful, says Brooks.

Here are a few of his behavioral red flags that can derail a knowledge-management effort:

- *Being seen as a whistle-blower or messenger of bad news.* Few people want to betray their boss, so they avoid presenting early warnings or disagreeing with internal documents. In organizations where "messengers get shot," sharing good news is fine, but sharing bad is not, which defeats the full value of sharing.

Phase	*Emphasis*	*Skills/People*	*Tools/Techniques*

Creation and Capture
Generate new
  knowledge
Make tacit knowledge
  explicit
Hire people with the
  right knowledge
Create culture of
  sharing
Encourage innovation
Incentives for sharing
	Human capital
	Customer capital
		Knowledge harvesters
		Knowledge owners
		Mentoring/coaching
		Partner with universities
		Teamwork
		Business intelligence
		Top management
			Easy-to-use capture tools
			E-mail
			Face-to-face meetings
			Knowledge tree
			Write-to-think
			Feedback

**Organization and
  Categorization**
Package knowledge
Add context to
  information
Create categories of
  knowledge
Create knowledge
  vocabulary
Create metadata tags
  for documents
Measure intellectual
  capital
	Structural capital	Academics
		Knowledge editors
		Librarians
		Knowledge architects
		Authors
		Subject matter experts
		IS
			Frameworks
			Cull knowledge from
			  sources
			Best practices databases
			Knowledge bases
			Knowledge thesaurus
			Knowledge indexes
			Measurement tools

**Distribution and
  Access**
Create links to
  knowledge
Create networks of
  people
Create electronic push
  and pull distribution
  mechanisms
Knowledge sharing
	Structural capital	Publishers
		Top management
		IS
			HTML
			Groupware, Lotus Notes
			Networks, intranets
			Navigation aids
			Search tools

Absorption and Reuse
Stimulate interaction
  among people
The learning
  organization
Informal networks
	Human capital	Group facilitators
		Organizational
		  developers
		Matchmakers
		Knowledge brokers
			Team processes
			Electronic bulletin
			  boards
			Communities of practice
			Yellow pages

FIGURE 13-2 Knowledge Management Stages

Source: Reprinted with permission from *Best Practices in Knowledge Management*, Giga Information Group, 1997.

- *Losing one's place as a knowledge gatekeeper.* Although knowledge brokers are important in organizations, their self-value comes from their controlling the knowledge they house and sharing it only with whom and when they choose. They may see a knowledge management system that encourages the free flow of ideas as decreasing their value, and therefore fight it.

- *Knowledge sharing really does take time.* Because sharing takes time, experts may hide so that they are not bothered by requests from others. Others may not participate in, say, presenting their ideas, which may benefit the organization as a whole but have no personal reward, so they think.

These reactions are human; therefore, knowledge-management efforts often need to build "cultural workarounds" so that these kinds of reactions do not block the work. Brooks offers some suggestions. For example, to reduce concerns about being a messenger, the system might allow only limited dissemination of some ideas or give people the ability to rank feedback comments based on their significance. To counter concerns about losing personal advantage, contributions could require authorship or comments might always be linked to the original items. To reduce time consumption, the reward structure could reward contributions based on their value.

In addition to cultural red flags, management red flags are also a concern. Three management red flags are

1. Saying the project is not cost-justifiable because the benefits are intangible
2. Concern that too much participation will reduce employee productivity
3. Concern that creating the taxonomy of knowledge categories will be just too expensive to undertake

Reducing these concerns is an important aspect of knowledge management. Some examples for mitigating these management roadblocks, says Brooks, include illustrating the value of serendipity that has occurred due to sharing, as illustrated in vendor case studies; ensuring that the new system promotes feedback to contributors, which can increase productivity; and drawing on vendor expertise to create knowledge taxonomies rather than start from scratch.

As Brooks points out, organizational culture is an important aspect of knowledge-management efforts and a key determinant of success.

Design the System to Match What the Users Value.   Thomas Stewart,[6] a well-known writer in the knowledge-management field, agrees and makes the important point that knowledge needs to be managed within the context where value is created. In short, the *system* needs to be designed to fit the people who will use it and gain value from it. He notes that many official knowledge-management efforts have come to naught because they did not create the place where people first look for knowledge. On the other hand, a number of grassroots, unofficial efforts have succeeded.

Stewart gives the example of three consultants who created an informal, unofficial Notes-based e-mail list in their company to have a place to collaborate online. Anyone could join the list; to date, it has attracted over 500 company employees. It has actually become the premier knowledge-sharing mechanism in the company even though it is difficult to search and generates a lot of messages, which fill up e-mail boxes. It works, notes Stewart, for four reasons:

1. It is demand driven. Some 80 percent of the traffic is members asking each other, "Does anyone know anything about. . . .?"
2. It roots out tacit knowledge. People contribute what they know, which might not be recorded anywhere in the company.

3. It is right in front of the members in their e-mail boxes every day.

4. It is full of intriguing and strongly held opinions, which the members find most interesting.

The system is like a conversation rather than a library; thus, it is about learning rather than teaching. That is a major difference, notes Stewart. It was designed to manage knowledge in the context where value is created. Given the high number of failed knowledge-management projects, Stewart suggests answering the following three questions before launching off:

1. Which group will use this knowledge space? Once determined, make them responsible for the content.

2. What kind of knowledge does the group need? Once known, that knowledge needs to be managed within that group's context because that is where the value arises. A knowledge-management system or resource should only deal with a single group that creates value in the same way.

3. What is the company culture; is it composed of reusers or originators? The difference matters. A repository of things promotes a reuse culture; an online chat room helps originators, but not vice versa.

Beware of creating a system that supports the wrong culture, warns Stewart. There is really no such thing as a generic knowledge-management system. Each one needs to fit a knowledge-sharing group. Answering these questions will help uncover the structure and content of a knowledge-management resource that will add value and actually be used.

As an example of a knowledge-management project that has worked and has followed many of the tenets espoused by Stewart, consider the work at Partners HealthCare System in Boston. Notice how it takes into account the health-care culture.

CASE EXAMPLE

PARTNERS HEALTHCARE SYSTEM

Not too long ago, Tom Davenport of Accenture's Institute for Strategic Change and John Glaser, CIO of Partners Health-Care System in Boston,[7] described how Partners HealthCare System is delivering just-in-time knowledge.

The problem the physicians at Partners HealthCare hospitals and physician groups face is the deluge of new knowledge they need to know but cannot possibly keep up with on their own. The solution has been to present physicians with the new knowledge they need when they need it through the information technology they already use in their work. In essence, this approach makes knowledge management part of their job, not a separate activity, and it can

(Case Continued)

deliver knowledge just when a patient really needs it.

The work at Partners HealthCare began on a small, doable scale: using the doctors' online order entry system to notify doctors of drug interactions when they enter a prescription order. The system checks the patient's medical record, looking for allergic reactions to the drug (or a similar drug) and alerts the physician. The doctor can inquire about the reaction, and, if it was mild, override the computer's recommendation to switch to another medication.

The system can also tell the doctor about a newer, more effective drug or inform him or her of another drug the patient is taking that can lead to a bad interaction. Or, if the doctor is ordering a test, the system can describe a newer, more effective test for the noted symptom. Or the system can warn the doctor that the prescribed medication could worsen a patient disease.

This integrated system is built on knowledge bases (databases of knowledge about the patient, drugs, tests, medical research, and such) and a logic engine (which, as its name implies, performs the logical interconnections between the various kinds of knowledge in the knowledge bases).

The system also has an event-detection mechanism, which alerts a physician when it learns of an event that can endanger the health of a patient. For example, when the patient's health indicators deviate from the norm while the patient is in the hospital, the doctor or a nurse is notified via pager. This capability brings knowledge management into real time, note Davenport and Glaser.

However, this system could not be bought. It had to be built by Partners HealthCare. It was a large investment, but it was made because too many patients at Partners were experiencing drug interactions. Management had to fix that problem. One of the steps it took was to form committees of top clinicians to identify the knowledge that needed to be in the knowledge bases and keep it up-to-date. The drug therapy committee makes the medication recommendations, whereas the radiology committee develops the logic to guide radiology testing. Participation in each committee is seen as prestigious, which is crucial to the success of the system, so that busy physicians give time to the committee work.

Another step Partners took was to only address the most critical processes. Furthermore, the system is simply seen as a recommendation system. It does not make final decisions. Those are left up to the physicians. The combined human–computer system seems to be working. Some 380 orders (out of 13,000 a day) are changed due to a computer suggestion. Some one-third to one-half of orders with drug interactions are cancelled, and some 72 percent of treatments are changed when the event-detection system sounds an alert. Partner's strong measurement culture helps it gather such statistics and see the benefits of the system.

In summary, Davenport and Glaser believe that embedding knowledge in the systems and work processes that professionals use is the way to achieve just-in-time knowledge management and dramatically improve an organization's performance. ∎

INTELLECTUAL CAPITAL ISSUES

Data, information, content, and intellectual capital all raise some thorny issues. These issues have prompted legislation in some countries, but not all, which causes even more problems in today's intertwined, global society. Their resolution is important for global e-commerce, and such resolution could be a long way off. We begin by looking at information value, usage, and sharing issues. Then we move on to the large, but rarely discussed, subject of computer ethics.

If information is to be viewed as an asset, as many companies now do, it must be treated differently from the traditional assets of labor and capital, notes Thomas Davenport[8] of Accenture and Babson College. For one thing, information is not divisible. Nor is it scarce. In addition, ownership cannot be clearly defined. Davenport discusses three categories of issues in managing information:

1. Value issues
2. Usage issues
3. Sharing issues

Value Issues

Information's value depends on the recipient and the context. In fact, most people cannot put a value on a piece of information until they have seen it. However, people do, indeed, place values on information. Look at all the information services that people buy. Information marketplaces exist, both inside and outside of companies. The only practical way to establish the value of information is to establish a price for it and see whether anyone buys it. Pricing possibilities include charging for the information itself rather than for the technology or the provider, charging by the document rather than a smaller unit, charging by length or time or number of users, or charging by value rather than cost.

A number of tools are being used within companies to increase the value of information.

- *Information maps.* These maps can be text-based charts or even diagrammatic maps that point to the location of information, whether in written material, experts' minds, and so forth. IBM, for example, created a guide to market information so that managers can find out where to get quick answers to their ad hoc questions. The result has been less money spent on duplicate information and increased understanding of the kinds of questions people typically ask.

- *Information guides.* Guides are people who know where desired information can be found. Librarians have traditionally played this role. Hallmark Cards, for instance, created a job guide in its business units to help employees find computer-based information on available jobs. These guides have substantially reduced the time needed to find information.

- *Business documents.* Business documents are yet another tool for sharing information. They provide organization and context. One fruitful way to embark on information management is to uncover what documents an organization needs. This process can be easier, and more useful, than defining common terms. One brokerage firm discovered that its brokers all used the same documents, over and over. Some 90 percent of these documents could be put on one CD-ROM, kept on local servers, and updated monthly, greatly facilitating information use.

- *Groupware.* Groupware is a tool for getting greater value out of less structured information. It allows people to share information across distances in a more structured manner than e-mail. Lotus Notes is such a product. Groupware can ease discussions and aid distribution of information, but its success depends upon the culture. For one, better access to information increases (not decreases) people's appetite for even more information. However, employees using sophisticated groupware products need to learn how the technology can be used to improve work habits and profits, neither of which flows naturally from the technology.

To have value, the databases need to be managed, even pruned and restructured. Knowledgeable people are needed to manage the information resource and its use. This need is true for intranets and Web sites as well.

Usage Issues

Information management is a management issue because it deals with how people use information, not how they use machines, says Davenport. Three points illustrate the importance and difficulty of managing information use.

One, information's complexity needs to be preserved. Information should not be simplified to be made to fit into a computer, because doing so truncates sharing and conversations. Information does not conform to common definitions. It is messy. It naturally has different perspectives, which are important and need to be preserved. A certain amount of tension between the desire for one common global meaning and numerous familiar local meanings is inevitable. Companies that want to settle on common corporate terms must do so with line people, not technical people, because line people will use the end results. The IS organization can facilitate these discussions, but the business people should determine the meanings.

Two, people do not easily share information, even though its value grows as it is shared. Culture often blocks sharing, especially in highly competitive organizational cultures.

Three, technology does not change culture. Just building an information system does not mean that people will use it. It is a false assumption that too many IS people make. To change the information culture of a company requires changing basic behaviors, values, attitudes, and management expectations.

Sharing Issues

If information sharing is the goal, a number of contentious challenges must first be resolved. Davenport explains that a sharing culture must be in place or the existing disincentives will thwart use of a sharing system.

Technical solutions do not address the sharing issue. For example, much talk has touted *information architectures*, where the definitions of stable types of corporate data, such as customers, products, and business transactions, can be specified ahead of time and used consistently across the firm. This approach may work for data, but it is problematic for information, because information architectures generally fail to take into account how people use the information. Managers get two-thirds of their information from conversations, one-third from documents, and almost none directly from computer systems. Therefore, a common computer-based information architecture is not likely to solve the information-management problem.

An issue in sharing is: Who determines who has legitimate need for the information? The "owning" department? Top management? And who identifies the owner? The process of developing the principles for managing information—how it is defined and distributed—is actually more important than the resulting principles because the touchy subject of information sharing is brought out into the open during the process. In short, working out information issues requires addressing entrenched attitudes about organizational control. That is where consensus needs to be built: in discussions, not through edicts.

Is sharing good? asks Davenport. Not in all cases. Forcing employees to share information with those above them can lead to intrusive management. Some executive support systems limit "drill down" for just this reason. Managers must think about these types of issues in information management.

Unlimited information sharing does not work. Limits are necessary. On the one hand, the sharing of corporate performance figures is beneficial, especially when corporate performance is poor, because it usually increases morale; uninformed employees usually guess the worst. On the other hand, the sharing of rumors (non-information) generally demoralizes people. Separating information from non-information is an information-management issue. Allowing employees to send messages to large distribution lists exacerbates the information-management problem. Managements have awakened to the fact that they need to address this issue. Vendors have developed filters and agents for e-mail systems. Such responses can help resolve corporate information management issues, but only when the correct underlying policies are put in place.

Even hiring practices play a role in information management. If promotions are based on circulation and publication of new ideas, a sharing environment exists. If these activities are not rewarded, sharing may be anathema to the culture.

In all, getting value out of information requires more than technology. Information is inherently hard to control. It is ever expanding and unpredictable. Only when executives view information in this light will they manage it for most effective use.

THE VAST ARENA OF COMPUTER ETHICS

To conclude this book, before looking to the future in the last chapter, we need to address an issue that is coming more to the fore: computer ethics. We can only touch on this vast subject, but this brief discussion will give a flavor of the issues involved. New technologies pose ethical issues when they open up new possibilities for human action—individual action as well as collective action—points out Deborah Johnson[9] of Georgia Institute of Technology in her book *Computer Ethics*. Nuclear power, the atom bomb, genetic engineering, and other technologies raise ethical questions, as do computers. Hence, the realm of computer ethics.

A Little History

In the first era of computing, when companies and governments used mainframes to collect personal information and store it in huge databases, the perceived threat was invasion of personal privacy, says Johnson. In the United States, that concern led to a major privacy study in 1976. At the time, no formal rules limited access to personal data in computers.

The second era of computing, mini- and microcomputers, turned attention to the democratizing aspects of computers and software and the ethical issues of property rights. Should software be owned? What sorts of intellectual property laws were needed to protect software owners? Such questions raised the ire of people who did not like the idea of property rights in software, those who believed software should be free. Issues of property rights also raised liability issues: Who is responsible for errors in code?

The third and latest era, the Internet, has brought "an endless set of ethical issues," notes Johnson, because it can be used in so many aspects of life. Thus, all the concerns of the past have resurfaced: privacy, the democratizing nature of the Internet, property rights on Web sites, the concept of free speech (is information on the Internet a form of speech or expression?), and now even global property rights.

What Is Computer Ethics?

In 1985, James Moor wrote the seminal piece, "What Is Computer Ethics?"[10] notes Johnson. Moor stated that new technologies raise ethical issues because they create policy vacuums. The ethical issues are these vacuums. The role of computer ethics is to fill the vacuums. Thus, areas of ethical concern include privacy, property rights, liabilities, free speech, and professional ethics. This notion implies that the technology appears first and the ethics follow. It might be better for IT to follow ethics, says Johnson, but that rarely happens in any technology. Two possible examples are freeware and the privacy-enhancing technology of anonymous remailers.

New technologies bring benefits and problems, which raise the ethical issues of how to shape a technology's use for good and minimize its use for harm. We need to make moral choices about how we are going to use IT, personally, organizationally, nationally, and even globally. The central task of computer ethics is to determine what our personal and social policies should be, states Moor.

Johnson provides a whole host of examples of IT ethical issues. Here are abbreviated samplings of a few of her examples to show the breadth of this subject.

- John buys a software package to help him invest in penny stocks. At a party, he mentions the software to Mary and she asks to borrow it. She likes it, so she copies it and then returns the original software to John. What did Mary do wrong, if anything? Why is it wrong? (Intellectual property rights)

- Inga has a small business and collects customer data from her customers directly and from their purchases. She wants to use data mining tools on this data to uncover patterns and correlations among her customers. The customers gave her the data to make a purchase; she wants to use that data for another purpose, even though individuals will not be uniquely identified in this use. Would she be doing anything wrong? (Privacy)

- Carl is a systems designer who is designing a system to monitor radar signals and launch missiles in response to those signals. He has become concerned that the system has not been made secure, for one thing, and that it cannot adequately distinguish between a missile and a small airplane, for another. His manager dismisses his concerns. What should he do? (Professional ethics)

- Grundner sent a message on an unmoderated listserv that contained the phrase "wives . . . and other informationally challenged individuals." Mabel sent him a private message reprimanding him for his sexist language. Grundner thought Mabel's message was sent to the entire listserv, so he broadcast a message that stated that online communications transcend barriers as long as "professional victim-mongers" do not "screw it up." Many members of the listserv felt Grundner's response was a personal attack on Mabel, and said so. Others sent messages on gender issues. Insulting spread around the listserv. What's wrong with this? (Flaming)

- Kimiko is a successful pension fund manager who uses an expert system to help her make investment decisions. Her experience tells her the market is going to turn down, so she wants to sell stock. However, the expert system recommends buying stock, even when Kimiko double-checks the economic indicator data she has entered. She does not understand the reasoning in the expert system, so she cannot check its logic. For all she knows, it could be malfunctioning. What should she do, buy or sell? (Accountability)

- Milo is an independent journalist and an expert on South American politics. He subscribes to an Internet-based service that sends him articles and news on areas of interest to him. Upon returning from a trip, he discovers a posting that says he is involved in illegal drug dealing and his articles protect drug cohorts. Milo is enraged by the lie. He wants to sue for defamation of character, but the bulletin board owner will not give him the address of the message poster, who used a pseudonym. So he sues the bulletin board owner instead. Are bulletin board owners liable for the contents posted on their board? (Accountability)

To address such issues, says Johnson, some people look to traditional moral norms and apply them to the new situations. They extend property law (copyrights, patent, and trade secret laws) to software. Similarly, certain kinds of spoken and written communications have traditionally been considered impolite or confidential. The same should hold for computer-mediated communications, some contend.

However, to apply past norms, we must first define, say, the *Internet* or *software*, which is difficult to do when both are still evolving. Is the Internet a highway? A shopping mall? A fantasy world? Each would have different laws, contends Johnson, which is one reason why computer ethics is so difficult. She questions whether we should be treating new opportunities like old situations. Although it is true that new uses of, say, computers, touch familiar ethical notions, we need to ask whether they pose new ethical issues. That is the main purview of computer ethics. IT creates a new species of traditional moral issues, with new variations and new twists, says Johnson.

So the question becomes, should we fill the vacuums with laws or something else? The answer should not begin nor end with laws. Rather, we need a shared sense of what is good and just. We need personal and institutional policies and social mores.

The ethical questions surround what people do to one another. Therefore, they involve such concepts as harm, responsibility, privacy, and property. In essence, says Johnson, IT creates a new *instrumentation* for human action, making new actions possible. As such, it can change the character of actions. For example, launching a computer virus on the Internet can wreak havoc for thousands, even tens of thousands of people and institutions. We need to account for this change in ethics, she contends.

Some actions are unethical only because they are illegal. Others are unethical whether or not they are legal. Much of the unethical behavior on the Internet is not controversial or complicated. It is just criminal behavior in a new medium. It is doing bad things in new ways. Computer ethics can thus be thought of as a new species of general moral issues that may not fit familiar categories. It has a global scope, which makes it unusual, and the actions have reproducibility in that they can be easily shared.

With this brief introduction to the realm of computer ethics, we now look at four areas that raise ethical and legal questions.

1. Information privacy
2. Intellectual property rights
3. Legal jurisdiction
4. Online contracting

Information Privacy

Privacy includes freedom from intrusion, the right to be left alone, the right to control information about oneself, and freedom from surveillance. It is a major issue in today's world because of the widespread availability of personal data and the ease of tracking a person's activities on the Internet.

The United States and many other countries have enacted laws to control certain types of personal information, such as medical, credit, and other financial information. These laws carry over to the online business environment. As companies have built large databases on their online customers, the value of this data makes selling it an attractive business option. That is one reason the United States now has a privacy law that requires companies to publish a description of how they treat the personally identifiable information they handle.

Internet technologies, cookies in particular, make tracking the browsing activities of individuals possible. Consumer concerns about this perceived invasion of privacy now require companies in some countries to post and adhere to privacy statements on their Web sites. The following hypothetical scenario found on zeroknowledge.com dramatizes these concerns.

> *Bob's father has just been diagnosed with cancer. In an effort to learn more about it, Bob visits cancer Web sites and posts several inquiries to a discussion group. A month later, Bob's insurance company informs him that he is no longer eligible for a certain rate given his "condition."*

Some companies use third-party cookies (i.e., cookies set by a firm other than the owner of the site being visited) to do *online profiling*. It is also known as profile-based advertising, and it is a technique that marketers use to collect information about the online behavior of Internet users and to facilitate targeted advertising. Profile-based advertising could easily be considered a form of online surveillance. What is worse, some third-party cookies are often placed on Web browsers' computers without their knowledge when banner advertisements appear. It is not necessary to click on the banner ad to generate a cookie.

Companies with cookies on their Web sites obviously want information about their customers to make better decisions about the types of products and services they should develop, says Johnson. On the other side of the coin is people's desire for privacy, their fear of who has information about them, and their mistrust of large, faceless organizations and governments.

Another technology that has privacy advocates concerned is RFID. They contend that these radio-frequency sensors on products will allow industry, governments, and thieves to monitor personal belongings after they have been purchased. As CNET's News.com reports, Debra Bowen, a California state senator, held a hearing on RFID technology and privacy to study what sorts of regulation might be needed to protect consumer privacy.[11] One example of privacy invasion mentioned at the hearing was, "How would you like it if you discovered that your clothes were reporting on your whereabouts?" Others presented other potential invasions of privacy from RFID tags on individual consumer items.

Still others suggested protection possibilities. One was to create a set of "fair use" guidelines for industry. One guideline might be that companies must label products that have RFID tags. Another might be to let consumers disable the sensors. A third could be to allow consumers to request and see the information collected about them from the sensors. Another suggestion was to require legal guidelines to be in place before deploying RFID.

Bowen has already introduced bills to regulate the use of other technologies that might invade privacy, including face recognition, data collected by cable and television companies on consumers' viewing habits, and shopper loyalty cards issued by supermarkets and other chains. Bowen is not alone in her concerns. Britain also is delving into RFID privacy issues.

However, the argument for personal information privacy has not "won the day," says Johnson. The following has not proven to be a strong argument: "*We control relationships by controlling the information we give to another party. When we lose control of our information, we lose control over how others perceive and treat us. The loss reduces our ability to establish and influence relationships.*" The reason that this argument is not strong is because when people must make a choice between a social good (such as police protection) and loss of control of information, they give up control.

A much stronger argument for the right to privacy can be made if privacy is seen as a social good, rather than as an individual good. This argument goes as follows, notes Johnson: "*Democracy is the freedom to exercise one's autonomy. If the consequences are too negative, few people will take the risk, and democracy will diminish. For example, people act differently when they know they are being watched. Thus, privacy is a social good in its own right. The less privacy, the more difficult it is to make social change. How information is gathered, exchanged, and used affects us all, not just those who have something to hide.*"

Johnson recommends five ways to increase information privacy protection:

1. *At the national level:* Treat privacy as a social good that lies at the heart of democracy, giving its protection more weight. Deal with privacy policy

nationwide rather than on an industry-by-industry basis, as it has been in the past. Citizens need protection from private institutions just as much as public ones, so include both public and private information gathering, with an eye toward global exchange. Treat personal information as part of the infrastructure of our society. It is better to manage this information outside the marketplace.

2. *Computer professionals:* Point out privacy matters to clients when they build databases that contain personal information.

3. *Technology:* Use privacy protection technologies, such as Web anonymity and tools for detecting the privacy level of a Web site.

4. *Institutions:* Adopt internal policies that protect privacy, such as restricting who can see personal information.

5. *Individuals:* Take personal actions to increase the privacy of information about you.

Intellectual Property Rights

The protection of intellectual property is critical in an Internet-based world because many products and services contain intellectual property, copies of such items are easy to make, and the copy is as good as the original. Examples of online activities in which intellectual property rights are critical include electronic publishing, software distribution, virtual art galleries, music distribution over the Internet, and online education.

Following are four types of legal protection of intellectual property: copyrights, patents, trademarks, and trade secrets.

Copyrights. Copyright law aims to protect an author's or artist's expression once it is in a tangible form. The work must be expressive rather than functional; a copyright protects the expression, not the idea. For example, a cartoon duck is an idea and cannot be copyrighted, but Donald Duck and Daffy Duck are expressions of that idea and are copyrighted. Registering a copyright is not a requirement; putting the expression into tangible form is sufficient. A copyright is valid for the life of the author plus 75 years.

Just about all original content on a Web site can be copyrighted by the creator of the site, from buttons to video, from text to a site layout. If a company hires someone to develop a site, by default the copyright belongs to the developer, not the company. The developer can then demand royalties from the company if it uses the Web site; therefore, it behooves companies to clearly define the ownership of the copyright in the contract.

The Internet raises many interesting issues for copyright law, which was developed for physical media. Placing copyrighted material, such as a photograph, on a Web site without permission of the copyright holder is a clear violation of the law. Less obvious is whether having a link to someone else's copyrighted material, say, a photograph, is a violation of copyright law. In this case, the answer is probably yes. However, if one includes a link to the homepage of the site rather than a direct link to the content, then probably no violation has occurred. Internet copyright issues are now being worked out in courts and legislatures.

Patents. Patent law aims to protect inventions—things or processes for producing things, where "things" are anything under the sun made by man but not abstract ideas or natural laws, according to U.S. copyright law. Valid for 20 years, patent protection is quite strong. In the United States, patents are granted by the U.S. Patent and Trademark Office after stringent thresholds on inventiveness have been met.

The United States recognizes patents for business processes. Although software, in general, cannot be patented—it must be copyrighted—certain business practices implemented in software can be patented. In the e-business area, Amazon.com has received a patent for "one-click purchasing." The company has enforced its patent rights against its main competitor, Barnes and Noble. Barnes and Noble cannot use one-click purchasing on its Web site. British Telecom has claimed to have invented the hyperlink. To obtain the patent, the company will have to show that no prior use of hyperlinks occurred before its use. Any prior use would invalidate the patent.

Trademarks.   Trademarks protect names, symbols, and other icons used to identify a company or product. Trademarks can be registered with the U.S. Patent and Trademark Office. A trademark is valid indefinitely, as long as it is used and does not become a generic name for the goods or services. The aim of trademark law is to prevent confusion among consumers in a market with similar identifying names or symbols. The standard for trademark infringement is whether the marks are confusingly similar.

The biggest area of trademark conflicts in e-business has to do with domain name registration. For a while, cybersquatters were registering domain names that clearly referred to known companies, realizing those companies would eventually want the domain name and would be willing to pay for it. Although this tactic worked for a while, anti-cybersquatting laws were passed and the practice is now illegal. To avoid potential problems, firms should obtain and register a trademark for its domain name. Note that most online services that register domain names do not check for trademark infringements. Firms are advised to do a search for possible trademark infringements before using a domain name to avoid future litigation.

Trade Secrets.   Trade secrets, as the name implies, protect company secrets, which can cover a wide range of processes, formulas, and techniques. A trade secret is not registered and is valid indefinitely, as long as it remains a secret. Although laws protect against the theft of trade secrets, it is not illegal to discover a trade secret through reverse engineering. Trade secrets are the area of intellectual property rights least applicable to e-business.

Legal Jurisdiction

Laws are written for particular jurisdictions with clear geographic boundaries, so how do those laws apply in cyberspace, which has no geographic boundaries? Take, for example, the case of trademark rights, which are limited to geographic areas. In the physical world, a sign over "Lee's Computer Services" in Singapore would not have a significant impact on "Lee's Computer Services" in Honolulu—neither in customers nor competition. However, in cyberspace the Web sites of the two companies would clearly overlap and, if the companies were to take advantage of the global reach of the Internet, competitive overlap could be an issue. The companies have little legal recourse for resolving their identical trademarks.

Gambling provides another example. Do Hawaiian laws against gambling apply to a Nevada company with a gambling site on its Web server located in Las Vegas? The Attorney General of Minnesota has asserted the right to regulate gambling that occurs on a foreign Web page that is accessed and "brought into" his state by a local resident.

Similar cases have involved sites dealing with pornography and securities trading. Alabama successfully prosecuted a California couple for bringing pornography into Alabama; their server was in California. Note that U.S. pornography laws are based on "community standards"; Los Angeles standards are clearly different from those of Mobile, Alabama. The state of New Jersey is attempting to regulate securities trading over the Internet if anyone in the state has access to it, and many states are trying to revise their tax codes to gain revenues from e-commerce.

At best, this trend is disturbing. At worst, it could greatly disrupt e-business. Faced with the inability to control the flow of electrons across physical boundaries, some authorities strive to impose their boundaries on cyberspace. When technological mechanisms, such as filters, fail, the authorities assert the right to regulate online trade if their local citizens may be affected. In essence, under this approach, all Internet-based commerce would be subject simultaneously to the laws of all territorial governments. Imagine a Hawaiian company setting up a Web site for retailing over the Internet needing to consider the laws of Hawaii, California, New York, and the other 47 states, plus Singapore, Peru, Syria, and any other place you might name. This situation would clearly cripple e-business.

The concepts of "distinct physical location" and "place where an activity occurred" fall apart in cyberspace; no clear answer is available to the question: Where did this event take place? Of relevance are the locations of the business's offices, warehouses, and servers containing the Web sites. Some of the uncertainty can be resolved by placing online contracts on the site specifying the legal jurisdiction that will be used for disputes. Users who agree to the contract designate so by clicking a button that says "I agree." In most cases, the contract will hold.

In the United States, states have adopted the Uniform Commercial Code (UCC), a wide-ranging codification of significant areas of U.S. commercial laws. The National Conference of Commissioners of Uniform State Law and the American Law Institute, who sponsor the UCC, are working to adapt the UCC to cyberspace.

Internationally, the United Nations Commission on International Trade Law has developed a model law that supports the commercial use of international contracts in e-commerce. This model law establishes rules and norms that validate and recognize contracts formed through electronic means, sets standards governing electronic contract performance, defines what constitutes a valid electronic writing and original document, provides for the acceptability of electronic signatures for legal and commercial purposes, and supports the admission of computer evidence in courts and arbitration proceedings.

Online Contracting

A contract is a voluntary exchange between two parties. Contract law looks for evidence that the parties have mutually assented to the terms of a particular set of obligations before it will impose those obligations on them. Before the law will recognize the existence of a binding contract, there must be

- A definite offer by one party, called the *offeror*
- A timely acceptance by the *offeree*
- Some consideration must pass between the offeree and the offeror

A widespread misconception holds that contracts must be in writing and signed before they are enforceable in court. The general rule is that offerees can show their acceptance of a contract offer by any means that are "reasonable under the circumstances." Reasonable acceptance includes oral agreements. Some exceptions do apply, however. For example, sales of real property require signed writings and, in the United States under the UCC, any contract for the sale of goods for a price greater than $500 requires a signed agreement.

In e-business, evidence of acceptance of a contract can be a simple click on a button saying "I accept" or "I agree." The case becomes more complex when the transaction involves payment greater than $500. The relevant questions are: Is our purely electronic communication "in writing" and have we "signed" the agreement? The answers are as yet unresolved. No cases have been presented regarding whether a file that exists in a computer's memory is "written" for purposes of contract law. Most commentators think the answer is probably "yes," but the final answer will have to wait until courts have reviewed the issue more closely.

In June 2000, President Clinton signed the Electronic Signatures in Global and National Commerce Act (E-Sign). Basically, E-Sign grants electronic signatures and documents equivalent legal status with traditional handwritten signatures. It is technology-neutral so that the parties entering into electronic contracts can choose the system they want to use to validate an online agreement. Many browsers contain minimal authentication features, and companies are developing pen-based and other types of technologies to facilitate online contracting. In addition, a number of companies already provide digital signature products using public key encryption methods.

The full impact of E-Sign may not be as revolutionary as some would hope. The act specifies that no one is obligated to use or accept electronic records or signatures—all parties must consent to using the method. The act does not apply to a wide range of situations, such as the creation and execution of wills, adoptions, divorces, any notice of cancellation or termination of utility services, or foreclosure or eviction under a credit agreement. In addition, the marketplace has to sort out some serious problems with varying electronic signature standards. For example, a number of companies issue digital certificates, but none of them can operate with the others. It would require parties interested in adopting electronic signatures for their business to provide several technologies or risk losing access to some customers.

CASE EXAMPLE

CLICKWRAP AGREEMENTS

On its Web site, the Cyberspace Law Institute[12] offers an interesting case. You subscribe to an electronic newsletter on a Web site with the following text:

You may obtain a 1-year subscription to our newsletter XYZ News for the special low price of $5.00 for each monthly issue, simply by filling in your

(Case Continued)

name and e-mail address on the form below and then clicking the SUB-SCRIBE button. By subscribing, you agree to the terms and conditions set forth in our Subscriber's Contract; to read the Subscriber's Contract, click on CONTRACT TERMS below.

Suppose you fill in your name and e-mail address and click SUBSCRIBE but, like most folks, you don't actually take the time to look at, let alone read, the Subscriber's Contract. Do you have a contract with XYZ?

Absolutely. You received an offer (to deliver the weekly newsletter to you); you took a specific action that the offeror deems to constitute acceptance of the offer (clicking on the SUBSCRIBE button); and you agreed to pay consideration for the contract (the offeror will deliver the newsletter to you for $5.00 per issue).

This clickwrap contract is an example of what the law calls a *contract of adhesion*—a contract that you did not really bargain over in any way, but which was presented as more of a take-it-or-leave-it offer. Generally speaking, adhesion contracts are legally enforceable.

The use of the term *clickwrap contract* is an extension to the shrinkwrap licenses used in purchased software. Mass-marketed software comes with the terms of the contract—the license agreement—packaged under clear wrapping, with the notice that by opening the package you are agreeing to the terms of that license. Clickwrap is the same idea: by clicking here, you similarly agree to the contract's terms. ∎

CONCLUSION

To properly support knowledge work, companies need to understand the life cycle of knowledge because each phase of the cycle is best supported by specific approaches. Two of the four phases discussed in this chapter are better supported using high-touch approaches, and two are better supported using high-tech approaches. There have been many undisclosed knowledge management failures, so it behooves executives to understand where IT fits in the overall knowledge-management and knowledge-sharing arena.

Likewise, it behooves management to understand the vast arena of computer ethics. IT adds new twists and, often, greater ramifications to long-standing ethical issues. New laws should not be the only recourse to address these ethical quandaries. Enterprises need to discuss these issues and make their own judgments.

Ethical use of IT is creeping into corporate policies, sometimes due to regulation. Companies in some countries now are required to state their privacy policies with respect to the personally identifiable information they handle. Many companies have also decided whether or not e-mail is company or private property and made their stance known to employees. It would be wise for CIOs to bring up other ethical issues and see that company policies are set, promulgated, and enforced, so that knowledge and other forms of intellectual property are properly used for good, not harm.

QUESTIONS AND EXERCISES

Review Questions

1. What is tacit knowledge? What is explicit knowledge?
2. What are the four phases of Giga's knowledge management model?
3. How do human capital, structural capital, and customer capital differ?
4. How has Buckman Laboratories encouraged knowledge creation and capture worldwide?
5. What is "the Rudy problem" and how did Seemann attempt to deal with it?
6. What are the two roles of the BP T-shaped manager in Egypt?
7. What did the pharmaceutical company do to create a knowledge infrastructure?
8. What approach did the energy company take to encourage knowledge sharing among its 15 business units?
9. Give three cultural roadblocks to knowledge management projects, as noted by Brooks.
10. What three questions does Stewart recommend be asked before launching a knowledge management project?
11. According to Davenport, what are three management issues in managing information? Briefly describe each.
12. According to Moor, what is the role of computer ethics?
13. Give some examples of IT ethical issues.
14. How does Johnson recommend increasing information privacy protection?
15. What are the four methods of legal protection of intellectual property?

Discussion Questions

1. Should IS take the lead in the development of knowledge management and sharing? Why or why not?
2. Knowledge management is a misnomer because knowledge only exists in people's heads. Thus, knowledge management is really just people management. Do you agree or disagree? Discuss.
3. An ethical question regarding e-mail is whether the contents belong to the sender or the corporation. What is your opinion? Explain your reasoning.
4. How do you think the flaming example on page 552 should have been handled by the listserv operator? By the listserv members?

Exercises

1. Find an article about a successful or failed knowledge management project. Why did it fail or succeed; that is, what were the "critical failure factors" or the "critical success factors"?
2. Visit a local organization that is developing a knowledge management system. Who is leading the development efforts? What benefits are being realized? What are their plans for the future?

3. Describe one or two computer ethics dilemmas either you or someone you know has faced. How was each handled? How could each have been handled better?
4. Describe your company's or school's policy on protecting information privacy. How easy was it to find this policy? Do you think it is being followed? If not, give examples of how it is being circumvented.

REFERENCES

1. Gartner EXP, 56 Top Gallant, Stamford, CT; www.gartner.com:
   a. Brewer, Tony, *Managing Knowledge*, Wentworth Research Program (now part of Gartner EXP), November 1995.
   b. Woolfe, Roger, Barbara McNurlin, and Phil Taylor, *Tactical Strategy*, Wentworth Research Program (now part of Gartner EXP), November 1999.

2. Giga Information Group, *Best Practices in Knowledge Management*, Norwell, MA, 1997.

3. Seemann, Patricia, "Building Knowledge Infrastructure: Creating Change Capabilities," Knowledge Imperative Symposium sponsored by Arthur Anderson and the American Center for Productivity and Quality, Houston, TX, September 1995.

4. Hansen, Morten, and Bolko von Oetinger, "Introducing T-Shaped Managers: Knowledge Management's Next Generation," *Harvard Business Review*, March 2001, pp. 107–116.

5. Brooks, Cyril, "KM Red Flags: Overcoming Cultural Barriers to Effective Knowledge Management," unpublished manuscript, 2000.

6. Stewart, Thomas, "The Case Against Knowledge Management," *Business 2.0*, February 2002, pp. 80–83.

7. Davenport, Thomas, and John Glaser, "Just-in-Time Delivery Comes to Knowledge Management," *Harvard Business Review*, July 2002, pp. 107–111.

8. Davenport, Thomas, "Saving IT's Soul: Human-Centered Information Management," *Harvard Business Review*, March/April 1994, pp. 119–131.

9. Johnson, Deborah, *Computer Ethics*, 3rd Ed., Prentice Hall, Upper Saddle River, NJ, 2001.

10. Moor, James, "What Is Computer Ethics?" *Metaphilosophy*, October 1985, pp. 266–275.

11. Gilbert, Alorie, "Privacy Advocates Call for RFID Regulation," CNET News.com, August 18, 2003. Available at news.com.com/2100-1029 3-5065388.html?tag=st rn. Accessed May 2004.

12. Lessig, Larry, David Post, and Eugene Volokh, "Lesson 68—Contract Law in Cyberspace," The Cyberspace Law Institute, Social Science Electronic Publishing, 1999.

PART IV
DISCUSSION CASE

HOW SHOULD LEGO PROTECT ITS TRADEMARK, OPERATING SYSTEM, AND APPLICATIONS?

Lego Company, with headquarters in Billund, Denmark, is the world's fourth-largest toy company. It makes the studded plastic Lego blocks that snap together. Sales are over $1.2 billion, and the CEO is the grandson of the founder, Kirk Christiansen, a carpenter who started Lego in 1932. Its name comes from "leg godt," which is Danish for "play well." The company does not publicize its toys, and it is privately held.

In 1998, Lego released Mindstorms Robotic Invention Systems. The Mindstorms kit includes hand-size programmable bricks covered with the familiar Lego "studs" and an integrated video camera so users can build robots. A robot is programmed on a computer screen by dragging and dropping virtual Lego bricks to form a list of instructions for the robot to follow, such as walk, run, throw an object, even chase something. These instructions are then transmitted to a programmable Lego brick using an infrared beam. Mindstorms costs $199 and is aimed at 12-year-olds.

Mindstorms was an instant success, selling 100,000 kits in 1998, rather than the 12,000 planned, states Paul Keegan.[1] It was developed over 10 years at the Lego lab at MIT (financed by Lego) based on the artificial intelligence programming language, Logo, that Seymour Papert, an MIT computer scientist, created for children. The toy was then named after Papert's 1980 book, *Mindstorms*, says Keegan. This 10-year development created enormous buzz among computer and robot enthusiasts; they could not wait to get their hands on the toy. So, much to Lego's surprise, it was not 12-year-olds who bought Mindstorms that first year, but twentysomethings—some 70 percent of Lego's initial customers.

The tinkerers immediately took Mindstorms apart (hacked it) to find out how it worked. They formed Mindstorms groups on the Internet and exchanged information. Less that 3 weeks after its release, part of Mindstorms' proprietary code had been hacked and posted on the Internet. The Mindstorms enthusiasts used this code to write more advanced software for their robots, says Keegan. One even created a new language, NQC, available on the Internet, that can be used to create, say, a robot that plays tic-tac-toe.

Another programmer went even further. He wrote his own operating system, which he had the chutzpah to call LegOS.

These hackers and their publicly posted extensions to Mindstorms fueled sales of the toy, making it even more versatile and fun to program. Today, 12-year-olds are the largest customer segment, accounting for 70 percent of sales, reports Keegan.

(Case Continued)

Lego's Dilemma

How should Lego management respond to these actions by hackers? On the one hand, the hackers helped market Mindstorms into being a hit. On the other hand, their software, which is offered free on the Internet, is out of Lego's control. What if some of it hurts Mindstorms' motors or infrared sensors? This might damage Lego's brand name and reputation. This third-party software infringes on Lego's intellectual property, but it makes the toy more versatile. The hackers are potentially Lego's biggest threat, and, at the same time, its biggest fans.

Should Lego sue these developers for infringement, earning their ire rather than their admiration? That is a tough question. But management faces an even more serious question: Should it sue the hacker who wrote an alternative operating system? Like the other hackers, he is not making money off his software; he offers it free on the Internet, believing that it is more powerful and flexible than the Lego software.

But, says Robert Johnston of the legal firm of Arnold and Palmer, if Lego does not control its operating system, how can it ensure that new generations of the operating system are compatible with the old ones? Furthermore, if Lego does not rein in its trademark, it will not be Lego's mark. Having an alternative operating system named LegOS is a trademark issue. If Lego doesn't offer some sort of certification program for applications, someone might go beyond the bounds. Once intellectual property is in the public domain, companies may lose the right to claim that it belongs to them. Doing nothing is not a wise move, Johnston argues.

Although the company is based in Denmark, the Mindstorms division is in California and has close ties to the hacker community in Silicon Valley. These Mindstorms executives do not want to become "the bad guy" nor fight with the hackers, says Keegan. They would argue that the hackers are not creating competing products. In fact, none of their software can be used without the Mindstorms kit. If company management does anger them, some might help a competitor. The hackers have helped Lego not only test Mindstorms but enhance it, make it smarter, create buzz about it, and give Lego new ideas faster and cheaper than Lego could do on its own.

Lego needs to decide where its source of profit lies: in the bricks, in Mindstorms' operating system, or in Mindstorms' applications. Management has decisions to make on three fronts: its operating system, its applications, and its trademarks.

Should Lego become a software company and discourage open source development? Or should it encourage third-party development within standards it establishes to protect its valuable brand? And what should it do about the hacker who appears to infringe on Lego's logo, calling his operating system LegOS?

It Is a Growing Dilemma

Lego's dilemma is not its alone. All software-based products and services potentially face the same issues.

Palm found itself in a similar situation. Management decided to give away its source code to people who wanted to create applications for its handheld devices. In doing so, Palm tapped a huge market. Over 150,000 developers created over 10,000 applications. However, Palm drew the line with its operating system; no one could touch it. That was its core business, and it licensed its operating

(Case Continued)

system to numerous other companies, such as Handspring.

To compete in both the software and hardware markets, Palm then divided into two companies. PalmSource develops and licenses the Palm OS operating system. PalmOne designs, builds, and markets handhelds and smart phones, and it bought Handspring.

Microsoft, on the other hand, believes companies should protect their copyrights and patents, and strongly urges others to follow its lead in taking infringers to court. Microsoft's argument is that not doing so will lead to chaos and ruin, states Keegan. Microsoft does not release its source code. It and others argue that when companies do not protect their intellectual property, it will be stolen. As a result, investors will not get a return on their investment, so they will not invest in future innovative products.

Other companies, such as IBM, embrace open source Linux and presumably would counsel Lego to utilize open source principles. Open source proponents argue that software can change faster when everyone knows the secrets.

Eben Moglen of Columbia Law School suggests that Lego set up a foundation to encourage free exchange of software among Mindstorms enthusiasts. He reasons that this approach would get even more consumers involved and could mimic the open source practice of users providing technical support. Mike Dooley, former Mindstorms team member, suggests that Lego patent parts of Mindstorms, such as its Vision Command, which is used by the robot's camera to detect motion and recognize color. Perhaps Lego could make royalties a new revenue stream to, say, videocamera makers. ∎

QUESTIONS

1. What should Lego management do to protect its trademark, operating system, and applications?

REFERENCES

1. Keegan, Paul, "Intellectual Property Is Not a Toy," *Business 2.0*, October 2001, pp. 90–96.

PART

V THINKING AHEAD

This part, which consists of just one chapter, is intended to stimulate thinking about the future and the roles IT could play. It begins by exploring some intriguing thoughts about potential organizing principles for an Internet-based world. These rules of the road do not extrapolate from the rules of the physical world, so they are worth considering carefully, especially when they appear to be counterintuitive.

The chapter also looks at the three people issues of moving ahead: gauging users' enthusiasm or reticence to embrace new technologies, non-IT executives' roles in leading the use of IT, and educating IS staff about the business.

In essence, this part is about leadership in the Internet-based economy. Thus, we end this book as we began it, highlighting the leadership box in our framework.

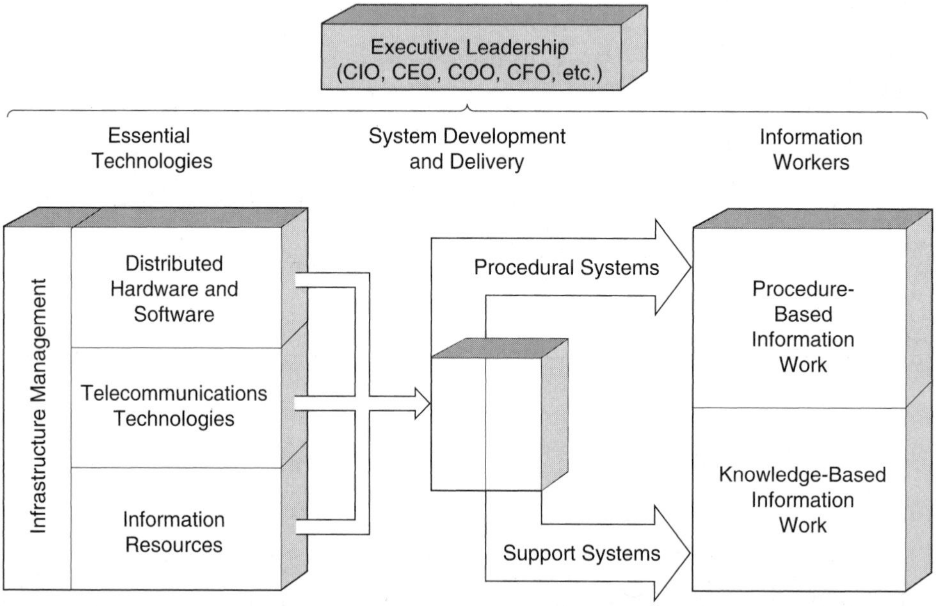

FIGURE P5-1 A Framework for IS Management

CHAPTER

14

THE CHALLENGES AHEAD

INTRODUCTION

It has become strangely out of fashion, even behind the times, to talk about the new economy, e-business, the e-world, or anything to do with *e*; yet, that is exactly the world we are moving into. The dot-com crash left a bad taste in the mouth of a lot of people, especially those who lost a lot of money in harebrained schemes. However, the end of that burst of frenzy does not mean that the e-world is going away. It has just gone underground. It is at work everywhere. Enterprises around the world are quietly redefining their strategies, work environments, and skills. This chapter looks at the challenges facing IS organizations worldwide by assembling a collage of opinions about possible principles underlying the e-world.

The computer is an amazing machine because it leverages people's brain power, not just their muscle power. This capability is being used to process data, and more importantly, to communicate in new ways. This communication, in turn, allows companies to compete in new ways. Following are some organizing principles being proposed for thriving in an Internet-based economy. The chapter ends by looking at ways to move forward.

ORGANIZING PRINCIPLES

This section is potentially the most exciting because we are in a time of grand exploration—a new economy is being born (perhaps by fits and starts). However, it is equally the most frustrating, because the tenets of this new economy are so different that the "rules" are just now being formulated, reformulated, and reformulated again. As the economy matures, some principles will prove true, others will fall by the wayside. The following opinions offer possible organizing principles. They point out the areas enterprises may need to focus on to succeed in an e-economy.

The Learning Organization

Peter Senge, director of the Systems Thinking and Organizational Learning Program at MIT's Sloan School of Management, wrote the influential book *The Fifth Discipline: The Art and Practice of the Learning Organization.*[1] No list of organizing principles for the new work environment would be complete without including his ideas.

Senge begins his book by noting that most organizations live only 40 years, which is only one-half the life of a person. The reason, he says, is because they have learning disabilities. In children, learning disabilities are tragic; in organizations, they are fatal. Therefore, he believes organizations will have to become learning organizations to survive.

Organizational learning disabilities are obvious, notes Senge. Here are just three. One, enterprises move forward by looking backward in that they rely on learning from experience. This approach means that companies end up solving the same problems over and over. Second, organizations fixate on events, such as budget cuts, monthly sales, and competitors' new announcements. Yet the real threats come from gradual changes that occur so slowly that no one notices them. Third, teamwork is not optimal, which is contrary to current belief. Team-based organizations operate below the lowest IQ on the team, leading to skilled incompetence.

Organizations that can learn faster than their competitors will survive. In fact, it is the only sustainable advantage, states Senge. To become a learning organization, an enterprise must create new learning and thinking behaviors in its people. That is, the organization and its people must master the following five basic learning disciplines:

1. Personal mastery
2. Mental models
3. Shared vision
4. Team learning
5. Systems thinking

Personal Mastery. People reach a special level of proficiency when they live creatively, striving for the results that matter most to them. In essence, their life turns into lifelong learning, in which they continually clarify and deepen their personal vision and focus their energies. This personal mastery forms the spiritual foundation for the learning organization. Unfortunately, few enterprises foster such aspirations; they are not committed to the full development of their people. Therefore, they foster burnout rather than creativity.

Mental Models. People's mental models are the deeply ingrained assumptions, generalizations, and images that influence how they see the world and what actions they take. Senge notes that Royal Dutch/Shell was one of the first organizations to understand the importance of mental models; that is, how its managers viewed the world and the oil industry. Shell learned how to surface its managers' assumptions and challenge their inaccurate mental models. In so doing, Shell was able to accelerate its organizational learning and spur the managers to investigate alternative futures by using scenarios. Then, when the 1974 oil crisis hit, its managers were able to react more appropriately than competitors because they had already explored the possibility of such a crisis and the best steps to take if one did occur. (Shell's current scenarios are explored in the Part 1 Discussion Case.) To change mental models, people must look inward, something few organizations encourage. However, those that do realize they have a powerful tool for fostering institutional learning.

Shared Vision. A shared vision is an organization's view of its purpose, its calling. It provides the common identity by which employees and others view it. Senge notes that Apple's shared vision has been to build computers for the rest of us. IBM's shared vision was exemplary service. A shared vision is vital to a learning organization because it provides the overarching goal as well as the rudder for the learning process. It becomes the force in people's hearts. It is the answer to: "What do we want to create?" Organizations with shared visions are powerful organizations.

Team Learning. When teams learn, they produce extraordinary results. One of the major tools for team learning is dialog, where people essentially think together. Senge distinguishes discussions from dialogs by saying that discussions occur when people try to convince others of their point of view. Dialogs, on the other hand, occur when people explore their own and others' ideas, without being defensive, to arrive at the best solution. Few teams dialog; most discuss, so they do not learn. Team learning, rather than individual learning, is essential in the learning organization, says Senge, because teams are the fundamental unit of the modern organization. If teams do not learn, neither does the organization.

Systems Thinking.   We live in a world of systems. To understand systems, people need to understand their underlying patterns. For example, people can only understand the "system" of an enterprise by contemplating its whole, not its parts. Today's complex enterprises are best understood by looking for patterns and viewing them as a whole entity. Systems thinking is a conceptual framework for making complete patterns clearer. Using and understanding systems thinking can help people see how to change the patterns effectively.

Of these five disciplines, Senge believes that systems thinking is the cornerstone. It is the fifth discipline. Until organizations look inwardly at the basic kinds of thinking and interacting they foster, they will not be able to learn faster than their competitors.

Processes Rather Than Functions

In *Beyond Reengineering*, the follow-up to *Reengineering the Corporation*, Michael Hammer[2] notes that the key point of the reengineering movement was not that changes needed to be dramatic (i.e., in terms of orders of magnitude), but that they needed to be made from a process-centered viewpoint rather than a task-centered one. The industrial revolution deconstructed processes into specialized tasks. As a result, the business world has focused on improving tasks. Tasks are about individuals; processes are about groups. We are now in a group economy, Hammer states.

Current organizational problems are process issues, he contends. They center around how specialized tasks fit together. Simple jobs require management and complex processes to get work done. When companies try to simplify these complex processes, they find simplification can only be done by creating complex jobs. A typical reengineering case in point is the move from a sequential workflow (where five people each perform just one or a few parts of a job) to a case-management approach (where one person performs the entire workflow). The result: simpler work process, more complex jobs. Employees manage themselves, eliminating the need for a supervisor.

Working and managing become part of everyone's job in a process-centered structure. Process-centered organizations can address today's organizational issues because the solutions require shifting perspective from tasks to processes. A growing number of enterprises are taking the process-centered approach, Hammer notes, with an emphasis on teams.

The shift to processes has a number of ramifications. One is the need for a new position, such as process owners. In every process, virtually every department is involved. So one person needs to have end-to-end responsibility. Rather than managing the people, process owners provide the knowledge of the process. They own the design of the process. Furthermore, processes need to be designed from a customer's perspective. Process design and process improvement become the essence of management in a process-centered organization.

The move to a process-centered structure also requires measures of processes, which are different from measures of tasks. Measuring a process (how long it takes to complete, its accuracy rate, its cost, etc.) means measuring its outcome from the customer's point of view. A task metric, on the other hand, would measure how many calls a customer service representative handles each hour. The process metric for the same job could be the percentage of problems (calls) handled completely on the first call, which is an outcome.

Process centering also turns people into professionals rather than workers, says Hammer, if you define a professional as someone who is responsible for achieving results rather than performing a task. The professional is responsible to customers, solving their problems by producing results. To do so means doing what it takes to complete a process. Workers, on the other hand, aim to please the boss, keeping busy with lots of activity, to perform what they are told to do. Workers are told not to be concerned with the totality of the work. The shift to professional from worker is profound. It makes factory employees concerned with customer satisfaction rather than number of parts produced per hour. It requires greater knowledge and a more holistic view by all the people involved.

Given this brief description of some of the principles underlying a process-centered organization, what would one look like? MeadWestvaco in Chapter 1 provides an in-progress example. Business process outsourcing provides another. For instance, order-to-cash is now a process being outsourced. It involves handling all the invoice-to-cash tasks. Thus, it turns an order for, say, a computer, into cash. Some outsourcers now specialize in performing this process for clients. These outsourcers are judged (and perhaps paid) based on how quickly they turn an invoice into cash.

Following are two other examples of process-centered operations. The first example, NYNEX, is based on an article in *Communications of the ACM* by Patricia Sachs,[3] then the technical director of the Works Systems Design group, and on work by Roger Woolfe.[4] The second example, a football team, is from Michael Hammer.[2]

CASE EXAMPLE

NYNEX

Due to the upheaval in the U.S. telecommunications industry, NYNEX, the New York-based telecommunications company, targeted 12 major processes for redesign in a companywide business process redesign initiative. Eleven used the traditional Rummler-Brache approach: looking at lines and boxes "as is" and "should be" in a 3-day off-site redesign effort.

The twelfth group used participative design and involved the Work Systems Design group, along with eight employees from across one provisioning process. The team spent 1 year from analysis to implementation, with everyone full-time. This project was the only one of the 12 implemented, and it yielded excellent results. (The other processes were addressed again in an intensive, large-scale process reengineering effort.)

The Work Systems Design group, whose charter was to create productive workplaces, was an interdisciplinary group with expertise in computer science, telephony, anthropology, and graphic art. It took a socio-technical view toward the analysis of work, which is fairly unusual in the industry. The quality movement in companies has aimed to correct processes to eliminate errors, whereas the socio-technical view equips people to handle problems, believing that all errors cannot be eliminated. Rather than

(Case Continued)

operate under the assumption that work can be automated and people can be downskilled, the group wanted to upskill employees.

Work is accomplished by people in working communities who possess all kinds of expertise nurtured by that community. The Work Systems Design group therefore looked at CoPs and their worlds of expertise. Redesigning processes required looking at an entire working community, its set of practices, its knowledge, and its expertise. To remain durable, such networks need to be nurtured, supported, and even made formal as teams or as CoPs, a notion they got from working with the people at the Institute for Research on Learning in Menlo Park, California.

In the provisioning redesign project, the goal was to redesign how NYNEX provided one type of high-speed telecommunications service to businesses. The team looked at how work was actually done, they created an implementable design, and then they disbanded. The operational members returned to their original provisioning work using the new process. That process was unique in NYNEX. Rather than pass a customer among specialized groups, all the people in the process worked together, in one area, as a multifunctional team. Thus, engineers worked alongside salespeople.

Because this multifunctional team structure was counter to NYNEX's culture and predominant work organization, it did cause problems. When new managers took over, they often did not understand this way of working. They wanted the group to return to the familiar "all the engineers in one group" structure. This weakened the group's more productive structure. A major difficulty with an innovative new process, NYNEX learned, was underrating how difficult it would be to keep it going when it is countercultural. ■

CASE EXAMPLE

A FOOTBALL TEAM

A football team is a good example of a process-centered organization, says Michael Hammer. It has two processes: offense and defense. It has process owners: offensive coordinators and defensive coordinators who select the players, train them, design plays, and script them.

Their concern is the performance of the process.

The team also has position coaches, such as the line coach, who act as counselors and mentors to train and develop the athletes for specific tasks. Their concern is the performance of the athletes.

(*Case Continued*)

Finally, the team has a head coach, the leader, who creates the organization, names the coordinators and coaches and then manages them, creates the team's culture and values, motivates the players to peak performance, and calls the plays during the game. However, once on the field, the team is self-directed; it adapts to the unfolding play. ■

Communities Rather Than Groups

Another organizing principle for the e-world is communities rather than groups. The distinction between the two is that communities form of their own volition. Groups are formed by design; their members are designated *a priori*, perhaps by a project manager, a select committee, or an executive.

As noted in Chapter 12, communities of practice (CoPs) are espoused by the Institute for Research on Learning in Menlo Park, California, a spin-off of Xerox PARC. As described by John Seely Brown, former director of Xerox PARC, and Estee Solomon Gray,[5] a founder of Congruity, a consulting firm, a CoP is a small group of people (rarely more than 50) that has worked together for a period of time, but not necessarily in an organized fashion. They may perform the same job or collaborate on a shared task or a product. They have complementary talents and expertise; they are held together by a common purpose and a need to know what the others know. Most people belong to several CoPs, and most important work in companies is done through them.

Communities are the building blocks of a knowledge-based company, state Brown and Solomon Gray, for three reasons. One, people, not processes, do the work. Big gaps separate official work processes and real-world practices (how things actually get done). The informal, perhaps impromptu, ways that people solve problems cannot be anticipated. When companies compete on knowledge, the name of the game is improvisation. The challenge is to keep processes elegantly minimal, so that they give room for local interpretation and improvisation; that is, for grassroots practices.

The second reason CoPs are important is that learning is about work, work is about learning, and both are social, say Brown and Solomon Gray. The crucial, unappreciated ingredient in companies is tacit knowledge — intuition, judgment, and common sense — which cannot be explained. Within groups, tacit knowledge exists in practices and relationships that are based on people working together over time. When people recognize the importance of tacit and collective dimensions of work, they realize that learning has to do with being part of a community rather than absorbing information.

Third, CoPs are important because organizations are webs of participation. When a pattern of participation changes, the organization changes. Participation is the core of the twenty-first-century company. Only people who make a commitment to their colleagues can create a winning company. Companies that realize the power of communities and adopt processes that allow them to emerge are moving toward e-world companies. National Semiconductor fosters CoPs.

CASE EXAMPLE

NATIONAL SEMICONDUCTOR

National Semiconductor has gone far in promoting CoPs, according to Brown and Solomon Gray. The company began encouraging such communities after its business model that built low-margin commodity chips collapsed. The new CEO restructured and rationalized the company, then put it on a growth path and changed its business model. Part of the strategy was to build a core competence in mixed signal technology, where chips function as the electronic interface between the real world of voice-video and the digital world of computing-communications.

CoPs are central to this plan. They energize and mobilize the firm's engineers. They even shape strategy and then enact it. A CoP on signal processing, for example, grew slowly over 18 months. It now includes engineers from numerous product lines and has been influential in strategy decisions.

Another CoP has grown up around phase lock loops (PLL), a technology critical in some important company products. For 20 years, PLL designers swapped ideas, insights, and solutions to problems, even though they worked in different business units that did not collaborate. Within this loose community, some PLL engineers began reviewing new chip designs as a group. When product teams around National Semiconductor heard about these reviews, they informally brought their designs to this group for advice. The more reviews the group did, the more effective it became; it earned a reputation for excellence.

These engineers cannot publish their design criteria, teach others how to do design reviews, or create a library of design because their knowledge is embedded within their experience as a CoP. The only way someone can learn how to critique a design is to become part of that community and interact with it.

This PLL CoP has now been formally recognized and has a charter: to make its design know-how accessible, to make successes and failures known, and to continue to build the firm's PLL competence. This community does not report to anyone; it is "run" by its members. It provides a means of collaboration among National engineers concerning their PLL designs. It has even received funding to develop two advanced PLL prototypes outside any National product line. It also has created a "PLL place," a lab that houses the equipment it buys.

National is extending CoPs by formally recognizing them, offering funding for their projects, and handing out a toolkit to help people form their own CoP. National also encourages CoPs to create homepages on the Web to communicate. ■

Virtual Rather Than Physical

The virtual organization has come to be the popular description of a new organizational form. The underlying principle is that time and space are no longer main organizing foundations. A virtual organization does not exist in one place or one time. It exists whenever and wherever the participants happen to be. As organizations expand globally but need to adapt to local conditions, virtual organizations have emerged inside them, just as have CoPs. As an example of a virtual organization within an existing company, consider Sun Microsystems as reported by Richard Rapaport.[6]

CASE EXAMPLE

SUN MICROSYSTEMS

John Gage, chief scientist of Sun Microsystems, gives an intriguing description of virtual organizations within an existing company. The network creates the company, "Your e-mail flow determines whether you're really part of the organization; the mailing lists you're on say a lot about the power you have." For example, Gage had been part of the Java group at Sun for 4 or 5 years when his name mistakenly was taken off. His flow of information stopped; he stopped being part of that organization. He got back on the list in a hurry, he says.

He notes that he uses Sun's alias file (the master list of its e-mail lists) to know what is going on in Sun. No one needs to tell him when a new project has started; he can see a new e-mail list. When he sees a list balloon from, say, 35 to 200, he knows something important is happening.

People even create their own aliases, he says. His own alias list is his personal view of the company's power structure on a project, no matter where the people work. The organization chart does not reflect the same list. These personal aliases have a secondary effect, too. They let others know whom you are keeping informed. In essence, each alias is a virtual organization. Web technology extends e-mail, says Gage, because it allows people to send "live" messages with embedded hyperlinks. So, rather than try to persuade people, you can just show them. ∎

Self-Organizing Rather Than Designed

Some of the most stimulating discussions about the form of future organizations are those centered around chaos theory, ecology, and biology. Meg Wheatley's highly influential book, *Leadership and the New Science*,[7] is one example. Two others are Kevin Kelly's mind-opening *Out of Control* and *New Rules for the New Economy*.[8] The basic tenet of these works is that nature provides a good model for future organizations; that is, organizations that must deal with complexity, share information and knowledge, and cope with continuous and discontinuous change. In seeming chaos, we can get order for free, according to both Wheatley and Kelly. As with natural phenomena, enterprises will do much better if they are self-organizing or emergent, rather than designed. Because it is easiest to illustrate these principles by example, we start there.

Examples of Self-Organization. Wheatley, in both *Leadership* and her more recent book with Myron Kellner-Rogers, *A Simpler Way*,[9] describes the famous chaos experiment by Stuart Kauffman, a theoretical biologist. He attached each of 200 light bulbs to two others and programmed them so that each one turned on or off depending on the behavior of the two partners. He was interested to see whether a pattern would emerge from the 10^{30} possible states. To his great surprise, a repeatable pattern emerged almost instantly, after 13 states. Even when he changed the connections, an organization (albeit a different one) emerged "instantly." His conclusion is that we get order for free, even without intelligence in the system.

Kevin Kelly, former executive editor of *Wired* magazine, gives many, many examples of order-from-chaos in both his books. Here are just three. The first concerns the movie *Batman Returns*, in which computer-generated bats were to flock through Gotham City. One computer-generated bat was created and allowed to automatically flap its wings. Then it was replicated, by the dozens, until there was a mob. Each was instructed to move on its own following just three rules: do not bump into another bat, keep up with your neighbors, and do not stray too far away. When the computer simulation of the mob of bats was run, they flocked just like real bats! Craig Reynolds had discovered the flocking rules, writes Kelly, and they were simple. So even though the bats were seemingly out of anyone's control, they flocked. The same happened with the marching mob of penguins in the same movie, which also drew on a simple Reynolds algorithm. Kelly says this kind of behavior indicates that order can be achieved from chaos in any distributed "vivisystem," combined biological mechanical systems, organic or man-made.

In an equally striking example, Kelly describes how Loren Carpenter, a computer graphics guru, demonstrated a similar kind of order-from-chaos in an auditorium with 5,000 computer graphics conferees. Each one had a cardboard wand, red on one side, green on the other. At the back of the auditorium, a computer scanned the wands when they were held up high, picking up the color on each wand. At the front of the auditorium was a huge screen that displayed the sea of wands, which looked like a candlelight parade. Attendees could find themselves in the sea and change their color on the screen by flipping their wand.

Carpenter then projected the game Pong (a videogame similar to table tennis) on the screen, telling the audience that those on the left controlled the left paddle, those on the right the right paddle. Within moments, the 5,000 were playing a pretty good game of Pong, with the movement of the paddle being the average of the several thousand players' intentions. When Carpenter speeded up the game, the crowd adjusted, almost instantly.

When an airplane flight simulator was projected on the screen, Carpenter told the audience that the left side of the room controlled the roll and the right controlled pitch. In essence, the pilot became 5,000 novices. They became silent as they studied the controls in the cockpit, wrote Kelly. The plane was headed for a landing, yet it pitched left and right because the signal was latent and the crowd continually overcompensated. When it was obvious that they would arrive wing first on the landing strip, they somehow pulled the plane up and turned it around, even though no one gave a command. They acted as one mind, turned wide, and tried a second landing. But again, the plane was not straight, so in unison, and again without verbal communication, they pulled up. On the way up, the plane rolled a bit, then a bit more, and then, "at some magical moment" the same thought seemed to occur to everyone, "I wonder if we can do a 360?" In unison, without speaking, they rolled the jet, fairly gracefully, and then gave themselves a standing ovation. Kelly notes that the conferees did just what the birds did: they flocked.

Five years later, Carpenter tried the same experiment at the same conference, states Kelly in *New Rules for the New Economy*. This time, the game was more sophisticated (the controls had more choices), and the task more challenging (to steer a 3D submarine in search of sea monster eggs). However, unlike previously, when the audience took control, nothing happened. The submarine did not move. Even after lots of fiddling with controls and shouting, still no movement took place. Finally, in exasperation, Carpenter said, "Why don't you go right?" Immediately, the submarine went right. He had unlocked the paralysis. The group needed leadership. It might only be a few words, but it was enough to initiate cohesion. From then on, the 5,000 copilots maneuvered the submarine deftly.

Finally, here is a business example from Kelly and *Business Week*[10] of a group acting as a self-organizing "swarm."

CASE EXAMPLE

CEMEX

Cemex (Cementos Mexicanos) delivers ready-mix cement in the state of Monterrey, Mexico. In the Guadalajara region of this state, delivering cement on time was extremely difficult due to traffic jams, poor roads, and contractors not ready for their orders. The situation was so bad that Cemex's on-time delivery rate was 35 percent. To improve, the company tried to enforce advanced reservations. However, that actually made matters worse because when contractors changed their orders just hours before delivery, as happened half the time, Cemex could not reschedule the delivery for another week or so.

To deal with its biggest problem of unpredictability of orders, management then took the opposite tack: no reservations required and delivery faster than pizza. They turned their attention to managing information rather than managing assets. To do so, they installed a companywide telecommunications system that included a global positioning satellite (GPS) system for the trucks and full information to all employees. Instead of dispatchers scheduling drivers, the drivers were to schedule themselves in real time as calls came in.

To ensure fast delivery, the drivers stationed themselves throughout the city, forming a kind of web. The driver closest to a call delivered the cement. The dispatchers played the new role of checking on customers' creditworthiness and making sure no customer call was being overlooked. The result of this self-organization was a 98 percent delivery rate, delivery times of 20 minutes (down from 3 hours), much less wasted (hardened) cement, 35 percent fewer trucks, lower fuel costs, and happier customers. ■

The Self-Organizing Point of View. Wheatley and Kellner-Rogers believe that organizations, like the light bulbs and many natural phenomena, can be self-organizing. They believe self-organization requires taking the perspective of "organizing-as-a-process" rather than "organization-as-an-object." Processes can do their own work if supplied with what the processes need to begin: resources, information, and access to new people.

Self-organizing systems create their own structure, patterns of behavior, and processes to accomplish the work. People within a process "design" what is necessary to do the work and "agree on" the relationships that make sense to them. System-wide stability depends on the ability of the members to change. As conditions change, the people change the process. As a result, the members do not need to plan things into existence; they only need to work with the unknowns, and an "organization" will emerge. Systems are relationships that are seen as structures, but those relationships cannot be structured; they can only emerge. Webs develop as the individuals explore their needs, if they are free to create the relationships they need. Freedom and trust are paramount for self-organizing systems to thrive. Such systems are healthiest when they are open to including diversity; it gives them strength and resiliency. (This discussion sounds like the open source movement discussed in Chapter 12, doesn't it?)

Kelly believes that the only way to create truly complex systems is to use biology's logic of self-governance, self-replication, partial learning, and some self-repair. He believes that the mechanical and biological worlds are merging, leading to bionic systems, which he calls "vivisystems." On the one hand, a nation's flight control system needs mechanical clockwork systems. However, when adaptability is needed, the best systems act as swarms, like a hive of bees. Kelly notes that when bees swarm, that is, move en masse to a new hive, the process is not command controlled. Instead, a few scouts check out possible new hive locations and report back to the swarm by dancing. The more theatrical a scout bee's dance, the better the bee liked the site. Deputy bees then check out one of the competing sites based on the dance that attracts them the most. If a scout concurs with the dancing bee's choice, the scout joins the dance. This activity induces others to check out the site and then join the dance if they concur. In this democracy, the favorite sites get more visitors, and, following the law of increasing returns, they get more dancing votes, and the others get fewer. In the end, one large snowballing dancing swarm dominates and flies off to the new site, taking the queen bee with it.

Can an example of an organization with such a self-organizing principle be found? Consider Semco of Brazil.

CASE EXAMPLE

SEMCO, S. A.

In his books *Maverick: The Success Story Behind the World's Most Unusual Workplace*, and *The Seven-Day Weekend*. Ricardo Semler,[11] CEO of Semco, describes how his company, a Brazilian manufacturer of industrial equipment, moved from fifty-sixth place to fourth place in its industry. To survive with Brazil's crippling

(Case Continued)

inflation rate, Semler felt he had to "break all the rules" to get costs down and productivity up.

As a result, factory workers at times set their own production quotas, help redesign products, formulate marketing plans, and even choose their own bosses. Bosses set their own salaries, yet everyone knows what they are, because workers have unlimited access to Semco's one set of books. All employees have been taught how to read balance sheets and cash flow statements. Finally, on the big decisions, such as relocating a factory, everyone decides. In one case, a factory was shut down for 1 day and buses took the employees to all three possible sites. Then the workers decided on a site that management would not have chosen.

One striking feature of Semler's most recent book, *The Seven-Day Weekend*,[11] is just how far self-management can go. At Semco, it goes a long way. Semler and the other top executives make few decisions. When there is a problem or issue—whether to have employee badges, if a group of employees unknowingly generates a high telecommunications bill one month, or what to do about a boss highly disliked by subordinates—the standard response from management is "to do nothing," notes Semler. It is the employees' job to handle their own problems in their own way, which may take longer and require a lot more discussion than a swift management decision, but it has a better lasting result. In fact, once a decision has been agreed on, its implementation is immediate—quite the opposite of top-down decisions that take time to be implemented by others (or not).

Semler believes the way to unleash innovation and have a motivated workforce is for top management to give up

control—a heretical thought in just about all other enterprises. Yet, Semco's financial success and low employee attrition rate attest to these principles, which have worked for the past 10 years.

Another self-organizing tenet at Semco is that *all* meetings are voluntary for *all* employees, including hiring meetings, budget meetings, team meetings, even board meetings (*any* employee can sign up to hold one of two open voting seats at the next board meeting). Meeting agendas are published ahead of time for everyone to see. If no one shows up at a meeting, then the company obviously should be doing nothing about that subject. Furthermore, people can leave a meeting when they are bored. This self-organizing discipline keeps the company focused on issues of importance to employees, notes Semler. Meetings that deal with issues of great concern draw many, many employees. People attend meetings they care about. Likewise, they work on what they care about. When they become unhappy, they are free to look for another job in the company.

Semco has no receptionists, secretaries, or perks, and Semler really does not know how many employees he has because some of his employees work part-time for him and part-time for competitors, others are contractors, and still others are vendor employees. When Semler took over the company after the death of his father, he threw out the rules because they discouraged flexibility and comforted complacency. For example, Semco sets no travel rules; employees are to spend whatever they think they should, as if it were their own money. The rationale: "If we're afraid to let people decide in which section of the plane to sit or how many stars their hotels should

(Case Continued)

have, we shouldn't be sending them abroad to do business in our name, should we?" writes Semler. Employees are considered partners; they are self-managing and self-governing. They even vote on how the profit-sharing pot will be split each year.

Things are rather messy around Semco, writes Semler. Machines are not in neat rows. They are set at odd angles, where the team that assembles a complete product puts them. Most workers do several jobs on a team, not just one, with the backing of the unions. Team members do not have to show up for work at the same time, but they do coordinate their schedules so as not to disrupt production. As the workers assumed more responsibility for their work, the number of supervisors decreased, as did corporate staff. Semco does not even have IS, training, or quality control departments. Three layers of management do the job that used to take 12, and those three are represented by three concentric circles.

Furthermore, departments can buy from whomever they choose. This competition keeps departments on their toes. Management encourages employees to start their own companies, even to the point of leasing Semco machinery to these start-ups at favorable rates. These companies sell to Semco and competitors. This strategy keeps Semco lean and agile.

The story goes on and on. The changes have been rough and were not undertaken in an orderly or coherent fashion, as Semler recounts, but the radical changes to a far more democratic workplace allowed the company to grow 600 percent at the same time that the Brazilian economy was faltering. It is a dramatic story, and illustrative of the benefits of self-organization in a chaotic business environment. ∎

Adaptable Rather Than Stable

In their provocative book *It's Alive: The Coming Convergence of Information, Biology, and Business*, Christopher Meyer and Stan Davis[12] speculate on future organizational structures. Actually, some of these structures exist today. The two authors contend that successful organizations will be structured to naturally support (perhaps even foster) volatility and continual surprises. Today, organizations are structured to maintain stability; change is minimized. Hence, change costs a lot. Firms built for stability are not adaptable.

IT is causing the world to become more connected, and connectivity increases volatility. To keep pace, companies will need to adapt more quickly. The only way to achieve adaptability is through distributed intelligence and action, contend Meyer and Davis. Thus, organizational models will be built around networks and will be designed to evolve.

The theories that drive biology will be used to model enterprises, the two authors believe. For example, agent-based models will become important because they help people understand individual and group behavior. Furthermore, such modeling gives people ways to see possible future consequences of their decisions by simulating these decisions and watching the agent-based model play out over time.

Individuals will become the focus of organizations because individuals are the agents of adaptation. Organizations will aim to influence the decisions that individuals make. A major strategy will be "seed, select, amplify," state Meyer and Davis, which means testing as many "seeds" (possible goods or services) as possible, selecting the ones that the market responds to, and then amplifying those winners. Such testing will be handled by the bottom of the organization, causing it to be run bottom up, rather than the top down. The leaders will govern the independent actions of the people in the organization by establishing the guidelines and constraints for their decisions and actions.

Capital One is a prime example of this future organizational structure, note Meyer and Davis.

CASE EXAMPLE

CAPITAL ONE

Capital One is in the credit business. Initially it issued credit cards and then it moved into consumer financing of automobiles, elective surgery, and dental work. IT enables Capital One's information-based strategy, which enables it to base decisions on the results of market tests. Capital One believes in "the law of large numbers;" that is, that high volumes of tests will yield an accurate reading of the marketplace. It therefore conducts tens of thousands of tests a year. It conducted 64,000 such tests in 2002, state Meyer and Davis.[12]

In fact, Capital One's core competency is its test design. The heart of the company's strategy is dreaming up credit programs that might have value to customers and then testing numerous variations of each program to see which yield the best results. Each new type of credit card or financing offer is tested on many factors. The results of the tests are then analyzed using algorithms and statistics. The winning variations are then modified and offered to more

consumers (once funding is acquired from management). It is "seed, select, and amplify," to use Meyers' and Davis' terminology. This strategy, which is akin to scientific experimentation, is not at all the convention in the industry. And it is far more IT based than competitors' strategies.

As one example, Capital One discovered from its first test that "balance transfer" was a winning offer. Consumers can use balance transfers to move credit card debt from another card to a Capital One credit card, which has a lower introductory interest rate. Capital One created this lucrative market and had it to itself for about 18 months, state Meyer and Davis. Once others jumped in, and profitability dropped, Capital One exited the market. But it has since reentered the market, once it became profitable again. Its continual testing has tracked that part of the market.

Capital One's strategy goes with its bottom-up culture, where decisions are made at the bottom based on the

(Case Continued)

market tests. Management controls funds for rolling out new products but not for conducting the testing. In general, management uses its veto power to approve or disapprove funding requests based on test results. Managers spend a significant amount of their time making hiring decisions using the same test-and-learn strategy, which has taught them which behaviors correlate with success in their environment.

The results speak for themselves. Capital One has become the sixth-largest credit card firm in the United States, note Meyer and Davis. It has the lowest net charge-off rate and the highest risk-adjusted margin in the industry, and it grew 45 percent in one year. ∎

Distributed Rather Than Centralized

Following are two views on how organizations of the future could become more distributed.

Distributed Capitalism.   Based on 10 years of research and thinking, Shoshana Zuboff, of Harvard Business School, and her husband, James Maxmin, former CEO and chairman of several companies, contend that the commercial purpose of organizations is changing. Hence, organizational structures will change. Here's a bit of their thinking from *The Support Economy: How Corporations Are Failing Individuals and the Next Episode of Capitalism.*[13]

Firms have believed that they create value by their production of goods and services. That belief has been the foundation of managerial capitalism, which has led to the deep structure of most organizations today. That structure includes the hierarchical and corporate forms of ownership so common today, and the centralized production of goods and services. This form of capitalism has provided a world with material prosperity, giving people affordable products. With this wealth has come a shift in consumers' desires: to individuality, which is apparent in the growing number of products and services aimed at smaller and smaller niches of consumers.

But managerial capitalism will not really satisfy today's consumers, state Zuboff and Maxmin, because there is a huge gap between consumers' desires and the goods and services for sale. That gap is all the hassles consumers encounter and have to battle themselves. What consumers really want is *deep support*; that is, they want someone to help them when they have a problem, not give them a hassle. They want someone who will take responsibility for an entire consumption experience, such as all the things that go with medical treatment that they now must handle on their own—hassles with insurance companies, hospitals, doctors' visits, and so on. They want the "concierge care" of the old family doctor.

Consumers are full of disappointment and rage because the terms and conditions of consumption are set by the producers, note Zuboff and Maxmin. Consumers want to set their own terms and conditions, which is why there is road rage, air rage, hotel rage, and so on. Likewise, on the sellers' side, employees face huge stresses in trying to satisfy seemingly unsatisfiable customers. That is why so many employees have opted out of the standard enterprise environment to start their own business.

The only form of capitalism that can actually provide deep support is *distributed capitalism*, state Zuboff and Maxmin, because it takes a very different view of the world. Primarily, it recognizes that economic value comes not from producers of goods and services, but from a relationship with an individual. Consumers are recipients of premade goods. Individuals have needs to be met. The difference is akin to being treated as a subject versus being treated as a citizen, state the authors.

To tap the value in individuals' needs, commercial processes will need to align with three "quests":

1. The quest for sanctuary (gaining control over time and activities)
2. The quest for voice (such as extreme sports that have no rules, self-published books and music, Internet blogs, and grassroots activism, all of which give individuals a direct voice rather than a voice through an intermediary)
3. The quest for connection with trusted others

Individuals will pay for the support that allows them to live their unique life.

One possible organizational structure for this distributed capitalism is federations, which offer a concierge service to each individual, as defined by that individual. Zuboff and Maxmin call this "the individuation of consumption." People will choose the level of support they want. Some may want self-service (via the Web); others may want the personal touch.

Providing deep support unique to each individual is highly complex, so federations would provide the support by collaborating with others and by coordinating the complexity using IT. IT allows them to create and keep track of highly complex relationships. The players in a federation get paid when the individual releases the money. In fact, individuals may actually own aspects of the means of production. Distributed production and ownership will be major tenets of this emerging distributed capitalism, state Zuboff and Maxmin.

Market-Based Organizations. Tom Malone, founder and director of MIT's Center for Coordination Science, also sees future organizational structures as being distributed in his book *The Future of Work, How the New Order of Business Will Shape Your Organization, Your Management Style, and Your Life.*[14] But he sees markets as being a major organizing tenet—inside and outside of enterprises.

The cost of communications has influenced the structure of organizations. When costs are high, organizations have centralized to keep these costs to a minimum. Now that IT is reducing the costs of communication, dramatically more decentralized ways of organizing work are possible. The benefits of large organizations (economies of scale and knowledge) can be achieved along with the benefits of small organizations (freedom, creativity, motivation, and flexibility). That's new. The new world of work will not have one center; it will have many. Loose hierarchies will have dense communications, lack of central control, and offer freedom to participate.

Organizations will structure themselves to operate more like democracies or markets. Some already do. Markets can be used in surprising ways, notes Malone. Here are just two examples. BP set up an internal market to reduce the greenhouse gases it produced. Business unit managers made their own decisions on buying and selling permits via electronic trading. The result was that BP achieved its 10-year goal in just 1 year. Likewise, H-P discovered that when it created an internal market of "idea futures," where any employee could guess, say, future printer sales, the futures market was more accurate than one produced by "the experts."

But companies need new infrastructures to bring in-house markets into being. For one thing, markets have incentive and trust problems, and they require lots of communication. Employees need new skills, and management needs new attitudes toward risk and control. Internal and external markets need legal frameworks to resolve disputes and regulatory systems to set and enforce the rules.

The job of management will shift from command and control to coordination and cultivation. Managers will define the rules of the game and manage the dependencies between activities. In fact, Malone goes so far as to say that some hierarchies may exist mainly to regulate internal markets—markets that allocate resources, schedule production, determine prices, and coordinate all kinds of work.

As can be seen, a number of these organizing principles seem to be moving in the same direction: toward organizations that are more self-organizing, demand driven, and distributed. This should not be too much of a surprise, because networking is such a major component to today's world—and it enables these new ways of organizing work. The next section explores aspects of a networked world.

UNDERSTANDING A NETWORKED WORLD

The world is becoming a networked world, and a networked world has different characteristics from the non-networked world many people are used to living in. This section presents three viewpoints of what these differences might be and why they are important.

The Internet Mindset

Just as PCs turned the mainframe data processing mindset upside down, the Internet wreaks havoc with businesses that do not understand and embrace the mindset of the global online world. The four components of this mindset are described by Elizabeth Ghaffari.[15]

1. Communication is personal, not mass market.
2. Customer contact is interactive, not broadcast.
3. The customer service time frame is theirs, not yours.
4. The culture is bottom-up, not top-down.

Communication Is Personal, Not Mass Market. The World Wide Web makes a significant break with the past. Its communication is "up close and personal," not top-down mass marketing. Personalized homepages differ substantially from those of major corporations. Many are personal vanity plates, resembling family photo albums where individuals tell their life story. These pages are alive, interesting, entertaining, humorous, personalized, and constantly changing. Their message to traditional marketing departments is, "Your ad copy is boring, dead."

Other Web sites are owned by frustrated writers who publish their own electronic magazines, called *e-zines*, or journals, called *blogs*. Their message to the publishing industry is, "Your editorial filters are too tight. If you won't pay us to publish our work, we will publish it ourselves." The Web demands that customers be viewed outside the traditional publishing frame of reference. Who is the customer of a magazine, really? Is it the reader? Or might it be the writer? What are people willing to pay for?

Some corporate Web sites are stuck in the traditional advertising model, merely duplicating the printed page but in the new graphical, dynamic, and global medium. Large brand name companies have littered the online world with digital equivalents of paper-based coupons. They are using the wrong mindset: mass market rather than personal.

Some companies have gotten the message and given people a way to create MySite personalized pages. Yahoo! was probably the first, allowing people to create a MyYahoo! homepage with whatever information they wanted to see: weather in a certain part of the country, sports, the stock market, and so on. Airlines, rental car companies, stock brokerages, and others now provide such personalized pages.

Customer Contact Is Interactive, Not Broadcast.   The single most important point of view to take toward the Internet is to view it as interactive, not broadcast: incoming, not outgoing. It is a get-the-message, listen-to-the-customer, capture-the-feedback milieu. In essence, the Internet is a customer's window to companies. It is substantially different from television because customers can initiate communications with a firm rather than merely react to their ads. They can express satisfaction or dissatisfaction with products. They can suggest improvements for products or co-design products with the company. Today's consumers are self-sufficient and intelligent. They want to define what custom-made means to them.

An excellent example of online consumer-initiated communications is in the area of medical self-help information. Every major ISP now has forums or conference areas where individuals can peruse medical information, outside the parameters of established medical associations. Even though the medical establishment bemoans "snake oil salesmen," the Internet gives consumers a way to search for the information they want on their own terms. Departments or groups that use the Internet for such interactions will succeed because they tap this huge, latent reservoir of customer needs, current thinking, and goodwill.

Customer-initiated dialog supported by the Internet significantly challenges marketing departments, customer support groups, and fulfillment folks. The 8-week turnaround from postcards in once-a-month magazines, for example, pales in comparison with just-in-time delivery of information via the Web.

The Customer Service Time Frame Is Theirs, Not Yours.   Through the Internet, customers are closer than most companies have ever experienced. In fact, they are closer than most companies can handle. For example, how can a company that serves its customers one at a time and answers its phones, "All our agents are busy . . . ," ever hope to handle tens of thousands of site hits or customer inquiries from online requests for the latest product and pricing data?

Being put on hold will increasingly irk customers. Companies that stay with this level of disservice use the wrong mindset. Today's consumers are busy folks. They have little patience with waiting. In the Internet world, they can do two or more things at once using multiple windows and fast comparison shopping. As with TV remote controls, customers who do not get immediate satisfaction will switch to the competition with a point and a click.

This more intimate customer environment means that companies can hear directly, "I couldn't find your product in three stores today. Where do I get it?" without the protective layers of intermediaries or other buffers. Firms that have the organization in place to listen and respond to these closer voices of customers will hold on to those customers. If not, they could lose them.

Thus, before an IS department can assist other departments in exploiting the Internet world, it needs to assess its proposed Internet business solutions using a new metric: "Will our firm's Internet strategy truly help all our customers communicate with us?"

The Culture Is Bottom-up, Not Top-down. The Internet is not the expert's world, where the few impart their knowledge to the many. In this information-intense world, "netizens" know that "together, we know more than any one of us alone."

This lesson even holds true for government officials who think they know what is best for their constituents. In Spokane, for example, local officials tried to levy a 6 percent tax on Internet providers. Citizens revolted and inundated city leaders with e-mail and phone calls. A Web site was established to gather their thoughts on the proposal.

The message is also clear for IS departments. IS cannot work in the top-down, broadcast mode, "I'm IS and I'm the expert, so here's your solution, customer." More than ever, IS must get input from its customers to determine the services they want, when they want them, and where they want them.

The traditional hierarchical expert model, where IS designed solutions followed by tests, migration, acceptance, and maintenance, no longer works as well. The customers of IS, too, can go elsewhere to find the expertise they need. They can browse the Internet to review lower-cost and lower-maintenance servers, view recommended best-business practices posted online, or download modeling software to compare alternative network costs in their market.

Furthermore, IS departments that are studying the feasibility of putting up an online parts catalog or are talking to marketing about designing online ads are using the outdated broadcast, top-down, mass-market mindset. Departmental customers are one step ahead. They are sending e-mails asking when the latest releases of Java and XML will be available because they want to develop Web Services applications so that suppliers can perform their own searches on the parts inventory.

Rather than merely dump traditional corporate copy onto the Internet, the IS department needs to create channels for its departmental customers to continually communicate with other parts of the firm and its partners. Furthermore, it needs to help its company view customers through a finer, more timely, mesh.

To hear from customers directly, without intermediaries, is both a gold mine and a massive challenge to those with a broadcast mindset. To truly take advantage of this gold mine requires viewing the Internet as an interactive medium and redesigning the corporate listening mechanisms to hear and understand customer feedback.

Where's the Value in a Network?

To know how to leverage the Internet (or any network), it helps to understand where value is created. Mohanbir Sawhney of Northwestern University and Deval Parikh of Pettiglio, Rabu, Toda & McGrath,[16] a consulting firm, offer some thought-provoking insights into how networks change sources of value. They note that when computers (or items containing computers) are not networked, each one needs to provide both front-end and back-end intelligence. Thus, stand-alone PCs have to bundle processing power, storage, and memory (the back end) with the display and interactive capabilities (the front end). This "coupled intelligence," to use Sawhney and Parikh's terminology, leads to compromises in both areas.

Introduce a network and these two forms of intelligence can be decoupled and better optimized. The back-end intelligence (to store and process data), which is best when centralized and made robust, stable, and standardized, can be housed in a core shared infrastructure, where it provides the most value. An example is Yahoo! and all the facilities it provides to online users, such as storage for their photos, e-mail, address books, and so on.

The front-end intelligence (for interacting with the user), which is most useful when it is decentralized, flexible, personalized, and sensitive to context (such as the type of display device), can be dispersed to a myriad of devices that can be small, mobile, customized, and specialized. These forms of front-end intelligence provide the most value. Examples are the handhelds and phones that permit Internet access as well as voice communication.

Value follows intelligence, state Sawhney and Parikh. Thus, in a networked world where everything is connected to everything else, value resides in four places: at the core and periphery, in common infrastructures, in modules, and from orchestration.

There Is Value at the Core and Periphery.   Value moves to the ends, the shared infrastructure and the specialized devices. The middle, the network, becomes an unintelligent conduit, as the Internet is. That is not at all like the voice networks. They presumed dumb telephones, so they had to embed intelligence in the network. As we now see, those old-line telephone companies are having a hard time adapting to the new IP-based world of dumb networks.

With intelligence and value diverging to the ends of networks, say Sawhney and Parikh, so, too, do companies, some to specialize on providing core infrastructure and others to focus on customer relationships (and controlling the user interface). The two require very different capabilities and strategies. Being decoupled, they can be optimized.

Another effect of value moving to the ends is the disappearance of middle management, state Sawhney and Parikh, because value is in the core (leadership and strategy handled by top management) and the periphery (customer-facing employees making decisions and taking actions). Middle managers were the information transporters between these two ends in the past. Digital highways now connect the two directly.

There Is Value in Common Infrastructures.   Elements of any infrastructure—an organization, a system, a business process—that were distributed now are being pulled together and operated as a utility, say Sawhney and Parikh. That is why we see companies centralizing their staff functions (such as HR, finance, accounting, and IT) in shared services groups. Companies are also outsourcing these functions and some business processes (such as order-to-pay, payroll and benefits, and others), believing that there is even more value in common infrastructures among companies. That is also why we see companies rationalizing their IT purchases, down to one or two desktop operating systems, a single network protocol, and a standard set of applications.

Sawhney and Parikh note that Avon is an example of a company that understands the value dynamics of networks (specifically the Internet) and is exploiting them. At first, Avon's Internet strategy was aimed at customers, allowing them to buy the company's cosmetics and other products online. However, this strategy undercut its independent sales representatives who sell friend-to-friend. Avon's second strategy was to give each sales rep a personal portal to submit orders, learn about new products, and even analyze their customers' buying patterns. This strategy gives the representatives a shared infrastructure that they can customize to better perform their customer-facing job. It also gives Avon headquarters valuable customer data that formerly was lost when a sales representative stopped selling Avon products. That data can now be consolidated to see buying patterns and can even be transferred to new sales representatives in open areas. Therefore, this strategy strengthened both the core (corporate) and the periphery (the sales representatives).

There Is Value in Modularity.   Software, devices, organizational capabilities, and business processes are being divided into self-standing modules, say Sawhney and Parikh, so they can be quickly and easily connected to form a value chain to respond to a circumstance. The more broadly a module can be used, the more value it has. This plug-and-play mentality is a chief tenet of Web Services.

There Is Value in Orchestration.   When modules are abundant, there is value in being able to bring them together, state Sawhney and Parikh. Competition will revolve around being the orchestrator in one's value chain, ecosystem, or industry because orchestration is the most valuable business skill in a networked world, they surmise. Value shifts from those who own intelligence to those who orchestrate it. That is why companies such as Cisco, H-P, and others are turning themselves into hubs that coordinate the information and interactions among their suppliers, customers, and channel partners. They garner more value from this coordination role than from performing the actions (such as building computers) themselves. This notion seems to defy our past beliefs of value creation. However, it is a notion that people in a networked world need to understand to tap this new form of network value.

Companies that understand these value dynamics are moving into four new kinds of businesses, say Sawhney and Parikh. The first is *arbitrage*, which means moving intelligence to areas where it is less costly to maintain. An example is providing online help to U.S. employees from Manila via the Internet to take advantage of the lower labor costs in the Philippines. Such offshore outsourcing is growing dramatically. A second new business is *aggregation*, which means combining formerly separate pieces of infrastructure. Sawhney and Parikh point to Loudcloud, which provides companies with an e-business infrastructure on very short notice. The service is a new kind of utility. Like electricity, it is "turned on" when a surge of Web site hits occurs and "turned off" when the hit rate subsides. The third new business is *rewiring*, which involves coordinating processes in a new way. An example is an exchange that links police departments and towing companies so that requests for police towing are handled much faster. The fourth new business is *reassembly*, state Sawhney and Parikh, which involves coordinating disparate pieces of intelligence to form personalized offerings. An example is providing individuals with a personal one-stop Web site for accessing all their personal information—bank balances, stock portfolio, travel reservations, credit card charges, calendar, and such—that is accessible from any type of browser. In fact, such a service could even securely allow different facilities to pass information to one another.

Sawhney and Parikh believe that companies that think about where intelligence resides in their network can extract the value of that intelligence by figuring out where it *should* reside and taking steps to migrate that intelligence to its most valuable locations.

The Rules of Networks

The Internet has turned the world into one giant network. Working in such a network means understanding the rules of networks. One of the best hypothesizers of the rules of networks is Kevin Kelly in his book *New Rules for the New Economy: Ten Radical Strategies for a Connected World*.[8] In it, he states that such a connected world has three distinguishing characteristics:

1. It is global.
2. It favors soft things—intangibles, such as software, information, ideas, and most importantly relationships—over hard things, such as trucks, steel, and cement.
3. It is intensely interlinked.

Kelly believes hard things will increasingly follow the rules of soft things, with the soft creating the context within which the hard operates. Thus, for example, a farmer will still plow a field, but he will have a portable office in his tractor cab linked to a GPS system. The soil will have sensors that talk to his system. He will electronically receive weather data, scientific findings, and pricing information and use all these kinds of information to increase his yields, use fewer resources, and get higher prices for his crops. In short, he will try to replace the hard with the soft.

To understand how to win in such a networked world, one must understand the laws of networks, recommends Kelly. His book lays out 10 such rules; here are 3:

1. Aim for relationship tech.
2. Follow the free.
3. Feed the web first.

Aim for Relationship Tech. Networks embody an amazing phenomenon: Connecting more devices to a network exponentially increases the value of the network for everyone on it because so many new possible connections are created. Thus, a network of 4 people has 12 one-to-one connections. Increasing the network to 5 people leads to 20 connections. Today's world is all about networks, which means it is all about connecting. Whereas the industrial age was about increasing productivity, the network age is about amplifying relationships; that is, increasing the quantity and quality of economic relationships.

With unlimited connections and abundant information, the organization of choice is peer-to-peer rather than hierarchical. New peer-to-peer relationships are forming—between customer and firm, between customer and customer—that question past ways of working. For example, when you pump your own gas, are you a customer or a non-paid employee? Both, answers Kelly. Producers and consumers become one, and when consumers have a hand in co-creating, they are likely to be happier with the result. The amazing aspect is that as a customer and a company create together, on a peer-to-peer basis, they both get smarter together, and they develop a closer relationship. Thus, the cost of switching to working with another company becomes high for a customer because the customer loses the time they have invested to teach the company their interests, and they lose what the company has learned about them. For example, if a florist sends a reminder of your Mom's birthday and says they will again send flowers to the same address and charge the same credit card as last year, how likely are you to call a different florist?

Technology that enhances such relationships is called *relationship tech*, says Kelly. These are the technologies companies should be investing in. One type is recommender systems, such as that used by Amazon.com. When you order a book from Amazon.com, it uses a recommender system to see what books other book buyers (who have bought that same book) have also bought, and then recommends those books to you. The power in this technology is that it can also be used to let people know of others who have similar interests, and thus spur new relationships.

It behooves companies to make their customers smarter, says Kelly, because the enterprise with the smartest customers wins. It is also wise to encourage customers to talk to each other, to even form affinity groups, because that increases loyalty. The greatest expertise about a product does not reside in the company; it resides with its fanatical customers. Companies should encourage these groups and tap their knowledge. Instead, most sue the groups to take down their fan Web sites.

However, having smarter customers requires more trust on both sides—the company trusting customers with information about product defects, for example, and customers trusting companies with information about themselves. At the heart of trust in the network economy is privacy. As a major issue, privacy should not be viewed by companies as an inconvenient obsession of customers that needs to be circumvented, but rather as a way to build a genuine relationship with customers. The concern is that customers do not know what a company knows about them nor how this information is being used, which creates mistrust. Restoring trust means restoring symmetry so that customers know who knows what about them (in detail), how that information was obtained, and who else has been given that information. Kelly believes that the network economy is based on relationships, which means trust must be a basic tenet.

This "shop for relationship tech" rule has obvious implications for CIOs. The main one is to take the point of view that IT is for processing, not communications, which may be quite a switch from the prevalent mindset. Even if CIOs share this network economy belief, they might have to convince their peers of its value.

Follow the Free.   One of the most fascinating aspects of the network economy can be seen today: The best get better and cheaper at the same time. It was not too many years ago when to get something better you had to pay more. Today, if you just wait a few months, you will either get the same quality for a lower price or better quality at today's price. The industrial age brought automation and cheap energy, initiating this phenomenon. Computers have accelerated it. In fact, Kelly notes that a transportation specialist told him that almost nothing in the information industry is moved by ships, everything is flown, so that the price will not drop during shipment. The underlying principle is that price drops with increased volume. The more that is manufactured, the cheaper each unit. Furthermore, quality increases due to the learning curve.

The network economy is founded on this principle of decreasing price for increasing quality. Smart companies anticipate this cheapness and offer products for free. Paradoxically, those that do can make a fortune. It is a tenet of the network economy. Kelly recounts an interesting story to demonstrate his point. It involves Robert Noyce and Jerry Sanders, the founders of Fairchild Semiconductor. In the 1960s, they were selling a transistor to the military that cost $100 to make. They wanted to sell the transistor to RCA for use in UHF tuners to replace the vacuum tubes RCA was using, which only cost them $1.05. Noyce and Sanders believed that learning and volume would decrease their production costs for transistors, so they boldly set their price at $1.05 from the start, even though they had not yet built the factory or the manufacturing processes they would use. They anticipated the cheap and got 90 percent of the UHF market and prospered. Within 2 years, they cut the price to 50 cents and still made a profit. Any item, soft or hard, that can be copied adheres to this inverted pricing principle, says Kelly, so follow the free. Technology creates an opportunity for demand and then fulfills it.

In the network economy, the most valuable goods and services are those that are most abundant because they increase the value of every other one. If they become cheaper as they become more plentiful, then the most valuable items are ubiquitous and free, he reasons. The fastest way to make something ubiquitous is to make it free. This strategy of the network economy is well tested, and it is the anathema of the strategy of the industrial age where scarcity was of the highest value. Netscape gave the browser away free and sold the servers. The strategy worked until Microsoft, with a larger network, did the same and took away market share.

So how do you make money in such a market? Kelly gives three answers. One, aim for free but only achieve cheap. It will have the same effect. Two, give away the core product and sell the service. This strategy has happened with cell phones and satellite dishes. They give the phones and dishes away free and sell the service. Three, structure the business so that you will be profitable when your product is free.

The reverse tenet of following the free is to see what is free today that could have value, and thus a price, tomorrow. One early example on the Web was the early indexes, which were free and became ubiquitous. Their value came from helping people find sites that might interest them via their categories. They drew people's attention, which is the scarce good in the network economy. Thus, they became valuable. Other free items that could have value in the future, surmises Kelly, are bots, remote cameras, catalogs, guides, distillations, and so forth. Thus, offering a good free and sharing with others can lead to ubiquity, which, in turn, can lead to having a valuable item.

The founding norm of the Internet was its gift economy mentality. Lots of information and knowledge were exchanged without money changing hands. In fact, software developers often asked for help by releasing their software as a beta version to be tested and improved by others. The most popular operating system for Internet servers—Apache— was developed this way; it is free. Linux, the freeware operating system, was, too. It makes you wonder whether CIOs could tap this gift economy. Of course, they would need to allow their developers to assist others in exchange. It is an interesting thought.

Feed the Web First.   In the industrial age, loyalty to one's enterprise was important. In the network age, it is more important to be on the right network or network platform. Kelly thus sees loyalty moving from enterprises to platforms. As an example, he asks: "Are you a Mac or a Windows person?" Both are examples of competing platforms. Being on one usually means being out of the other. Thus, Mac users originally could not use the software written for the PC, and vice versa. Similarly, in the network world, choosing the right platform makes an enterprise "in" or "out," so choice becomes important. Once the choice is made, it is important for the company to "feed" that choice to ensure that it grows so that they are on the right network; that is, the one that prospers. People who joined the Mac (closed, proprietary platform) network did not prosper; those who chose the PC (open, nonproprietary) did.

In the network economy, a company's success depends more than in the past on the standards it chooses. For example, many companies have chosen an ERP package. If they chose one selected by many other enterprises, third-party providers saw a larger market for their work, so more of them wrote "bolt-ons" to add new functions. This tendency, in turn, expanded the options for everyone using this ERP platform. Companies choosing a less-favored ERP package ended up having fewer bolt-ons to choose from, fewer peers to learn from, fewer consultants with expertise in the package, and so on.

Kelly contends that the destiny of firms and their "web" (the platforms they choose) are so intertwined that a company's first duty is to "feed the web," because the firm's prosperity is linked to the prosperity of the network. A company cannot prosper unless its network prospers.

Here is an example in the software industry. Software companies, such as Microsoft, pay as much attention to their web as they do to their software. Thus, they hold conferences for developers who use their products to write applications. They provide tools to these developers and co-promote their applications. They provide education to consultants to learn about their software. They give away software to schools to promote their name to future generations. In short, they feed the web (the ecosystem) that surrounds their products. The same is true in the video game industry, the music industry, and the movie industry. All three currently face challenges relating to providing their products over the Internet.

In the network economy, enterprises will shift their focus from maximizing their own value to maximizing the value of their network. Some networks will, of course, be more important than others. For example, choosing to support the laser disk rather than the DVD platform was obviously crucial to movie companies. It is too early to tell how important one wireless Internet access platform will be over another and to whom the choice will have the greatest value.

A corollary is that standards thus become ever more important in the network economy, notes Kelly. The prize is so large that many contend to become "the standard." That contest is now being waged in the wireless world. Which wireless protocol will win? It is still an open question. Companies that plan to offer services wirelessly must therefore decide before a clear winner is apparent. Then, they need to back it, promote it, and do all they can to ensure they have chosen the winner. The standard-making process becomes far more important in the network economy, so companies will devote much more time to it than in the past, says Kelly. In fact, technical standards will become as important as laws, he believes. Webs of relationships will be regulated by the technical standards they are built upon. Eventually, the Internet will encompass everything; everything will be interconnected. Furthermore, commerce will migrate to the Internet. Perhaps not all transactions will occur there, but some parts of all transactions will involve the Internet. Thus, Kelly recommends siding with the Internet: Invest in it, feed it, and promote its use by everyone in your ecosystem, because it will be the winner.

The important lesson for CIOs in this operating principle is that they need to inform their peers in top management of the importance of the IT platforms they choose, not just to run operations, but also to serve customers and enhance their products and services. These choices are not IT decisions; they are business decisions.

Given these potential operating principles for today's e-world, we present a few ideas on how to move forward.

MOVING FORWARD

The discussions in this chapter have been about processes, structures, and technologies; moving forward, though, is about people. It is about the people who lead us into this new business world and the people who are led. We start first with the followers; that is, the people who need to make use of the technologies in this emerging network-based business world. Not all people have the same inclinations to use technology. We end the chapter by talking about what business leaders need to know to be comfortable leading the use of IT and what IT leaders need to know about their business.

Understanding Users

Individuals, work groups, departments, and even business units have different levels of eagerness concerning any new technology. Therefore, if the IS department and other business leaders are truly going to help these groups use a new technology, they need to understand user comfort levels. Elizabeth Ghaffari,[15] an IT consultant in Los Angeles, cites the Yankee Group and Find/SVP, two market research firms, who distinguish levels of comfort with technology by using five "clusters." The Yankee Group uses these clusters to describe the 100 million U.S. households and how they view contemporary technology:

- 500,000 are innovators, constantly sniffing out new technologies.
- 5 million are early adopters of new technologies.
- 30 to 35 million are early majority households.
- 40 to 50 million are late majority households.
- 10 to 15 million are technically averse.

When graphed on a chart, these clusters look a lot like a two-humped camel, notes Ghaffari. It is lying on its stomach with its nose inside a tent, say, the Web Services technology tent. The first cluster is his nose as he nudges the flaps of the tent. The second is his slowly rising neck. The third and fourth are his two big humps; the fifth cluster is his rump. See Figure 14-1.

These five groups represent the spectrum from chomping-at-the-bit innovators (the camel's nose) to those who prefer to leave new technologies well enough alone (his rump). These concepts hold equally well for business users, departments, companies, and industries as well as for U.S. households.

For greatest success, IS departments would do well to benchmark their customers, partners, employees, and others in their business ecosystem against this camel, then introduce the new technology, such as wireless Internet access or Web Services, in a manner that reflects each cluster's willingness and ability to assimilate the new technology. Here are the different possible strategies for assisting each group at its comfort level.

Eager Beavers: The Innovators and Pioneers. The smallest group is the noisiest: the zealots, proselytizers, salespeople, writers, and service providers. Today, for example, they are ecstatic about 3G wireless network services and Web Services. Everything about these two emerging technologies, by definition, is pretty wonderful.

Most of these people are in software and hardware companies, where their enthusiasm and vision can be an asset. Some large IS departments have an advanced technology group charged with tracking new technologies and determining when and how to

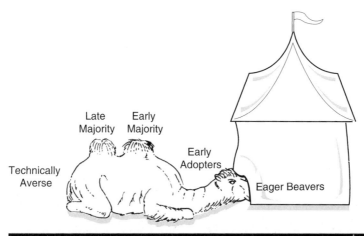

FIGURE 14-1 The Technology Camel

Source: Elizabeth Ghaffari and Barbara McNurlin, "The Technology Camel," unpublished paper, 1998.

begin testing and implementation. In the average corporation, though, eager beavers can be a money drain if they are given the reins to lead the company into new technologies too early.

The recommended approach to eager beavers is to support them with some funding and to learn from them. Perhaps 1 to 3 percent of the IS budget is enough for R&D, provided some business objectives are being supported. Let the market shake out the hype before investing much more in their ideas. However, if being at the bleeding edge of technology is a company's business, these folks need to be supported with more money. In other cases, companies take a big risk following these zealots.

Early Adopters: The First Consumers.   In the early Internet days, companies could barely constrain early adopters of Internet technology. They were the disciples, not too far behind the innovators. They were pushing to get corporate data on the Web. They probably even had their own homepages. They also bought a lot of BetaMaxs, eight-track tapes, and CB radios. Today, those excited about wireless doubtlessly have several generations of handheld devices and cell phone and subscribe to at least two wireless services—a 3G one if they can get it. Those into Web Services have already found ways to create some for their business group. They have a lot of discretionary income and tend to think their corporation does too.

Enterprises can miss a market by ignoring these folks, but they do need to be managed. They need IS's help and encouragement, but they should not be allowed to overwhelm their department or the company. Use them to generate showpieces, a few early successes, but do not let them run the company's mobile Internet presence or Web Services group because they will exceed any budget. In addition, they may not want to listen to the customer feedback their success might generate. Monitor their performance like a hawk. Make sure they invest their own money in their experiments.

Early Majority: The First Big Wave.   The first of the two big consumption waves includes the folks, departments, and companies that say they are willing to use new technologies but that they need some help. They are not the self-sufficient pioneers nor the risk takers. They have just bought a Web access handheld or will do so in the near future. They use instant messaging. They are willing to consider doing a Web Services pilot. They may be confused by the terminology and the proliferation of products and services. It may look like chaos to them, so they ask, "Is it worth my time, money, and support costs to go this route?"

These early majority folks tend to be in relatively important positions in the organization, so they can make or break the introduction of a new technology, even more so than top management. The real business impact of a new technology depends on what these early majority folks do with that technology. IS management needs to understand how these users view the company, customers, and competition, and then help them choose a strategy to expand their familiarity with, say, wireless Internet or Web Services offerings at a self-paced rate that can be incorporated into the way their group does business. If a Web Services offering does not help them compete better, it is not worth IS's time or money.

Thus, IS management must become adept at creating options that can be tested for acceptance or rejection. At the same time, IS needs to provide some education and explanations to these folks on the options. What Web Services do their customers want from the company? What kinds of wireless access might customers want? Is instant messaging important? Investments with this group are well placed. Before approaching these folks, IS needs to understand the non-technical products and services that consume these folks' time and attention. Learn about their business.

Late Majority: The Technology Skeptics. Late majority people, departments, and companies are not afraid of a technology, but they do have serious concerns about risks and costs. They are concerned about wasting time and money searching for information on the technologies and the kinds of investments needed to make solid, informed decisions about what it will do for them. Technology skeptics also ask questions about whether the company's customers and suppliers really will benefit from the technology or whether early users are just a bunch of looky-loos out for a free ride.

Late majority companies do not have Web Services on their radar screen. The technology is too new for them to see any benefit from jumping in until it is tested. They are likely to still be deciding whether to implement an ERP system. Even though their employees may not be able to live without cell phones, the company is not thinking about how consumers might want to access their Web site via a phone or handheld. For this group, 3G wireless is not really here, and until it is and proving itself, the late majority will not show an interest.

For these late majority folks, IS management needs to be as prepared to address risks and costs as they are to address technology opportunities. IS needs to show an appreciation of bottom-line concerns and answer security questions at the level that late majority people can appreciate. It is not necessary for corporations to allow their online presence to be accessed wirelessly via the Web. IS can point to examples, such as Lands' End and Eddie Bauer, where online information is an adjunct to traditional information delivery methods. Or they can cite Home Depot, which only shows the items stocked in the consumer's chosen nearby store. Web sites can be a sales sampling resource, isolated and independent of the private, internal corporate network. Or it can be a complementary source of advertising or education, providing a richer customer experience for customers, without sacrificing the reputation and the relationship nearby brick-and-mortar stores already have with customers.

Technically Averse: "Not on My Time You Don't."   The people, departments, and companies who resist technology are not currently considering doing anything about wireless access to their Web sites or implementing Web Services. In many cases, their concerns about loss of privacy, security, control, and possible exposure to competition override any perceivable benefits of these technologies.

Two industries that have traditionally been technology averse are real estate and publishing. Real estate has a sunk cost and protected monopoly position over multiple listing books. Publishing has a sunk cost and a protected monopoly position over media and advertising. It is rare, but the breakthrough cases in these two industries generally come from companies capturing niches by going outside the system. In real estate, for instance, a few have set up Web pages that permit wireless access by realtors as they are driving potential home buyers around looking at homes. Although traditional publishing media have begun to offer digitized content that can be downloaded from the Web, they are not thinking about wireless access from handhelds. In general, they do not know how to take advantage of it.

To guide the technically averse, IS first needs to understand their concerns. They have justifiable business fears that need to be identified and addressed before any thought of using a new technology for business purposes can be entertained. The challenge here is education, not applications. These people need the greatest amount of time to assimilate the changes taking place in their lives. Only then can IS help them explore potentials.

The message, then, is for the IS department and other leaders to recognize and acknowledge each cluster's concerns about new technology and then develop a multitiered approach to respond to those diverse concerns.

Increasing Executives' Understanding of IT

Finally, we end this chapter, and this book, as we began it, on the subject of leadership. As we have noted, business value comes from the use of IT, not from the technology itself, and IT use can only be guided by the users in the business. It follows that leadership of IT is no longer a technical challenge; it is a challenge for all business managers. An important action CIOs can take to move their enterprise forward in the e-world is to ensure that the business managers in their enterprise are staying abreast of the changes and new uses of IT; in short, that they understand and are comfortable with IT and its impact and potential value to the business.

Chuck Gibson,[17] a long-time top-level consultant and now a senior lecturer at the MIT Sloan School, points out some current reasons why business managers, particularly senior executives, need to understand IT as it is today. For one, although the ranks of IT-literate and IT-savvy senior executives are growing, most still do not have the depth of background in IT that they have in functions such as marketing, finance, HR, or manufacturing. As a result, they may not understand the issues that drive effective use of IT, such as the need to invest in infrastructure ahead of the need.

In addition, most executives are well aware of IT because computers have become so woven into the fabric of business. Therefore, they understand IT's operational importance. However, seeing IT used day in and day out may lull them into seeing IT *only* as an operational resource. They might not think of IT as a competitive resource, one that can be used innovatively on new business initiatives. Likewise, if the IS organization is only seen as keeping the back office running, business executives may not see the CIO as a potential peer and resource for new business initiatives.

The dot-com boom and bust have also had a damaging effect on collective opinions about IT, says Gibson, because many executives and venture capitalists believe the money they spent creating Web sites and funding new e-businesses was wasted. New channels to the customer did not pay off. As a result, many now de-emphasize the importance of e-commerce at the very time when early promise is being realized in many industries and sectors. "We are learning from the executives who come to our *IT for the Non-IT Executive* classes that there is an e-commerce boom taking place right now, even though the hype is gone. Companies are doing lots of work to streamline their operations by e-enabling them. In class, participants ask lots of questions about e-commerce. They clearly are beginning to integrate into their thinking its importance as an ongoing, viable part of doing business," says Gibson.

Behind this delayed realization lies an important lesson, itself worthy of executive learning: Although venture capitalists and many entrepreneurs jumped on the Web and its appendage businesses as soon as they became available, most of the rest of us did not, says Gibson. People undergo a gradual learning curve whether they are consumers or employees. Organizational and behavioral change takes time because acquiring new habits takes time. Only at a certain point in the curve does the network effect kick in: The more people who use a technology, the more necessary it becomes for others to use it due to the pressure they receive from the users and their need to be connected for their own benefit. Today, executives endanger their career when they ignore the growing, persistent, but somewhat underground e-commerce movement. During poor economic times, successful companies position themselves to thrive when the good times return. The time for executive learning on this manifestation of IT is now, or even yesterday.

For these reasons, CIOs need to be concerned with the potential gap between what their fellow business executives believe is important about IT versus what they really need to know to effectively guide the use of IT, believes Gibson. Executive learning on new ways of doing business using IT and new ways of solving old problems are thus more important than ever in both companies and nonprofit agencies. The technology continues to evolve, and the new information economy is emerging, albeit slower than we thought.

Executives' Leadership Roles.   Senior executives need to learn to carry out the following executive roles with respect to guiding the use of IT, notes Gibson.

Set the tone of the enterprise toward technology.   One of the most important jobs of executives is to set the tone of the organization toward IT and the IS organization, mainly through their actions. The importance of IT and information must be modeled by executives through their personal use of technology, their e-world knowledge, and their decisions. They may need education in performing this role well.

Envision how IT can serve business strategy.   Management must foresee how key business strategies can be enabled by IT. Business executives need to learn how to sense technology trends and discuss alternative scenarios of technological opportunities for their business. The goal is to achieve IT-business strategic thinking among all executives. However, some executives still believe that the IS function is a machine room, the CIO is a technician, and the IS function can stay a step behind business planning. Where these attitudes persist, organizations encounter problems aligning IS projects with business objectives. Understanding the role of the CIO and how to effectively integrate business and IT planning is part of the remedy.

Govern as well as lead.   Top executives look at the huge investment in IT resources and systems and the complex array of pervasiveness of IT and often wonder how they should get involved in managing it all. Should the CEO head the IT investment committee or delegate that role? Should divisions set their own IT strategy or should it be centralized? These kinds of questions require executives to understand IT governance as well as IT management decisions. As new research[18a,b] suggests, vital roles for top executives and board of directors are setting the right governance structure for IT as well as making particular situations part of IT decision making and planning.

Use IT to promote business change.   The emergence of e-business has exacerbated this leadership need. For one, change is occurring faster. Executives need to understand that implementation of a powerful package, such as ERP or creation of a transactional Web site, cannot bring about major business change on its own. But it can be a powerful catalyst and tool for top management to foster business change.

The IS department cannot be the driver of organizational change. Both top and line management must be the drivers. Line executives, in particular, are the real implementers of business change. This issue goes back many years, says Gibson, yet it is still with us. Time after time it has been shown that when line management does not lead a change, it does not stick. They need to learn how to implement IT-enabled change.

Assess costs and benefits.   This subject continues to be relevant because continuing tension characterizes the relationship between strategic objectives and the need to invest in IT infrastructure before people realize they need it. IS organizations must be ahead of requests for applications and have data available for unanticipated user needs. Business executives need to learn to use appropriate cost-benefit criteria to assess IT projects and understand the need to invest in IT infrastructure, even though it may have no easily measurable, near-term quantitative returns.

Current, Longstanding, and Upcoming IT Issues.   Based on his experience in MIT's *IT for the Non-IT Executive* program over the past 3 years, Gibson points out two new, three longstanding, and two upcoming IT issues that have arisen in class.

The impact of new regulations.   This is a current issue with a potentially huge impact, speculates Gibson. For example, U.S. government agencies are being required to become paperless. The U.S. pharmaceutical industry faces deadlines for creating a paperless trail of test results and patient experiences with new drugs because the U.S. Food and Drug Administration is exercising its statutory mandate to be able to track experiments and batches of medicines the minute a serious adverse reaction is uncovered. Privacy legislation is also likely to affect companies and might even fly in the face of the database consolidations so many companies are undertaking. To properly invest in IT, top and line management need to understand the regulations and their ramifications for their business.

Project management.   This is another topic of current interest. Business executives in the class want to know how to identify, initiate, and get involved in IT projects, says Gibson. They want to understand what the IS organization is doing and particularly how they can manage their part of projects—the implementation that requires business changes. A trade-off needs to be made, though. Involving businesspeople in systems projects elongates the projects, and the two parties need to work out a common language for talking about systems, architecture, change management, and infrastructure. The benefit, of course, is that successful implementation is much more likely when business people are involved from the outset.

Measuring the value of IT.   This is a longstanding topic of interest. Executives want to use familiar metrics such as ROI to justify projects. However, some business executives need education in this area. They become so focused on garnering value for cost that they do not realize they should be using a portfolio approach, recognizing that some kinds of IT investments require different kinds of metrics.

Basically, not all IT investments have comparable returns. Whereas some can be justified on savings (displacing labor), others can only be justified based on judgment (such as an executive dashboard). Still others can only be justified on indirect and future, hard-to-foresee returns (such as infrastructure). In the MIT course, participants are given a four-part framework for categorizing projects: strategic (experimental), information-giving, core processing, and infrastructure, based on the work of Weill and Broadbent.[19]

Change management.   This is a second longstanding issue because a number of companies really did not manage the business change required of ERP correctly. They do not want to undergo a similar disaster in implementing CRM. So at the MIT class, they want to know how to manage IT-induced change properly.

Organization and control of the IS organization.   This is a third longstanding issue. Currently, executives are grappling with balancing local needs with the need for standardization across the company. The other organizational issue over the past few years has been how to organize for e-commerce. Recent research on organizing for e-business by George Westerman,[18c] a research scientist at MIT, has shown that companies that wove in e-business organizationally have had greater long-term success that those that established and stuck to a separate e-business entity.

Cross-organizational e-processes.   This is an area of forthcoming importance. These processes, such as those that underlie e-business and supply chain management, are an area where we are on the verge of breaking through, speculates Gibson. The curve is now taking off. Some leading-edge companies are now truly taking advantage of their consolidation of customer information (given privacy restrictions) to provide the same look and feel to their customers through their numerous channels.

Obtaining services via the Web.   This is another forthcoming important area. In fact, it will be a real revolution, speculates Gibson. That is why executives need to understand such things as Web Services, application service providers, Web outsourcing, and such.

Means for Executive Learning.   There are numerous ways business executives can learn how to guide the use of IT. Here are three main ones, notes Gibson.

Learn by doing.   One of the cases presented in MIT's *IT for the Non-IT Executive* program is the case of Dow Corning. It illustrates learning by doing. When Dow Corning implemented ERP in 1995, the CIO was replaced with an experienced vice president who had spent his entire career in the company and was a well-respected business executive. He was given responsibility for IT and for the ERP project. He learned a lot about IT quickly; so did Dow Corning's executive team. They implemented SAP across the company in a few years' time and did so very successfully, even though it was hard on the people.

Another model is the example of Charlie Feld when he was head of IT at Frito-Lay in the 1980s, notes Gibson. Feld had a vision about the long-term potential of handheld devices for the Frito-Lay sales force. He sensed that information on store inventory and replenishment trends could lead to a new kind of executive management. Yet he knew useful systems would require years of infrastructure and, most critically, management acceptance through learning. He also knew he had to move forward in cost-justifiable pieces. So he initiated a pilot with a receptive friend, a manager in a district sales office. The pilot worked; the payoff was salespeople's time savings and data entry cost reduction at central headquarters. The innovation paid its way as it went, sales force and sales management found value, and eventually top executives came to use a new executive information system in a way that gave Frito-Lay a competitive edge in its markets.

Learn by governing.   An important learning forum for top business executives is steering committees and teams that include the CIO. Gibson notes that a CIO at Vanguard made his way to the executive suite in this way. Vanguard has huge investments in technology, and the Vanguard executive committee discussed major investment and technology issues as a regular part of its business. Being part of governance teams leads to executive learning.

Learn via educational programs.   Despite the pressures of business today, executives are currently making time for formal training programs in IT. For example, CEOs, COOs, heads of divisions, and other levels of managers are attending MIT's and other universities' executive education programs. "They come, in part, to get away from the pressures of their job and to engage in serious discussion. It's like a 2-day sabbatical to them. And because enrollment is open, they get to hear what's happening in other organizations—both profit and nonprofit," says Gibson.

Here is a brief description of MIT's 2-day program.

CASE EXAMPLE

MIT'S *IT FOR THE NON-IT EXECUTIVE* PROGRAM

The Sloan School at the Massachusetts Institute of Technology began its 2-day *IT for the Non-IT Executive* program in 1998 and has offered it three times a year since then. After the first few times, it has steadily attracted 60 to 100 executives.

(Case Continued)

The Attendees

In a recent session of 75 executives, 40 came from just 10 organizations and 20 came from organizations that had formerly sent participants to the program. There appears to be growing interest in creating a critical mass of people in many organizations who have this IT knowledge and can share vocabulary, frameworks, and approaches, notes Gibson.

In the last three programs, some 50 percent of the executives have come from the nonprofit sector, often because the U.S. government is tightening up on federal agencies to implement the privacy and paperless-government regulations that have been passed.

Interestingly, the executives often comment to the effect, "Our IS people should be here because I now have a way of looking at IT investments, architecture, and problems, and I want them to take that same view." However, MIT only wants executives who are in the same boat, so the program is closed to IS executives.

The Program

The program is not about technology. Rather, it presents frameworks and a vocabulary to help non-IT managers and executives understand, in business terms, what is going on with the technology. One framework,[18d] for example, is a pyramid for viewing IT systems in relation to the business. On the bottom of the pyramid is business strategy; at the top is business processes. In between are three IT components: IT architecture, infrastructure, and systems. This framework explains why IT is so important to being able to build business processes that support a business strategy.

A second framework is the portfolio framework mentioned earlier for categorizing IT projects. A third framework[18e] describes four recent stages of architecture: (1) decentralized to support functional needs, (2) integrated across businesses in an enterprise, (3) a wired company with the capability of exchanging data across divisions, and (4) modules, which is an architecture where enterprises can plug-and-play modules using Web Services offerings. A fourth framework provides an assessment of change management risks and approaches to manage the introduction of new systems in the organization.

The program is 80 percent lecture, 20 percent discussion. To encourage discussion, the attendees sit at round tables of 10. The topics are based on MIT research and are illustrated with articles and cases from a variety of sources.

In all, *IT for the Non-IT Executive* seems to be successful in spite of difficult economic times and thin ranks of managers, which indicates the continuing importance of IT in the eyes of business managers and the continuing value of certain relevant formal education programs. As one executive commented, "Great way to step back from the day-to-day and look at the role of IT from a business perspective," says Gibson. At the same time, the fact that many organizations are sending multiples of people, and in waves, suggests that formal learning in the classroom also needs reinforcement among groups of executives in their own culture and settings. Other forums of learning are at least as important as the classroom. ∎

Educating IS About the Business

"When it comes to educating users about IT, my philosophy is that we in IS should be educating ourselves about the business environment," says Nancy Markle, president of the Society for Information Management (SIM)—the professional society for CIOs and other senior IT leaders—and formerly CIO of Fannie Mae, Georgia Power, Home Savings of America, and Arthur Andersen, Americas. According to Markle, "IT is accepted when we use the language of the business and talk to users as business partners about what IT does. I've used several approaches to get my staff to understand the business."

Train in the Business.   Markle has long recognized the importance of training:

When I was CIO, I required my staff to take their 40 hours of training every year. In fact, one of the performance measures of my supervisors was whether or not all their subordinates had fulfilled their training requirement. Most of the developers, of course, wanted to take a Microsoft class, but we also offered them the option of spending a day or a week in a user department. Those times turned out to be the most important training they got.

I saw my staff make really meaningful contributions to the business when they got involved. The business saw them as assets because they think process: effectiveness and efficiency. In less than one week, I've seen IS staff members make important suggestions on how the business could be more efficient— right now, not sometime in the future. When they were not arrogant, the business loved their ideas. Sometimes the change involved a new technology, sometimes not. The key was that it was presented from a business standpoint.

Move into the Business.   Markle also encouraged some of her direct reports to move into the business:

There were always openings, and I found the business managers thrilled to get someone from within the company. They especially liked IS staff because they have an unusually broad view of the business from working on so many different projects. They also understand how departments interface with one another, and they are smart.

My main warning to my staff who moved to a business position was, "You probably think you know, but you don't. So don't be arrogant. Use this as an opportunity to grow. It's important for your career. Then, if you want to come back, I will welcome you back."

Generally, they went into operations. They rarely chose marketing or sales, unless it was marketing analysis. And generally they became involved in major projects that materially improved processes because the last thing an IS person wants to do is work that can be performed by a computer.

From my point of view, as CIO, having them in the business was a tremendous asset because they knew both IT and the business. We did not need a middleman to work with them. Even when they did not come back into IS, they were a huge asset to both the business and IS because of their expanded experience and process thinking.

However, a CIO should not encourage such moves if IS is not mature enough because the movers could end up criticizing IS and creating further friction. CIOs also should only move people they want to keep. Don't move someone you want to fire. Just fire them.

Lead with the Business.

Sometimes, learning the business involves getting the business to take the lead on an IT project, especially one that requires major business changes. Here is an example. When I was at Home Savings, a number of banks were introducing online banking. I talked to the president about what we should do. He said, "Our customers are 65 years old. Most won't be interested."

But I believed we needed to keep up with our competitors technologically, to attract younger customers. I thought online banking could do that. And we could introduce it differently, so as not to scare our older customers. We did not have to make a big splash and talk about how technology-enabled we had become. We could introduce it quietly, carefully, and cost effectively. The effort might end up only educating our people, but we needed to test it out.

When the president agreed, I told him it needed to be led by a businessperson, not me, because it had to be from a retail banking point of view, not an IT point of view. I was teamed with a woman who really understood retail banking. She took the customer side of the project, establishing the all-important new help desk, the in-depth training, even a new pay structure for the help desk staff. I was responsible for making the technology work; my business partner for introducing it and supporting it for the retail staff and customers. We put kiosks in the branches that had the younger clientele, and we gave the staff easy self-learning instruction so they could help the customers.

Our project grew slowly, but it became hugely successful. After the fact, our marketing people found out that many of our online customers were our most profitable customers—the 20 percent of our customers who generate the most profit. Had we not offered online banking, we would probably have lost them to our competitors who did.

The point of this story is that although we in IS came up with the idea, I did not present it in technology terms. I presented it in business terms. I talked about the need to attract younger customers, which was important to our business executives. And I insisted that it be a business initiative and be led by a business person.

Attend Business Programs.   "Our research has shown that CIOs in small-cap and mid-cap enterprises, especially, need more education in 'business-speak,'" says Markle. Thus, SIM, of which Markle is president, has introduced a Strategic Business Leaders Program to provide a forum for senior IT executives to interact with business leaders, to explore current issues from a business perspective, and to develop the vocabulary and concepts to expand their role from technical leader to business leader.

"When I was a CIO, I needed peers to talk to. That's why I joined SIM; its members are IT leaders. This new program is also built around communications, but with the twist of helping members communicate with business peers using business language.

Once IS people think in business terms, they are received by the business more positively," notes Markle.

Markle states that "Making the switch from technology-speak to business-speak can be difficult because technical people are most comfortable talking about technology. But that's not what businesspeople want to hear. As an analogy, most people who drive a car really do not want to hear about such technical details as engine torque or drive trains. IT is the same. Businesspeople want to know what a system can do for them, but not the technology details. When you make it simple and relevant, they listen; otherwise, their eyes glaze over."

As an example of a business-speak program for CIOs, following is a synopsis of SIM's first Strategic Business Leaders Program.

CASE EXAMPLE

SIM'S STRATEGIC BUSINESS LEADERS PROGRAM

SIM's 2-day program, presented by the Society for Information Management, gives senior IS leaders a place to interact with business leaders. The topic for the first program was "Navigating Uncharted Waters: The Global Economy and Business Strategy."

The five-session program is based around intense interaction and is co-facilitated by an IT specialist and a business leader.[20] It features 7 business and technology leaders and is limited to 25 attendees.

The five sessions progress from a general overview of current economic and global issues to specific actions that participants can take back to their organization.

Session 1: Informal Getting-to-Know-You Activities

Through a series of informal activities the evening before, the group (speakers and participants) gets acquainted with each other, discusses the forthcoming program, and suggests areas of particular interest to them.

Session 2: Establishing the Framework

The goal of this session is to provide participants with an overview of current economic issues and their implications for business. Bernard Baumohl presents a model of the economy to demystify its workings, along with key economic concepts, the vocabulary of economics, and an overview of current economic issues. He identifies critical issues for business and discusses directions the economy might take over the next year. Mr. Baumohl has been *Time* magazine's senior economics reporter for 15 years. He has covered the domestic and international economy from *Time*'s New York and Washington bureaus (as a

(Case Continued)

member of the White House press corps), and he has demonstrated a knack for being far ahead of the curve in assessing the direction of the U.S. and world economies.

Session 3: The Business Perspective

The goal of this session is to give participants some perspective on how business (and policy) executives view economic issues. Three frontline executives describe how they deal with global economic issues every day: Dr. William Fraser, Senior Director of Global Alliances for Dow Chemical, is responsible for identifying and executing large-scale alliances between Dow and partners. Edward B. Meyercord, III, is President, CEO and Director of Talk America, one of the nation's fastest-growing telephone companies. Dr. Herbert Taylor is Vice President and Corporate Secretary of the Federal Reserve Bank of Philadelphia. The Federal Reserve System, which serves as the nation's central bank, has the basic mission to create the financial conditions that foster economic growth: stable prices, sound banking practices, and a reliable payments system.

Session 4: Integration with the Technology Perspective

The goal of this session is to help participants understand how business-oriented technology executives integrate business thinking into their technology strategy. Three executives with IT and business backgrounds describe how they meld the two perspectives: Charles Anderson, Director of IT Planning at Air Products

and Chemicals, was formerly a lobbyist and an expert in organizational change. Bruce Brodie, most recently Senior Vice President of IT and Operations at start-up Arch Insurance, has been in the insurance business for 20 years handling mergers and acquisitions and has been CFO, CIO, and CAO. William Ledman, Senior Vice President of Information Systems at Freddie Mac, was formerly a lead systems executive at GEICO.

Session 5: Practical Take-Aways

The goal of the final session is to review the key ideas presented in the previous sessions and help the participants determine what practical steps they can take back to their organization.

IT and business views of the world can differ significantly, and although IT and businesspeople may not need to be fully comfortable in each other's world, they do need a common language and a working knowledge of each other's domain. The Strategic Business Leaders program offers one approach to giving IS executives a business foundation. The first Strategic Business Leaders program was attended by about 25 IS executives. Based on their feedback, they see educating IS on business principles as being important. Participants were most pleased by the practical focus of the sessions; they want future sessions to emphasize best practices. They found it particularly helpful to hear how the business-oriented technology leaders bridged the gap between the business and IS. ∎

CONCLUSION

What stands out in the discussions of organizing principles and the networked world at the beginning of this chapter is the repeated emphasis on naturally forming relationships. The talk actually centers around people-to-people contact rather than technology; technology is the underpinning. The principles talk about natural phenomena rather than human-made structures. They dwell on how to develop relationships that help people work effectively.

We are, indeed, in a business revolution. With it, the use of IT is changing in kind. It has shifted from amplifying thinking and processing to amplifying communicating and connecting. It is now much more about relationships than transactions (which happen in the background and are, indeed, becoming increasingly sophisticated). Now that this shift has been made, IT becomes about business and needs to be the responsibility of the business folks, not the technology folks.

IT professionals have always been enamored with the technical aspects of computer systems; the human side has been of less interest. However, it is people who make or break a system through their use or disuse of it. So even though the Internet-based economy relies heavily on IT, relationships and such mechanisms as CoPs play a major role. IT now allows such relationships to transcend time and space, and with the appearance of instant messaging, people can stay in on-demand contact. With cost-justifiable long-distance video, people will be able to communicate in richer ways across greater distances. In so doing, the foundations of past ways of working change. That is the exciting exploration that is going on right now as people grapple with creating the new work environment and the challenges it presents.

QUESTIONS AND EXERCISES

Review Questions

1. According to Hammer, how does a process-centered organization differ from a task-centered one?
2. According to Brown and Solomon Gray, why are communities the building blocks of knowledge-based companies?
3. What has National Semiconductor done to encourage CoPs?
4. According to Gage, how does he really know about the hot work being performed at Sun?
5. According to Kelly, what were the three rules given to the computer-generated bats in *Batman Returns*? What was the effect of these rules?
6. List some of the ways that Semco operates differently from most companies.
7. What is Capital One's core competency? Describe how it is used.
8. What do individuals really want, according to Zuboff and Maxmin? What are their three quests?
9. Give two examples of how a market has been used internally within a company, according to Malone.
10. What are the four mindsets of the Internet?
11. Explain the four places where Sawhney and Parikh find value in a network.

12. What are the three distinguishing characteristics of the e-economy, according to Kelly?
13. Why should companies invest in making their customers smart, according to Kelly?
14. Briefly describe the five groups in the technology camel.
15. List the roles executives need to play in managing the use of IT.
16. Briefly explain the four ways Markle educated her IS staff about the business.

Discussion Questions

1. Giving employees and small work groups the authority to make most of their own decisions seems to be of obvious benefit to companies. Why do you think this type of on-the-job self-management is not more prevalent? What are its drawbacks?
2. Kelly, Wheatley, and Kellner-Rogers talk about self-organizing systems. These ideas will not work in organizations because enterprises need defined structure, defined jobs, and limits. Do you agree or disagree? Describe your reasoning.
3. Executives over age 50 really do not "get it." They just do not understand nor appreciate the Internet. They have the wrong mindset, and they cannot be educated to have the right mindset. Companies need younger executives to provide the Internet-savvy leadership to thrive in the e-world. Present arguments for and against these ideas.

Exercises

1. Read several articles or scan several books on how IT is changing organizations and work. What management issues do these articles/books present with respect to work redesign? What potential roadblocks do they discuss?
2. Visit a local company and talk to an IS executive about how the company combines use of the Web with physical locations and the effect this combination has had on their organization's work environment. Ask for one or two examples of new ways of working. Ask the CIO's opinions on self-organizing work groups.
3. Describe the work environment you would like to work in. Present it to the class. Describe how you might reach your goal.

REFERENCES

1. Senge, Peter, *The Fifth Discipline: The Art and Practice of the Learning Organization*, Doubleday, New York, 1990.

2. Hammer, Michael, *Beyond Reengineering: How the Process-Centered Organization Is Changing Our Work and Our Lives*, HarperCollins Publishers, New York, 1996.

3. Sachs, Patricia, "Transforming Work: Collaboration, Learning, and Design," *Communications of the ACM*, September 1995, pp. 36–44.

4. Woolfe, Roger, *The Business of Innovation*, Wentworth Research Program (now part of Gartner EXP, Stamford, CT), May 1996.

5. Brown, John Seely, and Estee Solomon Gray, "The People Are the Company," *Fast Company*, November 1995. Available at www.fastcompany.com/magazine/01/people.html; Accessed October 2004.

6. Rapaport, Richard, "The Network Is the Company: An Interview with John Gage,"

Fast Company, April/May 1996. Available at www.fastcompany.com/online/02/gage.html; Accessed October 2004.

7. Wheatley, Margaret, *Leadership and the New Science: Learning About Organizations from an Orderly Universe*, Berrett-Koehler Publishers, San Francisco, 1994.

8. Kelly, Kevin, *Out of Control: The New Biology of Machines, Social Systems, and the Economic World*, Addison-Wesley Publishing, Reading, MA, 1994; *New Rules for the New Economy: Ten Radical Strategies for a Connected World*, Viking, New York, 1998.

9. Wheatley, Margaret, and Myron Kellner-Rogers, *A Simpler Way*, Berrett-Koehler Publishers, San Francisco, 1996.

10. Byrne, John, "The 21st Century Corporation: Management by Web," *Business Week*, August 28, 2000, pp. 84–96.

11. Semler, Ricardo, *Maverick: The Success Story Behind the World's Most Unusual Workplace*, Warner Books, New York, 1993. *The Seven-Day Weekend: A Better Way to Work in the 21st Century*, Random House Group Ltd., London, 2003; *The Seven-Day Weekend: Changing the Way Work Works*, Portfolio, New York, 2004.

12. Meyer, Christopher, and Stan Davis, *It's Alive: The Coming Convergence of Information, Biology, and Business*, Crown Business, New York, 2003.

13. Zuboff, Shoshana, and James Maxmin, *The Support Economy: How Corporations Are Failing Individuals and the Next Episode of Capitalism*, Viking Penguin, New York, 2002.

14. Malone, Thomas, *The Future of Work, How the New Order of Business Will Shape Your Organization, Your Management Style, and Your Life*, Harvard Business School Press, Boston, MA, 2004.

15. Ghaffari, Elizabeth, and Barbara McNurlin, "The Internet Mindset," unpublished paper 1998. Ghaffari can be reached at techplace@earthlink.net.

16. Sawhney, Mohanbir, and Deval Parikh, "Where Value Lives in a Networked World," *Harvard Business Review*, January 2001, pp. 79–86.

17. Communication with Chuck Gibson of Gibson and Associates, Concord, MA.

18. MIT's Center for Information Systems Research (CISR); Cambridge, MA, 3 Cambridge Center, 02139 web.mit.edu/cisr/www:
    a. Weill, Peter, Mani Subramani, and Marianne Broadbent, "A Senior Management Briefing on IT Infrastructure," CISR Research Briefing, Vol. 2, No. 1C, February 2002.
    b. Weill, Peter, and Richard Woodham, "Don't Just Lead, Govern: Implementing Effective IT Governance," CISR Working Paper No. 326, April 2002.
    c. Westerman, George, "Mixing Bricks and Clicks: Organization Designs for B2C E-Commerce in Incumbent Retailers," CISR Working Paper No. 332, October 2002.
    d. Rockart, John, and Jeanne Ross, "Reconceptualizing IT," CISR Working Paper No. 302, January 1999.
    e. Ross, Jeanne, and Peter Weill, "Stages of IT Architecture: Pursuing Alignment and Agility," CISR Research Briefing, Vol. 2, No. 2A, July 2002.

19. Weill, Peter, and Marianne Broadbent, *Leveraging the New Infrastructure: How Market Leaders Capitalize on Information Technology*, Harvard Business School Press, Boston, 1998.

20. SIM's first Strategic Business Leaders Program was designed and co-facilitated by Charlie Kreitzberg (the IT expert) and his wife Anne Pauker Kreitzberg (a former senior business executive and currently president of their company, Cognetics).

Glossary

3G Teams Teams of three generations (25+, 35+, 45+) that work together.

Action Labs An approach to planning where frontline employees identify and interactively refine local-level strategies by having to get them funded at action lab meetings with top management.

Advanced Technology Group A group within the IS department that is responsible for spotting and evaluating new technologies, often by conducting a pilot project.

Agent An electronic entity that performs tasks, either on its own or at the request of a person or a computer.

Aggregation Combining formerly separate pieces of infrastructure, providing companies with an e-business infrastructure on very short notice.

Analog Technology Signals sent as sine waves rather than ones and zeros (as in digital technology).

Applets Small single-function applications, often written in Java, that are pulled from the Internet when needed.

Application Program Interface (API) An interface created for a software product that, like a standard, allows programmers to write to, link to, and utilize that software's interface in their applications.

Application Service Provider (ASP) A company that rents out software over the Internet.

Architecture A blueprint that shows how a system, house, vehicle, or product will look and how the parts interrelate.

Artificial Intelligence (AI) A group of technologies that attempts to mimic our senses and emulate certain aspects of human behavior, such as reasoning and communicating.

Authentication Assuring that the digital signature of the user is valid.

Authorization Assuring that the correct user is accessing a network, application, or stored files or documents.

Backbone Systems Mainline corporate transaction processing systems.

Back-end Systems Computer systems that handle an enterprise's operational processing, as opposed to front-end systems that interact with users.

Back-end Tools Tools, such as code generators, in computer-aided software engineering suites that automatically generate source code.

Best-of-Breed Outsourcing Outsourcing specific functions, each to the most appropriate provider, rather than outsourcing all functions to one provider who may not be the best for all the functions.

Blogs Self-published journals posted electronically on the Web.

Bricks-and-Clicks Companies with a dual physical and Internet presence, becoming a hybrid of *Brick-and-Mortar* firms and *dot-com*s.

Bull-Whip Effect Where a small change by a customer results in a huge change upstream. For instance, a customer order triggers a company to generate an order to its supplier, who, in turn, generates its own larger order to its suppliers, and so on; moving upstream through the supply chain increases greater variance from the original order. If the customer then cancels the order, that cancellation ripples through the supply chain.

Business Continuity Involves not only disaster recovery (recovering data and programs from back-up and instituting communication links, for example) but also having back-up work procedures and office space for displaced employees to work with telephone lines and computers so that the business can continue operating.

Business Process Outsourcing (BPO) Outsourcing all or most of a reengineered process that has a large IT component.

Business Process Redesign/Reengineering (BPR) Significantly restructuring the operational business processes in a firm.

Business Visionary One of the CIO's roles where the CIO will need to believe, and then convince others, that the Internet will lead to new business models. This makes the CIO's role a main driver of strategy.

Case-Based Reasoning (CBR) Expert systems that draw inferences by comparing a current problem (or case) to hundreds or thousands of similar past cases. CBR is best used when the situation involves too many nuances and variations to be generalized into rules.

Champion A person inside or outside IS who has a vision and gets it implemented by obtaining the funding, pushing the project over hurdles, putting his or her reputation on the line, and taking on the risk of the project.

Change Management The process of assisting people to make major changes in their work and working environment.

Chaos Theory As applied to business, a theory that states that "order is free" when groups and organizations are allowed to be self-organizing because, as in scientific chaos theory, randomness (chaos) works within boundaries, which are called strange attractors. As a result, there is order in chaos.

Circuit Switching When a virtual (temporary) circuit is created between caller and receiver and that circuit is theirs alone to use; no other parties can share it during the duration of their telephone call. Most appropriate for voice calls.

Cleansed Data Data processed to make it usable for decision support; referred to in conjunction with data warehouses. Opposite is *dirty data* (data from different databases that does not match, has different names, uses different time frames, etc.).

Cleartext Nonencrypted versions of passwords and messages.

Clickwrap Contract A contract not really bargained over in any way, but presented as a take-it-or-leave-it offer. Generally speaking, these contracts are legally enforceable. The use of the term *clickwrap contract* is an extension to the "shrinkwrap licenses" used in purchased software.

Client-Server Splitting the computing workload between the "client," which is a computer used by the user and can sit on the desktop or carried around, and the "server," which houses the sharable resources.

Closed Network A network that is offered by one supplier and to which only the products of that supplier can be attached.

Collaborative Outsourcing Where one service provider becomes the prime contractor for numerous facets of an operation, but some of the work is provided by other external service providers (ESPs).

Communities of Practice (CoPs) Networks of people who work together in an unofficial way to get work accomplished using unofficial procedures that may be outside the company's formal corporate culture.

Competitive Local Exchange Carriers (CLECs) Telecom carriers that compete with incumbent local exchange carriers (ILECS) and provide new kinds of connection options to businesses and homes, such as cable modems, optical fiber, wireless, and satellite.

Connectivity Allowing users to communicate up, down, across, and out of an organization via a network.

Content Refers to information presented electronically in a variety of media: charts, text, voice, sound, graphics, animation, photographs, diagrams, and video.

Cookie A file in a Web user's computer that identifies the user to Web sites.

Cooperative Processing Computer systems that cooperate with each other to perform a task. The systems may span internal business functions or even span enterprises.

Copyright A law that aims to protect an expression in a tangible form; a copyright protects the expression, not the idea.

Corporate Memory The knowledge or information accumulated by a business, which is often stored in its software, databases, patents, and business processes.

Corporate Portal An intranet where employees, customers, and suppliers gain access to a company's information, applications, and processes. This approach moves the software from being decentralized (on PCs) to being centralized (on a server).

Countermeasures Mechanisms used by people and enterprises to protect themselves from security breaches, such as stealing data or machines, destroying files, redirecting traffic, shutting down Web sites, and unleashing computer viruses.

Critical Success Factors (CSF) The few key areas of an executive's job where things must go right in order for the organization to flourish.

Customer Capital The strength of a company's franchise with its customers and its relationships and networks of associates. This form of capital may be either human (relationships with the company) or structural (products used from the company).

Customer Relationship Management (CRM) Computer systems used to know much more about customers (and perhaps noncustomers). They are used to manage a firm's relationships with its customers; hence the name.

Cyberspace A "space" on the Internet where people "exist" in a virtual world.

Cybersquatting The act of registering domain names that clearly referred to known companies, anticipating that those companies would eventually want the domain name and would be willing to pay for it.

Cycle Time The amount of time it takes to accomplish a complete cycle, such as the time from getting an idea to turning it into a product or service.

Data Electronic information that is comprised of facts (devoid of meaning or context).

Data Dictionary The main tool by which data administrators control a company's standard data definitions, to make sure that corporate policy is being followed.

Data Integrity Data that maintains its integrity because it cannot be modified in transit or in storage.

Data Mart A subset of a data warehouse created for a specific set of users, such as the marketing department.

Data Mining Having computers explore huge repositories of data to uncover unknown patterns, trends, or anomalies.

Data Warehouse A huge repository of historical data used to answer queries and uncover trends; contains a snapshot of data at a point in time as opposed to operational databases that are updated with every new transaction.

Database Repository of data stored in a particular manner, such as a hierarchy or tables.

DDM Paradigm A part of the architecture of a DSS: the dialog (D) between the user and the system, the data (D) that supports the system, and the models (M) that provide the analysis capabilities.

Decision Support Systems (DSS) Computer applications used to support decision making.

Demand-Pull In this business model, companies offer customers the components of a service or product, and the customers create their own personalized versions, creating the demand that pulls the specific product or service they want through the supply chain; opposite is supply-push.

Denial-of-Service Attack Attack on a Web site from many coordinated computers that floods the site with so many empty messages that the site is overwhelmed and crashes and is therefore unable to process legitimate queries.

Digital Subscriber Line (DSL) A telephone subscription service that provides speed up to 1.2 Mbps (106 bits per second) over copper wire, as compared to modems' speed of 56 Kbps.

Distributed System A computer system that has components physically distributed around a company or among companies.

Document A unit of recorded information structured for human consumption. This definition accommodates "documents" dating back to cuneiform inscriptions on clay tablets—what has changed are the ways information is represented and the ways documents are processed.

Dot-coms Businesses based primarily or exclusively on the Web, and hence merging IS and business. The *dot-com crash* refers to the stock market slump in 2000–2002 of many of these start-up companies. They failed to live up to expectations, the value of their stock fell to zero, and the companies folded. Internet-only dot-com competitors have now become more reality based, and the integration of the Internet into how companies work has proceeded.

Dribbling Data Obtaining data for a new application from data in an existing application.

Dumb Terminals Desktop machines without processing or storage capabilities.

Eavesdropping Intercepting messages on a computer network.

E-business Outsourcing Outsourcing e-commerce and e-business aspects of one's company, such as Web-site hosting, application hosting, telecom management, and so forth.

E-commerce Buying and selling electronically, as in handling commerce transactions.

Ecosystem A web of relationships surrounding one or a few companies.

Edge Server Distributed databases on the edge of the Internet (close to a set of users), holding a copy of an organization's Web site.

E-enablement Integrating use of the Internet into how companies work; building e-enabled relationships with consumers and other enterprises, not simply performing transactions electronically.

Electronic Channel An electronic link used to create, distribute, and present information and knowledge as part of a product or service or as an ancillary good.

Electronic Data Interchange (EDI) Business transactions, such as orders, that cross company boundaries via a network using carefully defined protocols and data formats.

Electronic Tender An electronic communication capability in a product or service that allows that product or service to be tended; that is, cared for, attended to, or kept track of by a remote computer.

Electronic Vaulting An off-site data storage facility used by organizations for backing up data against loss in case of a disaster.

Encapsulation Combining data and procedures in an object.

Encryption Coding and decoding documents for security.

Enterprise Nervous System The technical means to a real-time enterprise; a network that connects people, applications, and devices.

Enterprise Resource Planning Systems (ERP) Systems that aim to provide companies with a single source of data about their operations. The systems have financial, manufacturing, HR, and other modules.

E-procurement Buying items via the Web using company-tailored electronic catalogs of items for which the company has negotiated prices with the seller; e-procurement generally uses a third-party marketplace to handle the coordination between buyer and seller.

E-tailing Retailing over the Web.

Ethernet A network protocol used in many local area networks that broadcasts messages across the network and rebroadcasts if a collision of messages occurs.

Exchanges Business-to-business electronic marketplaces where many buyers purchase goods from many sellers. These are generally organized by industry or by specialties within an industry.

Executive Dashboard A type of executive information system that allows executives access to a company's data warehouse (via a display screen that resembles a car dashboard), allowing real-time analysis of how well a division, region, or other part of the business is progressing on meeting its forecasts.

Executive Information System (EIS) A computer system specially built for executives to assist them in making decisions.

Expert Systems An automated type of analysis or problem-solving model that deals with a problem the way an "expert" does. The process involves consulting a base of knowledge or expertise to reason out an answer based on the characteristics of the problem.

Explicit Knowledge Knowledge that has been articulated, codified, and made public.

Extended Enterprise All of one's own organization plus those organizations with which one interacts, such as suppliers, buyers, and government agencies; interconnected single-organization networks that are not limited by industry and provide a type of electronic information consortium.

External Document-Based Information Electronic information that is available outside an organization and is text based, rather than numeric.

External Operational Measures Measures of computer operational performance that users can see, such as system and network uptime (or downtime), response time, turnaround time, and program failures. These directly relate to customer satisfaction.

External Record-Based Information Electronic information that is available outside an organization and is numeric, rather than text based.

External Service Provider (ESP) A company that provides services to a firm, often acting as an outsourcer. There are numerous types of ESPs, such as those that provide Web-site hosting, back-up and recovery, and application hosting.

Extract File A file extracted from a company's transaction database and placed in a decision support database or a data warehouse where it can be queried by end users.

Extranet A private network that uses Internet protocols and the public telecommunication system to securely share part of a business's information or operations with suppliers, vendors, partners, customers, or other businesses. An extranet is created by extending the company's intranet to users outside the company.

E-zines Web pages owned by frustrated writers who publish their own electronic magazines.

Federated Databases A way of organizing databases where each retains its autonomy, where its data is defined independently of the other databases, and where its database management system takes care of itself while retaining rules for others to access its data.

Feeding the Web Promoting the platform on which a firm bases its offerings because the firm's prosperity is linked to the platform's prosperity.

Fiber Optics/Optics Glass fiber that transmits voice or data signals via light pulses.

Filtering Using a software program (a filter) to automatically route messages or documents according to their content.

Firewall Software on Internet servers (or entire servers) that keeps the public from accessing the company's intranet.

Fourth Generation Language (4GLs) A computer programming language used by end users, as opposed to COBOL (a third generation language), or Assembler (a second generation language), or programming via plug boards (first generation programming).

Freeware Software given away for free, generally via the Internet but also on CD-ROMs.

Front-end intelligence An interface for interacting with the user, most useful when it is decentralized, flexible, personalized, and sensitive to context.

Front-end Tools Tools in a computer-aided software engineering suite that are used by analysts and designers to create the design of a computer system.

Gateway A data network connection that connects unlike networks.

Glocalizing Striking a balance between global and local needs.

Groupware Electronic tools that support teams of collaborators.

Hacking/Cracking The unauthorized access to a host computer. This access may be a direct intrusion or via a computer virus or Trojan horse.

Heuristics Rules that draw upon experience, common sense, ways of doing business, and even rules and regulations.

Homepage A person's or organization's base page on the World Wide Web.

Hubs One of three types of computers that route traffic, these forward packets of data from one machine to another. When a number of computers share a hub, data sent from one goes to all the others.

Human Capital Knowledge, skills, and innovativeness of employees as well as company values, culture, and philosophy.

Hypertext A style of presenting text in computer systems or networks where the reader can click on a highlighted word and jump to a related thought or site.

Hypertext Markup Language (HTML) The language multimedia Web pages are formatted in that uses the same technique to link graphical items on the World Wide Web.

Incumbent Local Exchange Carriers (ILECs) Formerly called Regional Bell Operating Companies (RBOCs), telecom companies spun off from AT&T in 1984.

Inference Engine A portion of an expert system's software that contains the reasoning methods used to search the knowledge base and solve the problem.

Information Data in context, which means the data has been given an explicit meaning in a specific context.

Information Age Though defined a multitude of ways, this book refers to the information age as when the number of U.S. information workers surpassed the number of U.S. workers in all other sectors combined (information workers exceeded 50 percent of the U.S. workforce).

Information Architecture A blueprint of definitions of corporate data—such as customers, products, and business transactions—that is used consistently across the firm's applications.

Information Repository The heart of a computer-aided software engineering (CASE) system that stores and organizes all information needed to create, modify, and develop a software system.

Information Resources The intangible information assets of a firm, including data, information, knowledge, processes, patents, and so on.

Infrastructure The implementation of an architecture, including in IT the processors, software, databases, electronic links, and data centers as well as the standards that ensure the components work together, the skills for managing the operation, and even some of the electronic processes themselves.

Insourcing Moving responsibility for specific services to a group within the company rather than to an external service provider. Commonly the insourcer is the shared services group.

Institutional DSS A decision support system built by DSS professionals using a DSS language that is intended to be used for the long term to support the organization's operations rather than to support an individual or small group for a short time.

Intellectual Capital A preferred term for knowledge, to distinguish it from the other kinds of capital that firms possess.

Inter-Exchange Carriers (IXCs) Long-distance telecom carriers.

Internal Document-Based Information Information that is available in-house and is text based, such as internal reports, memos, and so forth.

Internal Operational Measures Metrics of the performance of a firm's IT operations that are of interest to its computer operations staff, such as computer usage as a percentage of capacity, availability of mainline systems, disk storage utilized, job queue length, number of jobs run, number of jobs rerun due to problems, age of applications, and number of unresolved problems.

Internal Record-Based Information Information that is available in-house and is alphanumeric rather than textual.

Interoperate Different products working together, driven by the open systems movement.

Interorganizational Systems (IOS) Systems that require at least two parties with different objectives to collaborate on the development and operation of a joint computer-based system.

Intranet An internal company network that takes advantage of the Internet's infrastructure, telecommunication protocols, and browsers.

IT Governance The assignment of decision rights and the accountability framework to encourage desirable behavior in the use of IT. Governance differs from management in that governance is about deciding who makes decisions, while management is about making decisions once decision rights have been assigned.

Keiretsu Japanese term referring to the associations of independent and interdependent businesses working in concert.

Knowledge Information with direction or intent derived from strategies or objectives.

Knowledge Brokers A way to promote knowledge sharing by giving titles to employees who excel at knowledge sharing.

Knowledge Infrastructure A support system that manages information, enables understanding, and supports learning.

Knoware Advanced groupware information technology that helps people and organizations share knowledge.

Legacy Systems Mainframe computer applications that handle the day-to-day transactions of the company in a centralized, rather than distributed, manner. Alternatively, any system that does not use current technology.

Line Executive A business executive who manages a profit-oriented business unit, such as manufacturing, rather than a supporting staff unit, such as finance.

Linkage Analysis Planning A planning approach that studies the links between an organization and its suppliers and customers.

Local Area Network (LAN) A network that traverses a floor of a building, a work group, or a department (as opposed to a wide area network that crosses countries).

Local Exchange Carrier (LEC) Telecom companies that only handle local, not long distance, telephone calls.

Loosely/Tightly Coupled Groups Loosely coupled groups are where the activity of each member is relatively independent of the other members (such as salespeople who have their own sales territories). Tightly coupled groups are where the work of each member is tied closely to the work of the other members.

Mainframe A huge, very fast computer capable of handling all the computing for a large organization.

Marketspace A nonphysical marketplace where information substitutes for physical products and physical location.

M-commerce Conducting commerce via small wireless devices, such as buying an item from a vending machine using a cell phone or personal digital assistant (PDA).

Mead's Law Says that N transistors on a sliver of silicon yield N^2 performance and value.

Metadata Information about a data entity, such as its definition, how it was calculated, its source, when it is updated, who is responsible for it, and so forth.

Middleware Software that eases connection between clients and servers in a client/server system.

Mid-Tier Servers A network topology that has several tiers of servers, such as local work group servers, departmental servers, and an enterprise server (the corporate mainframe).

Moore's Law Computer processing power will double every 18 months. This law, stated by Gordon Moore, a founder of Intel, has proven true since 1959.

Multimedia The combination of text, graphics, sound, data, animation, and perhaps video in a message, a document, or at a Web site.

Network Army A set of individuals and communities aligned by a cause. They have moral and intellectual influencers as opposed to formal leadership, and are only as permanent as their common agenda. Their communications are open, in forums that anyone can join.

Network Effect When the value of a product or service offered on a platform (such as a gaming platform or an operating system) increases as the number of users increases, thereby creating a "virtuous" circle of upward spiraling product value and customers. The opposite is a downward spiraling "vicious" circle where a product continually loses its value and its customers.

Neural Networks A way to store knowledge and a type of decision-making system organized like the human brain, containing synapses and nodes that fire signals between each other. Neural networks are more intelligent than the other forms of knowledge representation discussed here because they can learn.

Nonrepudiation Not allowing a party in an electronic transaction to repudiate, which means claiming that the transaction never took place; nonrepudiation is an important cornerstone of electronic security.

Object In object-oriented programming, functions are packaged with data so that the two can be reused. These reusable components are called "classes," whereas at run time, each class can produce instances called "objects." Objects hold all the code and data in an object-oriented system.

Object-Oriented Programming A style of programming that encapsulates data and the operations that work on that data within an object, thus increasing the reusability of the code (as an object) and reducing the propagation of errors among objects.

Object-to-Object Communication The potential for objects such as smart tags to talk to one another.

Open Network or Open System Though the term "open" keeps expanding, this book refers to open networks/systems as those based on national or international standards so that the products of many manufacturers work with each other.

Open Source Software where the complete source code is distributed with any and all distributions, and where anyone can modify and redistribute the code.

Open/Closed Groups Open groups are where almost anyone can join. Closed groups are where membership is restricted. A "gray scale" between open and closed indicates the degree of difficulty to gain membership.

Outsourcing Contracting with another firm to perform work that had previously been performed in-house, generally requiring a multiyear contract and generally for "noncore" work.

Packet Switching Messages divided into packets, each with an address header, and each is sent separately—each packet may take a different path through the network.

Partnering Allying with another organization that has different core competencies, often on a strategic alliance basis, for mutual benefit.

Patent A law that aims to protect inventions (things or processes for producing things) but not abstract ideas or natural laws.

Peer-to-Peer (P2P) Computing Distributing a task over a wide number of computers (peers) connected to the Internet.

Personal Area Network (PAN) A network that allows computers in a "personal area" to communicate wirelessly, much like Wi-Fi.

Personal Digital Assistants (PDAs) Handheld computers that sometimes allow wireless connection to the Internet and contain personal productivity tools (such as calendaring, address book, to-do lists, and games).

Personalization Coordinating disparate pieces of intelligence to form personalized offerings.

Planning Developing a view of the future that guides decision making today.

Platform A major trend in interorganizational systems that provides the infrastructure for the operation of a business ecosystem, a region, or an industry. Examples are American Airlines' SABRE computer reservation system, or the video game industry's PlayStation, Nintendo, and Xbox platforms.

Privacy Includes the freedom from intrusion, the right to be left alone, the right to control information about oneself, and freedom from surveillance.

Private Programs Computer programs created and used by only one person.

Process Owner A person in an organization responsible for an end-to-end process such as the ordering process or a research and development process.

Process-Centered Organization A company whose perspective has shifted from tasks to processes; an approach to designing an organization where the business processes are the driving structures.

Proprietary Software Software sold only in its compiled state, undecipherable by humans, and whose code is not allowed to be changed except by the developer.

Prototype A computer program that is used to test a new computing concept, such as distributed Java applets, for learning and experimentation purposes.

Public Key Encryption A methodology for encrypting and decrypting text to ensure identity of the parties. A message sender uses the assigned private key to encrypt the message and the recipient uses the sender's public key (known to anyone) to decrypt it, thus validat-ing the sender's identity. The process also works in reverse; sending a message encrypted using a person's public key that can only be decrypted and read by that person using their private key.

Quality of Service Refers to the ability of a network to provide a range of assured levels of performance.

Quick Hit DSS A system that is quite limited in scope, is developed and put into use quickly, and helps a manager come to a decision. The term "ad hoc" has also been used to distinguish from institutional DSS, although some quick hit systems become regularly used.

Rationalized Data Using the same data name for all uses of the same data.

Real-Time Enterprise Where organizations can know how they are doing at the moment, rather than have to wait days, weeks, or months for analyzable data.

Reengineering Not to be confused with the term "business process reengineering," this term, "system or application reengineering," is much narrower and refers to rebuilding software for a new platform or new programming language.

Regional Bell Operating Company A regional telephone company formed by the 1984 deregulation of AT&T. Formerly, these companies were part of AT&T.

Relational Databases Databases that store data in tables.

Relationship Tech New peer-to-peer relationships that are forming—between customer and firm, between customer and customer—which question past ways of working (such as recommender systems).

Repudiation Refusing a computer-based transaction, such as when one party reneges on an agreement after the fact, the other party may be left paying for the transaction processing unless it is repudiated.

Routers One of three types of computers that route network traffic, these use a routing table to pass along a packet to the next appropriate router on a network, directing packets via the most efficient route and relaying packets around a failed network component. Routers also link network segments that use different protocols, and can connect to wide area networks (WANs).

Rules-Based Systems A common way to store knowledge in an expert system knowledge base, where rules are obtained from experts drawing on their own expertise. Rules generally present this knowledge in the form of if-then statements, and are appropriate when knowledge can be generalized into such specific statements.

Rummler-Brache Approach An approach for deciding how to reengineer an organization.

Scan-Based Trading (SBT) An arrangement between a retail store and product supplier whereby the scan data from point-of-sale checkout systems for products sold determines the amount the retailer pays the supplier.

Scenario A way to manage planning assumptions by creating a speculation of what the future might be like by drawing on trends, events, environmental factors, and the relationships among them.

Scope Creep Users asking for additional functions in applications as development proceeded.

Secure Sockets Layer (SSL) A protocol for providing security over the Internet.

Self-Managed Work Groups Groups or teams that handle most supervisory tasks on their own, without a supervisor.

Self-Organizing Systems Entities, such as ecosystems, organisms, or organizations, that deal with their environment by responding to each stimulus in an appropriate manner, rather than in a predetermined manner, so they self-organize when needed.

Sense-and-Respond Strategy Making An approach to strategy making that endorses keeping in close contact with the business world, continually sensing for important changes, and then responding quickly to changes by conducting experiments that test different possible futures—as opposed to betting on one strategy for the future.

Shared Services A department or division formed by consolidating and centralizing services formerly operated by business units. These services can include legal, travel, finance, IT, food service, fleet management, accounting, telecom, and others. It is a form of insourcing; business units draw on the expertise in shared services when needed.

Short Message Service An "always on" telecom service for communicating quickly and wirelessly using a small handheld device; the messages are typed using a shorthand, code words, abbreviations, or short phrases.

Smart Tags Communicating objects with a small chip that contains information and a radio frequency identification device (RFID). They can carry far more information than bar codes because they carry the history of an item.

Sniffing The interception and reading of electronic messages as they travel over the communication networks. Usually for attempting to unveil passwords to gain access to a system.

Spaghetti Code The way code in many legacy systems appears to a programmer because it has been patched so many times that the logic of the application weaves in and out like a plate of spaghetti.

Spiral Diagram A way of viewing the application development process as a spiral, as opposed to a waterfall.

Spoofing Masquerading as another party, such as a storefront, to collect thousands (or millions) of credit card numbers and other information from naive consumers.

Stages of Growth The four stages that many organizations go through in the introduction and assimilation of new technologies. These are *early successes* (leading to increased interest and experimentation), *contagion* (the learning period for the field), *control* (integration of systems is attempted but proves difficult), and *integration* (use of the particular new technology is mature). An organization can be in several stages simultaneously for different technologies.

Status Access System A system for monitoring what is going on in the company and in the outside world.

Straight-Through Processing A system where transaction data is entered just once in a process or a supply chain.

Strategic Having a significant, long-term impact on the growth rate, industry, and revenue of an organization.

Strategy Stating the direction you want to go and how you intend to get there.

Structural Capital The capabilities embedded in hardware, software, databases, organizational structure, patents, and trademarks that support employees as well as relationships with customers.

Structured Query Language (SQL) A database language for making queries of a database that has become the standard.

Supply Chain Management Systems Systems that integrate supply chains that compete against one another on their ability to reduce costs and time across their entire chains. Development of these interorganizational systems requires teams from the different organizations to work together.

Supply-Push In this business model, companies are organized to build a supply of products or services and then "push" them out to end customers, on store shelves, in catalogs, and such; the opposite is demand-pull.

Support Systems Systems that can help knowledge workers perform knowledge-based work.

Switches One of three types of computers that route traffic, these forward packets to the port of the intended computer, using the addressing information in each packet's header.

System Development The process of building a system, originally by writing code to create an application and then linking together applications to form a system; a newer process is system integration.

System Integration The current process of building systems by piecing together hardware components, software packages, database engines, and network products from numerous vendors into a single, cohesive system.

System-Wide Rules An operating discipline for distributed systems that is enforced at all times and governs security, communication between nodes, data accessibility, program and file transfers, and common operating procedures.

Tacit Knowledge Knowledge "known" but not easily explained to others.

Tech Clubs Cross-organizational groups that meet informally, but are supported and sanctioned by top management.

Technology Camel A way to distinguish levels of comfort with any technology using five clusters, which, when graphed on a chart, look a lot like a two-humped camel.

Telecommunications The sending of information in any form from one place to another, electronically.

Thin Clients Network computers that are used much like telephones; they have no hard disk or house applications, but rather just a browser, memory, keyboard, and a modem.

Third Generation Language A programming language used by a professional programmer, such as COBOL.

Timebox A methodology for building a system in which the developers promise to deliver specific portions of the system within a specific timeframe (a timebox); the intent is to better control project delivery schedules.

Total Quality Management (TQM) A management technique that focuses on managing the quality of a service or product, often through statistical quality control techniques, in order to achieve higher customer satisfaction and reduce costs as well.

Trademarks A law to protect names, symbols, and other icons used to identify a company or product.

Transitional Outsourcing The outsourcing of legacy systems for maintenance so that the in-house staff can focus on developing replacement client/server systems.

T-Shaped Managers Executives who have both a vertical role (such as running a business unit) and a horizontal role (such as sharing knowledge with their peers in other business units).

Value Assessment Framework A systematic way to separate potential benefits of IT investments by organizational levels.

Value Chain A technique for describing a chain of business processes from product/service conception through cessation of the product/service, where each of the processes adds some kind of value.

Virtual Circuit A temporary circuit created between caller and receiver where that circuit is theirs alone to use; no other parties can share it during the duration of their telephone call.

Vision A statement of how someone wants the future to be or believes it will be; it is used to set direction for an organization.

Visual Programming A technique for programming, such as creating a graphical user interface, by pointing and clicking on generic items—menus, dialog boxes, radio buttons, and other components of graphical displays—and then arranging them to create a screen.

Waterfall Approach A way to view the system development process as a series of steps that, when diagrammed, appear as a waterfall.

Waves of Innovation Primozic, Primozic, and Leben's presentation on how IT is used by industries and by enterprises, one view of the evolution of IT, and the escalating benefits it provides firms. They identify five waves of innovation, with *time* on the horizontal axis and *benefit* on the vertical access.

Web Cast Broadcast of a live event over the World Wide Web.

Web Services This second-generation Internet-based system environment gives software modules URLs (Internet addresses) so they can be called upon to perform their function as a service via the Internet.

Web Surfing (Surfing the Web) Slang term for continuously following hyperlinks hidden behind highlighted words on Web pages that, when clicked, jump to another Web page.

Web site A personal or organizational site on the World Wide Web. In just a few years, company Web sites have become standard business practice in most companies, large and small.

Wi-Fi The 802.11 family of wireless Ethernet standards. For instance, 802.11b transmits up to 11 megabits per second and behaves a lot like its wired cousin 10BaseT. Other members of this standard family exist and new ones are being developed.

Worknets Informal groups of people whose collective knowledge is used to accomplish a specific task.

Workscape The virtual workplace, which includes the Internet.

Zero Latency Reacting quickly to new information (with no wait time).

Acronyms and Abbreviations

1G/2G/3G/4G First, Second, Third, and Fourth Generation (of wireless systems)

3i Investors in Industry

4GLs Fourth Generation Languages

ACM Association for Computing Machinery

AI Artificial Intelligence

AIS Association for Information Systems

AM Amplitude Modulation

AmEx American Express

AMS/3 Third-Generation Automatic Order Matching and Execution System

ANSI American National Standards Institute

AOL America Online

AOP Advanced Optimization Planning

API Application Program Interface

ARPANET Advanced Research Projects Agency Network

ASP Application Service Provider or Active Server Page

AT&T American Telephone and Telegraph

ATM Asynchronous Transfer Mode or Automated Teller Machine

B2B Business to Business

B2C Business to Consumer

BCG Boston Consulting Group

BLISS Banking and Loan Insurance Software System

BMW Bavarian Motor Works

BPO Business Process Outsourcing

BPR Business Process Redesign/Reengineering

C/C + + Programming Languages Used with UNIX

CAD/CAM Computer-Aided Design/Computer-Aided Manufacturing

CAPS Center for Advanced Purchasing Studies

CAS Credit Authorization System

CASE Computer-Aided Software Engineering

CBR Case-Based Reasoning

CC Computer Center

CCITT Consultive Committee for International Telegraphy and Telephony

CDMA Code Division Multiple Access

CDPD Cellular Digital Packet Data

CD-ROM Compact Disc – Read Only Memory

CEMEX Cementos Mexicanos (a cement company)

CEO Chief Executive Officer

CFO Chief Financial Officer

CIO Chief Information Officer

CIR Corporate Information Resources

CIRANO Center for Interuniversity Research and Analysis on Organizations

CIS Corporate Information Services

CISR Center for Information Systems Research

CLEC Competitive Local Exchange Carrier

CMA Cash Management Account

COBOL Common Business Oriented Language

COE Common Operating Environment

COM Computer Output Microfilm or Component Object Model

COO Chief Operations Officer

CRAMM United Kingdom Central Computer and Telecommunication Agency Risk Analysis and Management Method

CRM Customer Relationship Management

CSC Computer Sciences Corporation

CSF Critical Success Factor

CTO Chief Technology Officer

CU Credit Unions

CXO A Group of "Chiefs" (CEO, CFO, CIO, COO, etc.)

DARPA Defense Advanced Research Projects Agency

DASD Direct Access Data Storage

DB Digital Business

DB2 Database 2 (an IBM product)

DBMS Database Management System

DDM Dialog, Data, and Modeling

DES Data Encryption Standard

DGMS Dialog Generation and Management System

DNS Distributed Name Service

DOS Disk Operating System

DP Data Processing

DPI Dots Per Inch

DSA Decision Support Application

DSL Digital Subscriber Line

DSS Decision Support System

DVD Digital Video Disc

EAI Enterprise Application Integration

EDI Electronic Data Interchange

EDM Electronic Document Management

EDP Electronic Data Processing

EDS Electronic Data System

EIS Executive Information System *or* Enterprise Information Solutions

EJB Enterprise Java Bean

E-mail Electronic Mail

EMR Electro Magnetic Radiation

EPRI Electric Power Research Institute

ERD Enterprise Reference Data

ERP Enterprise Resource Planning

ES Enterprise System

ESOP Employee Stock Ownership Plan

ESP External Service Provider

ESS Executive Support System

EUC End User Computing

EVP Executive Vice President

E-zines Electronic magazines

FAQ Frequently Asked Questions

Fax Facsimile

FBI Federal Bureau of Investigations

FDA U.S. Food and Drug Administration

FDDI Fiber Distributed Data Interface

FT *Financial Times*

FTC Federal Trade Commission

FTP File Transfer Protocol

GDSS Group Decision Support System

GOTOs Go-to's, in computer programming code

GPRS General Packed Radio System

GPS Global Positioning Satellite

GSM Global System for Mobile Communication

GSS Group Support System

GTE General Telephone Company

HEC Hautes Etudes Commerciales

HICSS Hawaii International Conference on System Sciences

HKEx Hong Kong Exchanges and Clearing

HP Hewlett-Packard

HR Human Resources

HTML HyperText Markup Language

HTTP HyperText Transfer Protocol

IBM International Business Machines Corporation

IC Intellectual Capital

ID Identification

IDE Integrated Development Environment

IDS Integrated Data Store or Intrusion Detection System

IEA Information Engineering Associates

IFTF Institute for the Future

IIML Indian Institute of Management, Lucknow

ILEC Incumbent Local Exchange Carrier

IM Information Management or Instant Messaging

INR Indian Rupes

IOS Inter-Organizational System

IP Internet Protocol

IPng Internet Protocol Next Generation

IR Information Resources

IS Information Systems

ISDN Integrated Services Digital Network

ISM Information Security Management

ISO International Standards Organization

ISP Internet Service Provider

ISS Internet Security System

IT Information Technology

IXC Inter-exchange Carrier

J2EE Java 2 Enterprise Edition

JAD Joint Application Design

JDS Job Diagnostic Survey

JIT Just-In-Time

Kbps Kilobytes Per Second
LAN Local Area Network
LEC Local Exchange Carrier
LLC Limited Liability Company
LN Local Network
LTL Less-Than-Truckload
Mac Apple's Macintosh Computer
MAN Metropolitan Area Network
MBMS Model Base Management System
Mbps Megabytes Per Second
MGM Metro-Goldwyn-Mayer
MIPS Millions of Instructions Per Second
MIS Management Information Systems
MIT Massachusetts Institute of Technology
MOM Message-Oriented Middleware
MU Multiple-User system
MVS Multiple Virtual System
NASA National Aeronautics and Space Administration
NBC National Broadcasting Corporation
NC Network Computer
Net, The The Internet
NetBIOS Network BIOS, a proprietary network transfer protocol
NFL National Football League
NIC Network Interface Card
NOC Network Operations Centers
NT Network Technology
NTT Nippon Telephone and Telegraph
NYNEX A New York-Based Telecom Company
OEM Original Equipment Manufacturer
OLAP Online Analytical Processing
OLTP Online Transaction Processing
OM Owens & Minor
OO Object-Oriented
OPEC Organization of Petroleum Exporting Countries
OR/MS Operations Research/Management Science
ORB Object Request Broker
OSI Open System Interconnection
OSS Open Source Software
OX Operations Expediter System
PAN Personal Area Network
PARC Xerox's Palo Alto Research Center
PBX Private Branch Exchange
PC Personal Computer
PCS Personal Communication Service
PDA Personal Digital Assistant
PDF Portable Document Format (proprietary file format in Adobe)

PIN Personal Identification Number
PL/1 Programming Language/1
PLL Phase Lock Loops
PODD Point of Delivery Device
POTS Plain Old Telephone Service
PPSR Personal Property Securities Register Service
PRA Passenger Revenue Accounting
PRAC Plymouth Rock Assurance Corporation
PROFS Professional Office System
PSTN Public Switched Telephone Network
PTT Postal, Telephone, and Telegraph Authority
PwC Pricewaterhouse Coopers
QoS Quality of Service
R&D Research and Development
RAD Rapid Application Development
RBOC Regional Bell Operating Company
RCA Radio Corporation of America
RF Radio Frequency
RFID Radio Frequency Identification
RIPP Rapid Iterative Production Prototyping
RN Remote Network
ROI Return On Investment
RPC Remote Procedure Call
RSA Encryption method named for developers Rivest, Shamir, & Adleman
RU Remote Utility
SAP Systeme Anwendung Produkte (System Application Product)
SAP R/3 SAP Release 3; the client-server version
SBT Scan-Based Trading
SCM Supply Chain Management
SEC U.S. Securities and Exchange Commission
SEI Software Engineering Institute at Carnegie Mellon University
SET Secure Electronic Transactions
SLBG Sara Lee Bakery Group
SLICE Simple Low Cost Innovative Engine
SMS Short Message Service
SNA System Network Architecture
SOAP Simple Object Access Protocol
SOHO Small Office/Home Office
SQL Structured Query Language
SSL Secure Sockets Layer
SSP Security Service Providers
STS Sociotechnical System
SU Single-User systems
SUMURU Single User, Multiple User, Remote Utility
TCO Total Cost of Ownership

TCP/IP Transmission Control Protocol/Internet Protocol

TDL Teleport Denver, Ltd.

TDMA Time Division Multiple Access

TQM Total Quality Management

TV Television

TVA Tennessee Valley Authority

UCC Uniform Commercial Code

UCLA University of California at Los Angeles

UDDI Universal Discovery, Description, and Integration

UHF Ultra High Fidelity

UMT United Management Technologies

UNIX "Unics" Operating System; an attempt at a pun

UPS United Parcel Service

URL Uniform Resource Locator

VAN Value Added Network

VoIP Voice-Over Internet Protocol

VPN Virtual Private Network

VSAT Very Small Aperture Terminal

WAN Wide Area Network

WAP Wireless Application Protocol

Web World Wide Web

Wi-Fi Wireless Fidelity

WiNS Wire Nova Scotia

WISP Wireless Internet Service Providers

WSDL Web Services Definition Language

XML Extensible Markup Language

Y2K Year 2000

Index